RULES OF THE GAME

AN INTRODUCTION TO CANADIAN POLITICS

Hamish Telford
University of the Fraser Valley

PEARSON

Toronto

Senior Acquisitions Editor: Matthew Christian
Marketing Manager: Jennifer Sutton
Program Manager: Söğüt Y. Güleç
Project Manager: Andrea Falkenberg
Senior Developmental Editor: Paul Donnelly
Production Services: Jogender Taneja/Aptara®, Inc.
Permissions Project Manager: Erica Mojzes
Photo Permissions Research: Zoe Milgram/QBS
Text Permissions Research: Varoon Deo-Singh/Electronic Publishing Services
Cover Designer: Alex Li
Cover Image: CP PHOTO/Tom Hanson

Library and Archives Canada Cataloguing in Publication

Telford, Hamish, 1964–, author
  Rules of the game: an introduction to Canadian politics / Hamish Telford,
  University of the Fraser Valley.

  Includes bibliographical references and index. ISBN 978-0-13-254685-0 (pbk.)

  1. Canada—Politics and government—Textbooks.   I. Title.

JL65.T44 2014   C2014-901881-9

320.971

ISBN   978-0-13-254685-0

To
Sally and Malcolm Telford,
with love and gratitude.

Brief Contents

Contents

Preface

Each time I teach introduction to Canadian politics, I invariably have one or more students confess to me that they know "nothing about politics." While I have no doubt these students are sincere in their belief, I am equally sure that they have underestimated their knowledge. Even the most politically disengaged student knows that Canada is a democracy, that there are elections with individuals from different parties competing to form the government. Virtually every student thus possesses a rudimentary understanding of the Canadian political system. This book will build on the knowledge base possessed by every student and develop it in a logical fashion. The overriding objective of this book is to provide a more accessible and engaging introduction to Canadian politics. To that end, I have employed a few broad strategies:

1. I have presented the material from the perspective of a first-time voter. Most people are introduced to the real world of Canadian politics when a candidate from a party comes and asks for their vote.

2. I have endeavoured to carry the narrative of this book—the rules of the game—throughout the text.

3. I have eschewed abstract theorizing. Instead, I have tried to weave theory, history, and questions of diversity throughout the narrative.

4. I have adopted a laddered approach to the material. The book starts quite simplistically, but the complexity of the material increases with each section of the text.

5. I have endeavoured to write the book in a conversational tone. My hope is that students will find this less formal approach more engaging.

In my view, a basic understanding of the rules is essential for participation in the political game. But I also hope to demonstrate that politics is not merely a game—it is the process by which we collectively attempt to realize some conception of the good life. It is thus crucial that citizens take an active interest in the game of politics. This book will provide students with the vocabulary and conceptual tools to follow politics in the media and to engage in political discourse with family and friends, and I hope it will motivate students to participate in the political process as critical citizens.

ORGANIZATION OF THIS TEXT

Part I of this book will establish the context of Canadian politics. Chapter 1 will provide a quick primer on the basic rules of the game as spelled out by the Constitution Act 1867 and the British parliamentary tradition. Chapter 2 will provide a brief survey of the enduring themes in Canadian political culture and the contours of Canadian political geography.

Part II will move on to examine the principles and practices of responsible parliamentary government from the perspective of a first-time voter. Most people enter the Canadian political system for the first time when a political party comes asking for their vote during an election. We examine parties (Chapter 3), elections (Chapter 4), and the formation of a government (Chapter 5). With a government formed, the next order of business in the Canadian political system is to convene Parliament, and that is the subject of Chapter 6. In this fashion, we are following what might be viewed as a natural political cycle from election to the formation of a government to the role of Parliament in governing the country and back to another election. This process can be mystifying for both new and experienced voters, so by proceeding in this fashion we can gain an appreciation of how the Canadian parliamentary system works.

In Chapter 7, we will turn our attention to federalism. Readers will note that the complexity of the material and narrative increases at this point. As federalism is inherently a constitutional concept, this chapter will serve as a bridge back to the constitution and provide the setup for Part III, which begins with the story of repatriating the constitution in Chapter 8. With the knowledge possessed from the previous chapters, students will more readily grasp the significance of the new rules of the game adopted with the Constitution Act 1982: the Charter of Rights and Freedoms and the recognition of Aboriginal rights, which will be the focus of Chapters 9 and 10, respectively.

In Chapter 11, we examine the challenges of political reform in Canada, and how debates over the rules of the game, especially in the 1990s, transformed Canadian politics in the twenty-first century. There are considerable advantages to closing the book with a discussion of constitutional reform: by giving students the opportunity to take possession of the political process in the first half of the book, they are able to situate themselves in Canada's constitutional debates as active participants and not alienated spectators. In Chapter 11, I also try to demonstrate how debates over the rules of the game have altered the party system and indeed the political culture of the country. In this way, the chapter attempts to link back to the material raised in the first three chapters of the book.

We shall conclude the book in Chapter 12 with an examination of the contemporary state of Canadian politics, with a special focus on the declining rates of participation in Canadian elections. Democracy requires actively engaged citizens, thus the long-term decline in voter participation is a worrisome trend, and it seems appropriate to consider ways to redress this development in the conclusion.

The organizational approach adopted in this text is somewhat unconventional, but it is grounded in praxis. In my experience, this approach works well for both politically engaged students and political neophytes. Novice students appreciate that the material is accessible, while politically engaged students enjoy having the opportunity to talk about politics from the get-go rather than getting bogged down in abstract theory. I have noticed that the enthusiasm for politics displayed by engaged students is contagious—it draws novice students into the course. This format thus unites students in a common purpose as citizens and enables them to journey together through the often strange but always wonderful world of Canadian politics.

PEDAGOGICAL FEATURES

This text is intended for a first-year, one-semester introductory course on Canadian politics. It is thus not intended to be wholly comprehensive. Instead, it is intended to provide students with a solid grounding in the basics of Canadian politics. I am more concerned that students remember a few overarching principles rather than a myriad details, and my objective is to get students talking about politics. If students can remember a few key points and terms, they will be in a position to begin following politics in the media and to discuss it with family and friends.

However, my students often complain about information overload, and they ask me what they need to remember. It is an impossible question to answer. They really need to learn all of the material, but it is difficult to cram it all in. With this in mind, each chapter will open with a few points that will provide students with a framework to help them organize the information in the chapter.

The key points are intended to be an *aide-mémoire*. Let me explain by way of analogy: When we create documents on a computer, we can save them all to the hard drive, but in short order we would have thousands of documents and it would be impossible to find them again. So we create folders and subfolders to remember where we have saved particular documents. This text may be viewed as the hard drive with all of the information, but it has 12 folders (chapters) with more focused information. The key points at the beginning of each chapter may be viewed as subfolders. If students can remember these subfolders, it should help them remember the information contained within each folder.

Key terms and concepts will be highlighted in bold, because for students to participate in politics *they must learn* the terms and concepts—the basic vocabulary—of the game. In most cases, the definition of the term will be embedded in the text, and in all cases a definition will be provided in the margin of the page. Each of these terms will also be included in the glossary at the end of the text.

In each chapter, the main text will be supplemented with two to three photographs depicting political figures and institutions. In some cases, it is easier to grasp information in a visual format. Thus, where appropriate, some material will be presented in tables, graphs, and figures. Special text boxes will provide additional or supplemental information. Since the book is focused on the rules of the game, the Constitution Acts of 1867 and 1982 are included in an appendix.

Each chapter will conclude with some "Questions to Think About." The goal is to transform the passive learning derived from reading the chapter into active participation in Canadian political debates. A question like "Should Canada change its electoral system?" forces students to review the mechanics of the major electoral systems, examine the pros and cons and assess the consequences of each system, then weigh all this to come to a conclusion. These are the sorts of questions faculty create for written exams or term papers (and in each chapter I have suggested some further readings that would help students in this respect).

Following the Questions to Think About, students will encounter a set of formal learning outcome so that students can ensure that they have learned what they were supposed to have learned in the chapter. At this point, students will be directed to the book's website to test their knowledge.

STUDENT SUPPLEMENTS

CourseSmart for Students

CourseSmart goes beyond traditional expectations—providing instant, online access to the textbooks and course materials you need at an average savings of 50 percent. With instant access from any computer and the ability to search your text, you'll find the content you need quickly, no matter where you are. And with online tools like highlighting and note-taking, you can save time and study efficiently. See all the benefits at www.coursesmart.com/students.

INSTRUCTOR SUPPLEMENTS

The following supplements can be downloaded from a password-protected location on Pearson Canada's online catalogue (http://catalogue.pearsoned.ca). Navigate to your book's catalogue page to view the list of available supplements. Ask your local Pearson Canada sales representative for details and access.

- The **Test Item File** test bank in Microsoft Word format contains a number of questions of different types (true/false, multiple choice, short answer) that test all the key concepts in the text.
- The **PowerPoint Presentations** summarize and illustrate the key concepts in each chapter.

CourseSmart for Instructors

CourseSmart goes beyond traditional expectations—providing instant, online access to the textbooks and course materials you need at a lower cost for students. And even as students save money, you can save time and hassle with a digital eTextbook that allows you to search for the most relevant content at the very moment you need it. Whether it's evaluating textbooks or creating lecture notes to help students with difficult concepts, CourseSmart can make life a little easier. See how when you visit www.coursesmart.com/instructors.

peerScholar

Firmly grounded in published research, peerScholar is a powerful online pedagogical tool that helps develop your students' critical and creative thinking skills. peerScholar facilitates this through the process of creation, evaluation, and reflection. Working in stages, students begin by submitting a written assignment. peerScholar then circulates their work for others to review, a process that can be anonymous or not, depending on your preference. Students receive peer feedback and evaluations immediately, reinforcing their learning and driving the development of higher-order thinking skills. Students can then resubmit revised work, again depending on your preference. Contact your Pearson Canada sales representative to learn more about peerScholar and the research behind it.

Learning Solutions Managers

Pearson's Learning Solutions Managers work with faculty and campus course designers to ensure that Pearson technology products, assessment tools, and online course materials are tailored to meet your specific needs. This highly qualified team is dedicated to helping schools take full advantage of a wide range of educational resources by assisting in the integration of a variety of instructional materials and media formats. Your local Pearson Canada sales representative can provide you with more details on this service program.

ACKNOWLEDGMENTS

An old African proverb suggests that it takes a whole village to raise a child. I can now attest that it takes an entire nation (or two or even three) to write a book on Canadian politics. I have a great many people to thank for their role in producing this book. I would first like to thank my very able research assistants, Jack Brown and Katie Schilt, for their work on the glossary in particular and feedback on the manuscript in general. I would also like to thank the following students for their comments on the book's conclusion: Beth Ashton, Stephen Barbour, Marin Beck, Rebekah Bergen, and Todd Hauptman. Dawn Emile did an excellent job proofreading the entire manuscript. Conversations with Dan Coulter have also been stimulating and extremely helpful. The students of POSC 410 all helped shape my thinking on Canadian politics, and I would especially like to thank the students of POSC 110: You have been a tough audience, but you have really forced me think about how to make the study of Canadian politics accessible and engaging.

The department of political science at the University of the Fraser Valley has been a very supportive home for many years now, and I would like to thank my colleagues individually for their various contributions and especially their friendship: Edward Akuffo, Ron Dart, Scott Fast, Fiona MacDonald, as well as my former colleague Rita Dhamoon. I owe a special debt of gratitude to Karli Menagh for attending to the administration of the department while I was preoccupied with writing this book (and other matters). I have also been supported and encouraged by many wonderful colleagues around the university, especially Jeffrey Morgan, Katherine Watson, Barbara Messamore, Alan Cameron, Irwin Cohen and Darryl Plecas (who is now my MLA; I would also like to thank my former MLA John van Dongen for sharing his insights on BC politics).

I am grateful for the financial (and emotional) support that I have received from the University of the Fraser Valley. In this respect, I would like to thank Jacqueline Nolte, Dean of the College of Arts; Diane Griffiths, Associate Vice-President of Human Resources, Adrienne Chan, the Associate Vice-President of Research as well as her predecessor Yvon Dandurand. Brad Whittaker also provided important logistical support.

Over the years, I have forged a great many friendships in the Canadian political science community. I am especially indebted to Tim Schouls for the many wonderful and engaging conversations we've had about Canadian politics over the last two-plus decades. Harvey Lazar and Keith Banting have been terrific mentors, and Barbara Arneil has been my role model—a teacher–scholar par excellence. I have also benefited tremendously from my friendships with Will Bain, Paul Howe, Gerry Baier, Adam Jones, and André

Lecours. The stalwarts of the BC Political Science Association have also provided considerable intellectual nourishment over the years: Tracy Summerville, Stephen Phillips, Paddy Smith, Mike Howlett, Fred Cutler, Matt James, Jamie Lawson, Derek Cook, Denis Pilon, Ayla Kilic, Greg Millard, Paul White, Marcel Dirk, Alex Netherton, Darin Nesbitt, and Paul Rowe.

I am very thankful for all of the support I have received from the entire production team at Pearson Canada. In particular, I would like to thank Laura Pratt for recruiting me to this project and Lisa Rahn for getting me launched. Megan Burns skilfully coached me through the first two-thirds of this marathon, while Paul Donnelly had the unenviable task of carrying me over the finish line. Leanne Rancourt did an excellent job with the copyediting. And Jogender Taneja skillfully directed the production process from his office in New Delhi. I am also grateful to the following reviewers for their feedback:

Christopher Alacantra	*Wilfrid Laurier University*
Cameron Anderson	*University of Western Ontario*
Dion Mark Blythe	*University of Alberta*
Geoffrey Booth	*Georgian College*
Amanda Burgess	*University of Windsor*
Allan Craigie	*University of British Columbia*
Alexandra Dumbrowolsky	*Saint Mary's University*
Greg Flynn	*McMaster University*
Paul Howe	*University of New Brunswick*
Alex Marland	*Memorial University of Newfoundland*
Stephen Phillips	*Langara College*
Ray Pillar	*Thompson Rivers University*
David Pond	*University of Toronto, Mississauga*
Elizabeth Smyth	*Concordia University*
John Soroski	*MacEwan University*
Ian Stewart	*Acadia University*
Lori Turnbull	*Dalhousie University*
Shauna Wilton	*University of Alberta*

I have also received support from many people not named here, but please know that I am grateful for your encouragement and friendship. With all of the assistance and support I have received producing this text, there really should not be any mistakes in the book, but I of course remain wholly responsible for all errors of fact or interpretation.

Finally, and most importantly, this book could not have been written without the support of my family. I would like to thank my son Ewan for his unconditional love and for insisting that we take the time to do fun things like skiing, swimming, or going to the park. And no one has supported—and endured—me longer than my parents. I cannot thank them enough for the love and encouragement they have provided me for the past half century. I thus humbly dedicate the book to them—Sally and Malcolm Telford.

Chapter 1
The Rules of the Game

Key Points

- Politics is a conflict over different conceptions of the "good life."

- Debates over the good life can be very intense, but there are well-established rules in Canada to handle political conflict in a civilized fashion.

- The rules of the game spell out who has won the right to form the government, how the government will operate, the limits of its authority, how the government can be changed, and the other players in the game along with their roles and responsibilities.

- The rules are set out in the constitution, which can be understood as Canada's master law.

- Responsible government and federalism are the founding principles of the Canadian political system.

- Some of the principles of responsible government and federalism are written down in the Constitution Act 1867, while other principles stem from the unwritten constitutional conventions inherited from Great Britain.

- The Canadian constitution was modified in 1982, but we'll get to that later.

The great thing about studying Canadian politics is that there is always something to talk about—new issues and events arise on a daily basis. In the past decade, Canada has endured a war in Afghanistan, a major economic recession, and the seemingly relentless march of global warming. The Government of Canada has also had to contend with the re-emergence of large fiscal deficits, the transformation of the manufacturing sector in central Canada, the pine beetle devastation in British Columbia, and the near collapse of the fishing industry in Atlantic Canada.

While these and other important issues have deeply affected the lives of Canadians, the Canadian political system has been in a protracted period of flux. There were four general elections between 2004 and 2011, the first three of which did not produce a clear winner. While a clear winner emerged after the election in 2011, the Canadian political system still appears to be in a period of profound transformation.

So what exactly happens on election day in Canada? On election day, we vote for people, who are usually members of a **political party**, to represent us in the **House of Commons**, which is the lower chamber of **Parliament**. The upper chamber of Parliament is called the **Senate**, but it is not a democratic chamber. Senators are appointed by the **governor general** on the advice of the **prime minister**. We will discuss the Senate further in Chapter 6. Getting back to election day, as a general rule the party that elects the most candidates "wins" the election and gets to form the government with its leader as prime minister (although there may be exceptions to this rule, as we will discuss in Chapter 5).

political party An organization designed to get its candidates elected to Parliament. Political parties are the primary connection between voters and Parliament.

House of Commons The lower chamber of parliament where there are 308 members who are elected by the people.

Parliament The legislative branch of government in Canada, consisting of the House of Commons, the Senate, and the Crown.

Senate The upper chamber of Parliament where there are 105 members who are appointed until age 75 by the Crown on the advice of the prime minister.

governor general The Queen's representative in Canada, and formally the head of the executive branch of government.

prime minister The leader of the government in Parliament. By convention, the prime minister is an elected member of the House of Commons.

In the game of Canadian politics, however, not all wins are equal. Some wins are better than others. The goal of every party is to win a *majority* of seats in the House of Commons. There are presently 308 seats in the House of Commons, so each party wants to elect at least 155 candidates. Why? Because all the laws made by Parliament have to be passed by a majority. If the governing party does not have a majority of seats, it has to rely on one or more of the opposition parties to pass its laws. Even more importantly, the Canadian system of government requires the government to maintain the **confidence** of Parliament; in other words, it must be able to command majority support in the House of Commons to stay in office.

When one party wins more than half the seats by itself, it forms a **majority government**. When a party forms the government with fewer than half the seats, it forms a **minority government**. Obviously, it is easier for the government to maintain the confidence of Parliament when it possesses a majority of seats. In the Canadian political system, majority governments are considered "normal," and they are usually very stable. By contrast, minority governments are less common, although some political scientists began thinking about them as the "new normal" after Canadians elected three consecutive minority governments in the 2004, 2006, and 2008 elections (see Table 1.1). Minority governments are typically unstable and relatively short lived, hence the four general elections between 2004 and 2011. With the election of a majority government in 2011, the Canadian political system returned to "normal" in some respects, although in other respects the political landscape looks entirely different, as we will discuss in Chapter 3.

For many Canadians, elections are the most obvious manifestation of politics. But this leads to a very simple question: What is politics? In most societies, politics involves a competition to assume control of the government. If we stop at this point, politics is very boring—it is a fight without a purpose. We must ask ourselves another question: Why would anyone want to assume control of the government? In some societies, it is entirely possible that people might want to take control of the government to acquire personal wealth or glory, but in Canada there are easier ways to get rich or famous. One could, for example, become a hockey player in the National Hockey League. There are 700 players in the NHL, but only one prime minister. The average hockey player makes more than $2 million per year and is adored by fans, while the prime minister makes about $300 000 per year and is abhorred by many voters.

confidence The ability of the government to command majority support in Parliament; it is the first rule of responsible government.

majority government When one political party wins more than half the seats in the House of Commons.

minority government When a political party forms the government with fewer than half the seats in the House of Commons.

Table 1.1 Federal Election Results, 2004–2011: Number of Candidates Elected (or seats won) by Each Party

Party	2004	2006	2008	2011
Conservative Party	99	**124**	**143**	**166**
Liberal Party	**135**	103	77	34
Bloc Québécois	54	51	49	4
NDP	19	29	37	103
Green Party	0	0	0	1
Independents	1	1	2	0
Total Seats	308	308	308	308
Outcome	Minority Liberal Government	Minority Conservative Government	Minority Conservative Government	Majority Conservative Government

So why do people go into politics in Canada? Why would anyone want to assume control of the government for relatively little financial reward and much personal abuse? The answer to this question was provided to us more than 2000 years ago by Plato and Aristotle, who suggested that politics is about a search for the "good life." People want to assume control of the government so that they can implement laws and policies that will enable people in society to live a good life. So the next question is: What is the good life? And this is where the fun begins, because different people have very different ideas about the good life. Should we have the death penalty? Should abortions be made illegal? Should we legalize marijuana? Should hunters have to register their rifles? Should gay and lesbian couples be allowed to marry? The Government of Canada now spends about $300 billion per year, but we still can't afford everything we might like, which leads to more debates. Should we spend more money on health care? Should we spend more on education so university students can graduate with less debt? Or should we cut back on health and education so we can spend more on the military? Should we raise taxes so we can pay for everything we want? Or should the government cut taxes and leave people with more of their own money to spend as they see fit, be it on health care, education, or a new car?

These are emotionally loaded questions with no easy answers. In fact, questions of this sort can lead to intense disagreements and protracted conflicts. Just imagine asking any one of these questions at the family dinner table over the holidays—there would undoubtedly be some pretty serious arguments. The same is true in our political system, both during election campaigns and in Parliament. Fortunately, there are well-established rules in Canada to handle these intense conflicts in a reasonably civilized fashion. The rules of the game, for example, help us determine who has earned the right to assume control of the government. Because these rules are widely accepted, the losers accept their fate and allow the winners to govern. And we follow the laws that are made by the government, even if we didn't vote for the party in power.

Canada is a democracy—meaning rule by the people—but it is not a free-for-all. Canada is a *constitutional* democracy; that is, we are governed by a set of laws. The law is more important than any individual, and the laws of the constitution are the most important of all laws. The constitution is Canada's *master law*—it describes how the entire political and legal system operates. And, just as importantly, all the laws made by the government must conform to the constitution. Laws, including criminal laws, that are found by the courts to be inconsistent with the constitution are null and void—they have no force or effect. Our constitution provides our system of government with stability. The constitution may be changed, but not easily and only by a special set of procedures, which we will discuss in Chapter 9. In Canada, the government not only makes the law, it must also follow the law. This is known as the **rule of law** and it is one of the fundamental characteristics of the Canadian political system. Having governments follow the rule of law is one of the hallmarks of a free society and it only happens in a select number of countries around the world.

The basic rules of the Canadian political game are found in the constitution, but not all of the rules of the game are in the written constitution. Some rules are **statutory laws** (laws made by Parliament) but they flow from the constitution and must be consistent with it. Other rules are part of the *unwritten* constitution inherited from Great Britain. These unwritten or informal rules of the constitution are known as **conventions**. "The informal rules of the constitution do vary considerably. Some rules are more important, more widely accepted, more frequently observed, and more precisely formulated than others."[1] Some conventions are fundamental and must be respected, while others may be viewed as nonbinding **rules of thumb**. Over time, some rules of thumb may emerge as conventions and some might eventually be enshrined in law or entrenched in the constitution, although most will likely remain as simple rules of thumb. Laws of the constitution are the most

rule of law The principle that governments must not only make the law but follow the law as well. It is one of the hallmarks of a free society.

statutory laws The laws made by Parliament.

conventions Unwritten rules of the Canadian political system. Many conventions were inherited from Great Britain's system of responsible government in 1867, while other conventions have emerged in Canada over time through political practice.

rules of thumb Nonbinding, informal unwritten rules. Some rules of thumb may emerge as conventions or become enshrined in law over time.

formal rules of the game and the hardest to change, while rules of thumb are the least formal and the easiest to circumvent (see Figure 1.1).

Constitutional Rules	Statutory Rules	Conventions	Rules of Thumb

<-->

| Most Formal | | Least Formal | |

Figure 1.1 The Rules of the Game

It is important to note that the rules of the game frequently have consequences; sometimes the rules of the game determine how the game is played and sometimes the rules influence the outcome of the game. For example, there are different types of electoral systems. In other words, there are different ways in which we can choose our representatives in Parliament. These different systems produce different results. For example, in the last few elections the Green Party has received more than half-a-million votes, but it has only ever elected one candidate to Parliament—leader Elizabeth May won a seat in the 2011 election. With a different electoral system, we could see as many as 20 or 30 members of the Green Party elected to Parliament, even if the Green Party did not appreciably increase its total number of votes. This may seem puzzling, but I will elaborate on this in Chapter 4. For the moment, let me just stress that *the rules of the game are not neutral*. The rules of the game shape how the game of politics is played, as we shall see as we work our way through the different aspects of the Canadian political system. Technically speaking, an analysis of the rules of the game and their effects is known as the **institutional approach** to the study of politics, in contrast to sociological, economic, or historical approaches. Good political analysis, however, incorporates all of these elements. It is a question of emphasis, rather than focusing on one dimension at the expense of the others.

There is a substantial consensus in Canada that our democracy is fundamentally sound and that the rules of the game work pretty well and are generally fair. But the game of politics is not perfect, and part of the political debate in Canada is about changing the rules of the game to make it more fair. Changing the rules of the game is not simple, and nobody knows exactly how rule changes will affect the game of politics—there is always the risk of unintended consequences. Changing the rules of the game is thus an extremely difficult proposition and much more important than ordinary policy decisions about taxation or new criminal laws. Rule changes are fundamental because they define the game—change the rules, and you change the game. Debates over rule changes in politics are thus very intense, emotional, and protracted. As this book progresses, we will examine a number of key political debates about policies and rule changes. While citizens frequently become frustrated and impatient with these never-ending debates, we should appreciate how civilized these debates are given the intensity of the subjects involved, such as the separation of Quebec from Canada or the creation of Aboriginal self-government.

There are frequently no right answers in politics. We debate issues at length not to get the "right" answer but to reach a sufficient social consensus so that we can proceed in a particular direction without tearing the country apart. In other societies, these issues can and do lead to civil war. While nobody expects civil war to erupt here, it is widely believed that Canada is a rather fragile country with not much holding it together. Despite its vast and rugged territory, in political terms Canada is not a vast country at all. The overwhelming majority of Canadians live within a few hundred kilometres of the US border. In a very real sense, the country is built on a string some 5000 kilometres long, and it is not beyond the scope of imagination to think that the string might be cut into several pieces. We thus need to proceed very cautiously when it comes to fundamental issues and rule changes.

In sum, politics is about conflicts over the good life and the right way to govern society. The rules of the game are designed to manage conflict in a civilized fashion, but they *are not designed to eliminate conflict*, because in a free society people are encouraged to voice their differing opinions. While Canadians are frequently turned off by the political fighting in Ottawa, it is helpful to remember that societies without political conflicts are governed by

institutional approach One type of approach used in the study of politics that analyzes the rules of the game and their effects on the political system.

totalitarian regimes. There is no political conflict in North Korea, for example, because anyone who speaks out is arrested and shot. There will always be disagreements over what constitutes the good life, and we need vigorous debates on the meaning of the good life to determine what path to follow. The key is to have these debates in a civilized fashion, and that is what the rules of the game are intended to accomplish.

totalitarian regimes Governments that maintain total control over the societies they govern. They are typically led by a single dictator.

So it is important for us all to learn the rules of the game. If we don't know the rules, we can't follow the game. And this is a game we need to know. Just about every facet of our life depends on politics. It determines university tuition fees and is responsible for providing health care and setting taxes (among many, many other things). The beauty of living in a democracy is that we get to have a say in how these issues will be resolved, which makes us enormously lucky and privileged to live in a democratic country. We derive all sorts of benefits from living in a democracy, but it requires engaged citizens to make it work. If citizens do not take an active interest in politics, democracy can stagnate and wither and we would lose all of the good things that come with living in a democratic political system. Citizens thus carry a huge responsibility, and each of us needs to play our part to make democracy work. For us to assume our democratic responsibilities we need to learn the basic rules of the game, we must follow the political news of the day, and we must discuss politics with our family, friends, and neighbours.

There are, of course, many players in the game of politics. Conceptually, the players in the game of politics may be divided into three groups. In the first group, there are voters, political leaders, and political parties. In the second group we have the bureaucracy, the courts, and other governments (most especially the provincial and territorial governments). In the last group, there are a variety of players, including the media, advocacy groups, religious organizations, unions, corporations and business associations, and nonprofit organizations. In this book, due to time and space limitations, we will focus primarily on the players in the first and second groups, but we must still bear in mind that the players in the third group are critically important in the game of politics. For example, much of the political game in Canada is played through the media, which shapes our very understanding of politics. The other players in the third group are equally important, albeit in different ways.

Confederation and the British North America Act of 1867

The constitution is at the heart of the Canadian political system. Unfortunately, the Canadian constitution is an enormously complex thing. It is partly a written document and partly unwritten, following British constitutional conventions. The modern written constitution consists of two main parts—the Constitution Act 1867 and the Constitution Act 1982 (see Appendices A and B)—but pre-Confederation documents such as the Royal Proclamation of 1763, the Quebec Act of 1774, the Constitutional Act of 1791, and the 1840 Act of Union still have symbolic importance in Canada, and in some cases legal significance, as we will discuss in later chapters. Most confusingly, perhaps, the Canadian constitution has always been a work in progress, and in important respects it remains an unfinished project. Quebec has never officially endorsed the Constitution Act 1982, which includes the Charter of Rights and Freedoms; Aboriginal peoples are still seeking the promise of self-government contained in Part II of the Constitution Act 1982; and there is considerable dissatisfaction among many Canadians with our national governing institutions, most notably the Senate.

Canada's constitutional history is very different from that of the United States. The Americans wrote a short and snappy constitution more than 200 years ago, and it is a highly valued document not to be toyed with. The American constitution was the product of its revolution—its clean break from the United Kingdom—and the unity of the American people. Canada has never had a revolution; it separated from Great Britain gradually and never completely. The Queen is still the head of the Canadian state. The Canadian constitution reflects this long linkage to the United Kingdom, and unlike the United States the people of Canada have never been completely united. We have been thrown together by history, and we are still not entirely sure that we constitute a single people.

If we do not *constitute* a single people, it is very difficult to design a *constitution* to govern us. Canada has debated its constitution for most of its existence. The constitutional debate in Canada is not merely a technical or legal question about this or that provision. At the root of these debates is the existential question "Who are we?" We will explore these debates more fully in later chapters. For now, all we need to know is that the cornerstone of the Canadian constitution is the British North America (BNA) Act, which came into effect on July 1, 1867; this is what we celebrate on Canada Day. The BNA Act is now officially called the "Constitution Act 1867." This constitutional document created the new country of Canada and outlined the two governing principles of the Canadian political system: **responsible government** and **federalism**. The Constitution Act 1982 added two more principles to the Canadian political order: a set of constitutionally protected rights and the recognition of Aboriginal rights.

Why was the new country born in 1867? As British colonies of North America moved into the 1860s, a couple of things were happening. Most alarmingly, a violent civil war erupted in the United States in 1861, which raged on until 1865 when the Union army finally defeated the Confederate army of the southern states. To defeat the south, President Lincoln had to amass a large army. When it became apparent that the Union was going to be victorious, many in the British North American colonies began to fear that Lincoln would turn his army north and invade them. While the prospect of an American invasion of Canada might seem far-fetched to us now, it was not beyond the imagination of British North American colonists in the 1860s. The American Revolutionary Army occupied the city of Montreal in the winter of 1775 before being chased away by the British the following spring; in the war of 1812 the Americans once again attempted to invade Upper Canada; in the 1840s the prospect of war rose again as the two countries argued over the border in the western part of the continent. In this last instance, war was only avoided when Great Britain and the United States agreed that the border should run along the forty-ninth parallel.

With fears of war looming again, the Maritime colonies (New Brunswick, Nova Scotia, and Prince Edward Island) decided to meet in Charlottetown in September 1864 to discuss the possibility of forming a political union. Sir John A. Macdonald and other representatives from

responsible government The Canadian system of government (inherited from Great Britain) in which ministers are responsible to Parliament and the Crown.

federalism A system of government with two constitutionally entrenched orders of government. One government is responsible for matters pertaining to the entire country, and the other order of government provides a range of services at a more local level. In Canada, the two orders of government are the 10 provinces and the federal government in Ottawa. (The territories are separate entities under the authority of the federal government).

The idea of Confederation was born in Charlottetown in September 1864, when John A. Macdonald (sitting centre) and his colleagues from Canada met their counterparts from the three Maritime colonies. It was an inauspicious beginning: The circus was in town and the politicians were all but ignored by the local population.

Table 1.2 Entrance of Provinces into Confederation

Province	Entry into Confederation
Ontario	1867
Quebec	1867
Nova Scotia	1867
New Brunswick	1867
Manitoba	1870
British Columbia	1871
Prince Edward Island	1873
Alberta	1905
Saskatchewan	1905
Newfoundland	1949

the United Province of Canada—at this time the combined Upper and Lower Canada or what we now know as Ontario and Quebec—invited themselves to the meeting and proposed that they collectively form a political union, and the Maritimes agreed. In October 1864, delegates from all the colonies met in Quebec City (Newfoundland came too) and drafted what became the British North America Act, although it took three more years to come into effect. We don't need to worry about all the twists and turns between 1864 and 1867, except to note that in the end Prince Edward Island and Newfoundland opted not to join the new country. On July 1, 1867, four provinces formed Canada: Ontario, Quebec, Nova Scotia, and New Brunswick. The other six provinces joined Confederation over the next 70 years (see Table 1.2).

The BNA Act has proven to be a very robust constitution, especially for a "country" that burned through four "constitutions" prior to Confederation. The BNA Act was the first constitution written *for* Canada *by* Canadians—this is one reason why it has been a relatively successful constitution. Previous constitutions (the Royal Proclamation of 1763, the Quebec Act of 1774, the Constitutional Act of 1791, and the 1840 Act of Union) were written *by* the British *for* Canadians. But while Canadians wrote the constitution for themselves, it is important to understand that the BNA Act was a law made by the Parliament of Great Britain. In short, the Fathers of Confederation drafted the constitution, took it to London, and the government of Great Britain passed it into law. Canada was thus one of the only "independent" countries in the world that did not own its own constitution. As a law of Great Britain, it could only be changed by the British Parliament. It also meant that a British court was the final authority for interpreting the Canadian constitution—even after the Supreme Court of Canada was created in 1875. Indeed, the Judicial Committee of the Privy Council in London remained the final court of appeal for Canadian cases until 1949, at which time the Supreme Court of Canada finally became the supreme interpreter of the Canadian constitution.

In many respects, then, Canada remained a colony of Great Britain long after 1867. This is how the Fathers of Confederation in Canada wanted it—they could not imagine that Canadians would ever want to be independent of the Mother Country. As we will see, the time came when Canadians did want to be independent from Great Britain and to bring the constitution back home, but that proved to be complicated. Britain was willing to give the constitution back to Canada after World War I, but Canadians were not ready to take it, for reasons that we will explore in Chapter 8. The constitution did not, in fact, come back home until 1982, and even then it almost tore the country apart. Canada has its own constitution now, but the country's master law remains unfinished, as we will see in Chapter 11.

Governing Principles of the Constitution Act 1867

As mentioned earlier, the Constitution Act 1867 (see Appendix A) is the cornerstone of the Canadian constitution. As such, it lays out the basic rules for the game of Canadian politics. So, before we can go any further, we need to see what the BNA Act says. The preamble to the BNA Act reads as follows:

> The Provinces of Canada, Nova Scotia, and New Brunswick have expressed their Desire to be federally united into One Dominion under the Crown of the United Kingdom of Great Britain and Ireland, with a constitution similar in principle to that of the United Kingdom.

What does it mean then to have "a constitution similar in principle to that of the United Kingdom"? It means mostly that Canada will be governed according to the conventions of the British parliamentary system of responsible government. As the British Parliament is located at Westminster, it is also called the Westminster form of parliamentary government. But the Constitution Act 1867 also indicates that we are to be "federally united" into one "Dominion." This means that Canada will have a federal form of government—that is, there will be a Government of Canada that is responsible for certain matters, but we also have 10 provincial governments responsible for other matters.

Responsible Government

The parliamentary form of government in Canada is almost identical to the British system of responsible parliamentary government, with a few modifications in accordance with the social reality of Canada. There is no aristocracy in Canada, so the second chamber of Parliament in Canada is styled as a Senate rather than a House of Lords, and the governor general serves in place of the Queen in Canada. The provisions for responsible government in Canada are found in Sections 9 to 57 of the Constitution Act 1867, but these sections do not spell out the various aspects of responsible government in great detail. (Sections 58 to 90 explain how the principles of responsible government are applied to each of the provinces.)

The British system of responsible government has existed for hundreds of years, and it operates largely according to tradition and convention. When Canada adopted the British parliamentary form of government, it adopted the same traditions and conventions. As these conventions were so well known, the Fathers of Confederation did not see any need to write them down in the constitution. But these traditions and conventions form part of the Canadian constitutional order—they are part of Canada's unwritten constitution.

Responsible government is a difficult thing to describe because it means quite a bit more than the actual words imply. The idea of responsible government embodies about 800 years of British history, and we can only really come to terms with the idea of responsible government by examining this history, albeit very briefly. We must first go all the way back to the start of the thirteenth century, when King John of England got in trouble with the aristocracy for spending too much money on war. In 1215, the aristocracy forced the King to make a deal, known as the Magna Carta, in which the King agreed not to tax the aristocracy without consultation. This consultation was to take place in a Great Council. By the end of the thirteenth century the Great Council had been transformed into a Parliament (which means a place to talk, from the French verb *parler*), but Parliament was still reserved for the aristocracy. Common people also wanted to be represented in Parliament because they were taxed as well, but it was not socially acceptable for ordinary people to sit with the aristocracy. So, a few decades later, Parliament was divided into a House of Lords for the aristocracy and a House of Commons for the commoners. We thus say that the British—and Canadian—Parliament is a **bicameral**, or two-chamber, legislature.

bicameral legislature A legislature that has two chambers. The Parliament of Canada is a bicameral legislature: The House of Commons is the elected lower chamber, and the Senate is the appointed upper chamber.

Up to the end of the seventeenth century, Britain was governed by the King in consultation with his ministers in Parliament. To make a long story short, the roles became reversed after the Glorious Revolution of 1688, after which Britain was governed by the ministers in Parliament in consultation with the King. It was as if the King said to his ministers in Parliament, "I am tired of governing the country, so I am going to give you the *responsibility* of governing the country in my name." When the King transferred responsibility of governing to his ministers, he said to them: "I will assume that you are governing responsibly so long as you maintain the *confidence* of Parliament." So long as the ministers could command the support of the majority in Parliament, the King would assume that they possessed the *confidence* of Parliament. Maintaining the confidence of Parliament is thus the first rule of responsible government.

This is not exactly how the Glorious Revolution unfolded, but it does explain how the idea of responsible government emerged and how Great Britain was transformed from an absolute monarchy to a constitutional monarchy. It is important to stress that the principles of responsible government and constitutional monarchy did not emerge in a single year; in fact, they were not fully articulated as we understand them today until about 150 years after the Glorious Revolution. During the eighteenth century and even into the nineteenth century, the prime minister and the other ministers of the government tended to sit in the more "dignified" House of Lords, as befitting the primary advisers to the Crown. Over the course of the nineteenth century, as Britain became more democratic, the convention emerged that the prime minister should sit in the House of Commons, along with most other ministers in the government. By the time Confederation happened in Canada in 1867, the principles of responsible government were well established, so there was no need to codify them in the constitution.

In sum, responsible government entailed the transfer of governing responsibility from the Crown to Parliament, or more accurately, to the Crown's ministers in Parliament. As the role of the Crown in Britain is spelled out mostly in constitutional conventions (and a few key documents), we can say that the Crown is now a constitutional monarchy. While in a modern democracy everyone wants the government to be responsible to the people, it is important to remember that the principles of responsible government speak mostly to the relationship between the Crown and Parliament. All government business in Canada is still done in the name of the Crown. The Crown is thus not an irrelevant figurehead from a bygone era. Indeed, the "invisible crown" has been described as the "first principle of Canadian government."[2]

What does responsible government mean for Canadians today in practical terms? After an election, as a general rule, the Crown designates the leader of the party with the most seats as the prime minister, and the prime minister chooses the other ministers. The job of the prime minister is to lead the government; the other ministers are responsible for particular aspects of the government. The Finance Minister is responsible for the government's finances, the Defence Minister is responsible for the military, the Foreign Affairs Minister is responsible for Canada's relations with other countries, and so on. In short, Canada has a government of ministers, and it is therefore formally referred to as a *ministry*.

As we have seen, the first principle of responsible government is that the ministry must maintain the confidence of Parliament. That is, the ministry must be able to command the support of a majority of the elected members of the House of Commons. As mentioned above, when the governing party wins a majority of seats in the House of Commons, it is relatively easy for the government to maintain the confidence of the House. When the governing party has less than a majority of seats, it requires the support of one or more of the opposition parties to maintain the confidence of the House. This is a trickier proposition, and consequently minority governments tend to be more short lived than majority governments. Historically, majority governments have lasted about four years, while minority governments typically last about 18 months. Under the system of responsible government, ministers also have individual and collective responsibilities, as we will discuss in Chapter 5. As mentioned, the principles of responsible government date back a couple of centuries, and at least some of these principles have come under a certain amount of strain in the modern context of Canadian (and British) politics. We will examine these stresses and strains more closely in Chapters 5 and 6.

Federalism

Although Canada was supposed to have a constitution similar in principle to that of the United Kingdom, the Constitution Act 1867 indicated that Canada was to be "federally united," even though modern constitutional federalism is an American invention. The Canadian political system is thus a blend of British and American institutions. What is federalism? In a federal political system, there are two constitutionally entrenched orders of government that are both supreme—or **sovereign**—in their spheres of jurisdiction. In Canada, we have the federal government in Ottawa that governs the whole country in certain matters, and we have 10 provincial governments responsible for other matters (we will talk about the territories below). The powers of the federal government (e.g., the military and making criminal law) are detailed in Section 91 of the Constitution Act 1867, and the powers of the provincial governments (e.g., education and health care) are listed in Section 92.

In most federal political systems, and Canada is no exception, it is inevitable that there will be conflicts between the two orders of government over who is responsible for certain laws. In part, this was because the Fathers of Confederation could not imagine everything that might happen in the future. How could the Fathers of Confederation assign responsibility for the Internet in 1867? The same goes for radio, television, and air transportation, among other things. Disputes over jurisdiction are resolved by the courts, ultimately the Supreme Court. The courts thus have an important role to play in Canada.

As in most federations, there are frequent disputes over money between the two orders of government in Canada. It is simply impossible to devise a system in which both orders of government have sufficient revenues to finance their various responsibilities independently. Federalism thus entails the sharing of fiscal resources between the two orders of government and the transfer of money from one to another, usually from the central government to the provinces. Federalism is most frequently adopted in diverse societies, and it is intended to provide *unity with diversity*. However, it is sometimes difficult to obtain the right balance between these two objectives. Canada has certainly struggled with questions of unity over the years.

Without dwelling too much on federalism now, we should stress that the two orders of government in Canada are wholly separate political authorities. We have elections to choose our representatives in the federal Parliament in Ottawa, and we have separate elections to choose representatives for the provincial legislatures. (Provincial elections are restricted to citizens residing in each province. For example, only Albertans vote for representatives in the legislature in Edmonton, and only Quebecers vote for representatives in the National Assembly in Quebec City.) Within their spheres of jurisdiction, both orders of government are sovereign. That is, each order of government reigns supreme in its area of jurisdiction, and neither order of government is subordinate to the other. The provincial premiers do not work for or at the behest of the prime minister of Canada. As we will see in Chapter 7, however, the two orders of government frequently have to work together collaboratively to provide services like health care to Canadians. This is the mysterious world of **intergovernmental relations**.

Before concluding this section, it should be noted that there are other types of government in the Canadian political system, such as territorial, municipal, and Aboriginal. The territorial and municipal governments, however, are *not* sovereign governments. In many respects, the three territorial governments look like the 10 provincial governments, but they exist under the authority of the federal government. Likewise, the municipal governments exist under the legislative authority of the provincial governments. The boundaries

sovereign Literally means "supreme power."

intergovernmental relations The interaction between the different governments in a federation, especially between the federal government and the provinces, but also between provinces and municipalities, Aboriginal peoples and governments of all levels, and even relationships across the border with state governments.

and powers of territorial and municipal governments can thus be changed by the federal government and the provinces respectively, whereas the boundaries and powers of the provinces flow directly from the constitution. As such, the provinces are much more significant players in the game of Canadian politics than the territories or municipalities, even though our biggest cities are larger than many of the provinces. The City of Toronto, for example, has a population greater than at least six of the provinces and an economy that is twice as big as Saskatchewan's, but it does not have constitutional status or power.

The question of Aboriginal government is more complicated. Under Section 91.24 of the Constitution Act 1867, the federal government is responsible for "Indians, and Lands reserved for the Indians." Band councils and Aboriginal people who live on reserves are governed by the **Indian Act**, which was first enacted by the Parliament of Canada in 1876 and has been revised from time to time since. Aboriginal people quite understandably resent this enduring colonial paternalism of the Canadian state, and many are seeking to establish their own sovereign governments under the Canadian constitution. The Constitution Act 1982 recognized and affirmed the existence of Aboriginal rights, and many legal scholars believe that this includes an inherent right to self-government, but little progress has been made to establish truly sovereign Aboriginal governments in Canada. The Nisga'a government of northwestern British Columbia is a notable exception. We will examine the issue of Aboriginal government in Chapter 10.

Indian Act Federal legislation that defines the legal status of Indian peoples in Canada and regulates the management of Indian lands and reserves.

A Brief Overview of This Book

The Canadian political system can be somewhat daunting for the uninitiated, so the first half of this book will examine the principles and practices of Canadian politics from the perspective of a first-time voter. Most people enter the Canadian political system for the first time when a political party comes asking for their vote during an election, so that is where we will begin. In the next chapter, we will briefly survey the enduring themes in Canadian political culture and the contours of Canadian political geography. Subsequent chapters will examine, in order, parties, elections, and the formation of a government. With a government formed, the next order of business in the Canadian political system is to convene Parliament, which will be the subject of Chapter 6. In this fashion, we are following what might be viewed as a natural political cycle from election to the formation of a government to the role of Parliament in governing the country and back to another election. In Chapter 7 we will turn our attention to federalism, the second major governing principle of the Constitution Act 1867. As federalism is a constitutional concept, Chapter 7 will serve as a bridge back to the constitution and will set up the third part of the book, which will examine the new governing principles introduced with the Constitution Act 1982 and the politics of constitutional reform. It is probably impossible to learn and remember all of the rules of the game from reading a single book since politics is ultimately a dialogue. The most effective way to learn the rules is to jump into the game by following politics in the media and discussing it with your family and friends. I encourage you to take the plunge now.

SUMMARY

Canada is a constitutional democracy. The British North America Act—now known as the Constitution Act 1867—provides the foundation for Canada's political system. While the constitution outlines the most important rules of the game, other rules are laid out in *statutory laws* made by Parliament, while others exist in the more informal realm of *convention*, and some are no more than *rules of thumb* that may or may not always be followed. The BNA

Act contains two governing principles: the British system of *responsible government* and *federalism*. The first rule of responsible government is that the government must maintain the confidence of Parliament. And with federalism we have two orders of government in Canada: the federal government for the whole country and 10 provinces, each with their own set of constitutional responsibilities.

Questions to Think About

1. What makes up the "good life" in Canada? What needs to be done to make the good life in Canada better?
2. Should voting in Canadian elections be mandatory?
3. What does the idea of "responsible government" mean to you?

Learning Outcomes

1. Explain the difference between a minority and majority government.
2. Define the rule of law.
3. Identify the different kinds of rules in the game of Canadian politics.
4. Describe the principal features of responsible government and federalism.

Additional Readings

Janet Ajzenstat et al., *Canada's Founding Debates* (Toronto, ON: University of Toronto Press, 2003).

Walter Bagehot, *The English Constitution* (Cambridge, UK: Cambridge University Press, 2001).

Anthony Birch, *Representative and Responsible Government: An Essay on the English Constitution* (London, UK: Allen and Unwin, 1964).

Donald Creighton, *The Road to Confederation: The Emergence of Canada, 1863–1867* (Toronto, ON: Macmillan, 1964).

Andrew Heard, *Canadian Constitutional Conventions: The Marriage of Law and Politics* (Toronto, ON: Oxford University Press, 1991).

David E. Smith, *The Invisible Crown: The First Principle of Canadian Government* (Toronto, ON: University of Toronto Press, 1995).

Notes

1. Andrew Heard, *Canadian Constitutional Conventions: The Marriage of Law and Politics* (Toronto, ON: Oxford University Press, 1991), 149. Professor Heard has classified five types of conventions on a sliding scale of importance: fundamental conventions, meso-conventions, semi-conventions, infra-conventions, and customary usages. The last two categories fall outside the standard definition of convention and are roughly analogous to what I am calling "rules of thumb."
2. David E. Smith, *The Invisible Crown: The First Principle of Canadian Government* (Toronto, ON: University of Toronto Press, 1995).

Chapter 2
The Political Culture of Canada

Key Points

- Political culture refers to the sum total of political values, attitudes, and beliefs in a country.

- Canadian political culture is characterized by a substantial consensus on the rules of the game: the rule of law, democracy, equality, individual rights, and respect for minorities.

- Canadians frequently disagree on what laws and policies governments should adopt based on their different conceptions of the good life.

- The different conceptions of the good life can be bundled into a few distinct groupings of ideas known as ideologies, such as liberalism, conservatism, and socialism.

- The main ideologies in Canadian politics are represented to a greater or lesser degree by political parties.

- The ideological landscape—and the support for the major political parties—varies from region to region across the country and among different subgroups in Canadian society, such as distinct linguistic, ethnic, or religious groups as well as groups defined by class and gender.

Canadian politics, like politics in other societies, is a public conflict over different conceptions of the good life. Canadians agree on some important matters (e.g., Canadians are overwhelmingly committed to the rule of law, democracy, equality, individual rights, and respect for minorities) and disagree on others. That Canadians share certain values represents a substantial consensus about how the political system should work. While Canadians generally agree on the rules of the game, they disagree—sometimes very strongly—on what laws and policies the government should adopt. Should governments spend more or less? Should taxes be lower or higher? Should governments build more prisons or more hospitals?

Fortunately for students of politics, different conceptions of the good life are not random. The different views on what laws and policies are appropriate to realize the good life coalesce into a few distinct groupings of ideas known as **ideologies**. These ideologies have names that are familiar to you, such as *liberalism*, *conservatism*, and (democratic) *socialism*, which are the principal ideologies in Canadian politics. More radical ideologies, such as Marxism, communism, and fascism, are at best only marginally present in Canada.

It is quite common to map ideologies on a continuum from left to right (see Figure 2.1). Newer ideologies like feminism and environmentalism do not fit comfortably on the left–right continuum. Many feminists and environmentalists are on the left side of the spectrum, but others are on the right side. There are certainly feminists and environmentalists in all of the major political parties in Canada, including the Conservative Party of Canada.

ideologies Specific bundles of ideas about politics and the good life, such as liberalism, conservatism, and socialism. Ideologies help people explain political phenomena, they allow people to evaluate good and bad, and they equip people with a program or agenda for political action.

Figure 2.1 The Ideological Spectrum

political culture The sum total of political beliefs in a country. It includes the attitudes, beliefs, and values that underpin the political system.

When we talk about the totality of political beliefs in Canada, we are talking about the country's **political culture**. The political culture of Canada, however, varies from region to region, and it also varies among identifiable groups of Canadians. The political culture of Quebec, for example, is very different from the rest of Canada. But, even in the rest of Canada, there are stark differences between the West, Ontario, Atlantic Canada, and the North. Urban and rural Canadians also see the world of politics in different terms; men and women exhibit different political beliefs, at least to some extent, as do Canadians of different religious and ethnic heritages; the rich and the poor clearly have different political interests; young and old Canadians also have different concerns and priorities. With all of these differences, Canadians are often deeply divided on major political issues. It is thus difficult for political parties to develop platforms (a set of policies) that will appeal to all Canadians, as will be discussed in the next chapter.

Ideologies

An ideology represents a particular conception of the good life. More precisely, an ideology is a relatively coherent and comprehensive set of ideas about the world of politics.[1] An ideology helps people *explain* political phenomena, it allows people to *evaluate* good and bad, and it equips people with a *program* or *agenda* for political action. Political phenomena are not intrinsically good or bad. Whether something is good or bad depends largely on one's prior beliefs, values, and principles. In sum, an ideology provides us with a way to understand the world and how to respond to it by elevating our gut feelings to more or less rational beliefs, thus providing us with a "worldview."

Before proceeding, three important points must be made: (1) ideologies are not perfectly logical or consistent, (2) ideologies can and do change over time, and (3) nobody adheres perfectly to a single ideology. A liberal, for example, might have some conservative beliefs and vice versa. This is especially true in Canadian politics, where the different ideologies tend to represent overlapping sets of ideas rather than radically distinct worldviews.

Liberalism and Conservatism

At the time of Confederation, liberalism and conservatism were the main political ideologies in Canada. These ideologies have evolved over the years, and they have spawned new variants, which we will discuss momentarily. For now, we will focus on the old liberalism and the old conservatism, or *classical* liberalism and *tory* conservatism as they are sometimes called. As you might guess, the essence of liberalism is *liberty*. Liberalism is about freedom—the freedom to live without interference from the government. For liberals, society is a collection of individuals, thus liberalism is the ideology of *individual freedom*. By contrast, conservatives historically focused on the *community*. Conservatism, as the name implies, is about *conservation*. More particularly, conservatives want to conserve a society's traditional way of life, and they are especially keen to maintain social *order* in the community. These differences are summarized in Figure 2.2.

Figure 2.2 The Foundations of Liberalism and Conservatism

There is more to liberalism and conservatism, as will be explored below, but already we can begin to see the sources of political conflict. Liberals want to maximize liberty for individuals, while conservatives want to ensure order in the community. Let's take a simple issue that has been debated in many communities across Canada. A number of cities in Canada have installed video surveillance cameras in public places with the objective of reducing crime. Do you think this is a good or bad idea? Your answer depends on your prior values. Liberals argue that public surveillance cameras constitute an unacceptable infringement on individual freedom, while conservatives argue that they are a perfectly legitimate way to maintain social order in the community. Liberals argue that the essence of living in a free society means being able to move around in public without the government watching or knowing about it; conservatives stress the importance of being able to move around the community safely. There are no right answers to this question; people evaluate the scheme by using their ideology.

Liberals and conservatives value more than just individual liberty and well-ordered communities. Liberals believe in the *equality* of all individuals. Historically, conservatives believed that there was a natural social *hierarchy*, with the King at the top and peasants at the bottom. In the conservative view, the pursuit of equality would upset this "natural" hierarchy and create disorder in the community. For conservatives, it was important for everyone to know his or her place in society and not to disrupt this natural order. Modern conservatives now generally believe in the principle of equality, although they still tend to be more deferential to authority than liberals. Liberals believe that knowledge is obtained through the power of *reason*, whereas for conservatives knowledge is derived from *tradition*.

Historically, liberals believed very much in *competition*—this was the route to progress. For liberals, wealth is generated by having entrepreneurs compete in the marketplace. How will a cure for cancer be found? By scientists competing to win a Nobel Prize. Conservatives, on the other hand, historically feared that competition would upset the natural order of things. Conservatives thus historically favoured *cooperation*. While conservatives expected those of low social standing to know their place in society and not disrupt the social order, they also expected the wealthy to contribute to the well-being of the less fortunate. This was the theory of *noblesse oblige*, or the idea that privilege entails responsibility. In short, conservatives viewed society organically, with each part playing its role. Liberals, on the other hand, tend to view society as a social construct—something created by people. In the liberal view, social injustices are not natural or organic, they are human made. If society was made by humans in the first place, humans can improve society by consciously eliminating injustices (see Figure 2.3).

Figure 2.3 The Principles of Liberalism and Conservatism

Now that we have a more complete picture of liberalism and conservatism, we are in a position to examine a more complex political conflict, such as same-sex marriage. When gay and lesbian couples were not permitted to marry, liberals argued that the state was not treating these individuals equally, and reason told them that no harm was done by two adult men or two adult women marrying each other. Conservatives, on the other hand, argued that marriage has traditionally been defined as a union between a man and a woman, and they feared that altering this definition of marriage would upset the natural order, which would have unknown consequences for the community. Liberals and conservatives, if they are being faithful to their respective ideologies, will never agree on the issue of same-sex marriage, because they are committed to different values and principles.

Some of you may not recognize the picture that has been drawn of liberals and conservatives. That's because ideologies change over time. Here we have sketched out the *old* versions of liberalism and conservatism. While many Canadians describe themselves as liberals or conservatives, few people now adhere strictly to the tenets of classical liberalism or tory conservatism. Ideologies change over time because new information causes people to change their worldview.

Democratic Socialism and Neo-Conservatism

Over the course of the twentieth century, new ideologies emerged in Canada. During the Great Depression in the 1930s the ideas of democratic socialism took root, and in the 1970s a new form of conservatism, neo-conservatism, emerged. In very simple terms, democratic socialism and neo-conservatism can each be understood as a different synthesis of classical liberalism and tory conservatism. Each of these ideologies, in other words, represents a different blending or combination of liberal and conservative principles. In the process, classical liberalism and tory conservatism were modified as well. Some would describe modern Canadian liberalism as a light version of democratic socialism; similarly, tory conservatism is now perhaps just a light version of neo-conservatism.

At the end of the nineteenth century, largely in response to Marxism, individuals with a concern for equality became distressed by the high levels of economic disparity in Canadian society. They feared that economic inequality would lead to social unrest and instability in the community. These individuals also reasoned that liberty was meaningless if people did not have the means to enjoy a good life. The freedom to own a house is no freedom at all unless you have the money to purchase it or at least to be in a position to borrow the money from a bank. Individuals inclined to this view therefore argued that the state ought to take positive steps to ensure that each individual had the means to realize a good life. This represented a rethinking of the theory of *noblesse oblige:* Instead of relying on the nobility to provide charity to the less fortunate, these individuals argued that the state had an obligation to look after the needs of all individuals equally and to instill a spirit of cooperation in the community. In short, these new thinkers borrowed elements from liberalism and conservatism to produce a new ideological synthesis, which we can call democratic socialism (as opposed to Marxist socialism or revolutionary communism; see Figure 2.4).

The ideas of democratic socialism flourished in the 1930s largely as a result of the Great Depression, when many believed that Marx's theory about the collapse of capitalism was

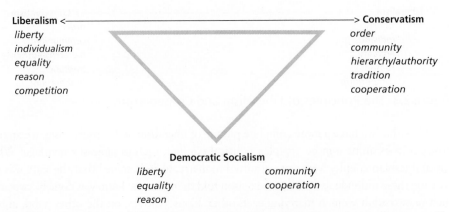

Figure 2.4 A Synthesis of Liberalism and Conservatism gave rise to Democratic Socialism in the late 19th Century

Source: Nelson Wiseman, "Political Parties," in *Canadian Politics in the 1990s*, eds. Michael S. Whittington and Glen Williams (Toronto, ON: ITP Nelson, 1995).

coming true. In response, the Government of Canada established a variety of programs including unemployment insurance and old-age pensions. After World War II, these programs were accompanied by hospital insurance, medical insurance, and a more elaborate pension plan. By the end of the 1960s, Canada had established a reasonably comprehensive social welfare state.

The development of the welfare state proved to be more expensive than anticipated, and the financial burden on the state was compounded in the 1970s when the economy took a turn for the worse. The Government of Canada was forced to borrow considerable sums of money to continue providing services to Canadians, which resulted in a large debt that still has not been paid off. In response, a new ideological synthesis emerged. Some people began to argue that the state could not afford to be an economic backstop for all members of society, and they argued that the government should seek to develop wealth by fostering competition in the marketplace. These ideas were drawn from the principles of classical liberalism, but at the same time there was also a moral backlash against what was perceived as the pleasure-seeking behaviour of the 1960s. The market principles of classical liberalism were thus joined with conservative notions of tradition and respect for authority. This is the ideology of neo-conservatism (see Figure 2.5). It should be noted that a small number of people advocated a return to market principles *without* the baggage of traditional conservative values. These individuals don't care who you sleep with or what you do in your spare time (as long as you don't cause harm to anyone else). In short, they are modern adherents of classical liberalism, but rather than being called old liberals they are known as **neo-liberals or libertarians**.

neo-liberals or libertarians
Modern adherents of classical liberalism.

Canada's debate over the future of health care demonstrates the conflict between the principles of democratic socialism and neo-conservatism. Health care in Canada is a responsibility of the provinces, although the federal government provides considerable financial support, as we will discuss in Chapter 7. In most provinces, health care now consumes almost half of the budget, and this proportion is steadily increasing. Social democrats argue that Canadians have a right to a universal, publicly financed health care system. They argue that a public system provides better health outcomes and is less expensive than a private health care system. Neo-conservatives, on the other hand, argue that the provision of a public health care system is

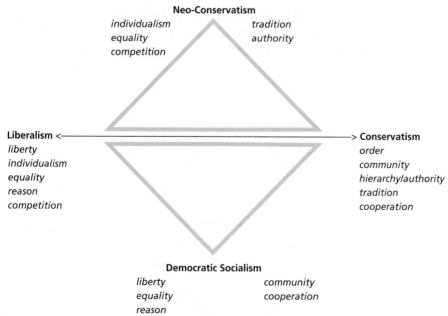

Figure 2.5 A Synthesis of Liberalism and Conservatism gave rise to Neo-Conservatism in the second half of the 20th Century

Source: Hamish Telford, "The Reform Party/Canadian Alliance and Canada's Flirtation with Republicanism," in *Canada: The State of the Federation 2001: Canadian Political Culture(s) in Transition,* eds. Hamish Telford and Harvey Lazar (Kingston, ON: Institute of Intergovernmental Relations, 2002).

increasingly a burden on government finances and that these costs must be brought under control, primarily by allowing more private health care options in the marketplace. If the social democratic view of health care is to prevail, taxes will surely have to increase, perhaps substantially. If the neo-conservative position prevails, the health care system may be privatized entirely.

Ideology and the Political Parties in Canada

The major ideological traditions at play in Canadian politics are represented by the main political parties, albeit imperfectly. Liberalism is, of course, represented by the Liberal Party, although the liberalism of the Liberal Party today is a cross between classical liberalism and democratic socialism. Many members of the Liberal Party lean "left" toward the principles of democratic socialism, but the Liberal Party has always had a "blue" contingent with strong ties to business. Former Prime Minister Paul Martin is a good example of a "blue" Liberal.

The conservatism of the Conservative Party is a mixture of classical toryism and neo-conservatism, although it leans much more to the latter than the former. (Neo-liberals do not have a natural or comfortable home in Canada, unless they join the very marginal Libertarian Party. Many neo-liberals probably end up supporting the Conservative Party because of its economic policies and general belief in limited government, even if they find the social conservatism of the party distasteful).

The New Democratic Party (the NDP) is the party of democratic socialism in Canada. Like the other parties, the NDP has its left and right wings. Those on the left side are proud to call themselves "socialists," while those on the right side of the party are not much different from left-leaning Liberals.

For the Bloc Québécois, the sovereignty of Quebec trumps ideology, although on most issues the Bloc conforms to the principles of democratic socialism. Similarly, for the Green Party the environment trumps ideology. Greens are typically described as a left-wing liberal–social democratic party along with the NDP, but it might be more accurate to view the Green Party's ideology of environmentalism as a cross between democratic socialism and toryism (see Figure 2.6).

In sum, ideologies enable people to explain and evaluate political issues, and they help people decide how to respond to these issues. In other words, they equip people with a program of action. Finally, an ideology allows each person to orient themselves with respect to the political system and to other political actors. It is, however, often difficult to situate yourself within the largely abstract ideological spectrum, particularly if you are new to

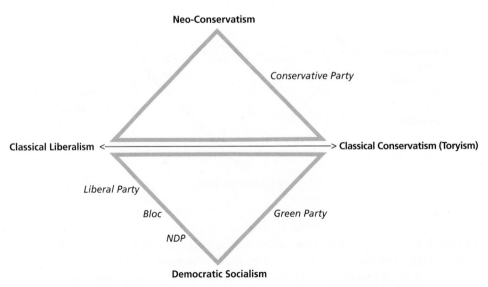

Figure 2.6 The Ideological Position of the Major Political Parties in Canada

politics. Over time, after watching the news, engaging in political conversations with family and friends, and participating in a few elections, you will eventually figure out where you are situated in the political spectrum. However, you can get a pretty good sense of where you stand with the help of a computer by taking an online quiz to help determine your ideology (although you should accept the results with more than just a few grains of salt).

The Canadian Political Landscape

While there are three major ideologies at play in Canada, it is important to note that these ideologies are not evenly distributed across the country. Just as Canada is divided into distinct geographical regions, the Canadian political landscape is similarly divided. Political scientists refer to these political divisions as **cleavages**. There are a number of enduring cleavages in the Canadian political landscape, such as language, region, and class. Each subgroup has a unique political culture and a particular set of concerns.

For some people, their group identity may be more important than their ideology. This gives rise to what political scientists call **identity politics**. Identity politics and social cleavages provide a variety of challenges and opportunities for political parties. Parties aiming to win an election and form the Government of Canada must find a way to bridge these distinct political communities into a winning coalition. This has long been the challenge for Canada's governing parties, the Conservative Party and the Liberal Party. Other parties, however, may find a niche in the Canadian political system by representing the concerns of a particular subgroup in the Canadian polity; the Bloc Québécois is the prime exemplar.

Language

Historically, the principal cleavage in Canadian politics has been language. The division between English-speaking and French-speaking Canadians predates Confederation by more than 100 years; it goes all the way back to the British Conquest of New France in 1759 on the Plains of Abraham in Quebec City. For some, Confederation represented a pact between English- and French-speaking peoples, who have been described as Canada's two founding nations. This theory of Confederation is more popular among Francophone Canadians, particularly in Quebec, who still tend to view the country as a union between two linguistic groups. While Anglophones recognize the linguistic duality of Canada, they generally view the country in different terms, perhaps because English-speaking Canadians have never viewed themselves as a single group. Even at Confederation in 1867, English-speaking Canadians were divided among English, Scots, and Irish, and these groups were themselves divided into Catholics and Protestants. In sociological terms, religion was a **crosscutting cleavage** among English-speaking Canadians of different national origins.

For many decades after Confederation, Quebec was a deeply conservative society. French-speaking Quebecers were overwhelmingly Catholic, and the Catholic Church held

cleavages The main political divisions in a country. Political scientists have long been concerned with a handful of enduring schisms in the Canadian political landscape, such as language, region, and class, among others.

identity politics A political orientation that is driven by one's identification with one's language, race, religion, gender, nation, sexual orientation, or some other aspect of the group one identifies with. Identity politics is often associated with groups seeking to free themselves from discrimination by dominant groups in Canadian society.

crosscutting cleavages A cleavage within a cleavage and an alliance across the main cleavage. The principal cleavage in Canada has historically been language: French and English. But the English-speaking community is further divided between Protestants and Catholics. And on some issues, English-speaking Catholics may have more in common with French-speaking Catholics than they do with English-speaking Protestants.

Quiet Revolution The transformation of Quebec from a deeply conservative society to a progressively liberal society in the 1960s.

revenge of the cradle A church-fostered policy known as *la revanche des berceaux*. The church encouraged women to have lots of babies to prevent the assimilation of the French by the English.

nationalism The passion some individuals display for their nation. It properly refers to an identifiable group of people rather than a country; love of country is properly known as *patriotism*. In Canada, many people in Quebec believe that Quebec is a separate nation.

sovereignists Quebecers who want Quebec to become a sovereign state, independent of Canada.

federalists Quebecers who are not in favour of separation. They are committed to Canada, although many of them want to see changes to the way the federation is governed.

sway over much of the province. In the 1960s, however, Quebec went through a profound social transformation known as *la Révolution tranquille*—the **Quiet Revolution**. While the winds of change had been sweeping through Quebec for some years, the revolution was precipitated by the death of Premier Maurice Duplessis, who led a political party called the *Union Nationale*, in 1959 and the election of a new Liberal government led by Jean Lesage in 1960. Duplessis governed Quebec with an iron fist from 1936 to 1939 and again from 1944 to his death. The Duplessis years are now known in Quebec as *les années noires*—the dark ages. Under Jean Lesage, by contrast, Quebec flourished. In the span of less than a decade, Quebec went from being the most conservative and religious province in Canada to being the most liberal and least religious. As the Catholic Church declined in Quebec, the government became considerably more active in Quebec society. Before the Quiet Revolution, Quebec had the lowest taxes among all of the provinces, but after the Quiet Revolution Quebec had the highest taxes in Canada. To this day, Quebec has the most generous social programs in Canada.

Perhaps most conspicuously, the Quiet Revolution had a dramatic impact on families in Quebec. Prior to the Quiet Revolution, Quebec had one of the highest birth rates in the Western world. The high birth rate was caused by a church-fostered policy known as *la revanche des berceaux*—the **revenge of the cradle**. By encouraging women to have lots of babies, the church hoped to prevent the assimilation of the French by the English. And some Quebec families were very large. Jean Chrétien, for example, was the second youngest of 19 children (10 of whom did not survive past infancy). Céline Dion is the youngest of 14 children.

In 1956, the overall fertility rate in Quebec was 3.98 children per woman, but by 1971 the figure was only 1.98 children per woman—one of the lowest in the Western world.[2] By 1981, the figure had fallen even further to 1.62 children per woman, well below the rate of 2.1 children per woman necessary to maintain the population at current levels. With the decline of church influence and after watching what their mothers had to endure, young women in Quebec eagerly embraced the advent of the birth control pill. The government of Quebec has subsequently taken steps to increase the birth rate in the province; between 1988 and 1997, the government actually gave women cash payments for each child they produced: $500 for her first child, $1000 for her second child, and $8000 for her third child and for each subsequent child. The program was controversial for a variety of reasons, but it succeeded in stimulating the birth rate.[3] Subsequently, the government of Quebec has introduced affordable public daycare, and in 2010 Quebec became the first jurisdiction in Canada to cover in vitro fertilization treatments under the public health system. The birth rate in Quebec is now slightly higher than the national average.

With the Quiet Revolution, many French-speaking Quebecers also developed a much stronger and more confident sense of themselves as a distinct nation in Canada. This passion for nation is known as **nationalism**. With the rise of nationalism in Quebec, many Quebecers began questioning their province's place in Canada, and some concluded that Quebec should seek to separate (or secede) from the Canadian federation. For many Quebecers, independence is the only way to protect and promote the French language and the distinct culture of the province. The question of secession now constitutes the principal cleavage in Quebec politics. Those who want Quebec to form a sovereign state are known as **sovereignists**, while those who remain committed to the Canadian federation are called **federalists**. This division, however, is not as great as it seems. Many federalists in Quebec want major changes to the way the federation works, while many sovereignists want to maintain strong links to Canada after independence.

Since the very narrow failure of the referendum on sovereignty in 1995, Quebecers have seemingly been less preoccupied by *la question nationale*. For Canadians outside Quebec, as well, the linguistic cleavage in Canadian politics also seems less urgent. Quebec's proportion of the Canadian population has been declining over the decades, while other parts of

Canada have been growing rapidly, especially the Greater Toronto Area, Alberta, and British Columbia. This population growth has been driven in large part by immigration, particularly from Asia. Consequently, for many Canadians Quebec seems less relevant in the scope of Canadian politics. On the other hand, there appears to be greater acceptance of the "French fact" in Canada, although this may not be an entirely positive development. Many Canadians outside Quebec now accept "French Canadians" as just another one of the numerous "multicultural" groups in the country, much to the dismay of many Quebecers who still view Canada as a union of two nations.

Region

Western Canada While the other regions of Canada are predominantly English speaking, they are also politically quite distinct. As a general rule, the older parts of the country are inclined to the older versions of liberalism and conservatism (as modified over time), and the newer parts of the country are more receptive to neo-conservatism and democratic socialism. Indeed, in Western Canada neo-conservatism and democratic socialism are the dominant ideologies, although there are important variations from province to province. In British Columbia, the principles of neo-conservatism and democratic socialism hold sway, with more people inclined to neo-conservatism. Alberta is almost wholly neo-conservative. Saskatchewan and Manitoba are more like British Columbia, except that democratic socialism runs deeper than neo-conservatism (although this may be changing in Saskatchewan). These are sweeping generalizations, of course. There are many liberals in Western Canada, mainly in the bigger cities, and there are old-fashioned tories scattered across the region.

A fierce egalitarianism cuts across the political spectrum in Western Canada. The West was settled by waves of immigrant groups, many of which came from outside the English–French and Protestant–Catholic cultural traditions, such as Ukrainians and Mennonites. A large number of Americans also settled in Western Canada, especially Alberta. Western settlers were thus culturally and ideologically distinct from the political elite in "Eastern" Canada, and many did not feel welcome or comfortable in the "old line parties." The West thus has a long history of creating new political parties—both on the left and the right—to challenge the elitism of the old parties, as we will discuss in Chapter 3. Western Canadian parties have generally been premised on the theory of **populism**. That is, they are committed to the principle that party policies should be determined by the members of the party and not by the leaders. In many respects, populism is a "truer" form of democracy, and the traditional political parties have embraced many of the principles and practices of populism. However, as we will discuss in the next chapter, populism can also be problematic.

populism A theory that extends the notion of democracy beyond the election of the government. It is the belief that major political decisions should be made by the people. Populism can be left-wing or right-wing, and is particularly prevalent in Western Canada.

Ontario With a population of about 13 million people, Ontario is the largest province in Canada and accounts for about 40 percent of the Canadian population. It is also geographically huge with a number of distinct regions. Indeed, from time to time there are calls to partition Ontario into one or more provinces. Some people argue that northern Ontario should be a separate province, while others say that Toronto should be a province unto itself. If the Greater Toronto Area were transformed into a province, it would have a population of almost 6 million people. It would probably be bigger than the rest of Ontario, and consequently it would constitute the second-largest province in the country behind Quebec, which would become the largest province in Canada if Ontario were partitioned. There are also persistent suggestions that Ottawa should be made into a separate "national capital region," like Washington DC and Canberra, the capital cities of the United States and Australia. As such, it is difficult to speak about *the* political culture of Ontario. In general, however, Ontario is inclined toward liberalism and tory conservatism, with solid doses of neo-conservatism and democratic socialism.

Atlantic Canada   If it is not fair to describe Ontario as a single region in Canada, it is even more unfair to lump the four provinces of Atlantic Canada into one group. Indeed, it might not even be fair to describe the three Maritime provinces—Nova Scotia, New Brunswick, and Prince Edward Island—as a single region. Newfoundland and Labrador is quite clearly a composite of at least two regions. Nevertheless, it is probably fair to say that politics in Atlantic Canada is dominated by old-fashioned liberals and tory conservatives. The principles of democratic socialism have not resonated strongly in Atlantic Canada, although the NDP had a breakthrough in Nova Scotia in the 2009 provincial election. But it was short lived. The NDP government in Nova Scotia was soundly defeated in the next election in 2013. Neoconservatism is almost totally absent in Atlantic Canada.

The North   The territories—Yukon, the Northwest Territories, and Nunavut—also constitute a distinct and very diverse region of Canada. Nunavut and the Northwest Territories are the only jurisdictions in Canada in which Aboriginal peoples constitute a majority of the population. The territories are rich in natural resources, and they are increasingly of strategic significance in world politics. However, the combined population of the three territories is about 100 000 people, or just slightly more than Kamloops, British Columbia. This is also about the same size as an average electoral district or riding in Canada. Thus, by the democratic principle of representation by population, the three territories should only have one representative in Parliament, but of course it would be impossible for one person to represent an area that is geographically larger than India. Consequently, each territory elects one member to Parliament. With a total of 308 people elected to Parliament, it is clear that the territories are not major players in the Canadian political system, notwithstanding their economic, strategic, and symbolic importance to the country.

Demography   When we are talking about regional political cultures in Canada, we must always be mindful of demography (see Table 2.1). Ontario and Quebec make up about two-thirds of the country, with the rest divided between the West and Atlantic Canada (with the West quite a bit larger than the Atlantic region). The political culture of Canada as a whole is thus largely determined by Ontario and Quebec, and this has meant in the past that Canada is broadly a liberal country. It also means that the West is very much an outlier in Canadian politics, both geographically and in terms of political culture, since it is more inclined to ideologies that fall decidedly to the right and left of the Canadian median established by the demographic weight of Central Canada. Moreover, many Westerners believe that the Government of Canada has made decisions, at least in the past, for the benefit of the majority in Central Canada but highly detrimental to Western interests. The West is thus acutely aware of its outlier status in Canadian politics and has often felt distant from the Canadian political system. Hence, we have the very real notion of **Western alienation** in this country.

Atlantic Canada is even more numerically disadvantaged than the West, but as we have seen the political culture of Atlantic Canada is relatively consistent with the Canadian norm, as defined by Central Canada or more particularly Ontario. Consequently, Atlantic Canadians have generally not felt alienated from the Canadian political system, with the possible exception of Newfoundland and Labrador, whose residents only voted to join Canada by a slim margin in 1949.

The 2011 election seemed to redefine the regional dynamics in Canadian politics. For the first time, Canadian politics was dominated by two parties rooted in Western Canadian populism: the Conservative Party led by Stephen Harper and the New Democratic Party led by the late Jack Layton, although the NDP is considerably more removed from its roots than the Conservative Party. Jack Layton was born and raised in Quebec and cut his political teeth in Toronto. In short, Ontario seemed to break with Quebec and Atlantic Canada in the 2011 election and aligned its interests with the West. It almost seemed as if the West remade Canada in its own image. As such, the notion of Western alienation began to ring a bit

western alienation The disconnection many Canadians in Western provinces feel to the rest of Canada, and the belief that the Government of Canada tends to make policies for the benefit of the majority in Central Canada to the detriment of the West.

Table 2.1 Population of Canada, 2011 Census

Region	Population of Region	Province/ Territory	Population of Province/ Territory	Seats in House of Commons per Province/ Territory	Seats in House of Commons per Region
West	10 661 200	British Columbia	4 573 300	36	92
		Alberta	3 779 400	28	
		Saskatchewan	1 057 900	14	
		Manitoba	1 250 600	14	
Ontario	13 373 000	Ontario	13 373 000	106	106
Quebec	7 979 700	Quebec	7 979 700	75	75
Atlantic	2 357 400	New Brunswick	755 500	10	32
		Nova Scotia	945 400	11	
		Prince Edward Island	145 900	4	
		Newfoundland and Labrador	510 600	7	
North	111 700	Nunavut	33 300	1	3
		Northwest Territories	43 700	1	
		Yukon	34 700	1	
Canada	34 483 000		34 483 000	308	308

Source: Statistics Canada, "Population by Year, by Province and Territory," www40.statcan.gc.ca/l01/cst01/demo02a-eng.htm.

hollow. With Ontario evidently aligned with the West, it is entirely possible that Atlantic Canada will feel increasingly alienated, particularly the provinces of New Brunswick and Prince Edward Island, which do not enjoy the luxury of natural gas revenues like Nova Scotia and Newfoundland. While Quebec abandoned the separatist Bloc Québécois in the 2011 election and threw its lot in with the federalist New Democratic Party, it also appeared more isolated than ever. The country thus seems as regionally divided as ever, even if the West is presently more content with the state of Canadian politics than it has been in the past.

Urban–Rural

Canada is one of the most urbanized countries in the world. Almost three-quarters of the Canadian population lives in one of 33 census metropolitan areas (defined as areas with more than 100 000 people), and the nine largest cities in Canada account for more than half the total population. Rural areas, however, are considerably overrepresented in Parliament, largely as a result of Canada's history as a rural society. Urban and rural Canadians may share mutual passions for things such as hockey or country music, but they often have different values and political interests. Urban Canada is relatively liberal, while rural Canada is more conservative. The economy of rural Canada depends largely on mining, forestry, agriculture, and fishing (at least in coastal areas), whereas the economy of urban Canada is based on financial and retail services, health and education, and manufacturing. The rural–urban cleavage can be seen in the debate over the long-gun registry, which was created in 1995. Urban Canadians believe that it is perfectly reasonable to insist that people register their hunting rifles, but rural Canadians tend to view it as an affront to their way of life. The long-gun registry was scrapped after the election of a Conservative majority government in 2011, much to the satisfaction of many rural Canadians and the dismay of many urban voters.

In the 2011 election, the major parties focused more than ever on the large and growing regions around the major cities—the suburbs and the more distant exurbs (new residential developments beyond the suburbs but still connected to major cities). In short, the big cities are expanding into previously rural areas, with new housing subdivisions being erected alongside old farm houses. These regions are often identified by separate telephone area codes (e.g., the "905 belt" around Toronto) and they tend to be settled by young families and immigrants looking for more affordable housing. The question is, will the suburbs and exurbs adopt the liberal values of urban Canada or the conservative values of rural Canada? How this question is answered in the next decade or two may well determine the course of Canadian politics for the rest of the century. In 2011, the Conservative Party swept through many suburban ridings and displaced the Liberals in a number of urban ridings, especially in Toronto but also to some extent in Vancouver. The NDP also picked up a couple of inner-city seats in Toronto.

A new electoral cleavage may have emerged in 2011. Both the Conservatives and the NDP won seats in urban and rural areas, but their respective victories seemed to follow a pattern. "The true divide, the new reality of Canadian politics, is between the economic heartlands that the Conservatives now dominate throughout the country and the economic hinterlands won by the NDP."[4] Put another way, the Conservative Party did well in the parts of the country that drive the economy, while the NDP tended to prevail in areas enduring economic hardship, although this relationship is not perfect. The Conservatives did win seats in northwest Ontario, Nunavut, and Labrador, while the NDP picked up seats in Victoria as well as the Vancouver suburb of Burnaby. The Liberal Party lost many of its more affluent seats in the 2011 election, and like the NDP has become something of a hinterland party, especially in Atlantic Canada. It will be interesting to see if this cleavage persists in future elections.

Religion and Multiculturalism

Canadians are generally rather reserved people, and they tend to look skeptically at the overt role that religion plays in American politics. Nonetheless, religion has played an important role in Canadian politics. In the past, at least, religion has been "the most powerful" predictor of party preferences among Canadian voters.[5] In short, research has revealed that Catholic voters have historically supported the Liberal Party in Canadian elections, whereas Protestants have been more likely to support the Conservative Party (although not to the same extent that Catholics favour the Liberal Party). The Catholic affinity for the Liberal Party remains a mystery,[6] but there is reason to believe that the Liberals have now lost this key constituency: "In 2006, Catholics were as likely to vote Conservative as Liberal. In 2008, they clearly actually preferred the Conservatives to the Liberals."[7] It is possible that the Liberal support for same-sex marriage shifted some Catholic voters, although it should be noted that Catholic support for the Liberal Party remained solid after the Liberal government legalized abortion in 1968. It is thus not clear why Catholic voters have suddenly changed their political allegiance.

Jewish voters also seem to have shifted their support from the Liberal Party to the new Conservative Party, and evangelical Christians overwhelmingly support the Conservative Party. It is too soon to know if these new affinities will be sustained in the long run, but the Conservative Party appears to have very skilfully employed coded language that appeals to certain religious groups without alarming secular voters or igniting the kind of impassioned discourse seen in the United States, although some Canadians have tried to raise an alarm.[8]

The Liberal Party of Canada has also historically been disproportionately supported by Canadians of non-European origin, especially after the Liberal government of Pierre Elliott Trudeau adopted a policy of official multiculturalism in 1971. Again, however, the Liberal Party appears to have lost its grip on this important constituency, especially among more recent immigrants.[9] Many immigrants arriving in Canada now come from socially conservative societies, and many new Canadians are highly entrepreneurial individuals with a strong interest in low rates of taxation and minimal government regulation of business. The Conservative Party has expended considerable energy courting these new voters, and these efforts seem to have paid off, especially with Chinese-Canadians in and around Vancouver. The Conservatives have also picked up some ridings with a significant number of Indo-Canadian voters, although Indo-Canadians, especially Sikhs, are politically active in all the major parties, probably as a result of the vibrant political culture of Punjab in northwest India.

While some new Canadians have clearly gravitated to the Conservative Party, there may be countervailing factors causing others to resist this lure. Some Muslim Canadians, for example, may well be suspicious of the Conservative government's enthusiasm for the "war on terrorism" and unwavering support for the state of Israel. Canada's population growth is driven largely by immigration, so the political views of new Canadians will have a strong influence on the future of Canadian politics.

Aboriginal Peoples

From Confederation right through to the early 1960s, Aboriginal peoples were legally excluded from the political process unless they relinquished their Aboriginal status and assimilated into the Canadian mainstream. Aboriginal peoples were finally given the right to vote in 1960, and their rights as Aboriginal peoples were recognized and affirmed in the Constitution Act 1982. But many of their rights have not been fulfilled, especially self-government. With about 1 million people in Canada, Aboriginal Canadians account for only about 4 percent of the population. It is also a deeply fragmented community. Aboriginal peoples include Status Indians (which is the official term used by the government; see Chapter 10), Inuit, and Métis. Status Indians are further divided into more than 600 bands scattered across the country. Many Aboriginal peoples live in remote parts of the country, and many communities are desperately poor. For all of these reasons, Aboriginal peoples have had considerable difficulty placing their issues and concerns on the political agenda of the country, and many are growing impatient with the political process in Canada.

The rights and issues of Aboriginal peoples are likely to become more salient in the future for two reasons. First, the governments of Canada have a constitutional obligation to fulfill the rights of Aboriginal peoples, as will be discussed at some length in Chapter 10. Second, the rights of Aboriginal peoples will have to be addressed if the governments of Canada want to further develop resource industries such as oil and gas on traditional Aboriginal lands.

Class

Class consciousness is not strong in Canada. While, theoretically, class cuts across some of the other cleavages we have discussed above, class consciousness in Canada has been too weak to cut through the more primordial allegiances such as language and region. Most Canadians tend to believe that they belong to the ubiquitous "middle class," apart perhaps from some ardent unionists and the ultra-rich. But class undoubtedly exists in Canada. It is not an easy concept to define, but broadly it relates to the economic stratification of individuals in society. Canada, like most industrial democracies, is characterized by a very large middle class, an unacceptably large group of poor Canadians, and a very small group of rich and ultra-rich individuals.

The middle class can be further divided into an upper middle class made up of doctors, lawyers, teachers, civil servants, and other white-collar professionals and a lower middle class or working class consisting of blue-collar workers and service workers. Only about 4 percent of Canadians earn more than $100 000 per year, while roughly 10 percent or approximately 3 million Canadians are defined as low income (the cut off for low income depends on the cost of living where one resides). Thus, about 85 percent of the population may be thought of as "middle class," although obviously there is a considerable income difference between the top and bottom segments of the middle class. Upper middle class Canadians are not only wealthier, they typically enjoy greater job and income security, whereas lower middle class Canadians are more vulnerable. Lower middle class Canadians may experience a reduction in work hours or even a loss of work when the economy dips. Over the last 20 years, the very rich have enjoyed higher incomes while incomes for everyone else have been relatively stagnant. In other words, the rich are indeed getting richer, while the poor are staying poor.

How can political parties exploit class cleavages when most Canadians are blissfully unaware of class? It becomes even more difficult for political parties to address class issues when you realize that many Canadians become uncomfortable when they hear people talking explicitly in terms of class. Political parties in Canada thus tend to speak about class euphemistically. The NDP will talk about "ordinary Canadians," while the Conservative Party has attempted to identify itself with fans of Tim Hortons instead of Starbucks, or people who shop at Canadian Tire rather than at Pottery Barn. In turn, the parties will attempt to devise policy that will appeal to their core constituencies.

Democracy is a game of numbers, so by and large the parties will promote policies that appeal to the middle class in Canada, but the middle class is really too broad to be wooed as a single group. The NDP tends to stress income security programs that will appeal to the lower segment of the middle class and low-income Canadians. The Conservative Party, on the other hand, tends to focus on the upper segment of the middle class by offering tax credits to enroll children in organized sports or music classes, and they also make appeals to wealthy Canadians. In the 2011 election, for example, the Conservative Party promised to introduce income splitting between spouses: A spouse who earns a high income would be able to transfer a portion of his or her income to a spouse who does not otherwise work to lower his or her overall tax burden. As high-income earners tend to be married, middle-aged men,[10] the policy would increase the take-home pay for rich men and create an incentive for their wives to stay at home.

The Liberal Party has historically attempted to straddle the class divide in Canada. The Liberal Party has always been a supporter of big business, but Liberal governments have also been responsible for introducing most of Canada's income security and other social programs. Of late, however, the Liberal Party has found it difficult to retain the support of both the rich and the poor. In sum, while Canadians are loath to talk about class, the major political parties all make class appeals, albeit most often with coded language.

Gender

While men and women are spread across the political spectrum from left to right, research has revealed that, at least to some extent, men and women view politics differently: "The sex differences are not huge, but in Canada they often rival or exceed the differences across the country's regional fault lines. And the differences in the political preferences and vote choices of women and men do not have to be dramatic to have a significant impact on the outcome of an election, especially in tight races."[11] As a gross generalization, women are interested in "sharing and caring" issues and men are more concerned about "money and guns." No doubt you know many exceptions to these stereotypes, but statistics show that men and women do vote differently. The Conservative Party is disproportionately supported by men, while the New Democratic Party garners more support from women; support for the Liberal Party is divided about equally. Political scientists refer to this phenomenon as the **gender gap**.

gender gap The differing support political parties receive from women and men.

While there is a very real gender gap at play in Canadian politics, it is important to remember a couple of points. First, the gender gap refers to the *relative* support parties receive from women and men. In terms of absolute numbers, there are more women on the right than on the left in Canada. Second, the relatively high support the NDP enjoys from women is more likely the result of men moving *away* from the NDP to more conservative parties. It is not clear why men have been moving to the right in Canada and other advanced democracies like the United States. It may reflect a cultural backlash against the feminist movement of the 1970s, or it may stem from changes in the economy, especially the decline of well-paying jobs for men in the manufacturing sector.

The main political parties are quite aware of the gender gap, and the Liberal Party and the NDP make a concerted effort to maintain support from women. The Conservative Party, to date at least, has done very little to increase its appeal to female voters. If parties want to improve their fortunes in future elections, they need to pick up support in areas where they are currently weak. The Conservatives would thus be well advised to pay more attention to female voters, and the NDP and the Liberals may want to think of ways of winning back male voters.

Age

It has often been observed that people become more conservative as they get older, and demographers have noted that Canada is an aging society. Indeed, by 2020 it is expected that there will be more people in Canada over the age of 65 than under 15. The rising population of senior citizens in Canada entails a number of policy challenges, such as ensuring economic productivity with fewer workers and financing pensions and health care. These demographic shifts and policy challenges will obviously have an impact on Canadian politics, at least to the extent that parties will have to design policies to address these fundamental issues. It is also possible that Canada's politics will become a little bit more conservative, although that proposition may not hold for the baby boomers now entering retirement. Younger voters are more open to political experimentation and supporting more radical political parties, such as the Green Party. However, younger voters are also much less likely to participate in Canadian elections, and they may become further alienated from the political process as parties increasingly talk about issues related to senior citizens.

SUMMARY

Politics is a conflict between different conceptions of the good life, but these conceptions can be bundled into a few distinct groupings of ideas known as *ideologies*. The main ideologies at play in Canadian politics—liberalism, conservatism, and democratic socialism—are clustered in the middle of the ideological spectrum. In some countries, these ideologies would represent radically distinct views of the world, but in Canada they tend to represent overlapping sets of ideas. Consequently, in Canada it is very common for a conservative to hold some liberal beliefs and vice versa. To confuse matters further, the character of the main ideologies in Canada has changed over time. Stephen Harper's conservatism at best only partially resembles the conservatism of Sir John A. Macdonald, even though they have both led the Conservative Party.

The Canadian political landscape is as varied as the country's geography. Historically, the principal cleavage in Canadian politics has been linguistic, and the political culture of Quebec and the rest of Canada—the so-called "two solitudes" of Canadian society—remain separate and distinct. But even outside Quebec the ideological dynamics of Canadian politics vary from region to region. By and large, the older regions of Canada are inclined to the older variants of liberalism and conservatism, while the West has been more receptive to new ideologies, notably democratic socialism and neo-conservatism. The political culture of the West has also been decidedly populist, and it has quite successfully exported some of the central tenets of populism to the rest of Canada. Recently, the urban–rural cleavage has become quite salient in Canadian politics, although it may have been supplanted in the 2011 election by an emerging cleavage between the regions in the economic heartland of Canada and the economic hinterlands. The political beliefs of Canadians also vary across religion, race, class, gender, and age.

Canada, in short, is characterized by multiple political cleavages, and it is consequently not an easy country to govern. It is the job of political parties to build bridges across the main cleavages in Canada and unite Canadians in a common purpose, which is no easy task, as we will see in the next chapter.

Questions to Think About

1. Should the governments of Canada raise taxes to sustain a universal health care system, or should governments cut health care spending to balance their budgets and pay down debt?

2. Why are younger voters less likely to vote? What impact does youth disengagement have on Canadian politics?

3. Does class exist in Canada? If so, what impact does it have on Canadian politics?

4. Does religion matter in Canadian politics?

5. Why is there a gender gap in Canadian politics?

6. How can political parties overcome all of the cleavages in Canadian society and govern Canada for the benefit of everyone?

Learning Outcomes

1. Describe the main principles of each of the major ideologies in Canada.

2. Describe the ideological orientation of the main political parties in Canada.

3. Describe the major cleavages in Canadian politics.

Additional Readings

Darrell Bricker and John Ibbitson, *The Big Shift: The Seismic Change in Canadian Politics, Business, and Culture and What It Means for Our Future* (Toronto, ON: Harper Collins, 2013).

Janine Brodie, *The Political Economy of Canadian Regionalism* (Toronto, ON: Harcourt Brace Jovanovich, 1990).

Elisabeth Gidengil, "Beyond the Gender Gap," *Canadian Journal of Political Science* 40:4 (December 2007), 815–831.

Ailsa Henderson, *Nunavut: Rethinking Political Culture* (Vancouver, BC: University of British Columbia Press, 2007).

Gad Horowitz, "Conservatism, Liberalism, and Socialism: An Interpretation," *Canadian Journal of Economics and Political Science* 22:2 (1966).

Paul Howe, *Citizens Adrift: The Democratic Disengagement of Young Canadians* (Vancouver, BC: University of British Columbia Press, 2010).

David Laycock, *Populism and Democratic Thought in the Canadian Prairies, 1910 to 1945* (Toronto, ON: University of Toronto Press, 1990).

Henry Milner, *The Internet Generation: Engaged Citizens or Political Dropouts* (Medford, MA: Tufts University Press, 2010).

John Porter, *The Vertical Mosaic: An Analysis of Social Class and Power in Canada* (Toronto, ON: University of Toronto Press, 1965).

Pierre Elliott Trudeau, *Federalism and the French Canadians* (Toronto, ON: Macmillan, 1968).

Jared J. Wesley, *Code Politics: Campaigns and Cultures on the Canadian Prairies* (Vancouver, BC: University of British Columbia Press, 2011).

Nelson Wiseman, *In Search of Canadian Political Culture* (Vancouver, BC: University of British Columbia Press, 2007).

Notes

1. Terence Ball et al., *Political Ideologies and the Democratic Ideal*, Canadian ed. (Toronto, ON: Pearson Education, 2006), 4. The discussion in this section draws heavily on the following sources: Gad Horowitz, "Conservatism, Liberalism, and Socialism: An Interpretation," *Canadian Journal of Economics and Political Science* 22:2 (1966); Nelson Wiseman, "Political Parties," in *Canadian Politics in the 1990s*, eds. Michael S. Whittington and Glen Williams (Toronto, ON: ITP Nelson, 1995); and Hamish Telford, "The Reform Party/Canadian Alliance and Canada's Flirtation with Republicanism," in *Canada: The State of the Federation 2001: Canadian Political Culture(s) in Transition*, eds. Hamish Telford and Harvey Lazar (Kingston, ON: Institute of Intergovernmental Relations, 2002).

2. Paul-André Linteau, *Quebec since 1930* (Toronto, ON: James Lorimer and Company, 1991), 155, 318.

3. Kevin Milligan, "Quebec's Baby Bonus: Can Public Policy Raise Fertility?" *Backgrounder* (Toronto, ON: CD Howe Institute, January 24, 2002).

4. Partrick Brethour, "Canada's New Electoral Divide: It's about the Money," *The Globe and Mail*, May 3, 2011.

5. Richard Johnston, "The Reproduction of the Religious Cleavage in Canadian Elections," *Canadian Journal of Political Science* 18:1 (March 1985), 99–113.

6. André Blais, "Accounting for the Electoral Success of the Liberal Party in Canada: Presidential Address to the Canadian Political Science Association, London, Ontario, June 3, 2005," *Canadian Journal of Political Science* 38:4 (December 2005), 821–840.

7. Elisabeth Gidengil et al., "The Anatomy of a Liberal Defeat," paper presented at the annual meeting of the Canadian Political Science Association at Carleton University, Ottawa, May 2009, 4.

8. Marci McDonald, *The Armageddon Factor: The Rise of Christian Nationalism in Canada* (Toronto, ON: Random House, 2010).

9. Gidengil et al., 3.

10. Brian Murphy, Paul Roberts, and Michael Wolfson, "A Profile of High-Income Canadians, 1982 to 2004," *Income Research Paper Series* (Ottawa, ON: Statistics Canada, 2007).

11. Elisabeth Gidengil, "Beyond the Gender Gap," *Canadian Journal of Political Science* 40:4 (December 2007), 816.

Chapter 3
Political Parties

Key Points

- The main ideologies in Canadian politics are represented to a greater or lesser degree by political parties.

- Political parties are organizations designed to get their candidates elected to Parliament.

- If a political party wants to win an election in Canada, it needs to be close to the middle of the ideological spectrum and able to transcend the linguistic and regional divisions in the country—at least this was the winning strategy for much of the twentieth century.

- In the twenty-first century, the winning formula might be quite different. At present, the party system is polarized and the influence of Quebec in Canadian politics seems to be diminishing.

- Canadian political parties are largely self-governing organizations, but Parliament has passed laws to regulate the financing of political parties among other things. Some people believe that stronger rules are needed to govern political parties.

political party An organization designed to get its candidates elected to Parliament. Political parties are the primary connection between voters and Parliament.

independent candidates Individuals running for election to the House of Commons who are not affiliated with any political party. There are many independent candidates in each election, but it is unusual for an independent candidate to win a seat in Parliament.

Political parties play an important role in Canadian politics. The different political parties in the system represent to a greater or lesser extent the different conceptions of the good life. Liberalism is represented by the Liberal Party, conservatism by the Conservative Party, and the New Democratic Party is the home of democratic socialism in Canada. The Bloc Québécois may be viewed as a social democratic party, although its primary mission is the independence of Quebec. The Green Party, of course, is the party of environmentalism. Almost everyone who gets elected to the House of Commons belongs to a **political party**. It is very difficult for **independent candidates**—candidates without a party affiliation—to get elected to Parliament, although it does happen occasionally. Political parties may thus be viewed as "electoral machines" geared to getting their candidates elected to Parliament. The party that elects the most candidates "wins" the election and (almost always) gets to form the government with its leader as prime minister.

How do parties win elections in Canada? What is the winning formula? There are, of course, a lot of factors that determine the outcome of an election—the popularity of the leaders, how long one party has been in government, and the state of the economy among others—but if a party wants to win an election and form the government it must be broadly congruent with Canadian political culture. In other words, it must be reasonably close to the centre of the ideological spectrum and it must be able to transcend the linguistic and regional divisions in the country. This was, at least, the winning formula through much of the twentieth century, but it is not clear that this will continue to be the winning formula in the twenty-first century. In the 2011 election, the Conservative Party demonstrated that it was possible to win a majority government *without* the centre or Quebec, and the NDP emerged as the official opposition, also without the centre (but *with* substantial support in Quebec). The Liberals sat in the centre of the ideological spectrum, but it was squeezed on both sides by the Conservatives and the NDP and finished in third place for the first time in its history. In short, the dramatic 2011 election may have signalled the start of a new political era in Canada.

The Canadian Party System

Before we turn our attention to election campaigns, we should briefly examine the history of political parties in Canada. When political scientists talk about political parties collectively, they refer to it as the **party system**. The party system changes from time to time as parties become weaker and stronger, appear and disappear. The party system, in fact, changes much more frequently than the underlying ideological landscape or political culture of Canada. Political culture evolves gradually over time, but changes in the party system can occur quickly and sometimes dramatically, as was observed in the 2011 election.

How should we talk about the Canadian party system? When political scientists talk about the party system, they are usually referring to the major parties—typically the parties that elect candidates to the House of Commons, especially those with a realistic chance of forming the government. There are actually many more parties in the system than most people know about. In the 2011 general election, there were 18 registered political parties (see Table 3.1). Canadians thus cannot complain about a lack of choice at election time, although admittedly the smaller parties typically do not run candidates across the country. Furthermore, the smallest 13 parties obtained just half of 1 percent of

party system The number of parties active in the political system at any one time. The party system may refer to only the dominant parties in the system or only the parties that elect candidates to Parliament or all of the parties, depending on the context.

Table 3.1 Registered Political Parties in Canada (2013)

1. Animal Alliance Environment Voters Party of Canada
2. Bloc Québécois
3. Canadian Action Party
4. Christian Heritage Party of Canada
5. Communist Party of Canada
6. Conservative Party of Canada
7. Green Party of Canada
8. Liberal Party of Canada
9. Libertarian Party of Canada
10. Marijuana Party of Canada
11. Marxist-Leninist Party of Canada
12. New Democratic Party
13. Online Party of Canada
14. Pirate Party of Canada
15. Progressive Canadian Party
16. Rhinoceros Party
17. United Party of Canada
18. Western Block Party

all the ballots cast in the election. They are thus very much **fringe parties**, although they are not unimportant. They often raise issues that the other political parties choose to ignore, for whatever reason, and they provide citizens with more options for active participation in the political system. Fringe parties thus enhance Canadian democracy. While fringe parties occupy an important niche in Canadian politics, we will focus on the major parties in this chapter.

The Parties of Confederation: The Conservatives and the Liberals

The Canadian party system has evolved in two broad phases. From Confederation to the 1920s, Canada had a simple *two-party system* with the Conservative Party and the Liberal Party as the only players in the game. Both parties came together as coalitions of pre-Confederation political factions. The Conservative Party was an amalgamation of Ontario tories and conservative *bleus* from Quebec. Until 1873, it was actually known as the Liberal-Conservative Party. Even though the Conservative Party has experienced a couple of distinct incarnations since Confederation, Conservatives still refer to themselves as tories and blue is still the party's primary colour. The Liberal Party emerged after Confederation as a coalition of liberal-minded reformers from Ontario (known as the Clear Grits) and liberal *rouges* from Quebec. The Liberals are still known as the Grits, and red is still the primary colour of the party.

The Founding Titans of the Conservative Party: Sir John A. Macdonald (on the $10 bill) and Sir Robert Borden (on the $100 bill)

Bank note image used with the permission of the Bank of Canada/Image de billet de banque utilisée avec la permission de la Banque du Canada.

For a long time after Confederation, the Conservative Party and the Liberal Party were both closely associated with a couple of dominant political figures. From 1867 to 1891, the Conservative Party was led by Sir John A. Macdonald. Through this period Macdonald was also Canada's prime minister, with the exception of the years from 1873 to 1878. After Macdonald's death in 1891, the Conservatives had a succession of short-term leaders. In 1901, Robert Borden, from Nova Scotia, became the leader of the party for the next 19 years. He was also Canada's prime minister from 1911 to 1920 and led Canada through World War I. His policy of conscription, however, was deeply unpopular in Quebec, and ever since then the Conservative Party has struggled to find support in that province. In any event, for 50 years the Conservative Party was the personal fiefdom of two major leaders.

After Borden, Canadian conservatives developed the unfortunate habit of feuding among themselves. The old-fashioned toryism of the Conservative Party was challenged by the rise of prairie populism in the 1920s. Three major populist parties have emerged at various times in Western Canada to challenge the orthodoxy of Central Canadian toryism, as we will discuss below. This tendency toward internal divisions among Canadian conservatives is known as the "tory syndrome." In short, since the 1920s, the Conservative Party has had a history of splitting and reconstituting itself (see Table 3.2). Every once in a while the party comes together under a dominant leader, wins a majority government, governs for a while, and then falls into a serious state of disrepair under a succession of unsuccessful leaders. It is too early to know if Stephen Harper has broken this pattern and positioned the new Conservative Party to be successful in the long term.

The Liberal Party, like the Conservatives, was also dominated by a few major leaders after Confederation. Initially, the leadership of the party alternated between Edward Blake and Alexander Mackenzie. Mackenzie actually defeated Macdonald in the 1873 election and served as Canada's prime minister for five years. The foundation for the Liberal Party's greatness in the twentieth century was laid when Sir Wilfrid Laurier became the leader of the party in 1887. In 1896, Laurier became Canada's first French Canadian prime minister. He held the position continuously until 1911, and he continued as the leader of the Liberal Party until his death in 1919. Laurier was succeeded by William Lyon Mackenzie King, who served as leader of the Liberal Party until 1948, with three separate stints as prime minister totalling more than 21 years. King led Canada

Table 3.2 Major Leaders of the Conservative Party (in its various incarnations)

Party	Leader	Years as Leader	Years as Prime Minister
Conservative Party (1867–1942)	John A. Macdonald	1867–1891	1867–1873 1878–1891
	Robert Borden	1901–1920	1911–1920
	R.B. Bennett	1927–1938	1930–1935
Progressive Conservative Party (1942–2003)	John Diefenbaker	1956–1967	1957–1963
	Brian Mulroney	1983–1993	1984–1993
Conservative Party of Canada (2003–present)	Stephen Harper	2003–	2006–

The Founding Titans of the
Liberal Party: Sir Wilfrid Laurier
(on the $5 bill) and William
Lyon Mackenzie King (on the
$50 bill)

Bank note image used with the permission of the Bank of Canada/Image de billet de banque utilisée avec la permission de la Banque du Canada.

through World War II, and he remains Canada's longest-serving prime minister. Thus, for more than 60 years the Liberal Party was led by just two men.

While the Liberal Party has never again had such a dominant leader (see Table 3.3), with the possible exception of Pierre Elliott Trudeau, it has enjoyed a much more stable history than the Conservative Party—every leader, from Mackenzie through to Paul Martin, served at least briefly as prime minister. However, the Liberal Party has suffered a serious decline since 2006, with two successive leaders—Stéphane Dion and Michael Ignatieff—failing to make it to 24 Sussex Drive (the official residence of the prime minister). In 2013, the Liberals elected Justin Trudeau to be their leader in the hope that he will be able to restore the party's fortunes, but it is a tall order.

The Rise of Prairie Populism

Canada's simple two-party system was shattered with the 1921 election, when the upstart Progressive Party emerged in Western Canada and elected 65 candidates to Parliament. The Progressives petered out very quickly, but the Social Credit Party emerged shortly thereafter as another right-wing prairie populist party. Additionally, the Co-operative Commonwealth Federation—the forerunner of the New Democratic Party—emerged on the prairies as a left-wing populist party. Consequently, for much of the twentieth century there were two major parties with a realistic chance of forming the government—the Liberal Party and (some version of) the Conservative Party—and

Table 3.3 Leaders of the Liberal Party of Canada

Leader	Linguistic Heritage	Years as Leader	Years as Prime Minister
No official leader		1867–1873	
Alexander Mackenzie	Anglophone	1873–1880	November 1873–October 1878
Edward Blake	Anglophone	1880–1887	Never became prime minister
Wilfrid Laurier	Francophone	1887–1919	July 1896–October 1911
William Lyon Mackenzie King	Anglophone	1919–1948	December 1921–June 1926 September 1926–August 1930 October 1935–November 1948
Louis St. Laurent	Francophone	1948–1958	November 1948–June 1957
Lester Pearson	Anglophone	1958–1968	April 1963–April 1968
Pierre Elliott Trudeau	Francophone	1968–1984	April 1968–June 1979 March 1980–June 1984
John Turner	Anglophone	1984–1990	June 1984–September 1984
Jean Chrétien	Francophone	1990–2003	November 1993–December 2003
Paul Martin	Anglophone	2003–2006	December 2003–February 2006
Stéphane Dion	Francophone	2006–2008	Never became prime minister
Michael Ignatieff	Anglophone	2008–2011	Never became prime minister
Justin Trudeau	Francophone	2013–	

one or more smaller parties also present in Parliament. Political scientists typically call this configuration a *two-party-plus system*.

The Progressive Party   The Progressives were populist farmers from Western Canada, although they had some support in Ontario as well. The party was nominally led by dissident Liberals, but in fact the party was highly resistant to leadership. In keeping with the principles of populism, "[e]ach electoral district was an autonomous unit in the party and as a result there was neither a national campaign nor an overall campaign strategy."[1] Once elected each Member of Parliament was free to represent the particular concerns of his constituents. These organizational principles demonstrate the virtues and perils of populism. On the one hand it represents a more direct form of democracy, but on the other it is a recipe for political suicide. In order to get things done in the Canadian parliamentary system, political parties must exhibit a high degree of unity—members can argue all they want behind closed doors, but in public they must speak with one voice. This is known as **party discipline**, and it is one of the informal rules of Canadian politics. A party is not obliged to be disciplined, but undisciplined parties are almost certainly destined to fail. The Progressive Party lacked any semblance of discipline, and thus it collapsed within a few elections after its inception.

party discipline The expectation that members of a party in Parliament will follow the directions of their leader.

In the early 1940s, after the Progressive Party had faded away, the Conservative Party adopted the mantle of progressivism and changed its name to the Progressive Conservative Party of Canada. The Progressive Party was the first reflection of Western alienation in

Canadian politics, even if it was an organizational failure. Western alienation, however, did not disappear with the demise of the Progressive Party. Indeed, two new populist parties emerged in Western Canada in the 1930s. Both parties were a direct response to the Great Depression, although they offered very different solutions to the economic problems facing the nation.

The Social Credit Party   The Social Credit Party was founded on the belief that the state should extend "credit" to citizens to increase their purchasing power in a time of economic need. Essentially, the party argued that the government should print and hand out money. The Supreme Court of Canada dismissed this radical plan, but nevertheless the Social Credit Party became the dominant party in Alberta and then in British Columbia. The party was first elected in Alberta under the leadership of William Aberhart in 1935. Aberhart was succeeded in 1943 by Ernest Manning, who governed the province until 1968. The Social Credit Party disappeared in Alberta shortly thereafter, but in British Columbia the Social Credit Party governed almost continuously from 1952 until 1991, with a brief but turbulent NDP interlude in the 1970s.

In federal elections, the Social Credit Party only twice captured more than 20 seats in the House of Commons, and by the late 1960s the party had been wiped out in Western Canada. The Quebec wing of the party, the *créditistes*, carried on the social credit legacy in the 1970s, and they played a major role in the demise of the short-lived Joe Clark Conservative minority government in 1979, but that was the party's last hurrah in federal politics.

The Co-operative Commonwealth Federation and the New Democratic Party   The Co-operative Commonwealth Federation (CCF) was the other populist prairie party to emerge during the Great Depression. Unlike the right-wing Social Credit Party, the CCF was a democratic socialist party. It believed that working Canadians would prosper only when the state owned the means of production. That would require the state to *nationalize*, or take over, private businesses. In 1944, the CCF won the provincial election in Saskatchewan, becoming the first socialist government in North America. Under the leadership of Tommy Douglas, it introduced the first universal health care program in Canada. In federal elections, however, the CCF had middling success. It generally captured about 10 percent of the vote, and on average it won about 16 seats. In 1961, the CCF joined forces with the Canadian Labour Congress to create the New Democratic Party, and Tommy Douglas was elected as the leader of the new party. The NDP was a more centrist party, but it was not much more successful than the old CCF. For 50 years after its creation the NDP captured about 15 percent of the vote and two dozen seats in Parliament. In 2011, however, it surged to 30 percent of the vote and 103 seats. This far surpassed the party's previous best of 43 seats won in the 1988 election.

The Destruction and Reconstruction of the Canadian Party System

By the 1980s, Canada had developed a stable two-party-plus system, with the dominant Liberal and Progressive Conservative parties plus the NDP. In the 1984 general election, the Progressive Conservative Party came to power under the leadership of Brian Mulroney with the biggest electoral landslide in Canadian history—they captured 211 of the 282 seats in the House of Commons, and Brian Mulroney won another majority government in 1988. Mulroney, a fluently bilingual Irish Quebecer, very skilfully built a winning team—or political coalition—among Quebec nationalists, Ontario tories, and Western neo-conservatives. While this coalition propelled Mulroney to two terms in office, it was inherently unstable.

Over Mulroney's eight years in office, it became increasingly difficult for him to forge a consensus between the Quebec nationalists and the Western neo-conservatives in his coalition. Even before Mulroney stepped down, two new political parties had been established to represent the interests of these constituencies. The Bloc Québécois was formed to champion the cause of Quebec sovereignty in Parliament and was led initially by Lucien Bouchard, the charismatic former Environment Minister in Brian Mulroney's government. In the West, the Reform Party was born. It was led by Preston Manning, the son of long-time Alberta premier and Social Credit Party leader Ernest Manning. In keeping with the political culture of Western Canada, the Reform Party was populist and decidedly neo-conservative.

The 1993 election was a watershed for the Canadian party system. When Mulroney stepped down that year, he was replaced by Kim Campbell as leader of the Progressive Conservative Party. She became the first (and to this day only) female prime minister of Canada, but within a few months she called an election and the PCs were wiped out, winning only two seats. Campbell even lost her own seat in Vancouver Centre. The Liberal Party led by Jean Chrétien won the election, taking 177 of 295 seats. The Bloc Québécois came second with 54 seats, paradoxically becoming "Her Majesty's Loyal Opposition" in Parliament. The Reform Party was a close third, with 52 seats. One Reformer was elected in Ontario; all the rest were from the West. Among the first wave of Reformers elected to Parliament was a young Stephen Harper, representing the constituency of Calgary West, but he quit four years later.

In this party system configuration, the Liberal Party was the only party with a realistic chance of forming the government. The Bloc Québécois only contested seats in Quebec, and therefore by definition it was not in a position to form the Government of Canada. In the 1990s, the NDP saw its support drop to historic lows. And neither of the conservative parties, albeit representing somewhat different types of conservatism, was sufficiently popular to challenge the Liberal Party. The Reform Party continued to do well in the West, but its neo-conservative populism held less appeal for Eastern Canadians. The old Progressive Conservative Party was consistently supported by 15 to 20 percent of the electorate, but its support was spread thinly across the country. Without a regional base of support, the Progressive Conservative Party continued to flounder. In sum, with the 1993 election Canada moved from a two-party-plus system to a *single-party dominant system*.

By the end of the 1990s, the Reform Party realized that it had no hope of winning an election. It thus made a concerted effort to broaden its appeal to more conservative voters, especially outside Western Canada, and it reconstituted itself as the Canadian Reform Conservative Alliance. The new party was led by Stockwell Day, the former Finance Minister in the government of Alberta. Voters, however, were not fooled. They viewed the Canadian Alliance as a simple continuation of the Reform Party. In the 2000 election, the Canadian Alliance won 66 seats in the House of Commons, an increase of six from 1997, but it continued to be a Western party. It only won two seats outside Western Canada, both in Ontario. Stockwell Day proved to be an ineffective leader, and he was replaced in 2002 by Stephen Harper, who had been persuaded to re-enter party politics after being away from Parliament for five years. In 2003, Harper managed to orchestrate the merger of the Canadian Alliance and the Progressive Conservatives, and he was chosen as the first leader of the new Conservative Party of Canada.

As leader of the Conservative Party, Stephen Harper attempted to reconstruct Brian Mulroney's winning coalition of Western neo-conservative populists, Ontario tories, and Quebec nationalists. Harper has referred to these groups as the "three sisters" of the conservative coalition in Canada. The new Conservative Party was strong in Western Canada from the get go, but its support in Ontario was limited mostly to rural areas, and it only had a smattering of support in Quebec (also in rural areas). This was sufficient to allow the Conservative Party to win minority governments in the 2006 and 2008 elections, but it

The late Jack Layton with his wife Olivia Chow (who was also a Member of Parliament from 2006–2014)

David Cooper/ZUMAPRESS/Newscom

remained notably weak in urban Canada; in three elections, it did not elect a single member in Montreal, Toronto, or Vancouver. So long as it remained weak in urban Canada, it was not in a position to win a majority government. In 2011, however, it made significant inroads in urban Canada, especially Toronto, which helped propel the new Conservative Party to its first majority government.

The 2011 election would appear to mark the beginning of a new party system. The unification of the two former conservative parties is now complete, and the new Conservative Party is clearly the dominant party in the system, although it remains weak in Quebec. The NDP made a dramatic breakthrough, especially in Quebec, and it is now positioned as the Official Opposition in Parliament. However, the NDP coalition appears fragile. The party is now dominated by Members of Parliament from Quebec, many of whom are new to the NDP. It is not clear at this point if the NDP can hang on to its newfound support in Quebec, especially after the death of leader Jack Layton in August 2011.

The Liberal Party suffered its worst defeat ever in 2011. The Liberals, for the first time, now find themselves as the third party in Parliament. It is not clear what will become of the Liberals: They may be able to mount a comeback, they may disappear entirely, or they may be destined to be perennially the third party in Parliament, much like the formerly great Liberal Party of Great Britain. The Bloc Québécois was also decimated. It was reduced from 47 seats before the election to just four. The *Bloquistes* now have to make a big decision: Do they rebuild the party? Or do they fold their tent and campaign for the provincial Parti Québécois?

On the other hand, the Green Party enjoyed a breakthrough: Elizabeth May became the first member of the Green Party to be elected to Parliament. She won the seat of Saanich–Gulf Islands in British Columbia (see Box 3.1). However, the Green Party still faces an uphill battle to become a major party in Canadian politics, as will be discussed in the next chapter.

The Evolution of the Green Party

Elizabeth May

The seeds for the Green Party were sown in the 1980 election when a dozen activists, including a very young Elizabeth May, ran for office on the environmental theme of "small is beautiful." They referred to themselves unofficially as the "Small Party." The Green Party of Canada was officially formed in 1983, and the party ran 60 candidates in the federal election the following year. For the next 20 years, the Greens remained a fringe party. The party went through a succession of leaders, never ran a full slate of candidates, and never received more than 1 percent of the vote, although it increased its vote incrementally in each successive election. Then, in 2004, the party ran a full slate of candidates for the first time and its vote total jumped to 4.3 percent. In 2006, Elizabeth May became the leader of the party and in the 2008 election the party received just under 1 million votes and captured nearly 7 percent of the vote. In 2011, the party's vote declined to under 600 000 and just under 4 percent, but Elizabeth May became the first Green candidate ever to be elected to the House of Commons. She was elected in the BC riding of Saanich–Gulf Islands, just northeast of Victoria.

So, how should we describe the party system after the 2011 election? For the moment, it would appear to be a two-party-plus system, but it seems unstable. If the NDP can consolidate its position or if the Liberals can mount a comeback, it may remain a two-party-plus system. On the other hand, the left side of the spectrum may remain divided, especially if the Bloc rebuilds, leaving the Conservatives as the only major party in the system. In this scenario, we would return to a single-party dominant system, but the opposite of the system we had in the 1990s when the Liberals were the only major party and the right side of the spectrum was divided between the two conservative parties. See Figure 3.1 for a summary of the history of the Canadian party system.

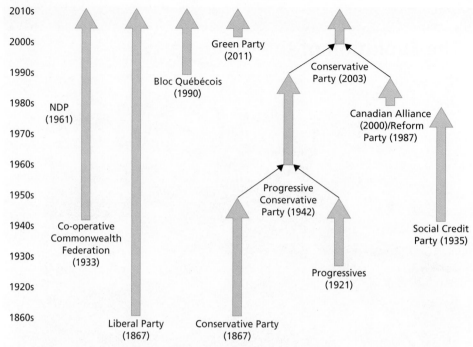

Figure 3.1 History of the Canadian Party System

Note: The Green Party of Canada was formed in 1983, but it did not elect any candidates until 2011 when leader Elizabeth May won the riding of Saanich–Gulf Islands in British Columbia.

Parties as Election Machines

Canadian political parties are commonly described as election machines—organizations designed to get their candidates elected to Parliament. But it is important to remember that parties are first and foremost associations of people—ordinary citizens with an interest in politics. All of the major parties have thousands of members. Furthermore, it is easy to become a member of a political party in Canada. Just go to the party website of your choice (see Box 3.2), fill out the form, pay a few bucks, and you're in. Conservatives will obviously join the Conservative Party, liberals will join the Liberal Party, democratic socialists will join the NDP, Quebec sovereignists will join the Bloc Québécois, and environmentalists will join the Green Party. Membership in a party has its privileges; as a member of a political party, you can participate in the selection of the party leader, you can attend party conventions and vote on the party's policies, you can help nominate the party candidate to run in your electoral district, and ultimately you can help your local candidate get elected by participating in the election campaign.

Canadian political parties are regarded as private organizations and are thus largely self-regulating, especially when it comes to leadership selection and the nomination of candidates for election and policy development. But there are also some statutory rules (laws of Parliament) governing political parties, particularly in relation to how parties finance their operations. During election campaigns, parties are also required to follow the Canada Elections Act, but some have argued that Canada needs stronger rules to govern political parties.[2]

Box 3.2

Canadian Party Websites

www.blocquebecois.org
www.conservative.ca
www.greenparty.ca

www.liberal.ca
www.ndp.ca
www.marijuanaparty.ca

Leadership Selection

The selection of the party leader is extremely important. The leader is the public face of the party, and many voters will decide how to vote based on the performance of the leader. In the old days, party leaders were selected by the members of the party in Parliament—the **caucus**. This selection process made sense; members of the caucus are presumably in the best position to know who is best able to lead them. This method of choosing a leader was also quick, cheap, and efficient, but over time it came to be seen as elitist and undemocratic.

caucus All the members of a political party elected to Parliament and appointed to the Senate.

In 1919, the Liberal Party selected Mackenzie King as their new leader at a party convention. This method of choosing a leader became the norm for all parties thereafter. It is probably not coincidental that this "more democratic" process took root after the emergence of the Progressive Party and the rise of populism in Western Canada. In this new process, party members would elect delegates to attend a leadership convention, and the delegates would choose the new leader. The delegate selection was frequently a rough-and-tumble affair, with lots of arm-twisting and backstabbing. Typically, a few thousand delegates would attend the convention, including members of the caucus and other party officials who were automatically granted delegate status.

At the convention, the winning candidate would need to be supported by 50 percent of the delegates. If, after the first round of voting, no candidate had passed the threshold, the candidate with the fewest votes was eliminated from the contest and a new round of voting would be held. It would often take multiple ballots, or rounds of voting, before a winner was determined. As candidates dropped off the ballot, their delegates would be "released" and free to support another candidate, although failed candidates would often attempt to direct their delegates to another candidate. It was always a very dramatic moment in a convention when a failed candidate crossed the floor with an entourage of supporters to form an alliance with a candidate still on the ballot. Eventually, one candidate would emerge with 50 percent support, at which point the convention president would ask the delegates to make the choice "unanimous" by shouting their approval. Leadership conventions were exciting and often bruising affairs—it made for excellent reality television.

The delegated leadership convention, however, was not entirely problem free. For one thing, many people would leave a convention with hurt feelings. The losing candidates would obviously be disappointed, but frequently delegates were wounded by the contest. While conventions were supposed to unite a party, all too often they would divide the party instead, sometimes for decades; the Liberal Party of Canada is still scarred by the 1990 leadership convention when Jean Chrétien triumphed over Paul Martin. Convention delegates are also the most passionate party members, and they may not be representative of the membership in general, let alone the voting public. They may thus make choices that do not resonate with the rest of the party or the public. Stéphane Dion, the former leader of the Liberal Party, is a case in point.

By the 1990s, with the rise of the Reform Party and another wave of populism, the delegated convention struck many as elitist and undemocratic. Many also viewed it as obsolete. In the age of the Internet, it was now conceivable for all members of the party to attend a virtual convention. The Reform Party (and Canadian Alliance), the Bloc Québécois, and virtually all parties at the provincial level shifted to a leadership selection model that gave every member of the party the opportunity to choose the new leader. When the leader is selected by all the party members, he or she is clearly more representative of the party membership and likely stands a greater chance of resonating with the public. However, the membership might still foist an ineffectual leader on the party's parliamentary caucus. Stockwell Day, the former leader of the Canadian Alliance, is a case in point.

This selection process also made the convention redundant. Parties, however, did not want to forgo the opportunity to bring members (and hopefully the television networks) together, but the sight of people waiting around for a computer to count the virtual ballots makes for very boring television. But there is a much more serious problem with direct leadership elections:

> Direct elections are much more atomistic than conventions. This is particularly true of telephone, mail, and Internet ballots that allow members to cast a vote without ever leaving home or perhaps even talking to another party member. In a country built on a tradition of parties seeking accommodative bridges across deep linguistic and regional divides, this is cause for concern.[3]

In the early 2000s, the Liberals and the Progressive Conservatives experimented with a "hybrid" model of leadership selection that attempted to combine a direct leadership election with the benefits of a delegated convention, but the experiment was short lived. All of the major parties have now converted to some version of direct election because it is "more democratic."

In sum, the selection of party leaders is now much more democratic than it was 100 years ago, but this may not be an entirely positive development. The selection of leaders by the party membership has made leaders considerably more powerful than in the past. When leaders were selected by the party caucus in Parliament, they could also be dumped by the caucus—this forced leaders to be responsive to their parliamentary colleagues. Now that leaders are chosen by the membership, the caucus is powerless to remove an ineffectual leader, and leaders can freely ignore the wishes of caucus if they so desire. Indeed, leaders, some more than others, now rule their parliamentary caucuses with iron fists. Members of caucus, who are the elected representatives of the people, are consequently restricted in their ability to express their views and represent the concerns of their constituents. The situation is compounded if the leader becomes prime minister. Over the past 40 years, there has been a steady centralization of power in the Prime Minister's Office, arguably reaching its peak with Prime Minister Harper. We will return to this issue in Chapter 5.

Candidate Selection

electoral districts The geographical constituencies in which Members of Parliament are elected in Canada's single-member plurality electoral system. There are currently 308 electoral districts in Canada, each with more or less comparable populations.

riding Another term for electoral district or constituency in Canada's single-member plurality electoral system. The term is uniquely Canadian.

The party also needs to choose individuals to run for the party in each election. Canada is divided into 308 **electoral districts** based largely on population. These districts are also known as constituencies or **ridings**. The national political parties organize themselves according to the ridings. When you join a political party, you belong to a particular constituency association. Candidates for the election are chosen by the members of the party in the constituency association. For example, Conservative Party members in the riding of Winnipeg South get to choose the candidate to run for the Conservative Party in Winnipeg South, and so on across the country.

When a party stands a good chance of winning the riding in the election, the nomination process is often hotly contested. Multiple individuals will seek the nomination, and each contestant will typically try to sell as many party memberships as possible and attempt to pack the nomination meeting with their supporters. On the other hand, if a party does not stand much chance of winning the riding, it may struggle to find a candidate to contest the election. While the major parties usually field a full slate of 308 candidates, the fringe parties are typically unable to do so. Once the candidate has been nominated by the members in the local constituency association, it is their job to help the candidate get elected, as we will discuss below.

The Aggregation of Political Demands and Party Platforms

If parties want to get their candidates elected, they must have some idea of what the public needs or wants. One of the most important tasks for political parties is to *aggregate* the demands of the electorate. Since no party can be all things to all people, parties package the demands of the electorate in different sets. Each party thus provides the electorate with a distinct program of what it would do if it were elected as the government. Since the electorate is very diverse, the parties may adopt different strategies in aggregating demands and building a party platform.

Some parties will try to provide a broad platform based on what the public *wants*, while other parties will offer a very narrow set of policies based on what they believe the country *needs*. Some parties will try to appeal to as many voters as possible, while other parties will tailor their platform to appeal to a specific segment of the electorate. The NDP, for example, aims its policies at "working class" voters, although now it usually speaks euphemistically about "ordinary" Canadians. In fact, the NDP now draws considerable support from middle class professionals in the public sector, such as civil servants, nurses, teachers, and university professors. The Bloc Québécois, of course, designs its policies to appeal only to one specific region of the country. Parties adopt their policies at party conventions held every second year. Ultimately, however, the campaign platform is determined by the leader and his or her campaign staff.

Party Organization and Financing

Canadian political parties are large organizations with tens of thousands of members. It takes a lot of work to run a political party, and the leader is far too busy to look after all of the logistical details in party operations. The major parties thus have an organizational wing and a parliamentary wing. We see the parliamentary wing in action regularly on television, particularly the leader, but the organizational wing works behind the scenes. Each party has a president, an executive, and a national council; these people are elected by the membership to run the party.

In short, the organizational wing is responsible for making sure that the party has enough money for the next election. In the 2011 election, each of the major parties spent about $21 million. Why so much? Because elections are very expensive. For a start, each party rents a jet airliner and crew for six weeks to fly the leader back and forth across the country. Then there are all the buses and hotels for the leader and his or her campaign staff. Advertising is also a huge expense: It costs a lot of money to make and air television commercials, and even newspaper and radio ads are expensive. Canadian political parties also spend a huge amount of money on opinion polling. During election campaigns, political parties—or more precisely the market research companies hired by the parties—poll Canadians every day by telephone. This gives parties a clear sense of what voters are thinking and how they are responding to the campaign. Raising money for the election is thus a major preoccupation for political parties.

Party fundraising was historically a sleazy business, and there was a perception that money would buy influence. One of Jean Chrétien's last acts in office was the introduction of public financing for political parties. Under the legislation, parties initially received $1.75 for each vote they received in an election. This figure was indexed to inflation, so after the 2008 election the parties received about $1.95 for each vote. This may not sound like much, until you realize that the Conservative Party received more than 5 million votes in the 2008 election, and the Liberal Party received almost 4 million. Even the Green Party, which did not elect a single candidate, received almost 1 million votes. This financing scheme, in general, was beneficial for smaller parties with a limited ability to raise funds. The public subsidy went a long way toward financing election campaigns for the major parties, but only the Bloc Québécois could live off the public subsidy because they only campaign in one province. Consequently, the major parties still have to raise millions of dollars to finance their election campaigns, but individual contributions were also severely limited under the new legislation. Jean Chrétien set the limit at $5000, but Stephen Harper's government consequently lowered it even further to $1100. The maximum contribution an individual can make is now $1200.

Over the last few years, the Conservative Party has mastered the art of raising small donations from numerous contributors. This is almost certainly a result of the Conservative Party's roots in the populist Reform Party. On the other hand, the Liberals and the NDP have struggled to adjust to the new financing environment. The Liberal Party historically relied on large corporate donations, while the NDP relied on large contributions from labour unions. Thus, ironically, Jean Chrétien's party financing laws have worked much more to the advantage of the Conservative Party. The Conservatives, in fact, have long argued that the vote subsidy should be abolished entirely, and after winning a majority government in 2011, the Conservative government did just that. While the subsidy will be eliminated in phases over a couple of years, the elimination of the subsidy will be highly detrimental to most parties in the system except the Conservative Party, which remains solvent thanks to its mastery of fundraising.

Prime Minister Harper argued for the abolition of the public subsidy saying that it was unfair for the public to finance political parties they did not support. However, this argument was flawed for a couple of reasons. First, each voter had the opportunity to direct his or her donation to the party of his or her choice in the election. Conservative voters were making $2 donations to the Conservative Party, Green voters were making a comparable donation to the Green Party, and so on and so forth. Second, the total bill for party subsidies was only $27 million—a tiny fraction of the government's $300 billion annual budget. And, more to the point, the Government of Canada continues to subsidize political parties with public money through tax credits for political donations. If someone gives the maximum $1200 donation to a political party, they receive a credit of about $600 when they file their next tax return. This public subsidization of parties actually tends to benefit the Conservative Party to a larger extent because they generally have more affluent supporters who can afford to make the maximum political donation to a party.

Election Campaigning

While parties spend years gearing up for an election, the formal campaign lasts just six weeks. Canadian election campaigns have two distinct parts. First, there is the national campaign, which is focused almost entirely on the leader. In the old days, the leader travelled by train and his speeches were reported by the local newspapers at each stop along the line. Today, the leaders criss-cross the country in chartered jetliners, and his or her campaign events are reported locally and nationally on television news and in local and national newspapers. Additionally, all of the parties air numerous commercials on the radio, television, and Internet. With the leader flying from here to there and party messages transmitted over the air waves, this part of the campaign is known in the media as the *air war*. The second part of the campaign takes part in each of the 308 electoral districts in the country, when party volunteers take to the streets in communities across the country to persuade citizens to vote for their candidate. This is known as the *ground war*.

The Air War   The national campaign is all about the leader, especially when the leader gives support to local candidates in ridings where the contest is close and the party has a fighting chance of taking the seat. National campaigns are run by professional political operatives, with little or no input from ordinary party members. National campaigns also tend to be driven by technology, and campaign dynamics have evolved with the development of new technology. Over time, Canadian political parties have become increasingly sophisticated electoral machines, although they lag behind their US counterparts.

The advent of television in the 1950s dramatically changed the nature of campaigns. It shifted the focus away from local campaigns to the leader, and the media's focus on the leader has only increased with time. With television, the campaign also became truly national, as the leader's daily activities were reported across the country on the nightly news. At the time, there were only a handful of television networks in the country, so anyone who owned a television would be sure to see these reports. Many families, of course, did not own a television, but they would hear about the campaign on the radio.

While election campaigns have been revolutionized in the twenty-first century by computers and the Internet, the national television debate between the leaders is still one of the most important parts of the campaign. With the proliferation of media options in the twenty-first century, many voters will not see or hear any of the campaign news, preferring instead to watch the sports channel or the cooking channel or catch up with friends on Facebook. The leaders' debate may, in fact, be the only time some voters tune in to the election campaign, and they may well decide how to vote based on a particular leader's performance. The stakes are thus very high for the leaders, and they are carefully coached for the debate by handlers, who are almost equally concerned with the leader's clothes as they are with how the leader should answer the questions. Winning the debate is hard, but losing it is very easy. An awkward grimace, a quivering lip, or a flat joke can destroy a party's chance of winning the election. There are two debates in every election, one in English and one in French, and the media are always on the lookout for a verbal slip when a leader is speaking in his or her second language. The leaders thus tend to be excessively cautious, and they stay very close to the script provided to them by their handlers, no matter what questions are asked.

In the twenty-first century, campaigns have been revolutionized by computers, although perhaps not fully. To date, surprisingly, Canadian political parties have not made very imaginative use of the Internet. For the most part, party websites have been used to "amplify traditional methods of campaigning."[4] While social media tools such as Facebook and Twitter were employed to a much greater extent in the 2011 election, some critics argued that Canadian political parties did not employ these tools to their full potential. In short, they failed to create an interactive electoral experience for voters.[5] On the other hand, parties are using computers behind the scenes to collect vast amounts of personal information about voters, and the potential exists for parties to send highly targeted messages to individual voters.[6] How is this possible? First, parties have access to our home addresses through the permanent voters list maintained by Elections Canada. Second, parties purchase market research information, like magazine subscription lists, and the two sets of information can be merged electronically. For example, if you have a subscription to a hunting and fishing magazine, you might get a letter from the Conservative Party outlining the party's pledge to scrap the long-gun registry. Parties are also slowly learning how to use computer technology to improve their fundraising efforts, although Canadian parties have a long way to go before matching the standard set by Barack Obama in the 2008 and especially the 2012 US presidential elections.

In many respects, the new technology has not changed political campaigning so much as it has made campaigning more fragmented and frenetic. Parties no longer have a captive audience, because voters are no longer camped out in front of their televisions watching one or two channels. Party messages must now be transmitted in numerous formats: in the newspaper, on the radio and television, on the party website, on Twitter and other social networking sites, and on YouTube. And, with smartphones at the ready, information now moves instantaneously. In the old days, if a leader made a mistake it would be reported in the paper the next day and the responses of the other leaders would appear in the paper the day after that. With the advent of television, the news cycle was cut from 48 hours to 24. Now, if Justin Trudeau says something silly in St. John's, Stephen Harper can respond immediately from Saskatoon, and the cable news networks will have the comments on the air within minutes. Politicians must also be aware of "ambush journalism"—citizens armed with smartphones hoping to catch a photo or video of a politician in an unguarded moment that they can upload to YouTube or Instagram. Canadian politicians have consequently become guarded because they are terrified that the tiniest mistake will cost them votes or even the election.

Ground War   The media tends to be highly focused on the air war, but ultimately Canadian elections are won and lost on the ground in the 308 electoral districts spread across the country. The real grunt work of Canadian politics happens on the ground through the volunteer efforts of ordinary party members who talk directly to voters. While the national campaign has become increasingly sophisticated, "this very local dimension of political life goes on much as it has for over a century."[7] And there is no better way to get to know your community than to participate in a local election campaign. You will discover places in your neighbourhood that you never knew existed, you will meet a diverse array of people, and you will come to understand their political concerns and hopes and aspirations for the country. It can be an eye-opening experience.

Party candidates, as discussed above, are chosen by the members of the local constituency associations, and when the election campaign formally begins the members are expected to help their candidate get elected. Many things have to be done if the candidate is going to get elected: the candidate will need a headquarters, usually a vacant storefront; lawn signs will have to be ordered; pamphlets will need to be written and printed; and buttons with the candidate's name and party logo will need to be produced. A big part of every local campaign is identifying potential supporters. Obviously, the campaign will want to contact all current and former party members in the riding, previous financial contributors to the party, individuals who have had a party lawn sign in past elections, as well as individuals who indicate to canvassers that they intend to support the party's candidate. Campaigns will also know from previous elections what parts of the community tend to be more disposed toward the party. In each riding, there will be a few dozen polling stations—at elementary schools, churches, and community centres—and the vote tallies from each polling station are announced after each election. Each party will therefore know where to place their greatest campaign efforts. Each candidate needs a telephone team to stay in touch with potential supporters, because it is important to make sure that identified supporters stay on side during the campaign. Finally, at the end of the campaign, it is essential to get the "vote out." Potential supporters will be called one more time and implored to vote, and a well-organized campaign will have volunteers available to drive seniors and shut-ins to the polling stations.

In contrast to the highly scripted and professional national campaigns, local campaigns are remarkably refreshing. In many ridings, the outcome of the election can be safely predicted at the outset, but nevertheless almost all candidates campaign vigorously and honestly, and candidates tend to be humbled when they live in the community and are meeting voters face to face. Anyone who has become cynical about politics should involve themselves in a local campaign, as they will likely find their faith in the democratic process restored.

The Golden Rules of Canadian Politics

What are the keys to success for Canadian political parties? That, of course, depends on the definition of success. Some parties are in the game of politics to win and form the government, while other parties have different goals. If a party wants to win an election, it must mould itself to the Canadian political landscape. It must be ideologically moderate or centrist, and it must be able to broker a political coalition across the diverse regions of Canada, especially across the linguistic divide. These are known as **brokerage parties**. In the twentieth century, the Liberal Party of Canada was a brokerage party *par excellence*, but in the twenty-first century the Liberal Party has encountered troubled waters. In short, the politics of brokerage may no longer be the key to success in Canadian politics. The rules of the political game in Canada may be very different in the twenty-first century.

Some political parties, however, are not necessarily in the game to win—they are in the game to offer a principled alternative to the pragmatic parties. These parties believe that they have the right ideas or policies for the country, and they are consequently not willing to compromise their principles for electoral advantage. These parties tend to be more rigidly ideological and focused on a particular mission, hence they are known as **missionary parties**. The Green Party and the Bloc Québécois are missionary parties. Greens are concerned about the environment, while the Bloc's mission is the sovereignty of Quebec. Other parties are even more particularistic. The Marijuana Party is devoted solely to the decriminalization of illicit drugs. These parties are known as **single issue parties**. Missionary parties can have some electoral success if their support is concentrated in particular regions. Single issue parties rarely elect candidates, but they can raise awareness about their issue.

brokerage parties Parties that are able to appeal to the different regions of Canada, especially the two major linguistic groups. Brokerage parties tend to be ideologically pragmatic, following the wishes of the voters rather than standing on a set of predetermined principles.

missionary parties Parties that are strongly committed to their political principles, and they are generally not willing to compromise their principles for electoral advantage. They stand in contrast to pragmatic brokerage parties.

single issue parties Parties that are preoccupied with only one issue. The Marijuana Party, for example, is concerned primarily with the decriminalization of drugs, especially marijuana.

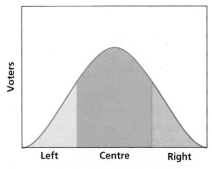

Figure 3.2 The Political Bell Curve: On the left-right spectrum, the largest number of voters are situated in the middle, with very few on the far left and the far right

Ideological Pragmatism

If a party wants to win an election, it must appeal to the largest number of voters. Where are most voters situated? If we attempted to measure the ideological temperament of Canadians, we would expect to see a *normal* distribution, or a *bell curve*. Most voters would be situated in the middle of the spectrum, either a little to the right or a little to the left, and there would be fewer voters as one moves further to the right or left. The far left and the far right have virtually no voters (see Figure 3.2). A party that wants to win an election will consequently attempt to position itself in the centre of the political spectrum. In order to do so, the party leader and its candidates may need to modify or compromise their political beliefs and principles. In other words, they need to be ideologically flexible or pragmatic.

Historically, the Liberal Party has been the most ideologically flexible party. It has been able to shift quite easily to the left or the right depending on the prevailing political winds. This is one advantage of sitting in the centre of the political spectrum. The old Progressive Conservative Party was also ideologically pragmatic, but it always had less room to manoeuvre. For the Progressive Conservative Party, there were not many votes to be had on its right side, and the left side was blocked by the Liberal Party.

On the other side, the NDP had little to gain by moving left, but it could not move to the right because the Liberals were an immovable force in the centre. New Democrats have long argued amongst themselves about the best strategy for the party. Some members want the party to be more pragmatic in a bid to enhance the party's electoral fortunes, while others want the party to be more resolutely socialist. A move to the left might relegate the party to third-place status in Parliament and perhaps right out of Parliament altogether, while a move to the centre would make the NDP look a lot like the Liberals but with less credibility in the business community, thus possibly making the NDP wholly irrelevant. Thus, by default, the NDP has become a *pragmatic missionary* party.

What about the Conservative Party? The Progressive Conservatives were ideologically pragmatic, but the Reform/Canadian Alliance was more of a right-wing missionary party. When Stephen Harper was a member of the Reform Party he was a principled conservative, and he evidently did not want the party to moderate its principles for electoral advantage. This, in fact, may be why he quit politics four years after being elected as an MP to become the president of the National Citizens Coalition, a right-wing think tank based in Calgary. As leader of the Conservative Party, however, Stephen Harper has attempted to position the Conservatives as a moderate centre–right party, but many voters are not convinced by his newfound pragmatism. They are still not sure who the real Stephen Harper is—the old reformer or the new tory—and they consequently fear that he has a "secret agenda." However, at the same time, the more Harper moves the party to the centre, the more he risks losing his most ardent conservative supporters, especially in the West.

Brokerage Politics

In addition to being ideologically flexible, a party that hopes to win an election must be able to *broker* a political coalition across the major regions of the country. This, historically, has required a party to bridge the linguistic divide in Canada. In the twentieth century, the Liberal Party mastered the art of brokerage politics. The Liberal Party was the first party to select a French Canadian leader, Sir Wilfrid Laurier, who subsequently became Canada's first French Canadian prime minister. This won the Liberal Party a huge following in Quebec. Since Laurier, the Liberal Party has exemplified its commitment to brokerage politics by its tradition of alternating between French- and English-speaking leaders. If a party wants to appeal to both French- and English-speaking Canadians, the party leader must be at least functionally, if not fluently, bilingual. This, of course, is not a legal requirement, but it is more than a rule of thumb—it is a requirement for winning the game.

The Conservative Party was a brokerage party under the leadership of Sir John A. Macdonald, but it lost Quebec when Prime Minister Borden introduced conscription during World War I over strong objections from Quebec. (Most able-bodied men in English-speaking Canada had already volunteered for the war by the time conscription was introduced, so conscription effectively forced French Canadian men into the war against their will.) After World War II, the Progressive Conservatives attempted to engage in brokerage politics, but they only succeeded twice: first under John Diefenbaker in the 1950s and more successfully under Brian Mulroney in the 1980s. The Conservatives did not choose their first French Canadian leader until after the 1993 election, when the party was reduced to two seats and one of those seats belonged to a Francophone, Jean Charest, who went on to become premier of Quebec. Stephen Harper made a sincere effort to reach out to Quebec, and he had some success in the 2006 election when the party won 10 seats in the province, but subsequently the Conservatives have not been able to increase their support in Quebec. In fact, the Conservatives were reduced to just five seats in Quebec in 2011 (even though they still managed to eke out a majority government).

In sum, historically at least, if a party wanted to win an election and form the Government of Canada, it needed to be a pragmatic brokerage party. In the twentieth century, the Liberal Party of Canada was a very successful brokerage party and was consequently a very successful political party—the most successful election machine in the world, in fact; the Liberals governed Canada for 69 of the 100 years during the twentieth century. The Liberal coalition has been ideologically cohesive from coast to coast, and the Liberal Party effectively appealed to large segments of Canadian society, notably Catholics, immigrants, and women. By the end of the twentieth century, the Liberal Party was known as Canada's *natural governing party*.

The Liberal Party, however, is now in crisis. Its glory days as a pragmatic brokerage party are gone, perhaps for good. After sweeping to power in 1968, Pierre Trudeau's Liberal Party lost virtually all of its support in Western Canada. By 1980, the Trudeau Liberals only had two seats in Western Canada, and the party remains conspicuously weak west of Ontario. Conversely, in 1980 the Liberal Party won all but one seat in Quebec. Since Trudeau retired in 1984, however, the Liberal Party has lost its base of support in Quebec. Presently, it is little more than a rump party in Quebec, concentrated in the non-Francophone areas of Montreal. In 2011, the Liberals lost much of their remaining support in urban Canada, and they even lost support in Atlantic Canada. It is not clear how the Liberals can rebuild a winning coalition.

The various conservative parties have all struggled with the politics of brokerage, at least subsequent to the successful tenure of Sir John A. Macdonald. Since Macdonald, conservative parties have only enjoyed short interludes in government after long periods of Liberal rule. Robert Borden (1911–1920), R.B. Bennett (1930–1935), John Diefenbaker (1958–1962), and Brian Mulroney (1984–1993) all won majority governments. Indeed, Diefenbaker and Mulroney orchestrated the largest electoral landslides in Canadian history. But none of the leaders was able to consolidate the Conservative Party's lock on power. Brian Mulroney was a brokerage politician *par excellence*, but the end result of his two terms in office was the complete destruction of his own party and the emergence of two regional parties, the Bloc Québécois and the Reform Party. In contrast to the Liberals, the Conservative's political coalition has been much more fragmented. Conservative tories in Atlantic and Central Canada do not always see eye to eye with conservative populists in Western Canada, and the various conservative parties have only occasionally and very briefly found support in Quebec, mostly among disaffected nationalists. In short, the "three sisters" in the conservative coalition don't really get along with each other well. Stephen Harper has managed to bring together two of the sisters, Western populists and Eastern tories, but Quebec has not warmed to the new Conservative Party.

In 2011, the people of Quebec threw their support to the NDP for the first time. The NDP scooped up 59 seats in Quebec in the 2011 election along with 44 seats outside Quebec. Does this mean that the NDP is now Canada's only brokerage party? It is too early to make that determination. The NDP's support in Quebec is very shallow. Some NDP candidates in Quebec won their seats without campaigning, and in some cases without even setting foot in the riding they were seeking to represent; they were just **paper candidates**—individuals who filed registration papers with Elections Canada as candidates so that the NDP could claim to be running a full national slate, and there was never any expectation that these individuals would actually be elected. Why so many Quebecers ended up voting for the NDP is not clear; it may simply have been a protest vote. The election of Thomas Mulcair, a fluently bilingual Quebecer, as the leader of the NDP may be viewed as an attempt to transform the NDP into a more traditional brokerage party.

paper candidates Members of a political party that file registration papers with Elections Canada as candidates even though they have no expectation of getting elected. They do this so their political party can claim to be running candidates across the nation.

Why has brokerage politics all but collapsed in Canada? We will come back to this question a number of times in later chapters, but it seems that Canada has become a more difficult country to govern. Now, as in 1867, the principal challenge to governing Canada is the ability to broker a coalition across the linguistic divide, but it may be that the two solitudes have nothing left to say to each other. The Conservative Party has demonstrated that it is now possible to win a majority government without much support in Quebec, and it may become easier to repeat that feat in the future. As the population of Canada grows, mostly around Toronto and in the West, Quebec's proportion of the Canadian population is steadily declining, and these demographic changes will be reflected in a new distribution of seats in the House of Commons. The number of seats in the House is slated to increase to 338 in 2014, with 18 new seats in Ontario, 5 in Alberta, and 7 in British Columbia. In short, as Quebec's demographic weight declines in the federation, the politics of brokerage becomes less imperative. This does not bode well for national unity, as we will discuss in later chapters.

From the Politics of Brokerage to Wedge Politics

The 2011 election produced a result not seen before in Canadian politics. For one thing, the Conservative Party demonstrated that it is now possible to win a majority government without substantial representation in Quebec. To the extent that the Conservative Party brokered a winning political coalition, it was between Ontario and the West and not across the linguistic divide. It is not clear how effectively the Conservative Party can govern the country with only five members elected in Quebec. Nor is it clear how people in Quebec will react to having so little representation in government, especially without the presence of the Bloc Québécois in Parliament to champion the province's cause. The collapse of brokerage politics is deeply troubling, as it raises the distinct possibility that Quebec and the rest of Canada may go their separate ways.

Can the politics of brokerage be re-established? With substantial support inside and outside Quebec, it is possible that the New Democratic Party will become Canada's main brokerage party. On the other hand, it is not certain that the NDP can retain its newfound support in Quebec. Before 2011, the NDP had never elected more than one candidate in Quebec, and its breakthrough in the 2011 election may have been a bit of a fluke rather than a significant transformation of Quebec's political culture.

What is Quebec's political culture? On the one hand, people in Quebec are generally left of centre and strongly committed to government social programs. On the surface, this is compatible with the NDP's commitment to democratic socialism. Indeed, on the left–right continuum, Quebecers are probably more comfortable with the NDP's brand of socialism than they are with Stephen Harper's style of conservatism.

But it might be too simplistic to look at Quebec in terms of left and right. There is another dimension to Quebec's political culture, what we might call the federal dimension. Quebec, historically at least, has not been comfortable with the federal government playing a strong role in Quebec society. In other words, many Quebecers would prefer Canada to be a relatively *decentralized* federation. On this dimension, the NDP, which has historically favoured a highly centralized federation, seems to be out of step with Quebec's political culture. The NDP has tried to square this circle by offering a program of **asymmetrical federalism**—treating Quebec as a province *unlike* the others. It is not clear that asymmetrical federalism will fly in the rest of Canada, though, as will be discussed in subsequent chapters.

The Bloc Québécois is the only party that appeals to Quebec on both dimensions (see Figure 3.3). So why did the Bloc fail so miserably in 2011? It is too early to know for sure. It is possible that the political culture of Quebec is shifting, or maybe Quebecers simply grew weary of Gilles Duceppe's style of leadership. While the displacement of the Bloc clears the way for another party to re-establish the politics of brokerage, it is not yet clear that any of the federalist parties can capitalize on this opportunity. And, if the political culture of Quebec has not appreciably changed, it is possible that the Bloc may be able to mount a comeback.

In 2011, the Conservative Party also seemed to produce a victory without necessarily occupying the broad middle part of the political spectrum. Instead, the Conservative Party captured power from the right. How did they do it? It has been suggested that the Conservative Party succeeded with a strategy of **wedge politics**—creating lines in the sand on particular issues so that the single largest group of people were standing with the Conservative Party while the rest of the electorate was more or less equally divided among the other parties.[8] Most notably, the Conservatives made crime a major wedge issue: Voters who supported tougher penalties for criminals overwhelmingly supported the Conservative Party, while those not so concerned about crime divided their support among four parties. The Conservative Party resisted the temptation to use "hot button" issues like abortion and capital punishment as

asymmetrical federalism A type of federalism in which the provinces exercise different powers.

wedge politics When a political party chooses to take one side of a particular "hot button" issue to attract more votes and divide the remaining electorate among the opposing parties.

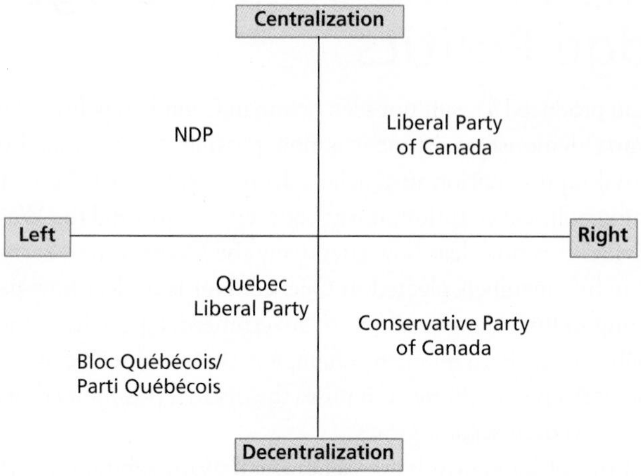

Figure 3.3 The Two Dimensions of Quebec's Political Culture

wedges, but its support for low taxes, the military, and Israel were effectively employed as wedge issues and enabled the Conservatives to capture new seats in the 2011 election.

The 2011 election may prove to be a critical turning point in Canadian electoral history as it may have signalled a transformation of the Canadian party system. The Liberal Party was seriously depleted in the 2011 election, and the Bloc Québécois was decimated; it is too early to know if either party will be able to recover. Thus, for the first time, the Canadian party system is dominated by two parties rooted in the populist tradition of Western Canada, with the Conservative Party firmly on the right and the New Democratic Party just as firmly on the left. With the decline of the broadly centrist Liberal Party, many Canadians are worried that politics will become considerably more polarized in the new party system. Tom Flanagan, a retired professor of political science at the University of Calgary and a former senior adviser to Stephen Harper, has suggested that Canadian politics will not become polarized in the future. Instead, he argues that the Conservatives and the NDP will both converge on the centre of the political spectrum because Canadian political culture is broadly centrist.[9]

Professor Flanagan's argument sounds plausible in theory, but it becomes a little difficult to swallow when he suggests that this is precisely what happens in the United States, Britain, Germany, and Australia. But we don't have to look beyond our borders to get a glimpse of what politics might look like in the new Canadian party system. With a Conservative majority government and an NDP opposition, the party system now bears a striking resemblance to the politics of British Columbia. Since the 1950s, BC politics has been dominated by a centre–right party (previously the Social Credit Party but currently the Liberal Party) with a socialist opposition party (first the CCF and now the NDP). Politics in British Columbia is ideologically polarized as in no other province (the federalist–sovereignist cleavage in Quebec is a different beast entirely). The BC Liberal Party and the Conservative Party of Canada are cut from the same cloth, while the NDP in British Columbia is tightly integrated with the federal New Democratic Party. There is thus every reason to believe that politics in the new federal party system, so long as it lasts, will come to resemble the polarized politics of British Columbia.

Stephen Harper does not have strong connections to British Columbia (he was born and raised in Toronto and moved to Alberta as a young man), but there is reason to believe that he has long desired to establish a polarized two-party system at the federal level, with the Conservatives and the NDP as the major parties. In the absence of a viable Liberal Party in the centre of the spectrum, Harper evidently believes that Canadians will opt to elect the Conservatives rather than the NDP more often than not. In this way, the Conservatives would become the "natural governing party" of Canada in the twenty-first century. If this plan succeeds—and so far it is working—politics in the twenty-first century may not resemble the pragmatic brokerage politics of the last century. Rather than trying

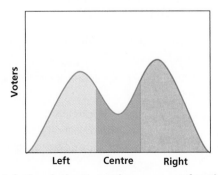

Figure 3.4 In the 2011 federal election, the support for the Liberal Party collapsed to an all time low with the NDP stronger of the left and the Conservative Party stronger on the right thereby creating a more polarized party system

to occupy the middle of the spectrum and pushing all contenders either to the left or the right, the Conservative Party will likely try to drive a wedge through the electorate and marginalize the NDP on the left. The NDP, of course, will try to push the wedge back to the right. In other words, rather than trying to capture the centre, politics will become a tug of war as the left and the right attempt to pull people over to their side (see Figure 3.4).

SUMMARY

Political parties represent different conceptions of the good life, although it must be stressed that the major Canadian political parties are not ideologically pure. While many factors determine the outcome of an election, a party needs to be broadly congruent with Canadian political culture if it wants to win an election. Historically, if a political party wanted to win an election and form the Government of Canada, it needed to situate itself close to the middle of the ideological spectrum and, just as importantly, it had to be able to transcend the linguistic and regional divisions in the country. Throughout the twentieth century, the Liberal Party of Canada mastered the art of moderate broker-age politics and it formed the Government of Canada most of the time; it was Canada's "natural governing party." The Conservative Party, in its different incarnations, struggled with brokerage politics and only occasionally formed the government. Exceptions were John Diefenbaker and Brian Mulroney, who led the largest majority governments in Canadian history.

The Canadian party system was dramatically redefined in the 2011 election, and the rules of brokerage politics may not apply in the twenty-first century. The Conservatives and the New Democrats are presently the dominant parties in the system, with the centrist Liberals positioned very much as the third party. For the first time, the Liberals are now the "plus party" in Canada's two-party-plus system. In other words, Canada's party system is now characterized by a distinctly conservative party and an equally distinct left-wing party, while the centre appears to have evaporated, at least temporarily. And wedge politics, the art of dividing the electorate into distinct ideological camps for electoral advantage, appears to have replaced the politics of brokerage—again, at least for the moment. As long as this party system is sustained, it would seem that Canadian politics will be decidedly more polar-ized in the coming years. However, as we have observed, party systems can change quickly, so it is a little too early to say definitively whether or not Canadian politics has been irrevo-cably transformed by the 2011 election.

Questions to Think About

1. If climate change is the biggest challenge of our time, why is the Green Party still a fringe party in Canada?
2. Should political parties stick to their political principles, or should they be ideologically flexible to meet the demands of voters?
3. Many Canadians have complained that the politics of brokerage forced all the parties to look and sound the same. In a more polarized political environment, the parties will offer much more distinct platforms. Do you think Canadians will appreciate having more distinct choices at election time?
4. What can parties do to re-establish the politics of brokerage?
5. How can parties more effectively use social media as a campaign tool?

Learning Outcomes

1. Describe the historical development of the major political parties in Canada.
2. Identify the major prime ministers in Canadian history and when they served.
3. Describe the main aspects of the air and ground campaigns in Canadian elections.
4. Explain the difference between brokerage and missionary parties.
5. Explain the concept of wedge politics and describe the features of a polarized party system.

Additional Readings

R. Kenneth Carty, William Cross, and Lisa Young, *Rebuilding Canadian Party Politics* (Vancouver, BC: UBC Press, 2000).

Stephen Clarkson, *The Big Red Machine: How the Liberal Party Dominates Canadian Politics* (Vancouver, BC: UBC Press, 2005).

William Cross, *Political Parties* (Vancouver, BC: UBC Press, 2004).

Thomas Flanagan, *Harper's Team: Behind the Scenes in the Conservative Rise to Power* (Montreal, QC: McGill-Queen's University Press, 2007).

Thomas Flanagan, *Waiting for the Wave: The Reform Party and Preston Manning* (Toronto, ON: Stoddart Publishing, 1995).

Brooke Jeffrey, *Divided Loyalties: The Liberal Party of Canada, 1984–2008* (Toronto, ON: University of Toronto Press, 2010).

David Laycock, *The New Right and Democracy in Canada: Understanding Reform and the Canadian Alliance* (Toronto, ON: Oxford University Press, 2002).

Christina McCall-Newman, *Grits: An Intimate Portrait of the Liberal Party* (Toronto, ON: Macmillan, 1982).

William L. Morton, *The Progressive Party in Canada* (Toronto, ON: University of Toronto Press, 1967).

George Perlin, *The Tory Syndrome: Leadership Politics in the Progressive Conservative Party* (Montreal, QC: McGill-Queen's University Press, 1980).

Reginald Whitaker, *The Government Party: Organizing and Financing the Liberal Party of Canada, 1930–1958* (Toronto, ON: University of Toronto Press, 1977).

Alan Whitehorn, *Canadian Socialism: Essays on the CCF-NDP* (Toronto, ON: Oxford University Press, 1992).

Lisa Young, *Feminists and Party Politics* (Vancouver, BC: UBC Press, 2000).

Lisa Young and Harold J. Jansen, eds., *Money, Politics and Democracy: Canada's Party Finance Reforms* (Vancouver, BC: UBC Press, 2011).

Notes

1. Walter D. Young, *Democracy and Discontent: Progressivism, Socialism and Social Credit in the Canadian West*, 2nd ed. (Toronto, ON: McGraw-Hill Ryerson, 1978), 30.
2. William Cross, *Political Parties* (Vancouver, BC: UBC Press, 2004).
3. Ibid., 100.
4. Tamara A. Small, "Canadian Cyberparties: Reflections on Internet-Based Campaigning and Party Systems," *Canadian Journal of Political Science* 40:3 (September 2007), 654.
5. Don Tapscott, "Why Did We Ignore Obama's Social Media Lesson?" *The Globe and Mail*, May 2, 2011.
6. R. Kenneth Carty, William Cross, and Lisa Young, *Rebuilding Canadian Party Politics* (Vancouver, BC: UBC Press, 2000), 200–205.
7. Ibid., 154.
8. Reg Whitaker, "Is the Government Party Over?" *The Globe and Mail*, May 16, 2011, A11.
9. Tom Flanagan, "We don't need a centre party to prevent political polarization," *The Globe and Mail*, May 4, 2011.

Chapter 4
Elections

Key Points

- Canada is a democracy, meaning that the government is elected by the people.
- Electoral systems are the rules by which votes are translated into seats in Parliament.
- There are different types of electoral systems, and each system produces a different result and changes the game of politics.
- Some political parties want Canada to adopt a different electoral system, but Canada still uses the electoral system it inherited from Great Britain in 1867. The debate over Canada's electoral system thus continues.
- If the rules of the game are changed—that is, if Canada adopts a different electoral system—the game of politics in Canada will change as well.

electoral systems The rules by which voter preferences are translated into seats in the legislature.

single-member plurality (SMP) electoral system An electoral system that provides for geographic representation in the legislature. The country is divided into geographic constituencies with approximately equal populations. A number of candidates will contest the election in each constituency, and the candidate with the most votes is elected to the legislature. This electoral system is very easy to use, but the distribution of seats in the legislature is not always proportional to a party's share of the vote in the election.

proportional representation (PR) electoral system An electoral system that ensures the distribution of seats in the legislature is proportional to a party's share of the vote in the election.

Political parties are election machines designed to get their candidates elected to the House of Commons. Some parties are in the game of politics to win, while others want to convey a particular message. The winning political strategy is well known in Canada: winning depends on how closely a party mirrors Canada's political culture and how well it appeals to voters in the different regions of the country, particularly the two linguistic communities. In the last chapter, we examined the dynamics of election campaigning. In this chapter, we are going to focus on the mechanics of the electoral system.

Electoral systems are the rules by which voter preferences are translated into seats in the legislature. Elections are one of the key aspects of democracy, but there are many types of electoral systems, or different ways in which voter preferences may be translated into seats in Parliament. Somehow, 15 million votes need to result in 308 candidates being elected to the House of Commons. And here's the key point: Different electoral systems produce different results. Since this is the case, political scientists say that electoral systems are not neutral. Psephologists—people who study elections—are fond of statistical analyses. The study of elections is by definition a study of numbers, so you may want to have your calculator on hand as you read this chapter.

In this chapter, we will first examine Canada's **single-member plurality (SMP) electoral system**. The SMP electoral system has served Canada well since Confederation, but there are good reasons to believe that it is not entirely fair. Some political parties are advantaged by the SMP electoral system, while other parties are disadvantaged by it. We will also see that the SMP electoral system reinforces some of the major political cleavages in Canadian politics, because SMP provides an imperfect translation of votes into seats. Second, we will consider what Canadian politics would look like if Canada had a different type of electoral system. Some of the electoral systems used in other countries, collectively known as **proportional representation (PR) electoral systems**, provide a more accurate translation of votes into seats, and thus many people believe that proportional representation systems are more fair. The question of electoral reform has consequently been a recurring theme in Canadian politics.

At this particular moment, the likelihood of electoral reform in Canada is slim, but it is still worthwhile to explore the topic for a couple of reasons. First, it provides a dramatic example of how changing the rules of the game would significantly change the game of politics in Canada. Second, there is reason to believe that electoral reform would reduce some of the major political cleavages evident in Canadian politics; for example, a system of proportional representation might serve to minimize the persistence of regionalism in Canada, as well as provide better representation for women and visible minorities. A system of PR might also improve voter turnout in Canadian elections. It is important to note that the rules of the electoral system are enshrined in statutory law enacted by Parliament, and it is thus within the power of Parliament to change the electoral system. The Canada Elections Act is the main statute governing federal elections in Canada.

When Do We Vote?

Before we can discuss Canada's electoral system, we need to know how and when an election is called. Constitutionally, an election is called by the governor general on the request of the prime minister. There are two instances in which a prime minister will ask the governor general for an election. First, the prime minister will ask for an election if the government loses the confidence of the House of Commons. It is unusual for a majority government to lose the confidence of Parliament, but a minority government may lose the confidence of Parliament at any time. On average, minority governments in Canada have lasted for about 18 months.

The second instance in which the prime minister will approach the governor general for an election is a bit more complicated to explain, because the situation has changed since 2006 and is still in flux. Historically, as long as the government maintained the confidence of Parliament, elections were called at the discretion of the prime minister. The Constitution Act 1867 indicates that an election must be held at least every five years, but by convention elections were held about every four years. Prime ministers would survey the political landscape to determine if it was a good time for their party to have an election; if things were not going well for the government, the prime minister would delay the election for as long as possible within the five-year time frame, but if things were going well the prime minister might ask the governor general for an election after just three or three-and-half years. The power to decide when to have an election gave the governing party a huge advantage over the opposition parties.

When the Conservative Party under Stephen Harper came to power in 2006, it introduced a law to fix the election date, and this law was approved by Parliament in November 2006. Under the new law, the election is still called by the governor general, and of course the prime minister would advise the governor general to call an election if the government loses the confidence of Parliament. But otherwise, under the new law, "each general election must be held on the third Monday of October in the fourth calendar year following polling day for the last general election."[1] The new law was intended to put a stop to prime ministers calling an election when it suited their party rather than the country. Under the new law, the next election was scheduled to take place in October 2011.

However, less than two years after the new law was passed by Parliament, Prime Minister Harper advised the governor general to call an election, even though his minority government continued to maintain the confidence of Parliament. In keeping with Canada's system of responsible government, the governor general accepted the prime minister's advice, and an election was set for October 14, 2008. In short, the new law on fixed election dates was ignored. The government was challenged in court for flouting its own election law, but the case was dismissed. The law thus appears to be toothless. The only check, it seems, on the power of the government—and it is a very important check—is public opinion and the power to change the government through voting. And in this instance, the people were not inclined to punish the government for ignoring the election law. Since the Conservatives won a majority government in 2011, one assumes that the next election will occur on October 19, 2015, as per the law on fixed election dates.

Do Fixed Election Dates Improve the Political Process?

The law on fixed election dates is consistent with the theory of populism. It is supposed to take power away from politicians and make elections more fair by giving all the parties the same opportunity to prepare for the election. On the other hand, it may sometimes be desirable to have an election before the scheduled date. An issue may arise in which it is appropriate for the government to ascertain the will of the people before proceeding. The new law, in conjunction with the new rules on party financing, also seems to have led to almost constant campaigning by political parties. This may have been related to the prolonged period of minority governments between 2004 and 2011, but it is also consistent with political practices in the United States, which has long operated with fixed election dates.

More fundamentally, fixed election dates are not necessarily compatible with Canada's system of responsible government. It is difficult to set an election date when the life of the government is dependent on maintaining the confidence of Parliament. More importantly, "the impetus for fixed election dates comes from the mistaken notion that governments are elected; governments, in fact, are appointed, and are responsible to the House of Commons; an election is the election of individuals to serve in the House of Commons."[2] To rephrase the last point, an election provides Canadians the opportunity to select an individual to represent them in Parliament. The government, in turn, is "chosen" by Parliament and appointed by the governor general. In sum, Canada's experiment with fixed election dates is still in its very early stages. It is perhaps too soon to know if the experiment will be successful. It should be noted that many of the provinces have moved to fixed election dates without adverse consequences, but arguably without any major benefits either.

The Single-Member Plurality Electoral System

The electoral system in Canada, for federal and provincial elections, is called the single-member plurality system, or SMP for short. It is also known informally as **first past the post**. SMP was adopted from Great Britain along with Canada's system of responsible government. SMP is a very simple electoral system: the country is divided into 308 electoral districts or ridings, and each party selects a candidate to run in each district. (The number of seats in the House of Commons has increased over time to keep pace with the population of the country; there will be 338 ridings for the election in 2015.) On election day, each voter marks an X beside the name of his or her preferred candidate (see Figure 4.1), and the candidate with a plurality—the most but not necessarily a majority—of votes wins and takes a seat in the House of Commons. All adult citizens are eligible to vote.[3] The party that elects the most candidates wins the election and has the right to form a government with its leader as prime minister. In effect, a Canadian election is really 308 mini-elections held on the same day.

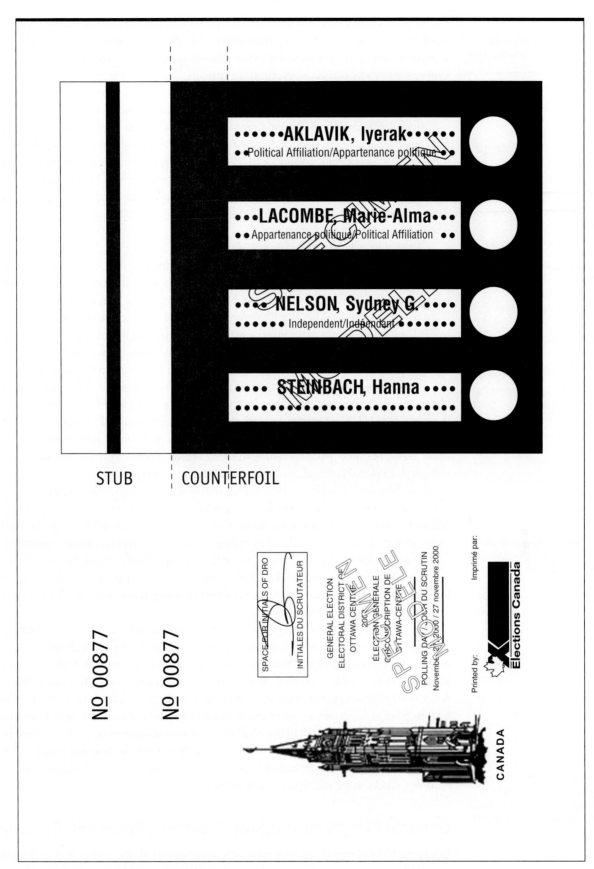

STUB COUNTERFOIL

Nᵒ 00877

Nᵒ 00877

Figure 4.1 Front and Back of an Elections Canada Ballot

Source: Elections Canada. This reproduction is a copy of the version available at www.elections.ca. Reproduced with the permission of Elections Canada.

In a Canadian election, there are 308 separate campaigns, and the battles vary considerably from one riding to the next. The major parties all have a certain number of **safe seats**—seats they can count on winning before the election is even called; for example, the Conservative Party can count on winning virtually all of the seats in Alberta. The regional political cultures of Canada, however, can play out in remarkably confined geographical areas. The Liberal Party, for example, has won the riding of Vancouver Centre in every election since 1993. But the NDP (and previously the CCF) has won the adjacent riding of Vancouver East in every election but two since 1935. And if you travel 60 kilometres east to the city of Abbotsford, you arrive in one of the safest Conservative seats in the country. Party leaders all tend to run in safe ridings; for example, Stephen Harper won his seat in Calgary Southwest in the 2008 election with more than 70 percent of the vote. The leaders simply do not have the time to engage in local campaigning during an election, so it makes sense for them to run in a safe riding.

Other ridings have a long history of electing candidates from different parties. These are known as **swing ridings**. In a swing riding, the election is very competitive, although the competition varies according to location. In Saskatchewan, the competition is primarily between the Conservative Party and the NDP. In Ontario, the Conservatives tend to fight it out with the Liberals. The Bloc Québécois dominated Quebec politics from 1993 through to 2011, with the Liberals providing the main opposition in Montreal and the Conservatives putting up some resistance around Quebec City. The NDP swept most of Quebec in 2011, and it is too soon to know who will provide the greatest challenge to the NDP in Quebec in the future. Some ridings will even have tight three-way races: in 2008, the election in Nunavut was extremely close: Conservative Leona Aglukkaq won by only 466 votes over the second place Liberal candidate, with the NDP candidate just 121 votes further behind.

Canadian elections are won and lost in swing ridings. Political parties will thus devote considerable resources to campaigning in swing ridings. Parties will advertise more in these ridings, professional political operatives from other areas may be brought in to run the campaign, and the leaders will visit these ridings during the campaign, often multiple times (the closer the competition, the more often the leaders will visit). Some swing ridings, known as **bellwether ridings**, have a unique habit of always electing a candidate from the winning party. In technical terms, bellwether ridings constitute a **representative sample** of the Canadian population. In other words, these ridings very closely mirror the political trends prevailing in the whole country. Political parties pay close attention to bellwether ridings. If the campaign goes well for a party in a bellwether riding, it may indicate that the national campaign, as a whole, is going well.

On election night, the party that elects the most candidates "wins" the election and gets to form the government with its leader as prime minister. The media, however, go a step further in their analysis of the election. The media want to know each party's share of the **popular vote** (see Table 4.1). How do you calculate the popular vote? You add up the number of votes received by each party in each of the 308 electoral districts then divide it by the total number of votes cast in the election and multiply by 100 to turn it into a percentage. The popular vote is irrelevant in the SMP electoral system, but it is typically reported by the media on election night because it provides a snapshot of the election in a simple headline. Unfortunately, a focus on the popular vote can lead to some misunderstandings about elections in Canada, as we will discuss momentarily.

General Effects of the SMP Electoral System in Canada

While the SMP electoral system is relatively straightforward, the results of the election are not purely random. Like all electoral systems, SMP influences the game of Canadian politics. If you were a candidate, where would you want to position yourself to get elected in the SMP system? To get elected, you need more votes than any other candidate, and since most

safe seats Ridings that political parties can generally count on winning in the election.

swing ridings Ridings with a long history of electing candidates from different parties.

bellwether ridings Ridings with a unique habit of electing a candidate to Parliament who belongs to the winning party.

representative sample A subset of the population that accurately reflects the entire population.

popular vote The total number of votes received by a political party across all constituencies divided by the number of votes cast in the election and multiplied by 100. It is expressed as a percentage of the vote. This information is irrelevant to the single-member plurality system used in Canada, but it is used by the media to judge the performance of the political parties in the election.

Table 4.1 Federal Election Results 2011, with Popular Vote

Party	Candidates Elected	Total Number of Votes	Share of Popular Vote	Share of Seats in House of Commons
Conservative Party	166	5 832 401	39.62%	53.90%
NDP	103	4 508 474	30.63%	33.44%
Liberal Party	34	2 783 175	18.91%	11.04%
Bloc Québécois	4	889 788	6.04%	1.30%
Green Party	1	576 221	3.91%	0.32%
Other	0	130 521	0.89%	0.00%
Total	308	14 720 580	100.00%	100.00%

votes are in the centre of the political spectrum, you need to put yourself there if you want to get elected. Similarly, if a party wants to win as many seats as possible, it will place itself in the middle of the ideological spectrum. So, in the SMP electoral system, the major parties will compete to occupy the centre ground. And, as a general rule, there is only space in the middle of the spectrum for two major parties. In Canada, only two parties have ever won an election: the Liberal Party and some version of the Conservative Party.

The single-member plurality system is also used in Great Britain and the United States. And in Great Britain, there are only two major parties: the Labour Party and the Conservative Party. Similarly, in the United States there are only two major parties: the Republican Party and the Democratic Party. In short, SMP drives a country toward a two-party political system. This trend was first noted by the French political scientist Maurice Duverger and is known today as **Duverger's law**. Duverger also noted that countries that employ the SMP system will typically have a one-party majority government as opposed to multi-party **coalition governments**, and that the two major parties will alternate in and out of government.

Duverger's law A law that stipulates the single-member plurality electoral system will result in a party system with two strong parties and most likely only two parties.

coalition governments Governments that are composed of two or more political parties.

The SMP system therefore works well when there are *only* two parties. With only two candidates in each riding, the person with the most votes will have a majority of the votes, and the party that elects the most candidates will likely have won a majority of votes. But things become more complicated with more parties. With three candidates in each riding, the winner may have less than a majority of votes, and likewise the winning party may form the government with less than a majority of votes. As the number of parties increase, the proportion of the vote required to win drops. A party, in fact, may win a majority of seats in the House of Commons with less than a majority of actual votes. Since 1921, only three governments have been elected with a majority of votes—the Liberals under Mackenzie King in 1940, the Progressive Conservatives under John Diefenbaker in 1958, and the Progressive Conservatives under Brian Mulroney in 1984. And these governments only barely received a majority of the vote: King received 51 percent of the votes, Diefenbaker got 54 percent, and Mulroney just squeaked over 50 percent by a few tenths of a percent. Majority governments in Canada are typically elected with 40 to 45 percent of the vote, so it is often said that the SMP system *manufactures* a majority for the winning party. In 2011, the Conservative Party won a substantial majority of seats with 39.6 percent of the vote. SMP most certainly gave the Conservatives a good bump.

With SMP, a party can actually win a plurality—even a majority—of seats with fewer votes than another party. At the federal level, Wilfrid Laurier's Liberals won a majority government with fewer votes than the Conservatives in 1896, and in 1957 John Diefenbaker's Progressive Conservatives won a minority government with fewer votes than the Liberals.

Table 4.2 In the 2004 Stanley Cup Finals, the Calgary Flames scored more goals in the series, but Tampa Bay won the cup because they won four of the seven games. Similarly, with the SMP electoral system, the key is winning games (ridings) not scoring goals (getting votes).

	Tampa	Calgary
Game 1	1	**4**
Game 2	**4**	1
Game 3	0	**3**
Game 4	**1**	0
Game 5	2	**3**
Game 6	**3**	2
Game 7	**2**	1
Total Goals	**13**	**14**
Games Won	**4**	**3**

In 1996, the NDP won a majority government in the BC provincial election with fewer votes than the BC Liberal Party, and the Parti Québécois won a majority provincial government in 1998 with fewer votes than the Quebec Liberal Party. How can a party "win" the election with fewer votes than another party? It has to do with the distribution of the votes. In these cases, the losing party wins some ridings by big margins, while the winning party wins more ridings but by smaller margins.

Still doesn't make sense? Here is an analogy: In the 2004 Stanley Cup final, the Tampa Bay Lightning beat the Calgary Flames. But over the seven-game series, Calgary scored 14 goals and Tampa only scored 13 goals (see Table 4.2). So why did Tampa win the Stanley Cup? Because the rules of the National Hockey League stipulate that the Stanley Cup is awarded to the team that wins four games in a seven-game series; the total number of goals scored in the series is irrelevant. Similarly, in the SMP electoral system, the total number of votes is irrelevant—what matters is the number of ridings won by each party. In other words, the party that elects more candidates to the House of Commons wins the election and gets to form the government; it doesn't matter which party gets the most votes overall.

However, what's fair in hockey may not be fair in politics. Is it fair for a party to win an election with fewer votes than another party? Maybe. The SMP electoral system arguably creates a more level playing field. Why did the Quebec Liberal Party win more votes than the Parti Québécois but lose the 1998 provincial election? Because the Quebec Liberal Party won a number of the Anglophone ridings on the west side of Montreal by enormous margins, but these ridings are not representative of the Francophone majority in Quebec. Similarly, the BC Liberal Party won some of the more affluent ridings in and around Vancouver in the 1996 provincial election by large margins, but the millionaires of Vancouver are hardly representative of people across the province. Would it have been fair to allow the millionaires of Vancouver to determine the outcome of the election? On the other hand, the notion of "one person, one vote" is central to the idea of democracy, so perhaps the election should be determined by the total number of votes won by each party overall rather than the number of ridings won by each party. Other electoral systems operate on this principle, as we will see shortly.

The Effects of SMP on Small Political Parties How does the SMP electoral system impact smaller parties? SMP works to the disadvantage of some small parties and to the advantage of other small parties, depending on the distribution of the party's support.

Smaller parties with regionally diffuse support are disadvantaged by SMP because their support is spread out too thinly across the country. This is the problem for the Green Party, which received almost 1 million votes in the 2008 election spread across 308 ridings; on average, the Green Party received about 3000 votes in each riding, which meant they were not competitive in any riding and consequently did not elect any candidates. Political scientists say that the Green Party's support was distributed very inefficiently, at least for the purposes of the SMP electoral system. With a different electoral system, the Greens would enjoy much more success; thus, the Green Party is a major advocate of electoral reform.

Smaller parties with regionally concentrated support can have success, because in these areas some candidates will have enough support to get elected. In the 2008 election, the vote total for the Bloc Québécois was only slightly greater than the Green Party, but it was concentrated entirely in the province of Quebec. The Bloc received just under 1.4 million votes, but it was spread across just 75 ridings. Thus, on average, the Bloc received almost 19 000 votes per riding in Quebec and was very competitive, winning 49 out of 75 ridings. In short, the Bloc's support was efficiently distributed (at least before it collapsed in 2011).

Before 2011, the NDP struggled with the SMP system. The NDP's support has been more efficiently distributed than the Green Party's, but it has never been as efficient as the Bloc's vote used to be. Historically, the NDP had pockets of support in Ontario, the prairies, and British Columbia. The NDP thus managed to elect some candidates in these areas, but not in proportion to their share of the popular vote. The NDP, like the Greens, was therefore also a major advocate of electoral reform. In 2011, however, the NDP's proportion of seats closely mirrored its share of the popular vote, and it is now positioned as the second party in the system. If the NDP consolidates its position as a major party in the system, it may become a beneficiary of the SMP system.

SMP did not produce a majority government in the 2004, 2006, and 2008 elections, but on each of these occasions the winning party obtained a proportion of seats in Parliament larger than their share of the popular vote. But, as noted, the system produced a majority government in 2011 in a big way (see Table 4.1). The smaller parties with diffuse support were penalized by SMP, especially the Greens. For a time, the Bloc Québécois benefited tremendously from SMP because its relatively smaller share of the popular vote was concentrated entirely in the province of Quebec. As always, fringe political parties, like the Communist Party and the Marijuana Party, were completely shut out of Parliament.

Strengths of the SMP Electoral System

The SMP electoral system has many virtues. For example, it is easy to understand and use. The SMP system is used in India, where two-thirds of the electorate is illiterate. Each party in India has a symbol, and these symbols appear on the election ballot beside the name of the candidate. The symbol for the governing Congress Party is a hand, and the party election slogan is "vote hand." Many voters simply look for the symbol of their preferred party on the ballot and vote accordingly. It is also easy to count the ballots in the SMP system. Even though ballots are counted manually in Canada, the unofficial results are tallied within a few hours of the polls closing. In other electoral systems, it can take days to count the ballots, even in much smaller countries. The outcome of the election—which party has won and will form the government—is also known within a few hours of the polls closing. In other countries that use different electoral systems the outcome of the election may not be known for weeks or even months as the parties all negotiate with each other to form a majority coalition government, as will be discussed further below.

With SMP, there is a strong connection between a riding and an elected Member of Parliament (MP). Each Member of Parliament has an obligation to represent the riding in parliamentary debates and to serve the needs of all the constituents who live in the riding. As a citizen, you are thus assured that your community will have a voice in Parliament, and you know exactly whom you should contact to voice your opinion on the issues of the day or to assist you with some government matter. And Members of Parliament are there to assist constituents when problems arise with government services, such as a delayed passport application, a rejected visa for a family member, or a problem with a student loan application.

With 18 registered parties, there is a lot of choice in Canadian elections, although admittedly only two parties have a realistic chance of winning an election. But is a strong two-party system really a problem? One could argue that the SMP system propels Canada toward the politics of moderation. In places with other electoral systems, like some countries in Western Europe, it is not uncommon for fascists and communists to be elected. In Canada, the two major parties compete to sit in the middle of the road, because that is where most voters are situated. In turn, the government does not lurch violently from left to right after every election, and people who did not vote for the government are content to live with the result because the two major parties are broadly similar. This is an important accomplishment, because this political stability allows Canada to grow and prosper. SMP has certainly served Canada well since Confederation.

Political stability is perhaps the greatest virtue of the SMP electoral system. Countries that use other electoral systems frequently suffer from political instability (some examples will be discussed later in this chapter). Most elections with SMP result in a majority government, and the party that wins usually has close to 50 percent of the vote. With fixed election dates, every majority government should last the full four years, while minority governments will usually only last about 18 months. In sum, the tradeoff of the SMP electoral system is a 5 to 10 percent deviation from the principle of majority rule, but the benefit is a stable and efficient government.

Weaknesses of the SMP Electoral System

There are some problems associated with the SMP electoral system. Recall that the purpose of an electoral system is to translate voter preferences into seats in Parliament. And herein lays the greatest problem with the SMP electoral system: It translates voter preferences imperfectly. SMP penalizes small parties with regionally diffuse electoral support and it gives the winning party a boost. Indeed, it often manufactures a majority for a party with less than a majority of votes, as discussed above. And as we already know, it is even possible for a party to "win" the election with fewer votes than the party that "loses" the election. When you realize that a majority of Canadians did not vote for the governing party, it is easier to understand why Canadians are often dissatisfied with the government of the day.

SMP translates votes imperfectly because there are a lot of so-called wasted votes in the SMP system. First, the winning party gets more votes than it really needs. It does not matter if a candidate wins by one vote or 10 000 votes, the candidate is elected either way. When a candidate wins by a large margin, the extra votes do not contribute anything. Conversely, many votes are directed toward smaller parties, but many of these votes are "wasted" as well. The Green Party received almost 1 million votes in the 2008 election, but it elected nobody.

Since many votes are wasted in the SMP electoral system, voters often choose to employ **strategic voting**. You may decide that you want to support a certain party, but you realize that the candidate for that party in your constituency does not stand a chance of being elected, so you vote for your second or even third choice in an attempt to block your least preferred candidate from winning. Let's say you're concerned about the environment: You may conclude that the Green Party is best for the environment, and the Conservative Party is the worst. But you realize that the Green Party stands no chance of winning in your riding. The NDP might be your second choice, but you end up voting for your third choice, the Liberals, because the Liberal candidate in your riding stands the best chance of defeating the Conservative candidate. This may be rational political behaviour, but voting for your third choice is not very satisfying.

strategic voting When a person votes for his or her second or third preference of party or candidate in an attempt to prevent the least favourite candidate or party from winning the seat. For example, a supporter of the Green Party might vote for a Liberal to prevent the Conservative from winning, or a Conservative might vote for the NDP to prevent a Liberal from being elected.

The problem of wasted votes, coupled with a perceived lack of choice in Canadian elections, might explain in part why Canada has experienced a long-term decline in voter participation. Prior to the 1980s, voter turnout in Canada averaged about 75 percent—in other words, about three-quarters of registered voters came out to vote on election day. But since the 1990s, voter turnout has hovered around 60 percent. The voter turnout in the 2008 election was 58.8 percent—the lowest on record. Most democracies have experienced a decline of voter turnout over the past three or four decades, but countries that employ the SMP electoral system have suffered the worst declines. The United States recorded its lowest turnout in a presidential election in 1996 when only 49 percent of eligible voters came out, and Great Britain reached rock bottom in the 2001 election at 59 percent. Both countries have seen turnout rebound somewhat in subsequent elections, but it is too early to tell if turnout will continue to increase in these countries or if these rebounds are just blips. The voter turnout in Canada edged up to 61.4 percent in 2011, but it is difficult to know if we have turned the corner. For now, voter turnout remains distressingly low.

Regionalism and the Canadian Electoral System

The "winner-take-all," first-past-the-post electoral system exacerbates the regional cleavages in the country. In the 2008 election, the Conservative Party obtained 26 percent of the vote in the city of Toronto, but this did not translate to any seats; the Liberal Party won 20 seats in Toronto, and the NDP won two. On the other hand, while the SMP system served the Liberal Party well in Toronto, the Liberals were disadvantaged in Western Canada, where they won 16 percent of the vote in the four Western provinces but only 7.6 percent of the seats. In Quebec, the Bloc obtained 38 percent of the vote in the 2008 election, but was over-rewarded by SMP and took 65 percent of the seats.

At times, the regional cleavages in Canadian politics have been starkly evident on the electoral map of Canada, with the West almost uniformly Conservative blue, Quebec until recently Bloc light blue but now mostly NDP orange, and Toronto uniformly red (at least up to 2011). After the 2011 election, the electoral map of Canada is predominantly Conservative blue and NDP orange with a few specks of Liberal red here and there. Since parties are designed to engage in political conflict, the map makes it look like the different regions of the country are pitted against each other. While the different parts of the country definitely have their rivalries, the SMP electoral system exaggerates the degree of political animosity between the regions by masking real voter preferences.

In sum, the SMP electoral system reinforces the major regional cleavages and makes the country more difficult to govern. In 2011, the Conservative Party finally elected some candidates in Toronto, but for five years the Conservatives governed with no representatives from Toronto. Consequently, when the Conservative Members of Parliament, the caucus, met to discuss policy, there was no one in the room from Toronto, Canada's biggest city. Similarly, the **cabinet** lacked representation from Toronto. The Conservatives are now vastly underrepresented in Quebec, and there is no one in the Conservative caucus from Montreal, another large city. Similarly, when the Liberals were in power, they had little or no representation from the West.

When the government lacks representation from one of the major regions of the country it is deeply problematic. It creates a perception, even if it is not always a fact, that policy has been designed to benefit one region of the country to the detriment of underrepresented regions. The problem here is not so much the fault of the political parties; it is a problem of an electoral system that does not translate votes to seats proportionately.

Nonterritorial Representation

We have seen that the major parties nominate candidates to run in all 308 ridings across the country. We might expect that, in a large and diverse country like Canada, this process would result in a diversity of candidates being elected to Parliament, but such is not the case. White men are considerably overrepresented in Parliament, and women, visible minorities, and Aboriginal peoples are all vastly underrepresented. Since women, visible minorities, and Aboriginal people live everywhere in Canada, political scientists often refer to them as *nonterritorial groups*. It is difficult to ensure

cabinet The central decision-making body in the Canadian political system. It is led by the prime minister and includes the other ministers of government.

representation for these groups in Parliament because the SMP is a territorial electoral system—it provides representation for 308 ridings or distinct geographic territories in Parliament, not for specific groups of Canadians. If the laws of Parliament, however, are to be truly representative of Canadians, it is important for these groups to be represented in Parliament more or less in proportion to their share of the population.

In 1970, women made up only 1 percent of the people elected to the House of Commons. By the 1980s, the figure had increased to about 20 percent. In the 2011 election, a record 76 women were elected to the House of Commons, up from 69 elected in 2008. However, women still only account for 25 percent of the people elected to the House of Commons. In other words, the proportion of women in Parliament has been frozen at more or less the same level for more than 20 years. Women account for slightly more than half the population, so if Parliament were truly representative of Canadian society, women would occupy half the seats in Parliament, or 154 seats. With only 76 seats, women thus have less than half the seats they should have according to their share of the population.

Visible minorities and Aboriginal peoples are similarly underrepresented in Parliament. In the 2011 election, 29 visible minorities were elected to Parliament, thus accounting for 9 percent of the House's membership. Visible minorities, however, account for 16.2 percent of the Canadian population, according to the 2006 census. Visible minorities are thus also considerably underrepresented in the House of Commons. The number of visible minorities in the House of Commons has been increasing steadily since 1993, "but they have not achieved any corresponding gains when their growing share of the population is taken into account."[4] In 2011, seven Aboriginal people were elected to the House of Commons, including Leona Aglukkaq from Nunavut (see photo on page 65). These seven individuals account for 2 percent of the seats in the House of Commons, whereas Aboriginal people account for about 4 percent of the Canadian population. Thus, like women and visible minorities, Aboriginal people are notably underrepresented in the House.

Why are there so few women and minorities in Parliament? It is because all the parties select their candidates locally, and every constituency association makes the same calculation when choosing candidates: Every constituency association wants a winning candidate. Who is a winning candidate? Someone who is well educated, successful, and connected in the community. In short, a winning candidate will probably be relatively affluent—and therein lies the problem. In 2004, according to a Statistics Canada study of tax returns, only 5 percent of the population made more than $89 000 a year. And guess what? Three-quarters of the people in that group were men.[5] It hardly seems coincidental that the gender breakdown in the House of Commons is virtually identical to the gender breakdown of the more affluent segment of Canadian society. As visible minorities and Aboriginal peoples tend to be less affluent than white Euro-Canadians, most candidates also therefore tend to be white. When political parties go looking for a relatively successful member of the community to run in the election, there is thus a good chance the individual will be a white male.

Visible minorities and Aboriginal peoples tend to enjoy electoral success only in constituencies where there are relatively high numbers of similar minorities. In 2011, an Indo-Canadian man was elected in Brampton–Springdale, a riding northwest of Toronto that has a large South Asian population; a Chinese Canadian woman was elected in Richmond, south of Vancouver, which has a large Chinese population; and an Inuit woman was elected in Nunavut, which is mostly Inuit.

The electoral opportunities for visible minorities and Aboriginal peoples could be improved within the context of the SMP electoral system by redrawing riding boundaries to increase the proportion of visible minorities or Aboriginal peoples as the case may be. The Supreme Court of Canada has affirmed this strategy, but to date there has been little political will to pursue it.[6]

The New Democratic Party and the Liberal Party have made concerted efforts to recruit more female candidates, but to date the Conservative Party has made no effort to improve the

The Canadian Press/Sean Kilpatrick

Leona Aglukkaq was elected to the House of Commons in 2008 to represent the riding of Nunavut. After the election, Stephen Harper selected her to be the Minister of Health. She was the first Inuk in Canadian history to be appointed to the cabinet. In 2013, she became the Minister of the Environment.

representation of women in politics. The NDP has had two female leaders: Audrey McLaughlin led the party from 1989 to 1995, and Alexa McDonough was the leader from 1995 to 2003. Under McDonough's leadership, the NDP ran more female candidates than all the other parties. In 1993 the Liberal Party resolved to ensure that 25 percent of its candidates were female. When Stéphane Dion was the leader of the Liberal Party, he pledged that women would make up at least one-third of all Liberal candidates, and in the 2008 election the Liberals ran more female candidates than any other party: 113 women, for a total of 37 percent of its candidates. Under the SMP electoral system, however, it is difficult to provide these guarantees, and it sometimes requires the leader to pre-empt or overrule the candidate selection process at the local level. The populist heritage of the Conservative Party prevents it from doing this, so the party has refused to establish a quota for female candidates. But there is a price to be paid for that refusal. In 2008, only 20.5 percent of Conservative candidates were women—last among the five major parties. This may help explain why the Conservative Party has trouble attracting female voters.

In sum, within the logic of the SMP electoral system, political parties are severely limited in their ability to improve representation for women, visible minorities, and Aboriginal peoples. In particular, the candidate selection process in the SMP electoral system works to the disadvantage of these nonterritorial groups. It is important to stress that this discrimination is not (necessarily) the product of racism or sexism; it is a product of the electoral system. When a system discriminates against particular groups of people it is referred to as **systemic discrimination**. Democratic politics is all about representation; for the law to be representative of the people, it is essential that all groups be represented roughly according to their share of the population. If the problem is systemic, it will probably require a systemic solution, such as a new electoral system.

systemic discrimination A form of discrimination produced by the operational logic of a system rather than individual intentions.

Proportional Representation Electoral Systems

The SMP system is very easy to use, and it has served Canada well. But, as we've seen, SMP also has some serious problems, most of which stem from the fact that it does not proportionately translate voter preferences into seats. Some electoral systems are designed to better reflect actual voting patterns and to prevent a party with less than half the vote gaining a

Table 4.3 Election Results, 2011: Actual Results with SMP versus Hypothetical Results with PR

Party	Actual Results with SMP		Hypothetical Results with PR
	% of Vote	Seats	Seats
Conservatives	39.6	166	122
NDP	30.6	103	94
Liberal	18.9	34	58
Bloc Québécois	6.0	4	19
Green	3.9	1	12
Other	1.0	0	3

proportional representation (PR) electoral systems Electoral systems that distribute seats in the legislature proportional to a party's share of the popular vote. If a party wins 20 percent of the vote, it is allocated 20 percent of the seats in the legislature. There are a number of different types of proportional representation electoral systems, including the simple list system, mixed member proportional, and the single transferable vote.

list system The simplest and purest form of all the proportional representation electoral systems. Each party produces a list of candidates equal to the number of seats in the government, with the leader ranked first and the most junior candidate last. On election day, citizens would vote for the party of their choice. Seats in the government are allocated to each party proportional to its share of the popular vote.

majority of seats. These systems are known as **proportional representation (PR) electoral systems**. Most European democracies use some form of proportional representation. There are many different PR systems, but we don't have to examine them all in detail, we just need to know that PR systems translate voter preferences more directly. In PR systems, there are no wasted votes—all votes work to get someone elected.

The **list system** is the simplest and purest form of PR. If Canada adopted a list electoral system, each party would produce a list of candidates equal to the number of seats in the House of Commons (currently 308), with the leader ranked first and the most junior candidate last. On election day, citizens would vote for the party of their choice, rather than an individual candidate. At the end of the night, the number of votes for each party would be tabulated and then divided by the total number of votes cast to determine each party's share of the popular vote. Let's look at an example: For ease of calculation, let's assume that the House of Commons has 300 seats. If the Conservative Party received 40 percent of the vote, it would receive 40 percent of the seats in the House of Commons, or 120 seats. The Conservative Party would then draw the first 120 names off its list, and these candidates would take their seats in the House of Commons. In short, parties would receive seats in the House of Commons proportional to their share of the vote (the smallest fringe parties would likely still be excluded from Parliament because they would still not have enough votes to elect any candidates).

Let's take the results of the 2011 election and compare the actual distribution of seats under SMP and the hypothetical distribution of seats under a system of PR. In Table 4.3, we can see that the parties that benefit from SMP lose seats with PR, and the parties disadvantaged by SMP gain with PR. The Conservatives would be reduced from 166 seats to 122 and would lose their status as a majority government. The NDP would also lose a few seats. On the other hand, the Liberal Party would gain almost twice as many seats. With PR, the Green Party would have won 12 seats (now you can see why the Green Party is a major advocate of electoral reform). With PR, it is also possible that some other small parties might elect candidates. (In this hypothetical situation, the results are based on the premise that everyone voted the same way they did in the actual 2011 election, but in fact some people might be more inclined to vote for smaller parties since there are no wasted votes with PR.[7])

General Effects of Proportional Representation

If Canada adopted PR, what effect would it have on Canadian politics? First, we would expect to see more small parties in Parliament. Second, there would be very few one-party majority governments, unless one party wins a majority of the vote, but that is unusual in Canada's multi-party democracy (as mentioned, this has happened only three times since 1921). Third, we would expect to see coalition governments emerge in Canada. In countries that currently use PR systems, coalitions are a common occurrence. When no party has a majority of seats in the legislature, parties need to work together in coalitions to get anything done.

The behaviour of political parties would also change considerably with PR. With SMP, the two major parties compete to occupy the middle of the political spectrum because a party needs to hold the middle ground to win the election. This means the major parties may agree on many of the issues during the election, but they typically do not agree on anything when they enter the House of Commons. Many Canadians complain about a lack of choice at election time, and they despair at the petty bickering displayed by the parties in Parliament, but the parties are simply following the logic of SMP. The logic of PR is very different: With PR, parties attempt to differentiate themselves from each other during elections and occupy distinct places on the ideological spectrum to obtain a share of the vote, as opposed to gathering up as many votes as possible in the centre. But when the parties enter the legislature in PR systems they must try to work together cooperatively. In sum, PR leads to a very different type of politics.

Strengths of Proportional Representation

Proportional representation electoral systems translate votes to seats very directly. With the simple list system, the distribution of seats in the legislature is exactly proportional to a party's share of the vote. The list system is also very easy to use and understand, and the votes can be tabulated quickly. There are no wasted votes with PR, and thus here is no need for strategic voting.—citizens can vote for their party of choice with the knowledge that their vote will help someone get elected. PR thus provides voters with more viable choices.

There are also no manufactured majority governments with PR. There will only be a one-party majority government if a party receives a majority of the vote. In a multi-party democracy, however, it is unusual for one party to accomplish this. With PR, a majority government is typically formed through a multi-party coalition. While coalition governments may be hard to form and maintain, they always represent the majority of the electorate. In Canada, with one-party government, the government typically represents only about 40 percent of the electorate. By contrast, Switzerland's four-party coalition government represents about 80 percent of the electorate.

PR may also help bridge the major cleavages in Canadian politics because parties would be awarded seats in each region according to their share of the vote. With PR, the major federalist parties would all receive more seats in Quebec, and the Liberals would receive more seats in the West. Each party would consequently be more representative of the country, and presumably its policies would be more sensitive to each region. To ensure this kind of regional balance, it would be necessary to modify the simple list system. Rather than a single list for the whole country, the parties would produce a list for each region of the country, or more likely one list for each province. If the Liberal Party received 11 percent of the vote in Alberta, as it did in the 2008 election, it would be awarded 11 percent, or three, of Alberta's seats.

There is also reason to believe that PR would be advantageous to women and minorities. In PR systems, especially the list system, candidates are typically chosen and ranked by central party offices. In this process, parties want to produce a winning list, as opposed to local associations that are trying to select a winning candidate. What would a winning list look like? It would probably look a lot like the country the party wants to govern. There would be a very strong incentive for parties to produce a list with a proportional number of men, women, Anglophones, Francophones, visible minorities, and Aboriginal peoples. There is, of course, no guarantee that parties would produce a demographically correct list, but countries that use PR generally have more balanced representation in their national legislatures.

Weaknesses of Proportional Representation

While PR would remedy many of the defects of SMP, it is not problem free. One of the primary virtues of SMP is the strong connection between a Member of Parliament and a particular geographic constituency; this connection is weakened with most forms of PR. With the pure list system, Members of Parliament are, in fact, not connected to any constituency. On the positive side, this allows members to make decisions in the best interests of the country as a whole, and it gives citizens more options. With SMP, citizens are normally expected to correspond with the member elected from their constituency when they have a political concern, even though they may not share this individual's political views. With PR, citizens may contact *any* Member of Parliament. In fact, they may contact different members depending on the issue. On the downside, it is possible that the concerns of some communities will be overlooked with PR because the electoral system is no longer tied to geography. This is not an issue for small countries that use list PR, such as the Netherlands, Switzerland, and Israel, but it is a concern in a large country like Canada.

More seriously, PR can *sometimes* lead to political instability. The proliferation of small parties is one of the effects of PR, and this can be problematic. It can result in too many parties occupying seats in the legislature, slowing down the business of government. PR can also facilitate the rise of extremist parties. For these reasons, it is often necessary to introduce a threshold before parties are awarded seats in the legislature. The election law might state, for example, that a party has to receive a certain percentage of the vote before it is allocated seats. These thresholds typically range from 1 to 5 percent of the popular vote. A higher threshold will reduce the number of parties in the legislature, and a lower threshold will lead to more parties.

Even with a minimum threshold in place, the politics of coalition building can be complicated. Let's look at the 2011 election results again. Under PR, the Conservative Party would still have the most seats (122), but it would be a long way from a majority in a 308-seat Parliament. The Conservative Party would therefore need the support of one or more parties to obtain a minimum majority of 155 seats. But the other parties might not be willing to join the Conservatives in a coalition; the Conservative Party and the Liberal Party might be ideologically compatible, but it is unusual for the two oldest parties in the system to enter a coalition together. This sort of grand coalition typically happens only in a crisis situation, such as war or possibly in the event of total legislative paralysis. The Conservative Party would also be unlikely to work with the NDP; the two parties are simply too far apart ideologically. The Conservatives might be willing to work with the Greens, but the Greens only have 12 seats, which would still leave the coalition short of a majority. Similarly, the Bloc would not have enough seats to help the Conservatives form a majority and, more fundamentally, it is unlikely that any of the federalist parties would enter a coalition with the party committed to the division of Canada. In this scenario, the Conservatives might not be able to form a governing coalition even though they are the largest party in the system.

The NDP and the Liberals might be able to work together, but they do not have enough seats between them to form a majority. They would have to invite the Greens to join the coalition to obtain a working majority. While an NDP–Liberal–Green coalition would have a majority of seats, it would obviously be something of a challenge for these three parties to agree on a common program.

As we can see, the politics of coalition building can be complicated. Sometimes the numbers just do not add up and it is impossible for the parties to form a viable coalition. In countries that use PR, it can often take weeks or even months following an election for the parties to reach an agreement. A party may drop key campaign promises to join a coalition, much to the disappointment of the people who voted for the party. And, at the end of the day, the coalition that emerges may be very fragile. It may have too many partners or the parties in the coalition may not agree on the major issues. In such cases, the government is destined to be short lived and the process begins again, often with the same result.

Some countries have had very poor experiences with PR, especially the pure list system. Italy and Israel are the most notable examples; both countries struggle with numerous small parties and unstable coalition governments. While some of the problems in Italy and Israel can be attributed to the shortcomings of PR, there is another factor at play in both countries. In Italy, the Communist Party typically received a large share of the vote and was consequently awarded a large block of seats in Parliament; however, during the Cold War none of the other parties was willing to invite the Communists into the government, which would have given the Communists access to NATO secrets. But when the Communists were excluded from the government, the arithmetic for coalition formation among the remaining parties became much more difficult. To a lesser extent, Israel has experienced the same problem with Arab political parties in the national legislature. On the other hand, Canada experienced a similar problem with SMP. When the Bloc Québécois was strong, it was always vastly overrepresented in Quebec, and of course no other party would ever agree to work with the Bloc in a coalition. In short, pariah parties can emerge in both types of electoral systems.

However, it is important to stress that PR does not always lead to political instability. Some countries that use PR are very stable and economically successful. Sweden, Switzerland, and Germany are cases in point.

Hybrid Electoral Systems

The single-member plurality system and the list system of proportional representation are in many respects mirror opposites of each other. With SMP, the distribution of seats among the parties in Parliament is not proportional to their share of the popular vote, whereas with the list system there is perfect proportionality. SMP typically results in a small party system, a one-party majority government, and a strong connection between voters and a Member of Parliament; the list system typically results in a larger party system, multi-party coalition governments, and a weaker connection between voters and Members of Parliament. With SMP, parties compete for the centre during elections, but move apart when they enter Parliament; with PR, parties attempt to differentiate themselves during elections but come together when they enter the legislature. In short, the strengths of one system are the weaknesses of the other.

It is, however, possible to mix and match these electoral systems. It is possible to have some Members of Parliament elected from geographical constituencies while other members are selected from lists. This is known as the **mixed member proportional (MMP) system**. With MMP, voters have two votes at election time. You vote for an individual to represent the constituency you live in, and then you vote for a political party and its list of candidates. Voters are free to vote for a candidate from one party but to cast a vote for another party's list. If Canada had MMP, you might vote for the Liberal candidate to represent your constituency but vote for the Green Party on the other ballot. Votes for the list are used to iron out the disproportionalities caused by the election of candidates through the first-past-the-post system.[8]

MMP has been used to good effect in Germany: It gives voters more choice, it establishes a linkage between the legislature and geographic constituencies, it provides proportionality, it is stable (with a 5 percent threshold needed to gain a seat), and most importantly it has enabled effective government. But it is not perfect. It creates a perception that there are two "classes" of representatives in the legislature—"real" representatives elected from a constituency and "freeloaders" selected from the lists. With half the representatives elected from lists, it means that the geographic constituencies are much larger than they would be with the single-member

mixed member proportional (MMP) electoral system An electoral system that combines the single-member plurality electoral system with the simple list electoral system. Each person votes for a candidate to represent the constituency he or she lives in and for a political party with its list of candidates. Votes for the list are used to iron out the disproportionalities caused by the election of candidates through the first-past-the-post system.

plurality system alone. More seriously, it adds complexity to the system. Many voters do not understand the formula employed to iron out the disproportionalities in the system.

single transferable vote (STV) electoral system The electoral system used in Ireland and Malta. With STV, the country is divided into a number of geographic constituencies in which multiple candidates will be elected. Constituencies with relatively small populations might only elect two candidates, but very large constituencies might elect as many as six candidates. Voters have the opportunity to rank order the candidates according to their preferences. Candidates are elected according to a complex electoral quotient.

There is one more electoral system that should be noted called the **single transferable vote (STV) electoral system**. This electoral system provides a high degree of proportionality without the use of lists. With STV, the country is divided into geographic constituencies in which multiple candidates will be elected. Constituencies with relatively small populations might only elect two candidates, but very large constituencies might elect as many as six. For each constituency it is necessary to calculate an electoral quotient (see Figure 4.2). For ease of calculation, let's assume that there are 100 000 voters in the constituency in which four candidates are to be elected. The number of voters would be divided by the number of candidates plus one, so in this case five. The electoral quotient would then be 20 000 votes plus 1.[9] When the ballots are counted, the scrutineers (individuals who examine an election poll) distribute the number of first preferences. Any candidate who has 20 001 votes is elected. Surplus votes are redistributed to other candidates, and candidates who come last are dropped. Second and third preferences are considered next, and when four candidates have received 20 001 votes the counting stops. At this point, the top four candidates have 80 004 votes, meaning that the next candidate can have no more than 19 996 votes and consequently cannot finish in the top four.

$$\text{Electoral Quotient} = \frac{\text{votes}}{\text{seats} + 1} + 1$$

Figure 4.2 The Electoral Quotient Formula for the STV Electoral System

STV provides proportionality, choice, geographic representation, a small party system, and relatively stable government. Some psephologists consider STV to be mathematically the most elegant electoral system, but it is undoubtedly the most complex system. It is not easy for voters to understand, it takes a long time to count the ballots, and it usually results in no party obtaining a majority of seats, so difficult coalition negotiations inevitably follow the election. Consequently, STV is only used in two countries—Ireland and Malta.

The Politics of Electoral Reform

Notwithstanding the very real deficiencies and somewhat undemocratic nature of SMP, there has been no movement toward PR at the federal level in Canada because it has not been in the interests of the (hitherto) dominant parties. The Liberals and the Conservatives both benefit from SMP, at least when they win. The two major parties are thus unlikely to endorse a shift to PR, unless they are forced to by circumstances. What could compel them to change their position? A groundswell of public support in favour of electoral reform *might* cause them to reconsider their positions. A couple of anomalous elections might spur some reconsiderations, such as one party winning more seats with fewer votes than the other party, or one party suffering a dramatic loss of seats without a corresponding collapse of popular support. Alternatively, the adoption of PR in one or more of the provinces could be a catalyst for reform at the federal level.

There has, in fact, been more serious consideration of electoral reform in some of the provinces, but to date none have switched from SMP. In 2004, a "citizens' assembly" was created by the government of British Columbia to consider the question of electoral reform. A total of 160 citizens were chosen at random—one man and one woman from each riding in the province. For the better part of a year, these citizens were tutored in the dynamics of electoral systems by two political scientists from the University of British Columbia. Ultimately, the assembly recommended the adoption of STV. All citizens had the opportunity to vote on the matter in a province-wide referendum in

May 2005. The proposal was endorsed by 58 percent of the population, but under the terms established by the government it needed 60 percent support before it could be adopted. With such a close result, the government announced that another referendum would be held in May 2009, but in the second vote the proposal was soundly rejected by a margin of 61 to 39 percent.

A similar assembly was established in Ontario, and it recommended the adoption of MMP. The citizens of Ontario, however, rejected the proposal 2 to 1 in a referendum in 2007. A referendum on MMP failed in Prince Edward Island by a similar margin in 2005. MMP was also recommended by a royal commission in New Brunswick, but a referendum on the issue was cancelled after a change of government. A commission in Quebec recommended MMP, but nothing has come of this recommendation. Thus, for now, electoral reform does not appear to be in the cards for Canada, although the issue will likely resurface in the future as Canadians contemplate how the game of politics could be improved.

Canadians have rejected PR for a number of reasons. First, we appear to be fearful of political instability. Second, many people appear to be suspicious of coalition governments. Canada has virtually no experience with coalition governments; they are simply not part of the country's political culture. There may also be a fear that small parties would extract concessions in exchange for supporting a coalition. Third, and perhaps most importantly, Canadians appear to value the connection established by SMP between Parliament and geographic constituencies and do not wish to have this connection weakened.

While Canadians have not been inclined to make the switch to PR, citizens in other countries have voted for change. New Zealand, another former British colony with responsible government and the SMP electoral system, adopted a form of MMP in 1996 after it was narrowly supported in a referendum. What have been the consequences of the switch? There has been an expansion of the party system and a change from one-party majority governments to multi-party coalition governments. And, after some initial growing pains, voters and parties seem to have made the necessary adjustments. In November 2011, New Zealanders voted 58 percent in favour of retaining the MMP system in another referendum.

SUMMARY

Canada's *single-member plurality electoral system* is very easy to use and it typically provides stable majority governments. In a multi-party democracy, however, SMP does not translate votes to seats accurately. Indeed, very often the system manufactures a majority government for one party that has less than a majority of the vote. While the winning party typically receives a boost from SMP, smaller parties with regionally diffuse support are penalized. There would appear to be something seriously wrong with SMP when a party can receive nearly 1 million votes across the country but fail to elect a single candidate. It also creates a perception that Canada's electoral system is not entirely democratic. SMP also exacerbates the major regional cleavages in Canada, and it appears to discriminate against women, visible minorities, and Aboriginal peoples.

Alternative electoral systems—generally known as *proportional representation systems*—provide a much more accurate translation of votes. With PR, the distribution of seats in Parliament is directly proportional to each party's share of the popular vote. In PR systems, however, there are typically more parties in the legislature and governments are normally formed through multi-party coalitions. As such, there is a greater risk of political instability in PR systems, especially with the simple list form of PR. Hybrid electoral systems are generally more stable than simple PR systems, but they are also more complex and confusing. The list system and hybrid systems typically result in better representation for women and minorities, and they would help ameliorate the regional political cleavages in Canada. It is within the power of Parliament to change the electoral system, but there needs to be a political or popular will to do so before Parliament will act.

While PR systems have some weaknesses, they more accurately reflect voter preferences and they generally provide better representation. For these reasons, some people believe that PR is more democratic than SMP. Canadians, however, have not been inclined to abandon SMP and adopt PR. Electoral reform has not been a top-of-mind issue for many people, and voters have rejected PR in referendums in three provinces. But with relatively high rates of political dissatisfaction in Canada, the debate over the electoral system is probably destined to continue. If Canada ever does adopt a proportional representation electoral system, the game of Canadian politics would be dramatically reshaped.

Questions to Think About

1. Is it democratic for one party to win a majority of seats in Parliament with less than a majority of the vote?
2. Why are coalition governments more democratic than a manufactured one-party majority government?
3. Why is it important for women, visible minorities, and Aboriginal peoples to be represented in Parliament roughly according to their share of the population?
4. How does the electoral system exacerbate the regional political cleavages in Canada?
5. Should Canada adopt proportional representation?

Learning Outcomes

1. Explain how the single-member plurality electoral system works.
2. Describe the advantages and disadvantages of the single-member plurality electoral system.
3. Describe the advantages and disadvantages of the proportional representation electoral systems.
4. Explain how the game of politics would change if Canada adopted a system of proportional representation.

Additional Readings

Cameron D. Anderson and Laura B. Stephenson, eds., *Voting Behaviour in Canada* (Vancouver, BC: UBC Press, 2010).

Amanda Bittner, *Platform or Personality? The Role of Party Leaders in Elections* (Oxford, UK: Oxford University Press, 2011).

André Blais, *To Keep or Change First Past the Post? The Politics of Electoral Reform* (Oxford, UK: Oxford University Press, 2008).

Citizens' Assembly on Electoral Reform, *Making Every Vote Count: The Case for Electoral Reform in British Columbia* (2004).

John C. Courtney, *Commissioned Ridings: Designing Canada's Electoral Districts* (Montreal, QC: McGill-Queen's University Press, 2001).

John C. Courtney, *Elections* (Vancouver, BC: UBC Press, 2004).

David M. Farrell, *Electoral Systems: A Comparative Introduction* (London, UK: Palgrave, 2001).

Elizabeth Gidengil et al., *Dominance and Decline: Making Sense of Recent Canadian Elections* (Toronto, ON: University of Toronto Press, 2012).

Arend Lijphart, *Electoral Systems and Party Systems: A Study of Twenty-Seven Democracies, 1945–1990* (Oxford, UK: Oxford University Press, 1994).

Richard Johnston, *Letting the People Decide: Dynamics of a Canadian Election* (Montreal, QC: McGill-Queen's University Press, 1992).

Law Commission of Canada, *Voting Counts: Electoral Reform in Canada* (2004).

Heather MacIvor, ed., *Election* (Toronto, ON: Emond Montgomery, 2009).

Henry Milner, ed., *Making Every Vote Count: Reassessing Canada's Electoral System* (Peterborough, ON: Broadview Press, 1999).

Ontario's Citizens' Assembly on Electoral Reform, *One Ballot, Two Votes: A New Way to Vote in Ontario* (2007).

Dennis Pilon, *The Politics of Voting: Reforming Canada's Electoral System* (Toronto, ON: Emond Montgomery, 2007).

Notes

1. Bill C-16, An Act to Amend the Canada Elections Act, as passed by the House of Commons, November 6, 2006; section 56.1(2).

2. Legislative Summary LS-530E, Bill C-16, An Act to Amend the Canada Elections Act, June 29, 2006 (Library of Parliament, Parliamentary Information Research Service).

3. The only citizens who are not permitted to vote are the chief electoral officer of Canada and the assistant chief electoral officer. Previously, individuals serving two or more years in prison were prohibited from voting while incarcerated, but that provision of the Election Act was struck down by the Supreme Court in 2002.

4. Jerome H. Black, "The 2006 Federal Election and Visible Minority Candidates: More of the Same?" *Canadian Parliamentary Review* (Autumn 2008), 31.

5. "High Income Canadians," *Perspectives on Labour and Income* 8:9 (September 2007).

6. Tim Schouls, "Aboriginal Peoples and Electoral Reform in Canada: Differentiated Representation versus Voter Equality," *Canadian Journal of Political Science* 29:4 (December 1996), 729–749.

7. In a pure form of PR, there would be no independent candidates. Citizens vote for parties rather than individuals. So, in this hypothetical scenario, the votes for independents have been combined with "other parties" for a total of 1 percent. That would translate to three seats in the House of Commons. This vote, however, would be split between many parties, and in all likelihood none of these parties would meet the threshold to obtain a seat in the House of Commons.

8. Most mixed member electoral systems use something called the "Hare formula" to iron out disproportionalities after the election. See David M. Farrell, *Electoral Systems: A Comparative Introduction* (London, UK: Palgrave, 2001).

9. This is known as the "Droop quotient." See David M. Farrell, *Electoral Systems: A Comparative Introduction* (London, UK: Palgrave, 2001).

Chapter 5
The Executive

Key Points

- Canadians elect people to represent them in Parliament—the legislative branch of government—but the political process is driven by the executive branch of government.

- Under the rules of the constitution, all executive authority is invested with the Queen, who is Canada's head of state. The duties of the Queen are normally handled by the governor general. They constitute the formal executive at the apex of Canada's political system.

- By convention, the power to make political decisions lies with the political executive: the prime minister and the other ministers in the cabinet. The prime minister is the head of government.

- The first rule of responsible government is that the prime minister must maintain the confidence of Parliament. Second, ministers must take individual responsibility for their departments. Third, the prime minister and the cabinet must assume collective responsibility. The rules of responsible government are guided by convention.

- The prime minister has always dominated the government, but over time the prime minister has become more powerful. In Canada's system of parliamentary government there is consequently a fusion of legislative and executive authority.

Let me summarize our progress so far. I have argued that politics is a competition between different conceptions of the good life. We examined these different conceptions of the good life when we discussed ideologies, and we saw how these ideologies are represented to a greater or lesser degree by political parties. We then had an election and learned that our single-member plurality electoral system steers us in a certain direction: toward two major parties, with one party usually having a majority of seats in Parliament. But before our elected representatives can take their seats in Parliament and begin the work of making legislation, we must first form a government. After an election, the governor general will (almost always) call upon the leader of the party that won the most seats to be prime minister and ask him or her to form a government.

The prime minister, in turn, will select the other ministers to sit with him or her in the government. So, before we can examine the operation of Parliament, we must consider the role of the **executive** in our political system. Once we have formed a government, we will be in a position to examine the rules of **responsible government** more fully.

executive The branch of government responsible for the execution of policy.

responsible government The Canadian system of government (inherited from Great Britain) in which ministers are responsible to Parliament and the Crown.

The Executive Branch of Government

In any political system, there are three branches of government: legislative, executive, and judicial. The legislature makes laws for the country, the executive enforces or executes those laws, and the judiciary interprets the law. An election gives Canadians the opportunity to choose their representatives to sit in the legislature, or Parliament, but voters do not directly elect the executive. Who makes up the executive in the Canadian political system? The answer to that question is a bit complicated. Under the Constitution Act 1867, all executive authority is vested with the Queen. The Queen is Canada's **head of state**, and more broadly the **Crown** embodies the entirety of the Canadian state; Canada's government is Her Majesty's government. Property owned by the Government of Canada is Crown property, and businesses owned by the Government of Canada are Crown corporations. As the Crown sits at the apex of the political system, it has been aptly described as the "first principle of Canadian government."[1] Because the Queen cannot be in Canada on a regular basis to conduct her duties, she has delegated her authority to the **governor general** of Canada and to the **lieutenant governors** of each province for matters relating to provincial affairs.

The Crown, however, does not govern alone. Under the constitution, there is a provision for the establishment of the **Queen's Privy Council for Canada** to advise the governor general. Privy councillors are chosen by the governor general (on the advice of the prime minister), and they are sworn into office for life. But the governor general does not consult with all of his Privy councillors. He relies on the advice offered to him by a special committee of his Privy Council—the **cabinet**, which is led by the **prime minister**. In the Canadian political system, the prime minister is the **head of government**. Usually the leader of the party that won the most seats in Parliament becomes prime minister, but it is not automatic. That leader must wait to be invited to form a government by the governor general. The prime minister in turn will choose the other **ministers** who will sit with him or her in the cabinet. The ministers collectively constitute the Government of Canada. As the government is a collection of ministers, it is properly called a **ministry**.

Before the ministry can take its place in Parliament, the ministers must be sworn in by the governor general. The formation of a government—the choosing of a prime minister, the selection of ministers, and the swearing in of ministers—all happens after the election but before Parliament begins the process of making new legislation. The formation of a government typically takes six to eight weeks. In other words, Parliament normally opens about two months after an election.

In the Canadian system of government, political authority is exercised by the prime minister and the other ministers in the cabinet on behalf of the Crown. For this reason, the prime minister and the ministers are known as the **political executive** while the Crown is known as the **formal executive**. The relationship between the Crown and the political executive and their respective roles and responsibilities are governed primarily by the rules or **conventions** of responsible government. Like all conventions, these rules are malleable—in other words, they evolve. In general, the power of the political executive has increased over time while the power of the formal executive has declined, so much so in fact that many people assume incorrectly that the Crown is now redundant. And, within the political executive, the power of the prime minister seems to have steadily increased over time. Indeed, some political scientists argue that we now essentially have a system of prime ministerial government, albeit still dressed in the trappings of responsible parliamentary government.

The Formal Executive

When the Queen is in Canada she can fulfill her role as head of state, but for the most part the duties of the Crown are handled by the governor general. The responsibilities of the governor general are outlined (briefly) in the Constitution Act 1867, and in the **Letters Patent**—a specific set of instructions from the Crown to the governor general. (Initially, each governor general received a unique set of instructions from the Crown, but after 1878 the Letters Patent became a standing letter. In 1947, the Letters Patent was significantly revised and the governor general was specifically authorized to exercise most of the Crown's powers on behalf of the sovereign.) The governor general's main responsibilities are to

head of state The official representative of the nation that is vested with all executive authority. The Queen is Canada's head of state.

Crown Refers to the entirety of the Canadian state. For example, property owned by the Government of Canada is Crown property and government-owned businesses are called Crown corporations.

governor general The Queen's representative in Canada, and formally the head of the executive branch of government.

lieutenant governors The Queen's representatives in each province.

Queen's Privy Council for Canada A largely ceremonial body that advises the Queen on matters of state related to Canada. It is made up of current and former cabinet ministers and other prominent Canadians. Individuals are appointed to the council by the governor general on the advice of the prime minister. It is a lifetime appointment, but only current members of the cabinet are entitled to advise the Crown directly.

cabinet The central decision-making body in the Canadian political system. It is led by the prime minister and includes the other ministers of government.

prime minister The leader of the government in Parliament. By convention, the prime minister is an elected member of the House of Commons.

head of government The official elected leader of the government. Canada's head of government is the prime minister.

ministers Members of Parliament, usually in the House of Commons, who have been appointed by the prime minister to sit with him or her in the cabinet. They collectively compose the Government of Canada.

ministry Refers to the Government of Canada, which is composed of ministers.

political executive The prime minister and the ministers in Canada.

formal executive The Crown in Canada.

conventions Unwritten rules of the Canadian political system. Many conventions were inherited from Great Britain's system of responsible government in 1867, while other conventions have emerged in Canada over time through political practice.

Letters Patent A specific set of instructions from the British Crown to the governor general.

appoint the prime minister, open and close each session of Parliament, and dissolve Parliament for elections. However, like the Queen, the governor general makes very few decisions on his or her own volition. By convention, the governor general almost always follows the advice of the prime minister.

But among the governor general's **prerogative powers** are important reserve powers that empower the governor general (in very rare circumstances) to disregard the advice of the prime minister. In 1926, Governor General Lord Byng did not accept Prime Minister Mackenzie King's advice to dissolve Parliament when his Liberal Party was facing a motion of censure in the House of Commons and was in danger of losing the confidence of Parliament. In this case, the previous election had occurred just eight months before, and the Liberal Party formed a minority government with fewer seats than the Conservatives. (King was able to carry on as prime minister in this unusual situation because he had the support of the Progressive Party in the House of Commons. This is the only occasion in Canadian history in which the governing party had fewer seats than the opposition parties, and it is a precedent unlikely to be repeated.) Under these circumstances, the governor general refused to accept King's request to dissolve Parliament. King consequently resigned, and the governor general invited the leader of the Conservative Party, Arthur Meighen, to form a government. But the new Conservative government lost the confidence of Parliament in very short order, so Meighen dutifully advised the governor general to dissolve Parliament and have an election. King campaigned vigorously against the actions of the governor general, and the Liberal Party was returned to Parliament with a minority government. This episode in Canadian history has been remembered as the King–Byng Affair.

A similar situation emerged after the October 2008 election, when Stephen Harper's Conservative Party was returned to power with another minority government. Parliament met the following month and the new government obtained the confidence of the House when its **Speech from the Throne**—its plan for the new session of Parliament—was accepted. But when the government presented Parliament with a dubious economic update a week later, the opposition parties threatened to withdraw their confidence in the government. The Liberal Party and the NDP formally agreed to establish a **coalition government** supported from the outside by the Bloc Québécois. Thus, if the government lost the confidence of Parliament, there was an alternative "government in waiting" for the governor general to call upon, if needed.

However, before a vote of confidence could be held, the prime minister asked the governor general to prorogue Parliament for two months. Governor General Michaëlle Jean was thus faced with a terrible dilemma. The government had effectively lost the confidence of Parliament, although the vote had not yet occurred, and now her prime minister was requesting a **prorogation** of Parliament to stave off the defeat of his government. Ultimately, the governor general opted to accept the prime minister's controversial advice for a proroga-tion, although she kept Stephen Harper waiting in the foyer at Rideau Hall, the governor general's residence, for a couple of hours while she made up her mind. Most constitutional experts believe that Madame Jean made the correct decision, but many Canadians (mostly those who did not vote Conservative) were disappointed that she did not refuse the prime minister's request under these conditions, as was her right.

The 2008 prorogation crisis revealed that "there are no firm rules to govern the use of the governor general's powers in summoning, proroguing, or dissolving Parliament."[2] In particular, it is not clear when a governor general might refuse the advice of a prime minis-ter to summon, dissolve, or prorogue Parliament. As long as the prime minister actually retains the confidence of Parliament, it seems likely that the governor general would accept the advice of the prime minister. And he or she would probably accept the prime minister's advice to dissolve Parliament if the government were defeated on a vote of confidence, unless it was very soon after an election, say within a few months, and there were a viable alternative government waiting in the wings. In other words, the governor general would probably want to know that there is another leader willing to be prime minister and that he or she has a reasonable possibility of obtaining and maintaining the confidence of Parliament at least for a few months before the country is plunged into another general election campaign. While political scientists enjoy speculating about these hypothetical scenarios, they are exceptionally unusual. There have only been two cases in the past 100 years, although it would certainly be helpful to clarify the rules surrounding the governor general's discretionary powers before the next crisis erupts.

Apart from these highly unusual scenarios, the governor general acts on the advice provided by her Privy Council, namely the prime minister and the other ministers in the cabinet. In this role, the governor general is required to sign off on all legislation duly passed by the House of Commons and the Senate and **orders in council** or legal decisions made by the cabinet. In this capacity, the governor general does not possess any discretionary power. Indeed, in these matters, the constitution refers to the governor general as the **governor in council**. Like the Queen, the governor general is fully briefed on all government matters, and he or she meets with the prime minister on a regular basis. In these meetings, which are completely private, the governor general is entitled to "advise, guide, and warn" the prime minister on matters he or she perceives to be of particular importance to the country. Queen Elizabeth II has been on the throne since 1952, and she has seen 12 prime ministers come and go, including such forceful personalities as Winston Churchill, Margaret Thatcher, and Tony Blair. So when the Queen issues a warning to her prime minister, it is not to be taken lightly. Obviously, the governor general of Canada does not have the same stature or wealth of experience as the Queen, but one assumes that his or her advice to the prime minister is not ignored, so long as it is offered judiciously.

It is true that much of the work of the governor general is ceremonial, but this work is important for a couple of reasons. First, the country needs to celebrate its accomplishments. Among other things, the governor general confers literary awards and awards for bravery as well as the Order of Canada, which is given to citizens for their contributions to Canadian life. These awards honour Canadians for their service and serve as an inspiration for other citizens. The governor general is also the ceremonial commander in chief of the Canadian forces, confers awards for military service, and visits Canadian military personnel at home and in service abroad. The governor general, as head of state, also represents Canada as he or she greets foreign dignitaries and receives the credentials of foreign ambassadors to Canada. The governor general may also attend state funerals for world leaders as Canada's representative. There is thus a pragmatic dimension to the ceremonial functions conducted by the governor general: It gives the prime minister more time to focus on the task of governing the nation. In contrast, US President Obama, who is both head of state and head of government, has to engage in purely ceremonial functions, which consumes precious time.

Who gets to be the governor general and how? The governor general is appointed by the Queen. Up until 1952, the governor general was dispatched from Great Britain to Canada by the Queen. This was originally done on the advice of the British prime minister, but gradually Canada's prime minister took the leading role in making the recommendation. Since 1952, the governor general has been a Canadian, appointed by the Queen on the advice of the prime minister of Canada. Over time, the position has been further "Canadianized." The position has rotated between Anglophones and Francophones since 1952, and it is now understood that the governor general should be bilingual.

In 1984, Jeanne Sauvé became the first woman to occupy the position, and in 1999 Adrienne Clarkson became the first visible minority to hold the position. As yet, no Aboriginal person has served as governor general, but a few Aboriginal Canadians have served as lieutenant governors, such as Steven Point in British Columbia and James Bartleman in Ontario. While no individual can embody every segment of the Canadian population, it is now accepted that the office of governor general should reflect the diversity of the country. In other words, over time all Canadians should be able to see themselves in the office of the governor general. The appointment of David Johnston in 2010 represents a return to a more traditional viceregal figure.

orders in council Decisions made by the cabinet that carry legal force.

governor in council The formal decisions of the governor general taken on the advice of cabinet.

Governor General David Johnston in the Senate before reading the Speech from the Throne.

© CHRIS WATTIE/Reuters/Corbis

Governors general have not only been symbolic of the nation, they have also provided some of the nation's most cherished symbols, such as the Stanley Cup and the Grey Cup; Lord Stanley was governor general from 1888–1893, and Lord Grey occupied the position from 1904–1911. Lady Byng, the wife of the aforementioned Lord Byng, also donated a trophy to the National Hockey League for the most sportsmanlike player. And in 2005, Adrienne Clarkson announced that henceforth there would be a new cup in her name awarded annually to the best women's professional hockey team.

Does Canada still need a governor general? Should the Queen still be the head of the Canadian state? Do these connections represent an old-fashioned tie to a colonial legacy? There are certainly many arguments that could be made to advocate for the elimination of the monarchy in Canada. However, one could also argue that it is important for a country to ground its political institutions in history, particularly if things have tended to work reasonably well. Leaving aside the historical argument, it is also not that easy to extricate the country from its ties to the monarchy. The Crown in Canada is not merely symbolic—it sits at the pinnacle of the Canadian political and legal system. The entire system of Canadian government and law is built around the Crown. Even if it can be undone, it needs to be replaced. Someone has to serve as Canada's head of state, and herein lies perhaps the greatest challenge. If Canada abolishes ties to the monarchy, who will become the head of the Canadian state? Should we have an elected president? If so, what is the relationship between the head of state and head of government? Or should the prime minister or perhaps Parliament appoint a president? In either scenario, the role of head of state is likely to become more politicized.

These are not hypothetical considerations. In 1999, Australia held a referendum to abolish ties to the monarchy in favour of a president appointed by a two-thirds majority vote of Parliament, but the referendum failed. While many Australians would like to abolish the country's ties to the monarchy, they could not agree on the appropriate alternative to the Crown. In sum, the Crown fulfills a critical function in Canada's political system, and all the alternatives seem problematic in one way or another.

The Political Executive

After an election, it is the responsibility of the prime minister to establish a ministry or, as most people call it, a **government**. The ministry includes the ministers of government as well as "junior ministers," or more properly **ministers of state or secretaries of state**. Ministers of state are attached to senior ministers—the Minister of State (Transport), for example, works under the Minister of Transport. The cabinet is the executive committee of the ministry, and it is responsible for setting the policies and legislative agenda of the government. The prime minister determines who will be in the cabinet. It typically includes all ministers, and it may include some or all of the ministers of state, at the discretion of the prime minister. Additionally, the prime minister appoints a number of **parliamentary secretaries** to assist ministers in Parliament. Parliamentary secretaries are not part of the ministry (see Figure 5.1).

government May refer broadly to the entire system of public administration that governs the country or more specifically to the governing party in Parliament.

ministers of state or secretaries of state Members of Parliament appointed by the prime minister to be a "junior minister" responsible for a particular department or agency under the auspices of a minister.

parliamentary secretaries Members of Parliament appointed by the prime minister to assist ministers in their parliamentary duties, such as answering questions when the minister is away.

CABINET			
Prime Minister	Ministers	Ministers of State	Parliamentary Secretaries
MINISTRY			

Figure 5.1 Relationship between the Ministry and Cabinet

In general, the prime minister selects his or her ministers from those who have been elected to the House of Commons and almost always from his or her own party. The prime minister may also appoint people from the Senate to the cabinet, although convention limits the number of senators that can be appointed to the cabinet. The prime minister may also appoint people to his cabinet who have no seat in Parliament. However, if someone is selected to be a minister who does not have a seat in Parliament, convention dictates that this individual must obtain a seat in short order, either through an appointment to the Senate or through a **by-election** to the House of Commons. If they are unable to secure a seat in Parliament within about six months, they are required (by convention) to resign their position as minister.

by-election An election to fill a vacancy in the House of Commons held between general elections.

Size of the Cabinet

The size of the cabinet is entirely up to the prime minister. New governments tend to have small cabinets to look organized and efficient, but this is often a question of optics rather than reality. The first government under Stephen Harper in 2006 had 27 cabinet ministers including the prime minister, down from 39 in the first Paul Martin cabinet (which included eight ministers of state). While the first Harper cabinet had fewer ministers, the number of portfolios remained more or less the same. In other words, a number of ministers wore two or three hats. The Minister of International Trade, David Emerson from Vancouver, was also the Minister of State for the Pacific Gateway and the Minister of State for the Vancouver Olympics. The Minister of Health, Tony Clement, was also the Minister of State for the Federal Economic Development Initiative for Northern Ontario. This kind of workload, however, cannot be sustained in the long term. By 2011, the Harper cabinet had increased to 39 individuals, including 11 ministers of state and an Associate Minister of National Defence. This is consistent with cabinets going back to the governments of Brian Mulroney in the 1980s.

The size of the cabinet, however, has grown over time. Sir John A. Macdonald had 13 ministers in cabinet including himself. Why has the cabinet tripled in size since Confederation? It has grown for at least three reasons. First, the population of Canada has increased tenfold since Confederation, and the number of provinces has increased from four to ten. Second, the business of government is now infinitely more complex than it was in 1867. Third, Canadian society has become considerably more complex and diverse. In 1867, many groups were excluded from the Canadian political process, notably women and Aboriginal peoples. And after Confederation many immigrants, particularly from Asia, were also excluded. Over the course of the twentieth century, people from all over the world came to Canada. As these previously excluded groups and new Canadians began to participate in the game of politics, it was necessary to afford them representation in the cabinet, at least to the extent possible among the individuals elected to Parliament and belonging to the governing party.

Rules of Cabinet Formation

A number of rules have emerged to guide the process of cabinet formation. For the most part these are rules of thumb, although there is often a price to be paid for ignoring these rules. The rules of cabinet formation revolve primarily around the question of representation—ensuring that all Canadians feel represented in the government. This is not always easy for the prime minister, because the governing party may not have elected many people from some groups or regions. However, if these groups or regions are underrepresented in the cabinet, the governing party may have trouble connecting with these groups or regions in the next election.

Linguistic Duality Since Confederation, the first rule of cabinet formation has been linguistic duality. The cabinet must represent the two major linguistic communities in fair numbers, at least to the extent possible with the members of the governing party elected to the House of Commons. French Canadians constitute about a quarter of the population, so one would expect to see about 10 Francophones in a 40-person cabinet. But it is more than just a numbers game. It is important that cabinet portfolios be divided fairly among the two linguistic groups. There must be Francophones and Anglophones at the top of the cabinet hierarchy and evenly distributed through the middle and lower ranks of the cabinet. The two linguistic communities have been famously characterized as composing "two solitudes." It is difficult for Anglophones from outside Quebec to understand the social and political dynamics of French Canada, and it is equally difficult for Francophone Quebecers to understand the rest of Canada. That's why it is so important for Francophone prime ministers to have an Anglophone deputy and vice versa. It is also symbolically important; it represents the partnership of the "two founding nations."

Historically, Anglophone prime ministers would ensure that a Francophone Quebecer was the number-two person in the government and vice versa. In 1867, Sir John A. Macdonald had Sir George-Étienne Cartier, for example. This pattern was generally maintained through to the 1990s with a few gaps here and there, but the advent of the Bloc Québécois followed by the NDP sweep of Quebec in 2011 has made it much more difficult for prime ministers to ensure adequate representation for Francophones in the cabinet because the governing party may simply not have a Francophone Quebecer with the necessary stature to assume the second position in the government.

Stephen Harper, perhaps more than any other recent prime minister, has faced this problem. Only 10 Conservatives were elected in Quebec in 2006. Four of these individuals were appointed to the cabinet, and in a rather unusual move the prime minister appointed another Quebecer to the Senate and gave him a seat at the cabinet table as well. And yet Francophones have been underrepresented in the Harper government, and none has been of sufficiently high stature to be considered the number-two person in the government. The Conservative Party has consequently struggled to increase its support in Quebec. Indeed, in 2011, the Conservative Party only elected five candidates in Quebec.

Representation of All Provinces According to Size   The second rule of cabinet formation is that every province must be represented in cabinet more or less according to its population. Thus, everything else being equal, Ontario should have the largest number of cabinet ministers followed by Quebec. The smallest provinces often only get one cabinet minister, and Prince Edward Island, with only four seats in the House of Commons, is sometimes not represented in the cabinet at all. A special problem arises when the governing party fails to elect any candidates in a province. When this has happened in the past, prime ministers have sometimes appointed a senator to the cabinet from the province where the party did not elect any candidates. However, when the Conservative Party did not elect any candidates in Newfoundland and Labrador in 2008, Stephen Harper did not follow this convention. In 2011, the Conservatives elected one candidate in Newfoundland and Labrador. Peter Penashue was the first Innu elected to the House of Commons; he resigned after two years when it was revealed that he had accepted illegal campaign donations.

With the regional cleavages in Canadian politics and the differential support bases for the two major parties, it can be quite difficult to ensure proper representation for each province. The West was underrepresented in the last few Liberal governments, but the West has been overrepresented in the Harper government, primarily at the expense of Quebec.

In the process of creating the cabinet, the prime minister will appoint some of his ministers to be responsible for particular provinces or regions in the country in addition to their ministerial duties and responsibilities for particular departments and agencies. These are known as **regional ministers**, and they have a responsibility to keep the cabinet informed of political developments in their regions and how the policies of the government might be received in their respective regions. Being a regional minister is more of a political role on behalf of the governing party rather than an official government role.

regional ministers Members of cabinet tasked by the prime minister to take the lead on issues related to a particular province or region. It is more of a partisan role than a government position.

Nonterritorial Representation   Prime ministers have increasingly attempted to provide representation in the cabinet for nonterritorial groups, such as women, visible minorities, and Aboriginal peoples. This can be a challenge for the prime minister, since these groups are generally underrepresented in the House of Commons. With the cabinet shuffle in July 2013, there were 12 women in the Harper cabinet: eight full ministers and four ministers of state. Women are thus represented in the cabinet more or less according to their proportion in the House of Commons, but they are significantly underrepresented in relation to their proportion of Canadian society. The women in the Harper cabinet, moreover, have generally been assigned to the "caring and sharing" portfolios such as, health, international cooperation, labour, and human resources, rather than the more "masculine" positions of finance, industry, and defence. There are also four visible minorities in Stephen Harper's cabinet. Visible minorities are thus represented in the cabinet in approximately the same ratio as they are represented in the House of Commons, but of course that is still less than their proportion in Canadian society. And only one is a full minister: Leona Aglukkaq, Minister of the Environment. There are no openly gay or lesbian individuals in the Harper government.

Party Harmony   The prime minister also has to be careful to promote harmony within the caucus and the party. The Liberals and Conservatives have historically been **big tent parties**, which encompass many groups and factions. Each of these groups and factions tends to have an unofficial leader in the parliamentary caucus of the party, and a prime minister ignores these groups and their leaders at his peril. Stephen Harper seems to understand this point intuitively. As we have seen, the Conservative Party was created in 2004 through a merger of the old Reform/Alliance Party and the Progressive Conservative Party; Stephen Harper was very careful to promote leading figures from both factions to the cabinet. Peter

big tent parties Diverse parties with multiple ideological factions.

MacKay was the last leader of the old Progressive Conservative Party, and he has been a leading member of the Harper cabinet. Similarly, Stockwell Day was previously a leader of the Canadian Alliance, and Stephen Harper turned to him for a number of important cabinet jobs before he retired from politics in 2011. Potential future leaders of the Conservative Party, people like Jason Kenney and James Moore, have also been kept busy with important cabinet posts.

There's an old adage in politics: Keep your friends close, and your enemies closer! As we will discuss below, cabinet ministers cannot publicly question the policies of the government. That means when enemies are in the cabinet they are required to be loyal to the prime minister, but if they are not in cabinet they are free to criticize the prime minister and the government. This is dangerous for the prime minister because these people are big figures in the party who command the loyalty of many party members. So it is very important for the prime minister to manage the egos around him for the good of the party and the success of his government.

Merit   Finally, the prime minister has to choose people who will be competent. After all the other variables are taken into consideration, the prime minister looks for merit: the most suitable candidates from each province, the most capable Francophone candidates, the best women, and the strongest visible minorities and Aboriginal candidates. It should be noted that there are virtually no formal qualifications for cabinet positions. By convention, the Justice Minister needs to be a lawyer because the Justice Minister also acts as the Attorney General of Canada—the government's top lawyer. For all other positions, it is about ability and not qualifications. The Finance Minister must be good with numbers and be able to read a balance sheet, but she or he does not have to be an accountant by training. In general, cabinet ministers need to learn quickly, be a good communicator, and have solid managerial skills. A cabinet minister must be able to learn complex policy problems quickly, communicate these complex policy issues to his or her cabinet colleagues accurately, and simultaneously manage a large department with thousands of employees.

It should be stressed that there is nothing new about ensuring that all cultural groups in Canada are represented in the cabinet. The issue is as old as Canada itself. Sir John A. Macdonald had a very difficult time putting together his first cabinet in 1867, as he struggled to get the right balance between English and French, Catholic and Protestant, and Irish and Scottish, as well as representation for all four provinces. Today, Canada is a much larger and more diverse country than it was in 1867, so the process of cabinet formation is even more complex, but the political pressures and calculations are the same. If Prime Minister Harper were to determine that the "best" ministers were all white men from Alberta, the rest of the country would not feel represented in the government, even if these men were objectively the most meritorious candidates for the cabinet. In a democracy, it is essential that the people—*all* of the people—feel represented in their government.

What Do Ministers Do?

Ministers are responsible for running the various departments of the government: Finance, Health, Transportation, Defence, Environment, Foreign Affairs, Labour, Justice, and Human Resources, among many others. There are also a variety of agencies with ministers assigned to them, such as the Royal Canadian Mounted Police (RCMP) and the Canadian Security Intelligence Service (CSIS). The various departments do not actually need a minister to do their work. All the departments have very capable **civil servants**—unelected employees of the government who usually know quite a bit more about the subject matter of the department than the minister. So why do we have ministers? Ministers are the buckle between the departments and the elected Parliament of the people. It is this relationship

civil servants Permanent employees of the government who assist the elected government with policy development and implementation as well as the administration of the state.

that crucially distinguishes a democracy from a dictatorship. We need ministers to ensure that departments respond to the wishes of the people and not their own interests. We also need elected representatives of the people to take responsibility for the actions of the various departments of government.

Ministers Connect the Departments of Government to Parliament

Government departments vary in size, but many of them employ tens of thousands of people. Each department is organized in a hierarchical fashion and is headed by a **deputy minister**, the top civil servant in the department. Additionally, there are a number of associate deputy ministers (ADMs) to assist the deputy. Below the ADMs there are a number of directors, policy analysts, and so on down the line (see Figure 5.2).

The job of the department is to assist the minister in developing and implementing the policies adopted by the government. There is, of course, a lot of give and take in the process. The department and the minister may not have the same priorities. Cabinet ministers rotate in and out of office every few years, but civil servants generally continue to work in the same department for many years. Cabinet ministers thus sometimes have short-term political objectives, while civil servants often have long-term objectives for the department. This uneasy relationship between ministers and civil servants was satirized in the British television series *Yes Minister* and the sequel *Yes Prime Minister*, which were on air in the 1980s. Today, you can see clips of the shows on You Tube, and you might find the DVDs in your local library.

As we have seen, ministers do not necessarily need specialized knowledge in the area of their portfolio. It may in fact be detrimental, because the knowledgeable minister may try to impose his or her ideas on the department rather than listen to the advice he or she receives from the department. Stephen Harper may have encountered this problem with one of his first choices for cabinet. When retired Brigadier General Gordon O'Connor was

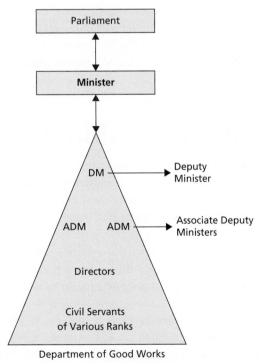

Figure 5.2 Ministers have been described as the buckle that fastens the departments and agencies of the government of Canada to Parliament

elected to represent the constituency of Carleton—Mississippi Mills on the outskirts of Ottawa, Stephen Harper evidently believed that he was ideally suited to be Minister of Defence; surely O'Connor would understand the major issues facing the military. Minister O'Connor's tenure at National Defence, however, did not go well. There were persistent rumours that he did not get along with his department or his generals. After about 15 months on the job, the prime minister shuffled him to the decidedly less glamorous position of Revenue Minister. No one outside of government really knows why O'Connor struggled as Minister of Defence, but, as a former general, he may have been better at giving orders than receiving advice. Or maybe his knowledge of military matters was out of date. Or maybe it was just a problem of being a rookie minister in a big department with many strong personalities. Either way, it did not seem to go well, even though he was presumably very knowledgeable about the subject matter of his department.

A story told by a former civil servant illustrates the kind of skills a minister must possess. In the early 1980s this civil servant worked for the Department of Energy, Mines and Resources, and his minister was Jean Chrétien. The department was trying to resolve a particularly complex issue relating to energy policy, but they did not have the expertise to resolve it on their own. They thus hired some expert consultants to assist them, and after almost a year of work they resolved the issue. Typically, ministers rely on **briefing notes** provided to them by officials in their departments. Ministers are busy people, and these notes must be *brief*, usually no more than two pages. Jean Chrétien, however, preferred to be briefed by his officials in person, so they arranged to give him a presentation. It took 30 minutes to explain the problem and its solution. When the presentation was over, Jean Chrétien said, "so what you're telling me is X, Y, and Z," and he summed it up in less than a minute and more effectively than the original presentation. At this point, the civil servant looked at him sheepishly and said, "yes, minister." No one ever accused Jean Chrétien of being an intellectual, but this story shows that he was a very quick study. He was able to grasp complex policy matters instantly, and he could explain them accurately and succinctly. It was these skills that allowed Chrétien to be a successful minister and ultimately a successful prime minister.[3]

In sum, ministers must be able to understand the complicated policy issues explained to them by the civil servants in their departments, accurately communicate that information to cabinet, advise cabinet on the best course of action on the basis of their judgment, and relay cabinet's decision to the department and ensure that the decision is implemented.

The Operation of Cabinet

The cabinet is the nerve centre of the Canadian government, but it is difficult for outsiders to know exactly how the cabinet works. The operation of cabinet is highly secret; when ministers are sworn into the Privy Council, they are sworn to secrecy for life, so even after they leave the government they are not permitted to discuss what happened in cabinet, and cabinet documents are only released to the public 30 years after the fact. It is all the more difficult to figure out how cabinet works since the operation of the cabinet is highly dependent on the managerial style of the prime minister. Some prime ministers like to talk and debate issues with their ministers, while other prime ministers tolerate very little discussion and debate in cabinet.

With more than three dozen members, the cabinet is too large to undertake all aspects of policy development. The cabinet consequently has a number of subcommittees with mandates to consider particular aspects of government policy. The number of cabinet committees, their mandates, and membership are all decided by the prime minister. Jean Chrétien had three cabinet committees and sat on none of them; Paul Martin had

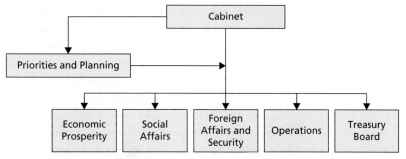

Figure 5.3 Cabinet Committees in the Harper Government

seven committees and sat on most of them; Stephen Harper has eight committees (including one subcommittee), but he sits on only one: the powerful Priorities and Planning Committee, which includes the chairs of all the other committees of cabinet as well as some of the other heavyweights in the government, such as the Finance Minister. This committee sets the government's agenda (see Figure 5.3).

How does cabinet work, and how does the Government of Canada make decisions? In brief, ministers bring proposals, which are developed in conjunction with the senior civil servants in the departments, to cabinet for consideration. These proposals are formally presented through a **memorandum to cabinet**. Each memorandum contains a policy recommendation supported by a detailed analysis of the problem. The cabinet will direct these memoranda to the appropriate subcommittee for more extensive consideration. The real grunt work of government decision making happens in these subcommittee meetings. When a committee has made a determination, it brings its decision to the full cabinet. What happens if the recommendation of the committee is not embraced by cabinet? It depends on the personality of the prime minister. Some prime ministers will encourage the full cabinet to debate the matter while other prime ministers will cut debate off quickly and send the matter back to the subcommittee for further consideration. Ultimately, however, the full cabinet will accept or reject the recommendation and it will be noted in a **record of decision**. The entire process is coordinated by the **Privy Council Office**, which is the apex of the civil service, as will be discussed further below.

The cabinet is not a democracy, and decisions are not made by voting. Rather, cabinet decisions are reached by consensus, and it is the prime minister's job to articulate the consensus. That does not mean the prime minister can decide anything—articulating the consensus of a meeting accurately is a special skill. It requires a delicate balance of sensitivity and firmness. The prime minister needs to listen to all points of view and to articulate a position that takes into account most, if not all, of the concerns raised by the ministers around the table. A prime minister who does this well will command the respect of his ministers and run an effective government. The consensus decision-making style of the cabinet reflects the basic institutional requirement of responsible government: The cabinet must speak with one voice.

memorandum to cabinet
A formal document used by a minister to present his or views to cabinet.

record of decision A formal document recording the final and official decisions of cabinet.

Privy Council Office (PCO)
The apex of the civil service and the office responsible for coordinating the actions of government and supporting the prime minister.

What Does the Prime Minister Do?

In contrast to other ministers, whose responsibilities are relatively well defined, the job of the prime minister is more vague. In theory, the prime minister is just another minister in the cabinet. In the British system of responsible government, the prime minister was historically described as *primus inter pares*—the first among equals. In a sense this is true; the prime minister and the other ministers are elected Members of Parliament, and the prime minister does not have a special status under the constitution. But the phrase *primus inter pares* overlooks the power dynamics in the government. The prime minister led his party to victory in the election; the prime minister chose the other ministers in the cabinet, who serve as long as they continue to have his blessing; and the prime minister leads the government in cabinet, in Parliament, in public, and in world affairs.

In order to understand the job of the prime minister, it may be helpful to contrast the prime minister's work with other ministers who are responsible for the various departments and agencies of the government. The other ministers tend to work vertically: They sit at the top of large departments and they are expected to transmit the work of their departments up to the cabinet and in turn they take the decisions of cabinet back to their departments. In the language of public administration, ministers operate in their own silos. They are expected to know everything that goes on in their silo, but they know very little about what goes on in the other silos of government. It is the job of the prime minister to know what goes on in *all* of the silos of government; in other words, the prime minister works horizontally.

How can one person possibly know what is going on across an organization as massive as the Government of Canada? Two offices provide the prime minister with logistical support. First, there is the Privy Council Office, or the PCO, as it is known throughout Ottawa. The PCO is the apex of the civil service because it is the coordinating office for all government departments. The **clerk of the Privy Council Office**, the top person at the PCO, is probably the second most powerful person in Ottawa just behind the prime minister. The clerk has three distinct roles. As the prime minister's deputy minister, the clerk "brings together the advice of the public service to support the prime minister in carrying out all his or her responsibilities as head of Canada's government."[4] As secretary to the cabinet, the clerk "provides support and advice to the ministry as a whole and oversees the provision of policy and secretariat support to cabinet and cabinet committees."[5] As head of the public service, the clerk "sets strategic direction and oversees all major issues for the public service."[6] In short, the clerk of the Privy Council is the deputy of all deputy ministers. About 1000 people work in the PCO, and they keep tabs on all the departments and agencies of the government on behalf of the prime minister, and they keep him fully informed.

clerk of the Privy Council Office
The top civil servant in the country. The clerk is also the deputy minister to the prime minister and secretary of the cabinet.

Wayne Wouters, Clerk of the Privy Council

How do you get to be the clerk of the Privy Council? Most clerks are career civil servants who have worked their way up through the system over the course of a couple of decades, but ultimately they are appointed to the top job by the prime minister. The prime minister also appoints all the deputy ministers in the federal government. The clerk of the Privy Council and the deputy ministers serve at the "pleasure" of the prime minister. In other words, they can be fired by the prime minister at any time without cause. The deputy ministers of the various departments and agencies in Ottawa work closely with their respective ministers, but they also report directly to the clerk of the Privy Council and through him or her to the prime minister. In the theory of responsible government, the primary allegiance of any deputy minister should be to his or her minister, but in reality many deputy ministers believe that they serve the prime minister. In short, the upper echelon of the bureaucracy is geared toward providing support to the prime minister, and this service is coordinated through the PCO by the clerk and the people who work for him or her.

In addition to the PCO, the prime minister has his own office—the **Prime Minister's Office (PMO)**. The PMO is a much smaller office—it consists of about 100 people, but they are typically members of the governing party and fiercely loyal to the prime minister personally. The PMO is extraordinarily powerful, and the prime minister's **chief of staff** is feared in the halls of Parliament almost as much as the prime minister. It is often said in Ottawa that "it's not what you know, it's *who* you know in the PMO that matters."

Why does the prime minister need his own office as well as the Privy Council Office? Because the two offices provide the prime minister with different sorts of advice. The PCO provides the prime minister with nonpartisan technical advice, because it works for the taxpayers of Canada and is only concerned about the impact of policy on Canada and not the governing party. The PMO, on the other hand, provides the prime minister with partisan political advice. The PCO might say, "Prime minister, if you spend $100 million on this project in Quebec it will create 450 permanent jobs in a region of the province that has a high rate of unemployment." Commenting on the same policy, the PMO might say, "Prime minister, if you proceed with this project the party will not pick up any seats in Quebec in the next election, and it will cost us votes in the West." In sum, the prime minister sits in the centre of a vast governing machine—largely of his own making—which affords him considerable power to direct the affairs of government (see Figure 5.4).

Prime Minister's Office (PMO) An office made up of the prime ministers top political staff. It provides the prime minister with partisan political support, unlike the Privy Council Office, which provides nonpartisan support. Each prime minister brings in his or her own staff, and they leave with him or her.

chief of staff The head of the Prime Minister's Office and the principal adviser to the prime minister. The chief of staff provides partisan advice to the prime minister, unlike the clerk of the Privy Council, who provides nonpartisan advice.

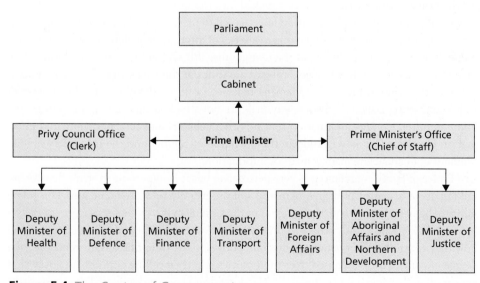

Figure 5.4 The Centre of Government

The Rise of Court Government

In the theory of responsible government, it should be the cabinet that informs the prime minister of what is going on across all government departments, but Donald Savoie, a highly distinguished professor of political science from New Brunswick, has argued that the PCO and PMO have effectively displaced the cabinet as the primary loci for decision making in the Canadian government. Since the 1960s, the PCO and PMO have become much larger and more robust institutions and they have been increasingly geared toward supporting the prime minister personally rather than the government as a whole. "The result," writes Savoie, "is that important decisions are no longer made in Cabinet. They are now made in federal–provincial meetings of first ministers, during 'Team Canada' trade visits abroad, where first ministers can hold informal meetings, in the Prime Minister's Office, in the Privy Council Office, in the Department of Finance, in international organizations and at international summits," or wherever else the prime minister might be at any moment in time.[7] In short, Professor Savoie argues, a new form of "court government" has been built up around the prime minister since the 1960s.

Savoie has provided three reasons explaining why this has happened. First, he argues that the election of the sovereignist Parti Québécois in 1976 sent shockwaves through Ottawa. Put bluntly, "no Canadian prime minister wants the country to break up on his or her watch."[8] To avoid this possibility, successive prime ministers have ensured that sufficient machinery has been in place to monitor the political situation in Quebec and to assess the impact of all government policies on "national unity." It is not that the Government of Canada will automatically avoid any policy that upsets Quebec; but if a policy has the potential to upset Quebec, the government wants advanced warning and a strategy to minimize the damage. Savoie also points out that all the other "provincial premiers have direct access to the prime minister and do not hesitate to pursue an issue with him. If the prime minister decides to support a minister, then the issue is brought to the centre of government in Ottawa for resolution."[9]

Second, the media has played a major role in empowering the prime minister since the 1960s. Savoie notes that "the attention of the mass media can, on very short notice, turn an issue, however trivial, into an important file," requiring the attention of the prime minister.[10] The media has always played a role in Canadian politics, but the advent of 24-hour news programming means that television producers have a lot of airtime to fill. Journalists thus work relentlessly to get new stories, and on-air personalities can spend hours and sometimes days analyzing an issue down to the smallest details, and ultimately journalists won't let the story go until they have heard from the prime minister on the matter, even though some other minister will typically be responsible for the issue. In these instances, it is hard for the prime minister to avoid getting sucked into the story.

Finally, the forces of globalization have served to increase the power of the prime minister. "Canadian prime ministers belong to a series of international clubs of heads of government, from the G7 to APEC, and the Commonwealth and la francophonie. Deals, even bilateral ones, between heads of government are struck at these meetings. The globalization of the world economy means that many more issues, or files, will fall to the prime minister's in-basket," writes Savoie.[11] Even when deals are not struck at international meetings, the prime minister acquires information that no other cabinet minister can obtain, and information translates into power. Indeed, the operation of cabinet and the machinery of government is all about the management of information.

Professor Savoie's argument is very persuasive, but it is important to stress that we are talking about a matter of degree here and not an entirely new phenomenon. The prime minister has *always* been a powerful figure in the Canadian government, as Herman Bakvis has noted: "One need only read accounts of John A. Macdonald and Wilfrid Laurier, and how they controlled their patronage machines down to the tiniest details, to appreciate the degree of control they exercised over their parties and their fellow ministers in a way that appears directly comparable to today."[12] Macdonald and Laurier dominated their respective governments to be sure, but the machinery of government has been redesigned since the 1960s to provide even greater logistical support to the prime minister and, in turn, power seems to have become more concentrated with each successive prime minister since Pierre Trudeau. This trend has continued unabated under Stephen Harper.

The power of the prime minister is not completely unfettered, however. The prime minister is constrained by the constitution and other laws, is surrounded in cabinet and caucus by ambitious individuals who seek to steer government decisions in their direction, and the top civil servants in the country are extremely smart and endeavour to get the prime minister to do what is best for Canada. And, of course, there is always the possibility that the governor general or the Queen herself (on the few occasions when she meets with the prime minister personally) might "advise or warn" the prime minister about particular issues. The regular meetings with the governor general serve to remind the prime minister that he or she works for the Crown and by extension the people of Canada.

But the major constraint on the prime minister is *time*. The prime minister simply does not have the physical capacity to be involved in all government decisions. At most, the prime minister can only be (deeply) involved in three or four major files at any one time. However, he gets to handle whatever files he wants; in other words, he can appropriate files from the responsible ministers almost at will.

Prime ministers in other parliamentary systems of government, such as Great Britain, have become more powerful over time as well, but the problem is especially acute in Canada. There are probably a few reasons why, but one is especially significant. In Canada, party leaders are elected by the members of the party at large, and it is virtually impossible to remove a leader involuntarily, especially a sitting prime minister. In other parliamentary systems, the elected members of the party in Parliament have a much greater—and sometimes exclusive—say in who will lead the party in Parliament. So in November 1990, the British Conservative Party dumped Margaret Thatcher just as Britain was set to join the United States in the first war against Iraq. And in 2010, the Australian Labor Party dumped its leader and prime minister in favour of Deputy Prime Minister Julia Gillard, who only

Box 5.1

The Working of Court Government

"Canadian prime ministers have in their hands all the important levers of power. Indeed, all major national public policy roads lead one way or another to their doorstep. They are elected leader of their party by party members, they chair cabinet meetings, establish cabinet processes and procedures, set the cabinet agenda, establish the consensus for cabinet decisions; they appoint and fire ministers and deputy ministers, establish cabinet committees and decide on their membership; they exercise virtually all the powers of patronage and act as personnel manager for thousands of government and patronage jobs; they articulate the government's strategic direction as outlined in the Speech from the Throne; they dictate the pace of change and are the main salespersons promoting the achievements of their government; they have a direct hand in establishing the government's fiscal framework; they represent Canada abroad; they establish the proper mandate of individual ministers and decide all machinery of government issues and they are the final arbiter in interdepartmental conflicts. The prime minister is the only politician with a national constituency, and unlike members of parliament and even cabinet ministers, the prime minister does not need to search out publicity or national media attention, since attention is invariably focussed on the person, the office or even the prime minister's residence, 24 Sussex Drive."

SOURCE: Donald Savoie, "The Rise of Court Government in Canada". Copyright © December, 1999 *Canadian Political Science Association*, 32:4. Reprinted with the permission of Cambridge University Press.

barely hung on to power after the election in August of the same year. Gillard, in turn, was dumped by her party just before the election in 2013 (which Labor lost). Such a scenario is unimaginable in Canada. Leaders stay in power in Canada until they decide to step down of their own volition. Thus, ironically, a more democratic way of selecting a leader results in a less democratic style of leadership. In sum, there is considerable merit to Professor Savoie's suggestion that *inter* and *pares* no longer exist in Canada; there is only *primus*.

The Principles of Responsible Government

Now that we have formed a government we are in a position to examine the rules of responsible government more fully. As we already know, the first rule of responsible government is that the government must maintain the confidence of Parliament—that is, it must always be able to command the support of a majority in Parliament. If Parliament loses confidence in the ministry, the prime minister must go to the governor general and in all likelihood would advise the governor general to dissolve Parliament and call an election (although theoretically he could recommend that another party be invited to form a government). If the governor general did invite another leader to form a government, its first test would be to obtain the confidence of Parliament.

The second rule of responsible government is that each minister must take individual responsibility for his or her department. By convention, a minister is supposed to resign if a mistake is made in his or her department, but the practicality of this convention has been called into question in the modern era. When the convention was formulated a few centuries ago, departments were very small and it was reasonable to assume that the minister knew all of the employees of the department and all its activities. Today, however, departments are huge and it is impossible for the minister to know everyone in the department and all of its activities. So what does the principle of individual ministerial responsibility mean today? Today, a minister is expected to resign if his or her personal conduct is called into question. If it is a question of departmental conduct, it is usually sufficient for the minister to say that he or she will get to the bottom of the problem and ensure that it does not happen again. In practice, however, a minister will continue to occupy his or her portfolio as long as he or she maintains the confidence of the prime minister. If the prime minister "asks" for a minister's resignation, the minister is gone.

Third, ministers must assume collective responsibility for the decisions of the government. If things go wrong, a minister cannot say that he or she argued against it, or it was the idea of this or that minister; there can be no blame shifting. If a minister cannot publicly defend a cabinet decision the minister must resign, but this rarely happens in Canada. Ministers usually manage to swallow their pride and stick with the government, because being in cabinet means staying where the action is in the Canadian political system.

The principles of responsible government are intended to ensure that the ministry is accountable to Parliament and through Parliament to the people of Canada. The prime minister, of course, would like the rules of responsible government to be applied in a relatively relaxed manner, but it is the job of the opposition parties in Parliament to ensure that these rules are followed as closely as possible. Indeed, the leaders of the opposition parties will appoint members of their respective parties to be **Opposition Critics**, who are expected to challenge ministers in parliamentary debates. The opposition critic for foreign affairs, for example, will follow developments in the Department of Foreign Affairs and in the international world of politics and ask the minister tough questions about these developments. It is often said that the critics of the Official Opposition party constitute a **Shadow cabinet**. In general, the leader of the opposition will employ the rules of cabinet formation to create his or her shadow cabinet, except that the official opposition has fewer members than the governing party, so the leader of the opposition has fewer people to draw on.

Opposition Critics Are selected by the leader of the official opposition party to critique the work of particular government ministers. Collectively, the opposition critics are known as the shadow cabinet.

Shadow cabinet Sits opposite the government in the House of Commons and holds the cabinet accountable. The shadow cabinet includes the leader of the official opposition party and its critics (who are appointed by the leader of the official opposition).

SUMMARY

Canada has a dual executive. *Formal executive* authority is invested in the Crown, but *political authority* lies with the prime minister and the other ministers in the cabinet. The relationship between the two executives and their respective roles and responsibilities are governed largely by the rules or conventions of *responsible government*. While the general public tends to view the Crown as purely symbolic and perhaps a touch anachronistic, the governor general fulfills a critical role in the Canadian political system on behalf of the Queen: as head of state, he or she appoints or dismisses the head of government. It may sound like a small point, but someone has to do that job, and for the most part British monarchs and Canadian governors general have performed the task impartially.

The Canadian prime minister, on the other hand, has considerable political authority: he or she chooses all the other ministers, establishes the committees of cabinet and their memberships, determines how cabinet meetings will be conducted, articulates the consensus of the cabinet, and appoints the top tier of the civil service, including the clerk of the Privy Council. Canadian prime ministers have always dominated their governments, but since the 1960s successive prime ministers have refocused the machinery of government to provide them with more direct logistical support. In many instances, the Privy Council Office and the Prime Minister's Office have displaced the cabinet as the central decision-making bodies in the Canadian political system, contrary to the principles of responsible government. Indeed, it increasingly seems that Canada now has a system of prime ministerial government.

Questions to Think About

1. Should Canada cut its ties to the Queen and establish a purely Canadian head of state?
2. Do prime ministers pay too much attention to representational issues and not enough to merit when forming the cabinet?
3. Do you know who is in your government? How many cabinet ministers can you name beyond the prime minister?
4. Do you agree with Donald Savoie that the prime minister has become too powerful? If not, why not? If so, what can be done about it?

Learning Outcomes

1. Describe the role of the governor general in Canada's political system and the relationship between the formal and informal executive.
2. Describe the informal rules used by most prime ministers to select cabinet ministers.
3. Describe the respective roles of the prime minister and ministers and the operation of cabinet.
4. Explain how the prime minister is able to dominate the government.
5. Describe the main principles of responsible government.

Additional Readings

Peter Aucoin, Mark D. Jarvis, and Lori Turnbull, *Democratizing the Constitution: Reforming Responsible Government* (Toronto, ON: Emond Montgomery, 2011).

Herman Bakvis, *Regional Ministers: Power and Influence in the Canadian Cabinet* (Toronto, ON: University of Toronto Press, 1991).

Eddie Goldenberg, *The Way it Works: Inside Ottawa* (Toronto, ON: McClelland and Stewart, 2006).

Lawrence Martin, *Harperland: The Politics of Control* (Toronto, ON: Viking, 2010).

Barbara Messamore, *Canada's Governors General, 1847–1878: Biography and Constitutional Evolution* (Toronto, ON: University of Toronto Press, 2006).

Gordon Robertson, *Memoirs of a Very Civil Servant: Mackenzie King to Pierre Trudeau* (Toronto, ON: University of Toronto Press, 2000).

Donald Savoie, *Governing from the Centre: The Concentration of Power in Canadian Politics* (Toronto, ON: University of Toronto Press, 1999).

Jeffrey Simpson, *The Friendly Dictatorship* (Toronto, ON: McClelland and Stewart, 2001).

David E. Smith, *The Invisible Crown: The First Principle of Canadian Government* (Toronto ON: University of Toronto Press, 1995).

Graham White, *Cabinets and First Ministers* (Vancouver, BC: UBC Press, 2005).

Notes

1. David E. Smith, *The Invisible Crown: The First Principle of Canadian Government* (Toronto, ON: University of Toronto Press, 1995).

2. Peter Aucoin, Mark D. Jarvis, and Lori Turnbull, *Democratizing the Constitution: Reforming Responsible Government* (Toronto, ON: Emond Montgomery, 2011), 9.

3. This anecdote was relayed to the author directly. The retired civil servant in question has asked to remain anonymous.

4. Privy Council Office, "The Role and Structure of the Privy Council Office," August 2010, www.pco-bcp.gc.ca.

5. Ibid.

6. Ibid.

7. Donald Savoie, "The Rise of Court Government in Canada". Copyright © December, 1999 *Canadian Political Science Association*, 32:4. Reprinted with the permission of Cambridge University Press.

8. Ibid., 637.

9. Ibid., 639.

10. Ibid., 641.

11. Ibid., 651.

12. Herman Bakvis, "Prime Minister and Cabinet in Canada: An Autocracy in Need of Reform?" *Journal of Canadian Studies* 35:4 (Winter 2004), 65.

Chapter 6
Parliament

Key Points

- Parliament consists of the Crown, the Senate, and the House of Commons.
- Parliament makes the law of the land and it holds the government accountable.
- The operation of Parliament is structured fundamentally by political parties.
- The social diversity of Canada is not fully represented in Parliament and consequently the law of the land may not be representative of the people.
- Efforts to reform Parliament, especially the Senate, have generally been unsuccessful.

Let's summarize our progress so far. I have argued that politics is a conflict between different conceptions of the good life. These different conceptions are embodied in bundles of ideas known as ideologies, which are represented by the main political parties to a greater or lesser extent. Parties are political machines designed to get their candidates elected to Parliament. Next we have an election, where the single-member plurality electoral system steers us in a certain direction: Toward two major parties, with one party usually having a majority of seats in Parliament. After the election, the governor general calls the leader of the party with the most seats and asks him or her to form a government. The prime minister, in turn, selects the other ministers who will join him or her in the government. Before the government can take its seat in Parliament, the prime minister and the other ministers must be sworn into office by the governor general at a ceremony at Rideau Hall (the governor general's office and residence, which is across the road from the prime minister's official residence at 24 Sussex Drive).

We are now ready to examine the operation of Parliament, which is the hub of the Canadian political system. The Canadian Parliament consists of three parts: the Crown, the Senate, and the House of Commons. We examined the role of the Crown in the last chapter, so we will focus on the House of Commons and Senate in this chapter. Members of the House of Commons are elected through the single-member plurality electoral system, and senators are appointed by the governor general on the advice of the prime minister. Parliament has two functions. First, it makes **legislation**, from the Latin word *legis*, which means *law*. In other words, Parliament makes law—the law of the land. Second, Parliament, especially the opposition parties in the House of Commons, is expected to hold the government accountable. The opposition parties question the government's policies, debate the government's legislation, and attempt to enforce the principles of responsible government.

legislation The formal process by which laws are enacted.

The two functions of Parliament are not entirely compatible. When the government has a majority, Parliament is quite an efficient legislative body but it is difficult for the opposition parties to hold the government accountable. When the government has a minority, accountability is considerably enhanced but the legislative process slows down and sometimes even grinds to a halt. Over the years, various proposals have been made to reform the House of Commons to achieve a better balance between legislative efficiency and accountability, but most proposals have fallen flat. More than any other branch of Parliament, the Senate has been an object of derision in Canada, but efforts to reform (or even abolish) the Senate have consistently failed.

The operation of Parliament is structured to a considerable extent by political parties. As we know, the first rule of responsible government is that the prime minister must maintain the confidence of Parliament, or more precisely the House of Commons (the government does not have to maintain the support of the Senate). When the government has a majority in the House of Commons, the prime minister relies on the support of his own party to maintain the confidence of Parliament. But when we have a minority government, the prime minister is required to obtain the support of other parties to continue governing.

But beyond the question of confidence, each new law must be passed by a majority in both the House of Commons and the Senate, and parties help expedite the legislative process. Without parties, Parliament would be a free-for-all and not much legislation would ever get passed. It is thus important for parties to be coherent and disciplined teams. And it is the job of party leaders to instill this discipline. However, many political scientists have come to believe that party discipline is now too rigid in Canada, and that our elected Members of Parliament are not sufficiently free to voice the concerns of their constituents. Why is party discipline more rigid now? It is tied directly to the increased power of the prime minister, as discussed in the previous chapter.

Parliament is the principal institution of representation in Canadian politics, but it is not especially representative of Canadian society. Some groups in Canadian society, such as women, visible minorities, and Aboriginal peoples, are consistently underrepresented in the House of Commons. For the most part, these groups are better represented in the Senate, which is an unelected chamber, although the average age in the Senate is 65 as opposed to 53 in the House of Commons and only 39 in the population at large. Members of both chambers are also generally more affluent than the average Canadian. When it comes to making legislation, Members of Parliament are guided by their ideology and their personal experience. Since Parliament does not reflect the full diversity of Canada, the law is arguably not representative of Canadian society. While some political parties have taken steps to run more female and minority candidates, it would seem that deeper systemic changes are needed to make Parliament more representative of Canadian society. In other words, the political system needs to be fixed to ensure that all Canadians feel properly represented in Parliament.

The House of Commons

jiawangkun/Shutterstock

The Start of a New Parliament

After a government is formed by the prime minister and sworn into office by the governor general, it is ready to take its position in Parliament. Before the government can begin the process of introducing new legislation, there are a few preliminaries that need to be dispensed with. First, it is necessary for the members to elect a referee from among themselves. The referee, known as the **Speaker**, then takes his or her seat in the big chair at the end of the House of Commons. The government, incidentally, always sits to the right of the Speaker. In the British parliamentary tradition, nobody is supposed to want this job, so when an individual is finally elected to serve as the Speaker he or she is grabbed by the prime minister and the leader of the opposition and dragged "unwillingly" to the Speaker's chair in an act of lighthearted political theatre. The Speaker is an elected member of the House of Commons, and like other members he or she represents a constituency. While the Speaker will handle matters on behalf of his or her constituents, the Speaker does not participate in debates in the House of Commons. The job of the Speaker is to moderate these debates: to keep order, enforce the rules of the House of Commons, and announce the results of votes. The Speaker only votes in the event of a tie, and on those rare occasions the Speaker is obliged by convention to vote in favour of the motion regardless of his or her personal position. It is just not considered appropriate for the Speaker, who has not participated in the debate, to terminate the life of a motion. There will always be another opportunity for Parliament to defeat a motion sustained by the Speaker—either in another round of voting in the House of Commons or in the Senate.

After the Speaker is elected, the parliamentary session is opened by the governor general with a **Speech from the Throne**. The Speech from the Throne represents the government's agenda for the new session of Parliament. The speech is read by the governor general, but it is written by the government. After an election, the speech will typically focus on the promises made by the party during the campaign. If the government later prorogues Parliament, another Throne Speech will be required and it will typically attempt to articulate a new set of priorities for the government. The speech is always read in the Senate and is a grand affair. Why does the governor general read the government's Throne Speech in the Senate? Because the Queen is not a commoner, so it would not be dignified for her

Speaker The person who moderates legislative debates. In Canada, the Speaker of the House of Commons is an elected Member of Parliament who in turn is elected by the other members to be the Speaker. There is also a Speaker in the Senate.

Speech from the Throne (or Throne Speech) A speech that opens each session of Parliament. The speech is written by the government but read in the Senate chamber by the governor general. It outlines the government's agenda for the new session of Parliament.

Andrew Scheer (Member of Parliament for Regina-Qu'Appelle) was elected Speaker of the House of Commons by the other elected members of parliament, in June 2011. After his election–following an old custom–he was escorted to the Speaker's chair by Prime Minister Stephen Harper and the leader of the opposition— the late Jack Layton.

REUTERS/Chris Wattie

representative in Canada to read the speech in the House of Commons. (In Britain, the Queen reads the Speech from the Throne in the House of Lords; the Queen even has her own door to Parliament—the Sovereign's Entrance).

The governor general will arrive on Parliament Hill with great pomp and ceremony and a 21-gun salute. Once in the Senate chamber, the governor general will occupy the seat of the Senate Speaker. The nine justices of the Supreme Court of Canada sit directly in front of the governor general, decked out in their red robes. The top brass from the military and the commissioner of the RCMP will also be in attendance. The prime minister, who is not a member of the Senate, will sit on a chair to the right of the governor general and somewhat out of view. Members of the House of Commons will be summoned to the Senate by the **Usher of the Black Rod**—the chief ceremonial officer of the Senate (usually a retired military officer). Members of the House are led to the Senate by the Speaker, but only a handful of members can fit into the visitors' area in the Senate entrance. Most members of the House consequently watch the speech on monitors in the hallway between the two chambers.

After the speech, the members return to the House of Commons, but before they debate the speech the prime minister is required to introduce Bill C-1, An Act respecting the Administration of Oaths of Office. This is a pro forma or "dummy" bill. (We will discuss bills more extensively later in this Chapter.) The reading of Bill C-1 empowers the House of Commons to conduct its business, and it is a practice that dates back more than 400 years in the British Parliament. Once the bill is read, the House of Commons can proceed to debate the Speech from the Throne or, as they say in the House of Commons, "reply" to the Speech from the governor general. Typically, a government supporter will move to thank the governor general for his or her speech. The government side of the House will praise the speech, while the opposition will criticize the speech and move amendments to "improve" it. At the end of the debate, which can last up to a week, the House of Commons will vote to accept or reject the speech. The vote is a matter of confidence. The speech represents the government's agenda for the entire session of Parliament, so if the House of Commons cannot endorse the government's action plan, by definition it does not have confidence in the government to govern and the prime minister would be required by convention to submit his resignation to the governor general. If the government commands a majority in the House of Commons, the Throne Speech will surely be endorsed. But even with a minority government, the opposition would be loath to defeat the government so soon after an election, at least over a Throne Speech.

The Legislative Process and the Making of Law

Once the Throne Speech has been accepted, Parliament can get down to work. The basic job of Parliament is to legislate—in other words, to make law. When the government introduces new legislation (proposes a new law), it is referred to as a **bill** (see Figure 6.1). When a bill is passed into law, it is known as an **act**. Each bill proceeds through Parliament in a series of stages called **readings**. In the **first reading**, the bill is introduced by the responsible minister. In this reading, the bill is numbered and printed in both official languages. Government bills introduced in the House of Commons are numbered from 1 to 200 with the prefix C for Commons. Bill C-1 is the pro forma bill introduced at the beginning of each new session of Parliament; the next bill is C-2, and so on. Bills introduced in the Senate begin with the prefix S, as in Bill S-2. With each new session of Parliament the numbers start again. In the first reading, there is no discussion or debate. The bill is put to a vote, and it needs a majority support to pass. In the **second reading**, the bill is debated *in principle*. At this reading, there is no discussion of the details of the bill, but the government will explain

Usher of the Black Rod The chief ceremonial officer of the Senate. The Sergeant-at-Arms is the chief ceremonial officer in the House of Commons.

bill A proposed new law. When it is finally passed by Parliament, it becomes known as an act.

act A statutory law of Parliament.

readings The stages that bills pass through in Parliament.

first reading The stage when a bill is introduced in Parliament and numbered. Bills introduced in the House of Commons begin with the prefix *C* followed by a number; bills introduced in the Senate begin with the prefix *S* followed by a number.

second reading The stage of the legislative process when the bill is debated in principle.

1st Session, 41st Parliament,
60 Elizabeth II, 2011

HOUSE OF COMMONS OF CANADA

BILL C-7

An Act respecting the selection of senators and amending the Constitution Act, 1867 in respect of Senate term limits

Preamble

Whereas it is important that Canada's representative institutions, including the Senate, continue to evolve in accordance with the principles of modern democracy and the expectations of Canadians;

Whereas the Government of Canada has undertaken to explore means to enable the Senate better to reflect the democratic values of Canadians and respond to the needs of Canada's regions;

Whereas in 1987 the First Ministers of Canada agreed, as an interim measure until Senate reform is achieved, that any person summoned to fill a vacancy in the Senate is to be chosen from among persons whose names have been submitted by the government of the province or territory to which the vacancy relates;

Whereas it is appropriate that those whose names are submitted to the Queen's Privy Council for Canada for summons to the Senate be determined by democratic election by the people of the province or territory that a senator is to represent;

Whereas it is appropriate that a framework be established to provide guidance to provinces and territories for the text of legislation governing such elections;

1re session, 41e législature,
60 Elizabeth II, 2011

CHAMBRE DES COMMUNES DU CANADA

PROJET DE LOI C-7

Loi concernant la sélection des sénateurs et modifiant la Loi constitutionnelle de 1867 relativement à la limitation de la durée du mandat des sénateurs

Préambule

Attendu :

qu'il est important que les institutions représentatives du Canada, notamment le Sénat, continuent d'évoluer de concert avec les principes d'une démocratie moderne et les attentes des Canadiens;

que le gouvernement du Canada s'est engagé à explorer des façons de permettre au Sénat de mieux refléter les valeurs démocratiques canadiennes et de mieux répondre aux besoins des régions du Canada;

qu'en 1987 les premiers ministres du Canada ont convenu, à titre de mesure provisoire jusqu'à ce que la réforme du Sénat soit réalisée, que les sièges vacants au Sénat soient comblés au moyen d'une liste de candidats sénatoriaux présentée par le gouvernement de la province ou du territoire visés;

qu'il est indiqué que les personnes dont la candidature est proposée au Conseil privé de la Reine pour le Canada en vue de leur nomination au Sénat soient choisies par voie d'une élection démocratique par la population de la province ou du territoire qu'elles représenteront;

Figure 6.1 First Page of Bill C-7, An Act Respecting the Selection of Senators and Amending the Constitution Act, 1867 in Respect of Senate Term Limits

why the bill is good policy and the opposition parties will argue that the bill is flawed. The bill is put to a vote again, and it needs a majority to pass.

If the bill passes second reading, it moves to the **committee stage**.[1] At this stage, the bill moves temporarily off the floor of the House of Commons and over to one of the

committee stage The stage of the legislative process when a bill is sent to a subcommittee of the House of Commons for detailed examination.

committee rooms in Parliament. There simply is not enough time for the House of Commons to consider each piece of legislation in great detail. And, with 308 members, the House of Commons is too large for that kind of detailed work. The House of Commons consequently has a number of subcommittees to examine bills in greater detail. There are 26 **standing committees**, which exist from one session of Parliament to the next, and typically there are a few ad hoc committees, which are created for a particular purpose and then disbanded. In a nutshell, there is a standing committee for each ministry that examines legislation coming from that ministry and other matters related to the ministry. So finance bills go to the standing committee on finance, and justice bills go to the standing committee on justice, and so forth. Each committee has 12 members, and the parties are represented in the committees more or less in proportion to their standing in the House of Commons. If one party has a majority in the House of Commons, it will have a majority on all the committees. Membership on each committee is determined by the party leadership. In the past, the chair of each committee was handpicked by the prime minister, but the chairs are now elected by the committee members themselves. In most cases, the chair comes from the governing party, "with the exception of five committees where the Chairs are chosen from the Official Opposition (i.e., the Standing Committees on Access to Information, Privacy and Ethics; Government Operations and Estimates; Public Accounts; Status of Women; and the Standing Joint Committee for the Scrutiny of Regulations)."[2]

The main task of each standing committee is to examine the details of bills brought before them. Committees usually hold public hearings to receive expert opinion on the legislation and to gather the opinions of interested groups and voters. After the public consultation phase of the process, the committee members study a bill clause by clause. Some bills may only be a couple of paragraphs or a few pages long, but other bills may be hundreds of pages long. After the bill has been scrutinized by the members clause by clause, the committee adopts a report on the bill and makes a recommendation to the House of Commons. The committee may recommend that the bill be accepted as drafted, accepted with amendments, or not be proceeded with further. Much of the legislative work of the House of Commons is done in committee, and consequently Members of Parliament typically spend more time in committee than in the Commons. In the period from April 2007 to March 2008, for example, "committees held 1,076 meetings, sat for 1,686 hours, and heard from 2,958 witnesses. In comparison, the House held 113 sittings during the same period."[3]

When the committee has finished its deliberations, it reports back to the House of Commons. This is the **report stage** of the legislative process. At this stage, motions to amend particular clauses of the bill are debated by the whole House of Commons. When the government has a majority, amendments will only be incorporated into the bill if the amendments are accepted by the government. But with a minority government, the opposition parties can secure amendments over the wishes of the government, at least if the opposition parties work together cooperatively. After all the amendments have been considered, a final draft of the bill is placed before the House of Commons for the **third reading**. At this stage, members of the House of Commons state why the bill as finally drafted should or should not be passed.

At each reading, the question of confidence is at play. Some bills are understood by way of convention to be matters of confidence. The Speech from the Throne and money bills (including the budget) are always matters of confidence. If a government loses a vote on these bills, it must resign. Confidence attaches to other bills at the discretion of the prime minister. If the prime minister decrees that a bill is a matter of confidence, he is indicating that the bill is extremely important to the government and he is putting his government on the line for it. If the government loses a vote on a bill that is not considered a matter of confidence, the bill dies but the government lives on.

standing committees Permanent committees that examine legislation in detail and consider other policy questions. There are approximately 26 standing committees in the House of Commons, one for each ministry.

report stage The stage of the legislative process when the standing committee reports back to the House of Commons on its deliberations about a bill.

third reading The stage of the legislative process when the bill is once again debated in principle and voted on in its entirety.

If the bill passes the third reading in the House of Commons, it proceeds to the Senate for *sober second thought*. Each bill must pass through the same legislative process in the Senate. Although the Senate tends to expedite the passage of most laws, Senate standing committees can and do hold public hearings on important laws and it can recommend amendments to the House. If the House of Commons rejects the amendments suggested by the Senate, the bill is referred to a joint committee of the two chambers for consideration. At the end of the day, each bill has to be passed by both chambers in exactly the same form. The Senate has the constitutional power to reject a bill passed by the House of Commons, but by convention the Senate does not block bills backed by the government.

After both chambers have passed a bill in identical form, it proceeds to the governor general for **royal assent**. It would be unimaginable for the governor general not to assent to a bill. The governor general may provide assent in a written declaration, or he or she may grant assent in a ceremony in the Senate chamber. At this point, the bill becomes an act of Parliament and it becomes the law of the land either on the day of royal assent or on the day indicated in the act.

As we can see, the process of making law is a very rigorous and time-consuming affair. How long does it take to pass a law? It depends on the scope of the law and its urgency. Short and simple bills can usually be passed in a few months, but longer and more complex bills may take a year or two. In some instances, complex bills can be dispatched quickly. After the terrorist attacks of 9/11, the Chrétien government moved swiftly to enact new anti-terrorism laws. The new Anti-Terrorism Act received royal assent before Christmas that year, even though it was more than 200 pages long. On the other hand, it took the Chrétien government more than six years to pass the Species at Risk Act. Three separate bills were introduced at various points to protect endangered species, but they all died when Parliament was either prorogued by the government or dissolved by the governor general for an election. Obviously, saving the Vancouver Island marmot was not a priority for the Chrétien government. (Curiously, when the Species at Risk Act was finally introduced in October 2002, it passed from first reading to third reading in the House of Commons in a single day. Obviously all of the ground work for the bill had been laid in previous sessions of Parliament. The Senate spent two months on the bill before it received royal assent.) The important thing to note is that the process is controlled by the governing party. Most bills introduced into the House of Commons are initiated by the government (specifically the cabinet) and, as long as the government has a majority, all government bills will eventually pass.

Types of Bills

All bills go through the same legislative process, but there are a few different types of bills. In the first instance, there are **public bills** and **private bills**. Public bills establish law for the whole of Canadian society, while private bills are passed for specific individuals or groups or other entities. A private bill, for example, might establish the incorporation of a new bank. However, the vast majority of bills passed by Parliament are public.

Public bills can be further divided into **government bills** and **private members' bills**. As the name implies, government bills are sponsored by the government and are introduced in Parliament by the responsible minister. Private members' bills are introduced by nongovernment Members of Parliament, as will be discussed more fully in this chapter.

Government bills come in two types: **money bills** and **non-money bills**. In Canada's parliamentary tradition, money bills are especially important and by convention are always a matter of confidence. Money bills cannot be introduced in the Senate; they must be introduced in the House of Commons by the responsible minister. Money bills, as the name implies, have to do with how the government spends money or gets money from taxpayers; non-money bills, on the other hand, are any piece of legislation that does *not* involve money (e.g., criminal laws). There are two types of money bills: **supply bills** and **ways-and-means bills**. Supply bills authorize the spending of money by the Government of Canada and its various departments and agencies. Ways-and-means bills involve taxation; they provide government with the money or the *means* to conducts its affairs. See Figure 6.2 for an overview of the types of bills.

The most important money bill is the **budget**. It outlines the government's spending and taxation plans for the whole year. Parties make a lot of promises during an election campaign, but the budget reveals the government's real priorities—as people say, money talks. As mentioned previously, by convention the budget is a matter of confidence. If it fails to pass in Parliament, the government falls. The Finance Minister usually presents the budget to Parliament in the spring, usually between February and April, and it is a big occasion. On budget day, Parliament is abuzz with anticipation, the media arrives in full gear, and many **interest groups** send representatives to hear the news first-hand and offer their spin on it to the media. Budget day also involves one of the more quirky traditions of Canadian politics: the Finance Minister traditionally wears a new pair of shoes and the media takes great interest in his or her choice of footwear. Occasionally, though, when the budget involves deep spending cuts the minister will make a point of wearing an old pair of shoes, demonstrating his or her commitment to austerity. The budget is always presented in the late afternoon after the stock market closes in Toronto to ensure that the budget does not disrupt the market. The Finance Minister will also typically provide a **fiscal update** in the fall. This too is an important day in the parliamentary calendar, but it does not have the same aura as budget day.

Private Members' Bills

While most legislation is controlled by the cabinet, the other members of the House of Commons are permitted to introduce bills without the support of the government. These are known as private members' bills.

It is not easy to get a private member's bill on to the legislative agenda; they are chosen by lottery at the start of each parliamentary session. Private members can introduce legislation

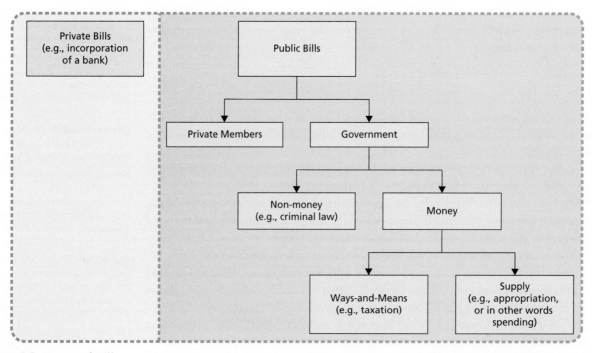

Figure 6.2 Types of Bills

on any subject except money bills. Most private bills die during the second reading and they are rarely passed into law—in fact, it is a newsworthy event when a private bill passes into law. A private member's bill will likely only succeed if it is supported by the government. Without the support of the government, a private bill does not usually stand a chance of being passed, although it is possible when there is a minority government.

While most private members' bills fail, they serve important purposes. First, they often raise issues that the government is ignoring. In 2001, long before same-sex marriage became legal in Canada, Svend Robinson, the NDP Member of Parliament for Burnaby and the first openly gay politician in Parliament, introduced a private member's bill to legalize same-sex marriage. It failed, but it brought considerable awareness to an issue that most politicians wanted to ignore. Private bills also give Members of Parliament the chance to demonstrate to their constituents that they are taking their riding's issues seriously. So even though they tend to fail, private members' bills serve an important function in our parliamentary system.

The Opposition Parties and Question Period: Holding the Government Accountable

If the legislative process is controlled by the government, what is the role of the other parties in Parliament? The Westminster parliamentary system is premised on institutional conflict. The adversarial character of the House of Commons shapes most of its operating rules and procedures. The Speaker—the referee—sits in the middle of the House of Commons with the government to the right and the opposition parties to the left, directly opposite the government (see Figure 6.3). Legend has it that the distance between the two sides is the equivalent of two sword lengths (a precaution to ensure that no one gets hurt if the debate gets too vigorous) but the story appears to be fictional (see Box 6.1). The party with the second-largest number of seats is known as the **Official Opposition** or, more grandiosely, *Her Majesty's Loyal Opposition*. The leader of the Official Opposition sits directly across from the prime minister in the middle of the first row of seats in the House of Commons. The Official Opposition has an obligation to the Crown to oppose the government and to insist that the principles of responsible government are respected.

Many Canadians are fed up with the constant conflict in Parliament. They just want the parties to cooperate, but the Westminster parliamentary system of government is not designed for cooperation. It is premised on conflict. The Westminster parliamentary system works much like the legal system. In a court of law, the prosecutor and the defence lawyer make starkly different arguments about the evidence. The cut and thrust of the legal system is an effort to get to the truth. By the same token, the adversarial nature of the Canadian system of parliamentary government is intended to reach the best possible policy outcome. The job of the opposition parties—most especially the Official Opposition—is to argue that government policy is wrong, or at least that it can be accomplished more effectively with another strategy. You have probably had the experience of doing something silly and saying later, "why didn't anybody say something before I made a fool of myself?" In the Canadian parliamentary system, the government can't say, "nobody told us it was a bad idea" because it has been warned by the opposition, and it must accept responsibility for how things turn out.

Our negative perceptions of the legislative process are reinforced by the fact that we do not see the normal law-making process on the nightly news. What we normally see on television are excerpts from what is known as **question period (QP)**. Question period is held daily whenever Parliament is in session, and it is 45 minutes of highly ritualized politics.

Official Opposition The second-largest party in Parliament that sits opposite the government in the House of Commons and holds it to account. Also known as *Her Majesty's Loyal Opposition*.

question period (QP) A 45-minute session held each day the House of Commons is in session in which Members of Parliament can ask the government questions and hold it to account.

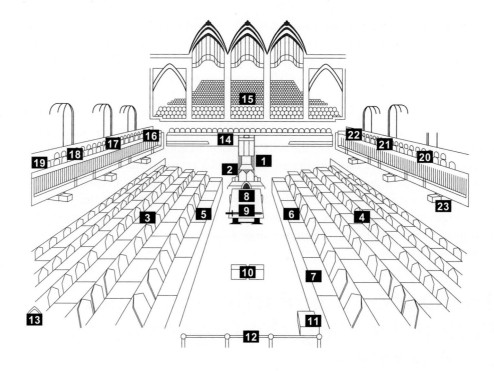

1. Speaker
2. Pages
3. Government Members
4. Opposition Members
5. Prime Minister
6. Leader of the Official Opposition
7. Leader of the Second Largest Party in Opposition
8. Clerk and Table Officers
9. Mace
10. Hansard Reporters
11. Sergeant-at-Arms
12. The Bar
13. Interpreters
14. Press Gallery
15. Public Gallery
16. Official Gallery
17. Leader of the Opposition's Gallery
18. Members' Gallery
19. Members' Gallery
20. Members' Gallery
21. Speaker's Gallery
22. Senate Gallery
23. T.V. Cameras

Figure 6.3 House of Commons Floor Plan

Library of Parliament / Bibliotheque du Canada. Reprinted by permission.

Legend has it that the distance across the floor of the House of Commons is equal to two sword lengths, but the story appears to be a myth. The distance between the government and opposition benches in the Canadian House of Commons is just under 4 metres, which is about four times the length of a standard sword. In the much smaller British House of Commons, the distance between the two sides is about 2.5 metres, or just over two sword lengths. However, there was never a time when British Members of Parliament were permitted to bring swords into the House of Commons. The origins of the sword story thus remain a mystery. Perhaps it originated as a joke after a particularly vigorous debate in the British House.

During QP the opposition parties grill the government on any subject of their choosing. More often than not, the opposition parties zero in on mistakes and perceived scandals, but the objective is to hold the government responsible for its actions. The ministers generally try to avoid the question altogether and taunt the opposition in return. And then members often come out of QP and go straight to the media to continue the fight. About 95 percent of the television coverage of the House of Commons is question period, but it is important to remember that this is not the real legislative work of the House of Commons. We rarely see a real legislative debate, and we almost never see a committee hearing, except when a committee is investigating an alleged scandal or in other exceptional circumstances, such as the drafting of new anti-terrorism laws after 9/11.

In ordinary circumstances, the media simply ignores the legislative process of Parliament. Why does the media ignore the real legislative work of Parliament? Because the media is a business, and it makes money by selling advertising. If a show does not produce an audience, then there is no one to see the commercials. And if people are not watching the commercials, the advertisers will pull them and the media will be out of business. The legislative process of Parliament does not produce an audience for television—making law is of interest only to lawyers. The media would much rather cover question period, which is the political equivalent of professional wrestling. However, while QP might be entertaining, the media coverage of it does not do us any favours as citizens, showing politicians at their very worst rather than doing the real work of making law. It is little wonder that Canadians have become jaded by the political process. However, the media alone is not to blame. Our politicians must accept some responsibility for the low opinion many Canadians have of Parliament. Since the introduction of cameras into the House of Commons in the 1970s, the members have increasingly played to the camera, and their behaviour has become increasingly theatrical to get onto the nightly news. Unfortunately, many of our politicians live by the motto, "no publicity is bad publicity."

Officers of Parliament: Outsourcing Accountability

It is not easy for the opposition parties to hold the government accountable. The elected Members of Parliament often lack the time, resources, and especially the information necessary to hold the government accountable. Fortunately for citizens, there are a few **officers of Parliament**, sometimes known as **agents of Parliament**, who act as independent watchdogs and report to Parliament on the activities of the government (see Box 6.2). These officers monitor whether or not public money has been well spent; that elections are conducted fairly and according to the rule of law; that the government is promoting bilingualism, protecting people's privacy, and ensuring access to information; and that Members of Parliament act ethically and are free from conflicts of interest. The auditor general in particular has emerged as the top government watchdog. From 2001 to 2011, the position was held by the highly capable and combative Sheila Fraser. The opposition parties and the

officers or agents of Parliament Independent watchdogs, such as the auditor general, who report to Parliament on the activities of the government.

media awaited her reports with anticipation, hoping that they would expose government wrongdoing. Perhaps most famously, a report by the auditor general in 2004 exposed serious corruption in government advertising contracts that were awarded in Quebec over the previous decade. This was the so-called sponsorship scandal.[4] The auditor general's report contributed to the collapse of the Liberal government led by Paul Martin, even though the scandal occurred under Jean Chrétien's watch. In 2013, the Conservatives earned the wrath of the new auditor general, Michael Ferguson, when he revealed that the government could not account for $3.1 billion spent on national security between 2001 and 2009.[5]

The 2006 general election was all about accountability, and the first piece of legislation introduced by the new Conservative government was the Federal Accountability Act, which sought to strengthen the powers of the officers of Parliament. Bill C-2 also established a new position: the parliamentary budget officer (PBO). Technically, the PBO is an officer of the Library of Parliament, but he or she acts very much like an officer of Parliament. Unlike the auditor general, who reports on how government money *was* spent, the PBO provides independent analysis of how the government *will* raise revenue and spend money. Kevin Page became Canada's first PBO in March 2008, and he quickly became a thorn in the side of government. He raised serious questions about the veracity of the government's budget figures: its projection of revenues, its estimation of the size of the deficit, how quickly the deficit can be eliminated, and the cost of certain items such as the new F-35 fighter jets. The opposition parties and the media relished these reports. Kevin Page retired in 2013 and was replaced by Jean-Denis Fréchette.

Party Discipline

Political parties have two main roles in the Canadian political system. First, parties operate as electoral machines designed to get their candidates elected to Parliament, as we discussed in Chapters 3 and 4. Now we can examine the second major role fulfilled by parties: they provide some structure to the operation of Parliament. Without political parties, the House of Commons would be a free-for-all and not much would ever get done. But when the 308 members elected to Parliament belong to a few relatively coherent teams, the legislative work of Parliament is expedited. Many Canadians may not believe it, but political parties make Parliament *more* efficient. In Canada's system of responsible government, it is essential for the government to maintain the confidence of the House of Commons, and parties play a central role in the question of confidence. The government uses its party to maintain the confidence of the House, while the Official Opposition bands together to oppose the government. Recall that the single-member plurality electoral system tends to manufacture a majority of seats for one party. When the government has a majority in the House, the prime minister can be certain that the government will always have the confidence of Parliament because the members of his or her own party will always support the government.

How does the prime minister know that the members of his or her party will always support the government? The prime minister wields considerable power over the members of his or her party to make sure that they support the government. In this role, the prime minister acts as the coach of a team, and he or she does a number of things to make sure the team follows his or her directives and stays united—this is known as **party discipline**. The prime minister is a busy person, so he or she appoints a member of the team to be responsible for party discipline. This person is known as the **whip**. The whip ensures that there will always be a sufficient number of people from the governing party in the House of Commons for the government to maintain the confidence of the House. It is also the whip's business to know how each member of the party *intends* to vote. If a member is not inclined to support the party, the whip will pressure the member to conform. If that fails, the whip will attempt to ensure that the member does not appear for the vote and embarrass the prime minister. Incidentally, all the parties have a whip, not just the governing party, but the government whip has a more important job. It is an especially difficult job when the government only has a minority.

Why do party members almost always support the leader, most especially when the leader is also the prime minister? Because party leaders exercise tremendous power over their members in Parliament. First, most party members owe their political existence to their leader. As we discussed previously, candidates are usually chosen by local party associations, but the leader of the party must approve of all the candidates before Elections Canada will put their names on the ballot under the party banner. If the leader refuses to sign a candidate's nomination papers, the candidate cannot run under the party banner. Since most voters choose to vote for a party, if a candidate has no party affiliation he or she will almost certainly not get elected. Since most Members of Parliament want to run again, they cannot afford to upset the leader because he or she might not re-sign their nomination papers at the time of the next election.

Second, the success of the party in the election is crucially dependent on the performance of the leader. If the party wins the election, the leader gets the credit. And, truthfully, most party members are elected on the coattails of the prime minister. The members consequently owe a large debt of gratitude to the prime minister.

Third, most members on the backbenches want to move up to the front benches and be a minister in the government. The backbenchers consequently need to stay in the prime minister's good books. But it is not just cabinet positions at stake. There are many other positions in Parliament, and they are all appointed by the prime minister or party leader. There are parliamentary secretaries, the people who assist the cabinet ministers, and these positions are good stepping stones to the cabinet. Members of standing committees in the House of Commons are also chosen by the party leaders. So any member who wants to do one of the interesting jobs in Parliament needs to stay on the good side of his or her leader. If a member does not support the party on a crucial vote, he or she will be relieved of his or her position as minister, cabinet secretary, or committee member. Ultimately, the party leader can toss a member out of the party and force them to sit as an independent in the back corner of the House of Commons. This is the kiss of death for most Members of Parliament, as some unfortunate souls have discovered.

Occasionally, the party leaders put away the whip and allow their members to decide how to vote. These are known as **free votes**, but they are not common. Free votes are generally reserved for private members' bills and matters of personal conscience, such as abortion and the death penalty. Some people have argued that there should be more free votes in the House of Commons, and to his credit Paul Martin did attempt to relax the reins of party discipline when he was prime minister, but his reforms did not catch on. Party discipline is deeply embedded in the Canadian political system, and leaders are reluctant to give it up.

Party discipline is much stronger in Canada than in Great Britain. There are at least two reasons why British Members of Parliament are more able to challenge the power of their leaders. First, as discussed in Chapter 3, party leaders in Canada are in a much stronger position than their British counterparts because they are elected directly by all of the members of the party, whereas in Britain the parliamentary caucuses play a much larger role in leadership selection. In the British Conservative Party, the caucus can actually call for a vote of no confidence

party discipline The expectation that members of a party in Parliament will follow the directions of their leader.

whip An individual appointed by a leader to be responsible for party discipline.

free votes Votes in Parliament in which members of a party may vote according to their conscience rather than having to follow the direction of the leader or whip.

in the leader and unseat him or her, as happened to Margaret Thatcher in 1990.[6] And she was a sitting prime minister when she was turfed by the members of her own party in Parliament! Second, many British Members of Parliament have very safe seats and the leaders have little power to dislodge them as party candidates. Third, because the House of Commons in Great Britain is much larger than the House of Commons in Canada, many members of the British House know that they will never be selected for cabinet, so they do not have to be as loyal to the leader. The British case shows that parliamentary government does not collapse with weaker party discipline. Indeed, it is probably desirable to give more voice to backbench Members of Parliament, but it seems unlikely that the Canadian Parliament will ever resemble the British Parliament because the political realities in each country are so different.

The virtue of party discipline is easier to grasp if we compare Canada to the United States. Barack Obama may be the president of the United States, but it is not easy for him to deliver on his election promises because he has very little power over his party in Congress. And no one in Congress can promise anything either, because the parties are not cohesive. A senator or representative may promise during an election campaign to *fight* for this or that, but he or she cannot necessarily deliver once in Washington because party discipline is weak to nonexistent in Congress. In contrast to Canadian Members of Parliament, US senators and representatives engage in horse trading on the floor of Congress: I will vote for your bill if you vote for my bill. In order to get support for their bills, members may even have to vote for things they campaigned against!

With strong party discipline, the legislative process in Canada is much more cohesive and efficient than in the United States. In Canada, the leader makes promises during the election, and if his or her party wins the election, especially a majority, he or she has the power to realize the promises made during the election campaign so long as he or she can maintain party discipline. Most Members of Parliament are elected on the basis of party affiliation and party platform. Voters thus have a checklist by which to measure the performance of the government. If the government fails to implement its promises, voters can hold it accountable. And it is the job of the leader to make sure that the party follows its platform. If we didn't have party discipline, we would not know who to hold accountable.

In sum, party discipline extends to virtually all aspects of business in the House of Commons, including the work of the legislative committees. Party discipline provides coherence to the legislative process, and it generally makes Parliament more efficient. The practice of party discipline, however, has generated considerable criticism in the public. There is a perception that our Members of Parliament are trained seals, barking when they are told to do so by their leaders. This perception was reinforced by former Prime Minister Pierre Trudeau when he famously quipped that backbench Members of Parliament are "nobodies" when they are more than 50 yards away from Parliament. Arguably, however, Trudeau got things backward. Members of Parliament are typically important figures in their local communities; they become nobodies when they take their seats on the backbenches of Parliament and vote as they are told rather than voting with their conscience or in the best interest of their constituency.

The Senate

So far in this chapter, we have focused mostly on the House of Commons—the democratically elected chamber of Parliament. By convention, most members of the government are members of the House of Commons; it is the hub of power in the Canadian political system. However, because of its roots in the British tradition, Canada has a bicameral, or two-chamber, Parliament. Since Canada does not have an aristocracy, the second chamber of the Canadian Parliament is called a Senate rather than a House of Lords, as in Britain. The idea of a senate dates from ancient Rome, and the term is derived from the Latin word *senatus*, meaning "council of elders." The Canadian Senate is an unelected chamber. It was designed to review legislation passed by the House of Commons. In short, it was to be a chamber of "sober second thought." It is also known as the "red chamber" because of its regal red carpeting, in contrast to the green carpeting in the House of Commons.

The Senate was one of the most contentious issues facing the Fathers of Confederation when they drafted the British North America Act, just as it was for the founding fathers in the United States. In the United States, each state has two senators no matter how big or small the state. California, with 37 million people (more than the entire population of Canada), has two senators, as does Vermont, which has just over half a million people. The lower branch of Congress, the House of Representatives, has representation by population. This was the American constitutional compromise: *representation by population* in the House of Representatives to please the big states and *representation by state* in the Senate to satisfy the small ones. In the United States, incidentally, senators were initially appointed by the state governments, but the constitution was amended in 1913 to allow for the direct election of senators by the people.

In Canada, the small Maritime provinces wanted an equal number of senators per province, but Ontario and Quebec did not agree. Ontario was especially adamant that the Canadian parliamentary system had to be based on representation by population, and it would not accept equal representation in the Senate for each province. So a different compromise was reached in Canada. The House of Commons has representation by population, but the Senate was designed to give equal representation to the different *regions* of Canada. At the time of Confederation, there were three regions: Ontario, Quebec, and the Maritimes (Nova Scotia, New Brunswick, and, after 1873, Prince Edward Island). Each region was afforded 24 senators. In the Maritimes, Nova Scotia and New Brunswick have 10 senators each, while Prince Edward Island has four. Subsequently, the West—Manitoba, Saskatchewan, Alberta, and British Columbia—was styled as a Senate region, and each province is represented by six senators for a total of 24 for that region as well. When Newfoundland and Labrador entered Confederation in 1949, it was granted six seats in the Senate; each territory also has one senator. Thus, there are 105 seats in the Senate in total.[7]

Qualifications for the Senate: Are Women Qualified Persons?

The Canadian Senate is not a democratic chamber. Senators are appointed by the governor general on the advice of the prime minister. Initially, senators were appointed for life, but the constitution was amended in 1965 and senators are now required to retire at age 75. Section 23 of the Constitution Act 1867 stipulates the qualifications for the Senate: among other things, senators must be at least 30 years of age, have real wealth exceeding $4000, and be a resident of the province for which "he" is appointed. With these qualifications in mind,

> The Governor General shall from Time to Time, in the Queen's Name, by Instrument under the Great Seal of Canada, summon qualified Persons to the Senate; and, subject to the Provisions of this Act, every Person so summoned shall become and be a Member of the Senate and a Senator (Section 24, Constitution Act 1867).

The qualifications for senators in the constitution are written in exclusively masculine terms. When women were given the right to vote and to be elected to the House of Commons in 1918, one might have assumed that the constitution would have been interpreted in inclusive or gender-neutral terms. But even after Agnes Macphail became the first woman elected to the House of Commons in 1921, the Government of Canada continued to maintain that only men were "qualified persons" for the purposes of sitting in the Senate. A group of five women—"the famous five" or "the valiant five"—challenged this interpretation of the constitution, but amazingly the Supreme Court of Canada concluded in 1928 that women were not, in fact, "qualified persons" for the purposes of sitting in the Senate. The case was appealed to the Judicial Committee of the Privy Council in London, England, which overturned the decision of the Supreme Court in 1929. This has forever been remembered as the *Persons Case*. In 1930, Cairine Wilson became Canada's first female senator.

The monument to the Famous Five women who fought the "persons case" was erected on Parliament Hill in 2000. The "Famous Five" were Emily Murphy (the first female judge in the British Empire), Irene Marryat Parlby (first female cabinet minister in Alberta); Nellie Mooney McClung (leading suffragist and member of the Alberta legislature), Louise Crummy McKinney (the first woman elected to a legislature in the British Empire), and Henrietta Muir Edwards (founding member of the Victorian Order of Nurses).
© Jim Varley Photography/Alamy

patronage The awarding of government perks and benefits by the prime minister to his or her supporters.

Getting a Seat in the Senate: It's Who You Know, Not What You Know

In 2010, senators received an annual salary of $132 300. So how do you get to be summoned to the Senate? Senate appointments have traditionally been governed by the politics of **patronage**—the awarding of benefits by the prime minister to political supporters. Obviously, for a big reward like a Senate seat, one must be a big supporter of the governing party. Occasionally a prime minister will break the model and appoint a distinguished Canadian with no partisan affiliation. Jean Chrétien appointed Frank "The Big-M" Mahovlich, a former star in the National Hockey League and a member of the Hockey Hall of Fame, and Roméo Dallaire, the former Lieutenant General of the Canadian Armed Forces who heroically attempted to prevent the mass genocide in Rwanda in 1994 when he was the commander of the United Nations Assistance Mission in that country. Stephen Harper has appointed a few celebrities as well, including Jacques Demers, the illiterate coach who guided the Montreal Canadiens to the Stanley Cup in 1993, and Nancy Greene Raine, the gold medal skier from the 1968 Olympic Games and Canada's female athlete of the twentieth century. But generally, Liberal prime ministers appoint Liberal Party loyalists, and Conservative prime ministers appoint Conservative Party loyalists. There are no New Democrats or Bloquistes in the Senate. (The NDP, which wants to abolish the Senate, won't allow its members to sit in the Senate as New Democrats, and no Bloquiste has ever been offered a Senate seat.)

With this highly partisan process, the Senate tends to become dominated by the governing party after a period of time. After a period of Liberal government the Senate is mostly Liberal, and after a time of Conservative government the Senate typically falls into Conservative hands. Thus, when a new Conservative government comes to power in the House of Commons, the Senate is usually dominated by Liberals, and when the Liberals come back into government some years later the Senate typically has a Conservative majority. When the House of Commons and the Senate are dominated by different parties, it is not uncommon for a certain amount of tension to exist between the two chambers. However, the Senate is not a confidence chamber; the government in the House of Commons does not require the support of the Senate, and the Senate typically will not defeat government legislation. But, understandably, Liberals in the Senate will generally not agree with Conservative government legislation and vice versa.

Powers of the Senate: Constitutionally Equal but Politically Subservient

As discussed the Senate is an integral part of the parliamentary process. All legislation must be approved by both chambers of Parliament before it can proceed to the governor general for royal assent. Although the Senate is an appointed chamber, its powers are virtually identical to the House of Commons. It can introduce legislation on any subject, except money bills, which must originate in the House of Commons, according to Section 53 of the Constitution Act 1867. While the Senate cannot introduce money bills, it can theoretically veto money bills passed by the lower chamber, including the budget. But, by convention, the Senate does not defeat government legislation passed in the House of Commons. The Senate has been known to proceed slowly and delay the passage of legislation when the majority of senators are from a different party than the majority of members in the House of Commons, much to the frustration of the government in the lower chamber. The Senate has also been known to veto private members' bills or bills that have passed through the House of Commons on a "free vote." However, even in these select circumstances, the Senate vetos legislation sparingly. In its entire history it has only rejected a handful of bills outright. The Senate simply does not have the legitimacy to thwart the legislation of the democratically elected government in the House of Commons.

Role of the Senate: The Chamber of Sober Second Thought

If the Senate lacks legitimacy and the ability to use its powers to their full extent, what does it do? Some people would argue that it does not do much of anything, but that would be unfair. Because senators are not elected and do not have constituents to look after, they have more time to consider legislation. Members of the House of Commons represent, on average, about 100 000 voters, and they have to attend to many requests for assistance from their constituents. The elected Members of Parliament spend a considerable amount of time in their ridings away from the nation's capital; members of the House of Commons are authorized to make 64 return trips between Ottawa and their constituencies each year. The travel may not be overly onerous for members from Montreal or Toronto, but it is extremely gruelling for the members from Whitehorse, Labrador, and other far-flung communities. And those members of the House of Commons who are also in the cabinet have large departments to manage on top of attending to their constituencies. By contrast, all senators have to do is review legislation.

Many senators are actually more experienced parliamentarians than the elected members of the House of Commons, and they frequently catch mistakes in the legislation passed by the House of Commons or they may otherwise suggest amendments that improve the legislation. In short, senators are the nation's legislative proofreaders. Some Senate committees have also done excellent research on subjects like health care and national security. In sum, the Senate was designed to be the chamber of sober second thought, and it fulfills this function reasonably well.

Senate Reform: The Bane of Canadian Politics

The Canadian Senate represents a compromise, and like many compromises it doesn't really satisfy anyone. Rather than a "thankless task," being a senator has cynically been described by some as a "taskless thanks." There have consequently been persistent demands to reform the Senate. Some people want Canada to adopt the American model: an elected Senate with an equal number of senators per province. These people, typically conservative populists in Western Canada, argue that an elected Senate would be more effective. Western conservatives have thus styled their proposal as the **Triple-E Senate**: elected, equal, and effective. Others, including the New Democratic Party and the Bloc Québécois, believe that the best way to reform the Senate is to abolish it entirely. Yet, after more than 140 years since Confederation, the Senate continues to work pretty much like it has always worked—or not worked, depending on your perspective.

Why has it been impossible to change the Senate? Because changing the rules of the game is fraught with challenges. The basic rules of the Senate are laid out in the Constitution Act 1867. Consequently, many of the proposals to reform the Senate require changing the constitution. For example, the regional pattern of representation in the Senate cannot be changed without first amending the relevant sections of the constitution. The Senate cannot even be abolished without constitutional change—it would require repealing all sections of the constitution related to the Senate. The politics of constitutional change in Canada is notoriously problematic, as we will discuss in subsequent chapters. Prior to 1982, Canada did not even have the ability to change its own constitution; the constitution could only be amended by the British Parliament, which is the Parliament that passed the British North America Act into law back in 1867. Since 1982, Canada has possessed the *legal* power to amend the constitution, but not necessarily the *political* ability to make significant constitutional changes. With respect to Senate reform, a major constitutional initiative called the Charlottetown Accord failed in 1992, as will be discussed in Chapter 11.

The Harper Plan for Senate Reform: One Step Forward and Two Steps Backward?

As a conservative from Western Canada, Stephen Harper has long supported the idea of a Triple-E Senate. Since it has been impossible to reform the Senate through constitutional change, the Harper government attempted to reform the Senate without changing the constitution (or with supposedly just minor constitutional amendments). But without a general constitutional amendment, Harper could only get two Es at best. The regional distribution of seats is entrenched in the constitution, and the government cannot unilaterally change this provision to give each province an equal number of seats. That would require the consent of at least seven provinces representing 50 percent of the population under the amending formulas in the Constitution Act 1982. And why would Ontario and Quebec consent to having their representation in the Senate drop from almost 25 percent of the seats to about 10 percent? Unless they are offered something in exchange, Ontario and Quebec are not likely to consent to an equal Senate, and with more than 50 percent of the country's population they are in a position to thwart a constitutional amendment in favour of an equal Senate.

The Harper government conceded that it could not unilaterally establish an equal Senate, but it introduced legislation that could have led to an elected Senate, at least indirectly. Bill C-7, An Act Respecting the Selection of Senators and Amending the Constitution Act, 1867 in Respect of Senate Term Limits, represented the fourth attempt by the Harper government to reform the Senate.[8] Under Bill C-7, the provinces and territories could have established an electoral process to allow candidates to campaign for a seat in the Senate of Canada, although the winners would not have automatically taken a seat in the Senate. Senate appointments would still have been made by the governor general on the recommendation of the prime minister, but one assumes that the prime minister would have recommended all candidates who had been duly elected by the people in a Senate election. But the constitution stipulates that Senate appointments last until age 75. Since no one wanted Senators to be elected for "life," Bill C-7 also proposed to limit Senate appointments to a single nine-year term. Thus, as the name of the bill stated, it would have been necessary to amend the constitution to establish a nine-year term limit for Senate appointments.

But can Parliament unilaterally change the constitution? Yes it can, in some cases. Under the Constitution Act 1982, "Parliament may exclusively make laws amending the Constitution of Canada in relation to the executive government of Canada or the Senate or the House of Commons."[9] Prime Minister Harper interpreted this section to mean that Parliament could unilaterally amend the constitution to introduce term limits for Senate appointments. But others argued that this change required the support of at least seven provinces representing at least 50 percent of the population. There was thus some constitutional uncertainty about the Harper plan for Senate reform. In February 2013, the government finally decided to refer the matter to the Supreme Court for a definitive ruling, and in April 2014 the Supreme Court ruled the Harper plan for Senate reform did indeed require the consent of at least seven provinces with 50 percent of the population. With the ruling, Bill C-7 was shelved, thereby bringing another attempt to reform the Senate to an unsuccessful conclusion.

When Stephen Harper came to power in 2006, he vowed not to appoint anyone to the Senate until the second chamber had been reformed. Over time, however, the Senate became seriously depleted, and there were no longer enough senators to staff the various committees of the Senate. Prime Minister Harper evidently grew frustrated with the slow pace of Senate reform, and thus decided to make a concerted effort to break the Liberal majority in the Senate with a rash of appointments. In December 2008, Prime Minister Harper announced 18 Senate appoints in one fell swoop, and he followed that up in August 2009 with nine more. With a total of 27 Senate appointments, Stephen Harper may have set a record for the most number of appointments within a 12-month span.[10] He also took the unusual step of securing a commitment from each appointee to support Conservative legislation on Senate reform as a condition of appointment. Most of the appointees were Conservative Party loyalists, but there were also a few sport celebrities and a couple of well-known journalists, including Pamela Wallin and Mike Duffy (both of whom were asked to leave the Conservative caucus in May 2013 after a controversy erupted over their expense claims). From December 2008 to May 2013, Stephen Harper appointed a total of 59 senators. By the end of 2010, the Conservative Party formed the majority in the Senate, and it used its power to veto a private members' bill passed by the House of Commons: Bill C-311, The Climate Change Accountability Act. The bill was killed at second reading, and it was probably the first time in history that the Senate had defeated a bill before it even went to committee for study.

The prime minister argues that he has to play by the rules to change the rules, but his actions with respect to the Senate have raised eyebrows, and some media commentators have been very critical. Writing in the conservative *National Post*, Don Martin fumed, "[i]nstead of reforming it, Mr. Harper has reconfirmed the Senate as the pigpen for party has-beens, cast-offs, bagmen and political pals with a couple of honourable mentions thrown in to make the Conservative rebalancing project go down a little easier."[11]

Do We Really Want an Elected Senate? In sum, the Senate has extensive legislative powers, but it does not exercise its full powers because it possesses very little political legitimacy. Many have argued that the Senate would be a considerably more effective legislative chamber if it possessed more democratic legitimacy. But, on the other hand, if the Senate gained legitimacy, it might be emboldened to use its full array of powers, which could put it on a collision course with the government in the House of Commons. If the Senate's legitimacy is to be enhanced, it would be prudent to reduce the power of the Senate to avoid the possibility of legislative gridlock. For example, the Senate's power to veto legislation, especially money bills, could be removed.[12] It would also be a good idea to establish a better mechanism for resolving disputes between the two chambers, as was the case with the plan for Senate reform in the Charlottetown Accord. In short, piecemeal reform of the Senate may do more harm than good.

It is also important to note that elections alone do not guarantee popular acceptance of an institution.[13] Indeed, elected politicians across the country are generally held in very low esteem by the public, whereas some nonelected figures, such as the governor general, are viewed very positively. Moreover, if the Senate becomes an elected chamber, senators will likely become just as busy as members of the House of Commons and therefore have less time to consider legislation and do research. While term limits are good in theory, they can be problematic in practice. If senators can only sit for nine years, it might be difficult to recruit good candidates to run for office. Who wants to take nine years out from the middle of their career? After nine years, they won't be qualified to go back to their old jobs, but they can't run for re-election either.

Just because democracy is one of our most cherished principles, it doesn't necessarily follow that "more democracy" is better. When one chamber of Parliament possesses democratic legitimacy and the other does not, there is no question as to which chamber should prevail in the event of an impasse. If both chambers are elected, both will likely claim to be the true champions of the people. And over time, senators may become the stars of the political system. They will be fewer in number than their counterparts in the House of Commons, and they will be able to claim to possess a mandate from the province that elected them rather than an individual riding. The establishment of an elected Senate could well result in a complete transformation of the Canadian political system. In short, the law of unintended consequences always looms large when major institutional reform is enacted.

Should the Senate Be Abolished?

If an elected Senate is problematic, would it be better to simply abolish the Senate? Maybe—or maybe not. As argued above, the Senate has been known to do good work. In 2002, for example, the Standing Senate Committee on Social Affairs, Science and Technology, chaired by Senator Michael Kirby, produced an excellent six-volume report on the future of health care in Canada. The committee interviewed more than 400 witnesses and held 76 meetings. The work of the committee was comparable to a royal commission. The Senate has also done very good work in the area of national security. The Senate should be encouraged and empowered to undertake forward-looking research. But this aside, it is also helpful to have a second set of eyes to examine legislation, which is the future laws of the land.

The abolition of the Senate, furthermore, is not so easy, especially after the Supreme Court ruled in April 2014 that abolition would require the consent of all the provinces (as well as the consent of the Senate itself). On the other hand, there is some precedent for the abolition of the Senate. Some of the provinces—Quebec, Manitoba, and those in the Maritimes—used to have bicameral legislatures, but gradually they were abolished and these provinces function perfectly well with a single democratic chamber. But an amendment to abolish the Senate is not likely to obtain the unanimous consent of the provinces. Most of the smaller provinces, especially in Atlantic Canada, appreciate that the regional representation of the Senate provides some counterweight to the democratic majority in Ontario and Quebec. So, while the NDP and the Bloc Québécois support the abolition of the Senate, it does not appear to be in the cards anytime soon.

Senate Reform: Is There a Third Option?

The Senate clearly has a legitimacy problem; the role and authority of an unelected legislature is ambiguous. "Yet to argue that elections are the sole source of political legitimacy is too broad a claim. . . . Elections are only one component of liberal democracy: constitutionalism, the rule of law and an institutional framework both to implement and to monitor representative government are equally important."[14] So the question is, can unelected political institutions have legitimacy? Clearly, the answer is yes. The governor general is an appointed figure and is well respected by most Canadians, as are other appointees, such as the chief of the defence staff and the commissioner of the RCMP. The judiciary in Canada is also appointed, and the courts do not have a legitimacy problem; on the contrary, the Supreme Court of Canada is highly respected. So what's the difference? Why do these institutions have legitimacy in the eyes of Canadians and not the Senate?

It all has to do with the appointment process. Senate appointments are overtly partisan, at least in most cases, whereas the appointments for the Supreme Court, the governor general, the military, and the RCMP are typically nonpartisan. When prime ministers search for a new governor general or a new justice for the Supreme Court, they typically look for people with merit. But when they look for new senators, they usually look for party loyalists.

Can Senate appointments ever be nonpartisan? Yes, they can. Liberal Prime Minister Paul Martin, for example, made an inspired choice when he appointed Hugh Segal—a Conservative Party loyalist—to the Senate in 2005. Senator Segal has devoted his life to public service. He was the associate secretary to the cabinet for the Progressive Conservative government of Ontario in the 1970s and 1980s, and in the 1990s he was chief of staff to Prime Minister Mulroney. Prior to his appointment to the Senate he was the president of the nonpartisan Institute for Research on Public Policy. Segal retired from the Senate in 2014 to become the master of Massey College at the University of Toronto. The Senate could do with more Segals, but this will only happen if the appointment process can somehow be de-politicized; however, the prospects for an improved and de-politicized Senate appointment process are not very good. Prime ministers are not in the habit of voluntarily relinquishing power. Experience in other countries, such as Great Britain and Australia, suggests that second chambers are only reformed after a political crisis of some sort. In other words, the Senate may have to do something truly objectionable before there is sufficient political will to reform the institution.

The Question of Representation

Now that we have some idea of how Parliament works, I want to turn to the question of representation. We saw in Chapter 4 that women, visible minorities, and Aboriginal people are all considerably underrepresented in the House of Commons. Visible minorities are equally underrepresented in the Senate, but women and Aboriginal peoples have much better representation in the second chamber (see Table 6.1). This data supports the suggestion that these groups face systemic discrimination in the single-member plurality electoral system. In keeping with the Roman notion of a Senate as a "council of elders," the average age in the Senate is considerably higher than it is in the House of Commons, which in turn has a higher average age than Canadian society. In sum, the Parliament of Canada is not really representative of Canadian society, at least in some important respects. The 2011 election saw a few more women and visible minorities elected to the House of Commons, and the average age has dipped a bit as a result of so many NDP "placeholder candidates" actually getting elected.

Does it matter that the diversity of Canadian society is not represented in Parliament? If the law of the land is to be truly representative of the people, arguably the people need to be represented in all their diversity when the law is being made. It is generally accepted that

Table 6.1 Representation of Various Groups in Parliament in Relation to their Proportion of the Canadian Population, 2010

	House of Commons (308 Members)	Senate (105 Members)	Canada
Women	22%	35%	50%
Aboriginal Peoples	2%	6%	4%
Visible Minorities	8%	8%	16%
Age	53 years	65 years	39 years

people with different life experiences will have different perceptions of the public good. Political theorists refer to this phenomenon as standpoint theory:

> The theory posits that the social groups to which one belongs affect one's perceptions of the world. Persons in different groups develop specific skills, norms of communicating, and values consistent with the needs of their lived group experiences. Therefore, the predominant culture in which all groups exist is not experienced in the same way by all persons or groups. The views of those who belong to groups with more social power (such as Whites, men, heterosexuals, or middle and upper classes) are validated more than those in marginalized groups. Those in marginalized groups must learn to be bicultural, or to "pass" in the dominant culture to survive, even though that perspective is not their own.[15]

We have to be careful not to overgeneralize standpoint theory. People from the same group do not all think the same way. Conservative women from Alberta, socialist women from Nova Scotia, and sovereignist women from Quebec obviously see the world in very different ways, but they may also have common experiences as women. They have probably all encountered sexism at some point in their life, discrimination in the workplace, and possibly unwanted sexual attention. Similarly, most visible minorities and Aboriginal peoples have probably experienced racism. By the same token, it is difficult for those in the dominant groups—those who have not personally experienced sexism, racism, or poverty—to really understand the challenges faced by disadvantaged groups on a daily basis. For the law to be fair to everyone, these perspectives need to be heard in Parliament.

A brief examination of Canada's laws against rape and sexual assault dramatically reveals the impact of a more diverse Parliament. These laws were completely overhauled in 1983, coinciding with a large influx of women into Parliament. Prior to 1983, there was a law against *rape*, defined as the "sexual penetration of a women's vagina with a man's penis without the woman's consent, outside of marriage."[16] Thus, by definition, women could not be raped by their husbands. The laws of evidence also allowed for a woman's sexual history to be called into question, thus requiring the woman to defend her "moral conduct" in court. The classic defence for rape used to be, "she slept with all these other guys, so I thought I could sleep with her too." And it was never easy to prove that penetration occurred, and without penetration it wasn't rape. The law also required witness corroboration of a woman's accusations against a man, which was problematic for a crime that was almost always committed in private, and women were required to report attacks almost immediately after they happened. With Bill C-127, introduced by the Trudeau government in 1983, the whole concept of rape was replaced with the notion of *sexual assault*, which did not require proof of penetration. The laws of evidence were also rewritten. A victim's sexual history was no longer admissible in court, witness corroboration was no longer required, victims no longer had to report crimes immediately, and spousal immunity was terminated. "Overall, the law was amended to emphasize the assaultive rather than the sexual nature of rape and to counter the sexist myth that rape, as an act of sex, cannot occur without at least some victim compliance."[17] It is hard to believe that the new law, which is considerably more sensitive to women, was unrelated to the influx of women into Parliament in the 1970s, although some still question if the law on sexual assault rather than rape was a positive development.[18]

It is not difficult to imagine that men and women might have different perspectives on a whole variety of subjects. Age matters, too. It is not surprising that a Parliament full of people in their fifties and sixties is preoccupied with health care and pensions. If there were more young people in Parliament greater attention might be paid to the environment and the cost of university.

The situation for Aboriginal peoples is even more acute. Since the late 1990s the Government of Canada has been trying to rewrite the Indian Act, which governs virtually all aspects of Aboriginal life in Canada, but there are very few Aboriginal voices in Parliament. Legislative committees of Parliament can always consult with Aboriginal people, but that reinforces a social divide between "us" and "them." The inclusion of more Aboriginal people *in* Parliament would make a world of difference, because policy is not simply debated on the floor of the House of Commons or in legislative committees. Policy is also discussed between members over coffee or dinner in the parliamentary restaurant or at the gym. Indeed, it is in these informal settings that people can really get to know each other and understand each other's concerns.

The question of representation is crucial in the making of the law. Put different people in Parliament and we will get different laws. But how do we get different people elected? Some of the parties have done more than others to address the issue of diversity, but there is only so much the parties can do within the confines of the current system. The problem is *systemic* (it is a problem of the system) and consequently not much will change without a *systemic* solution. A different, more proportional electoral system might improve the situation in the House of Commons, as argued in Chapter 4.

However, it is far from clear that a move to an elected Senate would improve diversity in the second chamber. There is much less diversity in the US Senate than there is in the lower House of Representatives. Why? Because when candidates must campaign statewide for a seat in Congress rather than in a single constituency within the state, they need to be more established figures with considerably more resources and deep connections. Without elections, the Senate in Canada is more diverse than the House of Commons. Unless special precautions are taken in Canada, one could anticipate that the current diversity in the Senate would be diluted with a move toward the popular election of senators. The politics of systemic reform are notoriously difficult, but Canada is becoming more diverse over time. For the law to be fair to all Canadians, it is thus essential for Parliament to become fully representative of this diversity.

SUMMARY

Parliament has two critically important functions in the Canadian political system: it makes the law of the land and it is supposed to hold the government accountable for its actions. When the government has a majority, Parliament is a very efficient legislative body but its ability to hold government accountable is compromised. When the government is in a minority situation, Parliament is very good at holding the government accountable but the legislative process often grinds to a halt or at least proceeds very slowly. There have been many proposals over the years to reform Parliament, but most of these proposals have fallen by the wayside. The Senate, in particular, has been remarkably immune to reform. And the prospects for Senate reform appear dim, now that the Supreme Court has ruled that major reform of the Senate requires the support of at least seven provinces with half the population and the abolition of the Senate requires unanimous provincial consent.

The operation of Parliament is structured to a considerable extent by political parties. In sum, *party discipline* extends to virtually all aspects of business in the House of Commons, including the work of the legislative committees. Party discipline provides coherence to the legislative process, and it generally makes Parliament more efficient. Without parties, Parliament would be a free-for-all and not much legislation would ever get passed. But party discipline is now arguably too rigid. Many political scientists believe that the elected Members of Parliament are not sufficiently free to voice the concerns of their constituents. The high level of party discipline in Canada's Parliament is tied directly to the increased power of the prime minister.

The other major challenge facing the Parliament of Canada is the question of representation. Canada is a highly diverse society, and becoming more diverse every year, but this diversity is not well represented in Parliament. Women, visible minorities, and Aboriginal peoples are consistently underrepresented, especially in the elected House of Commons, but things are not much better in the Senate. A move toward an elected Senate might actually erode the diversity already present in the second chamber. The lack of diversity in the House of Commons is primarily a function of the single-member plurality electoral system. There is reason to believe that a system of proportional representation would provide better representation in Parliament for disadvantaged groups. It would also help bridge some of the regional cleavages in Canadian politics by distributing seats to parties in accordance with their share of the vote in all areas of the country. If the law is to be truly representative of the people, Parliament needs to reflect the diversity present in Canadian society, and electoral reform would appear to be the most effective means to improve the representation of disadvantaged groups in Canada's Parliament.

Questions to Think About

1. Do you think the law-making process in Canada is too cumbersome?
2. Do you think party leaders have too much power over their members? Should members be given more freedom to represent the views of their constituents?
3. Do you think the Senate should be elected or abolished?
4. Do you think that Parliament adequately reflects the social diversity of Canada?
5. Do you think that electoral reform would improve the way Parliament works?

Learning Outcomes

1. Describe how a new session of Parliament unfolds.
2. Describe how bills are passed in Parliament.
3. Explain how Parliament holds the government accountable.
4. Evaluate the role of party discipline in Parliament.
5. Evaluate the role of the Senate and the various proposals for reforming the second chamber of Parliament.
6. Critically discuss the issue of representation in Parliament.

Additional Readings

C.E.S. Franks, *The Parliament of Canada* (Toronto, ON: University of Toronto Press, 1987).

David C. Docherty, *Mr. Smith Goes to Ottawa: Life in the House of Commons* (Vancouver, BC: UBC Press, 1997).

David C. Docherty, *Legislatures* (Vancouver, BC: UBC Press, 2005).

Robert J. Sharpe and Patricia I. McMahon, *The Persons Case: The Origins and Legacy of the Fight for Legal Personhood* (Toronto, ON: University of Toronto Press, 2007).

David E. Smith, *The Canadian Senate in Bicameral Perspective* (Toronto, ON: University of Toronto Press, 2003).

David E. Smith, *The People's House of Commons: Theories of Democracy in Contention* (Toronto, ON: University of Toronto Press, 2007).

Manon Tremblay and Linda Trimble, eds., *Women and Electoral Politics in Canada* (Toronto, ON: Oxford University Press, 2003).

Notes

1. The rules of the House of Commons were reformed in the 1990s to allow a bill to move directly from first reading to the committee stage of the legislative process. This procedure was presumably introduced to expedite the passage of legislation, but the practice has not caught on. It does seem a little premature for a committee to consider a bill in great detail before the House of Commons has declared its support for the bill in principle.

2. Parliament of Canada, *Committees Practical Guide* (Ottawa, ON: House of Commons, October 2008), 4.

3. Ibid., 1.

4. You can learn more about the sponsorship scandal by reading the report of the Commission of Inquiry into the Sponsorship Program and Advertising Activities chaired by Justice John Gomery. The report was entitled, *Who Is Responsible?* (2005) and can be accessed at www.cbc.ca/news2/background/groupaction/gomeryreport_phaseone.html.

5. *Report of the Auditor General of Canada*, Spring 2013, Chapter 8.

6. In the British Conservative Party, if more than two candidates seek the leadership of the party the parliamentary caucus will have a series of ballots to reduce the number to two before the vote is put to the members of the party at large. In the Labour Party, leadership candidates must first be nominated with the support of at least 12.5 percent of the caucus. And the final vote is weighted equally between the parliamentary caucus, the individual members of the party, and affiliated organizations (such as labour unions).

7. Under Section 26 of the Constitution Act 1867, the prime minister can increase representation in the Senate by an additional four or eight members to be distributed equally between the main four Senate divisions. However, this provision has only been used once: Prime Minister Brian Mulroney increased the number of senators by eight after the 1988 election to overcome Liberal opposition in the Senate to the goods and services tax (GST). These additional senators were not replaced when they retired, so the Senate gradually returned to its standard configuration over time.

8. Bills S-8, The Senatorial Selection Act, and C-10, An Act to Amend the Constitution Act, 1867 (Senate Term Limits), died when Parliament dissolved in March 2011 for the election. Previous bills died in September 2007 when Parliament was prorogued and again in September 2008 for the general election. Bill C-7, introduced in June 2011, combines what had previously been two bills: one to allow for the election of senators and the other to place a limit on Senate terms.

9. Constitution Act 1982, Section 44. Available at http://laws-lois.justice.gc.ca/eng/Const/page-16.html#h-53.

10. David Akin, "Harper Names Nine to Senate," *Leader Post* (Regina), August 28, 2009, B9.

11. Don Martin, "Harper to Senate," *National Post*, December 23, 2008, A4.

12. Campbell Sharman, "Political Legitimacy for an Appointed Senate," *IRPP Choices* 14:11 (September 2008), 20.

13. Ibid., 2.

14. Ibid., 2.

15. Victoria Pruin DeFrancisco and Catherine Helen Palczewski, *Communicating Gender Diversity: A Critical Approach* (Thousand Oaks, CA: Sage Publications, 2007), 51.

16. Bernard Schissel, "Law Reform and Social Change: A Time-Series Analysis of Sexual Assault in Canada," *Journal of Criminal Justice* 24:2 (1996), 137.

17. Ibid., 123.

18. See Kirk Makin, "How Canada's Sexual Assault Laws Violate Rape Victims," *The Globe and Mail*, October 5, 2013.

Chapter 7
Federalism

Key Points

■ Federalism is the second governing principle entrenched in the Constitution Act 1867.

■ Federalism establishes two orders of government in a country. In Canada, there is the federal government in Ottawa and 10 provincial governments. Each order has its own set of responsibilities outlined in Sections 91 and 92 of the constitution, respectively. Separate arrangements exist for the three territories.

■ There are four major challenges associated with federalism: conflicts over jurisdiction, gaps between jurisdictional authority and fiscal capacity, establishing institutions for intergovernmental relations, and maintaining a balance between unity and diversity.

■ Canada has managed the technical aspects of federalism rather well, but it has struggled with unity. Quebec presents the greatest challenge to Canadian unity, as we will discuss in the next chapter.

federalism A system of government with two constitutionally entrenched orders of government. One government is responsible for matters pertaining to the entire country, and the other order of government provides a range of services at a more local level. In Canada, the two orders of government are the 10 provinces and the federal government in Ottawa. (The territories are separate entities under the authority of the federal government).

sovereignty literally means "supreme authority." In Canada, sovereignty is divided between the federal and provincial governments.

intergovernmental relations The interaction between the different governments in a federation, especially between the federal government and the provinces, but also between provinces and municipalities, Aboriginal peoples and governments of all levels, and even relationships across the border with state governments.

While the provinces of Canada, Nova Scotia, and New Brunswick expressed their desire in the British North America Act to be governed by a constitution "similar in principle to that of the United Kingdom," the Canadian political system is a curious mixture of British and American constitutional principles. Canada's system of parliamentary government was drawn almost wholly from Britain, with minor modifications to make the system more compatible with Canadian circumstances, as we have discussed in previous chapters. But **federalism**, the second governing principle of the Canadian constitution, is an American invention.

Federalism is a system of shared rule. It establishes two orders of government in a country, each with its own set of responsibilities as outlined in the constitution. The Government of Canada, which has been the focus of our study so far, does not make all the laws or provide all the services and functions of government in Canada. It makes some of the laws and provides a select number of services, but other laws and services are the responsibility of the provincial governments. In technical terms, the **sovereignty** of Canada is divided and shared between the federal and provincial governments. While the Government of Canada is the largest government in the federation, over time some of the services provided by the provinces, such as health care and education, have become very important to Canadians. In theory, the two orders of government are supposed to operate independently, but in reality there is considerable interaction between them—this is the mysterious world of **intergovernmental relations**.

If you are concerned about health care, you need to know something about federalism and intergovernmental relations. If you are worried about the environment, you need to know something about federalism and intergovernmental relations. Really, if you want to know pretty much anything about Canadian politics, you need to know something about federalism and intergovernmental relations because so many important policy decisions that affect the lives of Canadians happen in meetings between the federal and provincial (and sometimes territorial) governments and not in the Parliament or legislature constitutionally responsible for the issue.

The Challenges of Federalism

When you hear the prime minister and the premiers bickering over money and other issues, it is easy to conclude that federalism is a frustrating and inefficient form of government. There are four challenges associated with the federal form of government. First, there are frequently conflicts between the two orders of government over the division of powers in the constitution. Second, there is often a gap between jurisdictional responsibility and fiscal capacity (it is difficult to ensure that each government has sufficient funds to finance its responsibilities). Third, many federations have struggled to establish satisfactory institutions for intergovernmental relations. Fourth, federalism is a system of government that seeks to ensure the unity of the country while allowing regional diversity to flourish, but this a difficult balance to establish and maintain.

Canada has struggled with all of these problems over the course of its history. Jurisdictional conflicts were common in the first 75 years after Confederation, and they still crop up from time to time. Since the end of World War II, the question of money has been at the centre of intergovernmental relations in Canada. And the very institutions of intergovernmental relations in Canada have been created in a purely ad hoc fashion with no constitutional or statutory authority. These technical dimensions of federalism will be the focus of this chapter.

Lurking behind these technical dimensions is the question of unity. We can think about unity as the overarching story of Canadian federalism. Quebec obviously provides the greatest challenge to Canadian unity, but it is not the only one. Western alienation runs deep, and this may account for the rise of anti-Ottawa populist parties in the West. But all of the provinces have participated in "fed-bashing" at one time or another to advance their particular causes. The social, cultural, and political dimensions of federalism will be the focus of the next chapter, most especially the challenge presented by Quebec. But first we must get a handle on the technical aspects of federalism because, as we will see in the next chapter, Quebec also has serious concerns about the formal and informal rules of Canadian federalism.

While federalism is a challenging form of government, we must not conclude that Canada is a difficult country to govern because we have a federal political system. On the contrary, we adopted federalism precisely because Canada is a difficult country to govern. Canada is regionally and culturally divided, and it is the job of federalism to hold the country together while allowing the distinct regions of the country to flourish in their own ways. It is not an easy task, and conflict is inevitable. However, it is important to remember that federalism is not the cause of regional conflict in Canada: it is a solution to regional conflict. Indeed, Canada would not exist without federalism. To understand this proposition, we must examine Canadian history.

Why Federalism?

In the debates over the constitution in 1865, Sir John A. Macdonald made it clear that he wanted a unitary system of government:

> I have again and again stated in the House that, if practicable, I thought a Legislative Union would be preferable. I have always contended that if we could have one parliament, legislating for the whole of these people, it would be the best, the cheapest, the most vigorous, and the strongest system of government we could adopt. . . . [However],

we found that such a system was impracticable. In the first place, it would not meet the assent of the people of Lower Canada, because they felt that in their peculiar position—being in a minority, with a different language, nationality and religion from the majority—their institutions and their laws might be assailed, and their ancestral associations . . . attacked and prejudiced. . . . [Furthermore] there was as great a disinclination on the part of the various Maritime Provinces to lose their individuality as separate political organizations, as we observed in the case of Lower Canada.[1]

Since Quebec and the Maritime provinces would not agree to enter Confederation without a measure of self-government, Macdonald was forced to accept the federal form of government. This was not easy for him; the United States was just concluding five years of Civil War, and Macdonald was convinced that federalism (at least the American form of it) was a contributing factor. The Americans, he argued, "commenced, in fact, at the wrong end. They declared by their constitution that each state was a sovereignty in itself, and that all the powers incident to a sovereignty belonged to each state, except those powers which, by the Constitution, were conferred upon the General government."[2] In Canada, he declared, "we have given the General Legislature . . . all the powers which are incident to sovereignty . . . we have thus avoided that great source of weakness which has been the cause of the disruption in the United States."[3]

While Macdonald was happy with the proposed constitution, others were less pleased. Antoine-Aimé Dorion, the fiery opposition *Rouges* leader from Lower Canada, denounced the constitution: "The whole scheme is absurd from beginning to end," he declared.[4] "I find that the powers assigned to the General Government enable it to legislate on all subjects whatsoever . . . because all the sovereignty is vested in the general government."[5] In sum, he concluded, "we shall be at its mercy."[6] While 37 delegates from Lower Canada voted in favour of the new constitution, the other 25 delegates voted against it. In Upper Canada, by contrast, the constitution was supported 54 to 8. The level of opposition to the constitution in Quebec was not an auspicious beginning for the new federation. And Quebec's acceptance of the constitution was conditional: they accepted on the condition that Quebec would have complete control over the matters assigned to provinces under the constitution.

Quebec was not the only province unhappy with Macdonald's constitution. Nova Scotia came very close to rejecting it, and one year after Confederation the government of Nova Scotia appealed to Queen Victoria for permission to separate from Canada; the appeal was denied. Prince Edward Island and Newfoundland refused to accept the constitution, and they remained as colonies of Great Britain. Prince Edward Island relented and joined Confederation in 1873, but Newfoundland held out until 1949, and then joined only after a bitter and divisive referendum. Manitoba entered the federation in 1870 but was denied ownership of its natural resources, unlike the other provinces. British Columbia was admitted the following year on terms similar to the original provinces. Saskatchewan and Alberta were created in 1905, but they were also denied ownership of the natural resources in their territories. Although the three Prairie provinces obtained ownership of their natural resources by an amendment of the constitution in 1930, many historians believe this initial injustice is one of the principal causes of Western alienation. The regional divisions in Canada clearly have deep historical roots.

The Division of Powers in the Constitution and the Formal Rules of Canadian Federalism

The responsibilities of the federal government are listed in Section 91 of the Constitution Act 1867, and the responsibilities of the provincial governments are enumerated principally in Section 92 (but also Sections 92A and 93). The federal government is responsible, among other things, for the military, trade and commerce, criminal law, and marriage and divorce, while the provinces are responsible for schools, hospitals, and the management of natural resources, among other things (see Appendix A). In some federations it is common for some matters to be subject to **concurrent jurisdiction**—shared between the two orders of government—but in Canada agriculture and immigration were the only shared powers in the original constitution, as per Section 95.[7]

In practice, however, things are not divided as neatly as Sections 91 and 92 would suggest. Both governments, for example, have broad powers of taxation. The federal government is permitted to raise revenue by "any Mode or System of Taxation," while the provinces are constitutionally restricted to "direct" taxation and various fees for licences, including the sale of wood and timber on public lands. In practice though, the federal government and the provinces rely on the same sort of taxes to a considerable extent: personal income tax, corporate tax, and sales taxes, as well as various "sin" taxes on items such as gasoline, alcohol, and tobacco. The federal government is broadly responsible for "trade and commerce," but the provinces have considerable powers to regulate commercial activity, such as incorporating companies and making laws related to property and civil rights. The federal government has the power to make laws with respect to marriage and divorce, but the provinces are responsible for the solemnization of marriage, or deciding who gets to perform marriage ceremonies. Finally, the federal government is responsible for making criminal law, but the provinces are responsible for the administration of justice. In short, there is considerable overlap between these two orders of government.

Why didn't the Fathers of Confederation devise a more rational **division of powers** so that each order of government would be truly independent? The various negotiators of the constitution all wanted the important powers of government, so they compromised and agreed to share them. More specifically, it was often necessary to accommodate Quebec's unique system of law and distinct cultural traditions. Sir John A. Macdonald was adamant that there should be only one criminal code for all of Canada (unlike in the United States, which has a separate code for each state), but Quebec was equally adamant that the provinces should be responsible for the administration of justice so as to preserve the province's **civil law** tradition. Similarly, Macdonald wanted one definition of marriage for all of Canada, but Quebec was just as concerned with ensuring that marriage in the province would be exclusively through the Catholic Church. In theory, it would have been possible to make one set of arrangements for Quebec and another set of arrangements for all of the other provinces. This is known as **asymmetrical federalism**, but generally the other provinces were anxious for all the provinces to be treated not just equally but identically, except in a few instances that need not concern us at this point. Macdonald was thus forced to give the provinces more powers than he would have liked.

Macdonald, however, was a savvy negotiator, and he did not give things away without getting something in return; he secured provisions that gave the federal government considerable power to control the provinces. Macdonald's claim that all sovereignty in Canada was vested in the federal government was surely an exaggeration, but there were a few features in the BNA Act that enabled the federal government to exercise considerably more control over the provinces than the US government could over the state governments. This led some constitutional experts to suggest that Canada was at best **quasi-federal** or only partially federal.

The Quasi-Federal Features of the BNA Act

There are a handful of measures in the constitution that may be viewed as quasi-federal, but three stand out. First, the federal government is authorized, by Section 58 of the Constitution Act 1867, to appoint the Crown's representative, the lieutenant governor, in each province. As far as the federal government was concerned, the lieutenant governors were supposed to keep an eye on the provincial governments and report back to Ottawa. The lieutenant

concurrent jurisdiction Refers to an area of responsibility that is shared between two or more orders of government. In Canada, agriculture and immigration are shared between the federal government and the provinces.

division of powers Refers to the separate and often overlapping areas of jurisdiction between the provinces and the federal government. The powers of each order of government are listed in Sections 91 and 92 of the Constitution Act 1867.

civil law A legal system that is descended from Roman law and is still used by the non-English-speaking parts of Europe and much of Africa. Rather than relying on judge-made precedent, civil law instead uses a comprehensive civil code that is written by a legislature. In Canada, Quebec still uses civil law, and thus maintains its own civil code—the *Code civil du Québec*.

asymmetrical federalism A type of federalism in which the provinces exercise different powers.

quasi-federal Refers to a country that is only partially federal. It might have certain qualities that federations have, but lack some others. In quasi-federal systems the central government is usually able to control and override the provinces or states.

reservation The constitutional power given to lieutenant governors to refer legislation passed by provincial legislatures to the federal cabinet for approval.

disallowance The constitutional power given to the federal government to override or negate any legislation passed by the provincial legislatures.

governors are still appointed by the federal government, but they are no longer expected to spy on the provinces.

Second, the powers of **reservation** and **disallowance** in Section 90 of the Constitution Act 1867 gave the federal government the constitutional authority to veto, or reject, any provincial law that it considered objectionable. In the first instance, if the lieutenant governor of a province was unsure of the propriety of a bill passed by the provincial legislature, he could *reserve* his decision to proclaim the law into effect and submit it to the federal government for consideration. But even if he signed a law into effect, the federal government could still *disallow* it. With these powers, the federal government possessed the ability to control the legislative autonomy of the provinces.

In fairness, under Sections 55 and 56 the governor general of Canada could also *reserve* laws passed by the Parliament of Canada for consideration by the British government, and the British government was similarly empowered to *disallow* Canadian laws it found objectionable, but the British government had little interest in Canadian affairs and only exercised these powers a couple of times. The Government of Canada, on the other hand, employed its powers of reservation and disallowance against the provinces with some regularity: between 1867 and 1942, the Government of Canada disallowed 112 provincial laws. Since 1942, however, the federal government has not disallowed any provincial bills, and the last bill to be reserved was in 1963. Even though the powers of reservation and disallowance remain in the constitution, many constitutional lawyers believe that these are now **dead letters**, meaning that they no longer have any force or effect.

dead letters A legal concept that refers to any constitutional provision that has fallen into disuse and consequently may no longer have force or effect.

As much as the provinces may have objected to the powers of reservation and disallowance and the role played by the lieutenant governors, these matters were unarguably constitutional. The third quasi-federal feature of the constitution, however, was considerably more contentious. As far as Sir John A. Macdonald was concerned, the federal government was granted a broad swath of power in the preamble to Section 91 of the constitution:

> It shall be lawful for the Queen, by and with the Advice and Consent of the Senate and House of Commons, to make Laws for the Peace, Order, and good Government of Canada, in relation to all Matters not coming within the Classes of Subjects by this Act assigned exclusively to the Legislatures of the Provinces.

POGG clause A clause that is located in the preamble to Section 91 of the Constitution Act 1867. It stipulates that the federal Parliament shall have the ability to make laws for the "peace, order, and good government of Canada."

This is called the **POGG clause**. It was this feature of the constitution that prompted Antoine-Aimé Dorion to declare that the constitution enabled the federal government to legislate on any matter "whatsoever," because presumably all laws are intended for peace, order, and good government.

The construction of Sections 91 and 92 is, however, highly ambiguous. The 29 enumerated powers of the federal government listed in Section 91 clearly trump the 16 provincial powers listed in Section 92. But does the federal government's general power to make laws for peace, order, and good government trump the power of the provinces to make laws in their exclusive areas of jurisdiction? Macdonald believed that POGG trumped the provinces, but not surprisingly the provinces held the opposite view. Ultimately it was up to the courts to determine which theory of the division of powers should prevail. The fight ensued first in the Canadian courts, but the final arbiter of the Canadian constitution was a British court—the **Judicial Committee of the Privy Council** (JCPC). The BNA Act was, after all, a British law.

Judicial Committee of the Privy Council The court of final appeal for all colonies in the British Empire; it remains the final court for some independent countries such as Jamaica and other islands in the Caribbean.

Conflicts over Jurisdiction and the Politics of Judicial Interpretation of the Constitution

Many of the cases that came before the JCPC were argued by the federal and provincial governments, often directly but sometimes indirectly as interveners in particular cases. And in many respects these various cases represented a second and more protracted

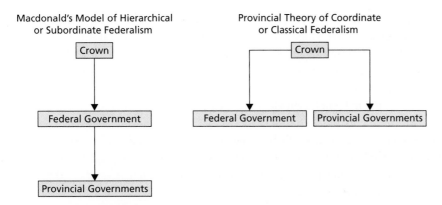

Figure 7.1 Two Conceptions of Federalism

debate between the two orders of government over Confederation and the true meaning of the British North America Act. At root, the debate revolved around two distinct conceptions of federalism (see Figure 7.1). Sir John A. Macdonald argued that the federal government derived its authority directly from the Crown and the provincial governments were *subordinate* to the federal government. In short, Macdonald had a very hierarchical conception of federalism, with the federal government at the top and the provinces below. The provinces, not surprisingly, did not enjoy being under the command and control of the federal government. They thus pressed for a very different conception of federalism: they argued that the federal and provincial governments both derived their authority directly from the Crown and consequently they were *coordinate*, or co-equal, authorities within their spheres of jurisdiction outlined by the constitution. This is the theory of **classical federalism**.

From the 1870s to 1900, the JCPC heard more than 30 constitutional cases from Canada and at least two dozen law lords were involved in these cases. Most of the judges remain faceless and anonymous figures in Canadian history; however, one figure does stand out above all others in this early period: Lord William Watson, a reclusive Scotsman. In 1892, Watson emphatically sided with the coordinate model of federalism advocated by the provincial governments. The object of the BNA Act, he wrote

> was neither to weld the provinces into one, nor to subordinate provincial governments to a central authority, but to create a federal government in which they should all be represented, entrusted with the exclusive administration of affairs in which they had a common interest, each province retaining its independence and autonomy.[8]

Four years later, Watson endorsed the provincial view that POGG could not be used to trump the power of the provinces. In short, Watson transformed the POGG clause from a general power to a purely **residual power**. The federal government could only use its POGG power if it related to a subject that was *not* related to the class of powers reserved exclusively for the provinces. And, in many cases, the JCPC concluded that the subject under dispute belonged to the vague and ill-defined provincial power to make laws with respect to **property and civil rights**. In other words, many cases went something like this: The federal government said "we are going to do X under the POGG power," and the JCPC said "no, you can't do that because X is a matter of property and civil rights and consequently is a provincial responsibility."

In the early 1920s, Lord Haldane ruled that the POGG clause could only be used in the case of a dire emergency. A decade later, in the midst of the Great Depression, the JCPC ruled that the federal government's unemployment insurance scheme was unconstitutional and therefore invalid because it encroached upon the power of the provincial governments to make laws with respect to property and civil rights. Many Canadian legal commentators

classical federalism The theory that each order of the government in the federation is legally equal and should each operate independently of the others.

residual power Refers to all matters not specifically enumerated in the constitution. Each federation has to determine which government will have responsibility for matters not explicitly allocated by the constitution.

property and civil rights The very broad swath of responsibility allocated to the provincial governments in Section 92, subsection 13, of the Constitution Act 1867. This is why people have to register their homes and cars with the provincial government. Civil rights also includes things like insurance and contract law.

were apoplectic. One prominent professor of constitutional law fumed, "it may be contended that an emergency power which the world economic crisis does not justify using is no power at all."[9] The legal establishment in English-speaking Canada was virtually unanimous in believing that the JCPC had destroyed Macdonald's constitution and emasculated the Government of Canada.

The response in French Canada was more positive; deliberately or otherwise, the JCPC sided with the theory of federalism espoused by Quebec. Indeed, before he became prime minister, Pierre Trudeau wrote "It has long been a custom in English Canada to denounce the Privy Council for its provincial bias; but it should perhaps be considered that if the law lords had not leaned in that direction, Quebec separatism might not be a threat today: it might be an accomplished fact."[10]

The Abolition of Appeals to the JCPC

The Parliament of Canada introduced legislation after World War II to abolish appeals to the JCPC. However, the legislation was challenged by some of the provincial governments, which had been generally quite satisfied with the JCPC's interpretation of the constitution. The Supreme Court of Canada was thus asked to determine if the federal government was empowered to abolish cases to the JCPC. The Supreme Court ruled in favour of the federal government, but the case was immediately appealed to the JCPC itself. Ultimately, the JCPC ruled that appeals to them from Canada could be abolished. The legislation to abolish appeals to the JCPC was finally passed by Parliament in 1949.

Over time, the JCPC transformed the political game in Canada. They rejected Macdonald's hierarchical model of federalism in favour of the provincial model of coordinate or classical federalism, thus establishing the provinces as co-equal authorities. Having done so, the federal powers of reservation and disallowance became untenable and fell into disuse. It is hard to imagine that these powers will ever be used again. The story of the JCPC is a dramatic example of the power of the courts to reshape the rules of the political game.

For better or worse, the JCPC largely resolved the tensions and contradictions in the division of powers in the Constitution Act 1867. Since the abolition of appeals to the JCPC, there have been relatively few jurisdictional disputes between the federal government and the provinces, although they crop up occasionally. The case of the long-gun registry is perhaps the most notable recent example.[11] In 1995, the Parliament of Canada passed the Firearms Act, which required owners of long guns to register their rifles and shotguns and to obtain a licence to operate them. Some of the provinces objected to the new law, saying the provinces were responsible for making laws with respect to property and civil rights (Section 92.13) and issuing licences for the purposes of raising revenue (Section 92.9). Guns, of course, are personal property, so on the surface the provincial argument seemed to have some merit. The federal government, on the other hand, argued that it was making criminal law, which it is empowered to do by Section 91.27 of the Constitution Act 1867. In other words, the federal government was saying that it would henceforth be a crime to be in possession of an unregistered long gun or to be in possession of a long gun without a licence.

pith and substance A legal term that refers to the essence of a law.

The Supreme Court thus had to determine the essence, or the **pith and substance**, of this law: Was it principally a property registration scheme for the purposes of raising revenue? Or was it legitimately a matter of criminal law? As guns are inherently dangerous, the Supreme Court ruled that the federal government was within its constitutional rights to enact criminal law to regulate the possession of long guns in the name of public safety. This jurisdictional dispute was a relatively uncommon occurrence in the modern world of Canadian federalism. Over the last 75 years, the two orders of government have argued mostly about money.

The Fiscal Arrangements of Confederation

Canada's system of fiscal federalism is complex and arcane. It is understood well by perhaps a few dozen people in government and an even smaller number in the academy and the think tanks.[12]

Fiscal federalism entails the constitutional division of revenue and the expenditure responsibilities of the federal and provincial governments, programs to ensure a fiscal balance between the two orders of governments, and measures to provide a degree of tax harmonization in the federation. While this may sound mind-boggling, behind this technical vocabulary are "issues that do matter to Canadians—issues like fairness and opportunity for individuals, the survival of the distinct peoples and nations that make up Canada, and indeed the very future of Canada as a country."[13] To really understand Canadian politics, it is thus essential to come to terms with the complex fiscal arrangements that make the federation work.

fiscal federalism Refers to both the distribution of taxation powers in the federation as well as the transfer of money between the federal and provincial governments.

The Division of Revenue in the Constitution Act 1867

Along with many other issues, the Fathers of Confederation struggled to devise workable fiscal arrangements for the two orders of government. At the time, the colonies of British North America had spent large sums of money developing railway lines and ports to transport people and goods into and out of the country and they were deeply in debt. Because the new Government of Canada would assume the debts of the colonies that joined the federation, and because they would also require large sums of money to build the railway to the Pacific coast, it was anticipated that the Government of Canada was going to require large sources of revenue. By contrast, the responsibilities assigned to the provinces were relatively inexpensive, and the provinces would therefore not need as much revenue. Section 91.1 of the Constitution Act 1867 accordingly provides the federal government with the sweeping power to raise "Money by any Mode or System of Taxation." The provinces are limited to the raising of "direct taxation," the sale of timber on public lands belonging to the province, and the sale of "shop, saloon, tavern, auctioneer and other licences."

Economists argue endlessly about what constitutes "direct" and "indirect" taxation. In short, direct taxation is applied to an individual or business and it cannot be passed off to anyone else. Income tax is the most obvious direct taxation—it is deducted directly from your paycheque and given to the government. Indirect taxes can be passed off to someone else. If you import goods for a living, you will pass the duties on to your customers by adding them to the sale price of your goods. At the time of Confederation, import and export duties were the primary sources of revenue, while direct taxation was negligible. Now, in an era of global free trade, import and export duties amount to very little while income and corporate taxes are the largest sources of revenue for government, along with sales taxes on goods and services. In many respects, the distinction between "direct" and "indirect" taxation has lost its meaning in Canadian fiscal federalism. The two orders of government now ostensibly share the most lucrative **tax fields**—income and corporate tax and sales taxes. However, the two orders of government do not share these fields equally. For historic and economic reasons, the federal government collects more income taxes than the provincial governments.

tax fields The categories of taxation where governments raise revenue. There are many different categories, but the most important ones today are personal income tax, corporate tax, and sales taxes.

Federal Subsidies for the Provinces

Even before Confederation became a reality, it was obvious that the provincial governments would not be able to function with the tax sources provided to them in the constitution, notwithstanding their relatively modest constitutional responsibilities. It was thus necessary for the federal government to provide the provinces with financial subsidies. While these subsidies helped they were generally insufficient, so over time the provinces introduced a variety of direct taxes: British Columbia and Prince Edward Island established property taxes in the 1870s, Quebec introduced a corporation tax in 1882, and Ontario imposed succession duties (death taxes) in 1892. And by World War I, most of the provinces had introduced a small income tax.

conditional grants Grants that are provided by the federal government to the provinces on the condition that the monies be used for particular purposes, such as financing health care.

While the provinces did find ways to raise revenue, they were still financially strapped and important social problems were often left unattended. So, starting in the 1910s, the federal government introduced a variety of targeted subsidies or **conditional grants**. The federal government would transfer money to the provinces on the *condition* that it be used in ways specified by the federal government. The first conditional grant in Canada was created in 1913 for agricultural instruction. In 1918, after World War I, conditional grants were provided for employment services, and the following year grants were provided for highway construction, technical education, and the prevention of venereal disease. In general, these grants were not very successful and most lapsed within a few years, but the federal government turned once again to conditional grants in the 1930s to help the provinces provide relief for the millions of people who lost their jobs as a result of the Great Depression.

By 1937, the federal government provided the provinces with $21 million in regular subsidies and $82 million in conditional grants, mostly for unemployment relief. While the sums are minuscule by modern standards, it is noteworthy that the ad hoc conditional grants were about four times greater than the subsidies established in the 1860s. Quite obviously, the fiscal arrangements of Confederation were now hopelessly inadequate and in desperate need of reconsideration. The Government of Canada thus established a Royal Commission on Dominion–Provincial Relations to examine the fiscal arrangements of the federation. The commission is also known as the *Rowell–Sirois Commission* after its two commissioners.

The commission's plan for a new system of fiscal federalism was derailed by the outbreak of World War II, but it is interesting to note that the commission was very critical of conditional grants. It concluded that "for permanent purposes, the conditional grant . . . is an inherently unsatisfactory device."[14] In short, the commission argued that strong conditions were inconsistent with the federal principle, while weak conditions were inconsistent with the principles of responsible government. However, the commission's advice was ignored. Most of the social programs initiated by the Government of Canada in conjunction with the provinces after the war were financed with conditional grants.

The Origins and Development of Tax Sharing

With the outbreak of World War II the Government of Canada desperately needed revenue, so in 1941 it compelled the provinces to accept a tax agreement in which the provinces would surrender their income, corporate, and succession taxes in exchange for an annual payment equivalent to what these taxes raised in 1940. In a sense, the provinces "rented" their tax fields to the federal government. This is known as the **wartime tax agreement**, or the first *tax rental agreement*, and it was scheduled to last for the duration of the war plus one year. The provinces expected the tax system to return to a federal structure after the war, but the story of fiscal federalism in the post-war era was considerably more complicated.

wartime tax agreement The first tax rental agreement that saw the provinces "rent" their tax fields to the federal government for set revenue over the life of the agreement.

When the war ended, the Government of Canada indicated that it would be necessary to renew the wartime tax agreement to finance the transition to a peace-time economy. The provinces agreed, but as usual they held out for better terms. Most notably, Quebec decided to collect its own income and corporate taxes, while the other provinces agreed to have their major taxes collected by Ottawa.[15] In 1957 the federal government and the provinces moved to a formal system of tax sharing. These early tax agreements provided three benefits. First, it was cheaper to have a single tax collection system. Second, it allowed for a high degree of **tax harmonization**, which is a huge issue in federal political systems; if the two

tax harmonization A measure required in federal political systems to ensure that the combined tax rates of the federal and provincial governments are not too onerous for taxpayers or that the two taxation systems are not working at cross purposes.

orders of government do not coordinate their tax policies, individuals and businesses can quickly become overburdened by taxation. Third, the wartime tax agreement established the dominance of the federal government in the major tax fields. This tax domination enabled the federal government to initiate and maintain Canada-wide social programs.

Over the second half of the twentieth century and into the twenty-first century, two long-term trends in Canadian fiscal federalism emerged: a steady reduction in tax harmonization and the decline of federal dominance in the major tax fields. The post-war system of tax sharing worked well for the provinces so long as federal taxes were increasing: as federal taxes increased so did provincial taxes. But in the late 1990s, the federal government began cutting taxes and this caused a corresponding decline in provincial revenues. So some of the provinces began to delink their income tax from the federal tax and imposed their taxes directly on income, although Ottawa continued to collect income tax on behalf of the provinces (except Quebec). The delinking of federal–provincial taxes has led to a reduction in tax harmonization.

The dominance of the federal government in the major tax fields was also seriously reduced in the latter half of the twentieth century. In 1950, the federal share of the tax pie was 69 percent, the provinces 18.6 percent, and local governments 12.4 percent. By 2000, the federal share had declined to 46.3 percent, the provinces were up to 38.6 percent, and local governments were down to 8.6 percent—the remaining 6.5 percent went to the Canada and Quebec Pension Plans (which did not exist in 1950). So, in 1950, the federal share of the tax pie was more than double the combined share of the provincial and local governments. In 2000, the federal share was exactly equal to the combined share of the provincial and local governments. The federal government is still the single largest player in Canada's system of fiscal federalism, but its capacity to initiate and sustain national social programs has been eroded.

Fiscal Federalism and the Post-War Social Union

Canada's system of fiscal federalism in the post-war era has been inextricably tied to the development of Canada's social union—the social programs enjoyed by Canadians across the country, including universal health care. Initially, the programs were started with considerable financial support from the federal government. However, since World War II, the provinces have seen their fiscal independence increase, as discussed above, but they still require **transfer payments** from the federal government to finance health care and other social programs that fall under their areas of responsibility. The politics of transfer payments have been highly contentious. In particular, the province of Quebec has long questioned the constitutionality of conditional grants, as will be discussed in the next chapter.

transfer payments Monies that are transferred from the federal government to provincial governments to pay for services. The Canada Health Transfer is one such transfer payment.

Origins and Development of Canada's Social Union

In 1867, the prevailing belief was that families should be responsible for their own welfare, and if they were unable to provide for themselves they should seek charity, primarily through churches. But in the 1920s public pressure mounted for government social programs, especially pensions for seniors because World War I took the lives of thousands of young men, leaving many senior citizens without any means of support. Here we begin to see the breakdown of the nineteenth-century mentality that families should be responsible for their own welfare. The state had sent their sons to war, and consequently the state felt obligated to provide assistance to seniors in need.

Pensions were a matter of provincial responsibility, but the provinces did not have sufficient revenue to finance pension programs. Thus, in 1927 the federal government offered to assume financial responsibility for half the cost of old-age pensions if the provinces agreed to supply and pay for the administration of such a plan. However, some of the provinces still could not finance the pension plan, so the federal government was forced to increase its support to 75 percent in 1930. A new pension program was brought into effect in 1951 with the Old Age Assistance Act. In 1963, the Government of Canada introduced the Canada Pension Plan (CPP)—and the corresponding Quebec Pension Program (QPP) managed by the province of Quebec—which provided seniors with a more robust means of support. These parallel pension programs are financed through payroll taxes—taxes deducted directly from your paycheque with corresponding contributions from your employer.

The origins of Canada's unemployment insurance program lie in the Great Depression, when millions of people were thrown out of work through no fault of their own. The federal government eventually felt compelled to act, and it transferred small amounts of money to the provinces to provide social assistance on an ad hoc basis. In 1935, the federal government proposed to create a national unemployment insurance plan, but the Supreme Court of Canada and ultimately the JCPC ruled that unemployment insurance was a matter of provincial responsibility. The constitution was consequently amended in 1940 to allow the federal government to introduce unemployment insurance. Like the Canada Pension Plan, unemployment insurance is financed through payroll taxes.

As World War II drew to a close, the Government of Canada revealed a plan to create a comprehensive welfare state, or what we now call the **social union**. The government's plan was outlined in a series of books with green covers, which are known as the **Green Books**. Among other things, the federal government wanted to establish a national health care system and a variety of social assistance programs. It believed that its proposals would make a threefold contribution: "they would provide a network of protection for the Canadian people that justifies itself on social and humanitarian grounds. They would provide an important degree of protection to buttress the nation's economy as a whole in times of stress and strain. Less tangible perhaps, but in some ways most important of all, they would make a vital contribution to the development of our concept of Canadian citizenship and to the forging of lasting bonds of Canadian unity."[16]

While the federal government possessed the financial resources necessary to realize the social union, the jurisdictional authority for most social programs lay with the provinces (see Table 7.1). Theoretically, the constitution could have been amended to give the federal government authority over social programs or to provide greater taxing powers to the provinces to finance social programs. But neither order of government was willing to relinquish power. So if Canada was going to have a social union, the two orders of government would have to work together cooperatively, and the age of **cooperative federalism** was born. The Green Book proposals were discussed by the two orders of government between August 1945 and 1946. Saskatchewan, led by Tommy Douglas, was enthusiastic, but Alberta, Ontario, and especially Quebec vigorously defended the principles of classical federalism and provincial autonomy. The negotiations finally collapsed in April 1946 when Quebec Premier Maurice Duplessis walked out. So, rather than creating a social union in one fell swoop, it was established piecemeal over the next 20 years.

social union The comprehensive set of programs and services that were established following World War II that today make up the modern welfare state in Canada. Programs like universal health care, the Canada Pension Plan, the public education system, and employment insurance are important pillars of the modern social union.

Green Books A series of reports by the federal government written at the end of World War II that proposed the creation of the modern welfare state in Canada.

cooperative federalism The cooperation of the federal government and the provinces in the delivery of programs and services to citizens. It stands in contrast to the theory of classical federalism, in which the two orders of government operate independently of each other in their areas of jurisdiction.

Table 7.1 The Constitutional Problem in Establishing a Social Union in Canada

Federal Government	Provincial Governments
Fiscal capacity to finance social programs	Constitutional authority for social programs
No constitutional authority for social programs	Insufficient fiscal capacity to finance social programs

In the 1940s and 1950s, a variety of assistance programs were created. In 1966, most of these programs were consolidated into the Canada Assistance Plan (CAP). In 1956, the Hospital Insurance Plan was introduced, with the condition that the services be universally available to all citizens of the provinces. Then, in 1966, the federal government passed the Medical Care Act, which provided universal health insurance to all citizens. In 1984, the five principles of medicare were incorporated into the Canada Health Act: Health care must be universal, comprehensive, accessible, portable, and under public administration. In other words, health care must be provided to all people in Canada, all medically necessary procedures must be covered, everyone should be able to access medical care, citizens and permanent residents must be able to obtain medical treatment anywhere in Canada, and the system must be administered by the government. Medicare was the last major social program created in Canada. These programs were created through federal–provincial negotiations; the federal government would normally outline the broad parameters of the programs, while the provinces would operate them. But there was always one big question: How would they be financed?

Conditional Grants

Most of the social programs established after World War II were initiated with conditional grants to the provinces from the federal government, usually on a 50–50 cost-sharing basis. After these programs were created, the size of the transfer payments and the terms of the conditions became the subject of continual negotiation and bargaining between the federal and provincial governments. As a rule of thumb, the provinces have wanted the most amount of money possible with the fewest conditions, while the federal government has wanted to transfer the least amount of money possible with the most conditions (see Table 7.2).

Once these programs were established, however, they proved to be very expensive. The provinces had very little incentive to control costs, since every dollar they spent would be matched by the federal government. Moreover, controlling costs would be unpopular. However, with the economic problems of the 1970s, the federal government could no longer sustain equal cost sharing. So, in 1976–1977, the federal government consolidated the funding for hospital and medical insurance and postsecondary education into the **Established Programs Financing Act (EPF)**. With EPF, the federal government started transferring fixed sums of money, or **block transfers**, to the provinces. With the block transfers, the provinces would have to absorb the rising cost of social programs (or find some way to control costs). The federal government attempted to sell the EPF scheme to the provinces with the promise that EPF transfers would be subject to fewer conditions.

With the introduction of EPF, the federal government also vacated a considerable amount of room in the major tax fields and allowed the provinces to move into this space. This was described by the federal government as a transfer of **tax points**. Ever since, the federal government and the provinces have argued over the exact level of federal support for provincial programs. In the early 2000s, before Jean Chrétien and Paul Martin poured a lot of money into health care, the provinces argued that the federal government was only contributing 15 percent to the cost of health care. The federal government rejected this accounting and insisted that its contribution to health care was more like 35 percent.

Established Programs Financing Act (EPF) An act introduced in 1976 as a new federal transfer to finance provincial social programs including health care. It introduced the concept of block transfers in Canadian fiscal federalism rather than cost sharing.

block transfers Fixed sums of money provided by the federal government to the provinces to finance social programs and health care. They were introduced with the Established Programs Financing Act in 1976.

tax points A means by which the federal government provides money to the provinces to finance provincial programs. With tax points, the federal government cuts its tax rates in one tax field (such as income tax) and the provinces increase their tax rates in this field by a corresponding amount.

Table 7.2 Federal–Provincial Negotiations over Conditional Grants

	Transfer Payments	Conditions
What the Federal Government Wants	Low	High
What the Provincial Governments Want	High	Low

How could the provinces and the federal government be so far apart on these numbers? The provinces only counted the **cash transfers** they received from the federal government, while the federal government calculated how much the provinces raised from tax points and added those figures to its cash transfers.

cash transfers Payments provided by the federal government to the provinces to finance provincial programs such as health care.

Canada Health and Social Transfer

While EPF helped reduce federal transfers for health care and education, the federal government was still on the hook for equal cost sharing under the Canada Assistance Program. So in 1991, the federal government placed a cap on CAP. However, the EPF and the cap on CAP were not sufficient to bring the federal deficit under control. Indeed, the deficit ballooned to almost $40 billion per year in the early 1990s. When Jean Chrétien took office in 1993, he concluded that drastic action was required to curb the deficit. In the 1995 budget, the federal government announced that the EPF and the CAP would be rolled into a single transfer: the **Canada Health and Social Transfer (CHST)**. With the CHST, the federal government cut its conditional transfers to the provinces from $18.5 billion per year down to $11.5 billion. The federal government tried to sugar coat the cut by telling the provinces that the CHST would be subject to fewer conditions, but the CHST was not entirely unconditional. There were two major conditions associated with the CHST: the provinces could not impose restrictions on welfare eligibility on residents arriving from other provinces, and the provinces were required to follow the five principles of the Canada Health Act.

Canada Health and Social Transfer (CHST) A single transfer that replaced the Established Programs Financing Act in 1995 as the primary federal transfer for provincial health and social programs.

The 1995 federal budget exacted a serious toll on the provincial coffers and exacerbated the vertical fiscal imbalance in the federation. When the federal government balanced its budget in 1998, the provinces demanded a restoration in CHST funding. Prime Minister Chrétien responded to these demands and ramped up funding for health care in 2000 and again in 2003, but with this increased support came new conditions. In particular, the federal government wanted more accountability from the provinces about how the money was spent, especially for health care. To that end, the CHST was divided into two separate programs: the **Canada Health Transfer (CHT)** and the **Canada Social Transfer (CST)** (or everything other than health care). Nevertheless, the cost of health care continued to soar.

Canada Health Transfer (CHT) and **Canada Social Transfer (CST)** Transfers created in 2003 to ensure more accountability surrounding how provinces spend money transferred from the federal government.

In September 2004, Prime Minister Martin met with the premiers to fix the "crisis" in health care for at least a "generation." By the end of the meeting, the premiers had extracted an additional $41 billion from the federal government over a period of 10 years; the deal also called for a 6 percent increase in federal health transfers each year for 10 years. However, the prime minister did not give the money away entirely for free. Among other things, he secured a commitment from the premiers to make "meaningful reductions" in wait times for important health procedures, notably cancer treatment, heart surgery, joint replacements, sight restoration, and diagnostic imaging. Working with the medical community, the provinces announced medically acceptable wait time "benchmarks" for these treatments in December 2005.

In the election campaign in the winter of 2005–2006, Stephen Harper stated that benchmarks were not good enough, and he promised to introduce a "wait time guarantee." When Harper became prime minister and presented his idea of a wait time guarantee to the provinces, the premiers asked for more money. When the prime minister indicated that no new money would be forthcoming, the premiers informed him that they would not be able to provide a wait time guarantee. The two orders of government engaged in difficult negotiations. In the absence of new money, the federal government made numerous concessions. First, it indicated that the provinces only had to provide a guarantee in one of the five priority areas. Second, it accepted quite long wait times. So, in the case of radiation treatments for cancer, the maximum acceptable wait time for treatment was set at eight weeks—double the benchmark established in 2005. British Columbia was already providing treatment for cancer within two weeks of diagnosis, so it was not difficult for the BC government to guarantee cancer treatment within eight weeks. Most of the other provinces found that they too were already offering at least one treatment within the guaranteed wait time. The Harper government in turn claimed that it had fulfilled its promise to negotiate a wait time guarantee with the provinces.[17]

The 2004 health accord with the provinces is set to expire in 2014. In the 2011 general election, Stephen Harper promised to maintain the annual 6 percent increase in health transfers to the provinces, but he did not say for how long. In December 2011, Finance Minister Jim Flaherty unilaterally announced a new 10-year health agreement. He indicated that the federal government would maintain the 6 percent increase through to 2016–2017, but thereafter federal transfers for health care would increase at the rate of "nominal GDP"— the rate of economic growth minus inflation. In other words, if the economy grows 4 percent but inflation is 2 percent, the nominal GDP is just 2 percent. The federal government did promise, however, to increase the health transfer by a minimum of 3 percent each year. Unlike previous health agreements, the provinces were not consulted on this new arrangement. But with federal transfers increasing at a lower rate, the provinces will have to find ways to curb the costs of health care, which now consume almost 50 percent of the budget in most provinces. However, with an aging population, the cost of health care is projected to rise exponentially in the coming decades. It would thus appear that the federal–provincial debate over health care and transfer payments is destined to continue far into the future.

Equalization

After the federal government initiated its rapid expansion of the welfare state after World War II, it quickly became apparent that some of the provinces did not have sufficient means to finance comparable social programs, even with the conditional grants offered by Ottawa. If Canada was going to have social programs with comparable standards from coast to coast, the federal government would have to top-up the less wealthy or so-called "have-not" provinces. Thus, in 1957, the Government of Canada introduced an **equalization program** as a means to establish horizontal equity across the provinces. It is now one of the federal government's largest expenditures ($14.5 billion in 2010).

The principle of equalization is very straightforward: Provinces that have less-than-average fiscal capacity will receive payments from the federal government to bring them up to the average fiscal capacity of all the provinces. The equalization program constitutes a pillar of social justice in Canadian society because it enables comparable social programs for all Canadians regardless of where they live at comparable rates of taxation. Unfortunately, the program is not well understood. So let's get a few things straight. First, as noted by the Expert Panel on Equalization, the equalization program is "funded entirely by the federal government using taxes paid by all Canadians across the country."[18] It is *not* a transfer from wealthy provinces to poor provinces. Second, while the federal government always tries to negotiate an equalization formula with the provinces, ultimately the federal government determines the formula for the program and how much money goes to each receiving province. Third, the federal government endeavours to create a formula to last for a five-year period, but it can and does change the formula midstream if circumstances demand it. Fourth, equalization payments are unconditional; they can be used by the provinces for any purpose.

equalization A federal expenditure program that is constitutionally entrenched in Section 36 of the Constitution Act 1982. It ensures that the provinces are able to offer comparable levels of service with roughly comparable levels of taxation, meaning that Canadians are ensured to receive roughly comparable levels of service for roughly comparable levels of taxation anywhere in the country.

Designing an Equalization Program

While the principle of equalization is straightforward, it is difficult to design a fair and stable equalization program. What exactly is a "have-not" province? How does one determine the average fiscal capacity of the provinces? There are a number of different ways to create an equalization program. The Canadian approach has always focused on the ability of the provinces to raise revenue. Because the provinces can and do have widely differing rates of taxation—Alberta, for example, has no provincial sales tax, while the sales tax in Nova Scotia is 10 percent—the equalization program does not rely on the actual revenues collected. Instead, it is necessary to determine the theoretical ability of the provinces to raise revenue through a **representative tax system**. In short, we need to identify all the sources of provincial revenue, calculate the average rate of taxation for these different sources, then determine how much money each province would raise if it taxed at the average rate for each revenue source: personal income tax, corporate tax, sales tax, health premiums, natural resources, alcohol and tobacco taxes, and so on. So even though Alberta has no provincial sales tax, it is still necessary to determine for the purposes of the equalization program how much Alberta *could* raise if it applied a sales tax at the average provincial rate of 7.15 percent. The same calculation is made for each province for each source of revenue. Ultimately, the figure for each province is divided by population to determine how much revenue is raised per capita; this is the only way to compare provinces of different sizes directly.

When the numbers are crunched, we can see that the fiscal capacities of the provinces vary enormously (see Figure 7.2). Alberta has the greatest fiscal capacity, while Prince Edward Island has the lowest. It is thus clear that if Prince Edward Island is going to offer comparable programs to its citizens with comparable provincial tax rates, it needs external fiscal support from Ottawa over and above conditional transfer payments for health and social services. Equalization payments bring those provinces with less-than-average fiscal capacity up to the average level (see Figure 7.3). Those provinces with higher-than-average fiscal capacity are unaffected; they are not brought down to the average level.

representative tax system An analytical tool used by the federal government to calculate the fiscal capacity of each province for the purposes of the equalization program.

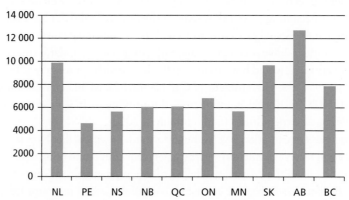

Figure 7.2 Fiscal Capacity of the Provinces per Capita

Source: Data are for the 2011–2012 fiscal year; obtained from the Department of Finance and through personal correspondence with the author.

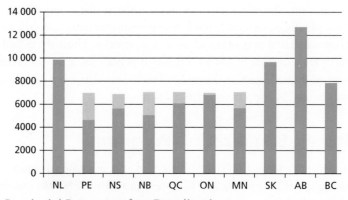

Figure 7.3 Provincial Revenue after Equalization

Source: Data are for the 2011–2012 fiscal year; obtained from the Department of Finance and through personal correspondence with the author.

Stresses and Strains in the Federal Equalization Program   The Expert Panel on Equalization described the equalization program as "the glue that holds our federation together."[19] However, the equalization program has been enormously difficult to operate. First, it has created tension between "have" and "have-not" provinces. Second, it has been difficult to establish a fair equalization formula. Third, it has often created budgetary problems for the federal government, so the equalization formula has been repeatedly adjusted to protect the federal government's budget position. All too often, the federal government works backwards: It determines how much it can afford to spend on equalization payments in total and then it devises a formula that will produce that number. The equalization program has thus often become the subject of haphazard economic and political tinkering.

The greatest challenge for the equalization program has been sudden jumps in the price of oil and gas at various times. When oil and gas prices surged in the late 1970s, the formula indicated that every province *except* Alberta should receive equalization payments. The federal government was not willing to accept that outcome, and the formula was rejigged to prevent Ontario from receiving equalization. In the 1980s, the discovery of oil and gas off the shores of Nova Scotia and Newfoundland created new problems: under the terms of the Constitution Act 1867, oil and gas underground belonged to the province, but oil and gas under the ocean belonged to the federal government. The Mulroney government consequently made deals with Nova Scotia and Newfoundland in 1985 and 1986, respectively, so that these provinces could keep the revenue generated from offshore oil and gas, although ownership of these resources legally remained with the federal government. However, as these resources began to generate revenue for Newfoundland and Nova Scotia, they began to lose equalization payments. Consequently, special accords were negotiated with these provinces to protect their resource royalties and equalization payments, at least for a period of time while the oil and gas industry was developed in these provinces. The **offshore accords** with Nova Scotia and Newfoundland continue to complicate Canada's equalization program.

When Paul Martin became prime minister in 2004, total equalization payments were projected to drop to $8.9 billion from a high of $10.9 billion in 2000–2001, much to the displeasure of the have-not provinces. The drop was "due to the combined impact of a slow-down in Ontario's economy and tax reductions in several provinces."[20] In what seemed like a calculated move to win political support in have-not provinces, the Martin government decided to cap the equalization program at $11 billion with annual increases limited to 3.5 percent. Many economists, however, were critical of this new framework. In response, the Martin government established an Expert Panel on Equalization, which recommended putting the equalization program back on a principled formula. The Harper government followed through on this recommendation in its 2007 budget. The new formula, however, led to a large increase in equalization payments, especially to Quebec. And then, as a result of the 2008 recession, Ontario became a have-not province. While Ontario's first equalization payment in 2009 was a relatively modest $347 million, it nearly tripled to $972 million in 2010, and it tripled again to about $3.2 billion in 2013–2014, after which it is projected to decline somewhat. Even so, at this rate, "the equalization program is likely to become unaffordable."[21] The Harper government has capped the program at $14.5 billion as a cost-control measure.

Canada's equalization program now faces some very serious challenges. First, there is a real risk that the provinces may become pitted against each other in a vicious zero-sum game for federal support. In a capped equalization system, as some provinces receive larger equalization payments, other provinces will inevitably receive smaller equalization payments. This has serious implications for national unity. Second, Canada's two largest provinces now receive equalization payments. It is not clear that the federal government can afford to provide equalization payments to Ontario and Quebec at current rates, but a drop

offshore accords Agreements negotiated between the federal government and Nova Scotia and Newfoundland. The accords enabled Nova Scotia and Newfoundland to receive royalty payments from offshore oil and gas resources as well as continue to receive a portion of their equalization payments.

in payments would have serious implications for the smaller have-not provinces like Prince Edward Island and New Brunswick. Third, the volatility of oil and gas prices is making it difficult for the economists in the federal Department of Finance to devise a fair and stable equalization formula. In short, Canada's equalization program appears to be at risk of becoming unglued.

Territorial Formula Financing

The territories have a different set of fiscal arrangements with the federal government. The territories receive CST and CHT payments on a per capita basis in common with the provinces, but the bulk of the federal government's financial support to the territories lies in the Territorial Formula Financing (TFF) program, which is like a separate equalization program for the three territories. Unlike the provincial equalization program, however, the TFF program takes into account the expenditure needs of the territories as well as their capacity to raise revenue. The territories possess many of the same revenue sources as the provinces: personal and business income taxes; tobacco, alcohol, and gasoline as well as general sales taxes; medical insurance premiums; property taxes; and lottery revenues. Natural resource revenues are handled separately for each territory and are thus not included in the territorial financing formula. Historically, the federal government collected royalties from natural resources located in the territories; however, in 2003 Yukon signed a devolution and resource revenue-sharing agreement with the federal government, the Northwest Territories signed a devolution agreement with the federal government in 2013, and as of 2013 the federal government was still negotiating a revenue-sharing agreement with Nunavut.

In sum, federal financial support for the territories is substantial, both in absolute terms and in relation to the fiscal capacity of the territories. The TFF is an unconditional transfer to the territories and it accounts for 66 percent of Yukon's total financial resources, 70 percent for the Northwest Territories, and 86 percent for Nunavut (as of 2013–2014). In 2013–2014, the territories received a total of $3.3 billion in TFF payments—that's $1.35 billion for Nunavut, just over a billion for the Northwest Territories, and $817 million for Yukon (see Table 7.3). That works out to a staggering $37 921 per person in Nunavut. The per capita transfers to the territories are much greater than for the provinces because of the relatively low fiscal capacity of the territories and very high expenditure needs associated with living in the north. The territories also have a plethora of social problems to deal with, such as high rates of unemployment, alcohol and drug dependency, and suicide. In short, the territories are heavily dependent on federal transfers to finance their activities. Fortunately, however, territorial financing does not seem to be as politically charged as equalization. The other governments in Canada seem to accept the challenges of governing in the north.

Table 7.3 Territorial Formula Financing 2013–2014

	TFF ($ millions)	TFF ($ per capita)	CHT ($ millions)	CST ($ millions)
Nunavut	1350	37 921	34	12
Northwest Territories	1100	25 287	27	15
Yukon	817	22 261	31	13

Source: Department of Finance Canada, "Territorial Formula Financing." Available at www.fin.gc.ca /fedprov/tff-eng.asp.

The Joys and Pathologies of Executive Federalism

In the nineteenth century, the federal government and the provinces lived in splendid isolation, but the economic challenges of the twentieth century compelled the two orders of government to work together to provide Canadians with a comprehensive set of social programs. But how would this collaboration be achieved? It became clear very quickly after World War II that intergovernmental coordination in Canada would be achieved primarily through the interaction of political executives, especially the prime minister and the provincial premiers—hence what the great political scientist Donald Smiley famously called **executive federalism**.

The emergence of executive federalism dramatically altered the nature of Canadian politics. Under the terms of the Constitution Act 1867, policy decisions are to be made either by the federal government under Section 91 or by the provincial governments under Section 92. The constitution did not envision a third space for policymaking, apart from agriculture and immigration (which were established as areas of concurrent jurisdiction). And yet almost all of the social programs valued by Canadians today, especially health care, were the products of executive federalism. And, as we will discuss in the next chapter, the repatriation of the constitution and the adoption of a Charter of Rights and Freedoms also happened through the processes of executive federalism.

Executive federalism has been a mixed blessing. It has generally produced pretty good policy outcomes, but it also problematic. It is important in a democracy for the political system to be transparent and accountable. The people should be able to see their politicians in action and debating major policy decisions publicly. But the world of intergovernmental relations is largely obscured from public view, even though huge policy decisions are being made on behalf of Canadians, often with major cost implications for taxpayers. Canadian political scientists have consequently been very critical of executive federalism. Donald Smiley offered the most damning indictment:

> My charges against executive federalism are these: First, it contributes to undue secrecy in the conduct of the public's business. Second, it contributes to an unduly low level of citizen-participation in public affairs. Third, it weakens and dilutes the accountability of governments to their respective legislatures and to the wider public. Fourth, it frustrates a number of matters of crucial public concern from coming on the public agenda and being dealt with by the public authorities. Fifth, it has been a contributing factor to the indiscriminate growth of government activities. Sixth, it leads to continuous and often unresolved conflicts among governments, conflicts which serve no purpose broader than the political and bureaucratic interests of those involved in them.[22]

Following Smiley's indictment, political scientists expended considerable energy imagining ways to address the pathologies of executive federalism. Three possible remedies were envisioned: (1) the disentanglement of the two orders of government, (2) reforming the Senate to better represent the interests of the provinces within the institutions of the federal government, and (3) improving the workability of executive federalism. However, the opportunities for disentanglement seem limited in an age of economic integration, and it has proven to be next to impossible to reform the Senate, as we discussed in the last chapter. Political decision makers thus turned by default (and perhaps preference) to the third option: making executive federalism work better. So while the pathologies of executive federalism were abundantly clear by the mid-1970s, executive federalism has continued to expand and deepen. The Canadian Intergovernmental Conference Secretariat typically coordinates more than 100 meetings per year between the federal and provincial governments, or about two per week.

executive federalism
The phenomenon whereby first ministers—the prime minister and the various provincial premiers—serve as the main nexus of interaction in intergovernmental affairs.

peak institutions The institutions that sit at the apex of Canada's system of executive federalism. The first ministers' meeting sits at the very top of this complex system.

managing institutions The institutions that sit below peak institutions in Canada's system of executive federalism. They coordinate various federal–provincial programs and initiatives.

The Institutions of Intergovernmental Relations in Canada

Over the decades, an elaborate network of intergovernmental relations has developed in Canada.[23] At the top of the network we have the **peak institutions** of intergovernmental relations with **managing institutions** below (see Figure 7.4). Some of these institutions are quite elaborate (or deeply institutionalized, as political scientists say) while some are still quite rudimentary. The **first ministers' meeting** or first ministers' conference, as it used to be called, is the most important peak institution in Canada's network of intergovernmental relations. At the end of the day, major policy decisions have to be taken in this forum—only the prime minister and the premiers have the authority to launch a major new initiative on behalf of their governments. First ministers' meetings, however, occur irregularly; they are scheduled

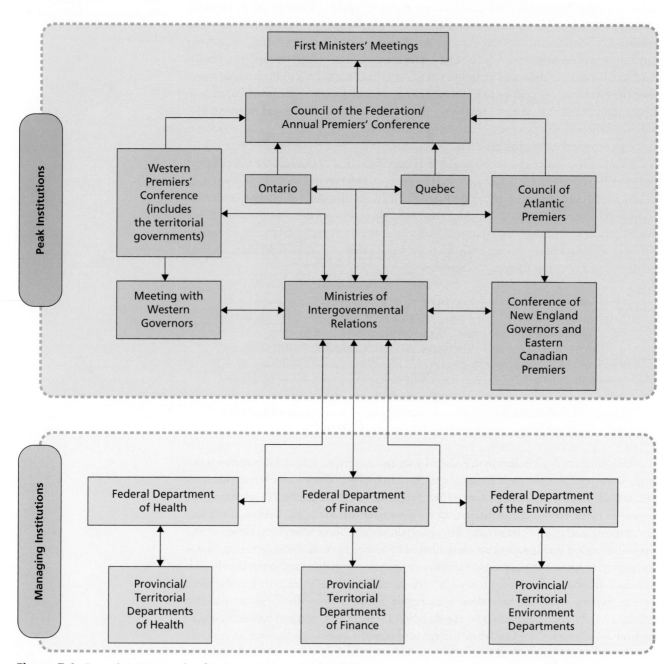

Figure 7.4 Canada's Network of Intergovernmental Relations

solely at the discretion of the prime minister. Some prime ministers enjoy meeting with the premiers, while other prime ministers generally try to avoid them. Jean Chrétien did not enjoy meeting the premiers, and Stephen Harper has been even less unenthusiastic. The number of first ministers' meetings has thus declined over the last two decades, and there has been a corresponding drop in intergovernmental coordination.

The provincial and territorial premiers, on the other hand, have ramped up their coordination over the last decade or two. The premiers started meeting annually in 1960, and in 2003 the premiers established the **Council of the Federation**, which maintains a permanent secretariat in Ottawa and generally organizes two meetings of the premiers each year. The premiers also meet regionally. The **Western Premiers' Conference** (with the three territorial leaders) has been meeting annually since 1973. The Maritime provinces have been meeting annually since 1972, and the **Council of Atlantic Premiers** (the three Maritime provinces plus Newfoundland and Labrador) was established in 2000. The Western and Atlantic premiers discuss matters of common concern and endeavour to establish a consensus on these matters before meeting with the larger Council of the Federation. When all 13 premiers meet at the council, they attempt to establish a consensus on the major issues before meeting with the federal government. Even if they do not reach a consensus—and Quebec often stands alone—it is helpful if they can go to the federal government with two or three positions rather than 13.

Below the peak institutions there are a number of managing institutions. Typically, these involve meetings between federal, provincial, and territorial ministers. Finance ministers, health ministers, environment ministers, and others across just about all ministries meet on a regular basis. Ministers, however, are not free agents. They are representatives of their governments and they must follow the direction of their respective first ministers—the prime minister and the premiers. Nevertheless, ministers can manage the routine business of the federation. Almost every policy area has an intergovernmental nexus with a few exceptions (e.g., the federal government exclusively handles foreign affairs and matters related to the military).

To facilitate the above meetings, all governments have specialized intergovernmental relations officials. They are situated in the middle of this vast network of intergovernmental relations and attempt to coordinate this immense buzz of activity. At the federal level, the Intergovernmental Affairs Ministry is located within the Privy Council Office. In other words, intergovernmental affairs are managed close to the centre of power in Ottawa. In most provinces, the intergovernmental ministers are similarly located within the premier's office. In fact, many premiers assume the role of Minister of Intergovernmental Relations themselves. And even when the first minister does not formally appoint him or herself to this role, premiers are typically very hands on with the key intergovernmental files. It is believed that Stephen Harper, for example, handles all important intergovernmental relations matters himself, notwithstanding the presence of a Minister of Intergovernmental Affairs in his cabinet.

In sum, we can see a vast network of intergovernmental relations, but the institutions of executive federalism seem to be moving in different directions. While the premiers have made a concerted effort to institutionalize collaboration, there is still a lack of overall coordination with the federal government. The federal government has been reluctant to deepen the institutions of executive federalism because it fears that more meetings with the provinces and territories would simply provide an opportunity for 13 premiers to extract ever larger transfer payments. While this has happened in the past, it may be the case that regular meetings between the prime minister and the premiers would diffuse tension in the federation and allow negotiations over transfer payments and other matters to occur in a more cordial fashion.

Defining the Rules of Executive Federalism

The institutions of executive federalism have developed in an ad hoc fashion: They have no constitutional or statutory authority, their operating rules are governed entirely by convention, participation is not mandatory, and decisions are not binding. While the institutions

first ministers' meeting
A meeting of the prime minister and all provincial premiers. It is the highest level of interaction in Canada's complex system of executive federalism. It is sometimes called the first ministers' conference.

Council of the Federation
The body of all premiers that meets roughly twice a year. It maintains a permanent secretariat to coordinate these meetings.

Western Premiers' Conference
A meeting of all four Western premiers plus the three territorial leaders. It occurs annually.

Council of Atlantic Premiers
A meeting of all four Atlantic premiers. It meets annually.

of executive federalism have generally led to good policy outcomes, the highly informal nature of the rules surrounding the processes of executive federalism leaves much to be desired. Consequently, there have been a few attempts over recent decades to provide some coherence to the processes of executive federalism.

The Social Union Framework Agreement   The provinces were devastated by the introduction of the Canada Health and Social Transfer in the 1995 budget. In response to the CHST, the provincial premiers sought to establish a framework for federal–provincial relations that would provide for greater consultation and predictability. In short, the premiers "wanted a new set of 'rules' that would enable them to plan their programs and financial affairs within a more stable policy and fiscal framework."[24] The federal government had little enthusiasm for this initiative, but the provinces were adamant that a set of rules had to be established to govern the processes of intergovernmental relations in Canada. The provinces and the federal government thus negotiated bitterly for two years until they finally signed the Social Union Framework Agreement in February 1999. Quebec refused to sign the agreement, for reasons that will be discussed in the next chapter.

The Social Union Framework Agreement (SUFA) opens with a series of motherhood statements (e.g., the governments of Canada will "treat all Canadians with fairness and equity"). Section 2 endorses the right of Canadians to move within the country; Section 3 addresses the question of accountability; Section 4 articulates some general principles for collaboration between governments, including reciprocal notice of finance changes. The premiers, in fact, secured a commitment from the federal government to inform the provinces at least one year in advance of anticipated program or funding changes. The federal government also agreed not to introduce new initiatives without the support of a majority of provinces.

SUFA did not materially advance any program or policy. It was intended solely to enhance the workability of executive federalism. Indeed, there was some hope that SUFA could act as a kind of constitution for executive federalism. However, SUFA has not lived up to expectations. Some people would argue that it is now just a footnote in the history of Canadian federalism. On the other hand, it remains a well-thought-out agreement, which could provide a useful framework for executive federalism.

Open Federalism   In its 2006 election platform, the Conservative Party stated that it was "time for the federal government to establish a new relationship of open federalism with the provinces."[25] The notion of **open federalism** sounded positive, and it likely helped the Conservatives pick up a few seats in Quebec and win the election. The promise of open federalism, however, has not been realized. The Conservative government has not established new institutions of intergovernmental relations, and it has not followed through on its promise to enact a Charter of Open Federalism. Indeed, the Harper government has not seemed interested in engaging with the provinces at all, and consequently important issues—like climate change and the environment—have languished because of insufficient attention. On so many policy fronts, the two orders of government must work together cooperatively to provide programs and services to Canadians. This has been the reality of Canadian politics since the end of World War II.

open federalism A campaign proposal made by the Conservative Party of Canada in the 2006 election to create a more positive relationship with the provinces, but little has been done to develop or institutionalize the concept since it was first proposed.

SUMMARY

Canada would not exist without federalism. In 1867, the different colonies that came together to form Canada insisted on keeping a measure of self-government to maintain and nurture the political and cultural aspirations of these distinct communities. And today it is impossible to imagine a Canada without the 10 provinces and three territories—the provinces and territories are integral to life in Canada.

Federalism, however, is a complex form of government and a certain amount of conflict between the two orders of government is inevitable. In the first instance, the two orders of government may have disputes over jurisdiction, or the formal division of powers in the constitution. In Canada, these disputes were common in the first 75 years after Confederation, but for better or worse the ambiguity surrounding the division of powers was clarified by the Judicial Committee of the Privy Council. Over the last 75 years, the governments of Canada have argued primarily about money. While the rules of fiscal federalism are confusing, they are much more flexible than the formal rules of federalism outlined in the constitution. Unfortunately, this adaptation all too frequently unfolds in the murky world of intergovernmental relations, with little input from citizens. Canada has struggled to create effective and transparent institutions for federal–provincial–territorial relations. While the formal and informal rules of Canadian federalism are undoubtedly confusing, we cannot afford to ignore them. Just about every policy subject in Canada has a federalism and intergovernmental relations nexus. More profoundly, these rules affect the overarching story of Canadian federalism: unity.

Questions to Think About

1. Does Canada still need federalism?
2. Why was the JCPC's interpretation of the constitution so controversial?
3. Should the federal government put more money into health care or should it let the principles of the Canada Health Act fall by the wayside and give the provinces more latitude to operate the health system in accordance with their fiscal realities?
4. How can intergovernmental relations be democratized in Canada? Is open federalism the answer?
5. What is the best way for the Government of Canada to promote unity in the federation?

Learning Outcomes

1. Explain the concept of federalism and outline the key features of the division of powers in the Constitution Act 1867.
2. Describe the main challenges associated with the federal form of government.
3. Outline the main conditional and unconditional transfer programs in Canada.
4. Describe Canada's system of executive federalism and its advantages and disadvantages.

Additional Readings

Janet Ajzenstat et al., *Canada's Founding Debates* (Toronto, ON: University of Toronto Press, 1999).

Keith Banting, *The Welfare State and Canadian Federalism*, 2nd ed. (Montreal, QC: McGill-Queen's University Press, 1987).

Alan C. Cairns, "The Judicial Committee and Its Critics," *Canadian Journal of Political Science* 4:3 (September 1971), 301–345.

Samuel LaSelva, *The Moral Foundations of Canadian Federalism: Paradoxes, Achievements, and Tragedies of Nationhood* (Montreal, QC: McGill-Queen's University Press, 1996).

Alex S. MacNevin, *The Canadian Federal–Provincial Equalization Regime: An Assessment* (Toronto, ON: Canadian Tax Foundation, 2004).

David Perry, *Financing the Canadian Federation, 1867 to 1995: Setting the Stage for Change* (Toronto, ON: Canadian Tax Foundation, 1997).

Richard Simeon and Ian Robinson, *State, Society, and the Development of Canadian Federalism* (Toronto, ON: University of Toronto Press, 1990).

Donald Smiley, *The Federal Condition in Canada* (Toronto, ON: McGraw-Hill Ryerson, 1987).

Jennifer Smith, *Federalism* (Vancouver, BC: UBC Press, 2004).

Garth Stevenson, *Unfilled Union: Canadian Federalism and National Unity*, 5th ed. (Montreal, QC: McGill-Queen's University Press, 2009).

Ronald L. Watts, *Comparing Federal Systems*, 3rd ed. (Kingston, ON Institute of Intergovernmental Relations, 2008).

Ronald L. Watts, *The Spending Power in Federal Systems: A Comparative Study* (Kingston, ON: Institute of Intergovernmental Relations, 1999).

Notes

1. Parliamentary debates on the subject of the Confederation of the British North American provinces, 3rd session, 8th provincial Parliament of Canada (Quebec: Hunter, Rose & Co., Parliamentary Printers, 1865; Ottawa, ON: Edmond Cloutier, 1951), 29.

2. Ibid., 33.

3. Ibid., 33.

4. Ibid., 255.

5. Ibid., 689.

6. Ibid., 690.

7. Pensions were added to the list of concurrent responsibilities by constitutional amendments in 1951 and 1964; see Section 94A.

8. *The Liquidators of the Maritime Bank of Canada v. The Receiver-General of New Brunswick (1892) A. C. 437;* I Olmsted *263*, 268.

9. F.R. Scott, "The Consequences of the Privy Council Decisions," *The Canadian Bar Review* 15 (1937), 489.

10. Pierre Elliott Trudeau, *Federalism and the French Canadians* (Toronto, ON: Macmillan Company, 1968), 198.

11. Reference re; Firearms Act (Can.), [2000] 1 S.C.R. 783.

12. Harvey Lazar, "In Search of a New Mission Statement for Canadian Fiscal Federalism," in Harvey Lazar, ed., *Canada: The State of the Federation 1999–2000: Toward a New Mission Statement for Canadian Fiscal Federalism* (Kingston, ON: Institute of Intergovernmental Relations, 2000), 3.

13. Ibid., 4.

14. *Report of the Royal Commission on Dominion–Provincial Relations*, Book 1 (Ottawa, ON: Queen's Printer, 1954), 259.

15. Ontario and Alberta collect their own corporate taxes.

16. Dominion–Provincial Conference on Reconstruction, *Proposals of the Government of Canada* (Ottawa, ON: August 1945), 28.

17. Sonia Norris, "The Wait Times Issue and the Patient Wait Times Guarantee," Parliamentary Information and Research Service (Ottawa, ON: Library of Parliament, 2009), paper PRB 05-82E.

18. Expert Panel on Equalization and Territorial Formula Financing, *Achieving a National Purpose: Putting Equalization Back on Track* (Ottawa, ON: Federal Department of Finance, 2006), 19.

19. Ibid., 2.

20. Ibid., 23.

21. Thomas J. Courchene, "Intergovernmental Transfers and Canadian Values: Retrospect and Prospect," *Policy Options* (May 2010), 38.

22. Donald Smiley, "An Outsider's Observations of Federal–Provincial Relations among Consenting Adults," in Richard Simeon, ed., *Confrontation and Collaboration: Intergovernmental Relations Today* (Toronto, ON: Institute of Public Administration of Canada, 1979), 105–106.

23. This section draws heavily on J. Peter Meekison, Hamish Telford, and Harvey Lazar, "The Institutions of Executive Federalism: Myths and Realities," in J. Peter Meekison et al., eds., *Canada: The State of the Federation 2002: Reconsidering the Institutions of Canadian Federalism* (Kingston, ON: Institute of Intergovernmental Relations, 2004).

24. Harvey Lazar, "The Social Union Framework Agreement and the Future of Fiscal Federalism," in Harvey Lazar, ed., *Canada: The State of the Federation, 1999–2000: Toward a New Mission Statement for Fiscal Federalism* (Kingston, ON: Institute of Intergovernmental Relations, 2000), 103.

25. Stand Up for Canada: Conservative Party of Canada Election Platform 2006, 42.

Chapter 8
Patriation

Key Points

- Governing highly diverse societies like Canada is a great challenge, and it is not easy to establish rules of the game that can stand the test of time.

- The Fathers of Confederation drafted a solid constitution for Canada, but by the 1920s it was beginning to look somewhat dated, especially given that it was legally a statute of the British Parliament.

- The effort to patriate—or bring the constitution from Great Britain to Canada—proved to be very difficult, and the political fabric of the country was severely strained.

- When the constitution was returned to Canada in 1982, it was renamed the Constitution Act 1867.

- At the same time, the Parliament of Canada enacted the Constitution Act 1982, which included a Charter of Rights and Freedoms and the recognition and affirmation of Aboriginal rights. These new governing principles have transformed the game of Canadian politics.

- Quebec did not support the new constitutional order. Canada thus still faces the challenge of governing a country with deep cultural divisions.

The BNA Act—now known as the Constitution Act 1867—has served Canada extremely well. It is one of the most successful constitutions in the world. But no constitution can stand the test of time. Countries grow and change, and constitutions must keep up. To a certain extent, constitutions can grow along with the country through gradual changes in practice and interpretation by the courts. From time to time, constitutions can also be formally changed or amended. Canada, however, was in the peculiar position of not owning its own constitution. The BNA Act was a statutory law of the British Parliament. Canadians were thus not in a position to change their own constitution; we had to ask the British Parliament to change it for us.

At a certain point (after World War I) Canadians grew weary of this constitutional paternalism and decided that it was time to take possession of their own constitution. But the effort to bring the constitution to Canada encountered many obstacles. The principal challenge was reconciling the divergent needs of Canada's two linguistic communities. Ultimately, the constitution was brought home in 1982 by Prime Minister Pierre Elliott Trudeau. At this time, two new governing principles were *added* to Canada's constitutional order: a Charter of Rights and Freedoms for all Canadians and the recognition and affirmation of Aboriginal rights and governance. This represented the most significant revision of the rules of the game since Confederation, and the game of Canadian politics has been profoundly transformed by these new governing principles, as we will see in the ensuing chapters.

The Canadian Constitutional Challenge: Maintaining Unity *with* Diversity

Canada is a highly diverse society. There are two official languages and a plethora of cultural communities, including Canada's Aboriginal peoples. Canadians celebrate this diversity today, but political theorists have long recognized the challenges—or even the impossibility— of governing diverse societies. Over 150 years ago, the great English philosopher John Stuart Mill argued:

> Free institutions are next to impossible in a country made up of different nationalities. Among a people without fellow-feeling, especially if they read and speak different languages, the united public opinion, necessary to the working of representative government, cannot exist.[1]

Mill's argument, however, did not go unchallenged. Indeed, Lord Acton, a contemporary of Mill, responded almost immediately: "the co-existence of several nations under the same state is a test, as well as the best security of freedom."[2]

Who's right? Mill or Acton? For Canada to succeed, we must all hope that Lord Acton was right. But there's lots of evidence to support Mill's argument. If free institutions are not possible in a culturally diverse society, there are limited options: Either you don't have free institutions or you seek to establish a more homogeneous society. How do you create a more homogeneous society? The options are all problematic: assimilation, partition, genocide. The main options for governing diverse societies are **consociationalism**, or shared governance, and federalism. Over the course of its long history, Canada has vacillated back and forth between Millian and Actonian options. While Canada is now firmly committed to preserving the country's diversity, the challenge of governing a diverse society continues to be a great test for all Canadians.

consociationalism A system of government whereby different ethnic or cultural groups share power, usually in the form of a coalition government with different parties representing the different cultural groups in the country.

A Brief History of Canada's Constitutional Arrangements

For many Canadians, Canada begins in 1867 with the British North America Act, or what we now call the Constitution Act 1867. Prior to 1867, however, there were a number of British colonies in the upper half of North America, and the British enacted a number of statutes to govern these colonies. After the conquest of New France in 1759, the British struggled to find a way to govern a society with deep cultural divisions. At times, they tried to preserve Canada's linguistic diversity, and at other times they attempted to assimilate the French-speaking minority. A brief examination of Canada's pre-Confederation constitutional arrangements will help us place Canada's constitution in historical context and understand the challenge of constitution-making in Canada.

The Royal Proclamation, 1763   The British conquest of New France in 1759 thrust English- and French-speaking people together in the upper half of North America and started what became Canada. Four years later, King George III issued a Royal Proclamation, which may be viewed as Canada's first constitution. The Royal Proclamation, in conjunction with the instructions given to Quebec's first British governor, was controversial among the French-speaking *habitants* of New France, or Quebec as the British renamed it. First, it abolished the French system of law and replaced it with the British system of common law. Second, it required Catholics to renounce their faith if they wished to participate in the processes of government. Third, it eliminated the taxes landowners paid to the Catholic

Church, which of course gravely threatened the church's ability to function. Fourth, and more positively, it laid the foundation for the establishment of representative institutions for the people of Quebec.

In short, the British enacted a resolutely British constitution for a colony that was not inhabited by British people. The Proclamation had two obvious objectives: to assimilate the French-speaking inhabitants of the colony into the English way of doing things and to establish the conditions to attract British settlers to the colony. (The latter objective, of course, would reinforce the objective of assimilation.) While the assimilation of the French was clearly the objective of the Proclamation, it should be noted that the Proclamation explicitly recognized and endorsed the rights of Aboriginal people to govern themselves freely in the British dominions of North America, as will be discussed more fully in Chapter 10.

When British immigration failed to materialize, the provisions for representative government in the Proclamation were never realized. Put simply, the British did not want to let the French-speaking inhabitants of the colony advise the governor and, indirectly, the King. Without representative government, the British governor of Quebec governed without taking advice from the people who lived in the colony. In short, the British established a dictatorship in Quebec—it may have been a benign dictatorship, but it was a dictatorship nonetheless. Needless to say, this did not go over well with the French-speaking people in Quebec! But it was also alarming to settlers in other North American colonies that did enjoy representative government. It led to fears that Britain was planning to establish direct rule in North America, and this fear (among others) led to the American Revolution a decade after the Royal Proclamation. As the revolution began to unfold in the United States, the British government realized it would have to do something to reassure its subjects in Quebec or risk having them join the revolution.

The Quebec Act, 1774   In the Quebec Act 1774, the British government explicitly recognized that the provisions of the Royal Proclamation were to a considerable extent "inapplicable to the State and Circumstances" of Quebec, and it revoked the most egregious provisions of the Proclamation. Under the new act, the people of Quebec were once again permitted to practise freely "the Religion of the Church of Rome," and Catholics were allowed to work for the government without having to renounce their faith. The act also resurrected the French system of civil law, although English criminal law was retained. In short, the Quebec Act reversed the policy of assimilation and restored the rights extinguished by the Royal Proclamation.

While the Quebec Act was a big improvement, it did not establish the institutions of representative government, although there were vague promises that it might later be established. At this time, French Canadians were not great democrats; what mattered to them were their civil rights. The question of representative government, however, became more pressing after the American Revolution. During the revolution, a large number of people left the American colonies and moved to Quebec and the Maritimes. These people, known as loyalists because they stayed loyal to Britain, had enjoyed the benefits of representative government in the United States and they expected to have it in Quebec as well. (The Maritime provinces already had representative government). But Quebec was now a culturally divided society—a sizable English minority was now living alongside the French majority. This presented a dilemma for British government: Were the institutions of representative government possible in a society with deep cultural divisions?

The Constitution Act, 1791   In 1791, the British government concluded that representative government couldn't work in a culturally divided society, so it decided to partition the territory. Most of the new English-speaking inhabitants of Quebec lived in the west along the north shore of Lake Ontario, while the French continued to live along the shores of the St. Lawrence River. The Constitution Act 1791 established two new provinces: Upper Canada and Lower Canada, which (roughly) correspond to what we now call Ontario and Quebec, respectively. However, the division was not perfect: There were some French Canadians in Upper Canada and some English Canadians in Lower Canada. But each minority was small, especially in Upper Canada. The British consequently felt comfortable introducing the institutions of representative government in each province.

The Constitution Act 1791 worked well until the 1830s, when there were rebellions in both Upper and Lower Canada. The rebellion in Upper Canada was led by William Lyon Mackenzie, while the rebellion in Lower Canada was led by Louis-Joseph Papineau. The Upper Canada rebellion is perhaps the most pathetic rebellion in the history of the world—the rebels dropped their guns and ran as soon as the British army showed up. The main battle in Toronto reportedly lasted less than an hour. In Lower Canada, the rebels stayed around long enough to fire a few shots, but the British army had no trouble quashing the rebellion in short order. Nevertheless, the British government was not pleased with these disturbances, and they dispatched a man named Lord Durham to investigate the political situation in the two Canadas.

Lord Durham's report on Canada is brilliant and deeply frustrating. Durham concluded that the rebellion in Upper Canada was the result of a flawed political system. In the British system of government, the governor is supposed to follow the advice provided by his ministers in the legislature, but this was not happening in Upper Canada. The governors sent over from Britain were small-time aristocrats (big-time aristocrats got better appointments). When the governors arrived in Toronto, they were typically pulled aside by the leading members of Upper Canadian society, the so-called "Family Compact," and given the lowdown on the political situation in the province. This was completely unacceptable, in Durham's opinion. He thus recommended that governors be mandated to accept the advice proffered by the ministers in the legislature. In other words, Durham recommended that Upper Canada be given **responsible government**.

responsible government The Canadian system of government (inherited from Great Britain) in which ministers are responsible to Parliament and the Crown.

When Durham turned his attention to Lower Canada, he could easily have made the same analysis. Governors in Lower Canada were equally under the spell of the local elite, the so-called *Château Clique*, but unfortunately Durham got distracted by the tense relations between the English- and French-speaking inhabitants in the province. In Lower Canada, Durham reported:

> I expected to find a contest between a government and a people: I found two nations warring in the bosom of a single state: I found a struggle, not of principles, but of races; and I perceived that it would be idle to attempt any amelioration of laws or institutions until we could first succeed in terminating the deadly animosity that now separates the inhabitants of Lower Canada into the hostile divisions of French and English.[3]

Durham therefore argued that a divided country cannot have representative institutions. So what do you do when you have two distinct communities living in the same space? Another partition of Quebec was not possible. For Lord Durham, there were only two solutions: Either forget about representative government and have authoritarian rule, or eliminate one of the communities. Durham was adamant that authoritarian rule was not the British way, so he set about concocting a plan to eliminate the national division of Lower Canada. Durham foresaw (correctly) that North America was destined to be an English-speaking continent, so he concluded that the French community in Lower Canada had to disappear. Fortunately, he did not advocate genocide, but he did insist that the people of Lower Canada had to become English. In short, Durham advocated a vigorous policy of assimilation (see Box 8.1). Needless to say, Lord Durham may be the most unpopular person in Quebec history. Nevertheless, the British government accepted his recommendations, as we will discuss momentarily.

In sum, Lord Durham is a very polarizing figure with a mixed legacy. On the one hand, he can reasonably be accused of advocating cultural genocide; on the other hand, Canadian democracy rests of the shoulders of Lord Durham because his report led directly to the

Box 8.1

Lord Durham's Plan for Constitutional Peace in Canada

A plan by which it is proposed to ensure the tranquil government of Lower Canada, must include in itself the means of putting an end to the agitation of national disputes in the legislature, by settling, at once and for ever, the national character of the Province. I entertain no doubts as to the national character which must be given to Lower Canada: it must be that of the British Empire; that of the majority race which must, in the lapse of no long period of time, be predominant over the whole North American continent. Without effecting the change so rapidly or so roughly as to shock the feelings and trample on the welfare of the existing generation, it must henceforth be the first and steady purpose of the British Government to establish an English population, with English laws and language, in this Province, and to trust its government to none but a decidedly English legislature.

Lord Durham, *Lord Durham's Report: An Abridgement of Report on the Affairs of British North America*, ed. Gerald M. Craig (Toronto, ON: McClelland and Stewart, 1963), 146.

introduction of responsible government in British North America, although it took a few years to be realized. We thus owe Lord Durham a huge debt of gratitude, but we cannot embrace him fully as a founder of modern Canada.

Act of Union, 1840   The British government attempted to realize Lord Durham's policy of assimilation with the Act of Union in 1840. Under this scheme, the provinces of Upper and Lower Canada were joined together as the United Provinces or simply the Province of Canada. The two sections were granted an equal number of representatives in the new legislature, even though the population of Lower Canada was much larger. In short, the scheme was undemocratic, but this was precisely the point: The objective was to establish a legislature in which a majority of the representatives were English speaking. Since there was a sizable English-speaking minority in Lower Canada (or Canada East, as it became known after the Act of Union), it was assumed that some of the representatives from that section would in fact be English and would unite with the English majority in Upper Canada (which became known as Canada West). In this fashion, so the thinking went, the French would have no choice but to assimilate.

The Act of Union failed in its bid to assimilate the French Canadians. On the contrary, the French representatives from Canada East remained French, and of course Canada East continued to be a French-speaking society. Furthermore, the legislature became wholly dependent on French–English cooperation. In fact, most legislation required majority support from both sections. This was not a legal requirement under the Act of Union—indeed it was contrary to its intended purpose. But out of necessity, a kind of informal consociationalism emerged, although it was highly unstable. The legislative process was also complicated by the various political factions in the legislature. In highly simplistic terms, the Tory–*Bleus* coalition and the Grit–*Rouges* coalition cancelled each other out, and the result was gridlock. A ministry would take office, govern for a while, and then lose the confidence of the legislature. The opposition would then form a ministry, govern for a while, and then lose the confidence of the legislature. An election would then be called, and the cycle would begin anew.

While it was clear by the late 1850s that the Canadian political system had to be redesigned, it took another decade to figure out a new constitutional arrangement. That arrangement, as we know, was the British North America Act. The new arrangement included New Brunswick and Nova Scotia, but the principal storyline of Confederation was the long struggle to accommodate both French- and English-speaking peoples. By 1867, the English outnumbered the French in the Province of Canada, and political leaders in Canada West like George Brown were adamant that the new constitution had to be placed firmly on the principle of "representation by population." That of course would leave French Canadians completely subject to the political whims of the English-speaking majority. French

Canadians could thus only accept representation by population if there were significant safeguards for the French minority. The solution was federalism.

Here's how the great constitutional scholar Peter Russell has characterized the bargain of Confederation:

> At its core was a recognition that if English Canadians and French Canadians were to continue to share a single state, the English majority could control the general or common government so long as the French were a majority in a province with exclusive jurisdiction over those matters essential to their distinct culture.[4]

For Quebec, the *sine qua non*—the indispensable condition—of Confederation was the promise that the provinces would possess *exclusive jurisdiction* in the areas assigned to them by the constitution. When this appeared to be threatened in the twentieth century, many Quebecers began to reconsider their commitment to Canada.

The British North America Act, 1867   The BNA Act has governed Canada since 1867 (as discussed in Chapter 7). It was the first constitution *for* Canada written *by* Canadians. This might explain why it has been so much more successful than previous constitutional arrangements. The BNA Act, however, did not make Canada an independent country. While the constitution was drafted by the Fathers of Confederation here in Canada, the BNA Act was a statutory law of the British Parliament. With the BNA Act, Canada continued to live under the monarchy, the final court of appeal for Canadian legal cases remained in Britain, and the Canadian constitution could only be amended by the British Parliament. This is precisely how the Fathers of Confederation—at least the English-speaking ones—wanted it. They believed that Canadians would forever want to be a part of the British Empire. Sir John A. Macdonald proudly declared, "A British subject I was born—a British subject I shall die."

For a long time after Confederation, Canadians were happy to be a part of the British Empire—so much so that when World War I erupted in 1914 many (English-speaking) Canadians rushed to the defence of the Mother Country. A strange thing happened, though, when they landed on the other side of the Atlantic: The British said, "Jolly good, the Canadians are here!" It was quite a shock for these young men. They weren't Canadians; Canadians spoke *French*. In their minds, they were *British* North Americans, but the British did not recognize them as such. And in due course, these young men from Canada began to realize that they were not in fact British; for the first time, English-speaking people in Canada began to think of themselves as *Canadians*.

As part of the British Empire, Canada was legally required to participate in World War I on behalf of Great Britain, and our country paid a terrible price: More than 65 000 men lost their lives (about 1 percent of the Canadian population) and another 150 000 were wounded. The social fabric of Canada was also deeply strained by the war. English-speaking Canadians were, at least initially, enthusiastic supporters of the war effort, while French Canadians were generally ambivalent. The war lasted much longer than anticipated, and the army was soon in need of more soldiers. So in 1917 Conservative Prime Minister Robert Borden introduced conscription. As most English-speaking men had already volunteered, conscription ended up pressing French Canadian men into the war against their will. This was immensely unpopular in Quebec, and it forever damaged the Conservative Party in that province. Since the war, Quebec has only twice elected large numbers of Conservatives: under John Diefenbaker in 1958 and under Brian Mulroney in the 1980s.

The war had additional impacts on Canada, psychologically, sociologically, and politically. When the war ended on November 11, 1918, it was clear to most Canadians that Canada would have to extricate itself from the British Empire and become truly independent. The British were willing to let Canada take back—or patriate—its constitution and become an independent state, but Canada was in fact not ready to receive its own constitution, for reasons that will be explained soon. Canada thus gained its independence incrementally. In 1931, the British government enacted the **Statute of Westminster**, which gave Canada independence in foreign affairs. Canada would thus never again be dragged into a war against its will. And in 1949 Canada was permitted to abolish appeals to the Judicial Committee of the Privy Council. Henceforth the Supreme Court of Canada would be truly *supreme* in all legal matters. Canada, however, did not become fully independent until 1982, when the BNA Act was brought back to Canada. In other words, it took Canada more than 60 years from the end of World War I to claim its independence. There were many challenges on the long road to patriation, not least of which was the social and political transformation of Quebec in the twentieth century.

Statute of Westminster A law passed by the British Parliament in 1931 that granted the dominions in the British Empire control over their own foreign affairs.

The Transformation of Quebec

The challenge of governing a society with deep cultural divisions has been the central theme in Canada's long constitutional odyssey. In the twentieth century, the challenge was complicated by the shifting identities in each of Canada's founding nations. We have already discussed how World War I transformed British North Americans into Canadians. In response, the original Canadians—*les Canadiens*—also went through a process of redefinition. If *les anglais* were now Canadians, many *Canadiens* wondered, "*qui sommes-nous?*" ("Who are we?") Their initial answer to that question was "we are *French* Canadians." But it soon became painfully obvious that most French Canadians lived in Quebec, and in short order a new *Québécois* identity emerged and effectively displaced the French Canadian identity. By the 1960s, many Québécois had come to believe that it was time for Quebec to separate from Canada. The emergence of a separatist movement in Quebec plunged Canada into a deep constitutional crisis.

Maurice Duplessis and *les années noires*

Starting in the 1930s, Quebec politics was dominated by one man for 30 years: Maurice Duplessis. He founded and led a party called the *Union Nationale*. He was first elected premier in 1936 but lost the election in 1940. He was re-elected in 1944, and then ruled the province with an iron fist until his death in 1959—a time remembered in Quebec as *les années noires* ("the dark years"). Duplessis was deeply conservative and an arch nationalist. He was not a separatist, but he quickly found himself on a collision course with the federal government. After World War II, as discussed in the last chapter, the Government of Canada was determined to create a comprehensive welfare state, and it outlined its plans for health care, pensions, and social security in a series of documents known as the Green Books. In August 1945 the federal government presented its plans to the provinces at the Dominion–Provincial Conference on Reconstruction. Duplessis was horrified by what he heard. He said wryly, "the appetite of the Federal Government has increased. This is not a good sign."[5]

Duplessis was not alone at the conference. He received strong support from the premiers of Ontario and Alberta. The conference ended in failure, but the federal government proceeded to establish the welfare state piecemeal over the ensuing decades. Duplessis vigorously opposed the federal government each step of the way. In 1953 he established a Royal Commission of Inquiry on Constitutional Problems, chaired by retired judge Thomas Tremblay. Duplessis was not expecting much from the commission; he just wanted some ammunition to use in his war with the federal government. But the commission deliberated for three years and delivered a monumental report on the state of Quebec and its position in Canada. The Tremblay report was grounded in an old-world Catholic view of society, and it painted a picture of Quebec as a quaint pastoral and church-abiding society.

classical federalism The theory that each order of the government in the federation is legally equal and should each operate independently of the others.

The Tremblay Commission   Tremblay's report was premised on the theory of **classical federalism**. He defined federalism as an "association between states in which the exercise of state power is shared between two orders of government, coordinate but not subordinate one to the other, each enjoying supreme power within the sphere of activity assigned to it by the constitution."[6] Of course, a jurisdiction cannot enjoy its power without adequate fiscal resources. For Tremblay, this was the key problem with Canadian federalism: "The provinces long ago won their autonomy on the political and juridical plane," he wrote, but they have "never enjoyed a sound financial and fiscal basis."[7] In fact, Tremblay asserted, the situation had grown worse since the 1930s. He argued, accurately, that the federal government had assumed a dominant fiscal position in Canada as a result of World War II and the Great Depression. And, of course, the federal government did not relinquish its dominant fiscal position after the war because it required huge resources to finance the new welfare state.

Tremblay was opposed to the new federal social policies for two reasons. First, he opposed state welfare on philosophical grounds. Social assistance, he believed, should be provided by the church and other charities. Second, he insisted that these new policies were matters of provincial jurisdiction:

> As for social policy, it seems to us that, in a federation composed of elements which are heterogeneous, from the cultural and religious point of view, it should not depend on the central authority. The Fathers of Confederation understood this perfectly well and it is, perhaps, on this point that the centralization policy of recent years has sabotaged their work most cruelly.[8]

While Tremblay was deeply distressed by the rise of the federal government's welfare program, he retained a faith in the ability of federalism to reconcile Canada's deep diversity. Tremblay's report, however, had no impact on the rest of Canada. On the contrary, the conflict between the governments of Canada and Quebec deepened *after* the death of Duplessis in 1959.

Jean Lesage and the Quiet Revolution

Quiet Revolution The transformation of Quebec from a deeply conservative society to a progressively liberal society in the 1960s.

In the 1960 provincial election, the Quebec Liberal Party came to power under the leadership of Jean Lesage. At the same time, Quebec experienced a profound social transformation that quickly became known as the **Quiet Revolution**, as discussed in Chapter 2. As Quebec became much more liberal, it also became more nationalist. Indeed, such a feeling of confidence emerged in Quebec that many people started believing that Quebec could be an independent country. While Lesage was not a separatist, the separatist movement in Quebec took off under his watch, as we will discuss shortly. With the separatist movement bubbling in the background, Lesage felt tremendous pressure to defend Quebec just as vigorously as Duplessis had done.

Jean Lesage, unlike Duplessis, was a strong supporter of the welfare state, but he wanted Quebec to create its *own* welfare state. Thus, like Duplessis, Lesage found himself on a collision course with the federal government. First, in order to finance his social programs Lesage needed to increase taxes, but the federal government was occupying the lion's share of the major tax fields, especially personal and corporate income taxes. Second, in order to create a comprehensive welfare state in Quebec, he argued that Quebec needed more constitutional powers. In other words, he wanted powers to be transferred from the list of federal powers in Section 91 of the BNA Act to the list of provincial powers in Section 92. If the federal government did not want to relinquish powers to all the provinces, Lesage indicated that Quebec would require a special constitutional status that would give it more powers than the other provinces. This is known as **asymmetrical federalism**. Unsurprisingly, the federal government and the other provinces did not embrace this idea. In sum, under Lesage, two expanding states—the federal government and Quebec—collided.

asymmetrical federalism A type of federalism in which the provinces exercise different powers.

Conditional Grants and the Federal Spending Power

For Duplessis and Lesage, the main issue in their battle with Ottawa was the federal government's use of conditional grants to establish shared-cost social programs. Soon after he became premier, Jean Lesage stated bluntly that conditional grants (federal transfer payments to the provinces to support provincial programs) were "absolutely unacceptable to Quebec."[9] In his view, the federal government was unconstitutionally spending money in areas of provincial jurisdiction. In response, the federal government argued that the constitution empowers it to raise revenue "by any mode or system of taxation," and thus it correspondingly has an unlimited **spending power**. However, the term *spending power* is not found in the constitution; it was defined unilaterally by the federal government as "the power of Parliament to make payments to people or institutions or governments for purposes on which it (Parliament) does not necessarily have the power to legislate."[10] This means that Parliament can spend money on something even if it cannot make legislation on that very same thing. For example, Parliament does not have the authority to create a national health care system through legislation, but it claims the right to spend money on health care.

Quebec has never accepted the federal government's position on the spending power, and it maintains that conditional grants are unconstitutional. Constitutional experts are divided on the matter, often along linguistic lines. The Supreme Court has indicated that the federal power to spend is wider than its power to legislate, but in my view it has not provided a definitive ruling on spending power. While the matter could be settled by a reference case, it is doubtful that any government wants to have a definitive answer because the stakes are too high: If the federal government lost the case, its ability to support social programs across the country would be undermined; if Quebec lost, its ability to set social policy in the province would be compromised.

Opting Out of Shared-Cost Programs

The federal spending power may or may not be constitutional, but in some respects it doesn't matter: It is a political problem. Ultimately, in 1965, the federal government agreed to allow Quebec (or any other province) to **opt out** of national shared-cost programs. Quebec immediately opted out of 29 programs, most notably hospital insurance. Opting out, however, is not a free pass. The federal government will only allow a province to opt out of a national program if it agrees to establish a comparable program with similar standards. In exchange, the opting out province will receive financial compensation from the federal government, either in the form of cash transfers or tax points. Opting out was a hollow victory; Quebec gained administrative responsibility for its social programs, but federal support for these programs was just as conditional as conditional grants. Thus, as far as Quebec is concerned, the issue of the spending power remains unresolved.

For many Quebecers, the spending power threatens Quebec's existence as a nation. It has thus been vigorously opposed by every political party in Quebec. For Quebec, the power to "exclusively make laws" in relation to all the matters enumerated in Section 92 was the *sine qua non*—the indispensable condition—of Confederation. From this perspective, the spending power breaks the federal bargain of 1867, thereby releasing Quebec from the obligations of the contract; in other words, it gives Quebec the right to separate from Canada. On the other hand, the spending power has built all the social programs that Canadians outside Quebec cherish. Indeed, many of these social programs, especially health care, are now at the core of our national identity. In sum, the federal spending power may be viewed as both an instrument of nation-building and nation-destroying.[11]

René Lévesque and the Rise of the Parti Québécois

In June 1966, Jean Lesage called a snap election and lost. The election was won by the Union Nationale, but it was the last victory for the party of Duplessis. Within two years, Quebec politics was transformed by the emergence of a new political party: the separatist

spending power The ability of the federal government to spend monies on programs and services that are outside its jurisdiction.

opt out The ability of provincial governments to remove themselves from national shared-cost programs and receive compensation from the federal government. However, provincial governments must still establish comparable programs with similar standards.

Parti Québécois (PQ). The new party was led by René Lévesque, who had been a star in the government of Jean Lesage (see Box 8.2). Lévesque said that he entered politics in 1960 to fight against "duplessism," but in government he became troubled by Quebec's confrontations with Ottawa. At first, he believed that Quebec's interests could best be served by insisting on the autonomy granted to the provinces under Section 92 of the constitution, but within a few years he came to believe that Quebec was "stifling within the framework of an old, obsolete federation." The federal government, he said, "was growing out of all proportion."[12] Thus, he concluded, "we must rid ourselves completely of a completely obsolete federal regime. And begin anew. . . . This means that Quebec must become sovereign as soon as possible."[13] When he failed to persuade the Quebec Liberal Party to adopt a separatist agenda, he decided to form the Parti Québécois.

After leaving the Liberal Party, Lévesque outlined his ideas for a new relationship between Quebec and the rest of Canada. On the one hand, he argued that Quebec should become completely independent and assume "complete mastery of every last area of basic collective decision-making."[14] On the other hand, he suggested, "there is no reason why we, as future neighbours, should not voluntarily remain associates and partners in a common enterprise."[15] Thus, he proposed, "Quebec should lay a project for association which would include: a monetary

The Life and Times of René Lévesque (1922–1987)

Pierre Roussel iPhoto Inc./Newscom

René Lévesque

René Lévesque was born in northern New Brunswick and raised in the Gaspé region of Quebec. He quit law school to become a journalist. He worked as a correspondent in Europe at the end of World War II, and he was with American troops when they liberated the survivors at the horrific Dachau concentration camp—the first such camp created by the Nazis. He was also a correspondent during the war in Korea.

Later, in the 1950s, he became the host of a very popular television news show in Quebec. He was consequently a household name when he entered politics in 1960s with Jean Lesage's Liberal team. As the Minister of Natural Resources, Lévesque modernized Quebec's hydroelectric system. Today, Hydro Québec is one of the world's largest producers of hydroelectricity.

After the defeat of the Liberal Party in 1966, Lévesque formed the Parti Québécois. The first-past-the-post electoral system was initially unkind to the new party. The party won 24 and 30 percent of the vote in the 1970 and 1973 elections, but only won seven seats and six seats, respectively. But in the 1976 election, the PQ stormed to victory. Lévesque led the party to victory again in 1981, but he was forced to resign in 1985 when his behaviour grew increasingly erratic and his commitment to sovereignty seemingly waned. Lévesque was a chainsmoker and prone to wearing rumpled suits, but he was flawlessly bilingual and extremely charming. Quebecers found him highly endearing. Indeed, he is regarded as the father of modern Quebec.

union and a common market, along with their logical complement, the co-ordination of fiscal policies."[16] In this fashion, he argued in conclusion, "we propose a system that would allow our two majorities to extricate themselves from an archaic federal framework in which our two very distinctive personalities paralyse each other by dint of pretending to have a third personality common to both."[17] In sum, Lévesque envisioned a new political arrangement between Quebec and the rest of Canada that he called **sovereignty-association**. Rather than a *federal* constitution in which two orders of government *share* sovereignty, Lévesque was calling for a *confederal* constitution in which two sovereign governments would collaborate on matters of mutual interest. While many Canadians outside Quebec have difficulty wrapping their minds around the idea of sovereignty-association, it is a perfectly legitimate model for governing a society with deep cultural divisions. However, it is clear that the emergence of the Parti Québécois deepened Canada's constitutional crisis considerably.

sovereignty-association The proposal made by René Lévesque for a new constitutional arrangement between Quebec and Canada, where Quebec would receive more powers and jurisdiction but would still be loosely affiliated with Canada.

Mega-Constitutional Politics and the Challenge of Patriation

The desire to take possession of our own constitution and become truly independent of Great Britain set in after World War I, but the patriation of the constitution proved to be more difficult than anyone imagined. Why did it take so long? Every constitution requires an **amending formula**, or a process for amendments after it has been enacted. As a statute of the British Parliament, the BNA Act could only be changed by the British Parliament. If Canada were going to be a truly independent country, a procedure would have to be established that would allow Canadians to change the constitution themselves. So, before the BNA Act could come back to Canada, Canadians had to concoct an amending formula. And therein lay the challenge: Canadians could not agree on how future constitutional changes should be made. This may sound like a mere technicality, but it was actually an enormously complex problem.

amending formula The procedure used to amend a constitution. Before patriation, Canada did not have its own amending formula but instead relied on the British Parliament for constitutional amendments.

Let's think about this for a minute: Who should have a say in changing the Canadian constitution? Clearly, the Parliament of Canada—the political embodiment of the country—should be included. Should anyone else have a say? Since Canada has a federal constitution, one assumes that the provinces should have something to say about constitutional amendments. But if all 10 provinces were required to consent to each and every amendment, the constitution would probably never be changed. So if unanimous provincial consent would make the amending formula too rigid, how many provinces should be on board to make a constitutional amendment? A majority of provinces, you say? Perhaps, but let's remember that the six smallest provinces—the four Atlantic provinces plus Manitoba and Saskatchewan—account for only 14 percent of the Canadian population. That would not be democratic. But we don't want to proceed simply on majority rule. That would mean that the four largest provinces, with 86 percent of the population, could dictate constitutional changes over a majority of provinces. So we need to devise an amending formula that balances the principles of both federalism and democracy. And what about the province *unlike* the others? Should the English-speaking provinces be allowed to change the constitution over the objections of the one province with a French-speaking majority? That of course would raise the spectre of assimilation. Finally, what about the people? Should we get a say? Now you can see why it took more than 60 years to patriate the constitution!

The effort to patriate the constitution opened up an existential debate about who we were as a people. This is what Peter Russell calls **mega-constitutional politics**. In Russell's words

> mega-constitutional politics goes beyond disputing the merits of specific constitutional proposals and addresses the very nature of the political community on which the constitution is based. Mega-constitutional politics . . . is concerned with reaching agreement on the identity and fundamental principles of the body politic.[18]

A constitution must necessarily rest on a definition of the people. With the rise of Quebec nationalism in the 1960s, Canadians began to wonder if they even constituted a single people anymore. This presented an enormous obstacle to the patriation of the constitution: If Canadians did not *constitute* a single people, it was going to be very difficult to draft a *constitution* for Canada.

So who are we? What is Canada all about? Canadians, in fact, have been asking these questions since Confederation because the governments of Canada needed to know the answers to determine how the federation would work, how the constitution would be interpreted by the courts, and how changes to the constitution would be settled (before making the formal request to the British Parliament for amendments to the BNA Act). Shortly after 1867, two major interpretations of Confederation emerged, both of which are known as the **compact theory**. Both versions of the theory posit that the BNA Act was a legal contract between consenting parties. The implication is that the contract cannot be changed without the consent of both parties. In the first version of the theory, the provinces are considered to be the consenting parties. The provincial compact theory originated in Quebec, but it was quickly embraced by the other provinces, especially Ontario. The second version of the theory suggests that Confederation was a compact between English- and French-speaking peoples; this is known as the **two nations thesis**. In this version of the theory, the English nation is not well defined, but the implication of the theory is clear: Both nations must consent to any amendment of the constitution. Since Quebec is the homeland of the French nation in Canada, Quebec's consent is required for all constitutional amendments.

We must also consider a third interpretation of Confederation. Recall the structure of Canada's Parliament: The House of Commons is based on representation by population, while the Senate gives representation to the different regions of Canada: the Maritimes, Quebec, Ontario, and the West each have 24 seats in the Senate (and Newfoundland and Labrador received six seats, while each territory has one). The Senate thus appears to institutionalize the notion that Canada is a country of regions, and it has been suggested that this could provide the basis for Canada's constitutional amending formula. This idea, however, has never been popular with those who favour the provincial compact theory because it does not treat all of the provinces equally. Two provinces, Ontario and Quebec, would each acquire a veto over constitutional change, while the Western and Atlantic provinces would be lumped together with only one a collective veto.

In sum, after Confederation there were a number of interpretations as to what the constitution represented: Was it a compact of nations? Was it a compact of provinces? Or was Canada a country of regions? No one ever suggested that the BNA Act rested on the sovereignty of the people—that would have been far too American for Canada. "Historians have had no difficulty in showing that, in a strict legal sense, Confederation could not have been a contract because, in 1867, neither the original provinces nor their people had sovereign legal power."[19] But historical accuracy is not the issue here. Every country needs a foundational myth to know how its constitution will work. As long as Canada's constitution remained a legal statute of the British Parliament, Canadians did not need to reach a consensus on the country's foundational myth. It only became imperative when we decided to bring the constitution home.

Pierre Elliott Trudeau and the Patriation of the Constitution

Pierre Elliott Trudeau was unlike any politician Canada had ever seen before. He was a suave intellectual from Montreal who spoke both French and English eloquently. He was personally recruited to enter politics by Prime Minister Lester Pearson. After his election to the House of Commons in 1965, Pearson appointed him as his parliamentary secretary. Trudeau instantly became Canada's most eligible bachelor (see Box 8.3). He was often seen

compact theory Two separate but related interpretations of the origins of the Canadian constitution. The first compact theory states that Canada was a creation of all of the provinces in the form of a contract. The second compact theory states that Canada was a creation of two peoples—English and French.

two nations thesis The second compact theory, which states Canada was a creation of two peoples—English and French.

driving around Ottawa in his immaculate 1957 Mercedes-Benz convertible wearing his trademark rose boutonniere in his lapel.

In 1967, Pearson appointed Trudeau to the cabinet as his Minister of Justice. In this capacity, Trudeau set about revising the Criminal Code. Although Trudeau was a devout Catholic, he introduced legislation to legalize abortion and contraception and to decriminalize homosexual acts between consenting adults. In defence of this historic legislation, he famously quipped, "there's no place for the state in the bedrooms of the nation." In 1968, Trudeau was elected as leader of the Liberal Party, and in the general election a few months later the party swept to victory on a wave of Trudeaumania.

Trudeau was a constitutional lawyer by training, and he had entered politics with the express goal of resolving Canada's constitutional predicament and thwarting Quebec separatism once and for all. And he had some very definite ideas about what needed to be done. First, he argued that Canada had to be a bilingual country. To this end, he introduced the Official Languages Act in 1969. Many Canadians, especially in Western Canada, were hostile to the idea of official bilingualism, but Trudeau maintained that bilingualism was necessary for Quebecers to feel at home in their own country—this was the price that Canadians outside Quebec would have to pay for national unity. It should be stressed that the Official Languages Act has a very narrow mandate. It means only that Canadians should be able to communicate with the Government of Canada in either English or French; it does not require any of the provinces to be bilingual (New Brunswick is the only officially bilingual province). French is the official language of Quebec, while all the other provinces operate only in English (although many offer selective services in French as well as other languages). And, of course, the act does not require individual Canadians to be bilingual.

Box 8.3

The Life and Times of Pierre Elliott Trudeau (1919–2000)

© Christopher J. Morris/CORBIS

Pierre Elliott Trudeau

Many young hearts were broken in March 1971, when 51-year-old Pierre Elliott

Trudeau married Margaret Sinclair, who was just 22 years old. They had three children together, Justin, Alexandre, and Michel, but within a few years their marriage spectacularly fell apart before the eyes of the nation. When Trudeau was fighting the election campaign in 1979, Margaret was spotted by the paparazzi dancing in New York's famous Studio 54 disco and partying with the Rolling Stones. Trudeau never married again, but much later in life he fathered a daughter, Sarah Coyne, who was born in 1991. Tragically, his son Michel was killed in 1998 when an avalanche swept him into Kokanee Lake in the interior of British Columbia; his body was never recovered. Trudeau was emotionally devastated by the death of his 23-year-old son, and he died just two years later. Millions of people watched the state funeral broadcast from Montreal's Notre-Dame Basilica. His son Justin, who is now the leader of the Liberal Party of Canada, gave a very moving eulogy.

Trudeau was equally adamant that Quebec would have to pay a price for constitutional peace: Quebec had to be a province like all the others. Many Quebec nationalists reacted negatively to this proposition because while they considered bilingualism to be necessary, it was not sufficient. Quebec is the only French-speaking jurisdiction in North America; if the province was going to stave off the threat of assimilation and remain a French-speaking society it would require a *statut particulier*—special constitutional status and powers. In Trudeau's view, special status for Quebec would violate the cardinal liberal principle of equality because it would create two kinds of citizenship: one for Quebecers and one for all other Canadians. Furthermore, he maintained, Quebec did not need special powers to protect the French language, because the Government of Canada was now completely committed to protecting the French language for all Francophone Canadians—those in Quebec and those living outside Quebec. If Trudeau's commitment to official bilingualism was a tough sell outside Quebec, his refusal to entertain special status for Quebec was an even harder sell in his home province.

Finally, Trudeau believed that Canada should have a bill of rights. Trudeau was a liberal in the philosophical and political sense of the term, and liberals believe in liberty, especially individual freedom. For liberals, the greatest threat to individual freedom is the immense power of the state—the combined forces of the federal and provincial governments. The state has identified us all with a number (our social insurance number), it knows where we live, who we are married to, how many kids we have, and how much money we make. It knows when we go to the doctor and what we were treated for. It knows when we get on an airplane, and it knows how many times we leave and re-enter the country. The state has vast investigative powers, including the police, immigration officials, border security, and tax inspectors. The state possesses a complete monopoly on coercive violence, and of course it makes all the laws and appoints all the judges.

Trudeau wanted to place some limits on the power of Parliament to better protect the rights of individuals. With a bill of rights, the rights of Canadians would be entrenched in the constitution. In other words, our rights would be put beyond the reach of Parliament. If Parliament enacted a law that compromised our rights, the courts would have the power to strike it down. Trudeau did not invent this idea. The Americans adopted a Bill of Rights in 1791, just two years after the ratification of their constitution. A bill of rights, however, was a novel concept in the British system of parliamentary government. Trudeau hoped that a bill of rights in Canada would do more than just secure the rights of the people; it was a key element in his plan for national unity. Trudeau wanted to break down our linguistic and regional identities and wanted Canadians to start thinking of themselves as rights-bearing citizens rather than as English or French, Westerners or Maritimers. In short, he wanted to establish a single Canadian identity and remake Canada. It was a bold undertaking, and it could only be contemplated by someone with Trudeau's massive intellect, charisma, and—to be frank—arrogance.

One final important policy the Trudeau government enacted was the **official policy on multiculturalism** in 1971. This, in my view, was not part of Trudeau's core constitutional vision, but rather was a response to Canadians not of English or French heritage that wanted some kind of official recognition after the adoption of bilingualism. It proved to be an expedient policy for the Liberal Party, which won considerable favour among immigrant voters for more than a generation.

official policy on multiculturalism A policy adopted by the Liberal Party of Canada in 1971 that declared Canada to be a bilingual and multicultural country.

The October Crisis

Front de libération du Québec (FLQ) A Quebec-based terrorist group that sought to establish an independent, socialist Quebec through an armed struggle.

Trudeau was a highly enigmatic figure, and he was sometimes contradictory. In October 1970, just two years after coming to power, Trudeau faced the biggest political crisis of his career when members of the **Front de libération du Québec (FLQ)**—a militant nationalist group—kidnapped a British diplomat and a minister of the Quebec government named Pierre

Box 8.4

Just Watch Him

Watch Pierre Trudeau's famous debate with a journalist on the War Measures Act on the front steps of Parliament:

www.cbc.ca/archives/categories/politics/civil-unrest/the-october-crisis-civil-liberties-suspended/just-watch-me.html

Laporte. The British diplomat was eventually rescued, but Laporte was murdered. Quebec Premier Robert Bourassa asked Prime Minister Trudeau to send the army into Quebec to restore order. Trudeau responded by imposing the **War Measures Act**, which suspended civil liberties in Canada. The press was not free, the police had enhanced powers to arrest and detain suspects, and the army patrolled the streets of Ottawa and Montreal. When asked by a journalist what else he might do to contain the crisis, Trudeau famously responded, "just watch me" (see Box 8.4). Canadians were gripped with fear, and most people wholeheartedly supported Trudeau's draconian measures. Only NDP leader Tommy Douglas had the courage to speak out against the War Measures Act. "The government," he said in the House of Commons, "is using a sledgehammer to crack a peanut." The **October Crisis** finally came to an end when the kidnappers surrendered in exchange for free passage to Cuba.

So what are we to make of Trudeau? The great advocate of civil liberties is also responsible for the greatest suspension of civil liberties in Canada during peace time. Perhaps Trudeau was just a hypocrite, or maybe the October Crisis reinforced his view that the power of the state needed to be limited by a bill of rights.

War Measures Act An act of Parliament that was invoked during wartime that curtailed civil liberties. It was invoked during the October Crisis in response to the kidnappings and bombings conducted by the FLQ. It has since been replaced with the Emergencies Act.

October Crisis A series of events that occurred in 1970 when the FLQ kidnapped a British diplomat and a Québec cabinet minister. The War Measures Act was invoked in response and lasted for the duration of the crisis.

The Victoria Agreement

In June 1971, at a meeting in Victoria, Pierre Trudeau reached an agreement with all of the provinces, including Quebec, to patriate the constitution. The agreement included an amending formula and a limited bill of rights. And, at Quebec's request, the agreement included some new powers for the provinces. The amending formula was premised on the regional view of Canada, as reflected in the Senate. Constitutional amendments under the Victoria formula need to obtain the consent of the federal Parliament, Ontario, Quebec, two of the four Atlantic provinces, and two of the four Western provinces representing 50 percent of the population. This formula seemed to touch all the bases: it was democratic because it required the support of a majority of the population, it also required the consent of a majority of provinces, and it gave Quebec a veto over constitutional change. When Premier Bourassa returned home, he quickly discovered that the agreement would not fly because it did not give Quebec special constitutional status. Bourassa thus withdrew his support for the agreement, and yet again Canada failed to bring its constitution home.

The First Quebec Referendum on Sovereignty

After the failure of the Victoria Agreement, Canada's constitutional crisis deepened. In November 1976, the Parti Québécois was elected and René Lévesque became the premier of Quebec. For the first time, Quebec was governed by a separatist party. The PQ was a thoroughly democratic party, and it was committed to achieving independence through the ballot box. The referendum was held in May 1980. The question, however, was rather convoluted. Rather than ask for independence outright, which surely would have failed, the PQ asked the people of Quebec to give it a "mandate" to negotiate "sovereignty-association" with Canada, to be followed by a second referendum to ratify the agreement. Nevertheless, it was interpreted by most people to be a vote on separation. On the eve of the referendum, Pierre Trudeau gave a powerful speech in Montreal, in which he stated emphatically

> the Government of Canada and all the provincial governments have made themselves perfectly clear. If the answer to the referendum question is NO, we have all said that this NO will be interpreted as a mandate to change the Constitution, to renew federalism. . . . I can make a most solemn commitment that following a NO vote, we will immediately take action to renew the Constitution and we will not stop until we have done that.[20]

Many people believe that Pierre Trudeau saved Canada that night. On referendum day, 60 percent of the people of Quebec voted no, and 40 percent voted yes. René Lévesque was gracious in defeat, and Pierre Trudeau was magnanimous in victory. While the referendum was defeated decisively, Trudeau recognized that a large number of Quebecers—including a slim majority of Francophone voters—had turned their backs on Canada. This was not a fact to be celebrated. On the contrary, it revealed the depths of Canada's constitutional crisis.

The Final Push toward Patriation and the Constitution Act 1982

Within weeks of the referendum, Trudeau invited the premiers to Ottawa to start negotiations on the constitution. Many of the premiers, however, did not seem to share Trudeau's sense of urgency. Only Ontario and New Brunswick supported Trudeau, while seven provinces lined up against him. After losing his referendum René Lévesque was politically isolated, but ultimately he joined forces with the group of provinces opposing Trudeau. This group became known as the **Gang of Eight**. When the Gang of Eight refused to cooperate with Trudeau, he threatened to go to Britain and get the constitution himself. The Gang of Eight insisted that the Government of Canada did not have the authority to patriate the constitution unilaterally. The battle to patriate the constitution proved to be epic and, in particular, the conflict between Trudeau and Lévesque is now a part of Canada's political mythology.

Gang of Eight The premiers of eight provinces that opposed Prime Minister Trudeau's plan to patriate the constitution. Only Ontario and New Brunswick supported Trudeau, and consequently they were not members of the Gang of Eight.

Reference Case on Patriation   When Trudeau refused to back down on his threat to act unilaterally, the Gang of Eight took him to court. Cases were launched in Manitoba, Quebec, and Newfoundland. The appeal courts in Manitoba and Quebec concluded that the federal government did not need provincial consent to patriate the constitution, but the court in Newfoundland took the contrary view. The issue thus had to be resolved by the Supreme Court of Canada. While there were some legal questions in this case, it was ultimately a political one, so the Supreme Court provided a very political answer. On the one hand, it ruled that there was no *legal* requirement for the federal government to secure the consent of the provinces. But, on the other hand, it indicated that Canada's *constitutional conventions* required the federal government to obtain a "substantial degree" of provincial consent before proceeding with a constitutional change of this magnitude. In a legal sense, it was an odd ruling. Constitutional conventions are not supposed to work against the law. They are, instead, supposed to be mutually reinforcing. For Trudeau, the court's decision "amounted to a legal green light and a political red light."[21] Trudeau could have proceeded with his plan to patriate the constitution unilaterally, because constitutional conventions are not enforceable by the courts. But, politically, Trudeau was forced to negotiate with the provinces one more time.

The Night of the Long Knives   Trudeau invited the premiers to Ottawa for a meeting in November 1981. Although the meeting happened before the eyes of the nation, it is still shrouded in mystery and intrigue. The perennial issues were on the table: the amending formula, the charter, and Quebec's status. On the question of the amending formula, Trudeau proposed the regional formula included in the Victoria Agreement. To repeat, under this formula constitutional amendments would require the consent of the federal Parliament, Ontario, Quebec, two of the four Atlantic provinces, and two of the four Western provinces representing 50 percent of the population. The Gang of Eight rejected this formula. The Western provinces, in particular, resented that Quebec and Ontario each had a veto while the other provinces did not. In their view, the provinces should all be afforded equal treatment. If each province had a veto, however, the amending formula would be too rigid—it would be impossible to ever amend the constitution. The Gang of Eight therefore suggested a different amending formula. It proposed that general constitutional amendments obtain the consent of the federal Parliament and 7 of 10 provinces representing 50 percent of the population.

René Lévesque took a huge risk when he joined the Gang of Eight. Quebec had always maintained that it historically possessed and politically deserved a veto over major constitutional change. Historically, the constitution was amended when the Government of Canada asked the British Parliament to make changes to the BNA Act. The consent of the provinces was generally sought when the amendment affected them, but the constitution was certainly changed on occasion without the consent of Quebec or the other provinces. So, empirically, it is fairly easy to refute Quebec's claim that it historically possessed a veto over constitutional change. However, as the one province unlike the others, a very good case can be made that justice requires Quebec's consent to make any major constitutional change. The Gang of Eight's formula, however, did not provide Quebec a veto.

Lévesque did not give away his veto for free. Quebec had long been concerned about federal encroachment into areas of provincial jurisdiction. So, in exchange for signing on to the Gang of Eight's formula, Lévesque negotiated a caveat: If the federal government acquired new powers from the provinces, any province not agreeing with the amendment would be afforded the right to opt out *with* financial compensation. So, for example, let's say the federal government wanted an enhanced role in postsecondary education and sought a constitutional amendment to that effect. Let's say further that all provinces agreed to the amendment except Quebec. Under the formula that Lévesque negotiated with the Gang of Eight, the amendment would proceed, but the federal government would have no authority over postsecondary education in Quebec, and it would have to provide Quebec with financial compensation.

The Gang of Eight also took issue with Trudeau's charter of rights. In their view, a charter was not consistent with Canada's parliamentary tradition. They argued that it would not be democratic to have unelected judges striking down the laws of democratically elected Members of Parliament or provincial legislatures. More to the point, the premiers feared that the Supreme Court of Canada—with all its judges appointed by the federal government— would not look upon provincial legislation favourably.

At this point, it seemed that another constitutional meeting would end in failure. To break the logjam, Trudeau privately approached Lévesque with a proposition: He suggested that they patriate the constitution and let the people decide the fate of the charter in a referendum. Lévesque agreed, and Trudeau announced that there was now a new Gang of Two. The other premiers in the Gang of Eight were furious with Lévesque—the last thing they wanted was a referendum on a charter of rights. Lévesque quickly backtracked on the referendum idea, but it was too late. The other provinces were now talking privately with the federal government.

The breakthrough in the negotiations was orchestrated by Trudeau's Minister of Justice, Jean Chrétien. One night after the first ministers had left for the day, Chrétien met with his counterparts from Ontario and Saskatchewan, Roy McMurtry and Roy Romanow respectively, in the kitchen of the conference centre. On the question of the amending formula,

general amending formula The general amending formula stipulates that most constitutional amendments require the consent of the federal government and 7 of 10 provinces representing 50 percent of the population. Also known as the 7/50 rule.

7/50 rule The term commonly used for the general amending formula in the constitution.

notwithstanding clause Refers to Section 33 of the Constitution Act 1982. It allows Parliament or a legislature to protect legislation that violates Section 2 and/or Sections 7 to 15 of the Canadian Charter of Rights and Freedoms. It expires after five years, and must be repassed if it is to remain in effect.

Chrétien indicated that the federal government would accept the amending formula proposed by the Gang of Eight as long as the provinces dropped their request for financial compensation for opting out of division of power amendments. This formula was ultimately adopted. Under this formula, most constitutional amendments require the consent of the federal government and 7 of 10 provinces representing 50 percent of the population. This is known as the **general amending formula** or more informally as the **7/50 rule**. There are additional formulas in the Constitution Act 1982 for more particular amendments, as we will discuss in the next chapter.

There was still the issue of the charter, however. Here was the nub of the problem: Trudeau wanted a charter, but the Gang of Eight feared that it would compromise the supremacy of Parliament and the provincial legislatures. Chrétien proposed that the charter include a mechanism that would preserve the supremacy of Parliament and provincial legislatures from the courts. It was called a **notwithstanding clause**. With a notwithstanding clause, Parliament or a provincial legislature could exempt a law from court challenge, or override a decision of the courts. Here's how it would work: Parliament or a legislature would say, "we think this law might violate the Charter, but we are passing it *notwithstanding*." A law passed "notwithstanding" could not be challenged in a court of law. Alternatively, if any other law was found by a court to be in violation of the Charter, the legislature or Parliament that passed the law could say, "we are keeping this law *notwithstanding* the decision of the court." Chrétien indicated that there would have to be some limitations placed on the "notwithstanding" clause, but it went a long way to appeasing the concerns of the provinces. In many respects, the "notwithstanding" clause undermines the whole purpose of a charter of rights: it allows Parliament and legislatures to do whatever they want notwithstanding what the courts might say. Romanow and McMurtry said, "if that's the kind of charter your boss wants, we can live with it."

Right after the meeting with Romanow and McMurtry, Chrétien called Trudeau and told him that Saskatchewan was now on board (Ontario had been on board from the beginning). Trudeau told Chrétien to talk to the other provinces. The next morning, Trudeau announced that a deal had been reached. But one province never received a phone call: Quebec. Premier Lévesque was livid. He warned that there would be "incalculable" consequences if the federal government proceeded with patriation over the objections of Quebec. In response, Trudeau said that the Supreme Court had ruled that he needed a "substantial" degree of provincial consent to patriate the constitution, and with nine provinces now on board Trudeau believed that he had met the necessary threshold to proceed. Quebec immediately challenged the patriation agreement in court, arguing that for the level of consent to be considered "substantial," Quebec, as the one province unlike the others, should be a party to the agreement. In April 1982, just 10 days before the Charter came into effect, the Quebec Court of Appeal ruled against Quebec, and in December 1982 the Supreme Court of Canada similarly dismissed Quebec's case. "It was not the Supreme Court's most convincing performance," says Peter Russell.[22]

René Lévesque felt betrayed by the other premiers. All the members of the Gang of Eight had signed a letter, which spelled out their position on a number of issues. If the Gang of Eight got everything it asked for, Lévesque figured Quebec could endorse the new constitution. But Lévesque was of the view that Trudeau would not agree to all of these points, and he was right: Trudeau could not accept the Gang of Eight's position on a few key points. As long as the Gang of Eight stood together, Lévesque had believed, it would be able to stop Trudeau's patriation plan. It was therefore to Lévesque's horror that the other members of the Gang of Eight compromised on some of their key points, such as opting out of constitutional amendments with compensation. It turned out that the other members of the Gang of Eight were not out to stop Trudeau, but rather to get a better deal. Trudeau had understood that Lévesque and the other premiers had different objectives, and so he tried, and succeeded, to split the Gang of Eight and isolate Lévesque. In fact, he broke Lévesque: while Lévesque led the Parti Québécois to victory again in 1981, his behaviour became increasingly erratic and he was forced out of office by his own party. He died in 1987 from a heart attack at only 65 years of age. The night the patriation deal came together in November 1981 is known in Quebec as the **night of the long knives**. This phrase is drawn from an episode in German history: *Nacht der langen messer* was the night in 1934 when Adolf Hitler unleashed the Gestapo to eliminate his opponents in the Nazi Party and secure his leadership.

night of the long knives Refers to the episode during the patriation negotiations during which all provincial premiers except Premier Lévesque of Québec were included in a late night, last-minute deal on patriation.

The Political Legacies of Patriation

On April 17, 1982, the constitution finally came back to Canada—115 years after Confederation, Canada was an independent nation. The Constitution Act 1982 contained a set of amending formulas, which we will examine more closely in the next chapter, but it also included a couple of new governing principles. First, in keeping with Trudeau's dream, a bill of rights was added to the constitution. The Charter of Rights and Freedoms has had a profound impact on Canadian politics, as we will also discuss in the next chapter. Second, the new Constitution Act "recognized and affirmed" the rights of Aboriginal peoples, which was a bit of a surprise. Trudeau had never expressed any interest in the rights of Aboriginal peoples, and none of the premiers had championed their cause either. But its inclusion in the constitution represents an enormous milestone in Canadian politics, although it remains more of a promise than a reality. It is important to stress that these new governing principles were added to Canada's constitutional order. Thus, henceforth, Canada would be governed by four constitutional principles: parliamentary democracy, federalism, a bill of rights, and Aboriginal rights and governance. For most Canadians, these were positive additions.

The legacy of patriation, however, is not entirely positive. The Quebec National Assembly formally rejected the Constitution Act 1982. This, however, was purely a political statement. As a matter of law, the new constitution applies fully in Quebec. But for Quebecers, the Constitution Act 1982 does not reflect the two nations vision of Canada: Quebec lost its constitutional veto, it didn't get financial compensation for opting out and the issue of the federal spending power was left hanging, the Charter overrides aspects of provincial jurisdiction on language, and it all happened over the objections of the government of Quebec. "A constitutional reform modifying Quebec's legislative powers to such an extent, without the explicit consent of the people, is profoundly illegitimate," writes a respected Quebec political scientist.[23] Indeed, he concludes, it represents the "end of a Canadian dream."

In sum, for many Quebecers the federal spending power and the Charter of Rights and Freedoms are instruments of assimilation because they are designed to provide Canadians with the same entitlements and rights. And to make matters worse for Quebecers, the new constitutional order was orchestrated by a French Canadian prime minister from Quebec—the same prime minister who ordered the army to patrol the streets of Quebec in October 1970. It was thus obvious that Canada's constitutional odyssey would not end with patriation. Quebec's concerns would have to be addressed in the future.

SUMMARY

Canada has long struggled with the challenge of governing a society with deep cultural divisions. The BNA Act, or what we now call the Constitution Act 1867, proved to be much more effective than the previous arrangements enacted to govern the colonies of British North America. But the BNA Act also had limitations, principally that Canada was still legally chained to the Mother Country. After World War I, Canadians concluded that it was finally time to become completely independent of Great Britain. However, the effort to patriate the constitution proved to be very challenging. Ultimately, the constitution returned to Canada in 1982, and at the same time a new Constitution Act entrenched a Charter of Rights and Freedoms. Aboriginal rights were also recognized and affirmed. These represent the most significant rule changes in the Canadian constitutional order since Confederation. The game of Canadian politics has been profoundly transformed by these changes, as we will see in the next few chapters. But these changes came at a high price. The political fabric of the country was severely strained by the protracted effort to revise the constitution. Indeed, the events that led to patriation were so acrimonious and divisive that when the constitution finally made it back to Canadian shores "no one cheered."[24] Quebec's refusal to endorse the new constitutional order ensured that Canada's constitutional odyssey would continue well into the future. Canada, in fact, is still grappling with the legacies of patriation.

Questions to Think About

1. Why is it so difficult to govern societies with deep cultural divisions?
2. Why has the Constitution Act 1867 been so successful?
3. Why did Quebec reject the Constitution Act 1982?
4. Did Pierre Trudeau do the right thing when he brought the constitution back to Canada over Quebec's objections?

Learning Outcomes

1. Name and briefly describe the constitutional arrangements prior to Confederation.
2. Explain the significance of the Quiet Revolution for Quebec society in particular and Canadian politics more generally.
3. Define the spending power and explain why it has been a source of controversy in Canadian politics.
4. Explain the concept of sovereignty-association.
5. Recount the story of patriation and the roles of the principal actors and explain why Quebec refused to endorse the final agreement to patriate the constitution.

Additional Readings

Janet Ajzenstat, *The Political Thought of Lord Durham* (Montreal, QC: McGill-Queen's University Press, 1988).

Michael D. Behiels, *Prelude to Quebec's Quiet Revolution: Liberalism versus Neo-Nationalism, 1945–1960* (Montreal, QC: McGill-Queen's University Press, 1985).

Conrad Black, *Duplessis* (Toronto, ON: McClelland and Stewart, 1977).

Alan Cairns, *Charter versus Federalism: The Dilemma of Constitutional Reform* (Montreal, QC: McGill-Queen's University Press, 1992).

Ramsay Cook, *Canada, Quebec, and the Uses of Nationalism* (Toronto, ON: McClelland and Stewart, 1995).

Graham Fraser, *PQ: René Lévesque and the Parti Québécois in Power* (Toronto, ON: Macmillan, 1984).

Guy Laforest, *Trudeau and the End of a Canadian Dream* (Montreal, QC: McGill-Queen's University Press, 1995).

Daniel Latouche, *Canada and Quebec, Past and Future* (Toronto, ON: University of Toronto Press, 1986).

Kenneth McRoberts, *Misconceiving Canada: The Struggle for National Unity* (Toronto, ON: Oxford University Press, 1997).

Kenneth McRoberts, *Quebec: Social Change and Political Crisis,* 3rd ed. (Toronto, ON: McClelland and Stewart, 1993).

Réjean Pelletier, *Le Québec et le Fédéralisme Canadien: Un Regard Critique* (Quebec, QC: Laval University Press, 2008).

Herbert F. Quinn, *The Union Nationale: A Study in Quebec Nationalism* (Toronto, ON: University of Toronto Press, 1963).

Peter H. Russell, *Constitutional Odyssey: Can Canadians Become a Sovereign People?* 3rd ed. (Toronto, ON: University of Toronto Press, 2004).

Dale C. Thomson, *Jean Lesage and the Quiet Revolution* (Toronto, ON: Macmillan, 1984).

Pierre Elliott Trudeau, *Federalism and the French Canadians* (Toronto, ON: Macmillan, 1968).

Notes

1. John Stuart Mill, *Considerations on Representative Government*, in H. B. Acton, ed., *Utilitarianism, On Liberty, and Considerations on Representative Government* (London, UK: J.M. Dent and Sons, 1987), 392.

2. Lord Acton, "Nationality," in *Essays on Freedom and Power* (Cleveland, OH: Meridian Books, 1948), 160.

3. Lord Durham, *Lord Durham's Report: An Abridgement of Report on the Affairs of British North America,* ed. Gerald M. Craig (Toronto, ON: McClelland and Stewart, 1963), 23.

4. Peter H. Russell, *Constitutional Odyssey: Can Canadians Become a Sovereign People?* 3rd ed. (Toronto, ON: University of Toronto Press, 2004), 18.

5. Dominion–Provincial Conference [on Reconstruction] 1945: Dominion and Provincial Submissions and Plenary Conference Discussions (Ottawa, ON: Government of Canada, 1946), 411.

6. *Report of the Royal Commission of Inquiry on Constitutional Problems,* vol. II (Quebec City, QC: Province of Quebec, 1956), 102.

7. Ibid., vol. I, 185.

8. Ibid., vol. II, 327.

9. Jean Lesage, "Québec Speaks," in J. Peter Meekison, ed., *Canadian Federalism: Myth or Reality* (Toronto, ON: Methuen, 1968), 222. This text was taken from Jean Lesage's budget speech to the Québec Legislative Assembly in 1963.

10. Pierre Elliott Trudeau, *Federal-Provincial Grants and the Spending Power of Parliament* (Ottawa, ON: Government of Canada, 1969), 4.

11. Hamish Telford, "The Federal Spending Power in Canada: Nation-Building or Nation-Destroying?" *Publius: The Journal of Federalism* 33:1 (Winter 2003).

12. René Lévesque, *My Québec* (Toronto, ON: Methuen, 1979), 20.

13. Quoted in Jean Provencher, *René Lévesque: Portrait of a Québécois* (Gage, 1975), 240.

14. René Lévesque, *An Option for Québec* (Toronto, ON: McClelland and Stewart, 1968), 27.

15. Ibid., 28.

16. Ibid., 39.

17. Ibid., 30.

18. Russell, *Constitutional Odyssey*, 75.

19. Ibid., 17.

20. Pierre Elliott Trudeau, Speech at the Paul Sauvé Arena, Montreal, May 14, 1980. Library and Archives Canada, http://www.collectionscanada.gc.ca/2/4/h4-4083-e.html, accessed August 10, 2011.

21. Russell, *Constitutional Odyssey*, 119.

22. Ibid., 129.

23. Guy Laforest, *Trudeau and the End of a Canadian Dream* (Montreal, QC: McGill-Queen's University Press, 1995), 148.

24. Keith Banting and Richard Simeon, eds., *And No One Cheered: Federalism, Democracy and the Constitution Act* (Toronto, ON: Methuen, 1983).

Chapter 9
The Charter and the Courts

Key Points

- The Constitution Act 1982, especially the Charter of Rights and Freedoms, is the handiwork of Pierre Trudeau, who hoped and believed it would be an instrument of unity.

- The amending formulas were the key to patriation, but the formulas are quite rigid, meaning it is difficult to obtain the necessary consensus to make constitutional changes.

- The Charter of Rights and Freedoms did not give Canadians new rights; instead, it offers more security by entrenching our rights in the constitution. The Canadian Charter of Rights provides both individual and group rights.

- The Charter has fundamentally changed the way the country is governed. Parliament and the Supreme Court are now engaged in a dialogue about the law.

- With the Supreme Court now making life and death decisions, the appointment process for the Supreme Court has come under scrutiny and steps have been taken to make the process more open and transparent.

- The old constitution and the new constitution are not entirely compatible. The Charter of Rights and Freedoms poses a challenge to federalism and Canada's parliamentary system of government.

- Quebec remains officially opposed to the new constitution, so to date the Charter of Rights and Freedoms has not united the country as Trudeau had hoped.

The Constitution Act 1982 is by far the most significant change in the Canadian political system since 1867. In a very real sense, Pierre Trudeau and the premiers of the day are the modern Fathers of Confederation. The new Constitution Act has four main components. First, there is a set of amending formulas, which at long last empower the governments of Canada to amend the country's constitution. Second, a comprehensive bill of rights called the Charter of Rights and Freedoms is entrenched in the constitution. The Charter has had an enormous impact on Canadian society, and it has made the Supreme Court of Canada a real player in Canadian politics. We will focus on these two components in this chapter. Third, again at long last, the constitution recognized and affirmed the rights of Aboriginal people; we will examine this part of the new constitution in the next chapter. Fourth, the equalization program, which we discussed in Chapter 7, was entrenched in the new Constitution Act; it is the only social program with constitutional status. It should also be noted that a new section was added to the Constitution Act 1867 as part of the patriation package. Section 92A clarifies the provincial ownership of nonrenewable natural resources. Regrettably, we do not have the space to examine the constitutional arrangements for the management of natural resources in Canada.

It is important to stress that the Constitution Act 1982 did not replace the old constitution. The British North America Act was renamed the Constitution Act 1867, and it operates alongside the new Constitution Act. These acts then form the foundation of Canada's modern constitutional order. Importantly, they made Canada—115 years after Confederation—completely self-governing. However, the two constitutional acts are not entirely compatible. The Charter of Rights and Freedoms in particular poses serious challenges to federalism and Canada's parliamentary system of government. This, of course, was Pierre Trudeau's intent. He was convinced that the old constitutional order was responsible, in part at least, for the deep regional cleavages in the federation, most especially between Quebec and the rest of Canada. He thus hoped and believed that the new Constitution Act would become an instrument of unity and overcome these longstanding cultural and political divisions. Quebec, of course, opposed Trudeau's patriation plan, and it continues to object to the new constitution, even though it must abide by its terms. Thus, while the new constitution has had a profound impact on Canada, it has not united the federation as Trudeau envisioned.

The Amending Formulas

The key to patriation was the amending formula. Without an amending formula, it would have been impossible to return the constitution to Canada. As we know from the last chapter, the negotiations over the amending formula led to an existential debate about the nature of the Canadian political community. Were we a compact of nations? Of provinces? Of regions? Ultimately, a series of formulas were adopted, but they were all premised on the provincial theory of Confederation (see Sections 38–49 of the Constitution Act 1982). A select number of amendments require the *unanimous* consent of the federal government and all 10 provinces. The unanimity procedure applies to the fundamental institutions of the Canadian political system: the Crown, the Supreme Court, bilingualism, the representation of the provinces in Parliament, and changes to this amending procedure itself (see Section 41). The unanimity amending procedure is very *rigid,* meaning it is a very high threshold to meet. Since 1982, no amendments have been made with this formula, although there were a couple of notable failures, as we will discuss in Chapter 11.

general amending formula
The general amending formula stipulates that most constitutional amendments require the consent of the federal government and 7 of 10 provinces representing 50 percent of the population. Also known as the 7/50 rule.

7/50 rule The term commonly used for the general amending formula in the constitution.

Most constitutional amendments are subject to the **general amending formula**: the consent of the federal government and 7 of 10 provinces representing 50 percent of the population. The general amending formula is also known as the **7/50 rule**. This formula flows from the principles of both democracy and federalism. It ensures that a majority of provinces are on board with a constitutional change along with a majority of the population. Effectively, it means that at least one of the two largest provinces must support the proposed change. If eight provinces are on side but Ontario and Quebec are opposed, the amendment will fail, since Ontario and Quebec constitute more than half the population of Canada. While the general amending formula represents a neat compromise between the principles of democracy and federalism, it has proven to be quite a rigid formula. Since 1982, the constitution has been amended only once with this procedure. Just one year after the new Constitution Act came into force, the provisions relating to Aboriginal peoples were strengthened.

By contrast, the other amending formulas are more *flexible*, and important constitutional changes have been effected with them. Amendments relating to just one or a few provinces can be made with the consent of the federal government and the province(s) concerned. So Quebec, with the consent of Parliament, replaced its system of denominational schools with linguistic schools; instead of Catholic and Protestant schools, Quebec now has French and English schools. Newfoundland and Labrador similarly abolished all denominational schools in the public sector and created one secular school system. In some instances, Parliament can amend the constitution itself. The Harper government believes that it can reform the Senate—with term limits and elected senators—with constitutional amendments approved only by Parliament, but many of the provinces argue that these reforms require the 7/50 rule. The Harper government has now referred the matter to the Supreme Court for a definitive determination; if the court sides with the provinces, it may prove forever impossible to reform the Senate.

With the Constitution Act 1982, Canada has possessed the legal ability to change its own constitution, but constitutional change has proven to be politically challenging. The unanimity formula and even the general amending formula are quite rigid. The governments of Canada have been unable to achieve the level of consent necessary to enact constitutional changes with these formulas. It would seem that the unanimity and the general amending formulas have placed Canada in a constitutional straightjacket, at least with respect to the more important provisions of the constitution. The other procedures have been more flexible, but they are also significantly more limited. The procedure that allows Parliament or a provincial legislature to amend the constitution with respect to itself is especially limited. Some important changes have been made at the provincial level, with the consent of Parliament and some of the provinces. But the possibility of constitutional change at the national level seems remote. And changing the amending formulas themselves is an even more remote possibility. So, after the arduous process to patriate the constitution, it would seem that Canada is destined to live with the same constitutional rules for the foreseeable future. Fortunately, there are other avenues for change. The instruments of fiscal federalism allow for adaptation in the federation, as discussed in Chapter 7, and the courts provide another avenue for change, as will be discussed later in this chapter.

If a rigid amending formula is the first legacy of patriation, the second legacy is the absence of a constitutional veto for Quebec. Pierre Trudeau always maintained that he offered Quebec a veto with his regional amending formula, and he insisted that René Lévesque gave away his veto when he joined forces with the Gang of Eight. The Supreme Court determined in the reference case after patriation that Quebec did not have a legal right to a veto. And, without any doubt, the Constitution Act 1982 applies fully to Quebec. But the law here is secondary to politics. Many people in Quebec believe that Pierre Trudeau stole Quebec's veto and that the rest of Canada stabbed Quebec in the back during the "night of the long knives." These beliefs do not bode well for the unity of the federation—which was the point of the patriation exercise. There were a couple of attempts in the 1990s to devise an amending formula (among other constitutional changes) to address Quebec's concerns, but both attempts failed, as will be discussed in Chapter 11. In sum, the issue of the amending formula, which seriously complicated the patriation of the constitution in the first place, continues to bedevil Canadians.

Rights and Freedoms in the English Legal System

With the Constitution Act 1982, Canada adopted a Charter of Rights and Freedoms. The purpose of the Charter is to prevent democratic majorities from using their political power to violate the rights of individuals, especially the rights of minorities. The Charter does this by entrenching rights in the constitution and putting them beyond the reach of Parliament (and legislatures of the provinces and territories). Since the constitution is Canada's *master law*, any law of Parliament (or a provincial or territorial legislature) that violates the constitution has no force or effect (see Section 52.1 of the Constitution Act 1982). Anyone who believes that their rights or freedoms have been infringed on or denied "may apply to a court of competent jurisdiction to obtain such remedy as the court considers appropriate and just in the circumstances" (see Section 24.1). It is important to stress that the Charter protects individuals from the actions of *government*; the Charter does not protect you from a boss who fires you for being gay. There are other remedies for that sort of injustice, such as a labour relations board, a human rights tribunal, or a civil lawsuit.

The fact that the Charter was adopted in 1982 suggests that Canadians only received rights recently, but that is not true. Canadians have long enjoyed rights under the system of common law inherited from England. The right of *habeas corpus*, which is the most basic human right, dates back to the fourteenth century. It prevents the state from snatching subjects off the street and locking them away indefinitely, or worse summarily executing them. *Habeas corpus* is an accusation against the state: It means literally "you must have the body." With a writ of *habeas corpus* signed by a judge, the state is required to produce a prisoner under arrest in a court of law. Over time, *habeas corpus* became too important to leave as a common law right. In England, the right of *habeas corpus* was written into law by Parliament in the seventeenth century. However, things like free speech and freedom of religion remained simply as common law rights.

Canadians have similarly long enjoyed these rights as a matter of common law and political convention. While these rights were supported by the weight of history, they were not constitutionally guaranteed. Common law rights could always be superseded by statutory laws of Parliament and even executive action. And, from time to time, there were real abuses by government, such as the detention of Japanese Canadians during World War II, the involuntary placement of Aboriginal children in residential schools, and the persecution of Jehovah's Witnesses in Quebec, among others.

Bill of Rights A statute enacted in 1960 by the government of John Diefenbaker. It enumerated the common law rights enjoyed by Canadians and prohibited discrimination based on race, national origin, colour, religion, or sex. The Bill of Rights was not entrenched in the constitution; it was a statutory law.

In light of these abuses, Prime Minister John Diefenbaker introduced a **Bill of Rights** in 1960 that was intended to eliminate racial discrimination and better secure the historical rights of all Canadians. The first section of the Bill of Rights prohibited discrimination "by reason of race, national origin, colour, religion or sex." It then proceeded to enumerate the common law rights Canadians had long enjoyed: the right to life, liberty, security of the person, the enjoyment of property and the right not to be deprived thereof except by due process of law, equality, freedom of speech and the press, religion, association and assembly, and all of the legal rights associated with English common law, including the right of *habeas corpus*.

The Bill of Rights, however, was not entrenched in the constitution; it was a statute of Parliament. Since the Bill of Rights was on the same legal footing as any other law of Parliament, the courts could not use it to strike down laws that violated the rights of Canadians. In other words, it was legally toothless. But the Bill of Rights did have an important impact on Canadian political culture. It made Canadians more receptive to the legal entrenchment of rights—something hitherto considered too American for Canada—and it started to redefine Canada as a multicultural society. It is not coincidental that the Bill of Rights was introduced by Diefenbaker, who was Canada's first (and still only) prime minister *not* of British or French heritage. As a Canadian of German origin, Diefenbaker endured many taunts as a young boy about his heritage. He was thus acutely sensitive to the concerns of minority groups in Canada.

The Charter of Rights and Freedoms did not give us new rights—it simply entrenched our historical rights in the constitution. It thus provides us with much greater protection from the actions of government. The courts have the responsibility of determining if the laws of Parliament (and the provincial and territorial legislatures) are consistent with the rights set out in the Charter. Before 1982, the courts played a much more limited role in the Canadian political process: from time to time, they were asked to determine if Parliament or a provincial legislature had the authority to make a particular law under the division of powers enumerated in Sections 91 and 92 of the Constitution Act 1867. Now, with the Charter of Rights and Freedoms, every law is subject to a possible court challenge. Consequently, the courts have become much more powerful players in the Canadian political system, as we will see later in this chapter.

Trudeau's Charter of Rights and Freedoms

Pierre Trudeau's role in the creation of the Charter of Rights and Freedoms cannot be overstated: we have a Charter because Pierre Trudeau believed it was imperative that we have one, pure and simple. There was no public demand for a Charter of Rights, and most of the provincial premiers were opposed to the concept of a constitutionally entrenched bill of rights. But Trudeau pushed it through over the objections of the premiers and an indifferent public. As a philosophical liberal, Trudeau believed that individuals need entrenched rights to protect them from the vast power of the state. He also hoped that the Charter would transcend the linguistic and regional cleavages that have divided the country for so long and forge a new Canadian identity. He most especially wanted to thwart the allure of nationalism in Quebec. The Charter, in his words

> established the primacy of the individual over the state and all government institutions, and in so doing, recognized that all sovereignty resides in the people. . . . In this respect, the Canadian Charter was a new beginning for the Canadian nation: it sought to strengthen the country's unity by basing the sovereignty of the Canadian people on a set of values common to all, and in particular on the notion of equality among all Canadians.[1]

To date, the Charter has not transcended the main political cleavages in the country and forged a new unity as Pierre Trudeau had hoped. On the other hand, the public has embraced the Charter wholeheartedly. Opinion polls have consistently shown that support for the Charter is very high across the country, including in Quebec. So, perhaps with more time, the Charter will emerge as an instrument of unity.

Individual Rights and Fundamental Freedoms in the Charter

The Charter of Rights and Freedoms very much reflects Pierre Trudeau's liberal philosophy. First, the Charter is written in the language of individual rights:

Everyone has the following fundamental freedoms . . .

Every citizen has the right to vote . . .

Every citizen has the right to enter, remain in and leave Canada . . .

Everyone has the right to life, liberty and the security of the person . . .

Everyone has the right to be secure against unreasonable search or seizure.

Everyone has the right not to be arbitrarily detained or imprisoned . . .

Everyone has the right on arrest or detention to be informed of the reasons therefor . . .

Any *person* charged with an offence has the right . . .

Everyone has the right not to be subjected to cruel and unusual treatment or punishment.

Every *individual* is equal before and under the law . . .

These are the rights and freedoms laid out in the first 15 sections of the Charter, and they represent the rights associated with classical liberalism. The origins of these rights lie with the emergence of the liberal state in the seventeenth century. Most of these rights were incorporated in the US Bill of Rights after the ratification of the American Constitution in 1789. (Equality and voting rights were added to the US Constitution after the Civil War in the 1860s, with a further extension of voting rights for women after World War I.)

Language Rights in the Charter

Unlike the US Bill of Rights, however, Canada's Charter is a thoroughly modern document. It goes beyond the rights of individuals associated with classical liberalism and recognizes group claims. For Trudeau, the language rights in Sections 16 through 22 constitute the heart of the Charter. In short, these sections entrenched his policy of official bilingualism in the constitution. But in Section 23 the Charter went even further and entrenched minority language education rights, at least for citizens who received their education in Canada. In short, English-speaking citizens in Quebec have the right to send their children to English schools, and French-speaking citizens outside Quebec have the right to send their children to French schools, so long as there are a sufficient number of people in each case to warrant the establishment of separate schools. People educated outside of Canada are not afforded the same right, even if they become Canadian citizens. The government of Quebec is thus within its rights to require the children of immigrants to attend French language schools, even if their mother tongue is English. (These children, of course, may attend private English language schools if their parents can afford the fees. There are very few French language schools outside Quebec, except for a couple of Francophone pockets here and there, so French-speaking immigrants in the rest of Canada are by and large forced to send their children to English language schools.) While Quebec has been able to work around Section 23 to some extent, it remains a source of great consternation for the government of Quebec, which maintains that education is a matter of exclusive provincial jurisdiction under the Constitution Act 1867. The entrenchment of language rights, however, was the cornerstone of Prime Minister Trudeau's project to remake Canada, hence their presence in the new constitution.

Group Rights in the Charter

While Trudeau was anxious to entrench language rights in the constitution, the Charter also recognized other group claims. This is a legacy of the process that led to patriation. When Prime Minister Trudeau was confronted by the firm opposition of eight premiers, he threatened to patriate the constitution unilaterally. As we know, the Gang of Eight took the federal government to court and obtained a partial victory. The court's decision forced Trudeau back to the negotiating table with the premiers. But while the premiers were fighting the federal government in court, Trudeau appealed to the court of public opinion with a proposal for a new "people's constitution." As part of his strategy to bypass the premiers, Trudeau offered the people a forum—a special parliamentary committee—to make their constitutional demands. And the people, at least some groups of people, responded enthusiastically. In the winter of 1980–1981, the special parliamentary committee on the constitution sat for 56 days and held 267 hours of hearings, all of which was broadcast on live television.[2]

While the people responded enthusiastically to Prime Minister Trudeau's appeal, the response was not what he was expecting. For the most part, the people who responded to the appeal represented various **advocacy groups**: religious groups, women's groups, gay and lesbian groups, multicultural groups, Aboriginal peoples, the disabled, business groups, labour groups, civil liberties groups, and environmental groups, among others. And they wanted the Charter to recognize group rights. While the demand for group rights was not consistent with Trudeau's philosophy, he could not very well reject these claims after encouraging the people at large to come forward with their constitutional demands—these groups, after all, were now the strongest supporters of his Charter. So, many of the claims made by these groups (although not all of them) ultimately made their way into the latter sections of the Charter. Curiously, they were grouped under the heading "General" as opposed to group rights or some other more descriptive heading. Sections 25 through 29 of the Charter represent the claims of Aboriginal peoples, multicultural groups, women, and religious groups.

advocacy groups Organizations representing the concerns of various social movements or economic interests. Rather than contest elections like a political party, advocacy groups seek to influence government policy from the outside. They are sometimes called interest groups, although it should be noted that this term is often used pejoratively.

The legal impact of these provisions has been limited. The equality provisions in Section 15 have proven to be of much greater significance, at least legally speaking. Politically, however, the group sections at the end of the Charter have been profoundly significant. The various groups mobilized by the patriation exercise identify strongly with their respective sections of the constitution. Political scientists refer to them as **Charter Canadians**. When the constitution was patriated in 1982 over the objections of Quebec, it was clear that Canada's constitutional odyssey was not over. But the Constitution Act 1982 forever changed the game. The federal government and the provinces were no longer the only actors with vested constitutional interests—Charter Canadians have taken ownership of particular sections of the constitution, and they have insisted on being party to subsequent negotiations so as to safeguard or expand their constitutional rights. In short, Charter Canadians are now players in Canada's game of constitutional politics.

Charter Canadians Minority groups with a vested interest in particular sections of the Charter of Rights and Freedoms, such as Section 27, which recognizes the multicultural heritage of Canada.

Section 33: The Notwithstanding Clause

As discussed in the last chapter, the **notwithstanding clause** was the key compromise that led to the patriation of the constitution and the adoption of the Charter of Rights and Freedoms. The Gang of Eight, which opposed Prime Minister Trudeau, was deeply concerned about unelected judges overturning the legislation of democratically elected governments. This concern evaporated when Trudeau agreed to include the notwithstanding clause in the new constitution. The notwithstanding clause gives government—federal, provincial, or territorial—the opportunity to protect a law from judicial challenge or to rescue a law struck down by the courts. The decision to include the notwithstanding clause in the Charter was extremely controversial. For many, it completely undermined the purpose of the Charter. Trudeau admitted that the Constitution Act 1982 was "not perfect," but he maintained that it was better to have "a charter with a notwithstanding clause than no charter at all."[3]

notwithstanding clause Refers to Section 33 of the Constitution Act 1982. It allows Parliament or a legislature to protect legislation that violates Section 2 and/or Sections 7 to 15 of the Canadian Charter of Rights and Freedoms. It expires after five years, and must be repassed if it is to remain in effect.

The notwithstanding clause is an important instrument for government, but it is not a free pass; the provision has serious limitations. First, it can only be applied against Sections 2 and 7 through 15 of the Charter. In other words, it *can* be used to limit our fundamental freedoms, our legal rights, and our equality rights, but it *cannot* be used to restrict our democratic rights, our mobility rights, our linguistic rights, or the rights of Charter Canadians. Second, the notwithstanding clause protects a law from court challenge only for five years; after five years the legislature that passed the law must invoke the notwithstanding clause again to continue protecting the law. There are no limits on how many times the notwithstanding clause can be invoked to protect a law, but there will be at least one election between each application of the clause.

Technically, the notwithstanding clause has been invoked numerous times, but that is because in 1982 Quebec passed all its laws notwithstanding as an act of political protest against Trudeau's Charter. Five years later, the new Liberal government of Quebec did not reapply the clause. Apart from Quebec's petulant protest, the notwithstanding clause has been employed only four times, and on three of those occasions it was moot. The Yukon government invoked the notwithstanding clause in 1982, but the statute in question was never brought into force. Saskatchewan used it in 1988 to end a strike by government workers, although the courts later determined that the law was consistent with the Charter, meaning that the override was not necessary. In 2000, Alberta applied it to a law outside its jurisdiction, and that meant the law in question was completely null and void.[4]

In real terms, the notwithstanding clause has been used only once. In 1989, the Supreme Court of Canada determined that Quebec's law requiring all commercial establishments in the province to have signs only in French was unconstitutional, on the grounds that it infringed on free speech. This was precisely why Quebec opposed the Charter in the first place: the ruling compromised the ability of the Quebec legislature to promote the French language in the province of Quebec. The Quebec National Assembly thus moved immediately to salvage the law with the notwithstanding clause. In turn, many people outside Quebec were furious with this limitation of free speech. The National Assembly did not renew the override when it expired five years later.

The federal government has never employed the notwithstanding clause, although it has been pressured to use it, especially by the Reform Party/Canadian Alliance—the forerunners to Stephen Harper's Conservative Party—and some conservative legal commentators. In 1999, the BC Court of Appeal concluded that some parts of Canada's law prohibiting the possession of child pornography were unconstitutional (this is known as the *Sharpe* case). Many people were outraged by the ruling, and the Reform Party pressured Jean Chrétien's Liberal government to override the decision with the notwithstanding clause. The Chrétien government resisted the pressure and appealed the case to the Supreme Court, which ultimately overturned the decision of the BC Court of Appeal and upheld the law (albeit with some creative interpretation).

Later in 2001, after the 9/11 attacks on the United States, the Chrétien government moved to introduce a new anti-terrorism law. The Canadian Alliance argued that the new law should be protected with the notwithstanding clause. The Alliance was concerned that accused terrorists would be set free if they managed to challenge the constitutionality of the law successfully. The Chrétien government maintained that the new law was fully constitutional, and therefore it was not necessary to invoke the notwithstanding clause. In fact, some sections of the anti-terrorism law have been found to be unconstitutional, although fortunately it has not resulted in the release of suspected terrorists. Jean Chrétien, of course, helped negotiate the notwithstanding clause in the first place, so there is some irony in his refusal to use it.

The Conservatives, at least in their former incarnations as the Reform and Canadian Alliance, have been more open to using the notwithstanding clause, but after almost a decade in government they have not used it. And it is not for lack of opportunity. In a unanimous decision in 2011, the Supreme Court ruled against the federal government on the controversial safe injection drug facility in Vancouver, known locally as Insite. While the Conservative government could not have been happy with the ruling, it did not move to override the decision. Similarly, the Harper government did not turn to the notwithstanding clause when the Supreme Court struck down parts of Canada's prostitution laws in 2013.

Clearly, the notwithstanding clause has a serious legitimacy problem, and understandably so. Think about it for a minute: when a government employs the notwithstanding clause, it is saying to the people, "we *know* this law violates your rights, but we're keeping it anyway." This is hardly a vote-winning slogan. Perhaps Pierre Trudeau understood that the notwithstanding clause would be impossible to use, and that's why he agreed to go along with it. If the notwithstanding clause is not used again soon, it may be on its way to becoming a dead letter in the constitution.

Section 1: The Limitations Clause

While Section 33 of the Charter of Rights and Freedoms was initially the subject of much notoriety, Section 1 has proven to be of much greater significance. Indeed, it is almost certainly the most important section of the Charter. It is known as the **limitations clause** and states:

limitations clause Section 1 of the Canadian Charter of Rights and Freedoms, which enables governments to place reasonable limits on the rights guaranteed by the Charter.

> The Canadian Charter of Rights and Freedoms guarantees the rights and freedoms set out in it subject only to such reasonable limits prescribed by law as can be demonstrably justified in a free and democratic society.

There is a lot packed into this single sentence. First, it says that the Charter *guarantees* the rights and freedoms of Canadians. But second, it says that *reasonable limits* can be placed on those rights if *prescribed by law*. In other words, it suggests that our rights are not absolute. That's obvious, to some extent: we have a right to free speech, but we can't go around spreading lies about people; the Charter does not make laws against slander and libel unconstitutional, so it is reasonable to limit free speech to protect people from the harm caused by slander and libel. Section 1 may thus be viewed as a constitutional loophole. It allows government to make laws that limit the rights guaranteed in the Charter as long as those limits can be *demonstrably justified* by the standards of a free and democratic society.

While the more infamous Section 33 has rarely been used, almost every Charter case boils down to Section 1. All Charter cases involve a two-step process. First, the judges must decide if the law in question places limits on the rights guaranteed by the Charter. So in the *Sharpe* case, for example, the Supreme Court asked, does the law prohibiting child pornography limit the freedom of expression? Clearly, the answer to that question is "yes." When the government says that you cannot write this or that story or take this or that picture, it is very obviously infringing on freedom of expression. Second, if the judges believe that the law violates the rights guaranteed by the Charter, they then ask if the limitation of the right is reasonable in a free and democratic society. The responsibility lies with the government to *demonstrate* that the law constitutes a reasonable limit on the rights of citizens. In the child pornography case, the government was able to demonstrate that the limitation of free speech was indeed reasonable. This may seem perfectly obvious, but judges cannot be guided simply by emotion or even common sense; we need a more rigorous method of determining when it is reasonable for the government to limit the rights guaranteed by the Charter. Even in the child pornography case, there were issues that were not so obvious—that's why the case went all the way to the Supreme Court in the first place.

When Section 1 first came into play in a real case, the Supreme Court needed to establish a test to determine what constitutes a reasonable limit on the rights guaranteed by the Charter. The test was devised in 1986 in the case of the Crown versus David Edwin Oakes (see Box 9.1), and it has been known ever since as the **Oakes test**. There are two

Oakes test A judicial test used by the Supreme Court of Canada to determine if a law is in accordance with Section 1 of the Canadian Charter of Rights and Freedoms.

Box 9.1

The Case of David Edwin Oakes (*R. v. Oakes* [1986] 1 S.C.R. 103)

In December 1981, David Edwin Oakes, a 23-year-old construction worker, was arrested outside a bar in London, Ontario, with eight one-gram vials of hashish oil in one pocket and $619.45 in the other pocket. Oakes told the police that the hashish was for his personal use (to control the pain from a work injury), and he said the money came from a workers' compensation cheque. The police did not buy his story, and he was charged with possession of a narcotic for the purpose of trafficking. The maximum sentence was life in prison. Under the old Narcotics Act, the prosecution only had to prove possession. If possession was proved, the accused was automatically deemed guilty of trafficking, unless he could prove otherwise.

At trial, the prosecution was easily able to prove that Oakes was in possession of hashish, at which point it was incumbent upon Oakes to prove that he was not trafficking the vials of hashish. In other words, Oakes had to prove his innocence on this point. His lawyer, fresh out of law school, argued that the presumption of innocence has been at the heart of Canada's system of common law for centuries. Moreover, it was explicitly protected by Section 11(d) of the new Charter of Rights and Freedoms. He thus argued that the

"reverse onus" section of the Narcotics Act was unconstitutional on the grounds that it violated Oakes's right to be presumed innocent. The trial judge agreed, and Oakes was convicted only of drug possession. The Crown appealed all the way to the Supreme Court of Canada. There, the Crown argued that the Narcotics Act constituted a reasonable limitation of the Charter right under Section 1.

Chief Justice Brian Dickson then had to determine what constituted a reasonable limit to our Charter rights. With the help of a couple of young legal assistants, Dickson came up with the "Oakes test," which has been described as "five of the most important pages ever written in Canadian constitutional law."[5] Dickson agreed with the Crown that the Narcotics Act was addressing a "pressing and substantial" problem (i.e., drug trafficking), but he concluded that it did not meet the rational connection test: "It would be irrational to infer that a person had an intent to traffic on the basis of his or her possession of a very small quantity of narcotics." Legal history was thus made by one sage judge, a couple of rookie lawyers, and a young construction worker. David Oakes now lives in Calgary; he does not relish his legal notoriety.[6]

Box 9.2

The Oakes Test

When the Supreme Court concludes that a law limits the rights guaranteed by the Charter, it applies the Oakes test. There are two parts to the test: the purpose of the law and the suitability of the means employed to pursue the law's objective.

1. Does the law in question address a "pressing and substantial problem"?

2. If so, are the means employed by the law proportional to the law's objectives?

Criteria of Proportionality

i. The measures adopted must be rationally connected to the objective and cannot be arbitrary, unfair, or based on irrational considerations.

ii. The means should impair as little as possible the right or freedom in question.

iii. Is the good that will be achieved by these means sufficient to outweigh the deleterious effects they will have on those individuals or groups whose rights are being set aside?

basic parts to the Oakes test (see Box 9.2). The first part concerns the purpose of the law; the second part concerns proportionality (i.e., the suitability of the means employed to pursue the law's objective). In the first instance, the Supreme Court wants to know if the law in question addresses a "pressing and substantial problem." Remember the question here: Under what conditions may government enact a law that limits the rights guaranteed in the Charter of Rights and Freedoms? The Supreme Court said the government may only limit our rights when it is tackling a pressing and substantial problem. The law prohibiting the production of child pornography clearly limits free speech, but just as clearly this law is addressing a pressing and substantial problem—the scourge of child pornography. But some laws fail to clear this hurdle. What pressing and substantial problem was government addressing when it denied the equality rights of gay and lesbian couples with respect to marriage? The courts concluded that there was no pressing and substantial problem here, so it ruled that the common law prohibition against same-sex marriage was unconstitutional.

If the government can persuade the court that the law is addressing a pressing and substantial problem, the government must then convince the court that the means employed to realize the law are proportionate to the law's objectives. There are three elements to this part of the test. First, the measures must be rationally connected to the objective. Second, the means should impair as little as possible the rights or freedoms in question. Third, the good effects of the law must outweigh the negative effects. If a law limits the rights guaranteed in the Charter but does not help the police catch bad guys, the courts will conclude that the limitation of the right is unreasonable.

Despite the court's desire to create an objective test, the test remains highly subjective. But that's all right; these matters cannot be determined with scientific precision. The Oakes test is important for three reasons. First, it is a rational test—judges are not making their decision on whims or emotions. Second, the same test is applied in each case. Our legislators in Parliament and provincial legislatures thus know how the courts will interpret the laws they make. Third, the test is flexible—it allows for changing circumstances. National security laws that may have been deemed completely unreasonable prior to 9/11 may now be considered perfectly reasonable.

What Happens When a Law Is Unconstitutional?

When a law is deemed unconstitutional, under the terms of Section 24.1 the Supreme Court may offer whatever remedy it considers "appropriate and just in the circumstances." Most often the Supreme Court will declare that a law is null and void. It is then up to Parliament to determine how to proceed. It could decide to enact a new law that would meet the concerns of the court, and the court will often give Parliament some tips on how to craft the new law. Parliament, however, may opt to do nothing and let the law go. When the Supreme Court struck down the law regulating abortion in the 1980s, the House of Commons voted for a new law but it was rejected by the Senate. Canada thus has no law regulating abortion. Finally, in some instances Parliament could employ the notwithstanding clause to overturn the court's decision, at least for five years, although as noted it has never taken advantage of this clause and may never do so.

In some cases, however, the Supreme Court takes matters into its own hands. In the *Sharpe* case on child pornography, the Supreme Court concluded that the law did not constitute a minimal impairment on the freedom of expression, as explained by Chief Justice Beverley McLachlin:

> The legislation prohibits a person from articulating thoughts in writing or visual images, even if the result is intended only for his or her own eyes. It further prohibits a teenager from possessing, again exclusively for personal use, sexually explicit photographs or videotapes of him- or herself alone or engaged with a partner in lawful sexual activity. The inclusion of these peripheral materials in the law's prohibition trenches heavily on freedom of expression while adding little to the protection the law provides children. To this extent, the law cannot be considered proportionate in its effects, and the infringement of [freedom of expression] contemplated by the legislation is not demonstrably justifiable under [Section] 1.[7]

The court, however, was not inclined to strike down a law addressing a problem as pressing as child pornography, especially when, in its view, the law was "substantially constitutional" and only "peripherally problematic." Thus, Chief Justice McLachlin wrote, "the appropriate remedy in this case is to *read into the law* an exclusion of the problematic applications" of the law.[8] Henceforth, self-created expressive material (for personal consumption only) and private recordings of lawful sexual activity (also for personal consumption only) would be exempt from the law prohibiting child pornography. Some commentators have been very critical of "legislating from the bench," as we will discuss below. However, there were no complaints in this case when the judges literally rewrote the law. On the contrary, people were relieved that the justices did not strike down this particular law, even if they took considerable liberties in their ruling.

Justices of the Supreme Court of Canada welcoming Andromache Karakatsanis (on the right) to the bench, November 14, 2011.

The Court System in Canada

The Supreme Court of Canada has played a much more significant role in Canadian politics since the adoption of the Charter of Rights and Freedoms. It has made hugely important decisions on subjects like abortion, same-sex marriage, euthanasia, and the death penalty. It is thus necessary to consider how the court system works in Canada, especially how justices are selected for the Supreme Court. But it must be stressed that the courts have always played an important role in the Canadian political system—this is a legacy of federalism. Federal political systems must have a written constitution, for as Albert Dicey noted more than 100 years ago, "The foundations of a federal state are a complicated contract. . . . To base an arrangement of this kind upon understandings or conventions would be certain to generate misunderstandings and disagreements."[9] And with a federal constitution it becomes necessary to have a court to interpret the constitution and resolve disputes between the two orders of government.

Federalism not only requires a written constitution and a judiciary, it also shapes the structure of the judiciary. The United States was the first modern federation, and its judiciary is quintessentially federal: federal courts interpret federal law and state courts interpret state law. The Supreme Court of the United States is the final court of appeal for both federal and state law (see Figure 9.1). Federal and Supreme Court judges are appointed by the federal government, and state court judges are selected at the state level.

The Canadian court system is more confusing than the American system. It might best be described as a federal system with unitary features. How did Canada end up with a quasi-federal court system? In the Confederation debates, Sir John A. Macdonald was adamant that criminal law should be a matter of federal responsibility, unlike in the United States where it is a state responsibility. But Quebec insisted that it wanted to maintain its unique system of **civil law**. Consequently, the administration of justice was made a matter of provincial responsibility. In other words, justice is effectively a matter of concurrent jurisdiction under the Constitution Act 1867. The Canadian court system reflects this political compromise. There are federal and provincial courts in Canada, much like in the United States, and the federal government appoints federal court judges and the provinces appoint provincial court judges. However, there is a third judicial branch in the Canadian court system: the provincial superior courts, which hear criminal cases. The provinces are responsible for the administration of the provincial superior courts, but the judges are chosen by the federal government because they are presiding over criminal law made by the

civil law A legal system that is descended from Roman law and is still used by the non-English-speaking parts of Europe and much of Africa. Rather than relying on judge-made precedent, civil law instead uses a comprehensive civil code that is written by a legislature. In Canada, Quebec still uses civil law, and thus maintains its own civil code—the *Code civil du Québec*.

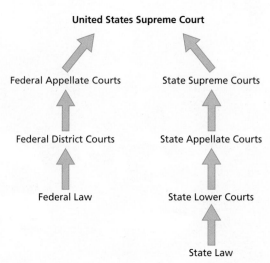

Figure 9.1 The American Court System

Chief Justice Beverley
McLachlin

Parliament of Canada. As in the United States, the Supreme Court of Canada is the final court of appeal for both federal and provincial courts, including the provincial superior courts (see Figure 9.2).

The Composition of the Supreme Court of Canada

The Supreme Court of Canada has nine justices. The only official requirement for becoming a Supreme Court justice is that the candidate must be a lawyer with at least 10 years of experience at the bar. Some have argued that justices on the Supreme Court should be fluently bilingual in French and English, but to date that has not been made an official requirement. Most often justices are selected from the federal or provincial appeals courts, but judicial experience is not required for an appointment to the Supreme Court. And, from time to time, a private practice lawyer is appointed to the Supreme Court. This is in fact desirable. Judges are frequently very far removed from the daily practice of law, so it is sometimes helpful to appoint a private practice lawyer to complement the judicial expertise already present on the bench.

Under the terms of the Supreme Court Act at least three justices must be from Quebec. This ensures that the Supreme Court has justices who are properly trained in Quebec's system

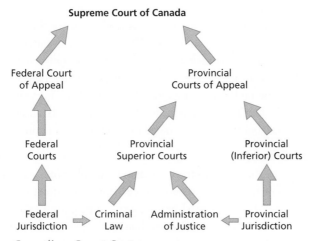

Figure 9.2 The Canadian Court System

of civil law. By *convention*, three justices come from Ontario, two from the West, and one from Atlantic Canada. Justices are allowed to serve until age 75. Traditionally, the most senior member of the court is appointed as the **Chief Justice**, although the governor general may appoint a different justice to this position on the advice of the prime minister. (By the way, if the governor general dies in office, the Chief Justice of the Supreme Court becomes the **Administrator of Canada** and temporarily assumes the duties of the governor general until a new governor general is appointed.) In 2000, Beverley McLachlin became the first female Chief Justice of Canada. She is now the longest serving Chief Justice in Canadian history. The other eight members of the court are known as *puisne* (an old French word for younger) justices.

How Does One Become a Justice on the Supreme Court of Canada?

Simply put, the justices are appointed by the governor general on the advice of the prime minister. The appointment process has always been more complex though, and it has been undergoing some much-needed reforms in the last decade. In order to understand these reforms, however, it is necessary to review how justices were appointed historically. In the past, when a vacancy emerged on the Supreme Court, the Minister of Justice would consult with members of the legal community in the province or region where the judge was to come from and solicit the names of potential justices. So, if a justice from the West retired, the Minister of Justice would talk with the attorney generals in the Western provinces, the chief justices in the provincial courts in the West, members of the provincial bar associations, and law professors at universities in the region. The process was very "old boy school." The Minister of Justice might say to his counterpart in Saskatchewan, "Do you know any decent chaps who might make a good Supreme Court justice?" From these conversations, the Minister of Justice would create a shortlist of candidates. The list would be submitted to the prime minister, and he would make his choice. The governor general would invariably accept the recommendation, and the candidate would take his or her seat on the court. The process was always shrouded in secrecy, until the announcement was made.

In the first half of the twentieth century, the judicial selection process was rife with patronage: Liberal governments would appoint judges with connections to the Liberal Party, and Conservative governments would appoint judges with connections of the Conservative Party. In the latter half of the twentieth century, though, the process became significantly less partisan, at least when it came to Supreme Court appointments. So, while the process was still informal and highly opaque, the people ultimately appointed to the Supreme Court of Canada in the latter half of the twentieth century were eminently qualified and went on to become excellent jurists. For some, there was thus no need for change: "If it ain't broke, don't fix it," they would say.

But others insist that a new selection process is required, since the Supreme Court now plays such an important role in Canadian politics. There are two very different lines of concern. Drawing on American practice, some have argued for a more transparent and accountable appointment process. We can call this the *republican critique*. Others, especially in Quebec, are more concerned about the underlying structure of the Canadian court system. These critics have demanded that the court system be federalized. Some progress has been made in response to the republican critique, but the concerns raised by Quebec remain unresolved.

The Republican Critique   With the adoption of the Charter of Rights and Freedoms and the enhanced role of the courts in the Canadian political system, some people began to call for a more democratic and transparent process for appointments, especially to the Supreme Court. Through the 1990s, the Reform Party—the forerunner to Stephen Harper's Conservative Party—demanded a complete overhaul of the judicial appointment process. It called for the provinces to nominate candidates for the Supreme Court of Canada, for the nominations to be considered and ratified by the Senate of Canada, and for justices to sit for a fixed 10-year term rather than allowing them to serve until age 75. In short, these proposals would move Canada closer to the American model of Supreme Court appointments, although justices on the US Supreme Court are allowed to serve for life once they are appointed to the bench. (It is not uncommon for justices on the US Supreme Court to serve well into their eighties, and a few carry on until they die.) In the United States, the president *nominates* candidates to be justices on the Supreme Court, but the Senate must *ratify* the nomination. The US Senate takes appointments to the Supreme Court very seriously: It holds public confirmation hearings, in which senators ask the nominees tough questions, and it quite often rejects potential candidates.

But if the Canadian process for appointing Supreme Court justices historically lacked too little scrutiny, the American process arguably involves too much scrutiny. In the confirmation process in the United States, senators routinely ask nominees to speculate about hypothetical cases. Most often, they focus on "hot button" issues such as abortion, the death penalty, gay marriage, and gun rights. Put bluntly, the senators want to know if the judges will be with them or against them on politically sensitive issues. Asking judges to speculate on such hypothetical cases is deeply problematic. Lawyers need real evidence before they can offer a sound legal opinion—without evidence it is a political debate, not a legal hearing. Second, the process may undermine the independence of the judiciary. When real cases subsequently arise in court, the justices may feel obligated to rule more or less along the lines they articulated during their confirmation hearing.

Worse, the confirmation process in the United States has become degraded by political muckraking. In 1987 Ronald Reagan nominated Robert Bork, a distinguished legal scholar, for the Supreme Court, but his nomination was rejected by the Senate because of his deeply conservative judicial philosophy. Henceforth, judicial nominees have typically possessed fairly banal legal track records, so the opposition party in the Senate and the media have turned to digging up dirt on the nominees. The process reached its lowest point in 1991, when George H.W. Bush moved to fill the vacancy created by the retirement of Justice Thurgood Marshall, who had the distinction of being the first black justice on the Supreme Court. For political reasons, President Bush wanted to replace Justice Marshall with another black judge, so he turned to the "most qualified" candidate he could find, a man named Clarence Thomas. After his nomination, there were allegations that Thomas had sexually harassed a former employee. Some senators revelled in the salacious details of the allegations, and the confirmation hearing was transformed into a daytime soap opera broadcast live on television. Thomas described the ordeal as a "high-tech lynching." He was eventually confirmed by the Senate by the narrowest of margins. The charges of sexual harassment, however, distracted everyone from the real issue: his very thin legal résumé.

The confirmation process in the United States has subsequently regained a modicum of civility, but some senators continue to focus on trivial matters for political advantage. In 2009, Sonia Sotomayor had to bat away questions about a single sentence she used in a speech to a group of law students a decade earlier. Sotomayor's nomination was confirmed by the Senate, and she became the first Hispanic American to sit on the US Supreme Court. In sum, when a nominee is put before a partisan committee, the process becomes partisan. Presidential candidates are now routinely asked what sort of justices they would nominate to the Supreme Court, further politicizing the judicial selection process. So while the American appointment process for the Supreme Court is much more transparent than the old Canadian appointment process, it is far from clear that it has led to superior judicial appointments, especially over the last three decades.

Reforming the Selection Process for the Supreme Court of Canada   With the Supreme Court of Canada literally making life and death decisions under the Charter of Rights and Freedoms on subjects like abortion, euthanasia, and capital punishment, the appointment of justices through an "old boys network" could no longer be justified, notwithstanding the fact that all appointments in living memory have been outstanding jurists. The door to the secretive appointment process was opened slightly in 2004 when Prime Minister Paul Martin asked the Minister of Justice to appear before the House of Commons Standing Committee on Justice to defend the nomination of Louise Charron and Rosalie Abella to the Supreme Court. *The Globe and Mail* described the new process as a "sham," and it was particularly scornful of the Minister of Justice: "Mr. Cotler was effusive in his praise of the government's choices. It was like sending your mother to your job interview."[10]

In 2005, Paul Martin unveiled a more elaborate and transparent process for Supreme Court appointments: The Minister of Justice would, as in the past, consult informally with the legal community and prepare a list of six to eight candidates. But instead of passing the list directly to the prime minister, the list would be submitted to an advisory committee consisting of a Member of Parliament from each recognized party in the House of Commons, an individual selected by the attorney generals from the region where the justice was to be chosen, a representative of the regional law societies, a retired judge, and two "prominent" citizens who were neither lawyers nor judges. The advisory committee was charged with reviewing the list of candidates and recommending three names to the prime minister, who would ultimately nominate one of the candidates. The Minister of Justice would go before the House of Commons Standing Committee on Justice and defend the government's nominee.

In the fall of 2005, an advisory committee was established to search for a new Supreme Court justice from Western Canada. The committee conducted its work, and it finally settled on three names. However, before the process could be drawn to a close, the minority Martin government lost a vote of confidence in the House of Commons. Parliament was duly dissolved, and an election was held that resulted in the Conservative Party winning a minority government in January 2006. Instead of initiating a new process, Stephen Harper nominated Marshall Rothstein from the list put forward by the advisory committee established by the Martin government. But, going beyond the process envisioned by the Liberal government, Prime Minister Harper asked Rothstein to appear with the Minister of Justice in front of the Standing Committee on Justice and answer questions from members of the committee. Judge Rothstein said he was "panic-stricken" before the hearing, but afterward he said, "The genie is out of the bottle . . . I don't think we will ever go back to a less public process for Supreme Court nominations."[11] But the very next nominee was spared the ordeal of a parliamentary hearing! Stephen Harper simply decided to skip the hearing when he appointed Thomas Cromwell of Nova Scotia to the Supreme Court in December 2008 in the midst of the prorogation crisis.

Since 2008 the appointment process seems to have arrived at a new normalcy. Stephen Harper has retained the idea of a judicial advisory committee, although it now only includes Members of Parliament (one member for each party with standing in the House of Commons). And justices Michael Moldaver, Andromache Karakatsanis, Richard Wagner, and Marc Nadon were all required to appear before the Standing Committee of Justice before taking their seats on the court. So, after a decade of experimentation, how well is the new appointment process working? The jury is split. *The Globe and Mail* has welcomed the new reforms,[12] but the Canadian Bar Association remains resolutely opposed to American-style confirmation hearings.[13] The selection of Marc Nadon in October 2013, however, reveals that the appointment process is still a work in progress. After Nadon took his seat on the bench, questions were raised about his credentials to sit on the Supreme Court. The Supreme Court Act states that justices from Quebec need to be superior court judges or members of the Quebec bar, but Nadon had been a federal court judge and had not been a member of the bar for more than two decades. The Supreme Court ultimately ruled that Nadon was not eligible to sit as a justice on the court. Clearly, the vetting process failed Justice Nadon. We should thus anticipate further reforms to the appointment process.

With the adoption of the Charter of Rights and Freedoms, it was necessary to adopt a more open process for appointing justices to the Supreme Court. Obviously, the governments of Canada have struggled to devise a process that is more transparent but also consistent with Canada's parliamentary system of government. To date, the judicial interviews conducted by the Standing Committee on Justice have been civil and modestly informative. But the American experience with confirmation hearings suggests that politicians have a great deal of difficulty remaining nonpartisan. In Canada, there is consensus that civility is on the decline in the House of Commons. There is thus reason to fear that hearings for Supreme Court nominees in Canada might go down the American road. And if this happens, the best candidates may not wish to be nominated. Why would someone agree to give up a good job and possibly considerable salary only to have their name dragged through the mud?

More importantly, American-style confirmation hearings may not be consistent with the principles of responsible government. In the Canadian system of government, the executive is supposed to assume responsibility for its decisions. Thus, in my view, it should be the Minister of Justice who is called before the Standing Committee on Justice to defend the government's nominees for the Supreme Court. The minister would surely be subjected to partisan questions, but at least the future justices of the Supreme Court would be spared from this political spectacle, thereby better preserving the principle of judicial independence. But I suspect there is no going back—the practice of interviewing nominees for the Supreme Court of Canada now appears to be a new convention in the Canadian political system.

The Federal Critique   While some progress has been made on the republican critique of the Canadian court system, the federal critique has proven to be much more challenging. It is a systemic critique—in other words, it focuses on the structure of the court system rather than its operation. In Canada, following the model in the United States, the final arbiter of the constitution is the Supreme Court. The problem with this arrangement was noted almost 200 years ago by Alexis de Tocqueville in *Democracy in America*, which is widely regarded as the best book ever written about American politics. Under the terms of the American constitution, whenever the power and the authority of the federal government is challenged by one of the states "a federal tribunal decides the question." This, he went on to say, "was a severe blow to the sovereignty of the states." The same is true in Canada, at least since the abolition of appeals to the Judicial Committee of the Privy Council. Think about it this way: in a high-stakes playoff game between Team Federal Government and Team Province, the federal government gets to choose the referees. The justices of the Supreme Court of Canada may well be independent and neutral, but they cannot eliminate the *perception* of bias, especially when they make rulings in favour of the federal government and to the detriment of the provinces.

All of the provinces are disadvantaged by the federal bias built into the structure of Canada's court system, but the apparent bias is especially troubling for Quebec. This issue was brought into sharp relief for many Quebecers by the processes that led to the patriation of the constitution. In the 1980 patriation reference case, the Supreme Court—which ruled that Prime Minister Trudeau's plan to patriate the constitution unilaterally was legal although not in the conventional sense—did not take into account Quebec's unique position in the federation as a province unlike the others. In the 1982 veto reference case, the Supreme Court again ignored Quebec's distinctiveness. In 1989, the Supreme Court struck down Quebec's sign law. These judgments, coupled with Trudeau's decision to patriate the constitution over the objections of Quebec, have created a serious legitimacy crisis for the Supreme Court in the province of Quebec. Guy Laforest, a prominent political scientist in Quebec, has stated bluntly, "the Supreme Court of Canada should not have any authority on the territory of Quebec."[14] This may sound like an extreme statement, but many in Quebec would agree. When the federal government asked the Supreme Court in 1998 if a province could legally separate from the federation, the government of Quebec refused to participate in the case, as will be discussed further in Chapter 11; Quebec simply didn't believe that it would get a fair hearing from a group of justices appointed by the federal government.

Over the past 20 years, Quebec has made a number of proposals to federalize the court system in Canada, especially the Supreme Court. While the Constitution Act 1867 gives the federal government the authority to establish a Supreme Court, the court itself has been governed historically by statutory legislation, the Supreme Court Act. As such, the Parliament of Canada could unilaterally reform—or even abolish—the Supreme Court. It could also change Quebec's representation on the Supreme Court. Quebec has thus long insisted that the Supreme Court should be entrenched in the constitution, including the provision from the Supreme Court Act that requires three of the nine justices to come from Quebec. The government of Quebec has also argued that the federal government should be required to name justices from lists submitted by the provinces. Many of these proposals were floated in the constitutional debates in the 1990s, but none were adopted, as will be discussed more fully in Chapter 11. However, some of these issues were addressed in the Supreme Court decision in the Nadon case in March 2014. In particular, the Supreme Court ruled that parts of the Supreme Court Act—especially the eligibility requirements for the top court—should henceforth be regarded as "the constitution of the court." As such, these provisions of the Supreme Court Act cannot be changed by Parliament without the unanimous consent of all the provinces. While Quebec can take some comfort in the court's decision, presumably it would still like to see these provisions formally entrenched in the constitution.

The Institutional Legacy of the Constitution Act 1982

The Constitution Act 1982 represents a significant transformation of the Canadian political system. Its significance goes well beyond the legal decisions made by the Supreme Court on topics like same-sex marriage, abortion, euthanasia, and the death penalty. The Constitution Act 1982—especially the Charter of Rights and Freedoms—poses fundamental challenges to the twin governing principles embedded in the British North America Act: federalism and responsible government. In short, it has threatened national unity, it has changed the way we are governed, and ultimately it has reshaped Canadian political culture.

The Charter versus Federalism

In the old constitution, the federal and provincial governments were positioned as the only players in the constitutional game. And the amending formulas entrenched in the new constitution are premised on federalism. So who can change the constitution? Only the federal and provincial governments. But, as Peter Russell notes, the Charter "produced a new set of players in the constitutional process—the interest groups whose rights claims gained constitutional recognition and whose perspective is distinctly indifferent to federalism."[15] In many respects, as Alan Cairns has detailed at length, Trudeau's people's constitution is pitted against the government's constitution of 1867. "Succinctly," writes Cairns, "the Charter states what the amending formula denies, that 'federalism is not enough'—that Canadians are more than a federal people."[16]

While many Canadians are distinctly indifferent to federalism, the province of Quebec has historically viewed federalism—or more precisely classical federalism—as an instrument of survival. The diminished salience of federalism in the new constitutional order, and more broadly in Canadian political culture, is deeply alarming to Quebec. Indeed, many people in *la belle province* believe that the Quebec nation has been marginalized in the new constitutional order. This, of course, was Pierre Trudeau's objective: He wanted to thwart Quebec's national aspirations permanently. It was a very high-stakes gamble. In the 1990s, it looked like the gamble would fail spectacularly, as Quebec appeared to be on the verge of leaving the federation. Now, with support for sovereignty at an all-time low, it looks like a better bet. But it is still too early to know if Pierre Trudeau's gamble has paid off. If 100 years from now Canada is a united and prosperous country with a vibrant French-speaking community in Quebec, historians will look back and credit Trudeau for saving Canada from the brink of dissolution. If, on the other hand, Quebec separates from the federation and the rest of the country splinters into a couple of regional fiefdoms, future historians will blame Trudeau for imposing a new constitutional order on the country over and above the vigorous opposition of Quebec. For the time being, the Charter will continue to pose a significant challenge to the saliency of federalism with uncertain consequences.

The Charter versus Responsible Government

In 1867, Canada adopted a constitution "similar in principle" to that of the United Kingdom. The British system of government is premised on the sovereignty of Parliament. In Canada, the principle of parliamentary sovereignty was limited from the outset by the adoption of a federal constitution. The Parliament of Canada cannot legislate on any matter whatsoever, because under the constitution some of the powers of government belong exclusively to the provinces. The Charter of Rights and Freedoms further circumscribes the power of government in Canada—both the federal Parliament and the legislatures of the provinces. The laws made by Parliament and the provincial legislatures must be consistent with the Charter of Rights and Freedoms, as determined by the courts. Thus, for some, the Charter of Rights and Freedoms is fundamentally undemocratic.

The critics of the Charter and judicial review argue that it is undemocratic for *unelected* judges to strike down legislation passed by *elected* legislators. In the Canadian system of government, however, responsibility does not begin and end with legislators. Legislators in Canada have always been guided by higher powers: the Crown, the constitution, and the rule of law. And judicial review has always been a part of the Canadian constitutional order: the courts have been empowered to determine if legislation is within the legislative competence of the government that made the law according to the division of powers in Sections 91 and 92 of the Constitution Act 1867. If the law in question were outside the legislative competence of the government, the courts would declare it *ultra vires* (beyond powers) and the law would consequently be null and void. Curiously, critics of the judicial review of the Charter generally do not seem to have a problem with the judicial review of federalism.

Canada, furthermore, is not an unqualified democracy: It is a *liberal* democracy. The core principles of liberalism—equality and individual liberty—are not always congruent with democracy. Unfortunately, democratic majorities have been known to deny liberty and equality to particular individuals, usually on the basis of some group affiliation such as race, religion, gender, or sexual orientation. The institutions of democracy are not well designed to protect minorities, because minorities are perpetually at risk of being outvoted in the electoral process. And Parliament is not well positioned to guarantee minority rights. Parliamentarians generally lack a comprehensive understanding of constitutional rights, they are susceptible to majority wishes, they are motivated by the next election, and they are subject to party discipline. The Charter of Rights and Freedoms is supposed to be a bulwark against the tyranny of the majority. And the courts, especially the Supreme Court, are in a much better position to guarantee minority rights. The justices of the Supreme Court have a comprehensive understanding of constitutional rights, they are not motivated by partisan concerns, they have security of tenure, and consequently they are buffered from public opinion. At least, their employment is not directly conditional on maintaining public support. In sum, the Charter is not inconsistent with Canadian political traditions; it simply attempts to afford a better balance between the sometimes mutually antagonistic principles of liberalism and democracy.

While it is fairly easy to dismiss the argument that the Charter is undemocratic, it is very true that the decisions of the Supreme Court very often have profound political implications. Why did Canada become one of the first countries to recognize same-sex marriage? Because the courts said that not recognizing same-sex marriage was unconstitutional. Some critics have thus suggested that the Supreme Court has wilfully engaged in "policymaking" in its judgments. In a strict sense, judges are not making policy; they are interpreting law. "Where a legal issue is properly before the court," Beverley McLachlin has said, "not deciding is not an option." And the law is not black and white—the answers are not necessarily obvious. Consequently, judgments of the Supreme Court are bound to be controversial from time to time. While judges are repeatedly criticized for entering the policymaking arena, one could just as easily (or even more easily) argue that parliamentarians have at times abdicated their responsibility to address difficult policy issues. Why take a stand on euthanasia and alienate many voters, some Members of Parliament may say to themselves, when the Supreme Court will almost certainly be asked to rule (again) on this explosive issue?

And finally, it must be stressed that the law begins and ends with Parliament. The law is made by Parliament in the first instance, and in the few instances when the law is tested in the courts and deemed to be unconstitutional, the law is returned to Parliament for reconsideration. It can redraft the law, it can let the law go, or it can (in some instances) invoke the notwithstanding clause. And the Supreme Court almost always offers some guidance on how the law could be revised to make it consistent with the Charter.

After more than 30 years of jurisprudence, Parliament is much more aware of the contours of the Charter. In short, Parliament and the Supreme Court are now engaged in a continual *dialogue* about the law.[17] It is a silent dialogue—the prime minister cannot pick up the phone and call the Chief Justice of the Supreme Court to get her opinion on a piece of impending legislation. But the Supreme Court and Parliament can and do send signals back and forth to each other about how the constitution should be interpreted. In so doing, the Supreme Court of Canada has not overstepped its bounds. On the contrary, it is fulfilling the task assigned to it by the constitution, which was drafted and adopted by the elected Members of Parliament. There is thus no conflict between the Supreme Court and Parliament, even if they don't always agree on the law.

SUMMARY

The Constitution Act 1982 was a new beginning for Canada. For the first time in its history, the governments of Canada possessed the legal ability to modify the country's constitution. The amending formulas, however, are quite rigid, meaning that it is fairly difficult to obtain the necessary consensus to effect a constitutional change, especially a major change. The political realities of the new amending formulas became painfully apparent in the 1990s, as will be discussed in Chapter 11. In a formal sense, Canada now exists in a constitutional straightjacket, and for the time being only small-scale constitutional amendments can be contemplated. For the most part, political reform will have to transpire through informal means, such as fiscal federalism and judicial review.

The Charter of Rights and Freedoms has had a profound impact on Canadian politics on two levels. On the first level, the Supreme Court of Canada has made significant judgments on matters like same-sex marriage, abortion, euthanasia, and the death penalty. In short, the Supreme Court is now a real player in the game of Canadian politics. Consequently, the selection of Supreme Court justices is now more important than ever, and successive governments of Canada have attempted to make the selection process more open and accountable. While the process is still evolving, it would seem that nominees for the

Supreme Court will henceforth be required to attend a parliamentary hearing. At this point in time, we do not know if these hearings will become unduly partisan and potentially undermine the independence of the judiciary.

At a deeper level, the Charter of Rights and Freedoms has presented a great challenge to Canada's historical governing principles of federalism and responsible government. It has made Canada a little less federal, and it has put new limits on the power of Parliament. The Supreme Court has been given the constitutional responsibility to ensure that the laws of Parliament are consistent with the constitution, especially the Charter of Rights and Freedoms. The Supreme Court and Parliament are now engaged in a continuous, if silent, dialogue on the law.

More broadly, the Charter presents a different image of the body politic. The Constitution Act 1867 reflected the old Canada of federalism, linguistic and religious dualism, and patriarchy (i.e., male dominance); the Constitution Act 1982 reflects the modern Canada of First Nations, multiculturalism, and gender equality. While many Canadians are comfortable with this new constitutional orientation, it has been distressing to many citizens of Quebec, who cannot help feeling that the nation of Quebec has been reduced from a full partner in the federation to just one of many multicultural groups vying for political attention. For some Quebecers, the new constitution represents the "end of a Canadian dream." In sum, the Constitution Act 1982 has changed the way Canada is governed, but it has not yet achieved the political unity sought by Pierre Trudeau.

Questions to Think About

1. Should the governments of Canada ever be allowed to limit the rights guaranteed by the Charter?

2. Do you think the notwithstanding clause was a reasonable compromise?

3. Do you think it is important to include language and group rights in the Charter of Rights and Freedoms along with traditional individual rights?

4. Is it undemocratic for unelected judges to strike down the laws enacted by elected legislators?

5. Do you think there should be parliamentary hearings for nominees to the Supreme Court?

6. Does the Charter of Rights and Freedoms undermine federalism and threaten Canadian unity?

Learning Outcomes

1. Describe the various amending formulas in the Constitution Act 1982 and explain why they seem to place Canada in a constitutional straightjacket.

2. Describe the different kinds of rights entrenched in the Charter of Rights and Freedoms.

3. Describe the notwithstanding clause of the Charter of Rights and Freedoms and explain why it was a controversial provision to include in the new constitution.

4. Describe the limitations section of the Charter of Rights and Freedoms and explain the Oakes test.

5. Describe the republican and federalist critiques of the appointment process to the Supreme Court of Canada and evaluate the recent reforms to the Supreme Court appointment process.

6. Explain how the Charter of Rights and Freedoms challenges the principles of federalism and responsible government.

Additional Reading

Dennis Baker, *Not Quite Supreme: The Courts and Coordinate Constitutional Interpretation* (Montreal, QC: McGill-Queen's University Press, 2010).

Ian Brodie, *Friends of the Court: The Privileging of Interest Group Litigants in Canada* (Albany, NY: State University of New York Press, 2002).

Ian Greene, *The Courts* (Vancouver, BC: UBC Press, 2006).

Janet L. Hiebert, *Charter Conflicts: What Is Parliament's Role?* (Montreal, QC: McGill-Queen's University Press, 2002).

Janet L. Hiebert, *Limiting Rights: The Dilemma of Judicial Review* (Montreal, QC: McGill-Queen's University Press, 1996).

James B. Kelly, *Governing with the Charter: Legislative and Judicial Activism and the Framer's Intent* (Vancouver, BC: UBC Press, 2005).

Emmett Macfarlane, *Governing from the Bench: The Supreme Court of Canada and the Judicial Role* (Vancouver, BC: UBC Press, 2013).

Kate Malleson and Peter H. Russell, eds., *Appointing Judges in an Age of Judicial Power: Critical Perspectives from Around the World* (Toronto, ON: University of Toronto Press, 2006).

Christopher P. Manfredi, *Judicial Power and the Charter: Canada and the Paradox of Liberal Constitutionalism*, 2nd ed. (Toronto, ON: Oxford University Press, 2001).

F.L. Morton and Rainer Knopff, *The Charter Revolution and the Court Party* (Peterborough, ON: Broadview Press, 2000).

Andrew Petter, *The Politics of the Charter: The Illusive Promise of Constitutional Rights* (Toronto, ON: University of Toronto Press, 2010).

Miriam Smith, *Lesbian and Gay Rights in Canada: Social Movements and Equality-Seeking, 1971–1995* (Toronto, ON: University of Toronto Press, 1999).

Donald R. Songer, *The Transformation of the Supreme Court of Canada: An Empirical Examination* (Toronto, ON: University of Toronto Press, 2008).

Notes

1. Pierre Elliott Trudeau, "The Values of a Just Society," in Thomas S. Axworthy and Pierre Elliott Trudeau, eds., *Towards a Just Society* (Toronto, ON: Penguin Books, 1992), 407.
2. Peter H. Russell, *Constitutional Odyssey: Can Canadians Become a Sovereign People?* 3rd ed. (Toronto, ON: University of Toronto Press, 2004), 114.
3. Pierre Elliott Trudeau, *Memoirs* (Toronto, ON: McClelland and Stewart, 1993), 328.
4. Peter W. Hogg, *Constitutional Law of Canada,* 5th ed. (Toronto, ON: Carswell, 2007).
5. Robert J. Sharpe and Kent Roach, *Brian Dickson: A Judge's Journey* (Toronto, ON: Osgoode Society for Canadian Legal History and University of Toronto Press, 2003), 334.
6. See Geoff Ellwand, "Routine Drug Arrest becomes Oakes Test," *The Lawyers Weekly* (May 20, 2011), 26–27.
7. *R. v. Sharpe*, [2001] 1 S.C.R. 45, 2001 SCC 2, para. 110.
8. Ibid., para. 114, emphasis added.
9. A. V. Dicey, *An Introduction to the Study of the Law of the Constitution*, 10th ed. (London, UK: Macmillan Press, 1959), 146.
10. "Chose Your Judge," Editorial, *The Globe and Mail*, September 1, 2005, A20.
11. "Judges in the Spotlight," Editorial, *The Globe and Mail*, October 30, 2006, A18.
12. "Supreme Court Nominee Review Needs More Time," Editorial, *The Globe and Mail*, October 20, 2011.
13. See Canadian Bar Association, "Supreme Court of Canada Appointment Process," March 2004; and "Federal Judicial Appointment Process," October 2005.
14. Guy Laforest, *Trudeau and the End of a Canadian Dream* (Montreal, QC: McGill-Queen's University Press, 1995), 191.
15. Russell, *Constitutional Odyssey*, 115.
16. Alan C. Cairns, *Charter versus Federalism: The Dilemmas of Constitutional Reform* (Montreal, QC: McGill-Queen's University Press, 1992), 8.
17. See Peter W. Hogg and Allison A. Bushell, "The Charter Dialogue between Courts and Legislatures," *Osgoode Hall Law Journal* 35:1 (1997), 75–124; and Peter W. Hogg, Allison A. Bushell Thornton, and Wade K. Wright, "Charter Dialogue Revised—Or Much Ado about Metaphors," *Osgoode Hall Law Journal* 45:1 (2007), 1–65.

Chapter 10
Aboriginal Rights

Key Points

- The rules of the game have always been different for Aboriginal peoples in Canada.

- Aboriginal peoples constituted self-governing communities in North America before the arrival of Europeans, and they entered into treaty arrangements with the Crown in many parts of Canada, although not everywhere (particularly British Columbia).

- Treaty arrangements with Aboriginal peoples were frequently ignored, and at Confederation Aboriginal peoples were subjected to a form of internal colonialism.

- In light of important court decisions in the 1960s and 1970s, the governments of Canada recognized and affirmed Aboriginal rights in the Constitution Act 1982.

- But the governments of Canada have been reluctant to negotiate a comprehensive settlement with Aboriginal peoples, so it has fallen to the Supreme Court to define the scope and meaning of Aboriginal rights, including self-government.

- The constitutional promises of 1982 are still not fulfilled, but it is clear that Aboriginal peoples constitute unique citizens in Canada.

- While Aboriginal rights are now constitutionally protected, many Aboriginal communities are still mired in poverty.

For many Canadians, the Charter of Rights and Freedoms is the cornerstone of the Constitution Act 1982, but Part II of the new constitution is potentially even more significant. Here we find, in one very brief section, the recognition and affirmation of Aboriginal rights. Section 35 was an afterthought for Pierre Trudeau and the provincial premiers, and it reads more like a promissory note than a plan for a new order of government. Nonetheless, for Aboriginal Canadians Section 35 represents the end of the colonial relationship between the Canadian state and Aboriginal peoples, just as the act of patriation marked the end of Canada's colonial relationship with Great Britain.

The significance of Section 35 cannot be overstated. It "renounces the old rules of the game," and calls "for a just settlement with aboriginal peoples."[1] Thus, paradoxically, a process that was intended to address the constitutional concerns of Quebec left Quebec feeling deeply alienated but it marked a new beginning for Aboriginal peoples, who did not participate directly in the process.

The governments of Canada, however, have been reluctant to fulfill the promises of 1982. In the absence of a political settlement, it has been left to the courts to interpret the scope and meaning of Section 35. While the Supreme Court has not been entirely consistent, it has defined the historical **treaty rights** of Aboriginal peoples, and it has also determined that **Aboriginal rights**, including **title** over land, exist independently of treaties. While many academics and

treaty rights Particular and uniquely Aboriginal rights stemming from the original treaties signed between Aboriginal peoples and the French and British Crowns.

Aboriginal rights Unique rights of Aboriginal peoples that stem from the original occupation and use of the land by Aboriginal peoples.

title An Aboriginal right to own land collectively as a result of the original occupation and use of the land by Aboriginal peoples.

A Note on Terminology

Terminology is a very sensitive matter in most discussions about race relations. With respect to Aboriginal peoples in Canada, we need to distinguish between legal terminology, anthropologically correct terminology, political terminology, and socially acceptable terminology. Under the Constitution Act 1982, Aboriginal people in Canada are defined as "Indian, Inuit and Métis." For the most part, I will refer to these legal terms in this chapter and throughout the book. That means I will use the word "Indian," even though the term is anthropologically incorrect and often socially unacceptable; clearly, the original inhabitants of Canada have never had any connection to India. "Indigenous" would be a better anthropological term to describe the original inhabitants of Canada. First Nations are groups of legal or "status Indians" living on a reserve or self-governing community, but it is not a legal term. It is the term adopted by Aboriginal peoples themselves for political reasons.[2]

self-government The right of Aboriginal peoples to establish, design, and administer their own governments under the constitution of Canada.

most Aboriginal people believe that Section 35 entrenches a right to **self-government**, the top court has been reluctant to make a definitive judgment on self-government.

The creation of an Aboriginal order of government is ultimately a political matter, but the governments of Canada have not pursued this issue with any urgency because they fear that it will be unpopular with non-Aboriginal Canadians, who constitute the democratic majority. However, it is important to recognize that the quest for Aboriginal self-government—unlike the movement for sovereignty in Quebec—is not about separating *from* Canada; it is about *joining* Canada as a partner in the federation. However, the idea of separate rights for Aboriginal peoples makes many people uncomfortable because it challenges the traditional definition of Canadian citizenship. Nevertheless, the governments of Canada now have a constitutional obligation to negotiate a just settlement with Aboriginal peoples, including self-government. The governments of Canada also have a moral obligation to alleviate the terrible poverty that remains endemic in many Aboriginal communities.

Aboriginal Peoples and the Crown

Aboriginal rights were not part of Pierre Trudeau's plan to secure constitutional peace, and none of the provincial governments had any interest in Aboriginal rights either. In order to understand how and why Aboriginal rights came to be included in the new constitution, we need to examine the historical relationship between Aboriginal peoples and the Crown. While this was a relationship of equals at the point of contact 500 years ago, it evolved over time into a relationship between colonial ruler and subject. After Confederation in 1867, the federal government embarked on a long and concerted effort to assimilate Aboriginal peoples and extinguish their traditional way of life. While the federal government believed it was offering Aboriginal peoples a better life, its policies were based on the deeply racist assumption that the Aboriginal way of life was not worthy. While the Constitution Act 1982 re-established Aboriginal peoples as partners in the federation, we are still in the process of undoing the damage inflicted by centuries of colonial domination over Aboriginal peoples.

The relationship between Aboriginal peoples and the Crown (first the French and later the British Crown) can be broken down into four stages: pre-contact, contact, colonial domination, and renewal (with the Canadian Crown), although it is not easy to mark each stage with precision.[3] There is considerable overlap between the stages, and the relationship started at different times across the country. Aboriginal groups in Eastern Canada experienced contact with European settlers earlier than groups in the West and North. While we are primarily concerned with the history of colonial domination and the current politics of renewal, the pre-contact and contact periods have assumed new legal and political relevance in the modern era. The politics of renewal commenced in 1982 with the new constitution.

Pre-Contact Era

Aboriginal peoples in Canada first made contact with Europeans when Viking explorers arrived on the shores of Newfoundland and Labrador around 1000 years ago, but these meetings were fleeting. Prior to the year 1500, Aboriginal and non-Aboriginal peoples largely inhabited separate worlds. Aboriginal peoples lived in communities all across the upper half of Turtle Island, as many Aboriginal people call North America. The first non-Aboriginal settlers in North America came from Europe. In their separate worlds, Aboriginal and European peoples developed very different political institutions as well as different belief systems and ways of life. While the pre-contact era was more than 500 years ago, it is not simply a matter of historical interest. Since 1982, the Supreme Court of Canada has tied contemporary Aboriginal rights to activities practised by Aboriginal peoples *prior* to contact with European settlers. The history of the pre-contact era is thus of considerable importance to both Aboriginal and non-Aboriginal peoples, as will be elaborated on below.

Contact and Cooperation

European settlers made contact with Aboriginal peoples in Eastern and Central Canada some 500 years ago, and European settlers slowly began to make their way across the continent, finally arriving on the Pacific coast about 200 years ago. Over this time, the relationship between Aboriginal and non-Aboriginal peoples changed dramatically. Initially, European explorers were dependent on the support of Aboriginal people. Europeans were unfamiliar with North America, and they relied on Aboriginal knowledge of the land and climate to survive. In exchange, Aboriginal peoples received European goods and technology. Later, the commercial links between Aboriginal and non-Aboriginal peoples deepened and political and military alliances were formed.

Royal Proclamation   Over time, Aboriginal peoples were drawn into expressly European conflicts. In the middle of the eighteenth century, Great Britain and France were engaged in a battle for global supremacy. After seven years of war, the British emerged victorious. In North America, the decisive battle was waged on the Plains of Abraham in Quebec City in 1759. Four years later, King George III issued a Royal Proclamation, in which he revealed how he intended to govern his newly acquired territory. George made it clear that he expected his French subjects to assimilate into the English way of life, as discussed in Chapter 8. But he adopted a very different tone with respect to Aboriginal peoples. The British government recognized that it needed the support of Aboriginal people to secure its new territory. With the Royal Proclamation, George sought to reassure Aboriginal peoples about his government's good intentions. He thus proclaimed that all lands not ceded or sold by the Indian "nations or tribes" with whom the British were connected were "reserved to them" (see Box 10.2).

Treaties   It is important to stress that France and later Britain did *not* conquer Aboriginal peoples in North America: they entered into cooperative relationships with Aboriginal nations, and these relationships were enshrined in treaties. The earliest treaties were signed between the French and British Crowns and First Nations along the St. Lawrence River and the Maritime colonies, respectively. These treaties were typically brief statements of friendship and cooperation. In the early nineteenth century, more elaborate treaties were signed with

Box 10.2

The Royal Proclamation

King George III

Queen Elizabeth II (the great, great, great granddaughter of George III)

And whereas it is just and reasonable, and essential to our Interest, and the Security of our Colonies, that the several Nations or Tribes of Indians with whom We are connected, and who live under our Protection, should not be molested or disturbed in the Possession of such Parts of Our Dominions and Territories as, not having been ceded to or purchased by Us, are reserved to them, or any of them, as their Hunting Grounds . . .

And. We do further strictly enjoin and require all Persons whatever who have either wilfully or inadvertently seated themselves upon any Lands within the Countries above described or upon any other Lands which, not having been ceded to or purchased by Us, are still reserved to the said Indians as aforesaid, forthwith to remove themselves from such Settlements . . .

Given at our Court at St. James's the 7th Day of October 1763, in the Third Year of our Reign.

King George III

First Nations in southern Ontario; treaties were also signed with First Nations on Vancouver Island at this time. After Confederation, a series of treaties—numbered 1 through 11—were signed with First Nations in northern Ontario, across the prairies, and most of the Northwest Territories. Treaty Number 8 also spills into northeastern British Columbia. The rest of British Columbia, apart from Vancouver Island, was not subject to any treaties. Most of British Columbia thus remains reserved for First Nations under the terms of the Royal Proclamation.

There may not have been much intention on the part of the Crown to honour the treaties it signed. For the Crown, treaties simply provided a legal veneer for the appropriation of Aboriginal land. Certainly, many Canadians today regard treaties as an historical anachronism with no contemporary relevance. But for many Aboriginal people the historical treaties are virtually sacred documents and must be honoured. The Canadian courts have determined that the historical treaties are in fact still legally valid. The governments of Canada subsequently recognized and affirmed the treaty rights of Aboriginal peoples in the Constitution Act 1982.

Colonial Domination

Cooperation with First Nations declined steadily through the nineteenth century as the European population expanded in Canada, but the era of colonial domination paradoxically commenced with Confederation in 1867. In other words, just as Canada gained a measure of independence from Great Britain, Canada embarked on long-term policy of **internal colonialism**. By this time, Aboriginal peoples were viewed as primitive savages, and the explicit policy objective of the Canadian state was to gradually prepare Aboriginal peoples for life in "civilized" society.

While most policies relied on Aboriginal peoples to volunteer for assimilation, the government frequently took it upon itself to determine what was in the best interests of Aboriginal people. Many Aboriginal children were taken from their families and forced into **residential schools** far from home, where they were often abused and thousands died (mostly from tuberculosis and other diseases). The Government of Canada started to phase out residential schools in the 1960s, but the last schools were not closed until the late 1990s. More than 150 000 Aboriginal children were forced to attend residential schools. The residential school policy has been described as an act of "cultural genocide."[4] Many residential school survivors were scarred for life, and their children have suffered too. In other cases, entire communities were forcibly relocated by the government, especially in the far north.

Under Section 91(24) of the Constitution Act 1867, the Parliament of Canada assumed responsibility for "Indians, and Land Reserved for Indians." In 1876, the Parliament of Canada enacted the **Indian Act**, which represented a consolidation of pre-Confederation Indian law. The original objective of the Indian Act was very clear: Aboriginal peoples should live under the control of the federal government on isolated reserves or they should abandon their traditional way of life and assimilate into the Canadian mainstream. The Indian Act effectively infantilized Aboriginal peoples and made them wards of the state.

The Indian Act continues to regulate just about every aspect of life for Aboriginal peoples, including the basic question of who is and is not "Indian." The Department of Aboriginal Affairs and Northern Development still issues **status cards** for people who meet the legal definition of "Indian." Indian status has always been a legal construct rather than an anthropological or racial construct. Historically, for example, Aboriginal women who married non-Aboriginal men *lost* their Indian status, but non-Aboriginal women who married Aboriginal men would *gain* Aboriginal status. These overtly sexist provisions of the Indian Act were eliminated in the 1980s, but the concept of a **Status Indian** remains problematic (Status Indians are also referred to as registered or legal Indians). There are an estimated 700 000 registered Indians in Canada, and another 500 000 people identify themselves as Aboriginal in the census. Aboriginal peoples thus make up 3 to 4 percent of the Canadian population.

The Indian Act also provides the governance framework for Aboriginal peoples in Canada, but again it is a legal construct. Aboriginal governance in Canada today only loosely corresponds with traditional Aboriginal government. Under the Indian Act, Status Indians belong to a **band** and live on a **reserve**. There are 614 bands in Canada and just over 2700 reserves. "In Eastern Canada each band is generally limited to one reserve, while in the West one band may encompass several reserves. British Columbia has over 1600 reserves but fewer than 200 bands."[5] Geographically, at 900 square kilometres the Blood Reserve in Alberta is the largest in the country; many reserves in British Columbia are just a few hectares. With over 8000 people, the Six Nations band near Brantford, Ontario, is the largest reserve in the country demographically. The average band has about 500 members.

Under the terms of the Indian Act, each band has a **band council**, with a chief elected by the members of the band. Band members also vote for councillors. The chief and the councillors serve two-year terms. Band councils are responsible for the public health of the community, law and order in the community, housing, and water, among other things.

internal colonialism The political and economic subjugation of a particular group of people within a country by the government of that country.

residential schools Schools that were established by the Government of Canada in conjunction with the Catholic and Anglican churches to forcibly educate Aboriginal children and assimilate them into mainstream Canadian society. The schools operated for more than a century, and the last residential school was closed in the 1990s. More than 150 000 Aboriginal children attended residential schools, where they were frequently physically and psychologically abused.

Indian Act Federal legislation that defines the legal status of Indian peoples in Canada and regulates the management of Indian lands and reserves.

status cards Cards issued by Aboriginal Affairs and Northern Development Canada to Aboriginal peoples registered under the Indian Act.

Status Indian An Aboriginal person who is registered under the Indian Act and consequently is entitled to certain legal rights.

band A group of Status Indians under the Indian Act. Many bands now prefer to be known as First Nations.

reserve An area of land owned by the Crown but reserved for the use of an Indian band. Some bands have more than one reserve.

band council The governing body of an Indian band under the Indian Act.

Many Aboriginal people today reject the band council system because it represents a colonially imposed system of governance.

As wards of the state, Aboriginal people were not permitted to vote in federal or provincial elections unless they relinquished their Indian status. This explicit policy of assimilation dates from before Confederation, with the passage of the Gradual Civilization Act of 1857. Under this act, "Indian men could seek enfranchisement. They had to be over 21, able to read and write either English or French, be reasonably well educated, free of debt, and of good moral character as determined by a commission of non-Indian examiners."[6] After Confederation, these terms were carried over to the Indian Act. However, only a few hundred Aboriginal people volunteered for enfranchisement—Aboriginal people were simply not willing to sacrifice their heritage to vote in Canadian elections. The Government of Canada exploited this resistance by threatening Aboriginal activists with **involuntary enfranchisement**. If someone was involuntarily enfranchised, he or she would be instantly ostracized in the community. It proved to be an effective way to thwart political activism in Aboriginal communities.

involuntary enfranchisement
The forcible enfranchisement of Indian individuals against their will, meaning that they lost their status as an Indian. Those who were involuntarily enfranchised were essentially divorced from their community. The Government of Canada used the threat of involuntary enfranchisement to curb Aboriginal activism.

The Great Wars and the Origins of Aboriginal Activism   When Great Britain declared war against Germany in August 1914, many Aboriginal peoples rushed to join the war effort, while French Canadians were mostly ambivalent about the war. While English Canadians may have been motivated by a desire to defend the "Mother Country," many Aboriginal peoples enlisted specifically to defend the Crown. More than 3500 Aboriginal peoples enlisted in World War I, and more than 300 were killed.[7] Aboriginal soldiers fought alongside non-Aboriginal soldiers in the Canadian Forces, and for the first time many Aboriginal people felt accepted as Canadian citizens. But after the war, when Aboriginal veterans returned home, it became "clear that the semblance of full citizenship had been only temporary."[8]

During the war, Status Indians on active duty were given the right to vote, and this right was extended to veterans after the war. But shamefully many Aboriginal veterans were denied the benefits offered to other soldiers. Some Aboriginal veterans consequently founded the League of Indians—modelled after the League of Nations, the forerunner of the United Nations—to defend the rights of Aboriginal peoples. In response, the federal government threatened the organizers with involuntary enfranchisement. The government also amended the Indian Act and made it illegal for Aboriginal people to raise funds for political purposes. In short, the federal government effectively squashed this early attempt at Aboriginal political mobilization.

While Aboriginal veterans were treated poorly upon their return from World War I, many Aboriginal peoples volunteered for World War II. Aboriginal veterans of World War II were given the right to vote, but they also encountered the same problems their elders experienced after the first war. Thus, as happened after World War I, many Aboriginal veterans began to organize politically. The Indian Association of Alberta was formed in 1939 and the Union of Saskatchewan Indians was established in 1946, as was the Indian Association of Manitoba and the Union of Ontario Indians. Also in 1946 a few bold activists attempted to form a continent-wide organization called the North American Indian Brotherhood.

Unlike the attempts at mobilization after World War I, the Government of Canada did not attempt to stifle the political activism by Aboriginal peoples after World War II. In fact, a joint committee of the House of Commons and the Senate was established to consider Indian affairs, but ultimately it did not propose sweeping policy changes. On the contrary, Parliament simply opted to revise the Indian Act in 1951. While some of the more odious elements of the Indian Act were eliminated or modified, the basic—and highly paternalistic—framework remained intact. While Aboriginal peoples did not participate in two world wars to rid the country of the Indian Act, Parliament's decision to revise the act was not much of a reward for the sacrifices made by Aboriginal peoples during these wars.

The Aboriginal Vote   British Columbia gave Aboriginal people the right to vote in 1949, and Aboriginal people were also allowed to vote in Newfoundland when it joined Confederation in 1949. In 1969, Quebec became the last province to extend the franchise to Aboriginal people. Curiously, Nova Scotia was the only jurisdiction in Canada that never prohibited Aboriginal people from voting. Aboriginal people received the right to vote at the federal level in 1960. The law was changed by Prime Minister Diefenbaker, who had long championed the rights of Aboriginal peoples. Two years earlier, he had appointed Chief James Gladstone of the Blackfoot First Nation to the Senate—the first Aboriginal Canadian to have a seat in Parliament. In 1968, Leonard Marchand of the Okanagan Indian Band became the first Aboriginal person elected to the House of Commons.[9]

Chief James Gladstone

Leonard Marchand

The White Paper   The Indian Act has been an instrument of colonial domination for almost as long as Canada has existed. One might think that the Indian Act should just be abolished, but it is not so simple, as Prime Minister Pierre Trudeau discovered much to his surprise in 1969, when his government released a position paper on Aboriginal affairs. This paper is properly called the *Statement of the Government of Canada on Indian Policy*, but it will be forever remembered as the **White Paper on Indian Policy**. The White Paper recognized the terrible plight of Aboriginal peoples, but it drew the wrong conclusions. "For many years," the statement read,

> Canadians believed that the Indian people had but two choices: they could live in a reserve community, or they could be assimilated and lose their Indian identity. Today Canada has more to offer. There is a third choice—a full role in Canadian society and in the economy while retaining, strengthening and developing an Indian identity which preserves the good things of the past and helps Indian people to prosper and thrive.[10]

The White Paper clearly assumed that Aboriginal peoples were just another cultural group in the Canadian mosaic. As such, it proposed to abolish the Indian Act and eliminate all references to Indians in the constitution.

White Paper on Indian Policy
A policy proposal made by the Trudeau government in 1969 to eliminate the Indian Act and Indian status and assimilate Aboriginal people into the mainstream of Canadian society. It was resolutely opposed by most Aboriginal peoples and organizations in the country.

While the Indian Act was—and continues to be—a reviled statute in Aboriginal communities, the White Paper was immediately rejected by Aboriginal peoples across Canada. The position of Aboriginal peoples was articulated clearly by Harold Cardinal, a young Cree leader from Alberta, when he wrote, "We do not want the Indian Act retained because it is a good piece of legislation. It isn't. It is discriminatory from start to finish. But . . . we would rather continue to live in bondage under the inequitable Indian Act than surrender our sacred rights."[11] In sum, the White Paper was viewed by Aboriginal peoples as another chapter in Canada's long policy of assimilation.

While the White Paper was a policy fiasco, it provided an opportunity for Aboriginal peoples to organize politically. They had, in fact, started organizing again in the early 1960s, after the earlier failures of the League of Indians and the North American Indian Brotherhood. In 1961, the National Indian Council was formed to represent Status Indians, non-Status Indians, and Métis people, but the interests of these distinct groups were too divergent and the organization collapsed. A few years later, Status Indians established the National Indian Brotherhood (NIB). In the early 1980s, the NIB was transformed into the Assembly of First Nations (AFN), which continues to be the principal voice for Status Indians in Canada. After the collapse of the National Indian Council, non-Status Indians and Métis formed the Native Council of Canada, but these groups separated after the patriation of the constitution in 1982. The Métis formed the Métis National Council (MNC), and non-Status Indians created the Congress of Aboriginal Peoples (CAP). In 1971, the Inuit Tapiriit Kanatami (ITK) was established, and in 1974 the Native Women's Association of Canada (NWAC) was created to represent the particular concerns of Aboriginal women.

The Calder Case and the End of Colonial Rule   While all court cases settle specific legal disputes, some cases shape the course of history. For Aboriginal peoples in Canada, the *Calder* case was a game changer. After the Supreme Court's landmark decision in 1973, the governments of Canada were forced to recognize the validity of Aboriginal legal claims and to rewrite the constitutional rules of the game. The origins of the *Calder* case lie in the late nineteenth century, when the Nisga'a (pronounced "Nishga") people in northwest British Columbia set out to establish title (i.e., ownership) over their ancestral lands. The Nisga'a, however, were thwarted at every turn. Before the Nisga'a could initiate legal action in a court of law, they needed to obtain permission—or a *fiat*—from the government of British Columbia, and it refused to grant permission. The Nisga'a then asked the federal government to refer the case to the Supreme Court of Canada, but the Government of Canada would not proceed without the consent of British Columbia. Unable to get their case into a Canadian court of law, the Nisga'a made a desperate appeal in 1913 to the Judicial Committee of the Privy Council, but the JCPC refused to hear the case without the consent of the Government of Canada. Then, in 1927, the Parliament of Canada amended the Indian Act and made it illegal for Aboriginal people to raise money to pursue land claims. The Nisga'a were thus prohibited from pursuing their case until Parliament amended the Indian Act in 1951 and again allowed Aboriginal people to raise money for land claims. The Nisga'a immediately resurrected their case, which at this time assumed the name of Frank Calder, the president of the Nisga'a Tribal Council and the lead plaintiff in the case (see Box 10.3).

When the *Calder* case finally made it to the Supreme Court of Canada, two questions needed to be answered: (1) Generally, did Aboriginal people in Canada ever possess title over their lands? (2) Specifically, did the Nisga'a have title over their land? In a historic decision, six of the seven justices of the Supreme Court answered the first question in the affirmative: "the fact is that when the settlers came, the Indians were there, organized in societies and occupying the land as their forefathers had done for centuries. This is what Indian title means."[12] On the second question, three justices argued that the Nisga'a lost the title over their land when British Columbia joined Confederation in 1871. Three other justices begged to differ. They argued

Box 10.3

Frank Calder

Frank Calder meeting with Prime Minister Trudeau and Jean Chrétien, Minister of Indian Affairs and Northern Development (circa 1973).

Frank Calder was born in 1915 in Nass Harbour, which is in the northwest corner of British Columbia. He was the first Status Indian to graduate from the University of British Columbia, and in 1949 he was elected to the Legislative Assembly of British Columbia as a member of the Co-operative Commonwealth Federation. He was the first Status Indian to be elected to a legislature anywhere in Canada, and he was re-elected eight more times with the CCF/NDP. In 1972, he became the first Aboriginal cabinet minister in British Columbia, but the premier fired him the following year after he was involved in a minor scandal. In 1975 he was re-elected to the legislature as a member of the Social Credit Party. He was finally defeated in the 1979 election—by just one vote. He died in 2006.

Once aboriginal title is established, it is presumed to continue until the contrary is proven. When the Nishga people came under British sovereignty they were entitled to assert, as a legal right, their Indian title. It being a legal right, it could not thereafter be extinguished except by surrender to the Crown or by competent legislative authority, and then only by specific legislation. There was no surrender by the Nisghas and neither the Colony of British Columbia nor the Province, after Confederation, enacted legislation specifically purporting to extinguish the Indian title nor did the Parliament of Canada.[13]

The seventh justice refused to take a position on title or extinguishment. He simply noted that the Nisga'a were required to obtain a *fiat* from the attorney general of British Columbia before suing the province; since they had not obtained it, he dismissed the case. While the Nisga'a lost their case on a technicality (failing to obtain the *fiat*), they ultimately won the war on behalf of all Aboriginal peoples by obtaining a clear statement from the highest court of the land that Aboriginal title was an **inherent right**, rooted in the fact that Aboriginal people owned and governed the land before the arrival of European settlers.

Following the *Calder* decision, the Trudeau government established a process to settle comprehensive and specific claims made by Aboriginal groups. **Comprehensive claims** focus on the parts of Canada where the claims of Aboriginal peoples have not been addressed by treaties or other legal means. **Specific claims**, on the other hand, focus on the failure of the governments of Canada to honour existing treaties. In both cases, however, progress has

inherent right Refers to Aboriginal rights, including title and self-government, stemming from the original occupation and use of the land by Aboriginal peoples.

Comprehensive claims Claims that address First Nations's rights to land and resources that are not subject to historic treaties.

Specific claims Claims that address issues that arise when the terms of specific Aboriginal treaties are not being recognized or fulfilled.

been painfully slow. To date, only 24 comprehensive land claims have been settled, including the Nisga'a Treaty of 1998 (which came into effect in 2000). While Trudeau was willing to settle land claims with Aboriginal peoples, he was reluctant to include them in the negotiations to patriate the constitution. But Aboriginal peoples recognized that their newfound rights would be jeopardized if they were not entrenched in the new constitution.

Aboriginal Peoples and the Patriation of the Constitution

As with much of the patriation story, the Aboriginal role in the constitutional negotiations of the early 1980s is shrouded in drama and intrigue. The idea of patriation was deeply troubling to Aboriginal peoples. The BNA Act spoke directly and indirectly to Aboriginal matters. While the *Calder* case indicated that Aboriginal rights existed independently of the Royal Proclamation, Aboriginal peoples continued to believe that they had a special relationship with the Crown. So long as the BNA Act remained a statute of the Parliament at Westminster, Aboriginal peoples believed, perhaps naively, that they could call upon the Crown in the United Kingdom to defend their interests. But if the constitution were returned to Canada, the governments of Canada would be free to amend it without regard to Aboriginal interests, or so many Aboriginal people feared. When the patriation negotiations commenced in the late 1970s, the National Indian Brotherhood (NIB)—the precursor to the Assembly of First Nations—demanded that Aboriginal and treaty rights be entrenched in the new constitution. Second, it insisted that Aboriginal peoples be included in the constitutional negotiations. The NIB "threatened that if these demands were not met, it would travel to England to ask the Queen to block patriation of the constitution."[14]

The patriation process was interrupted in the spring of 1979 when Pierre Trudeau lost the election to Joe Clark and the Progressive Conservative Party. But the negotiations resumed after the May 1980 referendum in Quebec. By this time Pierre Trudeau was once again prime minister. Aboriginal rights, however, were not a priority for Trudeau. All Trudeau was prepared to offer was a provision that would ensure that the Charter would not abrogate or derogate (cancel or reduce) Aboriginal and treaty rights, including rights recognized by the Royal Proclamation of 1763 or acquired through land claim settlements. This provision was ultimately entrenched in Section 25 of the Charter of Rights and Freedoms. As far as Trudeau was concerned, all other Aboriginal issues should be addressed in a second round of negotiations *after* patriation.

In his last term in office, Trudeau was determined to get a constitutional deal that would settle the Quebec issue once and for all. But, as we know from Chapter 8, the Gang of Eight stood in his way. Trudeau in turn decided to circumvent the premiers and appeal directly to the people of Canada for support, so he invited them to present their views on the constitution to a Special Joint Committee of the Senate and House of Commons, which was scheduled to start hearings in November 1980.

Some Aboriginal organizations decided to capitalize on this opportunity to participate in the constitutional debates. In October 1980, the Union of British Columbia Indian Chiefs announced their plan for a protest train to travel from Vancouver to Ottawa—the Constitution Express (see Figure 10.1). The train was scheduled to arrive in Ottawa in time for the hearings of the Special Joint Committee and an Assembly of First Nations organized by the National Indian Brotherhood. In late November, "five hundred Indians arrived in Ottawa on the constitution express . . . Two days later, the Assembly of First Nations met, with perhaps two thousand Indians in attendance . . . The Indians had established a remarkable presence in Ottawa at a crucial time in the constitutional reform process."[15] This pressure succeeded in producing the desired result, or so it seemed. In January 1981, the federal government agreed to recognize Aboriginal rights in the new constitution. In turn,

Box 10.4

The Constitution Act 1982, Part II, Rights of the Aboriginal Peoples of Canada

35. (1) The existing aboriginal and treaty rights of the aboriginal peoples of Canada are hereby recognized and affirmed.

(2) In this Act, "aboriginal peoples of Canada" includes the Indian, Inuit and Métis peoples of Canada.

the major Aboriginal organizations in Canada indicated that they would now support the plan to patriate the constitution from the United Kingdom.

But when the patriation package was finally revealed on November 5, 1981, after the infamous "night of the long knives," the section recognizing and affirming Aboriginal rights was missing. No one really knows why it got dropped. Some federal cabinet ministers blamed Aboriginal groups for not having a consistent position on the issue, Aboriginal groups blamed Pierre Trudeau, and Trudeau blamed the provinces. Regardless of who was to blame, Aboriginal groups were furious and they organized massive protests across the country. In the wake of these protests, the government of Alberta indicated that it was prepared to recognize "existing" Aboriginal rights, and one by one all the other provinces—except Quebec—came on board with this qualified recognition of Aboriginal rights. The federal government agreed too, and the Aboriginal rights section was reinstated in the constitution as Section 35, with the word "existing" inserted in it (see Box 10.4). But by this point just about every Aboriginal political organization in the country was now resolutely opposed to patriation, and they were going to take the fight to Great Britain to block it.

While the governments of Canada were haggling over the wording of Section 35, the Indian Association of Alberta appealed for an injunction to block patriation in a court in England. "The association argued that the treaties had been signed with the Crown and therefore responsibility for them remained with the Crown in the United Kingdom."[16] The case was dismissed, but a few weeks later, "Lord Denning, the maverick chief justice of the Court of Appeal, granted leave to appeal."[17] Lord Denning ultimately did not give Aboriginal people the judgment they were looking for, but he did send an important message to the Parliament of Canada. He argued that the rights and freedoms of Aboriginal people in Canada "have been guaranteed to them by the Crown—originally by the Crown in respect of the United Kingdom—now by the Crown in respect of Canada—but, in any case by the Crown. No Parliament should do anything to lessen the worth of these guarantees. *They should be honoured by the Crown in respect of Canada.*"[18]

After Denning's decision, the only recourse left to Aboriginal organizations was to lobby the Parliament of the United Kingdom. The British House of Commons set aside 30 hours for debate on the Canada Bill, and approximately 27 hours were spent on Aboriginal issues. About 80 percent of the debate in the House of Lords also focused on the "Indian question." But ultimately the bill was passed by both chambers, and the Queen granted royal assent in Ottawa on April 17, 1982. In her speech, the Queen indicated that she was pleased that "the rights of the aboriginal people are recognized *with full opportunity for further definition.*"[19] She is a wise sovereign, for indeed the Aboriginal rights entrenched in the Constitution Act 1982 needed—and still need today—further definition.

Amendments to Section 35

While the recognition and affirmation of Aboriginal rights was a major step forward in Canadian constitutional law, Section 35 was a very skeletal provision. The rights therein were

Figure 10.1 The Constitution Express

Union of B.C. Indian Chiefs

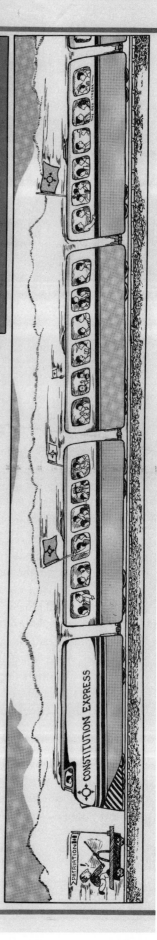

UNION OF BRITISH COLUMBIA INDIAN CHIEFS
CONSTITUTION EXPRESS

440 West Hastings Street, Vancouver, B.C. V6B 1L1

NOVEMBER 5, 1980

THE CONSTITUTION

Trudeau wants to go down in history as the man who made Canada an independent Nation. He wants to bring the B.N.A. Act to Canada, so that Canadian Governments don't have to ask the Queen everytime they want to change it.

This sounds fine, except that in the process our Indian Aboriginal Rights stand to be wiped out. The history of the Liberal Party's goal for the Indian people, Termination, leaves no doubt that this is deliberate. Indian Rights to lands, resources and self-determination are written into Declarations, Proclamations, Treaties and Agreements signed between the Queen and the Indian Nations. Section 91 (24) of the B.N.A. Act and the Indian Act deal with the Administration of those Agreements. Trudeau does not include those documents in the B.N.A. package. Our rights would not be protected in law.

At the same time Trudeau is introducing some new clauses that would further deprive people of their rights and freedoms.

THE CHARTER OF RIGHTS AND FREEDOMS

guarantees every individual equal rights. It does not recognise the rights of groups of people. We would no longer be Bands, Tribes or Nations. We would each be classified as Canadian.

Under the Charter of Rights and Freedoms, any non-Indian could point to Indian reserve lands, hunting rights, fishing rights, rights to no taxation on reserve lands and houses, and so on, and holler "discrimination": why couldn't he have those things? The Charter of Rights and Freedoms would be the supreme law over any other law regarding Indian People. The documents that recognise those rights in law would have become just museum pieces, with no effect in law. Section 24 of Trudeau's resolution that guarantees "traditional rights and freedoms" would just refer to our cultural rights.

NO ROLE FOR INDIAN NATIONS IN FUTURE CONSTITUTIONAL CHANGES

Another new clause that Trudeau has introduced would wipe out any Indian involvement in future changes to the B.N.A. Act. We could win our demand to have the Royal Proclamation and Declarations, etc. patriated with the B.N.A. Act, and once in Canada, the Federal and Provincial Governments could legislate them right out again.

PROVINCES RESPONSIBLE FOR SERVICES TO RESERVES

Under the new formula for sharing out the country's revenue to pay for services, Indian communities would be served by the Provincial Government, not the Federal Government. The recent victory over the Province brought about by our Indian Child Caravan would be worth nothing.

CONSTITUTION EXPRESS

Trudeau is very determined. He has railroaded his way through the House of Commons. He has not let the Provincial Premiers stop him. He has the machine for patriation in motion. He has established the proper Cabinet Committee to review his resolution, but it is stationary and can only make recommendations. It cannot stop him. The deadline for this committee is December 9th. The resolution then goes back to the House of Commons for final passage. Trudeau has a confirmed majority.

The only thing that could stop him now is another powerful machine: the Indian Constitution Express. The Constitution Express will take a thousand Indian people from Vancouver to Ottawa to tell Trudeau and the Canadian people that we will never stand for Termination of our Indian Aboriginal Rights. Thousands more will come on other trains, by bus and by air from across Canada to make sure this message is heard loud and clear. Trudeau would be violating every Proclamation, Treaty and Declaration and Agreement that Indian Nations have signed in the last 300 years.

Legal action has been started, but the courts are slow. Trudeau is counting on this to push through his resolution. We have to hold up the process in Ottawa. If there is no satisfaction in Ottawa, we must go to New York to demonstrate to the world that Trudeau has no regard for rights and freedoms in his country. This is a deadly serious mission. Unless we win this battle, everything that we believe in, everything that we have always fought so fiercely to defend, will be lost.

SCHEDULE

CONSTITUTION EXPRESS

Monday, November 24th

The first half of the Constitution Express, Train #104, leaves Vancouver for Ottawa at 8 p.m. via Calgary and Regina.

The second half of the Constitution Express, Train #102, leaves Vancouver for Ottawa at 9:45 p.m. via Edmonton and Saskatoon.

Wednesday, November 26th

Half of the Constitution Express (Train #102) arrives in Winnipeg at 17—25 p.m. The other half of the Express (Train #104) is scheduled to arrive one hour later at 18.25 p.m. Here in Winnipeg the two trains will join into one. The Constitution Express will continue its journey to Ottawa at 20:15 p.m.

Friday, November 28th

Constitution Express finally arrives in Ottawa at 9:30 a.m.

Saturday, November 29th

Workshop Sessions are scheduled in preparation for the All-Chiefs Conference.

Sunday, November 30th Monday, December 1st & Tuesday, December 2nd

Second All-Chiefs Conference

Wednesday, December 3rd Thursday, December 4th & Friday, December 5th

Workshop sessions to follow-up and prepare for International Lobby if necessary.

Saturday, December 6th

Constitution Express arrives in New York in afternoon.

**Monday, December 8th &
Tuesday, December 9th** International Lobby.

Wednesday, December 10th Participants of the Constitution Express head home.

CONSTITUTION EXPRESS STOPS AND PICK-UPS

Train #104 goes through Edmonton and Saskatoon.		Train #102 goes through Calgary and Regina.	
November 24th			
Vancouver	20.00 hours	Vancouver	21.45
New Westminster	20.55	New Westminster	22.45
Matsqui	21.49	Mission	23.25
Chilliwack	22.20		
Hope	23.05	**November 25th**	
		Agassiz	00.03
November 25th		Yale	00.50
Boston Bar	00.55	North Bend	02.10
Lytton	'01.55	Ashcroft (CP)	04.35
Ashcroft (CN)	03.30	Kamloops arrives	06.10
Kamloops arrives	05.10	leaves	06.25
leaves	05.40	Salmon Arm	08.25
Clearwater	07.30	Sicamous	09.05
Vavenby	07.55	Revelstoke arrives	10.35
Avola	08.50	leaves	11.05
Jasper (Alta.) arrives	15.10	Golden	15.15
leaves	15.40	Field	16.45
Edmonton (Alta.)	21.25	Banff	18.25
		Calgary arrives	20.35
November 26th		leaves	21.20
Saskatoon	07.20	Regina	08.45
	Winnipeg	Join Trains	

FARES:

Because our status cards give us half fare, we have hired two trains. The cost per ticket is $200, return Vancouver Ottawa.

Children under five travel free.

For those taking trains from Prince Rupert, Prince George, Fort St. John, Penticton, etc. to join the Constitution Express, these additional fares will be extra.

Elders can take a plane, as the train journey is very long. Return fare to Toronto is $188.00. We will get a bus for Toronto/Ottawa. Some young people will be accompanying the Elders. The two trains will only take 800 people. We will be hiring buses once the trains are full.

TICKETS FOR THE INDIAN CONSTITUTION EXPRESS ARE AVAILABLE FROM THE UBCIC OFFICE ONLY.

Contact Penny Billy or Phyllis George at 684-0231, as soon as possible to make reservations.

FOOD:

There are only two dining cars on each train, with facilities to feed less than 100 people. Cost of train meals is very high. **BRING YOUR OWN FOOD** for the three days on the train: dried meat and fish, bannock, fruit and vegetables, juice, etc.

CONSTITUTION EXPRESS ROUTE

ON THE TRAIN:

There will be workshops and strategy sessions. We hope to be showing some films. There will be story times for the children. **BRING YOUR OWN MUSIC:** Drums, guitars, and your songs. Bring things to keep you busy: it is a long ride.

ACCOMMODATION:

We have already sent staff to Ottawa to work with all Indian organisations to find accommodation for everyone. **BRING YOUR OWN SLEEPING BAGS** for both the train and billeting.

INDIAN DRESS

Our Elders have asked people to bring and wear Indian dress. The singers and dancers of the Kwakwewlth Nation will be coming to Ottawa and will be doing some fund-raising there.

DISCIPLINE:

Against such an action as this, the Government can only hope to make us look bad. We cannot tolerate any alcohol or drugs. This is a very serious journey that we are undertaking, to defend our existence as Indian people. Our security men will be going through strict physical and spiritual training.

Trudeau has challenged the Indian people to prove that we have our own rights and freedoms and these have meaning for us. We must show him in the courts and we must take him to his face. We must take as many Indian people to Ottawa as we possibly can.

ACTION!

POLITICAL ACTION

Every Chief and Council, Band organisation or group should telex or write to the Cabinet Committee established to look at Trudeau's resolution. This Committee is the only formal way we can make our strong feelings known to the House of Commons. It reports back to Trudeau on December 8th. Once this Committee is dissolved then there is *no way* to have direct involvement in stopping patriation of the Constitution.

This Committee must hear our demand that our Indian Aboriginal Rights must be firmly entrenched in the Canadian Constitution. The Committee must pay the fare to Ottawa of those whose case they consider should be heard. **This is the only public hearing being given on Trudeau's resolution.**

Write or telex:

Mr. Sandy Birch,
Clerk, Joint Committee of the Senate and House of Commons
on the Revision of the Canadian Constitution,
Parliament Buildings,
Ottawa, Ontario.

JOIN THE CONSTITUTION EXPRESS!

The Constitution Express will take thousands of Indian people to Ottawa to demonstrate to the Canadian Government. Canadian people, that we will not accept termination of Indian rights.

If it's not successful in Ottawa, the Constitution Express will go to New York to demonstrate to the United Nations that our Treaties, Declarations, etc., are being violated.

Fund-raising will be needed to get Band people to Ottawa. Billboards can declare our position. To gain support, we will have to educate the non-Indian population of our rights and concerns.

Buffy St. Marie will be giving a benefit concert December 15th at the Orpheum.

LEGAL ACTION

Join the court action launched by B.C. Bands to stop Trudeau from acting beyond his powers in trying to wipe out Indian rights.

Support the court action to be launched in Europe to ensure that Great Britain stands by the Proclamations, Treaties, etc.. which protect Indian Nations.

Individual people, as well as Bands, can join court actions.

More detailed information is being sent to all the Chiefs of Canada.

OUR FUTURE AS INDIAN PEOPLE IS NOW ON THE LINE.

not defined, and there were no explicit provisions for self-government. The Constitution Act 1982 recognized in fact that Section 35 required elaboration. Section 37, which is now repealed, called for a conference between Aboriginal peoples and the first ministers to be held within a year of the new Constitution Act coming into force to discuss "constitutional matters that directly affect the Aboriginal peoples of Canada, including the identification and definition of the rights of those peoples to be included in the Constitution of Canada." The conference took place in March 1983, and it resulted in some modest amendments to Section 35—the only constitutional amendments made to date with the general amending formula entrenched in the new constitution. While these amendments clarified some important points, they "fell well short of the growing constitutional aspirations of Canada's Aboriginal peoples."[20]

The governments of Canada held three more conferences with Aboriginal peoples between 1984 and 1987 to discuss self-government, but they all concluded in a philosophical impasse. "Aboriginal leaders regard the right of their peoples to govern themselves as a moral right that they had long before Europeans arrived, and one they have never relinquished."[21] In other words, Aboriginal leaders wanted the constitution to recognize their *inherent right to self-government*. The governments of Canada, by contrast, approached the issue "not from the perspective of philosophy but in terms of constitutional law. Putting an inherent right to self-government in the Constitution before at least roughing out the details involves too much uncertainty. Who knows what judges would make of such an abstract right?"[22] In the absence of a political agreement, Aboriginal peoples have turned to the courts to obtain "further definition"—as the Queen put it—of their constitutional rights. Thus, ironically, the governments of Canada have ended up with the thing they wanted to avoid: having judges determine the scope and meaning of Aboriginal rights.

The Honour of the Crown: The Judicial Interpretation of Aboriginal and Treaty Rights

As with the Charter of Rights and Freedoms, the recognition of Aboriginal rights in the new constitution led to a steady stream of court cases. By one count, the Supreme Court heard 65 Aboriginal cases between 1982 and 2006.[23] Unlike the Charter, however, Section 35 does not give the Supreme Court much to work with. The court has thus had to read meaning into Section 35. Now, some 30 years after patriation, it is possible to discern a hierarchy of rights for Aboriginal peoples: treaty rights, Aboriginal rights, title, and self-government.

Treaty Rights

In the early days of contact, the treaty was the principal instrument by which both the French and British Crowns established relationships with Aboriginal nations. Unfortunately, the historical treaties are often quite vague. It is thus not always easy to determine what the initial obligations entailed, and it is even more difficult to ascertain their contemporary significance and application. The Supreme Court has emphasized that treaties "should be liberally construed and doubtful expressions resolved in favour of the Indians." This rule stems from the fact that the treaties were written by representatives of the Crown, and the text "often differed from or did not fully express the Indians' oral understanding of the arrangements."[24]

The Marshall Cases   In *R. v. Marshall*—now known as *Marshall 1*—the Supreme Court revealed that it was prepared to interpret treaty rights very broadly. In this case, Donald Marshall, a Mi'kmaq Indian from Nova Scotia, claimed a right to catch and sell eels under the terms of a "peace and friendship" treaty signed in 1760. While the treaty did not specifically address the issue of fishing, the Supreme Court accepted Marshall's claim. Indeed, the court's decision "seemed to confer an aboriginal right over the commercial exploitation of most of the natural resources of Nova Scotia and New Brunswick."[25] The *Marshall* decision sparked a wave of protest by non-Aboriginal fishermen in Nova Scotia and New Brunswick. In response, the Supreme Court took the unprecedented step of clarifying its judgment. However, this second statement—now known as *Marshall II*—did not fundamentally alter the court's original decision.

In light of *Marshall I* and *Marshall II*, the Mi'kmaq decided to go into the logging business and began harvesting trees on Crown land without authorization from the governments of Nova Scotia or New Brunswick. They were consequently charged with illegal logging. In this case—*Marshall III*—the Supreme Court concluded that the "peace and friendship" treaty of 1760 did not extend to logging. Unlike eel fishing, the court argued that logging was not a traditional Mi'kmaq enterprise. While the justices have maintained that treaties should be "liberally construed," they have also indicated that there are limits to how broadly treaties can be interpreted.

Aboriginal Rights

Whereas Aboriginal treaty rights are rooted in historical documents signed between Aboriginal peoples and the Crown, Aboriginal rights are not spelled out in written documents. Aboriginal rights stem from the occupation and use of the land by Aboriginal peoples prior to the arrival of European settlers. The new constitution recognized the existence of these rights; it did not create them. However, it has not been easy to ascertain the specific nature of these rights.

The *Sparrow* Case   The Supreme Court's first opportunity to consider the meaning of Aboriginal rights under Section 35 came in 1990 with the *Sparrow* case. Ronald Edward Sparrow was a member of the Musqueam First Nation, which is located in southwest Vancouver. He was charged under the Fisheries Act in 1984 for fishing in the Fraser River with an oversized driftnet. Sparrow did not challenge the allegation, but he argued that "he was exercising an existing aboriginal right to fish and that the net length restriction contained in the Band's licence was invalid in that it was inconsistent with s. 35(1) of the *Constitution Act, 1982*."[26] The Supreme Court ultimately did not take a position on the guilt or innocence of Sparrow. Instead, it ordered a new trial with instructions on how Section 35 should be interpreted by the trial court.

Before examining the evidence in the *Sparrow* case, the court first had to determine the meaning of an "existing" Aboriginal right. The court concluded this word meant that Section 35 only applies to those rights that were in existence when the Constitution Act 1982 came into effect, but it stressed that the notion of "existing aboriginal rights" must be "interpreted flexibly so as to permit their evolution over time." However, the court stated emphatically that **extinguished rights** were not revived by the new constitution. In the *Sparrow* case specifically, the court concluded that "there is nothing in the *Fisheries Act . . .* that demonstrates *a clear and plain intention* to extinguish the Indian aboriginal right to fish."[27] In short, Aboriginal rights cannot be extinguished by stealth, erosion, or encroachment over time. If the right has not been explicitly extinguished by a duly constituted authority such as the Parliament of Canada, it remains an "existing" right by definition.

Turning to the evidence, the Supreme Court asked three questions: (1) Did the Musqueam possess an Aboriginal right to fish? (2) If so, was the right infringed on by the regulations set out by the governments of Canada and British Columbia? (3) If so, was the infringement justified? Before it answered these questions, the Supreme Court noted that Section 35 lies

extinguished rights Those Aboriginal rights that have been expressly terminated by a lawful authority, such as the Parliament of Canada.

outside the Charter of Rights and Freedoms; it is thus not subject to the reasonable limits clause in Section 1 of the new constitution. The constitution thus does not explicitly empower the governments of Canada to limit the rights of Aboriginal peoples, but the court argued that Aboriginal rights are not absolute. They can be infringed on, but only for justifiable reasons. The court then had to devise a test to determine if a particular law constitutes a justifiable infringement on Aboriginal rights.

The **Sparrow test** is analogous to the Oakes test, which was discussed in Chapter 9. Under the Charter, individuals may challenge a law, but it is incumbent upon them to demonstrate that it infringes their rights. If the court accepts that there is an infringement, the government must demonstrate that the law addresses a pressing and substantial problem, and then it must demonstrate that the law is proportional to its objectives. Similarly, Aboriginal people may challenge a law on the grounds that it compromises the rights protected by Section 35. As with Charter cases, the claimants must first demonstrate that their rights have been infringed by demonstrating that the infringement constitutes an undue hardship.

If the claimants can persuade the court that the law represents an infringement of Aboriginal rights, it is then incumbent upon the government to demonstrate that the limitation is justified. There are two parts to the justification test. First, is there a valid legislative objective? Here, the Supreme Court required the government to provide "compelling and substantial" objectives, such as the conservation of a natural resource for the benefit of Aboriginal peoples or the prevention of harm to Aboriginal peoples or the general population. But a valid legislative objective alone is not sufficient to justify the infringement of an existing Aboriginal right. The Supreme Court reminded the government that "the honour of the Crown is at stake in dealings with aboriginal peoples." In order to uphold the honour of the Crown, the government must demonstrate that it has consulted with the Aboriginal group in question before moving to limit their rights or offered compensation for the loss of the right. The duty to consult Aboriginal peoples when their rights might be affected is now a constitutional obligation on the part of the government. This has profound consequences for the development of many resource industries in Canada, especially in areas where there are unsettled land claims with Aboriginal peoples.

In sum, the *Sparrow* case was a major step forward for Aboriginal peoples because the Supreme Court endorsed a fairly expansive conception of Aboriginal rights. With *Sparrow*, the Supreme Court was sending the governments of Canada a strong message that the rights entrenched in Section 35 were as important as Charter rights, and like Charter rights they could only be infringed on for demonstrably sound reasons. Subsequently, the Supreme Court has moved to limit and qualify Aboriginal rights, as can be seen in the *Van der Peet* case, which involved another fishing dispute on the Fraser River.

The Van der Peet case   Dorothy Marie Van der Peet was a member of the Stó:lō First Nation, a community located near the city of Chilliwack on the Fraser River about 100 kilometres southeast of Vancouver. In 1987, she was charged with selling 10 salmon. Under the regulations of British Columbia, the Stó:lō were allowed to catch salmon for personal consumption, but they were not permitted to sell the fish. Van der Peet argued that the prohibition against the sale of fish was an infringement of the rights protected by Section 35. In *Sparrow*, the Supreme Court accepted without question that the Musqueam had an Aboriginal right to fish. The question now was, did Aboriginal people have a right to sell the fish they caught? In a split decision, the Supreme Court ruled against Van der Peet. In essence, the judgment filled in the blanks in the first part of the Sparrow test: It created the criteria for establishing an Aboriginal right.

The justices of the Supreme Court seemed perplexed by the task at hand. Writing on behalf of the majority, Chief Justice Antonio Lamer argued, "The task of this Court is to define aboriginal rights in a manner which recognizes that aboriginal rights are *rights* but

Sparrow test A test devised by the Supreme Court of Canada that seeks to determine if a particular law constitutes a reasonable infringement of an Aboriginal right. For the law to be a reasonable infringement, it must have a valid and important legislative objective, and the honour of the Crown must be upheld by ensuring that meaningful consultation has occurred with the affected Aboriginal group.

which does so without losing sight of the fact that they are rights held by aboriginal people because they are *aboriginal*."[28] In its efforts to connect the rights protected in Section 35 to notions of Aboriginality, the Supreme Court may have unduly tied Aboriginal peoples to their histories. Other Canadians are not required to tie their rights claims to their histories—indeed, many Canadians are trying to break the connection to history when they seek recognition of their rights claims. How else would same-sex couples obtain the right to marry? But in the case of Aboriginal peoples, the Supreme Court argued that rights must be directly related to the history of a particular Aboriginal community: "in order to be an aboriginal right an activity must be an element of a practice, custom or tradition integral to the distinctive culture of the aboriginal group claiming the right."[29] Specifically, the court elaborated, the practices, customs and traditions that "constitute aboriginal rights are those which have continuity with the practices, customs and traditions *that existed prior to contact [with European society]*."[30]

The **Van der Peet test** is enormously problematic. What makes an activity integral? If an activity only takes place once a year or once every few years, does that mean it is only incidental to the group's culture and therefore not an Aboriginal right? What does distinctive mean? If other Aboriginal groups have similar practices, does the right not exist? And what about Métis people? By definition, the Métis did not exist prior to contact with European peoples, but under Section 35 the Métis are Aboriginal peoples and have constitutionally protected rights. There is also a significant evidentiary challenge. How exactly do Aboriginal peoples prove that a practice existed prior to contact when there is no documentary evidence from the time period in question?

The decision in *Van der Peet* was a major setback for Aboriginal peoples across Canada. In *Sparrow*, the Supreme Court assumed a fairly broad and intuitive conception of Aboriginal rights, and it placed the onus on the governments of Canada to justify any infringement of Aboriginal rights. But in *Van der Peet* the court endorsed a "frozen rights" approach to Aboriginal rights that unduly chains Aboriginal people to their particular histories. And it transforms the justices of the Supreme Court of Canada into forensic anthropologists rather than umpires of the constitution. In *Van der Peet* and other cases, the Supreme Court concluded that the exchange of fish was "incidental" to their culture, but in *Gladstone* the court determined that the harvesting of herring spawn for trade and sale was "integral" to the cultural traditions of the Heiltsuk people (who live on the central coast of British Columbia).[31] The justices of the Supreme Court of Canada are not trained to make anthropological determinations of this nature, and it leads to a highly particularistic conception of Aboriginal rights. And, more fundamentally, the framework for Aboriginal rights established in the *Van der Peet* case has important implications for self-government, as well be discussed below.

Van der Peet test A test devised by the Supreme Court of Canada that establishes the criteria to determine the existence of an Aboriginal right. The Supreme Court has indicated that Aboriginal rights are those that have continuity with the practices, customs, and traditions of Aboriginal peoples that existed prior to contact with European society.

Aboriginal Title

The question of Aboriginal title was addressed just two years after the adoption of the new constitution in the *Guerin* case, which also involved the Musqueam First Nation of Vancouver. The *Guerin* case was the first major Aboriginal case to come before the Supreme Court after the adoption of the Constitution Act 1982, although it did not technically involve Section 35 since the facts of the case occurred before the new constitution came into effect. In the 1950s, the band voluntarily surrendered 162 acres of land to the federal government, which in turn leased it to a golf club. In the early 1980s, the Musqueam argued that the federal government did not secure the best possible deal for the land on behalf of the band. The band, led by Chief Delbert Guerin, thus decided to sue the federal government. The case was appealed all the way to the Supreme Court of Canada.

While the ownership of the land was not in question in this case, the Supreme Court took the opportunity to review the question of Aboriginal title. In *Guerin*, the Supreme

Court clarified and confirmed its decision in the *Calder* case: The court recognized Aboriginal title as a legal right stemming from the occupation of the lands by First Nations before the arrival of Europeans. This right, the court said, was recognized by the Royal Proclamation of 1763. In other words, the right to the land was not bestowed on First Nations by the Crown through the Royal Proclamation; the right predates the Royal Proclamation and exists independently of it. Nevertheless, Aboriginal peoples are not permitted to sell or lease their lands directly to third parties; they must first surrender it to the Crown. As the Crown took this responsibility upon itself in the Royal Proclamation, the Supreme Court argued that the Crown has an obligation to act in the best interests of Aboriginal people when it sells or leases land on their behalf. While the *Calder* and *Guerin* cases settled some important issues with respect to Aboriginal title, the Supreme Court did not have the opportunity to weigh in on the application of Aboriginal title until the famous *Delgamuukw* case in the 1990s.

The Delgamuukw Case

The *Delgamuukw* case was initiated in the early 1990s by the Wet'suwet'en and Gitksan peoples. The Wet'suwet'en and Gitksan reside respectively near the towns of Smithers and Hazelton in northwest British Columbia, between Prince George and the coastal community of Prince Rupert. The Wet'suwet'en and Gitksan claimed ownership of separate portions of about 58 000 square kilometres of land in this remote and pristine region of the province. The government of British Columbia rejected these claims, arguing that their right to this land was long ago extinguished. The Wet'suwet'en and Gitksan suffered a major setback in the BC Court of Appeal, but they persevered and took the case to the Supreme Court of Canada. The case assumed the name of *Delgamuukw*, the title of the Gitksan hereditary chief Earl Muldoe, a highly respected artist and carver. (His majestic totem poles are on display at Vancouver International Airport).

At the Supreme Court, the Wet'suwet'en and Gitksan claimed ownership of the land and a right to self-government. They rooted their claim to the land in their historic use and occupation of the territory, and they further substantiated their claims with traditional historical evidence from their communities. Each Gitksan house has an *adaawk*, "which is a collection of sacred oral tradition about their ancestors, histories and territories." And the Wet'suwet'en houses each have a *kungax*, "which is a spiritual song or dance or performance which ties them to their land." Additionally, the Wet'suwet'en and Gitksan have a "feast hall," where they "tell and retell their stories and identify their territories to remind themselves of the sacred connection that they have with their lands."[32] The BC Court of Appeal rejected this oral history out of hand, but the Supreme Court of Canada accepted these traditional stories as evidence. The acceptance of traditional evidence in *Delgamuukw* was thus an important corrective in the court's jurisprudence on Aboriginal rights, especially *Van der Peet*.

With the evidentiary issue settled, the Supreme Court proceeded in *Delgamuukw* to consider the question of title. The existence of Aboriginal title was recognized in *Calder* (1973), and it was reaffirmed in *Guerin* (1984). In *Delgamuukw*, the Supreme Court determined that Aboriginal title is a particular kind of Aboriginal right and is consequently protected by Section 35. While the court reaffirmed that Aboriginal title exists in theory, it was still not clear how an Aboriginal group proves that it owns a particular piece of land. On this point, the court argued that Aboriginal people must prove that they occupied the land in question *prior to the establishment of the Crown's sovereignty in North America*. In other words, the time frame to establish Aboriginal title is a little bit later than the time frame for Aboriginal rights more generally—the latter have to be grounded in practices that were established *prior to contact* with European settlers. The court's reasoning for this distinction is convoluted, to say the least.

In *Delgamuukw*, the Supreme Court confirmed that Aboriginal title was a right under Section 35, but it also indicated that the Aboriginal right to title is not absolute. Chief Justice Lamer stated that "Aboriginal title encompasses the right to exclusive use and

By Carrie Saxifrage for The Vancouver Observer

Chief Earl Muldoe
(a.k.a. Delgamuukw)

occupation of the land held pursuant to that title for a variety of purposes" but, he argued, those uses "must not be irreconcilable with the nature of the group's attachment to that land."[33] Elaborating, the Chief Justice wrote:

> if occupation is established with reference to the use of the land as a hunting ground, then the group that successfully claims aboriginal title to that land may not use it in such a fashion as to destroy its value for such a use (e.g., by strip mining it). Similarly, if a group claims a special bond with the land because of its ceremonial or cultural significance, it may not use the land in such a way as to destroy that relationship (e.g., by developing it in such a way that the bond is destroyed, perhaps by turning it into a parking lot).[34]

In sum, Aboriginal title is indeed an Aboriginal right under Section 35, but in the eyes of the court it is very much connected to some notion of Aboriginality. While non-Aboriginal Canadians must follow government regulations and bylaws, their use of the land is not tied to their cultural heritage. It would thus seem that Aboriginal title is more qualified than the title rights of other Canadians.

In sum, *Delgamuukw* advanced the rights of Aboriginal peoples in important ways. First, it allowed Aboriginal peoples to present traditional oral histories as evidence to support their claims. Second, the Supreme Court confirmed that title is a constitutionally protected right, although not an absolute right. Third, the Supreme Court adopted a more lenient standard for title claims than it did for general Aboriginal rights claims. However, in *Delgamuukw* the Supreme Court refused to make a judgment about self-government because "the appellants advanced the right to self-government in very broad terms." But the court was forced to consider the question of self-government in the *Pamajewon* case (which is discussed below), when the Shawanaga and Eagle Lake First Nations made it central to their defence.

Aboriginal Self-Government

While many academics and most Aboriginal peoples believe that Section 35 recognizes an Aboriginal right to self-government, the Supreme Court has been more circumspect. It has yet to confirm that self-government is an "existing Aboriginal right." The issue was addressed most directly in *Pamajewon*. In this case, two Ojibwa communities—the

Shawanaga First Nation of central Ontario and the Eagle Lake First Nation of northwest Ontario—were convicted of operating illegal gambling operations on their reserves. In their defence, both nations argued that their gambling operations were pursuant to their right to self-government under Section 35.

The Supreme Court did not actually make a definitive judgment about self-government in *Pamajewon*, but it revealed how it would approach the question. "Assuming without deciding that s. 35(1) includes self-government claims," Chief Justice Lamer wrote, "the applicable legal standard is that laid out in *R. v. Van der Peet*. Claims to self-government made under s. 35(1) are no different from other claims to the enjoyment of aboriginal rights and must be measured against the same standard."[35] Recall that in *Van der Peet* the Supreme Court determined that an Aboriginal right must be a practice, custom, or tradition "integral to the distinctive culture of the aboriginal group claiming the right." And, critically, the practice needs to have been established prior to contact with European settlers. In this case, the appellants were seeking to regulate gambling in their communities, but gambling, in the view of the Supreme Court, did not pass the *Van der Peet* test: Since gambling was not a traditional Ojibwa practice dating to the time prior to contact, the Shawanaga and Eagle Lake First Nations did not have a right to regulate or govern this activity.

Aboriginal peoples were disappointed by the decision to link the question of self-government to *Van der Peet*. The Supreme Court was obviously trying to make its judgments on Aboriginal rights line up with each other, but it seems unduly constraining to suggest that Aboriginal peoples can only govern matters integral to their culture. Aboriginal peoples were hoping that the Supreme Court would recognize self-government as a corollary of Aboriginal title, or better yet as an inherent right based on their prior occupation of the land. If Aboriginal peoples do have a collective right to the land, as the Supreme Court determined in *Calder*, then it would seem to follow that Aboriginal peoples would need a decision-making body to determine how to manage their land. In other words, they would need a governing body. But the Supreme Court was not willing to recognize such a broad right to self-government. Indeed, it indicated that self-government would have to be decided on a case-by-case basis, and it might not be applicable to all Aboriginal communities.

The Limitations of Jurisprudence

Since the adoption of the Constitution Act 1982, the Supreme Court has gradually adopted a more restrictive interpretation of Section 35, and it has notably refused to take a stand on the important question of self-government. It would seem that the Supreme Court has grown uncomfortable with making all of the important decisions with respect to the meaning of Aboriginal rights, with governments standing by idly. Indeed, in *Delgamuukw*, Chief Justice Lamer made an impassioned appeal to the governments of Canada to negotiate an honourable settlement with Aboriginal peoples: "Ultimately, it is through negotiated settlements, with good faith and give and take on all sides, reinforced by the judgments of this Court, that we will achieve what I stated in *Van der Peet* . . . to be a basic purpose of s.35(1)—the reconciliation of the pre-existence of aboriginal societies with the sovereignty of the Crown."[36]

Aboriginal peoples now seem to be caught between a rock and a hard place: the courts are unwilling to advance Aboriginal rights further because the unresolved issues are fundamentally political rather than legal, but the governments of Canada are reluctant to address these thorny issues because they fear a backlash from non-Aboriginal Canadians, who constitute the democratic majority. Canada would thus appear to be at a critical juncture in its relations with Aboriginal peoples. If both the legal and political avenues are closed to Aboriginal peoples, the only choices left to them are to give up or adopt a more confrontational and possibly extralegal strategy to secure self-government.

Social and Economic Conditions of Aboriginal Peoples in Canada

With the governments of Canada being reluctant to address Aboriginal rights and to negotiate self-government with First Nations, Aboriginal peoples were forced to pursue their claims in the courts. But pursuing claims in the courts has been costly, both financially and emotionally. Meanwhile, many Aboriginal people live in difficult, often deplorable, conditions. While conditions are slowly improving in some Aboriginal communities, Aboriginal peoples still lag behind the general population on just about every socioeconomic indicator.

There are so many social pathologies in Aboriginal communities across the country that it is difficult to know where to begin, but it is perhaps most appropriate to look first at the overall health of Aboriginal people in Canada. Infant mortality rates and average life expectancy are the two most important quality-of-life indicators. While these indicators have improved for Aboriginal peoples over the past two decades, they are both still below the Canadian average. And some diseases are much more prevalent in Aboriginal communities. Aboriginal peoples are three to five times more likely to suffer from diabetes than Canadians in the general population, and they are two times more likely to develop cardiovascular diseases. Tuberculosis has been virtually eliminated in Canadian society in general, but it is still prevalent in some Aboriginal communities, especially in the prairies. AIDS has been declining in the Canadian population overall, but it has been increasing in Aboriginal communities over the past two decades.[37] Many Aboriginal communities in Canada suffer from very high rates of drug and alcohol addiction, and in some remote communities where drugs and alcohol are difficult to obtain, Aboriginal youth sniff gasoline and other toxic substances.

Aboriginal people experience higher rates of violence than the general population, and they are much more likely to die from accidents than non-Aboriginal people. The death rates from car accidents, poisoning, and drowning are four times higher in the Aboriginal population, and the death rate from fire-related accidents is three times higher.[38] Victimization rates from intentional violence are even higher. Overall, the suicide rate in the Aboriginal community is about three times higher than the national rate and much higher for Aboriginal youth; in fact, suicide is the leading cause of death for Aboriginal youth and adults up to the age of 44.[39] Aboriginal peoples are also much more likely to be victims of homicide than non-Aboriginal people. Between 1997 and 2000, the homicide rate for Aboriginal people was almost seven times higher than that for non-Aboriginal people.[40] During the same time period, Aboriginal people were 10 times more likely to be accused of committing homicide.[41] While Aboriginal people only make up about 3 to 4 percent of the Canadian population, they make up about 20 percent of the people incarcerated in federal and provincial penitentiaries.

Many Aboriginal peoples, particularly on reserves, live in substandard and often appalling conditions. While conditions are improving in some communities, the housing situation on reserves still does not compare well with other communities in Canada. "Less than three quarters of Aboriginal homes have central heating, in contrast to over 90 percent of non-Aboriginal homes . . . crowding is also a problem for Aboriginal people. One in 43 non-Aboriginal homes was crowded, compared to the one in four proportion in Aboriginal homes. More than 15 percent of Aboriginal homes require major repairs. Overall, Aboriginal people have the least favourable housing conditions of any ethnic group in Canada."[42] Many houses on Aboriginal reserves are contaminated with mould, in many communities the water is not safe to drink, and some Aboriginal communities have been exposed to toxic wastes from various resource industries.

While the *absolute* economic conditions may be improving for Aboriginal peoples, in *relative* terms the disparity between Aboriginal peoples and non-Aboriginal peoples is growing. "In 1980 the average income for status Indians was 70 percent of that for all Canadians . . . by 2002, this had decreased to just over 50 percent of the average Canadian yearly earnings."[43] In 2002, the average income for a Status Indian family was $21 000, compared to $38 000 for the average family in Canada.[44] Moreover, Aboriginal peoples derive a larger share of their income from government transfers (unemployment insurance and welfare) than the general population. It should be noted and stressed that there are huge disparities *among* Aboriginal communities. In general, the economic and social conditions on reserves in remote regions of the country are worse than the conditions on reserves closer to urban areas.

The Royal Commission on Aboriginal Peoples

In light of the slow progress on land settlements and self-government and the deplorable social conditions endured by many Aboriginal peoples, Prime Minister Brian Mulroney appointed the Royal Commission on Aboriginal Peoples in 1991 to study the various concerns of Aboriginal peoples in Canada. The commission deliberated for five years, and its final report was more than 4000 pages long and contained more than 400 recommendations, which were directed toward five principal goals:

1. The reconstitution of Aboriginal nations
2. The transfer of political power to Aboriginal nations
3. A reallocation of land and resources to Aboriginal nations
4. Education in Aboriginal communities for governance and economic self-reliance
5. Economic development and the elimination of poverty in Aboriginal communities

The commission stressed that most of it recommendations could be accomplished without amending the constitution, but it also argued that some amendments were essential. In particular, it recommended "an explicit recognition that section 35 includes the inherent right of self-government as an Aboriginal right."[45]

The Royal Commission on Aboriginal Peoples recognized that its sweeping proposals were "*not without cost*."[46] Indeed, the commission called upon the Government of Canada to "invest" an additional $1.5–2 billion per year for 15 to 20 years—for a total of $30–40 billion—in Aboriginal communities. With the Government of Canada facing an annual deficit of $40 billion at the time, the commission knew it would be it difficult to persuade the government to accept its recommendation. It thus tried to emphasize that there was an even greater cost associated with doing nothing. The commission calculated that the plight of Aboriginal peoples costs the Canadian economy $7.5 billion per year, and it projected that this cost would rise to $11 billion per year by 2016. The Government of Canada was unmoved. It dismissed the recommendations "within an hour of the report's tabling in parliament."[47] The problems affecting Aboriginal peoples around the country have thus continued unabated.

A Down Payment on the Royal Commission: The Kelowna Accord

In November 2005, Prime Minister Paul Martin invited the provincial premiers, territorial leaders, and representatives from the main Aboriginal organizations in the country to a meeting in Kelowna, British Columbia, to discuss some of the issues raised by the Royal Commission on Aboriginal Peoples. Together they signed an agreement to address some of the most pressing issues affecting Aboriginal Canadians. The Kelowna Accord focused on five priorities: health, education, housing (including water), economic development, and restoring relations between Aboriginal peoples and the governments of Canada and Canadian society more generally.[48] The Government of Canada agreed to spend about $5 billion on these priority matters. This commitment was described at the time as a "down payment" on the royal commission's recommendations. However, three days later, the Martin government fell on a confidence vote (on an unrelated matter) in the House of Commons. In the ensuing election campaign, Stephen Harper indicated that he would not honour the Kelowna Accord if his party won the election—and he followed through on that promise when the Conservative Party formed the government in 2006.

Stephen Harper: Restoring the Relationship with First Nations?

While the Conservative government did not follow through on the Kelowna Accord, it has adopted some positive initiatives. Most notably, it has addressed the dreadful legacy of residential schools. In May 2006, the Harper government adopted the Indian Residential Schools Settlement Agreement, which set aside $1.9 billion as compensation for residential school survivors. Additionally, it established the Truth and Reconciliation Commission with a mandate "to promote public education and awareness about the Indian Residential School system and its legacy."[49] And on June 11, 2008, in a moving ceremony in Parliament, Prime Minister Harper offered a sincere apology to Aboriginal peoples on behalf of the Government of Canada for the damage caused by residential schools.

In general, however, the Conservative government has not pursued sweeping changes with respect to Aboriginal issues. On the contrary, it has demonstrated a preference for incremental reform. Rather than negotiate self-government, the Conservatives have focused on "modernizing" the Indian Act broadly by insisting on more accountability from band councils and making it easier for bands to pursue economic opportunities. While these changes may be beneficial, most bands have no interest in a new Indian Act, and frustration is mounting in many Aboriginal communities.

Aboriginal Radicalism and the Idle No More Movement   Aboriginal peoples have demonstrated an almost infinite degree of patience. They suffered through nearly a century of internal colonialism with nary a protest. Then, in 1982, Canada made a constitutional promise to forge a new relationship with its Aboriginal peoples, but the process of renewal has been painfully slow: Aboriginal peoples have had to fight for their rights under the constitution in the courts, little progress has been made on actualizing self-government, and various social and economic pathologies remain endemic in many Aboriginal communities. Aboriginal peoples have every reason to be angry, and occasionally their anger has been vented in violent confrontations with the authorities and surrounding communities. In 1990, the Mohawk First Nations in Kanesatake and Kahnawake near Montreal engaged in a summer-long standoff with the Sûreté du Québec (the provincial police force) and ultimately the Canadian Forces. Subsequently, other conflicts have erupted in places across the country: Gustafsen Lake in central British Columbia in 1995; Ipperwash Provincial Park on the shores of Lake Huron northeast of Sarnia in 1996; Burnt Church, New Brunswick, after the Supreme Court ruling on fishing rights in 1999; and on the Six Nations reserve near Caledonia, Ontario, southwest of Hamilton, in 2006. But these conflicts are relatively rare occurrences, notwithstanding the sensational media coverage they get.

In the fall of 2012, however, Aboriginal peoples initiated a thoroughly modern form of protest: a virtual protest. The Idle No More movement was launched specifically in response to measures included in the Conservative government's budget bills in 2012 (bills C-38 and C-45) that may infringe on Aboriginal treaty rights, but it was really born and sustained by the pent-up frustration in many Aboriginal communities across the country. Within weeks, the movement went viral on Twitter and Facebook, complete with other social media phenomenon such as flash mob protests in the West Edmonton Mall and Toronto's Eaton Centre. The movement linked Aboriginal peoples across the country—and indeed around the world—in a way previously unimaginable. Thirty years ago, during the patriation process, Aboriginal peoples had to charter a train from Vancouver to Ottawa to connect with each other. Now Aboriginal peoples are connected online and a new solidarity has been established. The Idle No More movement may wane or even disappear with time, but through it Aboriginal peoples have found their voice and established a presence in the world of social media. Aboriginal politics has been permanently transformed.

Aboriginal Peoples in Canada: *Sui Generis* Citizens

By now, it should be clear that the rules of the political game have always been different for Aboriginal peoples. Initially, and for more than 100 years, Aboriginal peoples were singled out for racist and discriminatory treatment by the Canadian state. Since the *Calder* decision in 1973, and especially since the patriation of the constitution in 1982, Aboriginal peoples have received more favourable treatment, although the process of building a new relationship is still a work in progress.

Whereas Aboriginal peoples were originally wards of the state and noncitizens, some people have now (approvingly) suggested that Aboriginal peoples are on their way to becoming "citizens plus" in Canada. Most Canadians now accept that the discriminatory treatment Aboriginal peoples received at the hands of the Canadian state was unjust, but many are not comfortable with the idea that Aboriginal peoples should have rights not available to other Canadians. Canadians typically believe in a particular type of equality— what political theorists call **procedural equality**—which insists that the state treat all citizens in the same way. From this perspective, the Indian Act should be abolished and Aboriginal Canadians should be treated like all other citizens. This was the logic behind Pierre Trudeau's ill-fated White Paper on Indian Policy. The White Paper was not simply rejected by Aboriginal people—it was inconsistent with the reality of Canada.

The reality is that Aboriginal Canadians are not like other Canadians. They occupy a unique position in the history and legal framework of Canada. Unlike other Canadians, Aboriginal peoples occupied the upper half of North America *before* the Crown established its sovereignty here. Aboriginal peoples formed self-governing societies prior to the arrival of European settlers, and contrary to popular opinion they were never conquered. On the contrary, the Crown entered into legal treaties with Aboriginal peoples. All of these facts "are exclusive to Aboriginal peoples in North America."[50] These facts were ignored for more than a century, but the governments of Canada recognized the unique position occupied by Aboriginal peoples in the Constitution Act 1982.

However, the term "citizens plus" may not be helpful. It suggests that Aboriginal peoples are better than or superior to other Canadians. The Supreme Court prefers the Latin term *sui generis*—meaning "of its own kind" or "unique"—when referring to Aboriginal citizens. This term is descriptive rather than judgmental, but it does require Canadians to reconceptualize their understanding of citizenship and the meaning of equality. The entrenchment of Aboriginal rights in the constitution requires a shift away from a singular understanding of citizenship in which all citizens have exactly the same rights to a model of **differential citizenship** in which citizens exercise different rights. This is a huge change; it would represent a major shift in Canadian political culture. The architects of the new constitution may not have realized the full implications of patriation, but Canadians now have a constitutional obligation to fulfill the promises made to Aboriginal peoples in 1982. The honour of the Crown is at stake.

procedural equality A type of equality that requires the state to apply the law in a similar fashion to all citizens regardless of differences such as gender or race.

differential citizenship A form of citizenship in which the state recognizes that disadvantaged groups, such as racial minorities, may require different treatment to realize their equality. Differential citizenship stands in contrast to the liberal principle of procedural equality.

SUMMARY

The Constitution Act 1982 recognized and affirmed the historical rights and treaty rights of Aboriginal peoples. With the new constitution, the governments of Canada pledged to build a new relationship with Aboriginal peoples, but they have been reluctant to negotiate a comprehensive political settlement with Aboriginal peoples (including the right to self-government) presumably because they fear that it would not be popular with non-Aboriginal Canadians who constitute the democratic majority.

In the absence of a political framework, it has fallen to the Supreme Court to define the meaning and extent of Aboriginal rights. But the Supreme Court has been reluctant to adopt a definitive position on the right of self-government. For the justices of the Supreme Court, self-government is a political matter rather than a legal issue. Aboriginal peoples are thus caught between the political branches of government on the one hand and the judicial branch of government on the other.

Meanwhile, many Aboriginal communities across the country continue to be plagued by various social and economic pathologies. Many Aboriginal Canadians believe that the constitutional promises of 1982 have not been fulfilled, and they are increasingly feeling betrayed. It would seem that Canada is stuck between the old colonial rules of the game with respect to Aboriginal peoples and the postcolonial rules of the game envisioned by the Constitution Act 1982.

Questions to Think About

1. Do you think Canada has overcome its history of internal colonialism with respect to Aboriginal peoples?

2. If Aboriginal peoples cannot obtain self-government through the courts or the political process, what are their options? What other routes can they take to advance their cause?

3. Do you think Canadians are ready to accept Aboriginal peoples as *sui generis* citizens and embrace the concept of differential citizenship?

4. What can be done to remedy the economic conditions for Aboriginal peoples in Canada? Is it necessary to settle land claims and self-government first? Or can economic development be pursued separately?

Learning Outcomes

1. Describe the historical relationship between Aboriginal peoples and the Crown and the Canadian state.

2. Describe the role of Aboriginal peoples in the patriation of the constitution.

3. Describe the different types of Aboriginal rights recognized and affirmed by Section 35 of the Constitution Act 1982.

4. Explain the source of Aboriginal rights in Canadian law and why these rights are exclusive to Aboriginal peoples.

5. Describe the social and economic conditions experienced by many Aboriginal peoples in Canada.

6. Describe the kind of relationship Aboriginal peoples would like to establish with the Canadian state.

Additional Readings

Taiaiake Alfred, *Peace, Power, and Righteousness: An Indigenous Manifesto* (Toronto, ON: Oxford University Press, 1999).

Taiaiake Alfred, *Wasáse: Indigenous Pathways of Action and Freedom* (Toronto, ON: University of Toronto Press, 2005).

John Borrows, *Canada's Indigenous Constitution* (Toronto, ON: University of Toronto Press, 2010).

John Borrows, *Recovering Canada: The Resurgence of Indigenous Law* (Toronto, ON: University of Toronto Press, 2002).

Alan C. Cairns, *Citizens Plus: Aboriginal Peoples and the Canadian State* (Vancouver, BC: UBC Press, 2000).

Thomas Flanagan, *First Nations? Second Thoughts* (Montreal, QC: McGill-Queen's University Press, 2000).

Patrick Macklem, *Indigenous Difference and the Constitution of Canada* (Toronto, ON: University of Toronto Press, 2001).

Patricia Monture-Angus, *Journeying Forward: Dreaming First Nations' Independence* (Halifax, NS: Fernwood Press, 1995).

Timothy Schouls, *Shifting Boundaries: Aboriginal Identity, Pluralist Theory, and the Politics of Self-Government* (Vancouver, BC: UBC Press, 2003).

Notes

1. Noel Lyon, "An Essay on Constitutional Interpretation," *Osgoode Hall Law Journal* 26 (1988), 100.

2. See *First Words: An Evolving Terminology Relating to Aboriginal Peoples in Canada* (Ottawa, ON: Communications Branch, Indian and Northern Affairs Canada, 2002).

3. Royal Commission on Aboriginal Peoples, *Report of the Royal Commission on Aboriginal Peoples, Volume 1: Looking Forward, Looking Back* (Ottawa, ON: Minister of Supply and Services Canada, 1996), 39.

4. David MacDonald and Graham Hudson, "The Genocide Question and Indian Residential Schools in Canada," *Canadian Journal of Political Science* 45:2 (June 2012), 427–449.

5. James S. Frideres and René R. Gadacz, *Aboriginal Peoples in Canada*, 8th ed. (Toronto, ON: Pearson Prentice Hall, 2008), 57.

6. Ibid., 271.

7. Ibid., 546.

8. Ibid., 547.

9. Métis leader Louis Riel was elected to the House of Commons three times in the early 1870s in the riding of Provencher in southeast Manitoba, but the Government of Canada declared that he was an outlaw and prohibited him from taking his seat in Parliament.

10. Department of Indian Affairs and Northern Development, *Statement of the Government of Canada on Indian Policy 1969, The White Paper* (Ottawa, ON: Queen's Printer, 1969), 11.

11. Harold Cardinal, *The Unjust Society: The Tragedy of Canada's Indians* (Edmonton, AB: M.G. Hurtig, 1969), 140.

12. *Calder v. Attorney-General of British Columbia [1973] SCR*, 328

13. Ibid., 316.

14. Douglas Sanders, "The Indian Lobby," in Keith Banting and Richard Simeon, eds., *And No One Cheered: Federalism, Democracy and the Constitution Act* (Toronto, ON: Methuen, 1983), 304.

15. Ibid., 313.

16. Ibid., 321.

17. Ibid., 322.

18. Ibid., 323; emphasis added.

19. Ibid., 324; emphasis added.

20. Peter H. Russell, *Constitutional Odyssey: Can Canadians Become a Sovereign People?* 3rd ed. (Toronto, ON: University of Toronto Press, 2004), 131.

21. Ibid., 131.

22. Ibid., 132.

23. Grace Li Xiu Woo, *Ghost Dancing with Colonialism: Decolonization and Indigenous Rights at the Supreme Court of Canada* (Vancouver, BC: UBC Press, 2011), see Appendix 4.

24. Peter W. Hogg, *Constitutional Law of Canada*, 5th ed., supplemented, vol. 2 (Toronto, ON: Carswell, 2007), 28–38.

25. Ibid., 28–29.

26. *R. v. Sparrow, [1990] 1 SCR 1075.*

27. Ibid., emphasis added.

28. *R. v. Van der Peet, [1996] 2 SCR 507,* para. 20.

29. Ibid., para. 46.

30. Ibid., para. 59.

31. See *R. v. Gladstone, [1996] 2 SCR 723.*

32. *Delgamuukw v. British Columbia, [1997] 3 SCR 1010.*

33. Ibid.

34. Ibid., para. 128.

35. *R. v. Pamajewon [1996] 2 SCR 821.*

36. *Delgamuukw v. British Columbia,* para. 186.

37. See Health Canada, "First Nations & Inuit Health: Diseases and Health Conditions," available at http://www.hc-sc.gc.ca/fniah-spnia/diseases-maladies/index-eng.php; and Heart and Stroke Foundation, "Aboriginal Peoples, Heart Disease and Stroke," available at http://www.heartandstroke.com/site/c.ikIQLcMWJtE/b.8732835/k.F615/Aboriginal_Peoples_Heart_Disease_and_Stroke.htm.

38. Frideres and Gadacz, *Aboriginal Peoples in Canada,* 84.

39. Centre for Suicide Prevention, *Suicide Prevention Resource Toolkit: Aboriginal* (2013). Available at https://suicideinfo.ca/LinkClick.aspx?fileticket=MVIyGo2V4YY%3D&tabid=516.

40. Jodi-Anne Brzozowski, Andrea Taylor-Butts, and Sara Johnson, "Victimization and Offending among the Aboriginal Population in Canada," Statistics Canada, Catalogue no. 85-002-XIE, vol. 26, no. 3, 1.

41. Ibid., 1.

42. Frideres and Gadacz, *Aboriginal Peoples in Canada,* 90.

43. Ibid., 103.

44. Ibid., 103.

45. Royal Commission on Aboriginal Peoples, *Report of the Royal Commission on Aboriginal Peoples, Volume 5, Renewal: A Twenty-Year Commitment* (Ottawa, ON: Minister of Supply and Services, 1996), 119–120.

46. Ibid., 55, emphasis added.

47. Peter O'Neil, "Ottawa Rejects Push for Extra $30 Billion: The Royal Commission on Aboriginal Peoples," *Vancouver Sun,* November 22, 1996, A3.

48. "First Ministers and National Aboriginal Leaders: Strengthening Relationships and Closing the Gap," Kelowna, British Columbia, November 24–25, 2005.

49. Aboriginal Affairs and Northern Development Canada, *Backgrounder: Indian Residential Schools Settlement Agreement.* Available at http://www.aadnc-aandc.gc.ca.

50. Patrick Macklem, *Indigenous Difference and the Constitution of Canada* (Toronto, ON: University of Toronto Press, 2001), 4.

Chapter 11
Constitutional Reform

Key Points

- The Constitution Act 1982 made Canada a self-governing country, and it has had a significant impact on Canadian society, especially the Charter of Rights and Freedoms—although the recognition and affirmation of Aboriginal rights is potentially even more significant.

- The patriation of the constitution over the strong objections of Quebec left a deep wound in the federation. Subsequent attempts to accommodate Quebec failed, and the province nearly voted to separate from Canada in the second referendum in 1995.

- After the second referendum, Parliament passed the Clarity Act, which spells out in law how a province can separate from the Canadian federation. With the Clarity Act, Canada has shown the world how the deeply divisive politics of secession can be pursued peacefully, democratically, and according to the rule of law.

- The constitutional debates in the 1990s represented a struggle to devise new rules of the game for a country in the throes of a profound social and political transformation.

- The politics of constitutional reform led to the decline of the traditional brokerage political parties and a major reorganization of the party system. Canada's parties are still trying to figure out how to adapt to the new realities of Canadian political culture.

The Constitution Act 1982 was the most significant institutional reform in the Canadian political system since Confederation. The Charter of Rights and Freedoms has already had a significant impact on Canadian society, and Part II of the new constitution (on Aboriginal rights) has the potential to transform the federation even more profoundly. The equalization program—entrenched in Part III of the new constitution—is not well understood by Canadians, but it is a critical instrument for horizontal equity. It enables the provinces to provide comparable levels of public services at reasonably comparable rates of taxation. And of course the amending formulas enable the governments of Canada to enact constitutional changes without appealing to the British Parliament in London—which was the key point of patriation in the first place. In other words, the Constitution Act 1982 made Canada completely self-governing for the first time in its history; April 17 really ought to be celebrated as Canada's independence day rather than July 1, but when the constitution finally made it back to Canadian shores "no one cheered."[1]

The manner in which the Constitution Act 1982 was realized—over the strenuous objections of Quebec—has prevented the new constitution from becoming an object of celebration and an instrument of unity, contrary to Pierre Trudeau's hopes and expectations. After the "night of the long knives" it was obvious that Canada's long constitutional odyssey was destined to continue. Quebec's objections to the new constitutional order could not be left unaddressed. Pierre Trudeau was not in a position to reopen the constitution; he had expended all of his political capital. But Brian Mulroney was in an excellent position to tackle this nettlesome file after he led the Progressive Conservative Party to the largest majority government in Canadian history in the fall of 1984. While Prime Minister Mulroney had the right intentions, his efforts at constitutional reform failed. By the time he left office in 1993, it was clear that Canadians in different parts of the country had very different constitutional perspectives, or what we might call **mega-constitutional orientations**.[2]

For much of the 1990s, Canadians were consumed by an intense debate over the rules of the political game, but the efforts to reform the constitution failed because the governments and people of Canada were working at cross-purposes. The governments of Canada were trying to resolve the constitutional dilemma of the twentieth century—namely, the accommodation of Quebec nationalism. Rather than extinguish Quebec nationalism, as Trudeau had hoped to do, Brian Mulroney sought to create some space in the constitution for Quebec's theory of two nations. While Mulroney was able to persuade the provincial governments to accept Quebec's demands, he discovered that many Canadians outside Quebec were not receptive to his constitutional vision. For many, Mulroney's vision represented the "old Canada" of linguistic duality and federalism and not the "new Canada" of Aboriginal peoples, multiculturalism, and the ethic of equality entrenched in the Charter of Rights and Freedoms. And as the constitutional debates unfolded, it became apparent that many people in the West had an entirely different constitutional philosophy. Ultimately, these constitutional conflicts led to a significant reorganization of the party system in the 1993 election. Most worrisomely, this critical election marked the beginning of the end of Canada's traditional brokerage parties. With the benefit of hindsight, we can see that the constitutional debates of the 1990s were emblematic of a federation in the throes of a profound social and political transformation.

mega-constitutional orientations Distinct perspectives— often associated with a particular region or group—on the identity and fundamental principles of the body politic.

The Meech Lake Accord

The Constitution Act 1982 was premised on Pierre Trudeau's political philosophy or mega-constitutional orientation. As discussed in Chapter 8, Trudeau wanted all Canadians to think of themselves as bilingual, rights-bearing individuals, rather than as Quebecers, Maritimers, or Westerners. In short, he hoped to establish a singular Canadian identity through the Charter of Rights and Freedoms. Trudeau, however, was also forced to recognize group rights for Aboriginal peoples, multicultural Canadians, and women—or so-called "Charter Canadians." Thus, alongside a traditional constitutional liberalism, the new constitution also made a political commitment to minority groups. This explicit support for minority groups represented an entirely new mega-constitutional orientation in Canadian political discourse. Both orientations were completely unacceptable to Quebec, but that was the point of the new constitution: Trudeau was attempting to extinguish Quebec's belief in the two nations thesis. As such, it is hardly surprising that Quebec rejected Trudeau's constitution.

Soon after the new constitution was enacted, the political landscape in Canada changed dramatically. First, in the spring of 1984 Pierre Trudeau retired, and in the election later that year Brian Mulroney led the Progressive Conservative Party to the largest electoral victory in Canadian politics. Second, in the summer of 1985 René Lévesque announced his retirement. In December 1985 the Quebec Liberal Party defeated the Parti Québécois, and Robert Bourassa became the premier of the province for the second time (Bourassa had previously led Quebec from 1970–1976). Although Prime Minister Mulroney was a Conservative and Bourassa was a Liberal, they got along well and they were both anxious to settle the unfinished business left over from patriation—namely, to secure Quebec's consent to the new constitution.

Prime Minister Brian Mulroney and Quebec Premier Robert Bourassa

Pierre Roussel/Images Distribution/Newscom

Premier Bourassa got the ball rolling on a new round of constitutional negotiations when he articulated Quebec's "minimum" conditions for supporting the new constitution:

1. The constitutional recognition of Quebec as a "distinct society"
2. A veto over future constitutional amendments
3. A role in selecting justices to the Supreme Court of Canada
4. Limits on the federal spending power
5. A role in the area of immigration

The constitutional recognition of Quebec as a distinct society was both symbolic and pragmatic. With the distinct society clause, Bourassa was hoping to secure some recognition from the rest of Canada that Quebec was, in fact, a nation. For Quebec, it was symbolically important to be accepted by the rest of the country on its own terms, especially after Pierre Trudeau had persuaded much of Canada to go along with a new constitutional order that treated Quebec as a province like all the others. The distinct society clause also had significant legal ramifications. Universal rights, such as those that exist in the Charter of Rights and Freedoms, are inherently homogenizing. If Canada was going to have a charter, Bourassa was saying, it was important to direct the Supreme Court to interpret the constitution in a manner consistent with Quebec's distinctiveness.

The other conditions articulated by Bourassa flowed from the recognition of Quebec as a distinct society. With the Supreme Court making important policy decisions under the Charter of Rights and Freedoms, Quebec—as the one province unlike the others—wanted some say in the selection of justices for the top court. Some of the other provinces have also long expressed the desire to have some role in the appointment of Supreme Court justices, as discussed in Chapter 9. And Bourassa's demand for a constitutional veto was not new. Quebec has always maintained that it needs—and has historically possessed—a veto over constitutional change. This point was all the more salient in light of the patriation of the constitution, the most significant constitutional change since Confederation, without Quebec's consent. Since the end of World War II, Quebec has maintained that the federal spending power circumvents the division of powers entrenched in the Constitution Act 1867 and thereby undermines Quebec's ability to protect and nurture its distinct society. Finally, Bourassa asked for a role in immigration, which under the Constitution Act 1867 is a matter of concurrent jurisdiction between the federal government and the provinces. Quebec has an interest in attracting immigrants who already speak French or who are at least committed to learning it. The influx of non-French-speaking immigrants would obviously undermine Quebec's distinctiveness.

Unlike Pierre Trudeau, Brian Mulroney did not have strong constitutional convictions, and he was considerably more pragmatic with respect to Quebec. In an essay published shortly before he became prime minister, Mulroney stated emphatically "I do not believe in a theory of two nations, five nations, or ten nations . . . Nor do I believe in any concept that would give any one province an advantage over any other." But, in the very next paragraph, he wrote:

> Quebec is different, very different. It is not strange or weird, it is just different. And the difference is rooted in language and culture. That is why the preservation and enhancement of these two instruments are so vital. That is why they must be protected and nurtured with a constancy and vigilance that can never be slackened. For English Canadians, comfortably ensconced in the protective linguistic cocoon that envelops all of North America, measures to ensure protection of the French language may sometimes seem silly and vexatious. But they are not. Such concerns are a deadly serious business.[3]

Thus, while Trudeau had always rejected Quebec's demands for a special constitutional status, Mulroney was obviously more receptive to the idea.

In April 1987, Prime Minister Mulroney invited the provincial premiers to the federal government's conference centre at Meech Lake in the Gatineau Hills north of Ottawa to discuss Premier Bourassa's conditions for accepting the new constitution. Before entering politics, Mulroney had spent some time as a labour negotiator. He was thus highly experienced in handling tense negotiations, and by the end of the day he secured an agreement with all of the provinces that became known as the **Meech Lake Accord**. Quebec's minimum conditions, however, were diluted over the course of the day. "In a nutshell," Peter Russell writes, "they had been provincialized. They had been made agreeable to the provincial premiers by respecting the principle of provincial equality and, with one exception, extending to all the provinces the powers sought by Quebec."[4] Even the clause recognizing Quebec as a distinct society was "Canadianized" to make it more palatable to people in the rest of Canada. In short, the clause attempted to situate Quebec's distinctiveness within the context of Canada's linguistic duality by referring to French-speaking Canadians outside Quebec as well as English-speaking Canadians in Quebec (see Box 11.1). Robert Bourassa was nevertheless prepared to accept these compromises to secure constitutional peace.

The public reaction to the Meech Lake Accord was initially underwhelming, but eventually many groups voiced strong opposition to the deal. Aboriginal peoples complained about being excluded from the process, some feminists worried that the distinct society clause might compromise the equality rights of women in Quebec, and social democrats feared that the limitations on the spending power would undermine social programs. These disparate opponents of the accord were galvanized into a unified opposition force when Pierre Trudeau emerged from retirement with a blistering critique of the agreement. Trudeau denounced every aspect of the accord and, breaking with political etiquette, he savagely attacked Prime Minister Mulroney, accusing him of putting Canada "on the fast track" to René Lévesque's dream of sovereignty-association.[5] Trudeau was convinced that the distinct society clause would lead to the breakup of Canada, as we can see from his statement to a special Senate Committee on the constitution:

> Canada henceforth will be governed by two Constitutions, one to be interpreted for the benefit of Canada and one to be interpreted for the preservation and promotion of Quebec's distinct society—two Constitutions, two Charters, promoting two distinct sets of values, and eventually two Canadas—well, one Canada and something else.[6]

Meech Lake Accord An agreement between the federal government and the provinces to amend the constitution. The recognition of Quebec as a distinct society was the centrepiece of the accord. The objective of the accord was to obtain Quebec's consent for the Constitution Act 1982, but the accord failed when it did not receive legislative support in Manitoba and Newfoundland.

The Meech Lake Accord

The distinct society clause was intended to be inserted as the second section of the Constitution Act 1867 as a directive to the courts for the interpretation of the whole constitution, including the Charter of Rights and Freedoms.

2.1 The Constitution of Canada shall be interpreted in a manner consistent with A) the recognition that the existence of French-speaking Canadians, centred in Quebec but also present elsewhere, and English-speaking Canadians, concentrated outside Quebec but also present in Quebec, constitutes a fundamental characteristic of Canada; and B) the recognition that Quebec constitutes within Canada a distinct society;

2.2 The role of the Parliament of Canada and the provincial legislatures to preserve the fundamental characteristic of Canada referred to in paragraph 1A is affirmed;

2.3 The role of the legislature and Government of Quebec to preserve and promote the distinct identity of Quebec referred to in paragraph 1B is affirmed.

Trudeau's hostility to the Meech Lake Accord flowed from a very rigid conception of equality. He believed that anything less than identical treatment of all individuals would compromise the principle of equality. Unfortunately, this conception of equality is blind to cultural differences, although Pierre Trudeau would beg to differ. While reasonable people can debate the meaning of equality, it is undeniable that Trudeau's vocal opposition to Meech Lake helped sink the accord.

The Collapse of the Meech Lake Accord

The Meech Lake Accord was a complex document. Some parts of the agreement, such as the distinct society clause, were subject only to the 7/50 amending formula, but other parts of the agreement, namely changes to the amending formula and the Supreme Court, required the unanimous consent of the federal government and all 10 provinces. And, under the terms of the formulas laid out in Sections 38 to 49 of the Constitution Act 1982, it was necessary to ratify the amendments in Parliament and the provincial legislatures. But because the accord was a tightly negotiated agreement, it was impossible to proceed with the amendments item by item; if the governments of Canada had proceeded in that fashion, some jurisdictions may have ended up with none of what they wanted and a bunch of things they opposed. The Meech Lake Accord thus became an all-or-nothing proposition that had to be ratified by Parliament and all 10 provincial legislatures.

On June 23, 1987, just weeks after the agreement was concluded, the Quebec National Assembly became the first legislature in Canada to ratify the Meech Lake Accord. Under the terms of Section 39(2) of the Constitution Act 1982, the other provincial legislatures and the Parliament of Canada were required to ratify the agreement within three years, but the other provinces were not as motivated as Quebec, and some delayed ratification. And, over the next three years, some of the governments that originally consented to the agreement were thrown out of office, and some of the new governments were not supportive of the agreement. While the new Liberal government in New Brunswick initially had some concerns about Meech Lake, the accord ultimately ran aground in two provinces: Newfoundland and Labrador and Manitoba. In Newfoundland and Labrador, Liberal

Premier Clyde Wells was a constitutional lawyer who shared many of Pierre Trudeau's concerns about the Meech Lake Accord. And, under his direction, the legislature of Newfoundland and Labrador repealed its support for the agreement just three months before the June 1990 deadline. Wells remained staunchly opposed to the accord to the bitter end, notwithstanding the enormous pressure placed on him by Prime Minister Mulroney to reverse his position.

The situation in Manitoba was more complicated. Premier Howard Pawley endorsed the agreement when it was negotiated in the spring of 1987, but his NDP government self-destructed the following year and, in the process, Pawley was replaced as leader by Gary Doer. In the subsequent election, the NDP was reduced to 12 seats in the 57-seat legislature. The Progressive Conservative Party led by Gary Filmon captured 25 seats and formed a weak minority government. Filmon was denied a majority by a resurgent Liberal Party led by Sharon Carstairs, who shared Trudeau's concerns about the accord and campaigned vigorously against it. The accord would now need the support of two parties to pass through the legislature, and none of them were enthusiastic about it.

With the June 23, 1990, deadline fast approaching, Prime Minister Mulroney moved to salvage the accord in the only way he knew how: he invited the premiers to Ottawa for a round of last-minute bargaining in true labour negotiator style. Premier Filmon from Manitoba was joined by Sharon Carstairs and Gary Doer, for the simple reason that he would ultimately need the support of either the opposition Liberal Party or the NDP to pass the accord through the legislature. The meeting lasted for a biblical seven days and seven nights. The media was camped outside the conference centre for the duration of the meeting, and citizens were glued to their television sets, awaiting updates from their political leaders at all times of the day and night. At close to midnight on June 9, the first ministers emerged to say that they had reached a new "agreement." In actuality, the premiers had only agreed to consider more constitutional amendments following the ratification of the Meech Lake Accord, such as a broader "Canada clause" to offset the distinct society clause, an elected Senate, stronger equality rights for women in the Charter of Rights and Freedoms, a review of the amending formulas, and a commitment to resume constitutional negotiations with Aboriginal peoples. So, in other words, Canada's constitutional odyssey was destined to continue even if the Meech Lake Accord was ratified.

The last-minute agreement to save Meech Lake was very tenuous. Clyde Wells agreed only to consider putting the accord to a new vote in the legislature. The trio of leaders from Manitoba were not enthusiastic about the new agreement either, although they at least agreed to push it through the legislature. However, time was now running out. And in order to fast track the agreement through the legislative process, it was necessary to suspend the normal operating rules of the legislature, but that required the unanimous consent of everyone in the legislature. And when this procedural issue was put to a vote, one member said no—Elijah Harper, a Cree from Red Sucker Lake in northeastern Manitoba. Harper was deeply concerned that Aboriginal peoples had been shut out of the Meech Lake negotiations. He also feared that a deal designed to secure Quebec's consent to the constitution would forever close the file on Canada's constitution, notwithstanding Prime Minister Mulroney's solemn promise to resume constitutional negotiations with Aboriginal peoples. As far as Harper was concerned, Aboriginal peoples in Canada had heard many nice promises but seen precious little action. Certainly, the recognition and affirmation of Aboriginal rights entrenched in Section 35 of the Constitution Act 1982 was still a hollow promise. Harper thus stood firm in his opposition to the Meech Lake Accord. When it became clear that there would be no vote in Manitoba, Clyde Wells opted not to put the accord to a vote in the legislature of Newfoundland and Labrador. The accord was consequently dead in the water.

Elijah Harper in the Manitoba
Legislature during the Debate
on the Meech Lake Accord

CP PICTURE ARCHIVE/Winnipeg Free Press/Wayne Glowacki

The Political Consequences
of the Meech Lake Accord

The objective of the Meech Lake Accord was to address Quebec's constitutional concerns, but at the end of the process Quebec was more alienated than ever. Indeed, the failure of the accord resurrected the sovereignty movement in Quebec. In the West, a new wave of conservative populism emerged in opposition to the Meech Lake Accord. Finally, the debate over the accord showed that Trudeau-style Canadian nationalists were still alive and well in many parts of the country, but a variety of new political forces also emerged. Charter Canadians demonstrated that they were now players in Canada's game of mega-constitutional politics, and the unleashing of these forces continues to reverberate throughout Canadian politics.

The Fallout in Quebec

The failure of the Meech Lake Accord had profound consequences in Quebec. The accord was intended to secure Quebec's consent to the constitutional reforms of 1982, and many Quebecers were stunned that the rest of Canada—or at least much of the rest of Canada—could not endorse Quebec's "minimum conditions" for endorsing the Constitution Act 1982. This led many Quebecers to feel rejected by the rest of Canada. The fact that Pierre Trudeau helped galvanize the opposition to the Meech Lake Accord enhanced the sense of betrayal. Support for sovereignty soared in the days following the collapse of the Meech Lake Accord. Indeed, "three days after Meech died, 200 000 Quebecers waving the Quebec flag and chanting 'in-dé-pen-dance' paraded through the streets of Montreal in the annual Jean-Baptiste Day celebrations."[7]

While the public reaction in Quebec to the failure of the Meech Lake Accord proved to be relatively short lived, the political consequences were much more enduring. In the run up to the June 23, 1990, deadline the Mulroney government was shaken by the resignation of Lucien Bouchard, the government's "Quebec lieutenant" and Mulroney's old friend from law school. Bouchard feared that Mulroney was planning to water down the Meech Lake Accord in a bid to appease the various critics of the agreement. For Bouchard, Quebec's "minimum conditions" for supporting the constitutional arrangements of 1982 had already been diluted in the Meech Lake Accord by extending most of the provisions to all of the provinces. If the accord were further diluted, Bouchard said, it would fall well short of Quebec's bottom line. Bouchard thus quit the cabinet in protest and assumed a seat in the back corner of the House of Commons as an independent member. He was soon joined by five more Progressive Conservative members plus two Liberals, who then collectively formed a *bloc* from Quebec. In short order, this informal coalition was transformed into the Bloc Québécois, which was committed to achieving Quebec's sovereignty. For the next two decades, the Bloc won a majority of seats in Quebec in each federal election, but the party inexplicably collapsed in the 2011 election, as will be discussed below.

Western Alienation

The Meech Lake saga also revealed that Western Canada has a distinct mega-constitutional orientation, although it has some affinities with Pierre Trudeau's liberalism, as many Westerners discovered much to their surprise when they found themselves agreeing with Trudeau's denunciation of the Meech Lake Accord. The political culture of the West rests on the region's frontier history. The West was settled by rugged individuals surviving on their own wiles with no government support beyond the Royal Canadian Mounted Police. From this experience emerges the theory of *rugged individualism*, which is characterized by a strong commitment to individual liberty and procedural equality.

At this point, we need to make a distinction between two conceptions of equality: **procedural equality** and **substantive equality**. With procedural equality, the state promises to treat each individual in the same way without discrimination; it is about equality of opportunity. Metaphorically, it is about ensuring that everyone gets to start the race of life on the same starting line. It does not matter who wins or loses the race—so long as everyone starts together, the result is fair according to the theory of procedural equality.

Supporters of substantive equality, by contrast, suggest that equality does not exist when there are winners and losers in life. With substantive equality, the goal is to ensure that *everyone* crosses the finish line together. Since some people are disadvantaged in the race of life, people may have to start the race at different places in order to finish together. Most people intuitively accept the theory of substantive equality, at least to some degree. For example, it is now widely accepted that people with disabilities should be afforded certain accommodations so that they can realize life opportunities, such as attending university or pursuing a career. And other sorts of disadvantages may also be debilitating. People from poor families, for example, may not have the means to attend university, so the state may provide loans or grants to help people from these families to realize their education. Similarly, people in various minority groups may face real barriers, such as discrimination, in the race of life. It may thus be necessary to provide these groups with special assistance. And other groups may face cultural challenges. Quebec, as the only French-speaking jurisdiction in North America, may have to do things differently than other provinces to ensure Quebec continues to be a vibrant French-speaking community.

Many Westerners do not buy into the notion that some cultural groups require special rights. From the perspective of rugged individualism, which is premised on the procedural conception of equality, the state is not treating individuals equally when it recognizes some but not others as distinct. Many Westerners were uncomfortable with Trudeau's commitment to bilingualism, because they viewed it as a special right for just one group in Canadian society. But Trudeau's critique of the distinct society clause struck a chord with many Westerners because it revealed that he had some affinities with the theory of rugged individualism.

While Westerners have typically been suspicious of group rights, they believe strongly in the *equality of provinces*. We saw this during patriation when the Gang of Eight, led by

procedural equality A type of equality that requires the state to apply the law in a similar fashion to all citizens regardless of differences such as gender or race.

substantive equality A type of equality that requires the state to apply the law differently to different groups based on their relative advantages or disadvantages so as to obtain an equal outcome or standard of living for all people.

Alberta, insisted on an amending formula that treated all provinces the same way. But the West has long wanted more. For most of the twentieth century, Westerners have felt that Central Canada has used its demographic weight in the federation to exploit the West, especially the region's natural resources. The sentiment was aptly illustrated in a political cartoon published in 1915 depicting a large cow standing over Canada, eating grass in the prairies but being milked by greedy capitalists in Ottawa, Montreal, and Toronto. This sentiment was revived by Trudeau's National Energy Program (NEP). The NEP was introduced in 1980 and it forced the West—mainly Alberta—to sell its oil and gas to the rest of Canada below world prices. While the program was intended to stimulate Canada's stagnant economy and reduce the country's reliance on oil and gas imported from volatile countries in the Middle East, it was damaging to Alberta's economy. The NEP consequently provoked considerable feelings of resentment across Western Canada, especially since it was introduced at a time when the governing Liberal Party held only two seats in Western Canada, both in Manitoba.

In order to counterbalance the population of Central Canada, the West has long wanted the idea of provincial equality to be embedded in the structure of Canada's political institutions. In many federations the constituent units (states or provinces, as the case may be) are represented equally in the second chamber of the national legislature. This is the case in the United States, where equal representation for the states in the Senate was deemed to be the *quid pro quo* (the tradeoff) for representation by population in the House of Representatives. The constitutional bargain in Canada was slightly different: federalism and provincial autonomy were the *quid pro quo* for representation by population in Parliament, including the Senate (more or less). Recall that the Senate of Canada is structured along regional lines: the Maritimes, Quebec, Ontario, and the West are each represented by 24 senators. (There are six senators for Newfoundland and Labrador, and one for each of the territories.) Moreover, as an appointed chamber the Senate typically defers to the will of the democratic majority represented in the House of Commons. Many Westerners have thus come to believe that Parliament is beholden to the wishes of Central Canada.

In the constitutional debates in the 1970s, Alberta floated the idea of transforming the Senate into a "house of provinces," with senators appointed by the provincial premiers rather

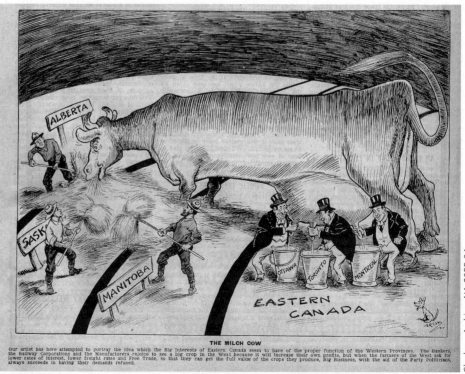

Cartoon 11.1 The Milch Cow, first published in the December 15, 1915, edition of the *Grain Growers Guide*. (Glenbow Museum, NA3055-24).

THE MILCH COW

Our artist has here attempted to portray the idea which the Big Interests of Eastern Canada seem to have of the proper function of the Western Provinces. The Bankers, the Railway Corporations and the Manufacturers rejoice to see a big crop in the West because it will increase their own profits, but when the farmers of the West ask for lower rates of interest, lower freight rates and Free Trade, so that they can get the full value of the crops they produce, Big Business, with the aid of the Party Politicians, always succeeds in having their demands refused.

than the prime minister, but this modest proposal did not find its way into the constitutional reforms of 1982. In the 1980s, the desire for a more democratic Senate took root in Alberta and across Western Canada more generally. In short, the goal was to transform the Senate into a more *effective* legislative chamber by making it an *elected* body with *equal* representation from each province. The idea quickly became known as the **Triple-E Senate**: elected, equal, and effective. In a Triple-E Senate, the representation of Ontario and Quebec would drop from nearly 50 percent to 20 percent (or even a bit less since the territories would also be entitled to some representation). Conversely, the representation for the other eight provinces would almost double from just over 40 percent to 80 percent. As an elected chamber, the Senate would possess the democratic legitimacy to reject legislation endorsed by the House of Commons. In this fashion, the less populated regions of the federation would be able to effectively counterbalance the demographic weight of Central Canada represented in the House of Commons.

While the concept of a Triple-E Senate has considerable merit, it is not without its problems. First, it creates the potential for legislative gridlock in Parliament. Gridlock is a regular occurrence in the US Congress, but in the United States, unlike Canada, the executive branch of government is wholly separate from the legislative branch and retains considerable authority to act independently of Congress. It is not clear that the advocates of a Triple-E Senate in Canada have adequately considered how it would operate in a parliamentary setting with the executive situated in and responsible to the lower chamber. Nevertheless, by the late 1980s a Triple-E Senate was at the very top of Western Canada's constitutional wish list, and many Westerners were bitterly disappointed when it became apparent that Senate reform would not be forthcoming with the Meech Lake Accord. Under the terms of Meech Lake, furthermore, Senate reform would have henceforth been subject to the unanimous consent of the federal government and all the provinces. Consequently, many Westerners rapidly came to the conclusion that, if the Meech Lake Accord went through, the Senate would never be reformed. Why would Ontario or Quebec agree to a constitutional amendment that would diminish their representation in the Senate from about 25 percent each to just 10 percent each?

The Rise of the Reform Party

The Meech Lake Accord left many Westerners feeling betrayed by their political leaders. Westerners had strongly backed Brian Mulroney's Progressive Conservative Party in two elections (and they were pleased when he scrapped the National Energy Program), but they could not help feeling that he had sold out their constitutional interests in a vain attempt to appease Quebec. By the late 1980s, many Westerners were coming to the conclusion that Brian Mulroney did not embrace their type of conservatism.

Some perceptive political entrepreneurs sensed the dissatisfaction in the West with the Progressive Conservative Party, and they decided to offer Westerners a new political alternative that would reflect the unique conservative populism of Western Canada. The inaugural meeting of the new Reform Party took place in May 1987, at exactly the same time that Brian Mulroney was unveiling the Meech Lake Accord in the Gatineau Hills. The leader of the new party was Preston Manning, the son of Ernest Manning, the former leader of the Alberta Social Credit Party and the premier of Alberta for a record 25 years (1943–1968). The Reform Party ran 72 candidates in Western Canada in the 1988 election, including a young "Steve Harper" in Calgary West, but it only captured 2.1 percent of the vote and it didn't win any seats. However, the party's popularity in Western Canada skyrocketed over the next two years with its staunch opposition to the Meech Lake Accord and its rallying cry "the West wants in."

Charter Canadians and the Politics of Constitutional Reform

A decade before the demise of the Meech Lake Accord, Pierre Trudeau had encouraged the people of Canada to take ownership of the constitution in a bid to thwart the recalcitrant premiers who opposed his plan to repatriate the British North America Act with a new

Steve Harper in the 1988
election campaign

David Lazarowych/Calgary Herald/Postmedia

Charter of Rights. Much to Trudeau's surprise, a variety of groups stepped forward and demanded specific rights to protect their group interests. As discussed in Chapter 9, the Charter of Rights and Freedoms went beyond the entrenchment of individual rights and included rights for linguistic groups, Aboriginal peoples, women, and multicultural groups. These groups now owned valuable constitutional real estate, and they were not happy about being excluded from the Meech Lake negotiations. Many were concerned that their newly found rights would be compromised by Meech Lake. And Aboriginal peoples feared that the governments of Canada would have no interest in negotiating a framework for self-government once Quebec's consent to the new constitutional order had been secured. In less than a decade, the political reality of Canada had changed as a result of the Charter. Canada was no longer just a federation of provinces; it was an entirely new political community with a multiplicity of collectives, each with their own set of constitutional values and interests to defend.

Charter Canadians objected to more than just the content (or lack of content) in Meech Lake—they objected to the very *process* that produced the accord. It was often said that Meech Lake was negotiated by 11 "white" men in suits, although this is perhaps somewhat unfair to Premier Joe Ghiz of Prince Edward Island who was of Arab descent. Leaving aside the ethnicity of the prime minister and premiers, it was undeniably true that Meech Lake was negotiated by the first ministers in private. This was completely in keeping with the longstanding practice of executive federalism in Canada. The British North America Act was negotiated by the leading politicians of the day, and constitutional negotiations in the twentieth century up to and including patriation were conducted almost exclusively by first ministers. So when Prime Minister Mulroney invited the premiers to Meech Lake to discuss the constitution, he was simply following past practice. But, as just mentioned, the political reality of Canada had changed in the few short years since patriation. The people of Canada had for the first time in the nation's history taken possession of the constitution. As such, Canadians were no longer prepared to tolerate the political elitism associated with executive federalism, at least when it came to mega-constitutional negotiations. On the contrary, the people were demanding the right to participate in Canada's constitutional negotiations. If it is difficult to get 11 first ministers to agree on a constitutional accord, it is obviously more challenging to get 33 million people to agree on a new set of constitutional reforms. The amending formulas may not require popular ratification of constitutional amendments, but this is firmly a part of Canada's constitutional amending process, at least for major constitutional changes.

The Charlottetown Accord

The Meech Lake Accord was motivated by a legitimate and genuine concern: to secure Quebec's consent to Canada's new constitutional order. But the accord did not reflect the new political reality of Canada. The Meech Lake Accord represented the old Canada of linguistic duality and federalism; it did not embrace the new Canada of Aboriginal peoples, multiculturalism, and the ethic of equality entrenched in the Charter of Rights and Freedoms. In Quebec, the failure of the Meech Lake Accord was regarded as a rejection of the province by the rest of the country, and many people in Quebec began to flirt again with the idea of sovereignty. In short, the failure of the Meech Lake Accord left Canada more divided than ever.

The Government of Canada could not allow the sovereignty movement to take root in Quebec again, but Prime Minister Mulroney was not in a position to launch a new round of constitutional negotiations. He had expended too much political capital with the Meech Lake fiasco. Mulroney thus handed the constitutional file to his old rival Joe Clark. Back in 1976, Joe Clark defeated Brian Mulroney to become the leader of the Progressive Conservative Party. Three years later, Clark defeated Pierre Trudeau in the general election to become the country's youngest prime minister. But Clark led a minority government, and it fell in a confidence vote after just six months; and Trudeau came back to win another majority government in 1980. Clark carried on as leader of the Progressive Conservative Party until Mulroney orchestrated his downfall in 1983. Clark, however, was determined to continue his political career, and he was returned to Parliament when the Tories swept to power in 1984 and became the Minister of External Affairs in Brian Mulroney's government. Clark is the only former prime minister to return to Parliament and assume a position as a cabinet minister. When Mulroney asked Clark to resolve Canada's constitutional conundrum, it was a backhanded compliment: on the one hand, the prime minister was entrusting Clark with the most important file on his desk, but he also seemed to be setting up his old nemesis for another failure.

Joe Clark was a "Red Tory" from Alberta, and his view of Canada was very different from that of Trudeau or Mulroney. Clark viewed Canada as a "community of communities"—he believed that all Canadians had roots in particular communities. As a young man he was convinced that his home town of High River "had the patent on that sense of being a place, a base, a defining community." But, he continued, "Canada is rooted in communities like that, places which, while you might leave them, keep drawing you back, at least

Prime Minister Joe Clark

emotionally and sometimes physically."[8] For Clark, then, the goal of constitutional reform was to give recognition to these distinct communities. He was also of the view that a new process was required for constitutional reform. In his opinion

> the opposition that mushroomed at the end of [the Meech Lake] process was not particularly anti-Quebec, nor even directed at the principles of the Meech Lake Accord. Instead, just as the 1982 agreement had become a symbol of exclusion of Quebecers, the Meech Lake Accord became a symbol of the exclusion of other Canadians—Aboriginals, Northerners, women, proponents of Senate reform, and a public that turned against the tradition of closed-door executive federalism.[9]

Further, he argued, Meech Lake had revealed that Canadians outside Quebec were not prepared to entertain a two-stage process whereby Quebec's concerns would be addressed before their concerns. The concerns of all Canadians would thus have to be addressed simultaneously. If Meech Lake had been the "Quebec round," the next attempt at constitutional reform would be the "Canada round."

For two-and-a-half years following the tumultuous demise of the Meech Lake Accord, Canadians were consumed by constitutional politics. There were royal commissions, Senate committees, constitutional conferences, and special party conventions to consider the constitution. But, following on the heels of Meech Lake, the different political constituencies across the land were pulling the federation in different directions. Whereas Quebec wanted constitutional recognition, the West rejected special recognition for anyone. Whereas the West wanted Senate reform, Quebec wanted to abolish the Senate. Whereas Quebec wanted limits on the federal spending power, social democrats in the rest of Canada wanted a charter to protect Canada's social programs. Whereas Aboriginal people wanted self-government, Canadian nationalists were left wondering "Who speaks for Canada?" If it had been difficult for Prime Minister Mulroney to bring 10 premiers on board for the Meech Lake Accord, it was going to be even more difficult to forge a constitutional consensus among a multiplicity of political actors. But, with executive federalism thoroughly discredited, Joe Clark had to find a way to bring the various constitutional actors together.

As with Meech Lake, Premier Bourassa got the ball rolling in the Canada round, but this time "the Meech process would be totally reversed: rather than negotiating first in private on the basis of Quebec's *minimum* demands, he would begin in public with Quebec's *maximum* demands for a restructuring of the federation."[10] Bourassa, furthermore, had no intention of negotiating with the rest of Canada. After being burned by Meech Lake, Bourassa indicated that he would only consider a proposal if it had already been ratified by the Parliament of Canada and all of the provincial legislatures. And, of course, he was free to reject the proposal if he didn't like it. And, to ensure that Canada did not drag its feet in producing a proposal, the Quebec National Assembly passed Bill 150 in May 1991, which stated that Quebec would hold a referendum on sovereignty either in June or October 1992. The rest of Canada was thus given about a year to come up with an offer for Quebec.

After a year of consultations, the governments of Canada were once again ready to negotiate a new, much more complex constitutional accord. The negotiations proceeded through the summer, culminating in a meeting of the prime minister and the premiers in Charlottetown in August 1992. The product of this meeting is known as the **Charlottetown Accord**. For Quebec, the new accord contained all of the provisions of Meech Lake, although those provisions were now offset by new provisions demanded by other constituencies. So, in Charlottetown, the recognition of Quebec as a "distinct society" was embedded in a much broader "Canada clause," which attempted to capture the social and political reality of modern Canada (see Box 11.2). The clause reaffirmed that Canada was committed to federalism and the parliamentary system of government—these, of course, were the original governing principles entrenched in the Constitution Act 1867.

Charlottetown Accord
An agreement between the federal government, the provinces, and Aboriginal organizations to amend the constitution. The primary objectives were to obtain Quebec's consent for the Constitution Act 1982, establish self-government for Aboriginal peoples, and reform the Senate. The agreement failed when Canadians rejected it in a referendum in October 1992.

Box 11.2

The Canada Clause in the Charlottetown Accord

1. The Constitution Act, 1867 is amended by adding thereto, immediately after section 1 thereof, the following section:

2.1 The Constitution of Canada, including the Canadian Charter of Rights and Freedoms, shall be interpreted in a manner consistent with the following fundamental characteristics:

a. Canada is a democracy committed to a parliamentary and federal system of government and to the rule of law;

b. the Aboriginal peoples of Canada, being the first peoples to govern this land, have the right to promote their language, cultures and traditions and to ensure the integrity of their societies, and their governments constitute one of the three orders of government in Canada;

c. Quebec constitutes within Canada a distinct society, which includes a French-speaking majority, a unique culture and a civil law tradition;

d. Canadians and their governments are committed to the vitality and development of official language minority communities throughout Canada;

e. Canadians are committed to racial and ethnic equality in a society that includes citizens from many lands who have contributed, and continue to contribute, to the building of a strong Canada that reflects its cultural and racial diversity;

f. Canadians are committed to a respect for individual and collective human rights and freedoms of all people;

g. Canadians are committed to the equality of female and male persons; and

h. Canadians confirm the principle of the equality of the provinces at the same time as recognizing their diverse characteristics.

It declared that Aboriginal governments would henceforth be one of the "three orders of government in Canada." It recognized Quebec's distinctiveness, the equality of provinces, individual and collective rights, the linguistic duality, gender equality, and the multicultural heritage of the country. The clause explicitly instructed the courts to interpret the constitution in a manner consistent with this depiction of Canada. Critics noted that some of these provisions are mutually exclusive, and they argued that it would thus be impossible for the courts to interpret the constitution in a manner consistent with the clause. Others replied that the clause reflected the modern reality of Canada, and they argued that the courts already do interpret the constitution in light of these realities.

The Charlottetown Accord contained a provision to limit the spending power, but it was offset by a new social charter to placate Ontario's NDP government. While the social charter was intended to protect Canada's cherished social programs, it was not going to be legally binding. The social charter was also further offset by provisions demanded by business to strengthen Canada's economic union. At the insistence of Western Canada, the accord contained provisions to reform the Senate. Under the terms of the accord, each province would be represented by six senators, and each province would have the option of electing senators directly by the people or indirectly by members of the provincial legislatures. Each territory would be represented by one senator. In exchange for an equal Senate, Ontario and Quebec would each gain 18 seats in the House of Commons to reflect more accurately their respective proportions of the population in the lower chamber. Quebec, furthermore, obtained a constitutional guarantee that it would always have 25 percent of the seats in the House of Commons. That was consistent with Quebec's share of the population at the time, although it was widely recognized that Quebec's share of the population was slowly declining. British Columbia was slated to gain four additional seats in the House of Commons, while Alberta would receive two more seats. Most importantly, the new Senate would have its powers reduced so as to maintain the primacy of the House of Commons in Parliament.

For the first time in Canada's long constitutional odyssey, representatives from the main Aboriginal organizations were invited to attend the meeting and negotiate alongside the first ministers. And, significantly, the accord proposed to amend the constitution to recognize that "Aboriginal peoples of Canada have the inherent right of self-government within Canada." As noted in the Canada clause, Aboriginal governments were henceforth to be regarded as one of the three orders of government in the new Canadian federation. The accord, furthermore, envisioned the integration of Aboriginal peoples in Canada's major institutions: the House of Commons, the Senate, and the Supreme Court. While the governments of Canada made a commitment to integrating Aboriginal peoples in the major institutions of the federation, the accord did not spell out precisely how this would happen. Some other important issues were also "not entirely resolved. One was the difficult ideological question of how the Charter of Rights should apply to the Aboriginal order of government. The other was the practical question of the fiscal basis of Aboriginal governments."[11] The Charlottetown Accord marked a promising new beginning for the relationship between Aboriginal peoples and the rest of Canada, but regrettably this promise has not yet been fully realized.

The Referendum

As the Charlottetown process was drawing to a close, Prime Minister Mulroney announced that the entire package would be put to a national referendum. The prime minister had clearly learned from Meech Lake that the accord would only be legitimate if it was ratified by the people. The people, however, were in a rather sour political mood in the fall of 1992. Some groups complained that they did not get enough in Charlottetown, while others were more upset by what other groups did obtain in the accord. While Robert Bourassa (weakly) endorsed the agreement, it was immediately denounced in Quebec as "less than Meech." All of the provisions from Meech were included in Charlottetown, but as a package the Charlottetown Accord represented a very different image of Canada. Whereas Meech represented a union of two nations, the Charlottetown Accord depicted a much more heterogeneous society. While Charlottetown may have captured the essence of modern Canada, many Quebecers could not help feeling that their nation was being demoted to just another cultural group in the tapestry of the federation.

While many people in Quebec felt that their province did not get enough in Charlottetown, other Canadians, particularly in the West, were of the opinion that Quebec got too much. Many Canadians outside Quebec were still not comfortable with the notion of recognizing Quebec as a distinct society, notwithstanding the much more inclusive "Canada clause." Social democrats outside Quebec were still skeptical about the limitations on the federal spending power, notwithstanding the inclusion of a social charter in the agreement. But more than anything else Canadians outside Quebec were gobsmacked when it was revealed that Quebec would receive 18 more seats in the House of Commons and forever be guaranteed 25 percent of the seats in the lower chamber, even though Quebec's share of the population was declining. (People in the West were none too pleased that Ontario was also slated to receive 18 more seats in the House of Commons.)

Westerners were not just upset with the provisions for Quebec; they were also of the view that the West got shafted again, notwithstanding the fact that the accord contained a significant plan to reform the Senate. Under the terms of Charlottetown, the Senate would be *equal* and *elected*, but in order to preserve the primacy of the House of Commons the new Senate would be smaller and possess fewer powers. This raised questions about the *effectiveness* of the new Senate. Preston Manning and the Reform Party dismissed the plan as a "two-and-a-half-E Senate." The new Senate may not have been everything the West wanted, but obviously Ontario and Quebec would want some concessions to move to an equal and elected second chamber; they were simply not going to give up their dominant position in the old Senate for nothing.

Many Canadians were also suspicious of the provisions for Aboriginal self-government, especially in Western Canada where the ramifications of Aboriginal self-government would be felt most acutely. On the other hand, many Aboriginal Canadians were of the view that the Charlottetown Accord did not go far enough. The accord did not spell out how Aboriginal governments would be financed, it was not clear how the Charter of Rights and Freedoms would operate in relation to Aboriginal self-government, and it was not clear when Aboriginal peoples would receive representation in Canada's governing institutions, such as Parliament and the Supreme Court. While the accord marked a step forward for Aboriginal peoples, it was a very tentative step.

The Charlottetown Accord did not represent an entirely coherent constitutional philosophy, but it did represent a genuine attempt to accommodate the constitutional interests of the main groups in Canadian society. It was a compromise. Nonetheless, Pierre Trudeau felt compelled to denounce the accord as a "mess," which deserved "a big NO."[12] The people, however, did not need Pierre Trudeau's encouragement to reject Prime Minister Mulroney's second attempt at constitutional reform. When the accord was put to a vote on October 28, 1992, the different mega-constitutional orientations across the country cancelled each other out. Overall, the accord was defeated by a margin of 55 percent to 45 percent. By and large, the accord was supported in Atlantic Canada and opposed strongly in Quebec and the West. Ontario was divided almost evenly (see Table 11.1). The Inuit voted in favour of the accord, but a majority of First Nations on reserve voted against it. Who knew that Canadians actually had such deeply entrenched constitutional positions? In the wake of the Charlottetown Accord, the country was bitter and deeply divided, but there was a consensus at least that the country should take a break from constitutional negotiations. But issues this big just don't disappear. They play out in different—and sometimes more dangerous—ways.

Table 11.1 The Charlottetown Referendum (by percent)

	Yes	No
Newfoundland and Labrador	63.2	36.8
Prince Edward Island	73.9	26.1
Nova Scotia	48.8	51.2
New Brunswick	61.8	38.2
Quebec	43.3	56.7
Ontario	50.1	49.9
Manitoba	38.4	61.6
Saskatchewan	44.7	55.3
Alberta	39.8	60.2
British Columbia	31.7	68.3
Northwest Territories	60.2	39.8
Yukon	43.4	56.6
Canada	**45.7**	**54.3**

Note: At the time of the Charlottetown referendum, Nunavut did not exist as a distinct territory. Nunavut was carved out of the eastern half of the Northwest Territories in 1999.

The Second Sovereignty Referendum in Quebec

As we have seen, the failure of the Meech Lake Accord was interpreted in Quebec as a "rejection" of the province by the rest of Canada. And, for many Quebecers, the Charlottetown Accord took Canada too far in the wrong direction. It is thus not surprising that the sovereignist Parti Québécois won the provincial election in 1994 under the leadership of Jacques Parizeau. Within months of taking office, Parizeau announced that the second referendum on sovereignty would be held on October 30, 1995. Parizeau was a hardline separatist, but he was persuaded by political allies to formulate a question along the lines of the 1980 referendum on sovereignty-association. Parizeau thus agreed that the referendum would propose a new "economic and political partnership" with the rest of Canada, with the understanding that if Canada rejected the proposal Quebec would separate from the federation. While Canadians outside Quebec complained that the question was convoluted, Quebecers understood the question perfectly. To make a long story short, Quebec nearly voted to leave Canada that day. With a 94 percent participation rate, Quebecers voted 49.4 percent in favour of the proposal and 50.6 percent against it. And among French speakers, a clear majority (approximately 60 percent) voted in favour. After decades of constitutional negotiations intended to reconcile the two solitudes in the federation, Canada had reached the brink of dissolution.

The Government of Canada Responds: Changing the Rules of the Game

The Government of Canada was sent reeling by the results of the second referendum on sovereignty in Quebec. Prime Minister Jean Chrétien moved almost immediately to address some of Quebec's longstanding issues with significant changes to the rules of the game. First, Chrétien put forward a motion in Parliament to recognize Quebec as a "distinct society." Parliamentary resolutions of this sort are not legally binding, but it was an important symbolic gesture, especially since Chrétien had long been a fierce opponent of Quebec nationalism.

Second, Chrétien moved to address Quebec's desire for a veto over constitutional change. The Government of Canada, of course, could not unilaterally change the amending formula in the constitution, but Prime Minister Chrétien offered to "lend" Quebec a veto. Under the amending formulas entrenched in the Constitution Act 1982, the federal government is required to consent to all constitutional changes—in other words, the federal government possesses a veto over constitutional amendments. In **Bill C-110, An Act Respecting Constitutional Amendments**, the Government of Canada stated that it would henceforth only support constitutional changes that were endorsed by the government of Quebec. If Quebec did not support the proposed amendment, the federal government would vote against the amendment and consequently it would fail. The Government of Canada, however, could not just lend a veto to Quebec—for many Canadians that would not be consistent with the prevailing belief across much of the country in the equality of provinces. The Government of Canada thus indicated in Bill C-110 that it would be prepared to lend its veto to all the "regions" in Canada. Thus, for Parliament to vote in favour of a constitutional amendment, it would need to be supported by at least two of the four Atlantic provinces (representing 50 percent of the region's population), Quebec, Ontario, and at least two of the four Western provinces (representing 50 percent of the region's population). This was the very amending formula Pierre Trudeau proposed back in the 1970s during the patriation negotiations—a formula that was rejected by the provinces because it did not treat the provinces equally.

Bill C-110, An Act Respecting Constitutional Amendments
A bill introduced and passed in Parliament after the Quebec referendum in 1995 that states the federal government will consent to an amendment of the constitution only if it is supported by the legislatures in the five regions of Canada: the Atlantic provinces, Quebec, Ontario, the Prairie provinces, and British Columbia.

When Bill C-110 was tabled in the House of Commons, there were howls of protest in British Columbia, which demanded to be recognized as a distinct region in the federation. The government thus quickly amended the bill and offered to lend its veto to British Columbia. By separating British Columbia from the rest of the West, Bill C-110 states that a constitutional amendment must be supported by at least two of the three Prairie provinces (representing 50 percent of the region's population). This provision effectively gives Alberta a veto over constitutional change, since it accounts for more than 50 percent of the population of the three Prairie provinces. Thus, in an effort to accommodate Quebec's longstanding desire for a veto over constitutional change, the federal government was forced to lend its veto to Ontario, Alberta, and British Columbia as well—so four provinces now effectively possess a veto over constitutional change.

It is important to stress that the 7/50 amending formula entrenched in the Constitution Act 1982 has not changed. However, with the Act Respecting Constitutional Amendments, the federal government now has a legal obligation to secure the consent of Canada's five regions before a constitutional amendment can be approved by the Parliament of Canada. As a statutory law, the Act Respecting Constitutional Amendments could always be amended or repealed by Parliament, but it is hard to imagine that ever happening since it would presumably strip some provinces of their de facto veto. So the law is presumably here to stay. However, it will make securing constitutional change even more difficult than it has been in the past, and it has never been easy for Canada to change its constitution.

The *Secession Reference Case* 1998

The Government of Canada hoped that recognizing Quebec as a "distinct society" and lending Quebec a veto would quell the secessionist fervour in *la belle province*, but the government of Quebec was unmoved. Quebec does not want to rely on the political goodwill of Parliament; it wants these sorts of protections written into Canada's "master law." In short, Quebec will only feel secure in the federation if these gestures are *entrenched* in the constitution. The government of Quebec thus continued to focus on creating the "winning conditions" for sovereignty in another imminent referendum. In response, the federal government decided to ask the Supreme Court if it would be legal for Quebec to unilaterally separate from the federation. The government of Quebec refused to participate in what is known as the **Secession Reference Case** because they argued that they would not get a fair hearing from judges appointed by the federal government.

Since the issue of secession is not explicitly addressed in the constitution, the Supreme Court was forced to read between the lines for an answer. In a masterful judgment, the justices identified four "fundamental and organizing principles" of the Canadian constitution: federalism, democracy, the rule of law, and respect for minorities.[13] While the Supreme Court concluded that Quebec did not have a *unilateral* right to separate from Canada, it argued that secession could be pursued *legally* by any province that abided by the principles of federalism, democracy, the rule of law, and respect for minorities. In short, it stated that a provincial government that obtained a "clear" majority in a referendum on a "clear" question on secession would have an important mandate to seek the constitutional amendments necessary to separate from Canada. And it insisted that the other governments of Canada would have a legal obligation to negotiate with the province in good faith. The Supreme Court did not define what a "clear question" or "clear majority" would look like, saying these were political not legal questions. In sum, the Government of Canada had the answer it wanted: Quebec did not have a unilateral right to secede. But the government of Quebec was equally pleased with the judgment, despite its initial misgivings about the case. As far as Quebec was concerned, the court had recognized the legality of Quebec's referendums on sovereignty.

Secession Reference Case A case referred to the Supreme Court by the Government of Canada to determine the legality of a province separating from the federation.

The Clarity Act

After the *Secession Reference Case*, the Government of Canada decided to introduce a law that would set out the process of separating from the country—the Clarity Act. It was introduced in 1999 by Stéphane Dion, the Minister of Intergovernmental Relations in Prime Minister Chrétien's government, and it was passed into law in 2000. The Clarity Act sets out a process for separation of a province from the federation. First, if a province (namely Quebec) decides to hold a referendum on separation, Parliament will immediately reconvene to determine if the question being asked is indeed "clear," although the act does not specify what a clear question would look like. It is a case of "show us the question, and we'll tell you if it's clear." If Parliament determines that the question is not clear, it will ignore the results of the referendum. If the referendum produces a "yes" vote on a "clear" question, Parliament would again reconvene to determine if the "majority" was in fact "clear," but again the act does not define what would constitute a clear majority. Once again, it is a case of "show us the numbers, and we'll tell you if it's clear." If everything is "clear," the governments of Canada would proceed to negotiate the terms of separation.

The Clarity Act was enormously contentious. Some complained that it provided Quebec with a "roadmap" for separation. The government of Quebec, however, was even less happy with the act. Sovereignists could not help feeling that after two referendums in the province—in which the federal government was an active participant—the federal government was moving the goal posts down the field now that Quebec was close to achieving sovereignty.

These concerns cannot be easily dismissed, but it is important to recognize the enormous significance of the Clarity Act. With the Clarity Act, Canada became the first—and still only—country in the world to spell out in law how a province can legally separate from the federation. In most other cases, the disintegration of countries with deep cultural divisions is usually associated with considerable violence. Canada has shown the world how secession can be pursued peacefully, democratically, and according to the rule of law. And the world has taken notice. Other countries struggling with cultural conflict routinely send delegations to Canada to study the Clarity Act, and invariably Canadians are on the ground in these countries helping to avoid a civil conflict or to rebuild after the conflict. In many respects, the Clarity Act represents the culmination of Canada's governing principles and political experiences.

The Demise of Mega-Constitutional Politics

With the Clarity Act, the era of mega-constitutional politics came to a close—at least for a period of time. The constitution had been patriated, but the country was far from united. Indeed, Meech Lake and Charlottetown left the country more disunited than ever. The best constitutional minds in the country had worked on the unity file and come up just a little bit short. By 2000, the experts were out of ideas. The governments of Canada thus determined that it would be appropriate to take a break from mega-constitutional politics. The break, however, has lasted more than a decade. The country has carried on, but it is highly unlikely that we can avoid the constitution indefinitely. All of the core issues remain unresolved, and the avoidance of the constitution is starting to have consequences. The Senate, for example, can at best only be partially reformed without major constitutional change. Unfortunately, we cannot proceed item by item: Canada still requires a comprehensive constitutional settlement. Launching a new round of mega-constitutional politics entails a certain degree of risk, but avoiding the constitution for too long also entails risk. Either way, the future of the country hangs in the balance.

Canada's Constitutional Debates and the Decline of Brokerage Politics

The constitutional convulsions of the 1990s had a profound impact on Canadian politics. After two rounds of constitutional failure (in conjunction with the goods and services tax and the Canada–United States Free Trade Agreement), Prime Minister Mulroney's popularity was severely damaged, and he wisely decided to retire in early 1993. Kim Campbell was elected as the new leader of the Progressive Conservative Party, and she was sworn in as Canada's first and still only female prime minister in June 1993. However, Kim Campbell was destined to be one of Canada's short-lived caretaker prime ministers. In the October 1993 general election, the Progressive Conservative Party was decimated. The party went from a commanding majority of 169 seats to just 2. Prime Minister Campbell lost her own seat in Vancouver Centre. It was the worst defeat any party has suffered anywhere in the world, and the Progressive Conservative Party never recovered. It was what political scientists call a **critical election**, where there is "a sharp and durable electoral realignment between parties."[14] But, more fundamentally, a critical election represents a realignment of the pre-existing political cleavages within the electorate.

When Brian Mulroney became the leader of the Progressive Conservative Party, he successfully united three disparate political constituencies: old-fashioned Tories in Ontario and Atlantic Canada, Quebec nationalists, and conservative populists in the West. With these groups united, the Progressive Conservative Party cruised to the largest majority government in Canadian history in 1984, and it comfortably won a second majority government in 1988. But it all fell apart as a result of the constitutional convulsions of the 1980s and 1990s. As noted above, the Bloc Québécois emerged as a direct response to the Meech Lake Accord, and the Reform Party secured a foothold in Western Canada with its resolute opposition to Meech Lake and subsequently the Charlottetown Accord. In the 1993 election, the Liberal Party of Canada secured a comfortable majority government with 177 seats, and the Bloc Québécois finished second with 54 seats. Thus, ironically, the Bloc formed Her Majesty's Loyal Opposition in Parliament. The Reform Party was just behind with 52 seats—all of them in the West save one seat in Ontario. The NDP dropped from 43 seats (the largest number of seats it had ever held at that point in the party's history) to just 9. And, as noted already, the Progressive Conservatives were reduced to just two seats, even though they secured 16 percent of the national vote. The Progressive Conservative Party limped along for another decade, but at this point it appealed only to old-fashioned Tories, mostly in Ontario, and a few diehard supporters in Atlantic Canada. Even with a succession of very able leaders—Jean Charest, Joe Clark, and Peter Mackay—the party was simply not able to broker a new political coalition. Consequently, one of the grand brokerage parties of Canadian politics faded into the annals of history.

In short, Brian Mulroney's political coalition shattered into its component parts in the 1993 election: Quebec went en masse with the Bloc Québécois and the West embraced the Reform Party (while old-fashioned Tories just faded away). The Bloc's charismatic leader, Lucien Bouchard, left the Bloc in 1996 to become the leader of the Parti Québécois and the premier of Quebec. He retired in 2001. The Bloc, however, continued to dominate federal elections in Quebec. In the five elections between 1997 and 2008, the Bloc, under the leadership of Gilles Duceppe, captured at least half of Quebec's 75 seats. The party inexplicably collapsed in the 2011 election, winning only four seats; Gilles Duceppe lost his own seat and consequently resigned as leader. It is too soon to know if the Bloc is gone for good or if it can stage a comeback or if it even wants to come back. Nevertheless, for two decades the people of Quebec believed that their interests were best served by the Bloc Québécois, even if it meant that Quebec—for the first time in living memory—was seriously underrepresented in the Government of Canada.

critical election An election with a sharp and durable realignment between political parties. It usually represents a more fundamental realignment of the pre-existing political cleavages within the electorate.

If Quebec has, at least temporarily, stepped out of the political life of the country, the West has moved in, although it took some time for the Reform Party to realize its goal. Along the way, moreover, the Reform Party felt compelled to reincarnate itself a couple of times. After the second Liberal majority government in 1997, Preston Manning concluded that the Reform Party needed to broaden its appeal. For Manning, it was not simply a matter of adopting new policies—he believed that the party itself needed to be rebranded. So in 2000 the Reform Party was transformed into the Canadian Reform Conservative Alliance. While the new party was generally known as the Canadian Alliance, the party's formal name indicates that Manning was attempting to establish an alliance between Reform Party supporters and other conservatives. Preston Manning wanted to lead this new entity, but the party's membership took the rebranding exercise to its logical conclusion and selected a new leader: Stockwell Day, the former finance minister of Alberta.

This massive rebranding exercise failed. In the 2000 election, the Canadian Alliance won a total of 66 seats, all of which were in the West except for two in Ontario. In short, the new Alliance party did not really do any better than the old Reform Party, which won 60 seats in the 1997 election. The Progressive Conservative Party under the leadership of Joe Clark dropped from 20 seats to 12. So once again conservative vote splitting, mostly in Ontario, allowed Jean Chrétien and the Liberal Party to cruise to its third consecutive majority government.

After another humiliating defeat at the hands of Jean Chrétien, both conservative parties selected new leaders. The Progressive Conservative Party elected Peter Mackay, and the Canadian Alliance chose Stephen Harper. Both men realized, though, that as long as the two conservative parties continued to split the right-of-centre vote, the Liberal Party would win every election. Thus, after a decade of destructive feuding, the two conservative parties decided to bury the hatchet and form a single united party simply called the Conservative Party of Canada. The Conservative Party was born in December 2003, and in March 2004 Stephen Harper became the leader of the new party. A few months later, Prime Minister Paul Martin surprised Harper with a snap election. Martin, however, may have been too clever by half: the Liberal Party was returned to power, but only with a minority government, while the Conservatives succeeded in winning 99 seats, including 24 seats in Ontario and 7 in Atlantic Canada. Although the Conservative Party fell short of forming the government, the decision to unite the two conservative parties had clearly paid dividends.

In 2006, Stephen Harper led the Conservative Party to victory. The Conservatives had a strong base of support in Western Canada, of course, but they also won 40 seats in Ontario. The Conservative Party also picked up 10 seats in Quebec and a further handful of seats in Atlantic Canada. While the Conservatives formed a minority government, they were conspicuously absent from Canada's three largest cities—Montreal, Toronto, and Vancouver. The Conservatives had a stronger showing in the 2008 election, although they continued to be shut out of the major cities. In 2011, Stephen Harper finally led the Conservative Party to a majority government, with strong support in the West and Ontario, including Toronto. But the Conservatives were reduced to just five seats in Quebec, which surprisingly abandoned the Bloc Québécois and embraced the New Democratic Party en masse. The significance of Stephen Harper's majority government cannot be understated: it is the first single-party majority government in Canadian history without substantial support in the province of Quebec. (Sir Robert Borden's Unionist government in 1917 had very little support in Quebec, but it was an exceptional wartime coalition government.) Quebec has never been more isolated in the federation than it is now.

While the Progressive Conservative Party was wiped out in 1993, the Liberal Party has receded in stages. The Liberal Party lost the West in the 1970s, it lost Quebec in the 1980s, and in it lost Ontario in the 2011 election. Without a base of support anywhere in the country, it is not clear that the Liberal Party can mount a comeback. The Liberal Party of Canada has turned to Justin Trudeau, the telegenic son of Pierre, to see if he can return the party to its glory days, but it will be a tall order for him to rebuild the party's old governing coalition. The new Conservative Party has succeeded in uniting the West with Ontario, but it is not clear how long that alliance can be sustained given the growing economic disparities between the two regions. Initially, Stephen Harper made a concerted effort to obtain support in Quebec, but ultimately he failed to win the province over and subsequently he has shown little interest in Quebec. So it would thus seem that the two parties of Confederation have lost the ability to bridge the linguistic cleavage in the federation—this does not bode well for "national" unity.

After the 2011 election, the New Democrats are the only party that looks anything like a brokerage party, but it is far too early to know if the NDP can hold its newfound base of support in Quebec. Does Quebec's embrace of the NDP represent a sudden conversion to the principles of democratic socialism? Or was the NDP simply the last remaining political option for Quebec, after abandoning the Liberal Party in the 1980s, the Progressive Conservatives in the 1990s, and concluding that the Bloc Québécois had outlived its utility? Only time will tell. In the meantime, the NDP has returned the favour to Quebec, selecting a fluently bilingual Quebecer as its new leader after the death of Jack Layton. Thomas Mulcair has his work cut out for him, however. The NDP has always put principles before politics, and it is not clear that the party can reinvent itself as an ideologically pragmatic brokerage party. Indeed, it is not clear *any* party can successfully engage in old-fashioned brokerage politics at the present time. The politics of brokerage may be gone for good.

SUMMARY

For the last three decades of the twentieth century, the governments and people of Canada engaged in an extensive debate over the rules of the Canadian political game. Over this time, there were some partial successes, such as the patriation of the constitution and the adoption of the Charter of Rights and Freedoms, and some notable failures, such as the Meech Lake and Charlottetown Accords, as well as two referendums on sovereignty in Quebec. Along the way, the amending formulas in the constitution have been effectively modified by Bill C-110, An Act Respecting Constitutional Amendments. And future referendums on secession in Quebec—or any other province, for that matter—will be governed by the Clarity Act. But the constitution itself remains unfinished. In hindsight, the constitutional convulsions of the 1990s reflected a country in the throes of a social transformation—from the old Canada of federalism and linguistic duality to the new Canada of Aboriginal peoples, multiculturalism, and the ethic of equality entrenched in the Charter of Rights and Freedoms.

The constitutional file, however, is now considerably more complicated. The different mega-constitutional orientations at play in the federation today are not wholly compatible. As such, the governments and people of Canada have to date been unable to put the final touches on the constitution. In the absence of a constitutional settlement, the debates over the constitution led to a major reorganization of the federal party system. The new party system has been characterized by the long-term decline of the Liberal Party and the demise of the Progressive Conservative Party. Thus, ironically, a four-decade process to *broker* constitutional peace resulted in the collapse of Canada's traditional *brokerage* political parties. The implications of this development are not at all clear at this time. Canada has always been governed by a brokerage party, and it is hard to imagine a country as large and diverse as Canada being governed any other way. The apparent decline of brokerage political parties is thus cause for great concern. Obviously, Canada's political parties are struggling to adapt to the new realities of the country's rapidly evolving political culture.

Questions to Think About

1. Do you think Quebec should be recognized as a "distinct society" in the constitution? With the benefit of hindsight, do you think Meech Lake should have been passed?

2. The Charlottetown Accord appeared to give something to everyone, so why do you suppose the accord was rejected by Canadians in the referendum?

3. Do you think the different mega-constitutional orientations can ever be reconciled? If so, how? What concessions do Canadians have to make to reach a final constitutional settlement?

4. What is the significance of the Clarity Act? Do you think the government made the right decision to adopt the Clarity Act?

5. Do you think it is important to re-establish the politics of brokerage in Canada? If so, how can this be accomplished?

6. What is the future of Canadian unity? Can the federation hang together, or is it destined to break up?

Learning Outcomes

1. Describe the major elements of the Meech Lake Accord and explain why it failed.

2. Describe the major elements of the Charlottetown Accord and explain why it failed.

3. Describe the concept of Western alienation and its impact on Canadian politics.

4. Explain the concept of Charter Canadians and describe their role in Canadian politics.

5. Describe the major elements of the Clarity Act and explain its political significance.

6. Describe how the politics of constitutional reform in the 1990s has shaped the Canadian party system in the twenty-first century.

Additional Readings

Cameron D. Anderson and Laura B. Stephenson, *Voting Behaviour in Canada* (Vancouver, BC: UBC Press, 2010).

Michael Behiels, ed., *The Meech Lake Primer: Conflicting Views of the 1987 Constitutional Accord* (Ottawa, ON: University of Ottawa Press, 1989).

Elisabeth Gidengil et al., *Dominance and Decline: Making Sense of Recent Canadian Elections* (Toronto, ON: University of Toronto Press, 2012).

Richard Johnston, ed., *The Challenge of Direct Democracy: The 1992 Canadian Referendum* (Montreal, QC: McGill-Queen's University Press, 1996).

Kenneth McRoberts, ed., *The Charlottetown Accord, the Referendum, and the Future of Canada* (Toronto, ON: University of Toronto Press, 1993).

Matthew Mendelsohn, "Public Brokerage: Constitutional Reform and the Accommodation of Mass Publics," *Canadian Journal of Political Science* 33:2 (June 2000), 245–272.

Patrick J. Monahan, *Meech Lake: The Inside Story* (Toronto, ON: University of Toronto Press, 1991).

Katherine Swinton and Carol Rogerson, eds., *Competing Constitutional Visions: The Meech Lake Accord* (Toronto, ON: Carswell, 1988).

Triadafilos Triadafilopoulos, *Becoming Multicultural: Immigration and the Politics of Membership in Canada and Germany* (Vancouver, BC: UBC Press, 2012).

Ronald L. Watts, ed., *Options for a New Canada* (Toronto, ON: University of Toronto Press, 1991).

Elke Winter, *Us, Them, and Others: Pluralism and National Identity in Diverse Societies* (Toronto, ON: University of Toronto Press, 2011).

Notes

1. Keith Banting and Richard Simeon, eds., *And No One Cheered: Federalism, Democracy and the Constitution Act* (Toronto, ON: Methuen, 1983).

2. Michael Lusztig, "Constitutional Paralysis: Why Canadian Constitutional Initiatives Are Doomed to Fail," *Canadian Journal of Political Science*, 27:4 (December 1994), 747–771.

3. Brian Mulroney, *Where I Stand* (Toronto, ON: McClelland and Stewart, 1983), 59.

4. Peter H. Russell, *Constitutional Odyssey: Can Canadians Become a Sovereign People?* 2nd ed. (Toronto, ON: University of Toronto Press, 1993), 136.

5. Donald Johnston, ed., *With a Bang, Not a Whimper: Pierre Trudeau Speaks Out* (Toronto, ON: Stoddart Publishing Company, 1988), 13.

6. Ibid., 99.

7. Russell, *Constitutional Odyssey*, 155.

8. Joe Clark, *A Nation Too Good to Lose: Renewing the Purpose of Canada* (Toronto, ON: Key Porter Books, 1994), 27.

9. Ibid., 5.

10. Russell, *Constitutional Odyssey*, 162; emphasis added.

11. Ibid., 201.

12. Pierre Elliott Trudeau, *A Mess that Deserves a Big No!* (Toronto, ON: Robert Davies Publishing, 1992).

13. *Reference re Secession of Quebec, [1998] 2 SCR 217.*

14. V.O. Key, "A Theory of Critical Elections," *Journal of Politics* 17:1 (February 1955), 16.

Chapter 12
We Are the *Demos*

Key Points

- The institutions of the Canadian political system have served the country extremely well. Canada is one of the most successful countries in the world, and it is politically stable and economically prosperous.

- Canadians have learned how to handle the highly divisive and emotional issue of secession (and mega-constitutional politics more generally) peacefully, democratically, and according to the rule of law. Canada provides a beacon of hope for other societies struggling with these difficult issues.

- But the enthusiasm for democracy in Canada seems to have waned. There has been a noticeable decline in voter participation over the past 30 years, and Canada now has a democratic deficit.

- The decline in voting rates has been caused primarily by the low rate of participation by young voters. It is not entirely clear why young people are less interested in politics than previous generations.

- It is a mistake to view the democratic deficit as just a youth problem. The democratic deficit is a much broader social, cultural, and economic issue.

- There is no institutional solution to the democratic deficit. New accountability acts, electoral reform, Senate reform, and constitutional reform more generally will not magically reverse the democratic deficit.

- The only solution is to restore Canada's democratic political culture. It comes down to us—we are the demos. If we do not participate in the political process, there will be no democracy. But before we can participate in politics, we must learn the rules of the game.

When we examine the institutions of Canadian politics, as we have done in this book, we see a high degree of continuity. The institutions of parliamentary democracy and federalism have evolved, but they have adapted mostly without formal constitutional amendment, apart from a few changes to the division of powers. The electoral system remains the same. The party system has fluctuated occasionally, but after 150 years only the Liberal Party and some version of the Conservative Party have ever formed the government. In light of the profound social and demographic changes in Canada since Confederation, the fact that the Constitution Act 1867 continues to be the bedrock of the Canadian political system is truly astounding. The Fathers of Confederation do not get the respect they deserve for establishing such a solid foundation for the country.

The Constitution Act 1982 represents the only major institutional reform in Canada's political system since Confederation. With it, two new governing principles were added to the Canadian political system: a Charter of Rights and Freedoms and the recognition and affirmation of Aboriginal rights. The Canadian Charter of Rights and Freedoms is a quint-essentially modern bill of rights. It recognizes group rights—Aboriginal peoples, linguistic and multicultural groups, and women—as well as individual rights. The Charter is perhaps the most cherished institution in Canada today, and it has become a model for many new and emerging democracies around the world. The impact of the Charter has been profound, but the recognition and affirmation of Aboriginal rights in Part II of the Constitution Act 1982 is potentially even more significant. Section 35 paves the way for the creation of a third order of government in the Canadian federation, although we are not there yet.

Together, the two Constitution Acts and the various conventions and associated rules of the game provide the foundation for the Canadian political system. And they have served the country well. Under this constitutional order, Canada has grown and become one of the most prosperous countries in the world. While Canada is still in search of a mega-constitutional consensus, it has learned how to handle the potentially explosive issues of secession and self-government peacefully, democratically, and according to the rule of law. Canada, in fact, is a global leader on these matters. We offer a beacon of hope for people around the world struggling with similar issues. Delegations from deeply divided societies routinely visit Canada to learn how we have managed our political cleavages with a modi-cum of civility, and invariably Canadians are on the ground in these countries helping them rebuild their political institutions. Yet something is not quite right *in* Canada. We seem to have become deeply disillusioned with our own political system over the last two or three decades. In short, Canada appears to be suffering from a **democratic deficit**.[1]

The emergence of a democratic deficit in the 1990s generated demands for political reform—and some reforms have been undertaken, particularly with respect to party financ-ing. The conflict-of-interest guidelines for parliamentarians have also been strengthened. A new Parliamentary Budget Office was established in 2006 to provide independent analysis of government revenue projections. The Harper government has pursued Senate reform, while other parties call for the replacement of the first-past-the-post electoral system with a system of proportional representation. But I am not convinced that our political malaise can be remedied through institutional reform. The democratic deficit is not an institutional or even political crisis—it is a social crisis. It is at root a product of late modernity. Other advanced industrial societies are experiencing a similar democratic malaise. The remedy for the democratic deficit ultimately lies with the people. *We are the demos*. If we do not partici-pate in our politics, there is no democracy; it cannot be done for us by others—we must do it. Collectively, we must make a commitment to restore Canada's democratic political culture.

democratic deficit Refers to a general public disinterest in politics and more specifically to the decline in voter participation.

The Democratic Deficit

The signs of political disillusionment are everywhere. We do not need large-scale surveys to tell us that Canadians hold politicians in very low esteem—we know this from everyday conversations. When we do turn to the surveys, the situation is perhaps worse than we even dared imagine. Politicians are the *least* respected professionals in Canada—even more reviled than car salespeople. We no longer view our politicians as community leaders. In short, there has been a measurable decline in deference in Canada over the last three decades.[2] The only comfort for Canadians is that politicians are held in even lower regard in the United States and Great Britain.[3] When politicians are so widely despised, it follows that many people are very cynical about the political system in general.

The high level of political cynicism now evident in Canada ironically comes at a time when the political system is more transparent and accountable than it has ever been. The conflict-of-interest code for the elected members of the House of Commons is more robust than ever. Ministers and parliamentary secretaries are subject further to the Conflict of

Interest Act for public officeholders. The act and the code are enforced by the ethics commissioner, who was appointed as an officer of Parliament under the Federal Accountability Act in 2006. At the same time, the parliamentary budget officer was created to evaluate the revenue and spending projections made by the government. And of course the auditor general continues to monitor how money is spent by the government. Yet, notwithstanding this intense scrutiny, many people believe that our Members of Parliament are overly self-interested actors and perhaps corrupt. It is a most unfortunate state of affairs, but it is not the only instance these days in which public perception does not necessarily match reality: people are more fearful of crime than ever before, even though crime rates have been steadily falling in Canada for decades.

If the democratic deficit was confined to grumbling about politicians with friends over coffee it would be perfectly understandable and perhaps even healthy and cathartic. Unfortunately, it extends far beyond grumbling. The democratic deficit has been manifested primarily at the ballot box. From 1867 to 1988, the average voter turnout in Canada was 72.2 percent, with a record high of 79.4 percent in 1958; the elections in 1962 and 1963 also cracked 79 percent, and the post-war average through to 1988 was 75 percent. The average has subsequently dropped more than 10 points. In the seven elections since 1988, turnout has averaged a meagre 63.4 percent. The four lowest turnouts in Canadian history have all happened in the twenty-first century, with a record low of 58.8 percent in 2008. Voter turnout in provincial elections is typically lower, especially in Ontario, Alberta, and British Columbia, where turnout now hovers around 50 percent. Prince Edward Island has historically had the best turnout rates, but it may also be declining: The 76.5 percent turnout in the 2011 was the lowest in 50 years—only the second time turnout has slipped below 80 percent on the island province. And turnout in municipal elections is abysmal, below 30 percent in many cities.

Canada is not alone. The average turnout in the United Kingdom in the post-war period through to the 1990s was 76.3 percent, but that has since dropped to 62 percent in the twenty-first century, with a record low of 59.4 percent recorded in 2001. Voter turnout in the United States has historically been lower than Canada and the United Kingdom, although it should be noted that the United States has a more stringent measure of turnout. If Canada used the same measure, the turnout figures here would be even lower.[4] But turnout in the United States has declined as well, with a record low of 49 percent in the 1996 presidential election. Turnout has subsequently rebounded somewhat in the United States, but it is still below the historic norm. Most advanced industrial democracies, in fact, have experienced a decline in voter turnout over the last three decades, although the problem is conspicuously more significant in the Anglo-American democracies that employ the old first-past-the-post electoral system; countries that use proportional representation have experienced smaller declines.

The steep decline in voter turnout is counterintuitive. Political sociologists discovered in the 1950s that voting was positively correlated with education. But as education levels have shot up in the last 50 years, voter participation has declined. Political knowledge is also an important component of voting. Back in the 1950s, there was radio, newspapers, and for those who were lucky and privileged there was also television. Today there are more media sources than ever. Virtually everyone has a television set now, and there are news stations operating 24 hours a day with lots of political content. And now, of course, people can follow the news on their smartphones at all times of the day or night, wherever they might be. But rather than tuning in to all of this political content, it seems that people are increasingly tuning politics out of their lives altogether.

What's happening to Canadian politics? Why has the rate of voter participation dropped so much? Many people believe that our political malaise relates to the operation of Canada's political institutions. There is a perception now that our votes do not matter. Lots of people certainly believe it doesn't matter *who* you vote for—the major parties all do the same thing in government, or so the thinking goes—and with Canada's single-member plurality electoral system it is true that the major parties converge on the centre of the political spectrum. But they are not exactly the same. They do represent different world-views and they have different policy priorities, and the policy differences can be profound. Others are concerned (more rightly) that the first-past-the-post electoral system does not afford voters much choice. The system privileges a couple of large parties and it punishes smaller parties, like the Green Party. But this is not new. Canada has always used the first-past-the-post electoral system, so it does not make sense to say that the electoral system is responsible for our political malaise. In social science terms, you cannot explain change with a constant variable.

It is true that the prime minister has become a more powerful figure in Canadian politics—or more accurately, the bureaucratic infrastructure supporting the prime minister has become more robust. A lot of people have also become frustrated with the seemingly excessive level of party discipline in Parliament. But once again this is not an entirely new phenomenon. Recall that Pierre Trudeau in the 1970s dismissed backbench Members of Parliament as "nobodies" once they were 50 yards off of Parliament Hill. Many people are disillusioned (or frankly turned off) by the behaviour of our Members of Parliament during question period, and there have been repeated calls for more decorum and civility in the House of Commons. But television cameras were introduced in the House of Commons in 1977, so Canadians have known for a long time that the proceedings of Parliament are a rough-and-tumble affair that is completely unlike any other workplace. Some people have campaigned for a reformed Senate, but the red chamber remains stubbornly resistant to change. All of these issues have been matters of contention for a long time, so it is difficult to fathom why people would suddenly reach the end of their tether in the 1990s and turn off politics entirely.

The Charter of Rights and Freedoms represents the biggest change in Canadian politics over the past 40 years, but the Charter itself is probably not responsible for the rise of political disengagement in Canada. Indeed, after more than 30 years the Charter remains very popular in Canada, including in Quebec, even after many controversial decisions by the Supreme Court. Some people have speculated that the high levels of political cynicism now evident in Canada might stem from the intense mega-constitutional negotiations that spanned more than a decade from the late 1970s to the early 1990s. But this explanation is also unpersuasive. If Canadians really were turned off by mega-constitutional politics, one would anticipate that participation rates would rebound as the constitutional battles of yesteryear recede further into history. But that is not what we have observed. Participation rates dropped *after* the constitutional debates were over, and they have remained low. Moreover, it seems that Canadians were actually engaged in the constitutional debates back in the 1980s and 1990s rather than turned off by them. There was a 72 percent participation rate in the Charlottetown referendum in 1992, and the turnout rate in the second Quebec referendum in 1995 was an astonishing 93.5 percent.

In sum, there does not appear to an *institutional* explanation for the democratic deficit. Institutions are static—they operate today more or less as they have always done. If anything has changed, it is our attitude about these institutions and our behaviour in them. We must therefore turn our attention away from the institutions and examine the actors in our political system: politicians, journalists, and voters.

Political Attitudes and Behaviour in the Twenty-First Century

As noted above, Canadians have a very low opinion of politicians, and they blame them for the sorry state of politics in Canada today. The public is right to be concerned about some of the tactics employed by modern political parties. Politics is, at root, a conflict over different conceptions of the good life. People can and do disagree strongly on some issues, and it is right and proper for politicians to engage in a vigorous debate on these issues; the public deserves to hear a full and frank exchange of ideas on controversial policies before they cast their votes. But good debates are few and far between these days. Politics has become overly partisan, scripted, and cynical.

For the longest time in Canada, the main brokerage parties appealed to the centre of the political spectrum. This followed the logic of Canada's first-past-the-post electoral system, as discussed in Chapters 3 and 4. The same was true in the United States, but less so in the United Kingdom with its sharper class divisions. The practice was so pronounced in Canada and the United States that political scientists generated one of the few plausible theories about political behaviour—the **median voter theorem**. But median voters are fickle—they are difficult to catch and harder to hold. Parties that pursue a median voter strategy, therefore, have to rebuild a political coalition with each election. Moreover, parties that attempt to appeal to median voters generally have to compromise their principles and adopt moderate policies, but this often upsets their strongest supporters, who are typically much more partisan than the median voter. Parties have recently discovered that it is much easier to mobilize their more partisan supporters, or what is known as the "base." You just have to throw them lots of "red meat"—that is, policies that appeal strongly to a party's fiercest supporters. The party that better mobilizes its base gets a leg up in the election, especially if its base is larger than other parties. This was the genius of Karl Rove, the mastermind behind George W. Bush's two successful presidential campaigns.

There is reason to believe, especially after the 2011 federal election, that Canadian parties are appealing increasingly to their base supporters. But there are consequences to this strategy. First, it polarizes the party system as brokerage parties move away from the centre and over to their supporters further to the right and left. Politics has also become overly polemical, as rabid partisans become the lead spokespeople for the party. More seriously, most parties do not have a sufficiently large base to win an election outright. But how can a party broaden its base of support if it does not offer policies that appeal to the fickle median voter? Increasingly, we have seen political parties adopt scare tactics to frighten the median voter away from other parties; in particular, parties resort to negative attack ads to demonize their opponents. If a party can successfully undermine the support for other parties, it stands a chance of winning the election by default. In short, the objective is to shrink the other party's base rather than broaden the base of your own party.

Political strategists swear that negative ads work—that's why they keep using them. But they leave many people feeling disillusioned about the political process. Indeed, Allen Gregg, a former strategist for Brian Mulroney and a noted political commentator, has argued that negative attack ads are ultimately self-defeating. This is why, he says, corporations do not employ negative attack ads: if McDonald's puts out a commercial suggesting that people will get sick if they eat a Burger King Whopper, it won't drive customers away from Burger King and over to McDonald's, it will turn people off hamburgers altogether and destroy the business of both companies. Modern political parties, however, do not mind if voters are turned off by the political process, so long as they can hold their base. In fact, many political strategists would probably like to remove median voters from the electoral process altogether, precisely because they are fickle and unpredictable. It might be good political strategy, but it is highly detrimental to the democratic process.

The political process in Canada and other democracies has not only become more partisan and polarized, it has also become considerably more cynical. Plato, the world's first political scientist, believed that the masses were fundamentally ignorant and incapable of realizing the truth. But, he argued, a few select individuals—philosophers—were capable of discovering the truth through the concerted application of thought. And, he insisted, these enlightened individuals have an obligation to lead their communities to a better place. For many people today,

<aside>
median voter theorem A theory that suggests political parties will appeal to voters in the centre of the political spectrum, especially in the single-member plurality electoral system.
</aside>

Plato's view of society smacks of elitism. By modern standards, it is not correct to suggest that the masses are ignorant or any less capable than our political leaders. But some political leaders and strategists today seem to accept Plato's premise, but draw another conclusion. In short, they seem quite willing to exploit the ignorance of the people for their own advantage. They make attractive promises to voters that really have very little chance of success. For example, over the last couple of decades in Canada parties of all stripes have promised the impossible: balanced budgets, low taxes, and robust social programs. But we can't have it all. At most, we can only have two of these three goods. But with the size and complexity of modern government, it is really quite easy for politicians to mislead the public.

With the rise of cable news channels and social media, communication specialists have also become an indispensable component of the modern political machine. Political leaders are now highly scripted and they rarely go off message. It doesn't matter what questions are put to them, they reply to every question with the "talking points" prepared for them by their communication specialists. The televised election debates among the party leaders have become especially rehearsed and completely devoid of spontaneity. The people want, expect, and deserve a frank exchange of ideas in these debates, but they are only getting pretested sound bites repeated ad nauseam. This, however, makes them look evasive. Over time, each successive prime minister has managed the media more tightly. In the 2011 election campaign, Stephen Harper would only answer five questions per day from the reporters travelling on his tour. At other times, he has attempted to control which journalists get to ask questions, rather than allowing the press gallery to determine the list of questioners. The days of a prime minister engaging a journalist in a spontaneous debate on the steps of Parliament, as Pierre Trudeau did during the October Crisis in 1970, are long gone.

In sum, there appears to be a crisis of authenticity in Canadian politics. Politicians are simply afraid of making a mistake, and for completely understandable reasons. When politicians go off script and speak bluntly to the people, they are all too often "crucified and roundly pilloried by journalists and opponents alike," writes Allen Gregg. The media will go on to "declare that a grievous strategic error" has been committed, and it will speculate for days on the damage caused to the party by the leaders impertinent remarks.[5] Few politicians will thus ever dare to deviate from the script laid out by their handlers, but this creates the impression that they are hiding something—it makes them appear shifty and untrustworthy. But there are counter examples. Rob Ford, the burly and gaffe-prone mayor of Toronto, connects with the public precisely because he is totally authentic. Many people question his judgment and his ability to govern the city, but his success demonstrates quite conclusively that many people are hankering for more authenticity in politics.

The Media

The media plays an essential role in democratic societies, but many people have become disillusioned with the media. In the United Kingdom, journalists are now viewed with almost as much contempt as politicians. Journalists are not so reviled in the United States, but their standing in public opinion has been falling over the last few decades. The situation is modestly better in Canada, but probably heading in the wrong direction.[6] This new disdain for the media is disconcerting. The media are the primary source of information about the political process, and one of the few independent sources of information available to the ordinary voter. Journalists have an ethical obligation to ask politicians tough questions and hold them accountable for their answers, and there are many fine political journalists in Canada doing an excellent job, but the media landscape has been changing rapidly over the last few decades and it seems to be serving Canadians less well even though there is much more of it. There are serious issues about the concentration of media ownership—a few major companies own most of the daily newspapers in Canada as well as many of the major television and radio stations—but I am mostly concerned about how politics is covered in the media and how people respond to this coverage.

The advent of television in the 1950s was a major development. On the one hand, it allowed ordinary voters to see their politicians in action for the first time, but on the other hand it made politicians considerably more image-conscious. The television landscape was changed again with the advent of cable news networks in the 1980s. CNN was launched in the United States in 1980, and CBC News Network followed in Canada nine years later; CTV News Channel came on air in 1997, and Sun News Network hit the airwaves in 2011. These stations are on air 24 hours a day, seven days a week. They consequently have a lot of airtime to fill, and often they fill the space with trivial or salacious political stories. While the stories are often irrelevant, the media makes them sound as significant as the Cuban missile crisis in order to hold the attention of viewers; I recall the American news networks debating President Obama's patriotism for days on end after he ordered a hamburger with *Dijon mustard* at a campaign event in May 2009. We are not immune from this kind of silly journalism in Canada. In the 2013 BC provincial election, the airwaves were abuzz for days when it was reported that Premier Christy Clark drove (harmlessly) through a red light at an empty intersection near her home at five o'clock in the morning when she was taking her 12-year-old son to a hockey practice. People piously declared that she "broke the law" and therefore was not fit to be the premier. It was just easier to talk about her driving skills than engage in a serious discussion about her party's policies. The media would much rather talk about the personal foibles of our politicians and who's up and who's down because "gotcha" and "horse-race" journalism—like reality television shows—produce an audience to see and hear commercials from sponsors.

Television is an expensive and competitive industry. Most networks have been trying to cut costs over the last number of years and make their operations more efficient, but they still have a lot of airtime to fill. But the networks have found an easy "solution," at least when it comes to the political shows like CBC's *Power and Politics* or CTV's *Power Play* or Sun's *Battleground*: political parties are only too happy to supply a representative for these shows and enjoy the benefits of free airtime. But these representatives are typically bombastic and always highly partisan. In the United States, the cable news networks have discovered that it is much easier to hold a segment of the audience if they speak to the ideological convictions of their viewers. Fox News is the station of choice for conservatives, while MSNBC has become the voice of the left. In other words, the media has come to mirror the political polarization in the American party system. Sun News Network has made a concerted effort to replicate the American experience in Canada. It has projected itself as the voice of conservatism, and it has attempted to portray the CBC (which it derisively calls the "state broadcaster") as a bastion of left-wing liberalism. It is too soon to know if Sun News will be successful with this strategy or if it will even survive, but these developments are disconcerting because it makes politics appealing only to hardcore partisans. It leaves ordinary voters—the median voters—feeling alienated from the political process. The political shows on cable news networks have very small audiences: They typically pull in about 50 000 viewers per episode, which is a tiny fraction of the 2 million people who tune in to watch *The Big Bang Theory* each week. But the political shows influence the coverage of politics in the rest of the media and shape the public perception of the political process.

Even when the media engages in solid investigative reporting, the barrage of coverage can have a distorting effect on public opinion. Take, for example, the sponsorship scandal that happened under Jean Chrétien's watch. After the 1995 referendum in Quebec, the Government of Canada launched a massive advertising campaign to win over the hearts and minds of Quebecers disaffected with the Canadian federation. Shortly thereafter rumours emerged that various advertising firms were lining their pockets with easy money from the federal government, and more seriously there were allegations that some of the money was being funnelled back to the Liberal Party of Canada. The auditor general eventually reported that as much as $100 million was spent over four years for little or no work. This is obviously a significant amount of money, but the Government of Canada is a very large operation. Over four years, it spent approximately $600 *billion*—that means the amount of money misspent on the sponsorship scandal amounted to about 0.0002 percent of government spending. Think about it this way: Let's say you left $6000 with a friend for safekeeping and when you returned to pick it up there was a dollar missing. What would you do? Ream your friend out for stealing your money, or thank him for keeping it so safe? That was the magnitude of the sponsorship scandal. And when the scandal was revealed by *The Globe and Mail* after months of dogged investigative journalism, the police were called, charges were laid, trials were held, and people went to jail. So what's the takeaway message from this story? That the Government of Canada is corrupt, or that our system of responsible government works? The sponsorship scandal was a very serious issue and *The Globe and Mail* should be applauded for uncovering it, but the media also has a responsibility to contextualize stories so that the public perception of the political process is not seriously distorted. Events like the sponsorship scandal are kind of like plane crashes: they happen once in a while, but they are not regular occurrences. It is essential for the media to keep these stories in perspective.

I want to stress that there are many fine media organizations in Canada in all formats—print, radio, television, and digital—with terrific journalists doing excellent political reporting. But quality journalism often seems to get drowned out by the noise created by sensational headlines and a few bombastic personalities. However, it may not be possible for the media to collectively do a better job. There may be too many competing interests in the marketplace to expect anything else. The tabloid journals and the ubiquitous call-in radio stations will always outnumber the serious media outlets. Ultimately, it is incumbent upon the people to separate the substance from the noise and seek out quality political journalism and spurn the gossip mongers in the business.

The People

With the rise of hyper-partisan politics and increasingly sensationalist and partisan media, it is not surprising that the public has become cynical and jaded about the political process in Canada and other advanced industrial democracies. The political situation in Canada now flies in the face of just about everything we used to believe about political behaviour: that more information and higher levels of education would promote political participation. But the reverse seems to have happened over the past four or five decades.

Perhaps the modern media environment sets up a barrier between the people and politicians. Before the advent of radio and television, politicians would travel from town to town during election campaigns and give a "stump speech"—they would stand on a tree stump or their own portable soapbox and give a public speech for everyone in town. Nowadays, people rarely get to meet political candidates in their community, and that's a great shame. People would likely have a more positive view of political candidates if they actually met them. In fact, it has been determined that even in the age of social media the most effective campaign technique is to canvas door to door and speak to voters directly, just as politicians did 100 years ago.[7] Candidates have learned this lesson and they are again knocking on a lot of doors, but they still only get to meet a small fraction of the electorate and their exchanges on the doorsteps with voters are fleeting. Many people are thus left feeling disconnected and helpless. In politics, as in life generally, the people should be able to reward the "good guys" and punish the "bad guys," but many people have come to the conclusion that *all* politicians are now behaving badly, so a vote for anyone rewards and reinforces poor behaviour. This does not really provide people with a strong incentive to get out and vote—on the contrary, it gives people an excuse *not* to vote at all.

But Canadian political scientists have discovered that the decline in voter participation over the past three decades is not a generalized phenomenon. "The single most important point to grasp about the decline in turnout since 1988 is that turnout has not declined in the electorate at large, but is largely confined to Canadians born after 1970."[8] Older voters are continuing to vote at more or less the same rates they have always voted, but of course the very oldest voters are passing away and they are not being replaced at the same rate by younger voters. So we know, and have known for some time, that voter "turnout is being dragged down by the increasing weight of the younger generations who are just less interested in politics than older generations."[9] It is estimated that only about one in three people under the age of 30 now vote (youth turnout is a bit higher in federal elections and a bit lower in provincial elections). While it is helpful to have the empirical data, we still do not have an explanation. We do not know why young people today are less interested in politics than previous generations of young people.

We do know, though, that the nonparticipation of young people is influencing electoral outcomes. In the 2011 federal election, opinion polls indicated that the Conservative Party was on track for a minority government, but it finished the night with a majority because too many younger voters who indicated that they would support the Liberals or the NDP did not show up to vote while older Conservative supporters did. Even more dramatically, in the BC provincial election in 2013 the polls predicated a large NDP majority government, but ultimately the Liberal Party secured a fourth majority under the leadership of Christy Clark. The polls showed that the NDP had a large lead in the 18 to 34 age group, but again the convictions of this demographic were not manifested at the polls. Polling companies are now learning how to "weight" the responses they get in their surveys according to how likely respondents are to vote. More importantly, for our purposes, political arties also now weight their platforms and campaigns accordingly. But the more parties speak to older voters, the more younger voters get turned off of politics—it is a vicious circle.

Youth Political Disengagement

Before I continue with a discussion about youth political disengagement, a few caveats are in order. First, I acknowledge that youth political disengagement may be perfectly rational. Some political scientists have argued for a long time that voting is irrational.[10] It takes a certain amount of effort to vote, and the effect of casting one of 15 million votes is negligible. In other words, the benefit of voting does not outweigh the cost. For young people today, who have grown up in an age of political cynicism, voting may make even less sense. Young people may be subconsciously saying to their parents, "If you think politics is corrupt and stupid, why do you vote? That's stupid." Second, I acknowledge that some young people abstain from formal electoral politics as a form of political protest. I have a lot of respect for conscientious objectors, but they are very few and far between. Conscientious objectors cannot possibly be responsible for the sharp drop in voter turnout over the last few decades. Third, I recognize that young people generally have more progressive values. In particular, they are more accepting of racial and sexual diversity than their parents and grandparents. Finally, I am not suggesting that all youth are disinterested in politics these days. On the contrary, lots of young people vote and are very active in politics and other forms of public service, such as volunteer work or organizing boycotts and buycotts and other kinds of protest.[11] But far too many young people are not engaged in politics at all, especially formal *electoral* politics. This is deeply distressing. Elections are how we get our government, so if too few people participate in the process the government will not be representative of the people. Voting, moreover, transforms "subjects into citizens," and that is an essential value in and of itself in a democratic society.[12]

Why are so many young people not voting? Many young people, when asked, say they do not vote because they are not interested in politics. But that only leads to another question: Why are so many young people totally disinterested in politics today? This is really a question for sociologists and perhaps ultimately psychologists rather than political scientists. It is also a historical question. We have to compare young people today with previous generations, and that is always a tricky and sensitive task. When political sociologists investigate the question of youth political disengagement, they typically focus on two related but distinct variables: a person's age and when they were born. When we know someone's age, we can make certain inferences about where they are in life. If someone is six, we know she is about to embark on Grade 1; if she is 16 we can assume that she is getting toward the end of high school; if she is 26, we might imagine that she has finished university and is about to launch her career. Sociologists refer to these developments as the **life cycle**. But we can draw other inferences about people when we know when they were born. For example, my mother was born in the Great Depression, raised as a child through World War II, and became an adult in the era of post-war food rationing in England. And all these years later she remains the thriftiest person I know—no scrap of food is too small to be saved for another day. The generation of people born *after* World War II—the so-called "baby boomers" who came of age in the 1960s—have typically displayed very different attitudes about life. In other words, each generation is distinct, although it is difficult to establish with any certainty when one generation ends and another begins. The unique characteristics of each generation are known as a **cohort effect**.

When we turn our attention to cohort effects, we know that some historical episodes shaped the values and attitudes of particular generations. Those who lived through the World Wars and the Depression have been dubbed "the greatest generation."[13] They were steadfast and stoical, and every subsequent generation has benefited tremendously from their sacrifices. We owe them a huge debt of gratitude. The post-war baby boomers were confident, ambitious, and generally liberal and anti-authoritarian. They opposed the Vietnam War and exposed the sometimes nefarious interests of the liberal state. They also brought us the sexual revolution and a general relaxation of social mores. The boomers were followed by Generation X, the cohort born in the 1960s and into the 1970s. Gen X has always lived in the shadow of the boomers. People in this generation generally share the same values as the boomers, but they missed out on all the fun because they were too young to join in the "summer of love" or go to Woodstock. Gen X also struggled more in the labour market because most of the good positions were occupied by the boomers, although some of Gen Xers are now finding their way to the top—people like Stephen McNeil (the premier of Nova Scotia), who was born in 1964, and Christy Clark (the premier of British Columbia) and Brad Wall (premier of Saskatchewan) who were both born in 1965. Robert Ghiz (premier of Prince Edward Island), who was born in 1974, might also be considered part of this generation. And Justin Trudeau (born December 25, 1971) may be poised to become the poster boy for all of Generation X.

Generation X was followed by Generation Y or the millennial generation. Millennials often feel that nothing important has happened in their lifetimes, at least compared to earlier generations that fought through or protested wars. But this argument is difficult to buy when you realize that millennials came of age politically in one day: September 11, 2001. Millennials have grown up with the cloak-and-dagger "war on terror," and the more traditional wars in Afghanistan and Iraq have unfolded before their very eyes. But these wars have not entered the public consciousness in the same way as past wars. We don't have a draft anymore, and the military industrial complex learned from the Vietnam War how to manage the public relations of war more effectively.

So what has seeped into the consciousness of the millennial generation? "While there is much to distinguish the world in which they entered adulthood from that of earlier generations, the omnipresence of the Internet is undeniably the most salient factor."[14]

life cycle A term used by psychologists and sociologists to describe the distinct phases of life each individual goes through regardless of generation, such as being a toddler, attending elementary school, going to university, working in a career, and retiring.

cohort effect A term used by sociologists to describe the unique characteristics of particular generations.

They can thus be called the "Internet generation," or *netizens*. Millennials tend to be technologically savvy, and they have tremendous amounts of information at the fingertips. But do millennials use the Internet to obtain political information about the world, or to follow tweets from the Kardashian sisters or to watch cat videos on YouTube? In short, as Henry Milner asks, "does growing up with the Internet foster engaged citizens or political dropouts?"[15] While some netizens may use the Internet for political purposes, the data on voter participation indicates that far too many young people have become political dropouts, although we cannot say for sure that the Internet has *caused* this state of affairs.

In the most comprehensive study of youth political disengagement in Canada, Paul Howe suggests that the cause of youth political disengagement is rooted in the way children are now raised. In other words, the *cohort effect* for young people today is a new and distinctly *modern life cycle*. "The most significant change in life course patterns over the past hundred years has been the consolidation of adolescence as a distinct stage of life, a feature of modern, industrial society that is historically unprecedented."[16] Up until the middle of the last century, adolescence was typically a very short stage in life. Boys and girls might have had a few carefree summers when they were 13 or 14 years old, but at this time many children did not finish high school and very few went to university. So, while they were still teenagers, boys went to work with men. Girls typically worked for a few years and then got married and looked after children with other women in their neighbourhoods. Thus, by their early twenties, boys and girls were grown up and had assumed their responsibilities as members of the community. They coached little league, paid taxes, and voted.

Now, of course, most young people complete high school and many go on to college or university. The rise in postsecondary education has been astounding. The proportion of 20–24 year olds in postsecondary education in Canada jumped from 16 to 66 percent between 1960 and 1989.[17] With the cost of education today, students are often taking more than four years to complete their first degree, and many have concluded that it is necessary to acquire a second degree to be competitive in the labour market. Consequently, many young people are in "school" right through their twenties and increasingly into their thirties. Upon graduation, often deeply indebted, many young people find themselves moving back in with their parents—that is, if they ever left home in the first place. Through this phase of their lives, they interact primarily with other members of their age cohort. "It is hard to imagine that young people spending the bulk of their time in educational settings surrounded by peers would not be subject to greater peer influence than young people who had left school behind to take their place manning the plough, helping to run the household, or toiling in the factories, mines, or office towers of the adult world."[18] In short, many young people today effectively live like adolescents through to their thirties, even though they have reached the age of adulthood. The term *adultolesence* has been coined to describe this new phase of life.

While the term may be new, the concept of adultolesence has been widely portrayed in contemporary popular culture, in films like *Failure to Launch* and *The 40 Year Old Virgin* and televisions shows like *Two and a Half Men*, *The Office*, *30 Rock*, and *Family Guy*. The immortal Homer Simpson is, of course, the quintessential adultolescent—the perennial boy living in a grown man's body. Curiously, though, it is almost exclusively men who are parodied for failing to grow up, although there are signs that might now be changing. A 30-something woman was gently mocked in the short-lived television show *How to Live with Your Parents (For the Rest of Your Life)* with Canadian actress Sarah Chalke (who shot to fame as the adorably neurotic Dr. Elliot Reid on the hit television show *Scrubs*). The fact that the show was cancelled after one year, though, suggests that we are not ready as a society to make light of a woman, especially a mother, who is struggling to find her way into adulthood. It is alright for men to be immature, but not women apparently. In the realm of popular culture, women are supposed to be adults, and their role is to exhort (which is usually depicted as nagging) the male buffoons around them to grow up—think of the long-suffering Marge Simpson or Liz Lemon. In real life, though, adultolescence affects men and women, probably about equally.

What does all this have to do with politics? How does adultolescence impact the political process? It has long been known that young people are less attentive to politics and more attuned to their own preoccupations rather than the broader concerns of the community. Politics is a public enterprise—it is about community, whether at the local, provincial, or national level. It is by definition about the "we" rather than "me." One of the abiding characteristics of youth is that they are *self*-regarding rather than *other*-regarding. Adultolesence prolongs this tendency, and it may prevent young people from developing a sense of civic duty and obligation. Various studies have concluded that young people generally do not share the duty-bound conception of citizenship valued by older generations.[19] For many young people, citizenship is seen as a *right* rather than an *obligation*, and consequently political participation is viewed as optional rather than mandatory.

Some have argued that young people would be more likely to participate if the process was more meaningful than simply ticking a ballot, but I am not so sure. I have never heard anyone say, "I don't bother to vote because I really want to spend my free time in more meaningful deliberative assemblies debating the finer points of public policy." I fear that a more demanding process would exacerbate the problem rather than solve it. Many younger citizens want the democratic process to be easier, as evidenced by the persistent calls for online voting, perhaps even from mobile devices. But online voting is probably not the solution to the democratic deficit either. Democracy requires more commitment than simply following someone on Twitter or liking someone's Facebook post. The Canadian writer Malcolm Gladwell has made this point in a provocative essay entitled "Small Change: Why the Revolution Will Not Be Tweeted"(a modern twist on the song "The Revolution Will Not Be Televised," recorded in 1970 by Gil Scott-Heron, the great progenitor of rap and hip hop music).[20]

So, where are we at now? Are young people political dropouts or are they on their way to becoming engaged citizens? It is perhaps too soon to answer that question definitively. There is a positive scenario and a negative one. If youth political disengagement is primarily a life cycle phenomenon, the problem should take care of itself: Young people will engage with politics when they get older. It is possible that we have just witnessed an engagement gap, one that should start to close as the cohort born in the 1970s reaches the age of political maturity. This is perhaps what we have seen in the United States. After reaching its political nadir in the late 1990s—about a decade before Canada hit rock bottom—engagement has inched up in the 2000s, especially in the 2008 and 2012 presidential elections. Unfortunately, we do not know if this higher turnout was generated by the "Obama effect" or if the United States has really turned the corner on democratic engagement.

In Canada, voter turnout has been depressed now for more than 20 years, and there are no signs it is about to be reversed anytime soon. We may thus be witnessing a cohort effect—a generation of people with little or no interest in politics. Regardless, we should be deeply concerned when young people do not embrace politics while they are still relatively young. Politics might be a lot like smoking: if you don't take it up at a young age, you probably won't get hooked on it later. Politics is a social activity that requires a certain degree of socialization. If people are not socialized into the world of politics when they are young, they will not have the conceptual tools—and more importantly the motivation—to take up the activity later in life. The consequences of youth political disengagement cannot be overstated: it puts into jeopardy the democratic foundation of the Canadian political system.

Politics and the Economics of Abundance

Even though the data are clear and young people are not voting at the same level as past generations, it would be a serious mistake to view the political disengagement of young people as a *youth* problem: It is a *social* problem. Youth disengagement is the product of large-scale social and economic changes over the last half century or more. These social and economic changes, in turn, have transformed Canadian political culture in important respects. And Canada is not alone—many advanced industrial democracies have experienced comparable transformations. Indeed, the transformation of Canadian political culture is intimately connected to the process of *becoming* an advanced industrial democracy.

The technological developments of the twentieth century were astonishing. My grandfather was born a dozen years before the Wright brothers flew their rickety little airplane 40 yards down a beach (at an altitude of 10 feet), and he died 16 years after Neil Armstrong walked on the moon. (Yes, he lived almost 94 years.) When he died in 1985, home computers were rare, the Internet was a military secret, and mobile phones existed only in the realm of science fiction. Way back in the middle of the nineteenth century, Karl Marx praised the productive capacity of capitalism in the *Communist Manifesto*: "The bourgeoisie, during its rule of scarce one hundred years, has created more massive and more colossal productive forces than have all preceding generations together."[21] The twentieth century was even more productive, and it improved the quality of life. At the beginning of the century life expectancy in Canada was about 50 years, and at the end of the century it was about 80 years. The dramatic increase in life expectancy stems from substantially improved maternal care and developments in health care more generally, more occupational safety, and a much better distribution of the essentials of life—food, shelter, and clothing. "Today," wrote American political scientist Ronald Inglehart almost four decades ago, "an unprecedented large portion of Western populations have been raised under conditions of exceptional economic security."[22]

Over the course of the twentieth century, the economy in most Western countries was transformed from one of *scarcity* to one of *abundance*. Poverty, hunger, and homelessness are, of course, still major issues. For a wealthy country like Canada, far too many people are reliant on food banks for their basic dietary requirements, and many others worry about making ends meet each month. But the bulk of the population "does *not* live under conditions of hunger and economic insecurity."[23] This fact has given rise to a new type of politics across countries in the West. Rather than focusing on basic *material* needs, such as food, shelter, and clothing, citizens in Western democracies have increasingly placed greater emphasis on *nonmaterial* values and priorities. Ronald Inglehart calls this the politics of **post-materialism**. For Inglehart, the politics of post-materialism is about "belonging, esteem and intellectual and aesthetic satisfaction."[24] It is about gender equality and sexual diversity, multiculturalism and racial tolerance, clean air and water and a healthy environment, and social justice. The politics of post-materialism is more about the *quality* of life rather than physical security. But there may be another side to the post-materialism coin. The economics of abundance may foster a sense of political detachment. When people do not need the state to meet their basic physical requirements, they may turn away from politics entirely and civic life more generally.

post-materialism The shift in political values in recent times away from basic economic concerns toward social justice and environmentalism.

Bowling Alone

In the 1990s, the American political sociologist Robert Putnam was deeply concerned about the falling voter turnout in the United States, and he set out to find out why it was in free fall. In short order, he found widespread evidence of civic disengagement: church attendance was down, union membership was down, parent–teacher associations were in decline, and membership in clubs and voluntary organizations was down as well. When he first published his findings, he famously wrote, the "most whimsical yet discomfiting bit of evidence of social disengagement in contemporary America that I have discovered is this: more Americans are bowling today than ever before, but bowling in organized leagues has plummeted in the last decade or so."[25] He proceeded subsequently to write a 500-page book called *Bowling Alone*, with reams of data supporting his hypothesis that the decline of civic engagement extends far beyond voting.

So what if Americans are bowling alone, you might ask. Why does it matter? How can it even remotely be connected to politics? Almost 200 years ago, the French political observer Alexis de Tocqueville marvelled at the civic enthusiasm of Americans in his book *Democracy in America*, which is widely regarded as the best book ever written about American society and politics. After travelling to the United States, Tocqueville came to believe that voluntary associations are an essential component of a democratic political system. He argued, "among democratic peoples all the citizens are independent and weak. They can do hardly anything for themselves, and none of them is in a position to force his fellows to help him. They would all therefore find themselves helpless if they did not learn to help each other voluntarily."[26] And he warned that if a democratic society lost its voluntary associations, it "would soon fall back into barbarism."[27]

Following in the footsteps of Tocqueville, Putnam argues in *Bowling Alone* that voluntary participation in civic associations establishes ties of reciprocity and trust among individuals.[28] "People," he elaborates, "who have active and trusting connections to others—whether family members, friends, or fellow bowlers—develop or maintain character traits that are good for the rest of society. Joiners become more tolerant, less cynical, and more empathetic to the misfortunes of others."[29] Putnam employs the term **social capital** to describe the benefit derived from voluntary participation in civic associations. Personally, I would prefer to talk about **civic virtue**, but Putnam uses the inelegant and clumsy term *social capital* because he wants to stress the relational dimension of civic engagement. I accept his point that a society of virtuous but unconnected individuals would be deeply problematic (not to mention deadly boring).

Social capital is significant not simply because it makes us nicer people or better neighbours. It is important because it generates the preconditions for the development and maintenance of democracy. Political scientists have spent a lot of time trying to identify the preconditions for democracy. It is not an easy task, but some things seem reasonably clear. First, democracy has typically flourished in liberal societies with free or capitalist markets. "A strong middle class," Inglehart writes, "seems to be a necessary but not sufficient condition for the rise of democracy."[30] But it also requires "the emergence among the general public of norms and attitudes that are supportive of democracy."[31] A sense of interpersonal trust is one of the most basic attitudes required for democracy. "One must view the opposition as a *loyal* opposition, who will not imprison or execute you if you surrender political power to them, but can be relied upon to govern within the laws, and to surrender political power reciprocally if your side wins the next election."[32] Unfortunately, the World Values Survey has indicated that the level of interpersonal trust has declined in Canada by about 15 percent over the last three decades. For Putnam, this erosion of trust is the inevitable result of declining civic associations. But the causal arrows could easily point in the opposite direction: civic associations may be stagnating as a result of declining rates of interpersonal trust in our society. Either way, one of the key conditions for democracy appears to be waning.

Bowling Alone has been widely praised and strongly critiqued. Putnam has been accused of wanting to return America to the era of his childhood—the idyllic time of *Father Knows Best* and *Leave It to Beaver*. This is unfair. Putnam recognizes and acknowledges that the "fifties and sixties were hardly a 'golden age,' especially for those Americans who were

social capital A term that describes the social benefits reaped from people participating in voluntary organizations.

civic virtue A term that encapsulates the notion that citizens have obligations to ensure the well-being of their communities.

marginalized because of their race or gender or social class or sexual orientation."[33] And he certainly does not lament the demise of the Ku Klux Klan and other socially intolerant organizations. But some serious problems have been exposed in his work. Barbara Arneil at the University of British Columbia, for example, has argued that there is a measurement bias in *Bowling Alone* that ignores the important contributions of women and visible minorities to American life over the last half century. Because Putnam wanted to show declining civic participation over time, he focused on national organizations with local chapters, but "it is exactly these criteria that limit a full understanding of women's *changing* civic participation in the twentieth century."[34] For example, she points out that there has been an explosion of women in all manner of organized sports (except maybe bowling) over the last four decades. The story of social capital in America is obviously more complex and multifaceted than Putnam imagined, but the fact remains that *voting* continues to be stubbornly and disturbingly low in the United States and other Anglo-American democracies, such as Canada and the United Kingdom.

Putnam has made a compelling case that the decline of democratic participation is correlated with (and perhaps caused by) a broader decline in civic participation and the erosion of trust in contemporary society. But what has caused the decline in social capital over the last 60 years? Putnam's explanation is not terribly persuasive. Broadly speaking, he attributes the decline in civic participation to our modern lifestyle. He argued that some of the decline could be attributed to the pressures of time and money that many families face, especially two-career families. With this explanation, some felt that Putnam was blaming the women's liberation movement for the ills of American democracy. Putnam was thus anxious to suggest that this factor only accounts for about 10 percent of the problem. He estimated that suburban sprawl and commuting accounted for another 10 percent. A more significant factor was the advent of television. He figured this could account for as much as 25 percent of the problem. But, in his view, the biggest problem has been "the slow, steady, and ineluctable replacement of the long civic generation by their less involved children and grandchildren."[35] He argued that generational change was responsible for at least half the problem, but he had no explanation for why young people might be less civic minded than their parents and grandparents. It would thus seem that we have to dig deeper for a convincing explanation.

The Demise of Liberalism?

The Canadian political philosopher Charles Taylor has argued that the decline in political participation in Western democracies might be inherent in liberalism itself. Taylor recognizes and appreciates that liberalism was a revolutionary ideology—it freed individuals from social tyranny and the despotism of royal absolutism (the dictatorship of kings). In a liberal society, "people have the right to choose for themselves their own pattern of life, to decide in conscience what convictions to espouse, to determine the shape of their lives in a whole host of ways that their ancestors couldn't control."[36] In a liberal society, in theory at least, people are free to choose their occupation, their partners, their religious beliefs, their hobbies, and where to live. But it is all about *individual* freedom. And Taylor warns that "the dark side of individualism is a centring on the self."[37]

In our modern consumer society, many people have become preoccupied with their own dreams. We are all familiar with the notion of the "American Dream," but many Canadians have the same dream: a nice house in the suburbs with a two-car garage, a home theatre, and a Jacuzzi. Just about everything has become "supersized" these days, not just fast-food servings. For example, we live in bigger homes, even though we have smaller families. The post-war bungalow in Canada was typically about 1000 square feet; new homes today are about twice the size of the traditional suburban bungalow, and of course they are much more luxurious, replete with all "mod-cons." I could go on, but I think you get my point—conspicuous consumption has become rampant in modern society. The politics of post-materialism is thus deeply ironic: just when we stopped worrying about our material survival for the first time in human history, we became more *materialistic* than ever, obsessed with the hottest brands, the latest gadgets, and designer fashion. Instead of lining up to vote, people now camp out overnight to be the first in line for the latest iPhone. We have become self-absorbed or, as Taylor puts it, "enclosed in our own hearts." And, he warns, a "society in which people end up as the kind of individuals who are 'enclosed in their own hearts' is one where few will want to participate actively in self-government. They will prefer to stay at home and enjoy the satisfactions of private life, as long as the government of the day produces the means to these satisfactions and distributes them widely."[38] In Taylor's view, modern society has become fragmented, or *atomized*, into its individual components.

Why did liberal societies seemingly fragment in the late twentieth century? With the defeat of fascism and communism, the American writer Francis Fukuyama provocatively argued that Western liberal societies had reached the "end of history."[39] There is nothing left to do except while away the time with trivial pursuits. Or, as Taylor puts it, "People no longer have a sense of a higher purpose, of something worth dying for."[40] But there are no shortages of existential threats to Western society at this time: There's globalization, climate change, and Islamic jihad, for starters.[41] There is thus plenty to be concerned about, if we were not so self-absorbed.

So why have we become so self-centred? It may have something to do with the economics of abundance, as discussed above, but it might also be related to developments in the ideological landscape in Anglo-American democracies in the last couple of decades of the twentieth century. In this regard, I would note that the fragmentation of liberal society and the associated decline in political participation in the Anglo-American democracies has coincided with the rise of neo-conservatism, or more accurately the adoption of neo-liberal economic policy by governments across Western democracies.

The ideology of neo-liberalism/neo-conservatism developed in the 1970s, and it culminated with the election of Margaret Thatcher in the United Kingdom in 1979, Ronald Reagan in the United States in 1980, and Brian Mulroney in Canada in 1984.[42] The neo-conservative movement in the Anglo-American democracies was a response to the liberal social mores of the hippy generation on the one hand and the economic conditions in the 1970s on the other hand. In order to understand the economic situation in the 1970s we have to go back to the Great Depression in the 1930s. The Depression shattered the nineteenth-century principle of personal responsibility—the belief that individuals and families were responsible for their own well-being. When millions of people were thrown out of work through no fault of their own, the state was obligated to provide relief. After the war, the federal government moved to create a comprehensive welfare state in cooperation with the provinces. A variety of assistance programs were created, the pension plan was enhanced, grants were provided to expand post-secondary education, hospital insurance was introduced in 1956, and finally medicare was created in the late 1960s. The development of the welfare state cost money, of course, but the citizenry consented to pay higher taxes in exchange for greater economic security.

As long as the economy was growing it was fairly easy for the government to raise the necessary revenue, but the welfare state came under considerable strain when the economy declined rapidly in the 1970s. The reasons for the recession are complex and multifaceted, but the principal shock occurred after the second Arab–Israeli war when the price of oil quadrupled almost overnight. When the price of oil increased, everything became more expensive, but the economy also slowed down dramatically. Western countries consequently experienced an entirely new phenomenon: rapid inflation and economic stagnation. In short order, *stagflation* became a new term in our economic lexicon. When the economy slowed, government revenue declined precipitously. In keeping with the economic lessons learned from the

Depression—at least as articulated by the British economist John Maynard Keynes—most industrial democracies including Canada borrowed money to make up for the shortfall. When a recession hits, Keynes argued, the state should continue to spend money to stimulate the economy or at least prevent it from falling further; it was believed that government spending would mitigate the recession and allow the economy to return to normal. But the recession lasted longer than people anticipated, and in Canada the federal budget was not balanced again until 1998. Over the course of 30 years, the federal debt grew exponentially.

Governments obviously cannot run deficits indefinitely, but all governments just as obviously have policy choices. A government could attempt to sustain the post-war social consensus, or alternatively it could pursue a different economic model entirely. Initially, most governments attempted to maintain the post-war welfare state, but it proved to be quite difficult, as noted above. With the arrival of Margaret Thatcher, Ronald Reagan, and Brian Mulroney, the Anglo-American democracies set about to establish a new economic model. The policies of these governments were inspired by neo-liberal economists like Milton Friedman in the United States and Friedrich Hayek in Great Britain.[43] In highly simplistic terms, neo-liberal economists argued that governments should scale back its activities and allow the marketplace to generate more wealth. Everyone benefits from a growing economy, or so goes the argument. In order to stimulate investment in the market and economic growth, governments should cut taxes, reduce regulation, and encourage competition. More generally, neo-liberals argued that the government does not allocate resources efficiently. It is better, in their view, for governments to leave more money in the pockets of individuals and let them determine how to allocate their resources. This new ethos represented a return to the old principle of personal responsibility. In the words of Margaret Thatcher, the "Nanny State" had to go and individuals had to become more self-reliant.

It is important to stress that *all* parties in Canada—the Conservatives, the Liberals, and the NDP (when they have formed provincial governments)—have pursued neo-liberal economic policies over the last few decades. The Canadian state consequently has been in retreat over the last three or four decades; it has quite literally shrunk. Not in absolute terms, of course, but in relative terms. Federal program spending has shrunk from a high of around 25 percent of GDP in the early 1980s to about 15 percent today, and the federal civil service has declined from a high of 1.2 percent of the population in 1975 to about 0.8 percent today. The welfare state has not been dismantled in Canada or any other advanced democracy— far from it—but it has been scaled down.

The downward trajectory of the Canadian state in our society is unprecedented. For more than 100 years the state was a driving force in Canadian society. After Confederation the government of Sir John A. Macdonald embarked on the national project: to build the country from coast to coast. The national policy required the state to facilitate the development of industry, build the railroad to the West coast, establish ports on both coasts, and to get immigrants to come to Canada, settle the West, and begin farming. Further, it required national institutions like the Royal Canadian Mounted Police. Subsequent governments led Canada through two World Wars and the Great Depression. And after World War II a new national project was initiated: the development of the welfare state. However, in the neo-liberal/neo-conservative world the state is no longer viewed as a positive force in society. On the contrary, it is seen as an impediment to prosperity and well-being. To the extent people internalize this sentiment, it works against political participation.

The point I am trying to make was poignantly illustrated in a remarkable article published after the death of Margaret Thatcher by bad-boy comedian Russell Brand, who describes himself as "one of Thatcher's children." He was born the year Thatcher became the leader of the Conservative Party, he was four when she became prime minister in 1979, and she remained in power until he was 15. In this most unusual "obit," Brand reflected on how Thatcher's ideology shaped his outlook on life. What is troubling, he wrote, "is my inability to ascertain where my own selfishness ends and her neo-liberal inculcation begins. All of us that grew up under Thatcher were taught that it is good to be selfish, that other people's pain is not your problem, that pain is in fact a weakness and suffering is deserved and shameful."[44] And significantly, for our investigation, he attributed his own "early [political] apathy and indifference" to Thatcher's dogmatic individualism and her insistence that "there is no such thing as society." Ultimately, he concluded, "If you behave like there's no such thing as society, in the end there isn't." At this point, the atomization of society is complete. It is a new Hobbesian world—life may not be "brutish and short" in the post-material world, but everyone is "enclosed in their own hearts" with little regard for the common good.

When a society becomes completely atomized, Charles Taylor warns that we are at risk of a distinctly modern form of despotism, something Tocqueville called "soft despotism." Soft despotism, Taylor elaborates

> will not be a tyranny of terror and oppression as in the old days. The government will be mild and paternalistic. It may even keep democratic forms, with periodic elections. But in fact, everything will be run by an "immense tutelary power," over which people will have little control. The only defence against this, Tocqueville thinks, is a vigorous political culture in which participation is valued, at several levels of government and in voluntary associations as well. But the atomism of the self-absorbed individual militates against this. Once participation declines, once the lateral associations that were its vehicles wither away, the individual citizen is left alone in the face of the vast bureaucratic state and feels, correctly, powerless. This demotivates the citizen even further, and the vicious cycle of soft despotism is joined.[45]

While our current state of affairs looks incredibly bleak, our only hope and option is to restore Canada's democratic political culture. There are no institutional or technological solutions to our predicament—it comes down to us. We have to turn it around.

Restoring Canada's Democratic Political Culture

The foregoing discussion makes it clear that the democratic deficit is not a youth problem; it is a deeply rooted social problem. It is the result of myriad social, cultural, political, and economic developments in the latter half of the twentieth century. And it is not unique to Canada. Other advanced industrial democracies have also experienced it. The democratic deficit is a byproduct of modernity; it is related to the process of becoming an advanced industrial democracy. In sum, the democratic deficit is a symptom of a much larger problem, thus it will not be reversed simply by exhorting young people to vote. Public service announcements from Elections Canada, rock the vote, or even mock elections for underage voters that parallel general elections won't do the trick either. All of these things have been tried with little effect. Even enhanced civic education in the schools has been inconsequential. Mandatory voting would surely drive up turnout, but it would not necessarily inculcate a democratic political culture. And that's our challenge. It won't be easy in light of all the social and cultural changes Canada has experienced over the last half century, but somehow we must find a way to reopen our hearts and reinvigorate democracy in Canada.

Some will no doubt argue that I am being unduly alarmist about the state of democracy in Canada. I certainly recognize that a counterargument can be made: we live in an age of unbelievable prosperity, Canadians enjoy longer life expectancies than ever before, and we live much more comfortable lives than previous generations. Our democratic disengagement may simply reflect a general political contentment. Why bother voting if we have no complaints? Because democracy is not primarily about fulfilling our immediate desires as *consumers*; it is not fundamentally about better government services and programs or lower taxes. It is primarily about *freedom*. If we do not participate in the democratic process, we are jeopardizing our own freedom.

The essential challenge for any liberal democracy was brilliantly captured by James Madison, the architect of the American constitution, in his famous *Federalist* essay *Number 51*:

> If men were angels, no government would be necessary. If angels were to govern men, neither external nor internal controls on government would be necessary. In framing a government which is to be administered by men over men, the great difficulty lies in this: You must first enable the government to control the governed; and in the next place, oblige it to control itself. A dependence on the people is no doubt the primary control on the government; but experience has taught mankind the necessity of auxiliary precautions.[46]

We have all sorts of auxiliary precautions in Canada: the official opposition, the officers of Parliament (the chief electoral officer, auditor general, parliamentary budget officer, ethics commission, privacy commissioner, and access to information commissioner), the Charter of Rights and Freedoms, an independent judiciary, as well as the media and various advocacy groups. But the *primary control* on the power of the government is a *dependence on the people*. Democracy is thus not optional—we have an *obligation* to participate in the democratic process to ensure our freedom. At the risk of being melodramatic, I would note that more than *100 000* Canadians sacrificed their lives in the two World Wars to preserve democracy in Canada and to guarantee our freedom. Comparatively speaking, it is really not much of a sacrifice to ask people today to vote once every few years to preserve democracy and the freedom of all subsequent generations.

How do we go about restoring Canada's democratic political culture? If there were a simple answer to this question, the democratic deficit would have been eliminated years ago or never materialized in the first place. As I have said, the democratic deficit is not fundamentally an institutional or technical problem, it is a social problem. It comes down to us. If we want to eliminate the democratic deficit, we must make a personal and collective commitment to do it. We need to create a new *social contract* between the people, our political representatives, and the media—and quickly.

We should start with our democratically elected representatives. While Canadian politicians are hardly responsible for the broad social and cultural changes that have occurred across most advanced industrial democracies over the last half century, they must accept some responsibility for the state of Canadian politics and assume a lead role in the restoration of Canada's democratic political culture. It is often said that one of the hardest things to do in politics is "speak truth to power," but it seems that politicians are equally afraid of levelling with the public. Politicians are obviously reluctant to say things that are unpopular, because they have to win a popularity contest every four years to keep their jobs. But politicians have to put the interests of the country first. They can and should campaign vigorously, but they must refrain from tactics and strategies that cause harm to the country's political institutions and democratic political culture. We now expect large corporations to exercise a degree of social responsibility while pursuing profits, so we must demand a comparable—or even stronger—sort of political responsibility from our elected representatives. In short, our elected representatives must make a new commitment to the principles of responsible government.

But politicians cannot do it alone. The media has an important role to play as well. The media has a lot of time and space to fill—and dwindling resources for solid investigative journalism—but it has to refrain from making mountains out of molehills. Even if a politician has done something terribly wrong, they can go on to serve with distinction. In 1977, for example, Quebec Premier René Lévesque drove over and killed a drunken homeless man lying in the street. The accident happened in the wee hours of the morning after a party. Lévesque was never tested for alcohol, but he was fined for not wearing his glasses while driving. He served another eight years as premier, and he is now viewed as an icon of Quebec politics. Today, the media goes crazy when a premier innocently drives through a red light in the wee hours of the morning taking her son to hockey practice. In the United States, Congressman Anthony Weiner was hounded out of office after it was revealed he enjoyed "sexting" female acquaintances. Maybe René Lévesque should have been charged with reckless driving and tried in a court of law (he did, after all, kill a man), but surely the media can overlook other minor infractions by our politicians and let them get on with their work. Most will never achieve the heights of René Lévesque, but they will do a better job if they are not being hounded by the media day and night on matters that are ultimately trivial and irrelevant. In any case, the late-night television comedians can take care of the Weiners of the world much more effectively than reporters on the political beat.

The people must play their part too. We can start by being a bit more empathetic and forgiving with our politicians. Politics is a tough job. It takes a certain kind of person to live his or her life on a public stage, to be away from home half the time, to subject her or his employment to a popular vote every few years, and to accept responsibility for the decisions and actions of anonymous civil servants whom they may have never even met. They will inevitably make decisions that we don't like. They may even make decisions that are unpopular and earn the wrath of the public. Canadians still don't like the GST, more than 25 years after it was brought in by Prime Minister Mulroney. But it is good public policy, as Jean Chrétien found out when he decided to keep the tax after promising in the election campaign to abolish it. I am not suggesting that we have to accept all government policies without comment or protest—we do get the chance to pass judgment on the performance of government every four years or so. But I am suggesting that we should not begrudge our elected representatives a good salary, a large severance when they lose office, and a generous lifelong pension. If our elected representatives know that they will be financially secure, win or lose, it affords them the opportunity to advance the interests of the country without regard for their personal well-being. We have to bear in mind that when people step forward to serve the public in an elected capacity, they may not be able to return to their old careers. Even after four years, many professionals will have lost their credentials to practise their trade or just be too dated to resume practice in a competent fashion. We need to create incentives for good people to step forward for elected office in the prime of their careers and to be able to pursue policies, even if they are unpopular, for the good of the country.

It will not be easy to bring about these kinds of attitudinal changes. In the twentieth century, various external threats served to unite Canadians in defence of democracy, but such existential threats do not currently exist and we certainly do not want to fabricate an enemy simply to resolve our democratic deficit. We will thus have to find our resolve internally. We could start by making election day a civic holiday. Once every four years, we can surely afford to close all businesses and schools so Canadians can collectively exercise their democratic franchise without having to worry about getting their kids to school or going to work (except perhaps for some essential service providers, like police officers, firefighters, and nurses). High school students could be employed as volunteers in the polling stations, and children could go along with their parents to vote. And everyone could watch the results roll in during the evening.

But we might have to do more. We might, for example, have to ask Canadians to affirm their citizenship before they can vote and perhaps even obtain a passport. We ask immigrants to take an oath of citizenship before they can vote or apply for a passport, but we have always believed that it was not necessary to ask naturally born Canadians to take the citizenship test and swear to fulfill their civic duties—we just assumed that Canadians would do so. And for the better part of a century Canadians did assume their obligations without question or complaint. But in light of the democratic deficit in Canada over the last three decades we might have to reconsider our assumptions. Perhaps at this time in our history Canadians need to be reminded about the importance of democracy—that democratic citizenship entails obligations as well as rights. The suggestion that naturally born Canadians might have to apply for citizenship would likely generate a storm of controversy, and it might raise constitutional questions, but it is not an onerous requirement. It is certainly not as onerous as the compulsory military service that is still required in advanced industrial democracies like Denmark, Finland, Norway, and Switzerland. It should thus be able to withstand a Charter challenge, especially to resolve a problem as "pressing and substantial" as the democratic deficit. I should note that Citizenship and Immigration Canada already has a program for people to voluntarily reaffirm their allegiance to the country and take the oath of citizenship. But it would be helpful to make this a more meaningful exercise by requiring it before one is able to access the benefits of citizenship, such as voting and applying for a passport. It would be a right of passage—a coming of age—and perhaps a way to restore Canada's democratic political culture.

In sum, we urgently need to renew our democratic vows, just as some couples choose to renew their marriage vows. We are the *demos*. If we do not participate in the democratic process, there is no democracy. I am not suggesting that we all have to rush out and join a political party and campaign for a candidate or run for office, but I am saying that we need to keep up on current events and talk about politics with our family, friends, and neighbours. I know it is not easy to follow politics in this day and age—there are so many distractions in modern society. Fifty years ago, there were only a handful of television stations in the country, and at certain times of the day they all showed the news; people couldn't avoid the news, even if they were not especially interested in politics. But in the age of the Internet and the 500-channel universe, many people will not absorb any news at all, preferring instead to watch the sports channel or the Food Network when the news comes on or catch up with friends on Facebook and Twitter or post their most recent photos to Instagram or videos on Vine. With all these distractions constantly around us, we have to make a conscious decision to choose politics. We must search it out and make it a part of our lives.

But there is a catch, as Robert Putnam notes: "Political knowledge and interest in public affairs are critical preconditions for more active forms of government. If you don't know the rules of the game and the players and don't care about the outcome, you're unlikely to try playing yourself."[47] But we have to play this game because there is plenty to be concerned about. Canada's prosperity is being challenged by globalization and the phenomenal rise of China, India, Brazil, and other emerging economies. We are also experiencing growing economic inequality at home, while at the same time we have witnessed the steady erosion of the welfare state. And, at least since 9/11, we have been deeply concerned about terrorism (and rightly so). But we should also be worried about the invasion of our privacy by the state's security apparatus. More broadly, the twenty-first century is shaping up to be the era of cyber-warfare, although there are still many thousands of conventional nuclear weapons in position and ready to go at the flick of a few switches. With more than 7 billion people in the world today (and projected to reach 10 billion by 2050) Earth's environment is coming under considerable strain. Now is the time for action on the environment, especially climate change. And here in Canada we must always be concerned about the welfare and dignity of Canada's Aboriginal peoples and national unity more generally. You are part of the *demos*. You have the opportunity to shape the future of the country. I hope this book has provided you with the conceptual tools to participate effectively and enthusiastically in the game of politics. *Carpe diem!*

Questions to Think About

1. Why do you think so many young people choose not to vote in Canadian elections? Do you think this is a problem?

2. What do you believe should be done to reverse the democratic deficit and restore Canada's democratic political culture?

Learning Outcomes

1. Define the democratic deficit and describe its key features.

2. Explain what sociologists mean by the "life cycle" and "cohort effects."

3. Describe the concept of post-materialism.

4. Describe the concept of social capital.

5. Explain what Tocqueville and Charles Taylor mean by a society in which individuals are "enclosed in their own hearts."

6. Outline how the democratic deficit might be reversed and how Canada's democratic culture can be restored.

7. Critically evaluate the thesis of this chapter.

Additional Readings

Barbara Arneil, *Diverse Communities: The Problem with Social Capital* (Cambridge, UK: Cambridge University Press, 2006).

Benjamin R. Barber, *Strong Democracy: Participatory Politics for a New Age* (Berkeley, CA: University of California Press, 1984).

Russell J. Dalton, *The Good Citizen: How a Younger Generation Is Reshaping American Politics* (Washington, DC: CQ Press, 2008).

Paul Howe, *Citizens Adrift: The Democratic Disengagement of Young Canadians* (Vancouver, BC: UBC Press, 2010).

Ronald Inglehart, *Culture Shift in Advanced Industrial Society* (Princeton, NJ: Princeton University Press, 1990).

Ronald Inglehart, *Modernization and Postmodernization: Cultural, Economic, and Political Change in 43 Societies* (Princeton, NJ: Princeton University Press, 1997).

Aaron Martin, *Young People and Politics: Political Engagement in the Anglo-American Democracies* (London, UK: Routledge, 2012).

Henry Milner, *Civic Literacy: How Informed Citizens Make Democracy Work* (Hanover, NH: University Press of New England, 2002).

Henry Milner, *The Internet Generation: Engaged Citizens or Political Dropouts* (Hanover, NH: University Press of New England, 2010).

Neil Nevitte, *The Decline of Deference: Canadian Value Change in Cross-National Perspective* (Peterborough, ON: Broadview Press, 1996).

Pippa Norris, ed., *Critical Citizens: Global Support for Democratic Government* (New York, NY: Oxford University Press, 1999).

Pippa Norris, *Democratic Deficit: Critical Citizens Revisited* (New York, NY: Cambridge University Press, 2011).

Pippa Norris, *Democratic Phoenix: Reinventing Political Activism* (New York, NY: Cambridge University Press, 2002).

Robert, D. Putnam, *Bowling Alone: The Collapse and Revival of American Community* (New York, NY: Simon & Schuster, 2000).

Notes

1. Pippa Norris, *Democratic Deficit: Critical Citizens Revisited* (Cambridge, UK: Cambridge University Press, 2011); Patti Tamara Lenard and Richard Simeon, eds., *Imperfect Democracies: The Democratic Deficit in Canada and the United States* (Vancouver, BC: UBC Press, 2012); William Cross, ed., *Auditing Canadian Democracy* (Vancouver, BC: UBC Press, 2010).

2. Neil Nevitte, *The Decline of Deference* (Peterborough, ON: Broadview Press, 1996).

3. Angus-Reid Public Opinion, "Nurses, Doctors Are Most Respected Jobs in Canada, US and Britain," October 2, 2012, http://www.angusreidglobal.com/polls/46931/nurses-doctors-are-most-respected -jobs-in-canada-u-s-and-britain.

4. In Canada, the turnout is the percentage of *registered* voters who cast a ballot. However, some people who are eligible to vote do not get registered to vote. The United States measures turnout against the number of *eligible* voters. The United States has a lower rate of voter registration as well. This is one of the legacies of the fractious race relations in the United States. For a long time, and even still to some extent, black Americans often had trouble registering to vote, even if they were eligible.

5. Allan Gregg, "On Authenticity: How the Truth Can Restore Faith in Politics and Government," 2011 Gordon Osbaldeston Lecture (Public Policy Forum, Ottawa, ON, November 19, 2011). Available at http://allangregg.com/on-authenticity-%E2%80%93-how-the-truth-can-restore-faith-in-politics-and -government.

6. Angus-Reid Public Opinion, October 2, 2012.

7. Donald P. Green and Alan S. Gerber, *Get out the Vote: How to Increase Voter Turnout* 2nd ed. (Washington, DC: Brookings Institution Press, 2008).

8. André Blais et al., *Anatomy of a Liberal Victory: Making Sense of the 2000 Canadian Election* (Peterborough, ON: Broadview Press, 2002), 46.

9. Ibid., 61.

10. Anthony Downs, *An Economic Theory of Democracy* (Boston, MA: Addison-Wesley, 1957).

11. Russell J. Dalton, *The Good Citizen: How a Younger Generation Is Reshaping American Politics* (Washington, DC: CQ Press, 2008).

12. Henry Milner, *The Internet Generation: Engaged Citizens or Political Dropouts* (Medford, MA: Tufts University Press, 2010), 9.

13. Tom Brokaw, *The Greatest Generation* (New York, NY: Random House, 1998).

14. Milner, *The Internet Generation*, 3.

15. Ibid., 3.

16. Paul Howe, *Citizens Adrift: The Democratic Disengagement of Young Canadians* (Vancouver, BC: UBC Press, 2010), 237.

17. Nevitte, *The Decline of Deference*, 24.

18. Howe, *Citizens Adrift*, 243.

19. Nicole Goodman et al., "Young Canadians in the 2008 Federal Election Campaign: Using Facebook to Probe Perceptions of Citizenship and Participation," *Canadian Journal of Political Science* 44:4 (December 2011), 859–881. See also Nevitte, *The Decline of Deference* and Dalton, *The Good Citizen*.

20. Malcolm Gladwell, "Small Change: Why the Revolution Will Not Be Tweeted," *The New Yorker*, October 4, 2010, http://www.newyorker.com/reporting/2010/10/04/101004fa_fact_gladwell?currentPage=all (accessed August 15, 2013).

21. Karl Marx, "Manifesto of the Communist Party," in Robert C. Tucker, ed., *The Marx-Engels Reader*, 2nd ed. (New York, NY: W. W. Norton & Company, 1978), 477.

22. Ronald Inglehart, *The Silent Revolution: Changing Values and Political Styles Among Western Publics* (Princeton, NJ: Princeton University Press, 1977), 3. See also Ronald Inglehart, *Modernization and Postmodernization: Cultural, Economic, and Political Change in 43 Societies* (Princeton, NJ: Princeton University Press, 1997).

23. Ronald Inglehart, *Culture Shift in Advanced Industrial Society* (Princeton, NJ: Princeton University Press, 1990), 68.

24. Ibid., 68.

25. Robert Putnam, "Bowling Alone: American's Declining Social Capital," *Journal of Democracy* 6:1 (1995), 70.

26. Alexis de Tocqueville, *Democracy in America*, trans. George Lawrence, ed. J.P. Mayer (New York, NY: Harper Collins, 2000), 514.

27. Ibid., 515.

28. Robert Putnam, *Bowling Alone* (New York, NY: Simon and Schuster, 2000), 19.

29. Ibid., 288.

30. Inglehart, *Culture Shift*, 22.

31. Ibid., 23.

32. Ibid., 23.

33. Putnam, *Bowling Alone*, 17.

34. Barbara Arneil, *Diverse Communities: The Problem with Social Capital* (Cambridge, UK: Cambridge University Press, 2006), 43.

35. Putnam, *Bowling Alone*, 283.

36. Charles Taylor, *The Malaise of Modernity* (Toronto, ON: Anansi Press, 1991), 2.

37. Ibid., 4.

38. Ibid., 9.

39. Francis Fukuyama, *The End of History and the Last Man* (New York, NY: Free Press, 1992).

40. Taylor, *The Malaise of Modernity*, 4.

41. See Samuel P. Huntington, *The Clash of Civilizations and the Remaking of World Order* (New York, NY: Simon and Schuster, 1996). See also Benjamin R. Barber, *Jihad vs. McWorld: How Globalization and Tribalism Are Reshaping the World* (New York, NY: Ballantine, 1995).

42. See James Farney, *Social Conservatives and Party Politics in Canada and the United States* (Toronto, ON: University of Toronto Press, 2012).

43. Milton Friedman, *Capitalism and Freedom* (Chicago, IL: University of Chicago Press, 1962); F.A. Hayek, *The Constitution of Liberty* (Chicago, IL: University of Chicago Press, 1960).

44. Russell Brand, "Russell Brand on Margaret Thatcher," *The Guardian*, April 9, 2013, http://www.theguardian.com/politics/2013/apr/09/russell-brand-margaret-thatcher (accessed January 27, 2014).

45. Taylor, *Malaise of Modernity*, 9–10.

46. James Madison, "Federalist Number 51," in Jacob E. Cooke, ed., *The Federalist* (Cleveland, OH: Meridian Books, 1961), 349.

47. Putnam, *Bowling Alone*, 35.

APPENDIX A Constitution Act, 1867[1]

Whereas the Provinces of Canada, Nova Scotia, and New Brunswick have expressed their Desire to be federally united into One Dominion under the Crown of the United Kingdom of Great Britain and Ireland, with a Constitution similar in Principle to that of the United Kingdom:

And whereas such a Union would conduce to the Welfare of the Provinces and promote the Interests of the British Empire:

And whereas on the Establishment of the Union by Authority of Parliament it is expedient, not only that the Constitution of the Legislative Authority in the Dominion be provided for, but also that the Nature of the Executive Government therein be declared:

And whereas it is expedient that Provision be made for the eventual Admission into the Union of other Parts of British North America:

I. Preliminary

1. This Act may be cited as the Constitution Act, 1867.
2. Repealed.

II. Union

3. It shall be lawful for the Queen, by and with the Advice of Her Majesty's Most Honourable Privy Council, to declare by Proclamation that, on and after a Day therein appointed, not being more than Six Months after the passing of this Act, the Provinces of Canada, Nova Scotia, and New Brunswick shall form and be One Dominion under the Name of Canada; and on and after that Day those Three Provinces shall form and be One Dominion under that Name accordingly.

4. Unless it is otherwise expressed or implied, the Name Canada shall be taken to mean Canada as constituted under this Act.

5. Canada shall be divided into Four Provinces, named Ontario, Quebec, Nova Scotia, and New Brunswick.

6. The Parts of the Province of Canada (as it exists at the passing of this Act) which formerly constituted respectively the Provinces of Upper Canada and Lower Canada shall be deemed to be severed, and shall form Two separate Provinces. The Part which formerly constituted the Province of Upper Canada shall constitute the Province of Ontario; and the Part which formerly constituted the Province of Lower Canada shall constitute the Province of Quebec.

7. The Provinces of Nova Scotia and New Brunswick shall have the same Limits as at the passing of this Act.

8. In the general Census of the Population of Canada which is hereby required to be taken in the Year One thousand eight hundred and seventy-one, and in every Tenth Year thereafter, the respective Populations of the Four Provinces shall be distinguished.

---

1. The complete and official versions of the Constitution Act, 1867 and Constitution Act, 1982 can be found at http://laws-lois.justice.gc.ca/PDF/CONST_E.pdf

III. Executive Power

9. The Executive Government and Authority of and over Canada is hereby declared to continue and be vested in the Queen.

10. The Provisions of this Act referring to the Governor General extend and apply to the Governor General for the Time being of Canada, or other the Chief Executive Officer or Administrator for the Time being carrying on the Government of Canada on behalf and in the Name of the Queen, by whatever Title he is designated.

11. There shall be a Council to aid and advise in the Government of Canada, to be styled the Queen's Privy Council for Canada; and the Persons who are to be Members of that Council shall be from Time to Time chosen and summoned by the Governor General and sworn in as Privy Councillors, and Members thereof may be from Time to Time removed by the Governor General.

12. All Powers, Authorities, and Functions which under any Act of the Parliament of Great Britain, or of the Parliament of the United Kingdom of Great Britain and Ireland, or of the Legislature of Upper Canada, Lower Canada, Canada, Nova Scotia, or New Brunswick, are at the Union vested in or exerciseable by the respective Governors or Lieutenant Governors of those Provinces, with the Advice, or with the Advice and Consent, of the respective Executive Councils thereof, or in conjunction with those Councils, or with any Number of Members thereof, or by those Governors or Lieutenant Governors individually, shall, as far as the same continue in existence and capable of being exercised after the Union in relation to the Government of Canada, be vested in and exerciseable by the Governor General, with the Advice or with the Advice and Consent of or in conjunction with the Queen's Privy Council for Canada, or any Members thereof, or by the Governor General individually, as the Case requires, subject nevertheless (except with respect to such as exist under Acts of the Parliament of Great Britain or of the Parliament of the United Kingdom of Great Britain and Ireland) to be abolished or altered by the Parliament of Canada.

13. The Provisions of this Act referring to the Governor General in Council shall be construed as referring to the Governor General acting by and with the Advice of the Queen's Privy Council for Canada.

14. It shall be lawful for the Queen, if Her Majesty thinks fit, to authorize the Governor General from Time to Time to appoint any Person or any Persons jointly or severally to be his Deputy or Deputies within any Part or Parts of Canada, and in that Capacity to exercise during the Pleasure of the Governor General such of the Powers, Authorities, and Functions of the Governor General as the Governor General deems it necessary or expedient to assign to him or them, subject to any Limitations or Directions expressed or given by the Queen; but the Appointment of such a Deputy or Deputies shall not affect the Exercise by the Governor General himself of any Power, Authority, or Function.

15. The Command-in-Chief of the Land and Naval Militia, and of all Naval and Military Forces, of and in Canada, is hereby declared to continue and be vested in the Queen.

16. Until the Queen otherwise directs, the Seat of Government of Canada shall be Ottawa.

IV. Legislative Power

17. There shall be One Parliament for Canada, consisting of the Queen, an Upper House styled the Senate, and the House of Commons.

18. The privileges, immunities, and powers to be held, enjoyed, and exercised by the Senate and by the House of Commons, and by the members thereof respectively, shall be such as are from time to time defined by Act of the Parliament of Canada, but so that any

Act of the Parliament of Canada defining such privileges, immunities, and powers shall not confer any privileges, immunities, or powers exceeding those at the passing of such Act held, enjoyed, and exercised by the Commons House of Parliament of the United Kingdom of Great Britain and Ireland, and by the members thereof.

19. The Parliament of Canada shall be called together not later than Six Months after the Union.

20. Repealed.

The Senate

21. The Senate shall, subject to the Provisions of this Act, consist of One Hundred and five members, who shall be styled Senators. (11)

22. In relation to the Constitution of the Senate Canada shall be deemed to consist of Four Divisions:

   1. Ontario;
   2. Quebec;
   3. The Maritime Provinces, Nova Scotia and New Brunswick, and Prince Edward Island;
   4. The Western Provinces of Manitoba, British Columbia, Saskatchewan, and Alberta;

   which Four Divisions shall (subject to the Provisions of this Act) be equally represented in the Senate as follows: Ontario by twenty-four senators; Quebec by twenty-four senators; the Maritime Provinces and Prince Edward Island by twenty-four senators, ten thereof representing Nova Scotia, ten thereof representing New Brunswick, and four thereof representing Prince Edward Island; the Western Provinces by twenty-four senators, six thereof representing Manitoba, six thereof representing British Columbia, six thereof representing Saskatchewan, and six thereof representing Alberta; Newfoundland shall be entitled to be represented in the Senate by six members; the Yukon Territory, the Northwest Territories and Nunavut shall be entitled to be represented in the Senate by one member each.

   In the Case of Quebec each of the Twenty-four Senators representing that Province shall be appointed for One of the Twenty-four Electoral Divisions of Lower Canada specified in Schedule A. to Chapter One of the Consolidated Statutes of Canada.

23. The Qualifications of a Senator shall be as follows:

   (1) He shall be of the full age of Thirty Years;

   (2) He shall be either a natural-born Subject of the Queen, or a Subject of the Queen naturalized by an Act of the Parliament of Great Britain, or of the Parliament of the United Kingdom of Great Britain and Ireland, or of the Legislature of One of the Provinces of Upper Canada, Lower Canada, Canada, Nova Scotia, or New Brunswick, before the Union, or of the Parliament of Canada after the Union;

   (3) He shall be legally or equitably seised as of Freehold for his own Use and Benefit of Lands or Tenements held in Free and Common Socage, or seised or possessed for his own Use and Benefit of Lands or Tenements held in Franc-alleu or in Roture, within the Province for which he is appointed, of the Value of Four thousand Dollars, over and above all Rents, Dues, Debts, Charges, Mortgages, and Incumbrances due or payable out of or charged on or affecting the same;

   (4) His Real and Personal Property shall be together worth Four thousand Dollars over and above his Debts and Liabilities;

   (5) He shall be resident in the Province for which he is appointed;

(6) In the Case of Quebec he shall have his Real Property Qualification in the Electoral Division for which he is appointed, or shall be resident in that Division.

24. The Governor General shall from Time to Time, in the Queen's Name, by Instrument under the Great Seal of Canada, summon qualified Persons to the Senate; and, subject to the Provisions of this Act, every Person so summoned shall become and be a Member of the Senate and a Senator.

25. Repealed.

26. If at any Time on the Recommendation of the Governor General the Queen thinks fit to direct that Four or Eight Members be added to the Senate, the Governor General may by Summons to Four or Eight qualified Persons (as the Case may be), representing equally the Four Divisions of Canada, add to the Senate accordingly.

27. In case of such Addition being at any Time made, the Governor General shall not summon any Person to the Senate, except on a further like Direction by the Queen on the like Recommendation, to represent one of the Four Divisions until such Division is represented by Twenty-four Senators and no more.

28. The Number of Senators shall not at any Time exceed One Hundred and thirteen.

29. **(1)** Subject to subsection (2), a Senator shall, subject to the provisions of this Act, hold his place in the Senate for life.

(2) A Senator who is summoned to the Senate after the coming into force of this subsection shall, subject to this Act, hold his place in the Senate until he attains the age of seventy-five years.

30. A Senator may by Writing under his Hand addressed to the Governor General resign his Place in the Senate, and thereupon the same shall be vacant.

31. The Place of a Senator shall become vacant in any of the following Cases:

(1) If for Two consecutive Sessions of the Parliament he fails to give his Attendance in the Senate;

(2) If he takes an Oath or makes a Declaration or Acknowledgment of Allegiance, Obedience, or Adherence to a Foreign Power, or does an Act whereby he becomes a Subject or Citizen, or entitled to the Rights or Privileges of a Subject or Citizen, of a Foreign Power;

(3) If he is adjudged Bankrupt or Insolvent, or applies for the Benefit of any Law relating to Insolvent Debtors, or becomes a public Defaulter;

(4) If he is attainted of Treason or convicted of Felony or of any infamous Crime;

(5) If he ceases to be qualified in respect of Property or of Residence; provided, that a Senator shall not be deemed to have ceased to be qualified in respect of Residence by reason only of his residing at the Seat of the Government of Canada while holding an Office under that Government requiring his Presence there.

32. When a Vacancy happens in the Senate by Resignation, Death, or otherwise, the Governor General shall by Summons to a fit and qualified Person fill the Vacancy.

33. If any Question arises respecting the Qualification of a Senator or a Vacancy in the Senate the same shall be heard and determined by the Senate.

34. The Governor General may from Time to Time, by Instrument under the Great Seal of Canada, appoint a Senator to be Speaker of the Senate, and may remove him and appoint another in his Stead.

35. Until the Parliament of Canada otherwise provides, the Presence of at least Fifteen Senators, including the Speaker, shall be necessary to constitute a Meeting of the Senate for the Exercise of its Powers.

36. Questions arising in the Senate shall be decided by a Majority of Voices, and the Speaker shall in all Cases have a Vote, and when the Voices are equal the Decision shall be deemed to be in the Negative.

The House of Commons

37. The House of Commons shall, subject to the Provisions of this Act, consist of three hundred and eight members of whom one hundred and six shall be elected for Ontario, seventy-five for Quebec, eleven for Nova Scotia, ten for New Brunswick, fourteen for Manitoba, thirty-six for British Columbia, four for Prince Edward Island, twenty-eight for Alberta, fourteen for Saskatchewan, seven for Newfoundland, one for the Yukon Territory, one for the Northwest Territories and one for Nunavut.

38. The Governor General shall from Time to Time, in the Queen's Name, by Instrument under the Great Seal of Canada, summon and call together the House of Commons.

39. A Senator shall not be capable of being elected or of sitting or voting as a Member of the House of Commons.

40. Until the Parliament of Canada otherwise provides, Ontario, Quebec, Nova Scotia, and New Brunswick shall, for the Purposes of the Election of Members to serve in the House of Commons, be divided into Electoral Districts as follows:

1. Ontario

Ontario shall be divided into the Counties, Ridings of Counties, Cities, Parts of Cities, and Towns enumerated in the First Schedule to this Act, each whereof shall be an Electoral District, each such District as numbered in that Schedule being entitled to return One Member.

2. Quebec

Quebec shall be divided into Sixty-five Electoral Districts, composed of the Sixty-five Electoral Divisions into which Lower Canada is at the passing of this Act divided under Chapter Two of the Consolidated Statutes of Canada, Chapter Seventy-five of the Consolidated Statutes for Lower Canada, and the Act of the Province of Canada of the Twenty-third Year of the Queen, Chapter One, or any other Act amending the same in force at the Union, so that each such Electoral Division shall be for the Purposes of this Act an Electoral District entitled to return One Member.

3. Nova Scotia

Each of the Eighteen Counties of Nova Scotia shall be an Electoral District. The County of Halifax shall be entitled to return Two Members, and each of the other Counties One Member.

4. New Brunswick

Each of the Fourteen Counties into which New Brunswick is divided, including the City and County of St. John, shall be an Electoral District. The City of St. John shall also be a separate Electoral District. Each of those Fifteen Electoral Districts shall be entitled to return One Member.

41. Until the Parliament of Canada otherwise provides, all Laws in force in the several Provinces at the Union relative to the following Matters or any of them, namely, — the Qualifications and Disqualifications of Persons to be elected or to sit or vote as Members of the House of Assembly or Legislative Assembly in the several Provinces, the Voters at Elections of such Members, the Oaths to be taken by Voters, the Returning Officers, their Powers and Duties, the Proceedings at Elections, the Periods during which Elections may be continued, the Trial of controverted Elections, and Proceedings incident thereto, the vacating of Seats of Members, and the Execution of new Writs in case of Seats vacated otherwise than by Dissolution, — shall respectively apply to Elections of Members to serve in the House of Commons for the same several Provinces. Provided that, until the Parliament of Canada otherwise provides, at any Election for a Member of the House of Commons for the District of Algoma, in addition to Persons qualified by the Law of the Province of Canada to vote, every Male British Subject, aged Twenty-one Years or upwards, being a Householder, shall have a Vote.

42. Repealed.

43. Repealed.

44. The House of Commons on its first assembling after a General Election shall proceed with all practicable Speed to elect One of its Members to be Speaker.

45. In case of a Vacancy happening in the Office of Speaker by Death, Resignation, or otherwise, the House of Commons shall with all practicable Speed proceed to elect another of its Members to be Speaker.

46. The Speaker shall preside at all Meetings of the House of Commons.

47. Until the Parliament of Canada otherwise provides, in case of the Absence for any Reason of the Speaker from the Chair of the House of Commons for a Period of Forty-eight consecutive Hours, the House may elect another of its Members to act as Speaker, and the Member so elected shall during the Continuance of such Absence of the Speaker have and execute all the Powers, Privileges, and Duties of Speaker.

48. The Presence of at least Twenty Members of the House of Commons shall be necessary to constitute a Meeting of the House for the Exercise of its Powers, and for that Purpose the Speaker shall be reckoned as a Member.

49. Questions arising in the House of Commons shall be decided by a Majority of Voices other than that of the Speaker, and when the Voices are equal, but not otherwise, the Speaker shall have a Vote.

50. Every House of Commons shall continue for Five Years from the Day of the Return of the Writs for choosing the House (subject to be sooner dissolved by the Governor General), and no longer.

51. (1) The number of members of the House of Commons and the representation of the provinces therein shall, on the completion of each decennial census, be readjusted by such authority, in such manner, and from such time as the Parliament of Canada provides from time to time, subject and according to the following rules:

Rules

1. There shall be assigned to each of the provinces a number of members equal to the number obtained by dividing the population of the province by the electoral quotient and rounding up any fractional remainder to one.

2. If the number of members assigned to a province by the application of rule 1 and section 51A is less than the total number assigned to that province on the date of the coming into force of the Constitution Act, 1985 (Representation), there shall be added to the number of members so assigned such number of members as will result in the province having the same number of members as were assigned on that date.

3. After the application of rules 1 and 2 and section 51A, there shall, in respect of each province that meets the condition set out in rule 4, be added, if necessary, a number of members such that, on the completion of the readjustment, the number obtained by dividing the number of members assigned to that province by the total number of members assigned to all the provinces is as close as possible to, without being below, the number obtained by dividing the population of that province by the total population of all the provinces.

4. Rule 3 applies to a province if, on the completion of the preceding readjustment, the number obtained by dividing the number of members assigned to that province by the total number of members assigned to all the provinces was equal to or greater than the number obtained by dividing the population of that province by the total population of all the provinces, the population of each province being its population as at July 1 of the year of the decennial census that preceded that readjustment according to the estimates prepared for the purpose of that readjustment.

5. Unless the context indicates otherwise, in these rules, the population of a province is the estimate of its population as at July 1 of the year of the most recent decennial census.

6. In these rules, "electoral quotient" means

  (a) 111,166, in relation to the readjustment following the completion of the 2011 decennial census, and

  (b) in relation to the readjustment following the completion of any subsequent decennial census, the number obtained by multiplying the electoral quotient that was applied in the preceding readjustment by the number that is the average of the numbers obtained by dividing the population of each province by the population of the province as at July 1 of the year of the preceding decennial census according to the estimates prepared for the purpose of the preceding readjustment, and rounding up any fractional remainder of that multiplication to one.

(1.1) For the purpose of the rules in subsection (1), there is required to be prepared an estimate of the population of Canada and of each province as at July 1, 2001 and July 1, 2011 — and, in each year following the 2011 decennial census in which a decennial census is taken, as at July 1 of that year — by such authority, in such manner, and from such time as the Parliament of Canada provides from time to time.

(2) The Yukon Territory as bounded and described in the schedule to chapter Y-2 of the Revised Statutes of Canada, 1985, shall be entitled to one member, the Northwest Territories as bounded and described in section 2 of chapter N-27 of the Revised Statutes of Canada, 1985, as amended by section 77 of chapter 28 of the Statutes of Canada, 1993, shall be entitled to one member, and Nunavut as bounded and described in section 3 of chapter 28 of the Statutes of Canada, 1993, shall be entitled to one member.

51A. Notwithstanding anything in this Act a province shall always be entitled to a number of members in the House of Commons not less than the number of senators representing such province.

52. The Number of Members of the House of Commons may be from Time to Time increased by the Parliament of Canada, provided the proportionate Representation of the Provinces prescribed by this Act is not thereby disturbed.

Money Votes; Royal Assent

53. Bills for appropriating any Part of the Public Revenue, or for imposing any Tax or Impost, shall originate in the House of Commons.

54. It shall not be lawful for the House of Commons to adopt or pass any Vote, Resolution, Address, or Bill for the Appropriation of any Part of the Public Revenue, or of any Tax or Impost, to any Purpose that has not been first recommended to that House by Message of the Governor General in the Session in which such Vote, Resolution, Address, or Bill is proposed.

55. Where a Bill passed by the Houses of the Parliament is presented to the Governor General for the Queen's Assent, he shall declare, according to his Discretion, but subject to the Provisions of this Act and to Her Majesty's Instructions, either that he

assents thereto in the Queen's Name, or that he withholds the Queen's Assent, or that he reserves the Bill for the Signification of the Queen's Pleasure.

56. Where the Governor General assents to a Bill in the Queen's Name, he shall by the first convenient Opportunity send an authentic Copy of the Act to One of Her Majesty's Principal Secretaries of State, and if the Queen in Council within Two Years after Receipt thereof by the Secretary of State thinks fit to disallow the Act, such Disallowance (with a Certificate of the Secretary of State of the Day on which the Act was received by him) being signified by the Governor General, by Speech or Message to each of the Houses of the Parliament or by Proclamation, shall annul the Act from and after the Day of such Signification.

57. A Bill reserved for the Signification of the Queen's Pleasure shall not have any Force unless and until, within Two Years from the Day on which it was presented to the Governor General for the Queen's Assent, the Governor General signifies, by Speech or Message to each of the Houses of the Parliament or by Proclamation, that it has received the Assent of the Queen in Council.

An Entry of every such Speech, Message, or Proclamation shall be made in the Journal of each House, and a Duplicate thereof duly attested shall be delivered to the proper Officer to be kept among the Records of Canada.

V. Provincial Constitutions
Executive Power

58. For each Province there shall be an Officer, styled the Lieutenant Governor, appointed by the Governor General in Council by Instrument under the Great Seal of Canada.

59. A Lieutenant Governor shall hold Office during the Pleasure of the Governor General; but any Lieutenant Governor appointed after the Commencement of the First Session of the Parliament of Canada shall not be removeable within Five Years from his Appointment, except for Cause assigned, which shall be communicated to him in Writing within One Month after the Order for his Removal is made, and shall be communicated by Message to the Senate and to the House of Commons within One Week thereafter if the Parliament is then sitting, and if not then within One Week after the Commencement of the next Session of the Parliament.

60. The Salaries of the Lieutenant Governors shall be fixed and provided by the Parliament of Canada.

61. Every Lieutenant Governor shall, before assuming the Duties of his Office, make and subscribe before the Governor General or some Person authorized by him Oaths of Allegiance and Office similar to those taken by the Governor General.

62. The Provisions of this Act referring to the Lieutenant Governor extend and apply to the Lieutenant Governor for the Time being of each Province, or other the Chief Executive Officer or Administrator for the Time being carrying on the Government of the Province, by whatever Title he is designated.

63. The Executive Council of Ontario and of Quebec shall be composed of such Persons as the Lieutenant Governor from Time to Time thinks fit, and in the first instance of the following Officers, namely, — the Attorney General, the Secretary and Registrar of the Province, the Treasurer of the Province, the Commissioner of Crown Lands, and the Commissioner of Agriculture and Public Works, with in Quebec the Speaker of the Legislative Council and the Solicitor General.

64. The Constitution of the Executive Authority in each of the Provinces of Nova Scotia and New Brunswick shall, subject to the Provisions of this Act, continue as it exists at the Union until altered under the Authority of this Act.

65. All Powers, Authorities, and Functions which under any Act of the Parliament of Great Britain, or of the Parliament of the United Kingdom of Great Britain and Ireland, or of the Legislature of Upper Canada, Lower Canada, or Canada, were or are before or at the Union vested in or exerciseable by the respective Governors or Lieutenant Governors of those Provinces, with the Advice or with the Advice and Consent of the respective Executive Councils thereof, or in conjunction with those Councils, or with any Number of Members thereof, or by those Governors or Lieutenant Governors individually, shall, as far as the same are capable of being exercised after the Union in relation to the Government of Ontario and Quebec respectively, be vested in and shall or may be exercised by the Lieutenant Governor of Ontario and Quebec respectively, with the Advice or with the Advice and Consent of or in conjunction with the respective Executive Councils, or any Members thereof, or by the Lieutenant Governor individually, as the Case requires, subject nevertheless (except with respect to such as exist under Acts of the Parliament of Great Britain, or of the Parliament of the United Kingdom of Great Britain and Ireland,) to be abolished or altered by the respective Legislatures of Ontario and Quebec.

66. The Provisions of this Act referring to the Lieutenant Governor in Council shall be construed as referring to the Lieutenant Governor of the Province acting by and with the Advice of the Executive Council thereof.

67. The Governor General in Council may from Time to Time appoint an Administrator to execute the Office and Functions of Lieutenant Governor during his Absence, Illness, or other Inability.

68. Unless and until the Executive Government of any Province otherwise directs with respect to that Province, the Seats of Government of the Provinces shall be as follows, namely, — of Ontario, the City of Toronto; of Quebec, the City of Quebec; of Nova Scotia, the City of Halifax; and of New Brunswick, the City of Fredericton.

Legislative Power

1. Ontario

69. There shall be a Legislature for Ontario consisting of the Lieutenant Governor and of One House, styled the Legislative Assembly of Ontario.

70. The Legislative Assembly of Ontario shall be composed of Eighty-two Members, to be elected to represent the Eighty-two Electoral Districts set forth in the First Schedule to this Act.

2. Quebec

71. There shall be a Legislature for Quebec consisting of the Lieutenant Governor and of Two Houses, styled the Legislative Council of Quebec and the Legislative Assembly of Quebec.

72. The Legislative Council of Quebec shall be composed of Twenty-four Members, to be appointed by the Lieutenant Governor, in the Queen's Name, by Instrument under the Great Seal of Quebec, one being appointed to represent each of the Twenty-four Electoral Divisions of Lower Canada in this Act referred to, and each holding Office for the Term of his Life, unless the Legislature of Quebec otherwise provides under the Provisions of this Act.

73. The Qualifications of the Legislative Councillors of Quebec shall be the same as those of the Senators for Quebec.

74. The Place of a Legislative Councillor of Quebec shall become vacant in the Cases, *mutatis mutandis*, in which the Place of Senator becomes vacant.

75. When a Vacancy happens in the Legislative Council of Quebec by Resignation, Death, or otherwise, the Lieutenant Governor, in the Queen's Name, by Instrument under the Great Seal of Quebec, shall appoint a fit and qualified Person to fill the Vacancy.

76. If any Question arises respecting the Qualification of a Legislative Councillor of Quebec, or a Vacancy in the Legislative Council of Quebec, the same shall be heard and determined by the Legislative Council.

77. The Lieutenant Governor may from Time to Time, by Instrument under the Great Seal of Quebec, appoint a Member of the Legislative Council of Quebec to be Speaker thereof, and may remove him and appoint another in his Stead.

78. Until the Legislature of Quebec otherwise provides, the Presence of at least Ten Members of the Legislative Council, including the Speaker, shall be necessary to constitute a Meeting for the Exercise of its Powers.

79. Questions arising in the Legislative Council of Quebec shall be decided by a Majority of Voices, and the Speaker shall in all Cases have a Vote, and when the Voices are equal the Decision shall be deemed to be in the Negative.

80. The Legislative Assembly of Quebec shall be composed of Sixty-five Members, to be elected to represent the Sixty-five Electoral Divisions or Districts of Lower Canada in this Act referred to, subject to Alteration thereof by the Legislature of Quebec: Provided that it shall not be lawful to present to the Lieutenant Governor of Quebec for Assent any Bill for altering the Limits of any of the Electoral Divisions or Districts mentioned in the Second Schedule to this Act, unless the Second and Third Readings of such Bill have been passed in the Legislative Assembly with the Concurrence of the Majority of the Members representing all those Electoral Divisions or Districts, and the Assent shall not be given to such Bill unless an Address has been presented by the Legislative Assembly to the Lieutenant Governor stating that it has been so passed.

3. Ontario and Quebec

81. Repealed.

82. The Lieutenant Governor of Ontario and of Quebec shall from Time to Time, in the Queen's Name, by Instrument under the Great Seal of the Province, summon and call together the Legislative Assembly of the Province.

83. Until the Legislature of Ontario or of Quebec otherwise provides, a Person accepting or holding in Ontario or in Quebec any Office, Commission, or Employment, permanent or temporary, at the Nomination of the Lieutenant Governor, to which an annual Salary, or any Fee, Allowance, Emolument, or Profit of any Kind or Amount whatever from the Province is attached, shall not be eligible as a Member of the Legislative Assembly of the respective Province, nor shall he sit or vote as such; but nothing in this Section shall make ineligible any Person being a Member of the Executive Council of the respective Province, or holding any of the following Offices, that is to say, the Offices of Attorney General, Secretary and Registrar of the Province, Treasurer of the Province, Commissioner of Crown Lands, and Commissioner of Agriculture and Public Works, and in Quebec Solicitor General, or shall disqualify him to sit or vote in the House for which he is elected, provided he is elected while holding such Office.

84. Until the legislatures of Ontario and Quebec respectively otherwise provide, all Laws which at the Union are in force in those Provinces respectively, relative to the following Matters, or any of them, namely, — the Qualifications and Disqualifications of Persons to be elected or to sit or vote as Members of the Assembly of Canada, the Qualifications or Disqualifications of Voters, the Oaths to be taken by Voters, the Returning Officers, their Powers and Duties, the Proceedings at Elections, the Periods during which such Elections may be continued, and the Trial of controverted Elections and the Proceedings incident thereto, the vacating of the Seats of Members and the issuing and execution of new Writs in case of Seats vacated otherwise than by Dissolution, — shall respectively apply to Elections of Members to serve in the respective Legislative Assemblies of Ontario and Quebec.

Provided that, until the Legislature of Ontario otherwise provides, at any Election for a Member of the Legislative Assembly of Ontario for the District of Algoma, in addition to Persons qualified by the Law of the Province of Canada to vote, every Male British Subject, aged Twenty-one Years or upwards, being a Householder, shall have a Vote.

85. Every Legislative Assembly of Ontario and every Legislative Assembly of Quebec shall continue for Four Years from the Day of the Return of the Writs for choosing the same (subject nevertheless to either the Legislative Assembly of Ontario or the Legislative Assembly of Quebec being sooner dissolved by the Lieutenant Governor of the Province), and no longer.

86. There shall be a Session of the Legislature of Ontario and of that of Quebec once at least in every Year, so that Twelve Months shall not intervene between the last Sitting of the Legislature in each Province in one Session and its first Sitting in the next Session.

87. The following Provisions of this Act respecting the House of Commons of Canada shall extend and apply to the Legislative Assemblies of Ontario and Quebec, that is to say, — the Provisions relating to the Election of a Speaker originally and on Vacancies, the Duties of the Speaker, the Absence of the Speaker, the Quorum, and the Mode of voting, as if those Provisions were here re-enacted and made applicable in Terms to each such Legislative Assembly.

4. Nova Scotia and New Brunswick

88. The Constitution of the Legislature of each of the Provinces of Nova Scotia and New Brunswick shall, subject to the Provisions of this Act, continue as it exists at the Union until altered under the Authority of this Act.

5. Ontario, Quebec, and Nova Scotia

89. Repealed.

6. The Four Provinces

90. The following Provisions of this Act respecting the Parliament of Canada, namely, — the Provisions relating to Appropriation and Tax Bills, the Recommendation of Money Votes, the Assent to Bills, the Disallowance of Acts, and the Signification of Pleasure on Bills reserved, — shall extend and apply to the Legislatures of the several Provinces as if those Provisions were here re-enacted and made applicable in Terms to the respective Provinces and the Legislatures thereof, with the Substitution of the Lieutenant Governor of the Province for the Governor General, of the Governor General for the Queen and for a Secretary of State, of One Year for Two Years, and of the Province for Canada.

VI. Distribution of Legislative Powers

Powers of the Parliament

91. It shall be lawful for the Queen, by and with the Advice and Consent of the Senate and House of Commons, to make Laws for the Peace, Order, and good Government of Canada, in relation to all Matters not coming within the Classes of Subjects by this Act assigned exclusively to the Legislatures of the Provinces; and for greater Certainty, but not so as to restrict the Generality of the foregoing Terms of this Section, it is hereby declared that (notwithstanding anything in this Act) the exclusive Legislative Authority of the Parliament of Canada extends to all Matters coming within the Classes of Subjects next hereinafter enumerated; that is to say,

1. Repealed.

1A. The Public Debt and Property.

2. The Regulation of Trade and Commerce.

2A. Unemployment insurance.

3. The raising of Money by any Mode or System of Taxation.

4. The borrowing of Money on the Public Credit.

5. Postal Service.

6. The Census and Statistics.

7. Militia, Military and Naval Service, and Defence.

8. The fixing of and providing for the Salaries and Allowances of Civil and other Officers of the Government of Canada.

9. Beacons, Buoys, Lighthouses, and Sable Island.

10. Navigation and Shipping.

11. Quarantine and the Establishment and Maintenance of Marine Hospitals.

12. Sea Coast and Inland Fisheries.

13. Ferries between a Province and any British or Foreign Country or between Two Provinces.

14. Currency and Coinage.

15. Banking, Incorporation of Banks, and the Issue of Paper Money.

16. Savings Banks.

17. Weights and Measures.

18. Bills of Exchange and Promissory Notes.

19. Interest.

20. Legal Tender.

21. Bankruptcy and Insolvency.

22. Patents of Invention and Discovery.

23. Copyrights.

24. Indians, and Lands reserved for the Indians.

25. Naturalization and Aliens.

26. Marriage and Divorce.

27. The Criminal Law, except the Constitution of Courts of Criminal Jurisdiction, but including the Procedure in Criminal Matters.

28. The Establishment, Maintenance, and Management of Penitentiaries.

29. Such Classes of Subjects as are expressly excepted in the Enumeration of the Classes of Subjects by this Act assigned exclusively to the Legislatures of the Provinces.

And any Matter coming within any of the Classes of Subjects enumerated in this Section shall not be deemed to come within the Class of Matters of a local or private Nature comprised in the Enumeration of the Classes of Subjects by this Act assigned exclusively to the Legislatures of the Provinces.

Exclusive Powers of Provincial Legislatures

92. In each Province the Legislature may exclusively make Laws in relation to Matters coming within the Classes of Subjects next hereinafter enumerated; that is to say,

1. Repealed.

2. Direct Taxation within the Province in order to the raising of a Revenue for Provincial Purposes.

3. The borrowing of Money on the sole Credit of the Province.

4. The Establishment and Tenure of Provincial Offices and the Appointment and Payment of Provincial Officers.

5. The Management and Sale of the Public Lands belonging to the Province and of the Timber and Wood thereon.

6. The Establishment, Maintenance, and Management of Public and Reformatory Prisons in and for the Province.

7. The Establishment, Maintenance, and Management of Hospitals, Asylums, Charities, and Eleemosynary Institutions in and for the Province, other than Marine Hospitals.

8. Municipal Institutions in the Province.

9. Shop, Saloon, Tavern, Auctioneer, and other Licences in order to the raising of a Revenue for Provincial, Local, or Municipal Purposes.

10. Local Works and Undertakings other than such as are of the following Classes:

    (a) Lines of Steam or other Ships, Railways, Canals, Telegraphs, and other Works and Undertakings connecting the Province with any other or others of the Provinces, or extending beyond the Limits of the Province:

    (b) Lines of Steam Ships between the Province and any British or Foreign Country:

    (c) Such Works as, although wholly situate within the Province, are before or after their Execution declared by the Parliament of Canada to be for the general Advantage of Canada or for the Advantage of Two or more of the Provinces.

11. The Incorporation of Companies with Provincial Objects.

12. The Solemnization of Marriage in the Province.

13. Property and Civil Rights in the Province.

14. The Administration of Justice in the Province, including the Constitution, Maintenance, and Organization of Provincial Courts, both of Civil and of Criminal Jurisdiction, and including Procedure in Civil Matters in those Courts.

15. The Imposition of Punishment by Fine, Penalty, or Imprisonment for enforcing any Law of the Province made in relation to any Matter coming within any of the Classes of Subjects enumerated in this Section.

16. Generally all Matters of a merely local or private Nature in the Province.

Non-Renewable Natural Resources, Forestry Resources and Electrical Energy

92A. (1) In each province, the legislature may exclusively make laws in relation to

    (a) exploration for non-renewable natural resources in the province;

    (b) development, conservation and management of non-renewable natural resources and forestry resources in the province, including laws in relation to the rate of primary production therefrom; and

    (c) development, conservation and management of sites and facilities in the province for the generation and production of electrical energy.

(2) In each province, the legislature may make laws in relation to the export from the province to another part of Canada of the primary production from non-renewable natural resources and forestry resources in the province and the production

from facilities in the province for the generation of electrical energy, but such laws may not authorize or provide for discrimination in prices or in supplies exported to another part of Canada.

(3) Nothing in subsection (2) derogates from the authority of Parliament to enact laws in relation to the matters referred to in that subsection and, where such a law of Parliament and a law of a province conflict, the law of Parliament prevails to the extent of the conflict.

(4) In each province, the legislature may make laws in relation to the raising of money by any mode or system of taxation in respect of

(a) non-renewable natural resources and forestry resources in the province and the primary production therefrom, and

(b) sites and facilities in the province for the generation of electrical energy and the production therefrom, whether or not such production is exported in whole or in part from the province, but such laws may not authorize or provide for taxation that differentiates between production exported to another part of Canada and production not exported from the province.

"Primary production"

(5) The expression "primary production" has the meaning assigned by the Sixth Schedule.

(6) Nothing in subsections (1) to (5) derogates from any powers or rights that a legislature or government of a province had immediately before the coming into force of this section.

Education

93. In and for each Province the Legislature may exclusively make Laws in relation to Education, subject and according to the following Provisions:

(1) Nothing in any such Law shall prejudicially affect any Right or Privilege with respect to Denominational Schools which any Class of Persons have by Law in the Province at the Union;

(2) All the Powers, Privileges, and Duties at the Union by Law conferred and imposed in Upper Canada on the Separate Schools and School Trustees of the Queen's Roman Catholic Subjects shall be and the same are hereby extended to the Dissentient Schools of the Queen's Protestant and Roman Catholic Subjects in Quebec;

(3) Where in any Province a System of Separate or Dissentient Schools exists by Law at the Union or is thereafter established by the Legislature of the Province, an Appeal shall lie to the Governor General in Council from any Act or Decision of any Provincial Authority affecting any Right or Privilege of the Protestant or Roman Catholic Minority of the Queen's Subjects in relation to Education;

(4) In case any such Provincial Law as from Time to Time seems to the Governor General in Council requisite for the due Execution of the Provisions of this Section is not made, or in case any Decision of the Governor General in Council on any Appeal under this Section is not duly executed by the proper Provincial Authority in that Behalf, then and in every such Case, and as far only as the Circumstances of each Case require, the Parliament of Canada may make remedial Laws for the due Execution of the Provisions of this Section and of any Decision of the Governor General in Council under this Section.

93A. Paragraphs (1) to (4) of section 93 do not apply to Quebec.

Uniformity of Laws in Ontario, Nova Scotia, and New Brunswick

94. Notwithstanding anything in this Act, the Parliament of Canada may make Provision for the Uniformity of all or any of the Laws relative to Property and Civil Rights in Ontario, Nova Scotia, and New Brunswick, and of the Procedure of all or any of the Courts in those Three Provinces, and from and after the passing of any Act in that Behalf the Power of the Parliament of Canada to make Laws in relation to any Matter comprised in any such Act shall, notwithstanding anything in this Act, be unrestricted; but any Act of the Parliament of Canada making Provision for such Uniformity shall not have effect in any Province unless and until it is adopted and enacted as Law by the Legislature thereof.

Old Age Pensions

94A. The Parliament of Canada may make laws in relation to old age pensions and supplementary benefits, including survivors' and disability benefits irrespective of age, but no such law shall affect the operation of any law present or future of a provincial legislature in relation to any such matter.

Agriculture and Immigration

95. In each Province the Legislature may make Laws in relation to Agriculture in the Province, and to Immigration into the Province; and it is hereby declared that the Parliament of Canada may from Time to Time make Laws in relation to Agriculture in all or any of the Provinces, and to Immigration into all or any of the Provinces; and any Law of the Legislature of a Province relative to Agriculture or to Immigration shall have effect in and for the Province as long and as far only as it is not repugnant to any Act of the Parliament of Canada.

VII. Judicature

96. The Governor General shall appoint the Judges of the Superior, District, and County Courts in each Province, except those of the Courts of Probate in Nova Scotia and New Brunswick.

97. Until the Laws relative to Property and Civil Rights in Ontario, Nova Scotia, and New Brunswick, and the Procedure of the Courts in those Provinces, are made uniform, the Judges of the Courts of those Provinces appointed by the Governor General shall be selected from the respective Bars of those Provinces.

98. The Judges of the Courts of Quebec shall be selected from the Bar of that Province.

99. **(1)** Subject to subsection (2) of this section, the judges of the superior courts shall hold office during good behaviour, but shall be removable by the Governor General on address of the Senate and House of Commons.

(2) A judge of a superior court, whether appointed before or after the coming into force of this section, shall cease to hold office upon attaining the age of seventy-five years, or upon the coming into force of this section if at that time he has already attained that age.

100. The Salaries, Allowances, and Pensions of the Judges of the Superior, District, and County Courts (except the Courts of Probate in Nova Scotia and New Brunswick), and of the Admiralty Courts in Cases where the Judges thereof are for the Time being paid by Salary, shall be fixed and provided by the Parliament of Canada.

101. The Parliament of Canada may, notwithstanding anything in this Act, from Time to Time provide for the Constitution, Maintenance, and Organization of a General Court of Appeal for Canada, and for the Establishment of any additional Courts for the better Administration of the Laws of Canada.

VIII. Revenues; Debts; Assets; Taxation

102. All Duties and Revenues over which the respective Legislatures of Canada, Nova Scotia, and New Brunswick before and at the Union had and have Power of Appropriation, except such Portions thereof as are by this Act reserved to the respective Legislatures of the Provinces, or are raised by them in accordance with the special Powers conferred on them by this Act, shall form One Consolidated Revenue Fund, to be appropriated for the Public Service of Canada in the Manner and subject to the Charges in this Act provided.

103. The Consolidated Revenue Fund of Canada shall be permanently charged with the Costs, Charges, and Expenses incident to the Collection, Management, and Receipt thereof, and the same shall form the First Charge thereon, subject to be reviewed and audited in such Manner as shall be ordered by the Governor General in Council until the Parliament otherwise provides.

104. The annual Interest of the Public Debts of the several Provinces of Canada, Nova Scotia, and New Brunswick at the Union shall form the Second Charge on the Consolidated Revenue Fund of Canada.

105. Unless altered by the Parliament of Canada, the Salary of the Governor General shall be Ten thousand Pounds Sterling Money of the United Kingdom of Great Britain and Ireland, payable out of the Consolidated Revenue Fund of Canada, and the same shall form the Third Charge thereon.

106. Subject to the several Payments by this Act charged on the Consolidated Revenue Fund of Canada, the same shall be appropriated by the Parliament of Canada for the Public Service.

107. All Stocks, Cash, Banker's Balances, and Securities for Money belonging to each Province at the Time of the Union, except as in this Act mentioned, shall be the Property of Canada, and shall be taken in Reduction of the Amount of the respective Debts of the Provinces at the Union.

108. The Public Works and Property of each Province, enumerated in the Third Schedule to this Act, shall be the Property of Canada.

109. All Lands, Mines, Minerals, and Royalties belonging to the several Provinces of Canada, Nova Scotia, and New Brunswick at the Union, and all Sums then due or payable for such Lands, Mines, Minerals, or Royalties, shall belong to the several Provinces of Ontario, Quebec, Nova Scotia, and New Brunswick in which the same are situate or arise, subject to any Trusts existing in respect thereof, and to any Interest other than that of the Province in the same.

110. All Assets connected with such Portions of the Public Debt of each Province as are assumed by that Province shall belong to that Province.

111. Canada shall be liable for the Debts and Liabilities of each Province existing at the Union.

112. Ontario and Quebec conjointly shall be liable to Canada for the Amount (if any) by which the Debt of the Province of Canada exceeds at the Union Sixty-two million five hundred thousand Dollars, and shall be charged with Interest at the Rate of Five per Centum per Annum thereon.

113. The Assets enumerated in the Fourth Schedule to this Act belonging at the Union to the Province of Canada shall be the Property of Ontario and Quebec conjointly.

114. Nova Scotia shall be liable to Canada for the Amount (if any) by which its Public Debt exceeds at the Union Eight million Dollars, and shall be charged with Interest at the Rate of Five per Centum per Annum thereon.

115. New Brunswick shall be liable to Canada for the Amount (if any) by which its Public Debt exceeds at the Union Seven million Dollars, and shall be charged with Interest at the Rate of Five per Centum per Annum thereon.

116. In case the Public Debts of Nova Scotia and New Brunswick do not at the Union amount to Eight million and Seven million Dollars respectively, they shall respectively receive by half-yearly Payments in advance from the Government of Canada Interest at Five per Centum per Annum on the Difference between the actual Amounts of their respective Debts and such stipulated Amounts.

117. The several Provinces shall retain all their respective Public Property not otherwise disposed of in this Act, subject to the Right of Canada to assume any Lands or Public Property required for Fortifications or for the Defence of the Country.

118. Repealed.

119. New Brunswick shall receive by half-yearly Payments in advance from Canada for the Period of Ten Years from the Union an additional Allowance of Sixty-three thousand Dollars per Annum; but as long as the Public Debt of that Province remains under Seven million Dollars, a Deduction equal to the Interest at Five per Centum per Annum on such Deficiency shall be made from that Allowance of Sixty-three thousand Dollars.

120. All Payments to be made under this Act, or in discharge of Liabilities created under any Act of the Provinces of Canada, Nova Scotia, and New Brunswick respectively, and assumed by Canada, shall, until the Parliament of Canada otherwise directs, be made in such Form and Manner as may from Time to Time be ordered by the Governor General in Council.

121. All Articles of the Growth, Produce, or Manufacture of any one of the Provinces shall, from and after the Union, be admitted free into each of the other Provinces.

122. The Customs and Excise Laws of each Province shall, subject to the Provisions of this Act, continue in force until altered by the Parliament of Canada.

123. Where Customs Duties are, at the Union, leviable on any Goods, Wares, or Merchandises in any Two Provinces, those Goods, Wares, and Merchandises may, from and after the Union, be imported from one of those Provinces into the other of them on Proof of Payment of the Customs Duty leviable thereon in the Province of Exportation, and on Payment of such further Amount (if any) of Customs Duty as is leviable thereon in the Province of Importation.

124. Nothing in this Act shall affect the Right of New Brunswick to levy the Lumber Dues provided in Chapter Fifteen of Title Three of the Revised Statutes of New Brunswick, or in any Act amending that Act before or after the Union, and not increasing the Amount of such Dues; but the Lumber of any of the Provinces other than New Brunswick shall not be subject to such Dues.

125. No Lands or Property belonging to Canada or any Province shall be liable to Taxation.

126. Such Portions of the Duties and Revenues over which the respective Legislatures of Canada, Nova Scotia, and New Brunswick had before the Union Power of Appropriation as are by this Act reserved to the respective Governments or Legislatures of the Provinces, and all Duties and Revenues raised by them in accordance with the special Powers conferred upon them by this Act, shall in each Province form One Consolidated Revenue Fund to be appropriated for the Public Service of the Province.

IX. Miscellaneous Provisions

General

127. Repealed.

128. Every Member of the Senate or House of Commons of Canada shall before taking his Seat therein take and subscribe before the Governor General or some Person authorized by him, and every Member of a Legislative Council or Legislative Assembly of any Province shall before taking his Seat therein take and subscribe before the Lieutenant Governor of the Province or some Person authorized by him, the Oath of Allegiance contained in the Fifth Schedule to this Act; and every Member of the Senate of Canada and every Member of the Legislative Council of Quebec shall also, before taking his Seat therein, take and subscribe before the Governor General, or some Person authorized by him, the Declaration of Qualification contained in the same Schedule.

129. Except as otherwise provided by this Act, all Laws in force in Canada, Nova Scotia, or New Brunswick at the Union, and all Courts of Civil and Criminal Jurisdiction, and all legal Commissions, Powers, and Authorities, and all Officers, Judicial, Administrative, and Ministerial, existing therein at the Union, shall continue in Ontario, Quebec, Nova Scotia, and New Brunswick respectively, as if the Union had not been made; subject nevertheless (except with respect to such as are enacted by or exist under Acts of the Parliament of Great Britain or of the Parliament of the United Kingdom of Great Britain and Ireland,) to be repealed, abolished, or altered by the Parliament of Canada, or by the Legislature of the respective Province, according to the Authority of the Parliament or of that Legislature under this Act.

130. Until the Parliament of Canada otherwise provides, all Officers of the several Provinces having Duties to discharge in relation to Matters other than those coming within the Classes of Subjects by this Act assigned exclusively to the Legislatures of the Provinces shall be Officers of Canada, and shall continue to discharge the Duties of their respective Offices under the same Liabilities, Responsibilities, and Penalties as if the Union had not been made.

131. Until the Parliament of Canada otherwise provides, the Governor General in Council may from Time to Time appoint such Officers as the Governor General in Council deems necessary or proper for the effectual Execution of this Act.

132. The Parliament and Government of Canada shall have all Powers necessary or proper for performing the Obligations of Canada or of any Province thereof, as Part of the British Empire, towards Foreign Countries, arising under Treaties between the Empire and such Foreign Countries.

133. Either the English or the French Language may be used by any Person in the Debates of the Houses of the Parliament of Canada and of the Houses of the Legislature of Quebec; and both those Languages shall be used in the respective Records and Journals of those Houses; and either of those Languages may be used by any Person or in any Pleading or Process in or issuing from any Court of Canada established under this Act, and in or from all or any of the Courts of Quebec. The Acts of the Parliament of Canada and of the Legislature of Quebec shall be printed and published in both those Languages.

Ontario and Quebec

134. Until the Legislature of Ontario or of Quebec otherwise provides, the Lieutenant Governors of Ontario and Quebec may each appoint under the Great Seal of the Province the following Officers, to hold Office during Pleasure, that is to say, — the

Attorney General, the Secretary and Registrar of the Province, the Treasurer of the Province, the Commissioner of Crown Lands, and the Commissioner of Agriculture and Public Works, and in the Case of Quebec the Solicitor General, and may, by Order of the Lieutenant Governor in Council, from Time to Time prescribe the Duties of those Officers, and of the several Departments over which they shall preside or to which they shall belong, and of the Officers and Clerks thereof, and may also appoint other and additional Officers to hold Office during Pleasure, and may from Time to Time prescribe the Duties of those Officers, and of the several Departments over which they shall preside or to which they shall belong, and of the Officers and Clerks thereof.

135. Until the Legislature of Ontario or Quebec otherwise provides, all Rights, Powers, Duties, Functions, Responsibilities, or Authorities at the passing of this Act vested in or imposed on the Attorney General, Solicitor General, Secretary and Registrar of the Province of Canada, Minister of Finance, Commissioner of Crown Lands, Commissioner of Public Works, and Minister of Agriculture and Receiver General, by any Law, Statute, or Ordinance of Upper Canada, Lower Canada, or Canada, and not repugnant to this Act, shall be vested in or imposed on any Officer to be appointed by the Lieutenant Governor for the Discharge of the same or any of them; and the Commissioner of Agriculture and Public Works shall perform the Duties and Functions of the Office of Minister of Agriculture at the passing of this Act imposed by the Law of the Province of Canada, as well as those of the Commissioner of Public Works.

136. Until altered by the Lieutenant Governor in Council, the Great Seals of Ontario and Quebec respectively shall be the same, or of the same Design, as those used in the Provinces of Upper Canada and Lower Canada respectively before their Union as the Province of Canada.

137. The words "and from thence to the End of the then next ensuing Session of the Legislature," or Words to the same Effect, used in any temporary Act of the Province of Canada not expired before the Union, shall be construed to extend and apply to the next Session of the Parliament of Canada if the Subject Matter of the Act is within the Powers of the same as defined by this Act, or to the next Sessions of the Legislatures of Ontario and Quebec respectively if the Subject Matter of the Act is within the Powers of the same as defined by this Act.

138. From and after the Union the Use of the Words "Upper Canada" instead of "Ontario," or "Lower Canada" instead of "Quebec," in any Deed, Writ, Process, Pleading, Document, Matter, or Thing shall not invalidate the same.

139. Any Proclamation under the Great Seal of the Province of Canada issued before the Union to take effect at a Time which is subsequent to the Union, whether relating to that Province, or to Upper Canada, or to Lower Canada, and the several Matters and Things therein proclaimed, shall be and continue of like Force and Effect as if the Union had not been made.

140. Any Proclamation which is authorized by any Act of the Legislature of the Province of Canada to be issued under the Great Seal of the Province of Canada, whether relating to that Province, or to Upper Canada, or to Lower Canada, and which is not issued before the Union, may be issued by the Lieutenant Governor of Ontario or of Quebec, as its Subject Matter requires, under the Great Seal thereof; and from and after the Issue of such Proclamation the same and the several Matters and Things therein proclaimed shall be and continue of the like Force and Effect in Ontario or Quebec as if the Union had not been made.

141. The Penitentiary of the Province of Canada shall, until the Parliament of Canada otherwise provides, be and continue the Penitentiary of Ontario and of Quebec.

142. The Division and Adjustment of the Debts, Credits, Liabilities, Properties, and Assets of Upper Canada and Lower Canada shall be referred to the Arbitrament of Three Arbitrators, One chosen by the Government of Ontario, One by the Government of Quebec, and One by the Government of Canada; and the Selection of the Arbitrators shall not be made until the Parliament of Canada and the Legislatures of Ontario and Quebec have met; and the Arbitrator chosen by the Government of Canada shall not be a Resident either in Ontario or in Quebec. (73)

143. The Governor General in Council may from Time to Time order that such and so many of the Records, Books, and Documents of the Province of Canada as he thinks fit shall be appropriated and delivered either to Ontario or to Quebec, and the same shall thenceforth be the Property of that Province; and any Copy thereof or Extract therefrom, duly certified by the Officer having charge of the Original thereof, shall be admitted as Evidence. (74)

144. The Lieutenant Governor of Quebec may from Time to Time, by Proclamation under the Great Seal of the Province, to take effect from a Day to be appointed therein, constitute Townships in those Parts of the Province of Quebec in which Townships are not then already constituted, and fix the Metes and Bounds thereof.

X. Intercolonial Railway

145. Repealed.

XI. Admission of Other Colonies

146. It shall be lawful for the Queen, by and with the Advice of Her Majesty's Most Honourable Privy Council, on Addresses from the Houses of the Parliament of Canada, and from the Houses of the respective Legislatures of the Colonies or Provinces of Newfoundland, Prince Edward Island, and British Columbia, to admit those Colonies or Provinces, or any of them, into the Union, and on Address from the Houses of the Parliament of Canada to admit Rupert's Land and the North-western Territory, or either of them, into the Union, on such Terms and Conditions in each Case as are in the Addresses expressed and as the Queen thinks fit to approve, subject to the Provisions of this Act; and the Provisions of any Order in Council in that Behalf shall have effect as if they had been enacted by the Parliament of the United Kingdom of Great Britain and Ireland.

147. In case of the Admission of Newfoundland and Prince Edward Island, or either of them, each shall be entitled to a Representation in the Senate of Canada of Four Members, and (notwithstanding anything in this Act) in case of the Admission of Newfoundland the normal Number of Senators shall be Seventy-six and their maximum Number shall be Eighty-two; but Prince Edward Island when admitted shall be deemed to be comprised in the third of the Three Divisions into which Canada is, in relation to the Constitution of the Senate, divided by this Act, and accordingly, after the Admission of Prince Edward Island, whether Newfoundland is admitted or not, the Representation of Nova Scotia and New Brunswick in the Senate shall, as Vacancies occur, be reduced from Twelve to Ten Members respectively, and the Representation of each of those Provinces shall not be increased at any Time beyond Ten, except under the Provisions of this Act for the Appointment of Three or Six additional Senators under the Direction of the Queen. (77)

APPENDIX B Constitution Act, 1982

Part I Canadian Charter of Rights and Freedoms

Whereas Canada is founded upon principles that recognize the supremacy of God and the rule of law:

1. The Canadian Charter of Rights and Freedoms guarantees the rights and freedoms set out in it subject only to such reasonable limits prescribed by law as can be demonstrably justified in a free and democratic society.

Fundamental Freedoms

2. Everyone has the following fundamental freedoms:
   (a) freedom of conscience and religion;
   (b) freedom of thought, belief, opinion and expression, including freedom of the press and other media of communication;
   (c) freedom of peaceful assembly; and
   (d) freedom of association.

Democratic Rights

3. Every citizen of Canada has the right to vote in an election of members of the House of Commons or of a legislative assembly and to be qualified for membership therein.

4. (1) No House of Commons and no legislative assembly shall continue for longer than five years from the date fixed for the return of the writs at a general election of its members.
   (2) In time of real or apprehended war, invasion or insurrection, a House of Commons may be continued by Parliament and a legislative assembly may be continued by the legislature beyond five years if such continuation is not opposed by the votes of more than one-third of the members of the House of Commons or the legislative assembly, as the case may be.

5. There shall be a sitting of Parliament and of each legislature at least once every twelve months.

Mobility Rights

6. (1) Every citizen of Canada has the right to enter, remain in and leave Canada.
   (2) Every citizen of Canada and every person who has the status of a permanent resident of Canada has the right
      (a) to move to and take up residence in any province; and
      (b) to pursue the gaining of a livelihood in any province.

(3) The rights specified in subsection (2) are subject to

   (a) any laws or practices of general application in force in a province other than those that discriminate among persons primarily on the basis of province of present or previous residence; and

   (b) any laws providing for reasonable residency requirements as a qualification for the receipt of publicly provided social services.

(4) Subsections (2) and (3) do not preclude any law, program or activity that has as its object the amelioration in a province of conditions of individuals in that province who are socially or economically disadvantaged if the rate of employment in that province is below the rate of employment in Canada.

Legal Rights

7. Everyone has the right to life, liberty and security of the person and the right not to be deprived thereof except in accordance with the principles of fundamental justice.

8. Everyone has the right to be secure against unreasonable search or seizure.

9. Everyone has the right not to be arbitrarily detained or imprisoned.

10. Everyone has the right on arrest or detention

   (a) to be informed promptly of the reasons therefor;

   (b) to retain and instruct counsel without delay and to be informed of that right; and

   (c) to have the validity of the detention determined by way of *habeas corpus* and to be released if the detention is not lawful.

11. Any person charged with an offence has the right

   (a) to be informed without unreasonable delay of the specific offence;

   (b) to be tried within a reasonable time;

   (c) not to be compelled to be a witness in proceedings against that person in respect of the offence;

   (d) to be presumed innocent until proven guilty according to law in a fair and public hearing by an independent and impartial tribunal;

   (e) not to be denied reasonable bail without just cause;

   (f) except in the case of an offence under military law tried before a military tribunal, to the benefit of trial by jury where the maximum punishment for the offence is imprisonment for five years or a more severe punishment;

   (g) not to be found guilty on account of any act or omission unless, at the time of the act or omission, it constituted an offence under Canadian or international law or was criminal according to the general principles of law recognized by the community of nations;

   (h) if finally acquitted of the offence, not to be tried for it again and, if finally found guilty and punished for the offence, not to be tried or punished for it again; and

   (i) if found guilty of the offence and if the punishment for the offence has been varied between the time of commission and the time of sentencing, to the benefit of the lesser punishment.

12. Everyone has the right not to be subjected to any cruel and unusual treatment or punishment.

13. A witness who testifies in any proceedings has the right not to have any incriminating evidence so given used to incriminate that witness in any other proceedings, except in a prosecution for perjury or for the giving of contradictory evidence.

14. A party or witness in any proceedings who does not understand or speak the language in which the proceedings are conducted or who is deaf has the right to the assistance of an interpreter.

Equality Rights

15. (1) Every individual is equal before and under the law and has the right to the equal protection and equal benefit of the law without discrimination and, in particular, without discrimination based on race, national or ethnic origin, colour, religion, sex, age or mental or physical disability.

(2) Subsection (1) does not preclude any law, program or activity that has as its object the amelioration of conditions of disadvantaged individuals or groups including those that are disadvantaged because of race, national or ethnic origin, colour, religion, sex, age or mental or physical disability.

Official Languages of Canada

16. (1) English and French are the official languages of Canada and have equality of status and equal rights and privileges as to their use in all institutions of the Parliament and government of Canada.

(2) English and French are the official languages of New Brunswick and have equality of status and equal rights and privileges as to their use in all institutions of the legislature and government of New Brunswick.

(3) Nothing in this Charter limits the authority of Parliament or a legislature to advance the equality of status or use of English and French.

16.1(1) The English linguistic community and the French linguistic community in New Brunswick have equality of status and equal rights and privileges, including the right to distinct educational institutions and such distinct cultural institutions as are necessary for the preservation and promotion of those communities.

(2) The role of the legislature and government of New Brunswick to preserve and promote the status, rights and privileges referred to in subsection (1) is affirmed. (85)

17. (1) Everyone has the right to use English or French in any debates and other proceedings of Parliament.

(2) Everyone has the right to use English or French in any debates and other proceedings of the legislature of New Brunswick.

18. (1) The statutes, records and journals of Parliament shall be printed and published in English and French and both language versions are equally authoritative.

(2) The statutes, records and journals of the legislature of New Brunswick shall be printed and published in English and French and both language versions are equally authoritative.

19. (1) Either English or French may be used by any person in, or in any pleading in or process issuing from, any court established by Parliament.

(2) Either English or French may be used by any person in, or in any pleading in or process issuing from, any court of New Brunswick. (91)

20. (1) Any member of the public in Canada has the right to communicate with, and to receive available services from, any head or central office of an institution of the Parliament or government of Canada in English or French, and has the same right with respect to any other office of any such institution where

(a) there is a significant demand for communications with and services from that office in such language; or

(b) due to the nature of the office, it is reasonable that communications with and services from that office be available in both English and French.

(2) Any member of the public in New Brunswick has the right to communicate with, and to receive available services from, any office of an institution of the legislature or government of New Brunswick in English or French.

21. Nothing in sections 16 to 20 abrogates or derogates from any right, privilege or obligation with respect to the English and French languages, or either of them, that exists or is continued by virtue of any other provision of the Constitution of Canada.

22. Nothing in sections 16 to 20 abrogates or derogates from any legal or customary right or privilege acquired or enjoyed either before or after the coming into force of this Charter with respect to any language that is not English or French.

Minority Language Educational Rights

23. (1) Citizens of Canada

(a) whose first language learned and still understood is that of the English or French linguistic minority population of the province in which they reside, or

(b) who have received their primary school instruction in Canada in English or French and reside in a province where the language in which they received that instruction is the language of the English or French linguistic minority population of the province, have the right to have their children receive primary and secondary school instruction in that language in that province.

(2) Citizens of Canada of whom any child has received or is receiving primary or secondary school instruction in English or French in Canada, have the right to have all their children receive primary and secondary school instruction in the same language.

(3) The right of citizens of Canada under subsections (1) and (2) to have their children receive primary and secondary school instruction in the language of the English or French linguistic minority population of a province

(a) applies wherever in the province the number of children of citizens who have such a right is sufficient to warrant the provision to them out of public funds of minority language instruction; and

(b) includes, where the number of those children so warrants, the right to have them receive that instruction in minority language educational facilities provided out of public funds.

Enforcement

24. (1) Anyone whose rights or freedoms, as guaranteed by this Charter, have been infringed or denied may apply to a court of competent jurisdiction to obtain such remedy as the court considers appropriate and just in the circumstances.

(2) Where, in proceedings under subsection (1), a court concludes that evidence was obtained in a manner that infringed or denied any rights or freedoms guaranteed by this Charter, the evidence shall be excluded if it is established that, having regard to all the circumstances, the admission of it in the proceedings would bring the administration of justice into disrepute.

General

25. The guarantee in this Charter of certain rights and freedoms shall not be construed so as to abrogate or derogate from any aboriginal, treaty or other rights or freedoms that pertain to the aboriginal peoples of Canada including

  (a) any rights or freedoms that have been recognized by the Royal Proclamation of October 7, 1763; and

  (b) any rights or freedoms that now exist by way of land claims agreements or may be so acquired. (94)

26. The guarantee in this Charter of certain rights and freedoms shall not be construed as denying the existence of any other rights or freedoms that exist in Canada.

27. This Charter shall be interpreted in a manner consistent with the preservation and enhancement of the multicultural heritage of Canadians.

28. Notwithstanding anything in this Charter, the rights and freedoms referred to in it are guaranteed equally to male and female persons.

29. Nothing in this Charter abrogates or derogates from any rights or privileges guaranteed by or under the Constitution of Canada in respect of denominational, separate or dissentient schools.

30. A reference in this Charter to a province or to the legislative assembly or legislature of a province shall be deemed to include a reference to the Yukon Territory and the Northwest Territories, or to the appropriate legislative authority thereof, as the case may be.

31. Nothing in this Charter extends the legislative powers of any body or authority.

Application of Charter

32. (1) This Charter applies

  (a) to the Parliament and government of Canada in respect of all matters within the authority of Parliament including all matters relating to the Yukon Territory and Northwest Territories; and

  (b) to the legislature and government of each province in respect of all matters within the authority of the legislature of each province.

  (2) Notwithstanding subsection (1), section 15 shall not have effect until three years after this section comes into force.

33. (1) Parliament or the legislature of a province may expressly declare in an Act of Parliament or of the legislature, as the case may be, that the Act or a provision thereof shall operate notwithstanding a provision included in section 2 or sections 7 to 15 of this Charter.

  (2) An Act or a provision of an Act in respect of which a declaration made under this section is in effect shall have such operation as it would have but for the provision of this Charter referred to in the declaration.

  (3) A declaration made under subsection (1) shall cease to have effect five years after it comes into force or on such earlier date as may be specified in the declaration.

  (4) Parliament or the legislature of a province may re-enact a declaration made under subsection (1).

  (5) Subsection (3) applies in respect of a re-enactment made under subsection (4).

34. This Part may be cited as the Canadian Charter of Rights and Freedoms.

Part II Rights of the Aboriginal Peoples of Canada

35. **(1)** The existing aboriginal and treaty rights of the aboriginal peoples of Canada are hereby recognized and affirmed.

(2) In this Act, "aboriginal peoples of Canada" includes the Indian, Inuit and Métis peoples of Canada.

(3) For greater certainty, in subsection (1) "treaty rights" includes rights that now exist by way of land claims agreements or may be so acquired.

(4) Notwithstanding any other provision of this Act, the aboriginal and treaty rights referred to in subsection (1) are guaranteed equally to male and female persons. (96)

35.1 The government of Canada and the provincial governments are committed to the principle that, before any amendment is made to Class 24 of section 91 of the "Constitution Act, 1867", to section 25 of this Act or to this Part,

(a) a constitutional conference that includes in its agenda an item relating to the proposed amendment, composed of the Prime Minister of Canada and the first ministers of the provinces, will be convened by the Prime Minister of Canada; and

(b) the Prime Minister of Canada will invite representatives of the aboriginal peoples of Canada to participate in the discussions on that item. (97)

Part III Equalization and Regional Disparities

36. **(1)** Without altering the legislative authority of Parliament or of the provincial legislatures, or the rights of any of them with respect to the exercise of their legislative authority, Parliament and the legislatures, together with the government of Canada and the provincial governments, are committed to

(a) promoting equal opportunities for the well-being of Canadians;

(b) furthering economic development to reduce disparity in opportunities; and

(c) providing essential public services of reasonable quality to all Canadians.

(2) Parliament and the government of Canada are committed to the principle of making equalization payments to ensure that provincial governments have sufficient revenues to provide reasonably comparable levels of public services at reasonably comparable levels of taxation.

Part IV Constitutional Conference

37. Repealed.

Part IV. I Constitutional Conferences

37.1 Repealed.

Part V Procedure for Amending Constitution of Canada

38. **(1)** An amendment to the Constitution of Canada may be made by proclamation issued by the Governor General under the Great Seal of Canada where so authorized by

(a) resolutions of the Senate and House of Commons; and

(b) resolutions of the legislative assemblies of at least two-thirds of the provinces that have, in the aggregate, according to the then latest general census, at least fifty per cent of the population of all the provinces.

(2) An amendment made under subsection (1) that derogates from the legislative powers, the proprietary rights or any other rights or privileges of the legislature or government of a province shall require a resolution supported by a majority of the members of each of the Senate, the House of Commons and the legislative assemblies required under subsection (1).

(3) An amendment referred to in subsection (2) shall not have effect in a province the legislative assembly of which has expressed its dissent thereto by resolution supported by a majority of its members prior to the issue of the proclamation to which the amendment relates unless that legislative assembly, subsequently, by resolution supported by a majority of its members, revokes its dissent and authorizes the amendment.

(4) A resolution of dissent made for the purposes of subsection (3) may be revoked at any time before or after the issue of the proclamation to which it relates.

39. **(1)** A proclamation shall not be issued under subsection 38(1) before the expiration of one year from the adoption of the resolution initiating the amendment procedure thereunder, unless the legislative assembly of each province has previously adopted a resolution of assent or dissent.

(2) A proclamation shall not be issued under subsection 38(1) after the expiration of three years from the adoption of the resolution initiating the amendment procedure thereunder.

40. Where an amendment is made under subsection 38(1) that transfers provincial legislative powers relating to education or other cultural matters from provincial legislatures to Parliament, Canada shall provide reasonable compensation to any province to which the amendment does not apply.

41. An amendment to the Constitution of Canada in relation to the following matters may be made by proclamation issued by the Governor General under the Great Seal of Canada only where authorized by resolutions of the Senate and House of Commons and of the legislative assembly of each province:

(a) the office of the Queen, the Governor General and the Lieutenant Governor of a province;

(b) the right of a province to a number of members in the House of Commons not less than the number of Senators by which the province is entitled to be represented at the time this Part comes into force;

(c) subject to section 43, the use of the English or the French language;

(d) the composition of the Supreme Court of Canada; and

(e) an amendment to this Part.

42. (1) An amendment to the Constitution of Canada in relation to the following matters may be made only in accordance with subsection 38(1):

(a) the principle of proportionate representation of the provinces in the House of Commons prescribed by the Constitution of Canada;

(b) the powers of the Senate and the method of selecting Senators;

(c) the number of members by which a province is entitled to be represented in the Senate and the residence qualifications of Senators;

(d) subject to paragraph 41(d), the Supreme Court of Canada;

(e) the extension of existing provinces into the territories; and

(f) notwithstanding any other law or practice, the establishment of new provinces.

(2) Subsections 38(2) to (4) do not apply in respect of amendments in relation to matters referred to in subsection (1).

43. An amendment to the Constitution of Canada in relation to any provision that applies to one or more, but not all, provinces, including

(a) any alteration to boundaries between provinces, and

(b) any amendment to any provision that relates to the use of the English or the French language within a province, may be made by proclamation issued by the Governor General under the Great Seal of Canada only where so authorized by resolutions of the Senate and House of Commons and of the legislative assembly of each province to which the amendment applies.

44. Subject to sections 41 and 42, Parliament may exclusively make laws amending the Constitution of Canada in relation to the executive government of Canada or the Senate and House of Commons.

45. Subject to section 41, the legislature of each province may exclusively make laws amending the constitution of the province.

46. (1) The procedures for amendment under sections 38, 41, 42 and 43 may be initiated either by the Senate or the House of Commons or by the legislative assembly of a province.

(2) A resolution of assent made for the purposes of this Part may be revoked at any time before the issue of a proclamation authorized by it.

47. (1) An amendment to the Constitution of Canada made by proclamation under section 38, 41, 42 or 43 may be made without a resolution of the Senate authorizing the issue of the proclamation if, within one hundred and eighty days after the adoption by the House of Commons of a resolution authorizing its issue, the Senate has not adopted such a resolution and if, at any time after the expiration of that period, the House of Commons again adopts the resolution.

(2) Any period when Parliament is prorogued or dissolved shall not be counted in computing the one hundred and eighty day period referred to in subsection (1).

48. The Queen's Privy Council for Canada shall advise the Governor General to issue a proclamation under this Part forthwith on the adoption of the resolutions required for an amendment made by proclamation under this Part.

49. A constitutional conference composed of the Prime Minister of Canada and the first ministers of the provinces shall be convened by the Prime Minister of Canada within fifteen years after this Part comes into force to review the provisions of this Part.

Part VI Amendment to the Constitution Act, 1867

50. (The text of this amendment is set out in the Constitution Act, 1867, as section 92A.)

51. (The text of this amendment is set out in the Constitution Act, 1867, as the Sixth Schedule.)

Part VII General

52. (1) The Constitution of Canada is the supreme law of Canada, and any law that is inconsistent with the provisions of the Constitution is, to the extent of the inconsistency, of no force or effect.

(2) The Constitution of Canada includes

(a) the Canada Act 1982, including this Act;

(b) the Acts and orders referred to in the schedule; and

(c) any amendment to any Act or order referred to in paragraph (a) or (b).

(3) Amendments to the Constitution of Canada shall be made only in accordance with the authority contained in the Constitution of Canada.

53. (1) The enactments referred to in Column I of the schedule are hereby repealed or amended to the extent indicated in Column II thereof and, unless repealed, shall continue as law in Canada under the names set out in Column III thereof.

(2) Every enactment, except the Canada Act 1982, that refers to an enactment referred to in the schedule by the name in Column I thereof is hereby amended by substituting for that name the corresponding name in Column III thereof, and any British North America Act not referred to in the schedule may be cited as the Constitution Act followed by the year and number, if any, of its enactment.

54. Part IV is repealed on the day that is one year after this Part comes into force and this section may be repealed and this Act renumbered, consequentially upon the repeal of Part IV and this section, by proclamation issued by the Governor General under the Great Seal of Canada.

54.1 Repealed.

55. A French version of the portions of the Constitution of Canada referred to in the schedule shall be prepared by the Minister of Justice of Canada as expeditiously as possible and, when any portion thereof sufficient to warrant action being taken has been so prepared, it shall be put forward for enactment by proclamation issued by the Governor General under the Great Seal of Canada pursuant to the procedure then applicable to an amendment of the same provisions of the Constitution of Canada.

56. Where any portion of the Constitution of Canada has been or is enacted in English and French or where a French version of any portion of the Constitution is enacted pursuant to section 55, the English and French versions of that portion of the Constitution are equally authoritative.

57. The English and French versions of this Act are equally authoritative.

58. Subject to section 59, this Act shall come into force on a day to be fixed by proclamation issued by the Queen or the Governor General under the Great Seal of Canada.

59. (1) Paragraph 23(1)(a) shall come into force in respect of Quebec on a day to be fixed by proclamation issued by the Queen or the Governor General under the Great Seal of Canada.

(2) A proclamation under subsection (1) shall be issued only where authorized by the legislative assembly or government of Quebec.

(3) This section may be repealed on the day paragraph 23(1)(a) comes into force in respect of Quebec and this Act amended and renumbered, consequentially upon the repeal of this section, by proclamation issued by the Queen or the Governor General under the Great Seal of Canada.

60. This Act may be cited as the Constitution Act, 1982, and the Constitution Acts 1867 to 1975 (No. 2) and this Act may be cited together as the Constitution Acts, 1867 to 1982.

61. A reference to the "Constitution Acts, 1867 to 1982" shall be deemed to include a reference to the "Constitution Amendment Proclamation, 1983".

Glossary

7/50 rule The term commonly used for the general amending formula in the constitution.

Aboriginal rights Unique rights of Aboriginal peoples that stem from the original occupation and use of the land by Aboriginal peoples.

act A statutory law of Parliament.

Administrator of Canada A position held by the Chief Justice of the Supreme Court of Canada if the governor general dies in office.

advocacy groups Organizations representing the concerns of various social movements or economic interests. Rather than contest elections like a political party, advocacy groups seek to influence government policy from the outside. They are sometimes called interest groups, although it should be noted that this term is often used pejoratively.

amending formula The procedure used to amend a constitution. Before patriation, Canada did not have its own amending formula but instead relied on the British Parliament for constitutional amendments.

asymmetrical federalism A type of federalism in which the provinces exercise different powers.

band A group of Status Indians under the Indian Act. Many bands now prefer to be known as First Nations.

band council The governing body of an Indian band under the Indian Act.

bellwether ridings Ridings with a unique habit of electing a candidate to Parliament who belongs to the winning party.

bicameral legislature A legislature that has two chambers. The Parliament of Canada is a bicameral legislature: The House of Commons is the elected lower chamber, and the Senate is the appointed upper chamber.

big tent parties Diverse parties with multiple ideological factions.

bill A proposed new law. When it is finally passed by Parliament, it becomes known as an act.

Bill C-110, An Act Respecting Constitutional Amendments A bill introduced and passed in Parliament after the Quebec referendum in 1995 that states the federal government will consent to an amendment of the constitution only if it is supported by the legislatures in the five regions of Canada: the Atlantic provinces, Quebec, Ontario, the Prairie provinces, and British Columbia.

Bill of Rights A statute enacted in 1960 by the government of John Diefenbaker. It enumerated the common law rights enjoyed by Canadians and prohibited discrimination based on race, national origin, colour, religion, or sex. The Bill of Rights was not entrenched in the constitution; it was a statutory law.

block transfers Fixed sums of money provided by the federal government to the provinces to finance social programs and health care. They were introduced with the Established Programs Financing Act in 1976.

briefing notes Short documents prepared by the civil service to inform ministers of key developments or to advise them on policy.

brokerage parties Parties that are able to appeal to the different regions of Canada, especially the two major linguistic groups. Brokerage parties tend to be ideologically pragmatic, following the wishes of the voters rather than standing on a set of predetermined principles.

budget The government's annual plan for raising revenue and spending revenue. It is the most important money bill of the year and by definition is a matter of confidence. It is usually introduced in the spring.

by-election An election to fill a vacancy in the House of Commons held between general elections.

cabinet The central decision-making body in the Canadian political system. It is led by the prime minister and includes the other ministers of government.

Canada Health and Social Transfer (CHST) A single transfer that replaced the Established Programs Financing Act in 1995 as the primary federal transfer for provincial health and social programs.

Canada Health Transfer (CHT) and Canada Social Transfer (CST) Transfers created in 2003 to ensure more accountability surrounding how provinces spend money transferred from the federal government.

cash transfers Payments provided by the federal government to the provinces to finance provincial programs such as health care.

caucus All the members of a political party elected to Parliament and appointed to the Senate.

Charlottetown Accord An agreement between the federal government, the provinces, and Aboriginal organizations to amend the constitution. The primary objectives were to obtain Quebec's consent for the Constitution Act 1982, establish self-government for Aboriginal peoples, and reform the Senate. The agreement failed when Canadians rejected it in a referendum in October 1992.

Charter Canadians Minority groups with a vested interest in particular sections of the Charter of Rights and Freedoms, such as Section 27, which recognizes the multicultural heritage of Canada.

Chief Justice The senior member of the Supreme Court of Canada.

chief of staff The head of the Prime Minister's Office and the principal adviser to the prime minister. The chief of staff provides partisan advice to the prime minister, unlike the clerk of the Privy Council, who provides nonpartisan advice.

civic virtue A term that encapsulates the notion that citizens have obligations to ensure the well-being of their communities.

civil law A legal system that is descended from Roman law and is still used by the non-English-speaking parts of Europe and much of Africa. Rather than relying on judge-made precedent, civil law instead uses a comprehensive civil code that is written by a legislature. In Canada, Quebec still uses civil law, and thus maintains its own civil code—the *Code civil du Québec*.

civil servants Permanent employees of the government who assist the elected government with policy development and implementation as well as the administration of the state.

classical federalism The theory that each order of the government in the federation is legally equal and should each operate independently of the others.

cleavages The main political divisions in a country. Political scientists have long been concerned with a handful of enduring schisms in the Canadian political landscape, such as language, region, and class, among others.

clerk of the Privy Council Office The top civil servant in the country. The clerk is also the deputy minister to the prime minister and secretary of the cabinet.

coalition governments Governments that are composed of two or more political parties.

cohort effect A term used by sociologists to describe the unique characteristics of particular generations.

committee stage The stage of the legislative process when a bill is sent to a subcommittee of the House of Commons for detailed examination.

compact theory Two separate but related interpretations of the origins of the Canadian constitution. The first compact theory states that Canada was a creation of all of the provinces in the form of a contract. The second compact theory states that Canada was a creation of two peoples—English and French.

comprehensive claims Claims that address First Nations's rights to land and resources that are not subject to historic treaties.

concurrent jurisdiction Refers to an area of responsibility that is shared between two or more orders of government. In Canada, agriculture and immigration are shared between the federal government and the provinces.

conditional grants Grants that are provided by the federal government to the provinces on the condition that the monies be used for particular purposes, such as financing health care.

confidence The ability of the government to command majority support in Parliament; it is the first rule of responsible government.

consociationalism A system of government whereby different ethnic or cultural groups share power, usually in the form of a coalition government with different parties representing the different cultural groups in the country.

conventions Unwritten rules of the Canadian political system. Many conventions were inherited from Great Britain's system of responsible government in 1867, while other conventions have emerged in Canada over time through political practice.

cooperative federalism The cooperation of the federal government and the provinces in the delivery of programs and services to citizens. It stands in contrast to the theory of classical federalism, in which the two orders of government operate independently of each other in their areas of jurisdiction.

Council of Atlantic Premiers A meeting of all four Atlantic premiers. It meets annually.

Council of the Federation The body of all premiers that meets roughly twice a year. It maintains a permanent secretariat to coordinate these meetings.

critical election An election with a sharp and durable realignment between political parties. It usually represents a more fundamental realignment of the pre-existing political cleavages within the electorate.

crosscutting cleavages A cleavage within a cleavage and an alliance across the main cleavage. The principal cleavage in Canada has historically been language: French and English. But the English-speaking community is further divided between Protestants and Catholics. And on some issues, English-speaking Catholics may have more in common with French-speaking Catholics than they do with English-speaking Protestants.

Crown Refers to the entirety of the Canadian state. For example, property owned by the Government of Canada is Crown property and government-owned businesses are called Crown corporations.

dead letters A legal concept that refers to any constitutional provision that has fallen into disuse and consequently may no longer have force or effect.

democratic deficit Refers to a general public disinterest in politics and more specifically to the decline in voter participation.

deputy minister The top civil servant in a department. A deputy minister is an employee of the government rather than an elected Member of Parliament.

differential citizenship A form of citizenship in which the state recognizes that disadvantaged groups, such as racial minorities, may require different treatment to realize their equality. Differential citizenship stands in contrast to the liberal principle of procedural equality.

disallowance The constitutional power given to the federal government to override or negate any legislation passed by the provincial legislatures.

division of powers Refers to the separate and often overlapping areas of jurisdiction between the provinces and the federal government. The powers of each order of government are listed in Sections 91 and 92 of the Constitution Act 1867.

Duverger's law A law that stipulates the single-member plurality electoral system will result in a party system with two strong parties and most likely only two parties.

electoral districts The geographical constituencies in which Members of Parliament are elected in Canada's single-member plurality electoral system. There are currently 308 electoral districts in Canada, each with more or less comparable populations.

electoral systems The rules by which voter preferences are translated into seats in the legislature.

equalization A federal expenditure program that is constitutionally entrenched in Section 36 of the Constitution Act 1982. It ensures that the provinces are able to offer comparable levels of service with roughly comparable levels of taxation, meaning that Canadians are ensured to receive roughly comparable levels of service for roughly comparable levels of taxation anywhere in the country.

Established Programs Financing Act (EPF) An act introduced in 1976 as a new federal transfer to finance provincial social programs including health care. It introduced the concept of block transfers in Canadian fiscal federalism rather than cost sharing.

executive The branch of government responsible for the execution of policy.

executive federalism The phenomenon whereby first ministers—the prime minister and the various provincial premiers—serve as the main nexus of interaction in intergovernmental affairs.

extinguished rights Those Aboriginal rights that have been expressly terminated by a lawful authority, such as the Parliament of Canada.

federalism A system of government with two constitutionally entrenched orders of government. One government is responsible for matters pertaining to the entire country, and the other order of government provides a range of services at a more local level. In Canada, the two orders of government are the 10 provinces and the federal government in Ottawa. (The territories are separate entities under the authority of the federal government).

federalists Quebecers who are not in favour of separation. They are committed to Canada, although many of them want to see changes to the way the federation is governed.

first ministers' meeting A meeting of the prime minister and all provincial premiers. It is the highest level of interaction in Canada's complex system of executive federalism. It is sometimes called the first ministers' conference.

first past the post The informal name for the single-member plurality electoral system.

first reading The stage when a bill is introduced in Parliament and numbered. Bills introduced in the House of Commons begin with the prefix C followed by a number; bills introduced in the Senate begin with the prefix S followed by a number.

fiscal federalism Refers to both the distribution of taxation powers in the federation as well as the transfer of money between the federal and provincial governments.

fiscal update An update on the government's budget situation that is given each fall by the Finance Minister. It may include new tax and spending measures.

formal executive The Crown in Canada.

free votes Votes in Parliament in which members of a party may vote according to their conscience rather than having to follow the direction of the leader or whip.

fringe parties Political parties that garner only a small percentage of the overall vote. However, they play an important role in Canadian politics because they often raise issues that major parties choose to ignore and thus provide citizens with more options to participate in the political system.

Front de libération du Québec (FLQ) A Quebec-based terrorist group that sought to establish an independent, socialist Quebec through an armed struggle.

Gang of Eight The premiers of eight provinces that opposed Prime Minister Trudeau's plan to patriate the constitution. Only Ontario and New Brunswick supported Trudeau, and consequently they were not members of the Gang of Eight.

gender gap The differing support political parties receive from women and men.

general amending formula The general amending formula stipulates that most constitutional amendments require the consent of the federal government and 7 of 10 provinces representing 50 percent of the population. Also known as the 7/50 rule.

government bills Bills that are supported by the cabinet and introduced by the responsible minister.

government May refer broadly to the entire system of public administration that governs the country or more specifically to the governing party in Parliament.

governor general The Queen's representative in Canada, and formally the head of the executive branch of government.

governor in council The formal decisions of the governor general taken on the advice of cabinet.

Green Books A series of reports by the federal government written at the end of World War II that proposed the creation of the modern welfare state in Canada.

head of government The official elected leader of the government. Canada's head of government is the prime minister.

head of state The official representative of the nation that is vested with all executive authority. The Queen is Canada's head of state.

House of Commons The lower chamber of parliament where there are 308 members who are elected by the people.

identity politics A political orientation that is driven by one's identification with one's language, race, religion, gender, nation, sexual orientation, or some other aspect of the group one identifies with. Identity politics is often associated with groups seeking to free themselves from discrimination by dominant groups in Canadian society.

ideologies Specific bundles of ideas about politics and the good life, such as liberalism, conservatism, and socialism. Ideologies help people explain political phenomena, they allow people to evaluate good and bad, and they equip people with a program or agenda for political action.

independent candidates Individuals running for election to the House of Commons who are not affiliated with any political party. There are many independent candidates in each election, but it is unusual for an independent candidate to win a seat in Parliament.

Indian Act Federal legislation that defines the legal status of Indian peoples in Canada and regulates the management of Indian lands and reserves.

inherent right Refers to Aboriginal rights, including title and self-government, stemming from the original occupation and use of the land by Aboriginal peoples.

institutional approach One type of approach used in the study of politics that analyzes the rules of the game and their effects on the political system.

interest groups Groups that represent particular interests in Canadian society and typically lobby or pressure the government for measures that benefit their members.

intergovernmental relations The interaction between the different governments in a federation, especially between the federal government and the provinces, but also between provinces and municipalities, Aboriginal peoples and governments of all levels, and even relationships across the border with state governments.

internal colonialism The political and economic subjugation of a particular group of people within a country by the government of that country.

involuntary enfranchisement The forcible enfranchisement of Indian individuals against their will, meaning that they lost their status as an Indian. Those who were involuntarily enfranchised were essentially divorced from their community. The Government of Canada used the threat of involuntary enfranchisement to curb Aboriginal activism.

Judicial Committee of the Privy Council The court of final appeal for all colonies in the British Empire; it remains the final court for some independent countries such as Jamaica and other islands in the Caribbean.

legislation The formal process by which laws are enacted.

Letters Patent A specific set of instructions from the British Crown to the governor general.

lieutenant governors The Queen's representatives in each province.

life cycle A term used by psychologists and sociologists to describe the distinct phases of life each individual goes through regardless of generation, such as being a toddler, attending elementary school, going to university, working in a career, and retiring.

limitations clause Section 1 of the Canadian Charter of Rights and Freedoms, which enables governments to place reasonable limits on the rights guaranteed by the Charter.

list system The simplest and purest form of all the proportional representation electoral systems. Each party produces a list of candidates equal to the number of seats in the government, with the leader ranked first and the most junior candidate last. On election day, citizens would vote for the party of their choice. Seats in the government are allocated to each party proportional to its share of the popular vote.

majority government When one political party wins more than half the seats in the House of Commons.

managing institutions The institutions that sit below peak institutions in Canada's system of executive federalism. They coordinate various federal–provincial programs and initiatives.

median voter theorem A theory that suggests political parties will appeal to voters in the centre of the political spectrum, especially in the single-member plurality electoral system.

Meech Lake Accord An agreement between the federal government and the provinces to amend the constitution. The recognition of Quebec as a distinct society was the centrepiece of the accord. The objective of the accord was to obtain Quebec's consent for the Constitution Act 1982, but the accord failed when it did not receive legislative support in Manitoba and Newfoundland.

mega-constitutional orientations Distinct perspectives—often associated with a particular region or group—on the identity and fundamental principles of the body politic.

mega-constitutional politics The practice of debating the existential basis of the country and its fundamental law.

memorandum to cabinet A formal document used by a minister to present his or views to cabinet.

ministers Members of Parliament, usually in the House of Commons, who have been appointed by the prime minister to sit with him or her in the cabinet. They collectively compose the Government of Canada.

ministers of state or secretaries of state Members of Parliament appointed by the prime minister to be a "junior minister" responsible for a particular department or agency under the auspices of a minister.

ministry Refers to the Government of Canada, which is composed of ministers.

minority government When a political party forms the government with fewer than half the seats in the House of Commons.

missionary parties Parties that are strongly committed to their political principles, and they are generally not willing to compromise their principles for electoral advantage. They stand in contrast to pragmatic brokerage parties.

mixed member proportional (MMP) electoral system An electoral system that combines the single-member plurality electoral system with the simple list electoral system. Each person votes for a candidate to represent the constituency he or she lives in and for a political party with its list of candidates. Votes for the list are used to iron out the disproportionalities caused by the election of candidates through the first-past-the-post system.

money bills Bills that allow the government to collect taxes and spend revenues. In Canada's system of parliamentary government, money bills are by definition matters of confidence.

nationalism The passion some individuals display for their nation. It properly refers to an identifiable group of people rather than a country; love of country is properly known as *patriotism*. In Canada, many people in Quebec believe that Quebec is a separate nation.

neo-liberals or libertarians Modern adherents of classical liberalism.

night of the long knives Refers to the episode during the patriation negotiations during which all provincial premiers except Premier Lévesque of Québec were included in a late-night, last-minute deal on patriation.

non-money bills Bills that entail all matters of legislation except the raising of taxes or the spending of revenue.

notwithstanding clause Refers to Section 33 of the Constitution Act 1982. It allows Parliament or a legislature to protect legislation that violates Section 2 and/or Sections 7 to 15 of the Canadian Charter of Rights and Freedoms. It expires after five years, and must be repassed if it is to remain in effect.

oakes test A judicial test used by the Supreme Court of Canada to determine if a law is in accordance with Section 1 of the Canadian Charter of Rights and Freedoms.

October Crisis A series of events that occurred in 1970 when the FLQ kidnapped a British diplomat and a Québec cabinet minister. The War Measures Act was invoked in response and lasted for the duration of the crisis.

officers or agents of Parliament Independent watchdogs, such as the auditor general, who report to Parliament on the activities of the government.

Official Opposition The second-largest party in Parliament that sits opposite the government in the House of Commons and holds it to account. Also known as *Her Majesty's Loyal Opposition*.

official policy on multiculturalism A policy adopted by the Liberal Party of Canada in 1971 that declared Canada to be a bilingual and multicultural country.

offshore accords Agreements negotiated between the federal government and Nova Scotia and Newfoundland. The accords enabled Nova Scotia and Newfoundland to receive royalty payments from offshore oil and gas resources as well as continue to receive a portion of their equalization payments.

open federalism A campaign proposal made by the Conservative Party of Canada in the 2006 election to create a more positive relationship with the provinces, but little has been done to develop or institutionalize the concept since it was first proposed.

Opposition Critics Are selected by the leader of the official opposition party to critique the work of particular government ministers. Collectively, the opposition critics are known as the shadow cabinet.

opt out The ability of provincial governments to remove themselves from national shared-cost programs and receive compensation from the federal government. However, provincial governments must still establish comparable programs with similar standards.

orders in council Decisions made by the cabinet that carry legal force.

paper candidates Members of a political party that file registration papers with Elections Canada as candidates even though they have no expectation of getting elected. They do this so their political party can claim to be running candidates across the nation.

Parliament The legislative branch of government in Canada, consisting of the House of Commons, the Senate, and the Crown.

parliamentary secretaries Members of Parliament appointed by the prime minister to assist ministers in their parliamentary duties, such as answering questions when the minister is away.

Parti Québécois (PQ) The main sovereignist party in Québec. It is a provincial party that is dedicated to making Quebec a sovereign country.

party discipline The expectation that members of a party in Parliament will follow the directions of their leader.

party system The number of parties active in the political system at any one time. The party system may refer to only the dominant parties in the system or only the parties that elect candidates to Parliament or all of the parties, depending on the context.

patronage The awarding of government perks and benefits by the prime minister to his or her supporters.

peak institutions The institutions that sit at the apex of Canada's system of executive federalism. The first ministers' meeting sits at the very top of this complex system.

pith and substance A legal term that refers to the essence of a law.

POGG clause A clause that is located in the preamble to Section 91 of the Constitution Act 1867. It stipulates that the federal Parliament shall have the ability to make laws for the "peace, order, and good government of Canada."

political culture The sum total of political beliefs in a country. It includes the attitudes, beliefs, and values that underpin the political system.

political executive The prime minister and the ministers in Canada.

political party An organization designed to get its candidates elected to Parliament. Political parties are the primary connection between voters and Parliament.

popular vote The total number of votes received by a political party across all constituencies divided by the number of votes cast in the election and multiplied by 100. It is expressed as a percentage of the vote. This information is irrelevant to the single-member plurality system used in Canada, but it is used by the media to judge the performance of the political parties in the election.

populism A theory that extends the notion of democracy beyond the election of the government. It is the belief that major political decisions should be made by the people. Populism can be left-wing or right-wing, and is particularly prevalent in Western Canada.

post-materialism The shift in political values in recent times away from basic economic concerns toward social justice and environmentalism.

prerogative powers The powers of the governor general that have been reserved from the time when the monarch exercised absolute authority in the British political system.

prime minister The leader of the government in Parliament. By convention, the prime minister is an elected member of the House of Commons.

Prime Minister's Office (PMO) An office made up of the prime ministers top political staff. It provides the prime minister with partisan political support, unlike the Privy Council Office, which provides nonpartisan support. Each prime minister brings in his or her own staff, and they leave with him or her.

private bills Bills that are passed for specific individuals, groups, or entities, such as the incorporation of a new bank.

private members' bills Bills that are introduced by the private members of the House of Commons, that is, all members who are not part of the government (i.e., who are not cabinet ministers or ministers of state).

Privy Council Office (PCO) The apex of the civil service and the office responsible for coordinating the actions of government and supporting the prime minister.

procedural equality A type of equality that requires the state to apply the law in a similar fashion to all citizens regardless of differences such as gender or race.

property and civil rights The very broad swath of responsibility allocated to the provincial governments in Section 92, subsection 13, of the Constitution Act 1867. This is why people have to register their homes and cars with the provincial government. Civil rights also includes things like insurance and contract law.

proportional representation (PR) electoral systems Electoral systems that distribute seats in the legislature proportional to a party's share of the popular vote. If a party wins 20 percent of the vote, it is allocated 20 percent of the seats in the legislature. There are a number of different types of proportional representation electoral systems, including the simple list system, mixed member proportional, and the single transferable vote.

prorogation A temporary closing of Parliament between elections. It marks the end of one session of Parliament and gives the government the opportunity to plan for the next session.

public bills Bills that establish law for the whole of Canadian society. Most bills passed by Parliament are public bills.

quasi-federal Refers to a country that is only partially federal. It might have certain qualities that federations have, but lack some others. In quasi-federal systems the central government is usually able to control and override the provinces or states.

Queen's Privy Council for Canada A largely ceremonial body that advises the Queen on matters of state related to Canada. It is made up of current and former cabinet ministers and other prominent Canadians. Individuals are appointed to the council by the governor general on the advice of the prime minister. It is a lifetime appointment, but only current members of the cabinet are entitled to advise the Crown directly.

question period (QP) A 45-minute session held each day the House of Commons is in session in which Members of Parliament can ask the government questions and hold it to account.

Quiet Revolution The transformation of Quebec from a deeply conservative society to a progressively liberal society in the 1960s.

readings The stages that bills pass through in Parliament.

record of decision A formal document recording the final and official decisions of cabinet.

regional ministers Members of cabinet tasked by the prime minister to take the lead on issues related to a particular province or region. It is more of a partisan role than a government position.

report stage The stage of the legislative process when the standing committee reports back to the House of Commons on its deliberations about a bill.

representative sample A subset of the population that accurately reflects the entire population.

representative tax system An analytical tool used by the federal government to calculate the fiscal capacity of each province for the purposes of the equalization program.

reservation The constitutional power given to lieutenant governors to refer legislation passed by provincial legislatures to the federal cabinet for approval.

reserve An area of land owned by the Crown but reserved for the use of an Indian band. Some bands have more than one reserve.

residential schools Schools that were established by the Government of Canada in conjunction with the Catholic and Anglican churches to forcibly educate Aboriginal children and assimilate them into mainstream Canadian society. The schools operated for more than a century, and the last residential school was closed in the 1990s. More than 150 000 Aboriginal children attended residential schools, where they were frequently physically and psychologically abused.

residual power Refers to all matters not specifically enumerated in the constitution. Each federation has to determine which government will have responsibility for matters not explicitly allocated by the constitution.

responsible government The Canadian system of government (inherited from Great Britain) in which ministers are responsible to Parliament and the Crown.

revenge of the cradle A church-fostered policy known as *la revanche des berceaux*. The church encouraged women to have lots of babies to prevent the assimilation of the French by the English.

riding Another term for electoral district or constituency in Canada's single-member plurality electoral system. The term is uniquely Canadian.

royal assent The final stage in the legislative process, when a bill that has been passed in both the House of Commons and the Senate goes to the governor general for proclamation.

rule of law The principle that governments must not only make the law but follow the law as well. It is one of the hallmarks of a free society.

rules of thumb Nonbinding, informal unwritten rules. Some rules of thumb may emerge as conventions or become enshrined in law over time.

safe seats Ridings that political parties can generally count on winning in the election.

Secession Reference Case A case referred to the Supreme Court by the Government of Canada to determine the legality of a province separating from the federation.

second reading The stage of the legislative process when the bill is debated in principle.

self-government The right of Aboriginal peoples to establish, design, and administer their own governments under the constitution of Canada.

Senate The upper chamber of Parliament where there are 105 members who are appointed until age 75 by the Crown on the advice of the prime minister.

Shadow cabinet Sits opposite the government in the House of Commons and holds the cabinet accountable. The shadow cabinet includes the leader of the official opposition party and its critics (who are appointed by the leader of the official opposition).

single issue parties Parties that are preoccupied with only one issue. The Marijuana Party, for example, is concerned primarily with the decriminalization of drugs, especially marijuana.

single transferable vote (STV) electoral system The electoral system used in Ireland and Malta. With STV, the country is divided into a number of geographic constituencies in which multiple candidates will be elected. Constituencies with relatively small populations might only elect two candidates, but very large constituencies might elect as many as six candidates. Voters have the opportunity to rank order the candidates according to their preferences. Candidates are elected according to a complex electoral quotient.

single-member plurality (SMP) electoral system An electoral system that provides for geographic representation in the legislature. The country is divided into geographic constituencies with approximately equal populations. A number of candidates will contest the election in each constituency, and the candidate with the most votes is elected to the legislature. This electoral system is very easy to use, but the distribution of seats in the legislature is not always proportional to a party's share of the vote in the election.

social capital A term that describes the social benefits reaped from people participating in voluntary organizations.

social union The comprehensive set of programs and services that were established following World War II that today make up the modern welfare state in Canada. Programs like universal health care, the Canada Pension Plan, the public education system, and employment insurance are important pillars of the modern social union.

sovereign Literally means "supreme power."

sovereignists Quebecers who want Quebec to become a sovereign state, independent of Canada.

sovereignty Literally means "supreme authority." In Canada, sovereignty is divided between the federal and provincial governments.

sovereignty-association The proposal made by René Lévesque for a new constitutional arrangement between Quebec and Canada, where Quebec would receive more powers and jurisdiction but would still be loosely affiliated with Canada.

Sparrow test A test devised by the Supreme Court of Canada that seeks to determine if a particular law constitutes a reasonable infringement of an Aboriginal right. For the law to be a reasonable infringement, it must have a valid and important legislative objective, and the honour of the Crown must be upheld by ensuring that meaningful consultation has occurred with the affected Aboriginal group.

Speaker The person who moderates legislative debates. In Canada, the Speaker of the House of Commons is an elected Member of Parliament who in turn is elected by the other members to be the Speaker. There is also a Speaker in the Senate.

specific claims Claims that address issues that arise when the terms of specific Aboriginal treaties are not being recognized or fulfilled.

Speech from the Throne (or Throne Speech) A speech that opens each session of Parliament. The speech is written by the government but read in the Senate chamber by the governor general. It outlines the government's agenda for the new session of Parliament.

spending power The ability of the federal government to spend monies on programs and services that are outside its jurisdiction.

standing committees Permanent committees that examine legislation in detail and consider other policy questions. There are approximately 26 standing committees in the House of Commons, one for each ministry.

status cards Cards issued by Aboriginal Affairs and Northern Development Canada to Aboriginal peoples registered under the Indian Act.

Status Indian An Aboriginal person who is registered under the Indian Act and consequently is entitled to certain legal rights.

Statute of Westminster A law passed by the British Parliament in 1931 that granted the dominions in the British Empire control over their own foreign affairs.

statutory laws The laws made by Parliament.

strategic voting When a person votes for his or her second or third preference of party or candidate in an attempt to prevent the least favourite candidate or party from winning the seat. For example, a supporter of the Green Party might vote for a Liberal to prevent the Conservative from winning, or a Conservative might vote for the NDP to prevent a Liberal from being elected.

substantive equality A type of equality that requires the state to apply the law differently to different groups based on their relative advantages or disadvantages so as to obtain an equal outcome or standard of living for all people.

supply bills Bills that authorize the spending of money by the government.

swing ridings Ridings with a long history of electing candidates from different parties.

systemic discrimination A form of discrimination produced by the operational logic of a system rather than individual intentions.

tax fields The categories of taxation where governments raise revenue. There are many different categories, but the most important ones today are personal income tax, corporate tax, and sales taxes.

tax harmonization A measure required in federal political systems to ensure that the combined tax rates of the federal and provincial governments are not too onerous for taxpayers or that the two taxation systems are not working at cross purposes.

tax points A means by which the federal government provides money to the provinces to finance provincial programs. With tax points, the federal government cuts its tax rates in one tax field (such as income tax) and the provinces increase their tax rates in this field by a corresponding amount.

third reading The stage of the legislative process when the bill is once again debated in principle and voted on in its entirety.

title An Aboriginal right to own land collectively as a result of the original occupation and use of the land by Aboriginal peoples.

totalitarian regimes Governments that maintain total control over the societies they govern. They are typically led by a single dictator.

transfer payments Monies that are transferred from the federal government to provincial governments to pay for services. The Canada Health Transfer is one such transfer payment.

treaty rights Particular and uniquely Aboriginal rights stemming from the original treaties signed between Aboriginal peoples and the French and British Crowns.

Triple-E Senate An idea promoted by conservatives in Western Canada to make the Senate of Canada an elected chamber with an equal number of representatives from each province, with the hope of creating a more effective counterbalance to the House of Commons.

two nations thesis The second compact theory, which states Canada was a creation of two peoples—English and French.

Usher of the Black Rod The chief ceremonial officer of the Senate. The Sergeant-at-Arms is the chief ceremonial officer in the House of Commons.

Van der Peet test A test devised by the Supreme Court of Canada that establishes the criteria to determine the existence of an Aboriginal right. The Supreme Court has indicated that Aboriginal rights are those that have continuity with the practices, customs, and traditions of Aboriginal peoples that existed prior to contact with European society.

War Measures Act An act of Parliament that was invoked during wartime that curtailed civil liberties. It was invoked during the October Crisis in response to the kidnappings and bombings conducted by the FLQ. It has since been replaced with the Emergencies Act.

wartime tax agreement The first tax rental agreement that saw the provinces "rent" their tax fields to the federal government for set revenue over the life of the agreement.

ways-and-means bills Bills that enable the government to collect taxes.

wedge politics When a political party chooses to take one side of a particular "hot button" issue to attract more votes and divide the remaining electorate among the opposing parties.

western alienation The disconnection many Canadians in Western provinces feel to the rest of Canada, and the belief that the Government of Canada tends to make policies for the benefit of the majority in Central Canada to the detriment of the West.

Western Premiers' Conference A meeting of all four Western premiers plus the three territorial leaders. It occurs annually.

whip An individual appointed by a leader to be responsible for party discipline.

White Paper on Indian Policy A policy proposal made by the Trudeau government in 1969 to eliminate the Indian Act and Indian status and assimilate Aboriginal people into the mainstream of Canadian society. It was resolutely opposed by most Aboriginal peoples and organizations in the country.

Index

Social Credit Party, 36, 51
wait time guarantee, 130
British Conquest of New France, 19
British Conservative Party, 59, 89, 105–106
British North America Act, 5–7, 107, 118, 141, 142, 145, 146–147, 164
see also Constitution Act, 1867
Brittain, Donald, 159
brokerage parties, 46, 240
brokerage politics, 48–49, 231–233
Brown, George, 145
budget, 100
Bush, George H.W., 177
Bush, George W., 240
by-election, 79
Byng, Lord, 76

cabinet, 63, 75
committees, in Harper government, 85
Francophone Quebecers in, 80
linguistic duality, 80
memorandum to cabinet, 85
merit, 82
nonterritorial representation, 81
operation of cabinet, 84–85
party harmony, 81–82
representation of all provinces according to size, 81
rules of cabinet formation, 80–82
shadow cabinet, 90
size of, 79–80
Cairns, Alan, 180
Calder, Frank, 192
Calder case, 192–194, 202, 204
Campbell, Kim, 37, 231
Canada
constitution. See constitution
constitutional democracy, 3
constitutional history, 5–7
court system, 174–180, 175f
health care, 17–18
ideologies and political parties, 18–19
immigrants, 25
journalists, 241
population, 2011, 23t
social union, 127–129, 128t
social welfare state, 17
United Kingdom, linkage to, 5–6
voter turnout, 238, 247
Canada Assistance Plan (CAP), 129, 130
Canada clause, 224, 226
Canada Elections Act, 40
Canada Health Act (CHT), 129, 130
Canada Health and Social Transfer (CHST), 130, 138
Canada Pension Plan (CPP), 127, 128
Canada Social Transfer (CST), 130
Canadian Action Party, 31t

Canadian Alliance, 37, 41, 47, 81, 82, 170, 232
Canadian Bar Association, 178
Canadian Charter of Rights and Freedoms. See Charter of Rights and Freedoms
Canadian Intergovernmental Conference Secretariat, 135
Canadian Labour Congress, 36
Canadian party system. See party system
Canadian political landscape, 19–27
Aboriginal peoples, 25
age, 27
class, 25–26
gender, 26–27
language, 19–21
multiculturalism, 24–25
region, 21–23
religion, 24–25
urban-rural, 23–24
Canadian Reform Conservative Alliance, 37, 232
Canadian Security Intelligence Service (CSIS), 82
candidate selection, 42
Cardinal, Harold, 192
Carstairs, Sharon, 217
Cartier, George-Étienne, 80
cash transfers, 130
Catholic Church, 19–20, 121, 142, 143
Catholic voters, 24
caucus, 41
CBC News Network, 242
Chalke, Sarah, 246
The Champions, 159
change to rules of the game, 4
Charest, Jean, 48, 231
Charlottetown Accord, 110, 111, 223–227, 231
Charron, Louise, 178
Charter Canadians, 169, 213, 221–222
Charter of Open Federalism, 138
Charter of Rights and Freedoms, 5, 135, 141, 237
entrenchment in constitution, 163, 165–166
vs. federalism, 180–181
fundamental freedoms, 167
group rights, 168–169, 222
impact on Canadian politics, 159
individual rights, 167
language rights, 168
limitations clause, 170–172
notwithstanding clause, 158, 169–170
popularity of, 239
provisions, 281–285
purpose, 165–166
vs. responsible government, 181–182
Trudeau, role of, 167–170
Château Clique, 144
Chief Justice, 176
chief of staff, 87

China, 256
Chinese-Canadians, 25
Chow, Olivia, 38f
Chrétien, Jean, 35t, 37, 41, 43, 44, 84, 99, 104, 108, 129, 130, 137, 157–158, 170, 228, 230, 232, 242–243
Christian Heritage Party of Canada, 31t
Churchill, Winston, 77
Citizenship and Immigration Canada, 256
civic virtue, 249
civil law, 121, 174
civil servants, 82
civil war, 4, 6, 143
Clarity Act, 230
Clark, Christy, 242, 244, 245
Clark, Joe, 36, 194, 223–224, 223f, 231
Clarkson, Adrienne, 77
class, 25–26
classical conservatism. See tory conservatism
classical federalism, 123, 124, 128, 148
classical liberalism, 14, 16, 17, 18f, 21, 22
Clear Grits, 32
cleavages, 19
Clement, Tony, 79
clerk of the Privy Council Office, 86–87
Climate Change Accountability Act, 111
CNN, 242
Co-operative Commonwealth Federation (CCF), 34, 36, 51
coalition building, 68
coalition governments, 59, 76
cohort effect, 245, 246
Cold War, 69
colonial domination, 189–190
committee stage, 97
communism, 13
Communist Manifesto (Marx), 248
Communist Party of Canada, 31t, 61
Communist Party of Italy, 69
community, 14
compact theory, 152
competition, 15
comprehensive claims, 193
concurrent jurisdiction, 121
conditional grants, 126, 129–131, 129t, 149
Confederation, 5–7, 6f, 7t, 19, 120, 125–127, 145–146
confidence, 2, 9
conflict management, 4–5
Conflict of Interest Act, 237–238
Congress of Aboriginal Peoples (CAP), 192
Congress Party (India), 61
conservation, 14
conservatism, 13, 14–16, 17f
and Conservative Party, 18, 30
neo-conservatism, 17, 17f, 18f, 21, 251
old conservatism, 14
tory conservatism, 14, 16, 18f, 21, 22

McMurtry, Roy, 157, 158
McNeil, Stephen, 245
media, 88, 241–243
median voter theorem, 240
Medical Care Act, 129
Medicare, 129
Meech Lake Accord, 213–222, 231
    collapse of, 216–217
    distinct society, 214–215, 216
    fallout in Quebec, 218–219
    political consequences, 218–222
    public reaction to, 215–216
    Reform Party, rise of, 221
    Western alienation, 219–221
mega-constitutional orientations, 213
mega-constitutional politics, 151–152, 230
Meighen, Arthur, 76
Member of Parliament (MP), 61
memorandum to cabinet, 85
Métis, 25, 186, 192, 201
    see also Aboriginal government
Métis National Council (MNC), 192
middle class, 25–26
Mill, John Stuart, 142
millennial generation, 245–246
Milner, Henry, 246
Minister of Justice, 178, 179
ministers, 9, 75
    associate deputy ministers (ADMs), 83
    deputy minister, 83
    government departments, 83–84
    role of, 82–84
    swearing in, 93
ministers of state, 79
ministry, 9, 75
minority government, 2, 9, 56, 59, 232
missionary parties, 46
mixed member proportional (MMP)
    system, 69–70, 71
modern life cycle, 246
Mohawk First Nations, 207
Moldaver, Michael, 178
money bills, 99
Moore, James, 82
MSNBC, 242
Mulcair, Thomas, 49, 233
Mulroney, Brian, 33t, 36–37, 48, 59, 113,
    133, 146, 206, 213, 215, 221, 222,
    223, 231, 240, 251, 252, 255
    see also Meech Lake Accord
multiculturalism, 24–25, 154
municipal government, 10–11
Murphy, Emily, 108f
Muslim Canadians, 25

Nadon, Marc, 178
Nanny State, 252
National Citizens Coalition, 47
National Energy Program (NEP),
    220, 221
national governing party, 48

National Indian Brotherhood (NIB),
    192, 194
National Indian Council, 192
nationalism, 20
Native Council of Canada, 192
Native Women's Association of Canada
    (NWAC), 192
"natural governing party," 51
natural resources, 120, 133, 163
NDP. See New Democratic Party (NDP)
negative attack ads, 240
neo-conservatism, 17, 17f, 18f, 21, 251
neo-liberals, 17, 18, 251, 252
the Netherlands, 68
netizens, 246
New Brunswick, 21
    see also Atlantic Canada; provinces
    alienation, 23
    Confederation, 7, 7t
    electoral reform, 71
    Meech Lake Accord, 216
    senators, number of, 107
New Democratic Party (NDP), 31t, 36, 43
    brokerage party, 233
    class issues, 26
    creation of, 36
    democratic socialism, 18, 30
    election, 1993, 231
    election, 2008, 232
    election, 2011, 22, 24, 30, 38, 50, 51, 51f
    female candidates, 64
    female leaders, 65
    financing, 43–44
    gender and, 26, 27
    ideological pragmatism, 47
    Quebec, 23, 49
    in 1990s, 37
    safe seats, 58
    Senate, abolishment of, 108, 110, 112
    and SMP system, 61
New France, 19, 142
New Zealand, 71
Newfoundland and Labrador, 21
    see also Atlantic Canada; provinces
    cabinet ministers, 81
    Confederation, 7t, 120
    Meech Lake Accord, 216–217
    natural gas revenues, 23
    senators, number of, 107
night of the long knives, 156–159, 212
Nisga'a, 192
Nisga'a Treaty, 194
noblesse oblige, 15, 16
non-money bills, 99
non-Status Indians, 192
nonterritorial representation, 63–65, 81
normal distribution, 47, 47f
North American Indian Brotherhood,
    190, 192
the North (Canada), 22
North Korea, 5

Northwest Territories, 22
Norway, 256
notwithstanding clause, 158, 169–170
Nova Scotia, 21
    see also Atlantic Canada; provinces
    Confederation, 7, 7t, 120
    natural gas revenues, 23
    senators, number of, 107
Nunavut, 22, 58

Oakes, David Edwin, 171–172
Oakes test, 171–172, 199
Obama, Barack, 77, 106, 242, 247
O'Connor, Gordon, 83–84
October Crisis, 154–155
officers of Parliament, 103–104
Official Languages Act, 153
Official Opposition, 98, 101
official policy on multiculturalism, 154
offshore accords, 133
oil and gas resources, 133
Old Age Assistance Act, 128
old conservatism, 14
    see also tory conservatism
old liberalism, 14
    see also classical liberalism
older voters, 26
Online Party of Canada, 31t
Ontario
    see also provinces
    cabinet ministers, 81
    Confederation, 7, 7t
    demography, 22
    electoral reform, 71
    Green Book proposals, 128
    ideologies, 21
    party competition, 58
    seats in House of Commons, 49
    senators, number of, 107
open federalism, 138
opposition critics, 90
opposition parties, 101–103
opt out, 149
Order of Canada, 77
orders in council, 77

Page, Kevin, 104
Pamajewon case, 203–204
paper candidates, 49
Papineau, Louis-Joseph, 144
Parizeau, Jacques, 228
Parlby, Irene Marryat, 108f
Parliament, 1
    accountability, 101–104
    bicameral, 8
    confidence, 2, 9
    conflict in, 101
    functions of, 93–94
    legislative process and the making of
        law, 96–101
    officers of Parliament, 103–104